W9-AAG-838

Maturational Windows and Adult Cortical Plasticity

Maturational Windows and Adult Cortical Plasticity

Editors

Bela Julesz
Rutgers University
Piscataway, NJ 08854

Ilona Kovács
Rutgers University
Piscataway, NJ 08854

Proceedings Volume XXIII

Santa Fe Institute
Studies in the Sciences of Complexity

Addison-Wesley Publishing Company
The Advanced Book Program

Reading, Massachusetts   Menlo Park, California   New York
Don Mills, Ontario   Wokingham, England   Amsterdam   Bonn
Sydney   Singapore   Tokyo   Madrid   San Juan
Paris   Seoul   Milan   Mexico City   Taipei

Publisher: *David Goehring*
Executive Editor: *Jeff Robbins*
Production Manager: *Michael Cirone*
Production Supervisor: *Lynne Reed*

Director of Publications, Santa Fe Institute: *Ronda K. Butler-Villa*
Production, Santa Fe Institute: *Della L. Ulibarri*

This volume was typeset using TEXtures on a Macintosh IIsi computer. Camera-ready output from a Hewlett Packard Laser Jet 4M Printer.

Copyright © 1995 by Addison-Wesley Publishing Company,
The Advanced Book Program, Jacob Way, Reading, MA 01867

All rights reserved. No part of this publication may be reproduced, stored in a retrieval system, or transmitted in any form or by any means, electronic, mechanical, photocopying, recording, or otherwise, without the prior written permission of the publisher. Printed in the United States of America. Published simultaneously in Canada.

ISBN 0-201-48367-X (Hardcover)
ISBN 0-201-48370-X (Paperback)

1 2 3 4 5 6 7 8 9 10-MA-9998979695
First printing, August 1995

About the Santa Fe Institute

The *Santa Fe Institute* (SFI) is a multidisciplinary graduate research and teaching institution formed to nurture research on complex systems and their simpler elements. A private, independent institution, SFI was founded in 1984. Its primary concern is to focus the tools of traditional scientific disciplines and emerging new computer resources on the problems and opportunities that are involved in the multidisciplinary study of complex systems—those fundamental processes that shape almost every aspect of human life. Understanding complex systems is critical to realizing the full potential of science, and may be expected to yield enormous intellectual and practical benefits.

All titles from the *Santa Fe Institute Studies in the Sciences of Complexity* series will carry this imprint which is based on a Mimbres pottery design (circa A.D. 950–1150), drawn by Betsy Jones. The design was selected because the radiating feathers are evocative of the outreach of the Santa Fe Institute Program to many disciplines and institutions.

Contributors to This Volume

Allman, J. M., *California Institute of Technology*

Antonini, A., *University of California*

Bachevalier, J., *University of Texas Medical School*

Braginn, A., *Rutgers University*

Buzsáki, G., *Rutgers University*

Cargo, J. E., *University of Alabama at Birmingham*

Chapman, B., *University of California at Davis*

Chrobak, J. J., *Rutgers University*

Jenkins, W. M., *W. M. Keck Center for Integrative Neurosciences, University of California at San Francisco*

Jeo, R. M., *California Institute of Technology*

Johnson, M. H., *MRC Cognitive Development Unit*

Julesz, B., *Rutgers University*

Karni, A., *National Institutes of Health*

Katz, E., *Cornell University Medical College*

Konishi, M., *California Institute of Technology*

Kovács, I., *Rutgers University*

Merzenich, M. M., *W. M. Keck Center for Integrative Neurosciences, University of California at San Francisco*

Nádasdy, Z., *Rutgers University*

Polat, U., *The Weizmann Institute of Science*

Pons, T. P., *Bowman Gray School of Medicine*

Purpura, K., *Cornell University Medical College*

Ramachandran, V. S., *University of California, San Diego*

Sagi, D., *The Weizmann Institute of Science*

Shrager, J., *Carnegie Mellon University*

Stiles, J., *University of California, San Diego*

Stryker, M. P., *University of California*

Tallal, P., *Rutgers University*

Taub, E., *University of Alabama at Birmingham*

Ungerleider, L. G., *National Institutes of Health*

Victor, J. D., *Cornell University Medical College*

Webster, M. J., *National Institutes of Health*

Yonebayashi, Y., *California Institute of Technology*

Santa Fe Institute Editorial Board
June 1993

Dr. L. M. Simmons, Jr., *Chair*
Vice President for Academic Affairs, Santa Fe Institute

Prof. Kenneth J. Arrow
Department of Economics, Stanford University

Prof. W. Brian Arthur
Dean & Virginia Morrison Professor of Population Studies and Economics,
Food Research Institute, Stanford University

Prof. Michele Boldrin
MEDS, Northwestern University

Dr. David K. Campbell
Head, Department of Physics, University of Illinois and
Director, Center for Nonlinear Studies, Los Alamos National Laboratory

Dr. George A. Cowan
Visiting Scientist, Santa Fe Institute and Senior Fellow Emeritus, Los Alamos
National Laboratory

Prof. Marcus W. Feldman
Director, Institute for Population & Resource Studies, Stanford University

Prof. Murray Gell-Mann
Division of Physics & Astronomy, California Institute of Technology

Prof. John H. Holland
Division of Computer Science & Engineering, University of Michigan

Prof. Stuart A. Kauffman
School of Medicine, University of Pennsylvania

Dr. Edward A. Knapp
President, Santa Fe Institute

Prof. Harold Morowitz
Robinson Professor, George Mason University

Dr. Alan S. Perelson
Theoretical Division, Los Alamos National Laboratory

Prof. David Pines
Department of Physics, University of Illinois

Prof. Harry L. Swinney
Department of Physics, University of Texas

Santa Fe Institute
Studies in the Sciences of Complexity

Lectures Volumes

Vol.	Editor	Title
I	D. L. Stein	Lectures in the Sciences of Complexity, 1989
II	E. Jen	1989 Lectures in Complex Systems, 1990
III	L. Nadel & D. L. Stein	1990 Lectures in Complex Systems, 1991
IV	L. Nadel & D. L. Stein	1991 Lectures in Complex Systems, 1992
V	L. Nadel & D. L. Stein	1992 Lectures in Complex Systems, 1993
VI	L. Nadel & D. L. Stein	1993 Lectures in Complex Systems, 1995

Lecture Notes Volumes

Vol.	Author	Title
I	J. Hertz, A. Krogh, & R. Palmer	Introduction to the Theory of Neural Computation, 1990
II	G. Weisbuch	Complex Systems Dynamics, 1990
III	W. D. Stein & F. J. Varela	Thinking About Biology, 1993

Reference Volumes

Vol.	Author	Title
I	A. Wuensche & M. Lesser	The Global Dynamics of Cellular Automata: Attraction Fields of One-Dimensional Cellular Automata, 1992

Contents

This volume is dedicated to George A. Cowan

Bela Julesz :
Rutgers University, Psychology Building—Busch Campus, Piscataway, NJ 08854

Preamble

On February 17, 1993, I wrote an open letter to a large number of colleagues whom I regarded as top experts in cortical plasticity, inviting them to participate in a workshop at the Santa Fe Institute (SFI) for Complex Adaptive Systems. I expressed the interest of members of SFI in the topic of learning before and after the maturational windows closed for certain perceptual and cognitive tasks. Then I continued as follows: *Indeed, much of the literature on maturational windows tells us of missed opportunities. We read about stereo blind children who were operated too late on their strabismus, and their "lazy eye" condition remained for life; babies with severe astigmatism who cannot be helped when correction was attempted too late; or "wolf children" who were unable to learn correct human speech after some years of neglect. The pessimistic tenor of these findings was based on the rigidity of the central nervous system (CNS) in adults.*

However, in recent years there is some accumulating evidence that the CNS is more plastic than believed earlier. From songbirds (Konishi and Nottebohm) to rapid neural sprouting (Darian-Smith and Gilbert) there are novel insights that show the plasticity of CNS. Recent studies of learning in early vision, e.g., texture discrimination (Karni and Sagi), and increasing Panum's fusional area (Julesz and Kovács) in stereopsis also show robust learning (coupled with a good night's sleep) in human adults. The classic findings by Merzenich, Kaas, and his colleagues on "filling in" of "silenced" neural sites by neighboring cortical areas, with Ramachandran's findings on "phantom limbs" all point to a new way to look at learning and rehabilitation in humans.

As a member of the Advisory Board of SFI I feel it is my duty to organize with your help such a workshop in order to find out whether a more optimistic look at rehabilitation and/or learning of new skills by humans is warranted. I did not consult with all of you yet, but hope that you accept this invitation."

Most of the colleagues to whom we wrote accepted our invitation or recommended some other prominent replacement. (Our workshop coincided with a memorial symposium in the honor of Otto Creutzfeld—whom I knew and admired—an outstanding neurophysiologist who just died, and several of our prospective invitees attended this memorial symposium instead.)

For years I was ruminating to find a topic in psychobiology that I would find proper to introduce to the large group of prominent scientists (including several Nobel laureates and MacArthur Fellows) at SFI. At one end of the spectrum there are mathematical problems in psychobiology (e.g., how many connections are needed to a synapse to have the brain fully connected: using some probability estimates from graph theory, or to understand the many sonar systems in bats: using analogies from various radar systems), but I felt that these problems were too specialized and of limited use for mankind. I thought that the high-powered theoretical physicist should instead work on more significant problems of economy or population growth, as they do, at SFI. At the other end of the spectrum there are the enigmatic problems of psychobiology (e.g., "why we sleep or dream?," "the role of consciousness," "the mind-body problem," "can machines develop feelings," and the nagging problems of mental health) that of course are of utmost interest to everyone, but in my opinion cannot be attacked yet. During my three decades in physiological psychology I was well acquainted with a seeming paradox in my specialty: *stereopsis.* Here we had infants whose strabismus prevented the fine-tuning of binocularly corresponding points during a critical period, and after this window of opportunity has been missed no corrective surgery could restore the loss of stereopsis. On the other hand, after I introduced the computer-generated random-dot stereograms I was startled of how many observers had difficulty with their fusion at the first time, but after they succeeded, years later they could see depth in a jiffy. So, here was a skill that required acquisition at infancy, nevertheless could be improved on in adulthood. Obviously, the brain had some plasticity left in adults, but of a limited kind. And then came the interesting news alluded in my letter. Finally I knew a topic that interested me, and was sure that it would interest members of SFI, particularly George Cowan, ex-president of SFI, with a keen interest in the possible rehabilitation of handicapped and underprivileged children. Furthermore, with my background as a physiological psychologist I had many past interactions with both perceptual and cognitive psychologists, linguists, neurophysiologists, and neuroanatomists who usually do not talk together. I thought a workshop on appraising the field of cortical plasticity as seen from various perspectives would be also of use to the participants. To my satisfaction all the participants seem to have agreed with this philosophy, were willing to come to Santa Fe in the second part of May 1993, and accepted our request to contribute a written article to be refereed for the workshop proceedings.

Before the actual workshop convened I suddenly realized the difficult organizational task that confronted me, particularly since I was amidst writing my second monograph *Dialogues on Perception*, published in 1995 of 1994 by MIT Press. Luckily, a close associate of mine, Dr. Ilona Kovács volunteered to help with the symposium, not only in its administration, but in the deepest scientific sense, including two novel scientific contributions of ours, in which she played a major part. Without her help this volume had never reached the present stage. The workshop convened at SFI in the second part of May, 1993, as planned and though there were many colleagues who already knew each other, there were many who met the first time, exactly as we wanted events to unfold.

Now that almost all the manuscripts are together do I write this preamble. It is a difficult task to oversee these multifaceted contributions in a quickly moving field. Just to give an example: during the workshop there was a heated debate whether the anatomy of plasticity was observable in the electron microscope as neural sprouting, or was some other mechanism responsible for long-term learning and/or reorganization. Just in the last month did Darian-Smith and Gilbert[1] find neural sprouting accompanying neural reorganization in the adult cat. So, at least the mechanism that might enable long-term changes has been found.

Already Mark Konishi found in male songbirds new activity in their brain in the spring related to new songs. He also reported that he noticed mitosis (cell division) in these newly developed areas. However, he does not know whether these new cells are responsible for the learning of new songs. Furthermore, when we asked him, whether such birds with mitosis being observed did develop cancer soon after, he had no answer. However, he emphasized that the act of flying requires great strength, and there are no senile birds, thus the question of linking the observed mitosis in the bird's brain with cancer is a difficult problem to research.

However, what does this plasticity prove to us, beyond questioning the exaggerated dogma that the adult brain cannot grow and the only change is the constant death of neurons. After all we all experience learning in adult organisms, sometimes even one-instance learning. From the pioneering experiments on conditioned reflexes by Pavlov to the gill movement conditioning of Aplasia (sea slugs and other mollusks) by Kandel and his co-workers there is ample evidence of plasticity, whether called slow learning, conditioning, long-term potentiation (LTP), and so on. Indeed, there are a few anecdotal reports of all kinds of learning. For instance, it is usually claimed that frogs cannot learn any new behavior; however, it is rumored that if a frog is ever strung by a wasp, it will avoid from then on catching wasps. It is also said that Brenda Milner's famous patient (whose two hippocampi have been surgically removed and thus could not learn new events or lexical subjects after surgery), reportedly could still learn procedural skills, such as the Towers of Hanoi game.

There is another kind of plasticity, usually associated with embryogenesis. The nervous system develops (similarly to other organs in embryogenesis) by both rapid cell growth and perhaps even more rapid cell death. These two forces are the sculptors of complex structures. However, after birth one might assume that rapid cell death would be less the carrier of learning. Yet, we know from the work of Peter Eimas that in the linguistic centers of Japanese infants in the first year most of the syllabic detectors are present, but soon after many of them, for instance, related to the "r"-sound (that is not used in the Japanese) these analyzers slowly disappear.

I wrote this preamble merely to link my role with cortical plasticity, with the Santa Fe Institute, with the selection of some of the participants, with my interest in visual learning, with George Cowan, and with Ilona Kovács, and in the Introduction I hope we will be able to establish some framework into which these contributions might fit in.

But most importantly, I wanted to put down some milestones that enables both us, the editors and the reader, to evaluate the progress made at the workshop, and particularly, now, after the contributed papers finally came in, and we had the opportunity to judge ourselves the great changes that were made in our own thinking and in the participants thinking, to be stated in the next paragraphs in the Introduction. By the way, my *Dialogues* to be published in the Fall have a chapter on maturational windows, and the reader can evaluate the great progress that was made during the year-long interval between the closing of my monograph and this volume.

REFERENCES

1. Darian-Smith, C., and C. S. Gilbert. "Axonal Sprouting Accompanies Functional Reorganization in Adult Cat Straite Cortex." *Nature* **368** (1994): 737–740.

Bela Julesz and Ilona Kovács
Rutgers University, Psychology Building–Busch Campus, Piscataway, NJ 08854

Maturational Windows and Adult Cortical Plasticity

INTRODUCTION

Paradoxically, this Introduction is the Summary to this Proceedings volume. How else? It took over a year until the last articles trickled in. Two participants reneged on their promise, so we asked others to contribute papers so that the most important problems all should be covered.

In addition to such a happenstance that editors are usually confronted with, we had three pleasant surprises. One, alluded to in the Preamble, was the first direct evidence of neural sprouting in the cat cortex by Darian-Smith and Gilbert,[2] whose possibility was constantly debated during the workshop. In a way without a cortical sprouting mechanism, much of the psychobiological findings and models were based on some shaky evidence, probable but not proven. With this new evidence everything started to fall into its correct place. It is nice to see how several of the neurophysiological papers are already giving reference to this pioneering paper.

The second surprise was a paper by Merzenich and Jenkins that arrived among the last, but was worth waiting for. We assumed that Merzenich (a pioneer in studying how cortical receptive fields of digits in monkeys' hands would fill in by neighbors as a digit in between was amputated) would write about his paradigm, but instead he wrote a paper on the psychobiological meaning of perceptual deficits in slow learning infants with their possible rehabilitation. This project was pioneered by Paula Tallal and to see a cooperative effort being started between Merzenich's group and Tallal's group on such an interesting new project justifies by itself the hard work of having this workshop brought into existence. We are particularly pleased by this fortuitous event, since Merzenich's epoch-making paradigm is well known, and several authors in this volume are referring to his classic work, while his paper with Jenkins in this volume heralds a much broader view of the central nervous system (CNS) fortified with the deep neuroanatomical and neurophysiological insights of their authors. The notion of plasticity from the perspective of developmental and clinical neuropsychology is further explained by Stiles and by Taub in our volume.

And the third pleasant event: the work of two workshop participants, who were brought together at our meeting for the first time, were recently referred to under the slogan of "Learn while you sleep" that (*Science* **256** (1994): 603–604; 679–681) has been enforced both by György Buzsaki from the physiological, and by Avi Karni from the human psychophysical perspectives. These are key studies for the understanding of the mechanisms of memory consolidation.

The 15 papers in this volume, together with the many references by their authors, cover a wide area of the most up-to-date findings in cortical plasticity. It is also gratifying that the authors took the slogan of the workshop seriously and tried to emphasize the optimistic outlook of their work where this was possible. The way we divided the material into four main areas reflects merely our own opinion. Needless to say, other editors might have combined the articles into different groups according to their own tastes. Luckily, the way the material is subdivided is immaterial to its valuable contents, and the reader should follow her own interests as she browses through this material. Furthermore, because the material is so vast and novel, it would be a pity to put it in the straightjacket of our own evaluation. So, we leave that to the reader, the more so because there are only a few, if any at all, who could penetrate the many fields of psychobiology from electron microscopy, and anatomy to cognition and linguistics.

The surface of the body—the interface between the organism and the external world—is represented in the primary sensory cortices of different modalities in a topographic fashion. Several chapters of this book (Shrager and Johnson; Antonini at al; Ramachandran) deal with the formation of somatotopic and visuotopic maps during embryogenesis, during a critical period after birth, and in adult life. The accepted view is that these maps evolve in the course of dynamic, largely self-organizing processes, and maintain some adaptability even in the adult brain.

One way to look at the dynamic self-organizing process followed by adaptability is to assume that the brain has its "deep structures," but the "fine tuning" of these deep structures requires interactions with the environment during a "critical period." This view was originated with Humboldt two centuries ago to explain human infants' unique and remarkable ability to learn a language, where the fine tuning with the environment (mother) referred to the very language (Chinese, English, etc.). In this framework it is believed that the genetic information is inadequate to specify the nature of the language in detail, and only the bootstrapping features are genetically provided.

However, for some simpler skills, such as the perception of orientation or stereopsis, the genetic information might seem to be adequate to specify the entire behavior of the organism, yet the fine tuning by the environment during the critical period or even after is crucial for the animal to be able to adapt to some bodily harm (e.g., loss of one eye, or limb) or to some special feature of the environment (e.g., learning to read Braille). Furthermore, the body of the organism grows (e.g., the interocular distance, or size of the limbs) that have to be compensated for by the brain. Reorganization phenomena (even in adults) may follow both the architectural changes of the organism itself (growth or injuries) and changes in local stimulation of the intact skin surface or the retina. Adaptation to these changes is a slow learning process, involving long exposure to the new conditions and leading to long-term changes in the distributed properties of cortical areas. The basic mechanisms of activity-dependent synaptic plasticity, competitive learning and correlated activity of neighboring neurons that shape cortical representational structures, are believed to account for the majority of adaptation and learning phenomena in the cortex. This view has been heralded by Pavlovian conditioning and Hebbian learning rules over a generation ago, yet the idea to trace the cortical sensory map in finding out cortical plasticity for all modalities is rather novel, and will certainly be enhanced by the new PET and MRI technologies as they mature.

While many of these modifications require slow learning in order to prevail for a long time, there are some long-lasting perceptual changes that might be called "one-shot" learning effects. One of the most challenging questions of brain research is how do these fast learning effects occur. Memory circuits behind recognition memory (Webster et al.) and neural mechanisms underlying the memory for cognitive contours (Jeo et al.) are discussed in our volume.

After these general comments that seem to us the consensus of the opinions of most authors in this book, we turn to plasticity effects in stereopsis.

PLASTICITY OF STEREOPSIS

Our reliance on stereopsis in this introductory chapter is based on two facts: (a) that stereopsis is a model system for cortical plasticity in early vision as attested by the binocular sensitivity columns (slabs) in V1 and their robust alteration by perceptual manipulations, and (b) authors' intimate familiarity with binocular vision.

First, it is known, based on strabistic (cross-eyed) adults who were not operated on during a critical period, that they remain stereo blind. On the other hand, we know[1,11] that in normal human infants, stereopsis matures 3.5 months after birth as revealed with dynamic RDS and cortically evoked potentials. It is less known that wrong stimulation (such as strabismus) is not the same as *no* stimulation at all. Indeed, if one uses a haploscope (a mirror stereoscope) and binocularly stimulates those close areas that are in the shadow of one's nose, stereopsis can be obtained, even though these areas were never stimulated binocularly before. So wrong stimulation causes amblyopia exanopsia ("lazy eye") condition, while *no* stimulation of binocular cortical units does not lead to their atrophy. This seems an adaptive cortical strategy since double vision is very disturbing, and it is better to have only one, but correctly functioning eye. The intact vision for binocularly virgin areas should not be confused with monocular deprivation, since in the former case both eyes are correctly stimulated by the incoming light, but not in a binocularly correlated way.

Stereopsis exhibits some interesting learning phenomena that are based on quite different mechanisms and illustrate how cautious one has to be when studying cortical plasticity. When a computer-generated random-dot stereogram (RDS, Figure 1.1, from Julesz[4]) is fused the first time, the viewer often requires a minute or more to see the hidden (cyclopean) object jump out in vivid depth, but after successful fusion the same RDS can be fused in a jiffy even years later. Obviously something has been learned in an instant that prevails over several years. This phenomenon is particularly dramatic for cyclopean targets with large disparities (outside of Panum's fusional area, since, for targets within, fusion can be obtained in less than 60 msec; see Julesz and Chang[9]). What happens is that for large disparities the stereograms have to be placed within Panum's limit by the convergence mechanism of the eyes, that in the absence of monocular contours, comply with great difficulty. It takes minutes to learn the proper convergence strategy, mostly an unconscious process, that remains with the observer for a long time.[6,7] It is like learning a mechanical skill, such as riding a bicycle, which lasts for years and the processes involved in learning it are related to the coordination of many body movements, acts of balancing, and the correct sequencing of these processes are hidden from our consciousness. This long-term "one-instant learning" is very different from the cortical learning studied by Ramachandran and Braddick[13] who showed orientation-sensitive learning of stereopsis after prolonged stimulation. In the following we show yet another kind of cortical learning, the dramatic extension of Panum's fusional area under prolonged learning.

That Panum's area can be as large as 120 arcmin has been first shown by Fender and Julesz[3] under retinal stabilization and by slowly pulling an already fused RDS apart. The hysteresis effect of Fender and Julesz established that a small RDS with a Panum's limit of 6 arcmin could be slowly pulled apart without breaking fusion before 120 arcmin disparity was reached (and convergence eye movements were prevented by close fitting contact lenses and a mirror system attached to the lenses). Of course, after the breaking of fusion, observers had to view the small (1 arcdeg × 1 arcdeg) RDS again at 6 arcmin disparity to reestablish fusion. In our learning studies the trained observer can start from scratch with, say, a 120-arcmin disparity target and immediately can fuse these RDS.

One of us (B.J.) noticed decades ago in his laboratory at Bell Labs as he worked with summer students that the range of binocular disparity can be increased many-fold after hundreds of trials. However, he never had an adequate number of students and adequate time to follow up these anecdotal findings, until four years ago when Ilona Kovács joined his new laboratory at Rutgers University. The purpose of the following experiment was to explore the extent one can increase the maximal binocular disparity threshold with prolonged practice, but without eye-movements (see Figure 1). Of the four observers who participated in the experiments, three showed significant learning during the training periods covering 3 to 12 months. The fourth observer showed a slight stereo-deficiency, and improvement during her short (1-month) training period could not be measured.

The observed learning effects are as follows: (a) Maximal binocular disparity limit (above which reporting the correct depth of the cyclopean target drops to chance) *can be extended by at least a factor of four* in adult human observers (from 15 arcmin even to 120 arcmin, with an average of 60–70 arcmin). (b) Learning *does not occur within a session* (of 100–150 trials) as shown in Figure 2(a). Thus there is no immediate learning effect observable during practice. (c) A moderate improvement is observed on the time scale of days; that is, performance systematically *increases between sessions* that are completed in consecutive days (Figure 2(b)). Learning proceeds slowly. Significant learning requires *at least 4 weeks* of training (24 sessions, 1 to 2 hours each). After the first month, performance still improved and observers did not reach a steady level. (d) Learning is *long term*: retests show that enhanced disparity thresholds are retained several months after terminating the training period (see Figure 2(c)).

The time scale of these learning effects is consistent with recent findings reported by Karni and Sagi, in our volume, who found that for the *consolidation of perceptual memory*, long hours need to be spent, and the effect of learning becomes significant on a days-to-weeks scale. The dynamic, rapidly adapting cortical response properties within the span of minutes to hours, where consolidation is not involved yet, are discussed by Katz et al. (this volume). Learning occurs step-by-step not only in the temporal but also in the spatial sense, proceeding from small to large disparities. A main characteristic of cortical remapping of stereopsis is that the extent of Panum's fusional area is increased by a slow progressive learning, one cannot start with a large disparity and wait till depth appears at the end. This property agrees with Polat and Sagi's findings (in this volume) who have shown that *local (neighbor) interactions* between cortical units are necessary to produce long-range spatial interactions that lie behind perceptual learning. We find that disparity increase is gradual, between a manifold of overlapping binocularly sensitive neurons. That such cyclopean neurons exist, firing for RDS in layer IVb of V1 in macaque monkey, has been shown by Gian Poggio.[12] So the learning is between cortically overlapping cyclopean receptive fields, thus also belonging to the kind of cortical plasticity revealed in the somatosensory cortex.

FIGURE 1 Stimulus for the depth discrimination task of the learning paradigm. The RDS had the extent of 9 arcdeg × 8 arcdeg containing a 1.6 arcdeg × 1.6 arcdeg cyclopean square, presented for 160 msec, and followed by a zero disparity RDS mask. (Such short presentations ensure that eye movements cannot be initiated during a trial.) Viewing distance was 1.4 m. The observers were wearing alternating liquid crystal-shutter-type goggles that stimulated each eye with the proper stereo half-pair, respectively, without any cross-talk. Observers were instructed to fixate at a central mark, and a chin rest was used to keep the head position constant. In a forced choice procedure, observers were asked to tell whether the cyclopean square was seen in front or behind the fixation plane. To avoid depth fixation preferences, besides the RDS with crossed and uncrossed dispariities, we introduced some catch trials using uncorrelated RDS. (Without such uncorrelated control, the observer could "cheat" by fixating, say, at the front target, and calling the nonfused target as being "behind." Since the uncorrelated target is seen always behind [if not fixated on the zero depth plane], the catch trials force observers to fixate on the marker for best possible performance.) The "front," "behind," and "uncorrelated" targets were presented at random. A staircase method (invented by von Békésy) was used to determine the maximal disparity thresholds. Separate staircases were used for the "front" and "behind" presentations. After a few practice sessions, each observer took part in 1- to 2-hour training sessions at least for 24 days in succession, and the changes in their depth-discrimination performance were monitored.

We hope that our experiment is a good introduction into the many exciting plastic effects found in the somatosensory and visual cortex by our distinguished collegues throughout this book. Obviously, these experiments on human adults show the cortical plasticity of binocular vision, and reinforce the optimistic view.

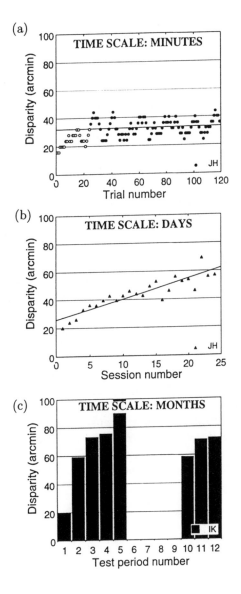

FIGURE 2 Typical learning curves of the depth-discrimination task. (a) On the time scale of minutes there was no observable improvement in depth discrimination performance. Data points are values of one of the two interleaved (front and behind) staircases, representing front disparities. Disparity values of consecutive trials signed with filled symbols are alternating around the threshold. The session was started at a minimal disparity of 16 arcmin. Empty symbols represent the first 25 trials that were taken by the subject to approximate threshold. (b) Disparity thresholds of 25 sessions completed in consecutive days. A slow, day-by-day improvement can be observed. (c) An enormous improvement is observed on the time scale of months. Preformance is retained even after several months separation between test periods. The columns represent disparity thresholds measured on the first day of each test period (months).

REFERENCES

1. Braddick, O., J. Atkinson, B. Julesz, W. Kropfl, I. Bodis-Wollner, and E. Raab. "Cortical Binocularity in Infants." *Nature* **288** (1980): 363–365.

2. Darian-Smith, C., and C. S. Gilbert. "Axonal Sprouting Accompanies Functional Reorganization in Adult Cat Striate Cortex." *Nature* **368** (1994): 737–740.

3. Fender, D., and B. Julesz. "Extension of Panum's Fusional Area in Binocularly Stabilized Vision." *J. Optical Soc. Am.* **57(6)** (1967): 819–830.

4. Julesz, B. "Binocular Depth Perception of Computer-Generated Patterns." *Bell System Tech. J.* **39** (1960): 1125–1162.

5. Julesz, B. *Foundations of Cyclopean Perception.* Chicago, IL: University of Chicago Press, 1971.

6. Julesz, B. "Global Stereopsis: Cooperative Phenomena in Stereopsis Depth Perception." In *Handbook of Sensory Physiology, VIII: Perception,* edited by R. Held, H. W. Leibowitz, and H. Teuber. Berlin: Springer-Verlag, 1978.

7. Julesz, B. "Stereoscopic Vision." *Vision Res.* **26(9)** (1986): 1601–1612. Twenty-fifth Anniversary Issue.

8. Julesz, B., and J. E. Miller. "Independent Spatial Frequency Tuned Channels in Binocular Fusion and Rivalry." *Perception* **4** (1975): 125–143.

9. Julesz, B., and J. J. Chang. "Interaction Between Pools of Binocular Disparity Detectors Tuned to Different Disparities." *Biol. Cybern.* **22** (1976): 107–119.

10. Karni, A., D. Tanne, B. S. Rubenstein, J. J. M. Askenasy, and D. Sagi. "Dependence on REM Sleep of Overnight Improvement of a Perceptual Skill." *Science* **265** (1994): 679–682.

11. Petrig, B., B. Julesz, W. Kropfl, G. Baumgartner, and M. Anliker. "Development of Stereopsis and Cortical Binocularity in Human Infants: Electrophysiological Evidence." *Science* **13** (1981): 1402–1405.

12. Poggio, G. F. "Processing of Stereoscopic Information in Primate Visual Cortex." In *Dynamic Aspects of Neocortical Function,* edited by G. M. Edelman, W. E. Gall, and W. M. Cowan, 613–635. New York: Wiley, 1984.

13. Ramachandran, V. S., and O. Braddick. "Orientation Specific Learning in Stereopsis." *Perception* **2** (1973): 371–376.

Acknowledgments

We thank the Science Board of SFI and particularly George A. Cowan for their support of this conference. We appreciate the invaluable aid that Andi Sutherland, Ronda K. Butler-Villa and Della L. Ulibarri of the Institute provided in making the workshop and the book a reality.

Synapses and Plasticity

G. Buzsáki,† A. Bragin, J. J. Chrobak, and Z. Nádasdy
Center for Molecular and Behavioral Neuroscience, Rutgers, The State University of New Jersey, 197 University Avenue, Newark, NJ 07102
†To whom correspondence should be addressed:
György Buzsáki, Center for Molecular and Behavioral Neuroscience, Rutgers University, 197 University Avenue, Newark, NJ 07102; Tel: (201)648-1080, ext. 3131; Fax: (201)648-1588

Memory Consolidation in the "Nonaroused" Brain: A Physiological Perspective

Although it is commonly accepted that the hippocampus is a key structure in memory formation, it is also known that permanent memory traces are probably stored in the neocortex and not or not only in the hippocampus. Understanding how memories are formed in the hippocampus and how they are transferred to the neocortex is a major challenge in modern neuroscience. The goal of this chapter is to summarize current knowledge in this field and, in particular, to point out that consolidation of declarative memory traces is a slow process and requires the sleeping brain. A similar view is presented in the chapter by Karni and Sagi in connection with procedural memory.

The idea that modification of synaptic function can provide a basis for memory arose shortly after the discovery of the synapse.[3,68,74] During the past decades several memory models have been proposed in which information is represented by combinations of the firing patterns of individual neurons. In most of these models, memory is due to activity-dependent changes in neuronal connections and the resulting change preferentially enhances subsequent occurrences of that activity pattern during recall.[27,37,42,43,51,58] A candidate neurophysiological model for such use-dependent modification of synaptic connections is long-term potentiation (LTP).[9,10] The three main requirements for the induction of LTP are intensity, frequency, and pattern of stimulation. The numerous *in vitro* studies carried out over the past decade have laid down the rules and requirements of long-term synaptic plasticity,

Maturational Windows and Adult Cortical Plasticity, Eds. B. Julesz & I. Kovács,
SFI Studies in the Sciences of Complexity, Vol. XXIII, Addison-Wesley, 1995

which include: (a) conjunctive pre- and postsynaptic activity, (b) specific modification of those afferents that were coactivated with the postsynaptic depolarization of the cell, and (c) neither postsynaptic depolarization alone nor weak afferent excitation in the absence of postsynaptic depolarization results in LTP.[41,47,88]

Whatever cooperative patterns of neuronal activity in the brain may eventually prove to be the mechanism for inducing LTP, they should meet the basic requirements for the elicitation of LTP, provided that LTP is indeed a valid neurophysiological model for memory trace formation. Physiological patterns in the intact nervous system provide a logical starting point to examine whether the requirements of LTP are present in the behaving animal.[19,31,51,65] Accordingly, the main objectives of this review are (a) to consider that memory traces may be formed during "nonaroused" states of the brain, (b) to examine physiologically occurring neuronal patterns that might meet the experimentally defined criteria of LTP, and (c) to propose possible rules which may allow "noisy" neuronal activity to carry highly specific information.

TWO ANTAGONISTIC PATTERNS IN THE NERVOUS SYSTEM: FROM CHANNELS TO SYSTEMS

The notion of activation is a Newtonian concept implying the necessity of external sources to energize and set into motion an inert system. The sleeping or "nonaroused" brain, however, is clearly not inert. It is not active in the sense that the information-carrying capacity of both the afferent and efferent systems is at its minimum. The "nonaroused" nervous system is in a "closed-loop" state but it is by no means inactive and without intrinsic activity. The dichotomy of open- vs. closed-loop states appear to be present at all levels of the central nervous system (see Table 1).

Recent developments of recording techniques *in vivo* combined with *in vitro* methods have offered new insights into the operations of nerve cells. These enable us to begin to distinguish the intrinsic biophysical characteristics of individual neurons from network-derived response properties as well as to reveal their relationships. The majority of neurons in the mammalian brain have two basic modes of operation: steady firing and burst discharge. The burst discharge mode appears to be an intrinsic feature of several neuronal types, including thalamic, neocortical, and hippocampal projection neurons.[49] Since the burst mode is an intrinsic property of neurons, the information transmitted by the cells to their respective targets will be rather independent of their inputs in this mode of discharge. In other words, the bursting mode of cell activity is probably the least optimal state for high-fidelity pattern transfer. In contrast, sustained firing appears to be the characteristic neuronal pattern in the awake, behaviorally responsive animal. The reason for the

TABLE 1 Dichotomy of operations at different levels of neuronal organization.

Level	Activated	Nonactivated
behavior	aroused[1]	nonaroused
field (EEG)	desynchronized[1]	synchronized
population (network)	asynchronous	synchronous
cellular	continuous firing	burst firing
control	extrinsic	intrinsic
state	open-loop	closed-loop
function	information processing	memory formation

[1] REM sleep is regarded as an activated state at the thalamic and neocortical levels, although clearly no behavioral arousal is present.

refractoriness of the neuron in the burst mode state is that a burst of action potentials is associated with a long-lasting afterhyperpolarization (AHP) of the cell (an intrinsic mechanism). In addition, the burst pattern recruits strong recurrent inhibition. Both mechanisms then prevent the occurrence of further spikes in response to synaptic inputs. A major part of the AHP is due to a Ca^{2+}-mediated K^+-conductance change. The long-lasting nature of AHP favors the summation of outward currents of individual pyramidal cells resulting in a large local field positivity in deep layers. Such extracellularly summated currents form the basis of slow delta EEG waves recorded during sleep.

Several subcortical neurotransmitters with widespread cortical projections, including acetylcholine, histamine, and noradrenaline, attenuate the AHP of pyramidal cells[28,36,52,55] making the synaptic responsivity of the neurons more efficient. As a result, cortical cells can respond briskly and without failure to afferent information.

The dual mode of discharge patterns has several important implications for the network (population) behavior of neurons (Table 1). First, the long-lasting nature of AHP following burst discharges in individual neurons considerably facilitates the emergence of population synchrony.[18,84] As hypothesized above, synchronous occurrence of AHP in a large number of neurons results in summed extracellular currents and consequent slow delta waves in the EEG record. In contrast, blockade of the AHP by acetylcholine and other monoamines of subcortical origin reduce the probability of population synchrony and results in desynchronized EEG.[17] Population synchrony is largely a closed-loop phenomenon of the neuronal network,[84] while the desynchronized (or "activated") state is dependent on external, arousing inputs in thalamus, neocortex, and hippocampus.

The activation process implies a switching action between the two fundamental modes of forebrain operations. In the activated state the brain is in a continuous interaction with the environment. A distinguishing feature of the nonaroused state of cortical networks is the significant calcium influx into the cells during the burst mode, a prerequisite for the induction of biochemical and molecular changes in neurons. Until recently, no function has been assigned to the noninteractive mode of brain activity. We have suggested, however, that population bursting, the characteristic pattern of the closed-loop state, is a likely candidate for the induction of long-term plastic changes underlying memory formation.[19] From this perspective the activation process is not simply a shift from the passive state into an active one but is viewed as a fundamental change from the storage mode into the information processing mode of brain operation.

THE ANATOMICAL SUBSTRATE

A summary of the interconnectivity in the hippocampal system is schematized in Figure 1. The entorhinal cortex and septum serve as nodal points, the entorhinal for descending neocortical inputs, the septum for subcortical. Neurons in the superficial layers of the pre- and parasubiculum, and primarily the entorhinal cortex innervate the major subfields of the hippocampus. The most extensive innervation is of the dentate granule cells, which provide the mossy fiber innervation of the CA3 subfield; the CA3 pyramids in turn innervate the CA1 region. The CA1 and the contiguous subicular pyramids provide the major output of the hippocampus to the deep layers of the pre- and parasubiculum, and prominently the entorhinal cortex. Pre- and parasubicular neurons also innervate the entorhinal cortex, primarily the medial entorhinal cortex. It is important to note that the entorhinal cortex is bidirectionally connected to vast areas of the cortical mantle,[80,87] and is thus poised to route information into the hippocampus and return hippocampally processed information back to these cortical targets.

Medial septal and contiguous diagonal band neurons innervate all areas of the hippocampus, as well as the pre- and parasubiculum and entorhinal cortex. Other subcortical afferents, directly or largely via an influence on hippocampopetal septal neurons, can orchestrate activity in the hippocampus and entorhinal cortex and thus effectively gate processing of information in the hippocampus.[13,33]

From the above brief description of the anatomy it appears that the hippocampal cortex is special in many ways. Highly processed information about the external world (the content) reaches the hippocampus via the entorhinal cortex, whereas information about the "internal world" (the context) is conveyed by the subcortical

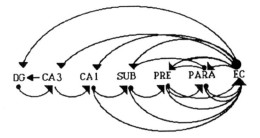

FIGURE 1 Interconnectivity of hippocampal and retrohippocampal structures. Neocortical inputs access hippocampal circuits via the entorhinal cortex (EC), hippocampal circuits return inputs to neocortical structures via the entorhinal cortex. Subcortical inputs, largely via the septum, innervate this complex from the dentate area (DG) to EC (not shown). The septal input orchestrates the excitability of distinct intra- and extrahippocampal pathways. For simplicity, all inhibitory connections are omitted. Abbreviations: subiculum (SUB); presubiculum (PRE); parasubiculum (PARA).

inputs. In contrast to neocortical areas, the main output targets of the hippocampus are the same as its main inputs (i.e., the entorhinal cortex). Thus, the hippocampus can be conceived as an "appendage" of the large neocortex. From this strategic position it may already be deduced that the main function of the hippocampal formation is to modify its inputs by feeding back a processed "reafferent copy" to the neocortex. As will be described in some detail below, transfer of neocortical information to the hippocampus and the modification process in neocortical circuitries by the hippocampal output takes place in a temporally discontinuous manner and might be separated by minutes, hours, or days from the initial acquisition phase.

The entorhinal input can reach each of the main cell types of the hippocampus directly and indirectly via a mainly unidirectional, excitatory pathway. Numerically, the major target is the one million granule cells in the rat. The granule cells and the various subtypes of hilar neurons[2] are reciprocally connected. In addition, CA3 pyramidal cells also project back to the hilus and onto granule cells,[48] although this feedback is sparse in the septal part of the hippocampus. The dentate area is perhaps the most important to the function of the hippocampal formation, since this arrangement is not replicated anywhere in the neocortex.

Each CA3 pyramidal neuron receives inputs from only a few dozen granule cells (< 60) and each granule cell innervates less than a hundred pyramidal cells in a narrow septotemporal lamella. Thus, the large mossy fiber synapses, the axon terminals of the granules cells, comprise only a very small fraction of the total number of synapses ($> 50,000$) on the dendrites of CA3 pyramidal cells. The largest number of contacts on CA3 pyramidal cells derive from other CA3 pyramidal cells. Although the extensive axon collateral system of the CA3 region was already appreciated in

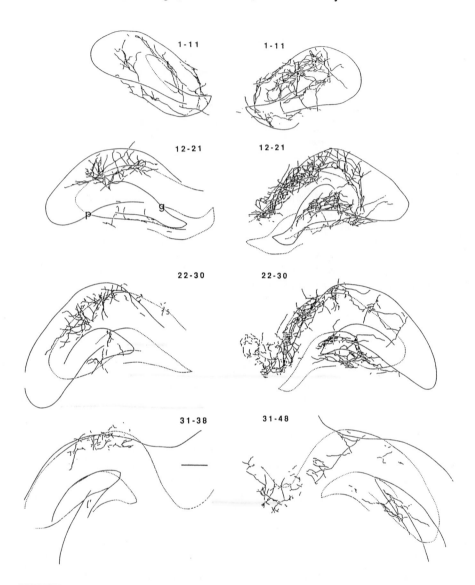

FIGURE 2 Axon arbor of a CA3c pyramidal cell in the ipsilateral and contralateral hippocampi. Distribution of axons are superimposed on the outlines of the pyramidal layer (p) and granule cell layer (g). The numbers of the sections (100 μm each) condensed into each of the drawings is indicated by the figures medial to the sections. The cell body is indicated by a black triangle (sections 22–30). Note high fiber density in stratum radiatum of CA1 in both hemispheres. Note also the lack of axonal connections between CA3 and CA1 regions in the more caudal sections and the paucity of fibers in CA3b. Calibration: 500 μm. (Reprinted with permission from Li et al.[48])

early Golgi studies,[50,72] its longitudinal extent and topographic organization have only recently been studied in any detail.[39,48,81] The total length of axon collaterals of completely filled cells in the ipsilateral hippocampus vary from 150 to 300 mm (see Figure 2). Based on the average interbouton distance (5 μm), we estimated that CA3 pyramidal cells establish between 30,000 to 60,000 synapses in the ipsilateral hippocampus which is translated to a total of ten billion synapses for the 200,000 CA3 pyramidal cells in the rat. These anatomical observations suggest that the matrix connectivity of the CA3 pyramidal neurons meets two important requirements of an "ideal" storage device: widely distributed but sparse connections combined with high-density "patches."[85]

A major difference between pyramidal cells of the CA3 and CA1 regions is the extremely limited interconnectivity of CA1 pyramidal cells.[24,83] The question to ask, then, is what new processing is taking place in the CA1 region that is lacking in CA3? One suggestion is that the CA1 pyramidal cells are a type of "and" neurons that discharge only if several CA3 pyramidal neurons converge on them.[51,63] As will be described in detail below, we believe that a highly organized pattern emerges from the interaction between CA1 pyramidal cells and their inhibitory interneurons, which serves to transfer information from the CA3 region to the neocortex for permanent storage.

POPULATION PATTERNS IN THE HIPPOCAMPAL FORMATION

Various population patterns, as reflected by spontaneous field potentials and rhythms, are present in the hippocampal formation, including theta activity and associated gamma pattern (40–100 Hz oscillation), hippocampal sharp waves (SPW), and associated high-frequency (200 Hz) oscillation ("ripple"), two types of dentate spikes, sleep spindles, and delta waves of sleep.[7,8,12,19,20,21,64]

THETA PATTERN

Hippocampal rhythmic slow activity (RSA or theta) is the most studied pattern and has been implicated in several functions, ranging from sensory processing to the voluntary control of movement.[12,86] In the rat, hippocampal theta activity occurs during exploratory behaviors, such as sniffing, rearing, walking, and the paradoxical phase of sleep[86] (see Table 2 and Figures 3 and 4(a)). During theta activity the vast majority of pyramidal neurons and granule cells are virtually silent.[12,32,69,83] Only a limited number of pyramidal and granule cells, representing, for example, the spatial position of the animal, show a marked increase in firing as the animal moves into unique spatial locations.[40,64] These concurrently active "spatial" cells are also phase-locked to the extracellularly recorded field theta pattern.

TABLE 2 Behavioral and cellular correlates of the major hippocampal EEG patterns.

	THETA	SHARP WAVE
behavioral and sleep states	locomotion sniffing attentive to stimuli REM sleep	awake immobility eating drinking slow wave sleep
septal neurons	rhythmic bursting	unknown
granule cells	short bursts	SPW-associated increase
interneurons	rhythmic activity	SPW-associated increase
CA3, CA1, SUB pyramidal cells (HPC outputs)	majority silent (spatial and other selective activity)	SPW-associated increase
entorhinal superficial layers (II-III) (input to HPC)	phase-related increase	majority silent
entorhinal deep layer (V) (output to neocortex)	not related to theta increase	SPW-associated

Hippocampal theta activity may have two interdependent functions. First, its large-scale oscillation in the entorhinal-hippocampal network makes it possible for hippocampal neurons to be activated with the least amount of energy because the intrinsic "resonant" properties of hippocampal neurons are sharply "tuned" to theta frequency.[1,45] Second, theta activity increases the "signal-to-noise" ratio by silencing most principal cells and keeping their membrane voltage close but below the firing threshold. As a result, a relatively few active perforant path fibers from the entorhinal cortex (CA1 and CA3) and mossy fibers of the granule cells (CA3) are sufficient to discharge the pyramidal cells. Because theta activity induces a fluctuation in cellular excitability, the probability that spatially distant and otherwise noninteractive neurons discharge nearly simultaneously is substantially increased.

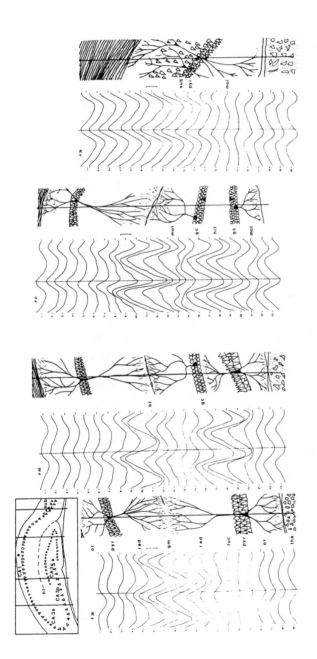

FIGURE 3 Spatial distribution of hippocampal theta activity. The individual traces are averages of 64 theta epochs (256 msec) recorded during running. Since the behavior was "clamped" by an operant conditioning task, the successively recorded traces can be viewed as if all of them were recorded simultaneously. Theta obtained from a stationary electrode in the stratum oriens of CA1 (black dot in inset) was used to normalize the averages. The microelectrodes tracks are illustrated by vertical lines in the inset. Abbreviations: or, stratum oriens; pyr, pyramidal layer; rad, stratum radiatum; gm, stratum lacunosum-moleculare; luc, stratum lucidum; thal, thalamus; hf, hippocampal fissure; mol, molecular layer; gc, granule cell layer; hil, hilus; sub, subiculum (Reprinted with permission from Buzsaki et al.[15])

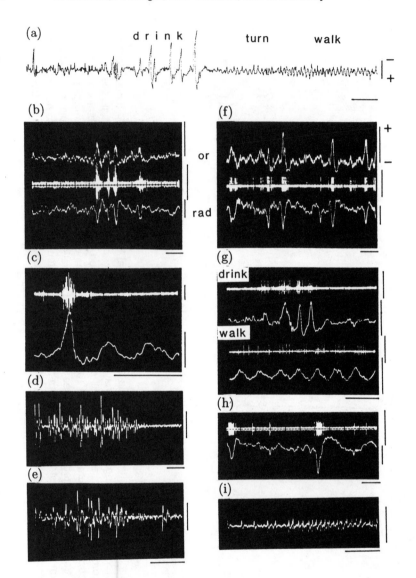

FIGURE 4 SPWs are associated with synchronous bursts of neuronal activity in the hippocampal formation. (a) EEG activity recorded from stratum radiatum of CA1 during drinking and walking. Note the presence of large amplitude SPW during drinking and rhythmic theta waves during walking. (b)–(e) SPW-associated population burst of CA1 pyramidal cells. (f)–(g) SPW-associated firing of interneurons in various regions of the CA1 field. (i) Detail of the burst shown in (h). Note frequency increase up to 800 Hz. Calibrations: 20 μV (units), 1 mV (EEG); 1 sec (a), 0.2 sec (b, c, f, g, h), 10 msec (d, e, i). (Reprinted with permission from Buzsáki et al.[12]).

GAMMA RHYTHM

Concurrent with theta waves, a fast (40–100 Hz) oscillatory pattern is present in the hilus and occasionally in the vicinity of the pyramidal cell layer of CA1 and CA3.[8,12,46,77] The power of gamma activity substantially decreases following surgical removal of the entorhinal cortex. This finding is compatible with the view that the perforant path synapses on the dendrites of granule cells and hilar neurons play an important role in the generation of gamma field activity. In line with this suggestion are the observations that gamma field oscillations and associated firing of neurons are present in the superficial layers of the entorhinal cortex of the anesthetized[22] and awake rat during theta behaviors.[25,26] The intimate relationship between theta and gamma patterns is shown by the phase-locking of gamma waves to the theta pattern as well as by the relationship between changes in theta frequency (6–10 Hz) and gamma frequency (40–100 Hz).

The behavioral significance of the hippocampal gamma pattern is not known.[46] However, given the hypothesized relationship between features of the input signal (the "binding" problem) and gamma oscillations in the sensory areas of the neocortex[35] one may speculate that a transiently emerging high coherence of gamma oscillations in the neocortex and hippocampus may signal the binding of the perceived and stored attributes of objects and events.

SHARP WAVES AND HIGH FREQUENCY OSCILLATION (200 HZ)

At the end of exploration, decreased activity of subcortical inputs will terminate theta activity. The absence of subcortical activation will change the firing properties of hippocampal pyramidal cells with an increased tendency for burst firing. At the network level, this change is expressed as sharp waves (SPW) of 40 to 120-ms duration. SPWs occur irregularly during slow wave sleep, awake immobility, drinking, eating, face washing, and grooming.[12,19,79] The frequency of SPWs ranges from 0.02 to 3/sec. Cellular correlates of theta and SPWs are characteristically different. The firing pattern of pyramidal cells changes substantially at the cessation of theta-associated exploratory behavior. Importantly, groups of pyramidal cells in CA1-3, subiculum and deep layers of the entorhinal cortex now fire in synchronous population bursts associated with the field SPW (Figures 4 and 5). Furthermore, pyramidal cells fire complex-spikes (calcium spikes) more often during SPW states than during theta.[12] SPWs in CA1 region reflect synchronous excitation (EPSP) of pyramidal cells by the Schaffer collaterals of CA3 neurons.

In conjunction with the stratum radiatum SPWs, fast field oscillations ("ripples") are invariably present in the CA1 pyramidal layer.[21] Ripples consist of packets of 5 to 15 sinusoid waves with approximately 200-Hz intraburst frequency. The amplitude maxima of the ripples are found in the pyramidal layer with polarity reversal in stratum radiatum, suggesting that the main current source of the ripples is the synapses that terminate on the somata of pyramidal cells.

(a)

(b)

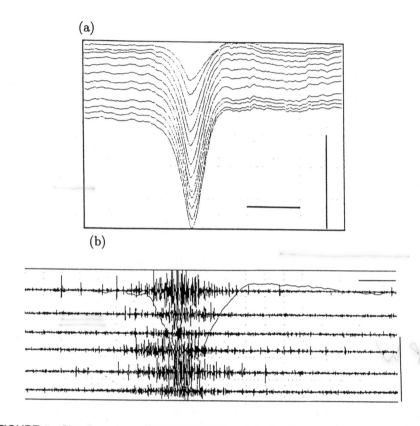

FIGURE 5   Simultaneous recording of SPW activity in the stratum radiatum of the CA1
region (a) and pyramidal cell activity (b) along the longitudinal axis of the hippocampus.
Electrode spacing was 300 μm. Note synchronous firing of multiple pyramidal cells
around the negative peak of the locally derived SPW from a stratum radiatum electrode.
The amplitude variation of SPWs (a) is due to slight differences of the electrode
locations in the dorsoventral axis. Averages of 50 repetitions. Calibrations: 2 mV;
100 msec (a), 50 msec (b).

Simultaneous recordings from several dozen CA1 pyramidal cells reveals that
the probability of discharge of any given cell was significantly greater during the
negative peaks of the oscillatory field potential than on the positive peaks (Figures 6 and 7). In contrast to CA1 pyramidal cells, a group of physiologically identified interneurons fired rhythmically at ripple frequency. Simultaneous recording
from multiple sites along the longitudinal axis of the hippocampus (2.4 mm) showed

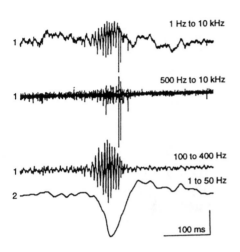

1 Hz to 10 kHz

500 Hz to 10 kHz

100 to 400 Hz

1 to 50 Hz

100 ms

FIGURE 6   Fast field oscillation in the CA1 region of the dorsal hippocampus. Simultaneous recordings from the CA1 pyramidal layer (electrode 1) and stratum radiatum (electrode 2; bottom trace). Uppermost trace of electrode 1 is wide band recording (1 Hz–10 kHz). Second and third traces are digitally filtered derivatives of the wide band trace: unit activity (500 Hz–10 kHz) and fast field oscillation (100 Hz–400 Hz). Note simultaneous occurrence of fast field oscillation, unit discharges, and sharp wave (2). Electrode 2 was 200 μm below the pyramidal layer. Calibrations: 0.5 mV (trace 1), 0.25 mV (traces 2 and 3) and 1.0 mV (trace 4). (Reprinted with permission from Buzsáki et al.[21])

very high coherence of the extracellularly recorded fast oscillation with zero mean time lag. These observations indicated that the fast oscillation is not simply a sum of nearby fast discharging cells but an emerging pattern of a large number of interactive pyramidal cells. During the fast network oscillation, pyramidal cells at distant locations within the CA1 region can discharge with a synchrony of better than 3 msec.

Intracellular observations of SPW and fast ripples in the anesthetized rat reveals that they correspond to strong dendritic depolarization and somatic GABAA-receptor-mediated hyperpolarizing potentials, respectively.[89] From these and other observations, we suggested that the high-frequency oscillation is a network-driven rhythm with critical participation of inhibitory interneurons. During the SPW burst the Schaffer collateral system also activate interneurons in a feedforward manner.[11] This barrage of depolarizing inputs will sustain a depolarizing plateau in the interneurons. Such a sustained (20 to 80 msec) depolarization may activate voltage-dependent currents that produce repetitive firing and membrane oscillations in these interneurons at ripple frequency. We speculate that the primary event of the high-frequency oscillation is a voltage-dependent fast firing of interneurons brought about by the depolarizing CA3 input and the feedback excitation of these cells by the recurrent collaterals of the CA1 pyramidal neurons. Phase-locked firing of a large enough number of interneurons would then produce a hyperpolarizing rhythm in pyramidal cells superimposed on the coexisting depolarization brought about by the excitatory CA3 input.

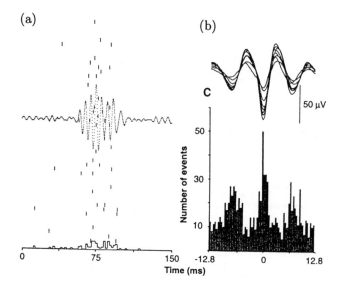

FIGURE 7 High-frequency oscillation of the CA1 network. (a) Fast field oscillation-associated discharges of 50 simultaneously recorded pyramidal neurons by a 24-site silicon probe. Middle trace is an average of simultaneously recorded field activity (100–400 Hz) from eight sites. Vertical lines are discriminated actions potentials. In this single trace only 32 of the 50 units emitted action potentials. Histogram presents averaged momentary firing of pyramidal cells. (b) Superimposed averaged traces from eight different recording sites (maximum interelectrode distance was 1.8 mm). Averaged traces are virtually synchronized. (c) Cross-correlogram of all 50 units with the negative peaks of fast field oscillatory waves as time zero. Time scale is as in (b). Neurons fire on the negative peaks of fast field oscillatory cycles. (Reprinted with permission from Buzsáki et al.[21])

Recently, we began to investigate neuronal activity in retrohippocampal structures, including the entorhinal cortex during hippocampal SPW activity.[25,26] We found that deep-layer retrohippocampal (entorhinal and presubicular) and subicular neurons all exhibit a concurrent increase in activity during SPWs, while superficial-layer neurons exhibited no alteration in activity during the SPW. In contrast, neurons in layers I to III of the entorhinal cortex were virtually silent or fired independent of SPW and increased their firing rates during theta.[62,67] From these studies we concluded that theta and SPW states of the same hippocampal neurons correlate with the activity of distinct neuronal populations in the entorhinal cortex. Neurons that give rise to the perforant path (layers II and III) are active predominantly during theta, whereas neurons in layer V, the main output cells of the entorhinal cortex, are activated mostly in association with hippocampal SPW.

These findings indicate that the hippocampal output may exert a powerful impact on distant neocortical areas during SPW bursts.

SHARP WAVE-ASSOCIATED POPULATION BURSTS AS A PHYSIOLOGICAL CANDIDATE OF LTP

Whatever electrophysiological patterns may eventually prove to be the substrate of LTP, they should meet the basic requirements for the elicitation of LTP, such as the necessity of strong synaptic bombardment, preferably in bursts, and cooperative activity of a number of converging afferent fibers.[30,29,47,56] From the behavioral point of view these conditions must be present at times when an important behavior that led to reward or punishment is to be reinforced.[34,38,73,75] As will be discussed below the cellular events underlying hippocampal SPWs may satisfy these requirements.[19]

The three main variables for the induction of LTP are intensity, frequency, and pattern. The intensity of synaptic drive during the SPW may be estimated by the firing frequency of interneurons, since the discharge rate of fast-firing interneurons is correlated with their depolarization. Bursts of action potentials above 600/sec have been observed in interneurons in association with SPWs.[12] Because LTP magnitude is directly proportional to the depolarization of the post-synaptic membrane,[10,53,56] this finding suggests that the induction of LTP in pyramidal cells is most likely during the SPW-burst.

The overall frequency of synaptic inputs on a given pyramidal cell during the SPW-bursts is difficult to estimate. The highest frequency in a given afferent fiber is equal to the frequency of action potentials in pyramidal cells during a complex-spike burst of 2 to 7 spikes and is in the range of 50 to 300 Hz.[68] This repetition rate is similar to the frequency of the high-frequency field oscillation (200-Hz ripples) and the optimum frequency range for the induction of LTP.[29] Pyramidal cells often fire complex-spike bursts (i.e., a combination of Na^+ and calcium spikes) during SPWs but they rarely do during theta-behaviors.[12,78]

In summary, complex-spike (burst) firing and large depolarization of a group of pyramidal cells, and convergent coactivation of these neurons during the SPW-population burst make this neuronal pattern a likely candidate for producing long-lasting synaptic modifications in the hippocampal circuitry. A formal model of this hypothesis will be elaborated below.

TEACHING INPUTS: DO THEY EXIST IN THE HIPPOCAMPUS?

An essential element in the Hebbian model of association is a teaching input (supervised learning process). The teaching or detonator input to a postsynaptic cell possesses two main features: (a) it always discharges the postsynaptic neuron, and (b) it is nonmodifiable.[54,58] A major problem with the concept of the teaching input is that most hippocampal excitatory synapses are both extremely weak and rather unreliable[57,61] and to date, all synapses examined in the intrahippocampal circuitry proved plastic.[10]

We suggest that separate detonator synapses neither exist in the hippocampus nor are necessary for synaptic plasticity. Instead, we hypothesize that the strong convergence of excitatory actions on some cells of the neuronal network from otherwise "normal" afferents may produce depolarizations of sufficient magnitude and duration in those neurons and trigger the LTP mechanism. Thus, we conceive the detonator or teaching "synapse" as a collective property of the network and propose that the "strong input" requirements of the Hebbian model may be substituted with the population excitatory events underlying hippocampal SPW.

SYNAPTIC MODIFICATIONS DURING SHARP WAVES

In an attempt to answer the question whether the same or different sets of neurons contribute to successive SPW-bursts, we tried to influence the structure of the population bursts by afferent stimulation. We have described elsewhere that in rats with fimbria-fornix lesion, large-amplitude (up to 8 mV) short-duration EEG spikes occur spontaneously and their incidence may be influenced by stimulation of the perforant path.[18,20] We used multichannel recordings from the CA1 area to study how high-frequency trains affect population bursts along the longitudinal axis of the hippocampus.

In Figure 8 we illustrate such an experiment. First, evoked potentials were recorded in response to perforant path stimulation. Next, high-frequency conditioning trains were delivered to the perforant path and the spontaneously occurring EEG spikes were detected following the trains. We found that as a result of the high-frequency stimulation the shape and spatial distribution of the EEG spikes became very similar to the evoked responses. A major difference between the evoked and spontaneous patterns was the lack of the volume-conducted dentate potential in the spontaneous EEG spikes. These findings are interpreted by assuming that the perforant path conditioning trains led to the potentiation of a subgroup of CA3 neurons which, in turn, became the "initiators" of the subsequently occurring population bursts. This explains why the spontaneously occurring population events became identical with the evoked ones.

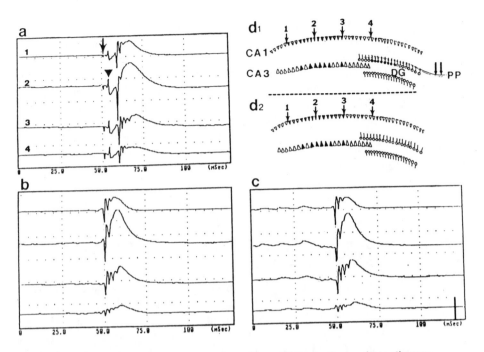

FIGURE 8 Stimulation-induced EEG spikes. Recording electrodes (1 to 4) were positioned in the pyramidal layer of CA1 along the longitudinal axis of the hippocampus. Distance between electrodes: 500 μm. In this animal the subcortical input to the hippocampus were removed by aspiration. Single pulse stimulation of the perforant path (arrows in (a) and (d1); PP) evoked monosynaptic population spikes in the dentate gyrus and trisynaptic responses in CA1. Triangle in (a) indicates volume-conducted population spike from the dentate gyrus. Following high-frequency tetanization of the perforant path (8 times 200 Hz, 100-ms bursts) large-amplitude spontaneous EEG spikes occurred after the trains ((b): 1 min; (c): 5 min). Note virtually identical configuration of the evoked responses (a) and spontaneously occurring EEG spikes (b, c) in all four leads. Note also the absence of the dentate component in the EEG spikes. (d1, d2):. Possible circuit diagram of the events in (a) to (c). Single pulse stimulation of a subset of perforant path (PP in (d1)) sequentially activated subgroups of granule cells, CA3 and CA1 pyramidal neurons (black circles and black triangles). Tetanization of PP-induced heterosynaptic potentiation of the recurrent axon collaterals of the CA3 cell group. These potentiated CA3 pyramidal cells then served as "initiator" neurons of the subsequent spontaneous population bursts (d2). Postsynaptic activation of CA1 pyramidal neurons (mainly in the vicinity of electrode 2) by the bursting CA3 cells resulted in EEG spikes. Potentiation of a subpopulation of CA3 pyramidal neurons (initiator cells) is thus assumed to be responsible for triggering the uniform EEG spikes. Calibration: 3 mV. (Reprinted with permission from Buzsáki.[19])

In order to explore the possible involvement of SPWs in physiologically occurring LTP, we artificially induced population bursts in the hippocampal slice preparation. Population bursts in the CA3 region were triggered by single pulse stimulation of the Schaffer collaterals in the presence of local application of bicuculline onto the CA3 pyramidal cells. The single volleys evoked a series of small amplitude spikes in the CA3 region, similar to the population bursts during the SPW. The population bursts in CA3 induced a large increase of the population spike of the test responses in CA1.[16] The potentiation outlasted the local effects of bicuculline on the CA3 pyramidal cells and thus represented a true long-term synaptic change.

SYNAPTIC MODIFICATION DURING THETA: ROLE OF DENTATE GRANULE CELLS

It has been repeatedly demonstrated that destruction of granule cells prevents an animal's ability to learn a spatial task. Based on these behavioral studies it was suggested that the cause of the learning impairment is the interruption of the trisynaptic circuitry and the consequent inability of the remaining hippocampus to process spatial information. This notion, however, has been recently challenged by a series of experiments by McNaughton et al.[59] They examined the spatial properties of CA1 and CA3 pyramidal neurons in a radial arm maze after colchicine-destruction of nearly all granule cells. Contrast to expectation, the absence of granule cells had remarkably little effect on the spatial selectivity of "place cell" discharge in the maze, as compared to recordings from control animals. The results of these experiments suggest that (a) granule cells are not required for the maintenance of spatial properties of pyramidal cells, and (b) spatial information is conveyed directly to the pyramidal cells via the perforant path bypassing the dentate gyrus.

A conclusion of these behavioral and physiological experiments involving the destruction of principal cells of the dentate gyrus is that granule cells are not necessary for providing spatial information to the hippocampus but are essential for the acquisition of a new spatial task. A logical progression of thought is to assume that the functional role of granule cells is to assist induction of this plastic process in hippocampal pyramidal cells.

How might granule cells change the interactive patterns of pyramidal cells during the acquisition of a new spatial task so that the animal can remember the new contingencies? As discussed earlier, granule cells contact CA3 pyramidal cells via the mossy synapse, one of the most powerful excitatory synapses in the central nervous system. Intuitively, a powerful input such as the mossy fiber afferents of granule cells can efficiently and selectively alter the functional connectivity of the CA3 network. Recent *in vitro* experiments suggest that this is indeed possible. When single pulses delivered to the association fibers of CA3 pyramidal cells were coupled with strong trains of high-frequency bursts to the mossy fibers at theta frequency, a lasting potentiation of the associational terminals was observed. The potentiation effect, however, was absent or the synapses were even depressed when stimuli to the two afferent systems were delivered out-of- phase.[23] Thus, functional connections among the CA3 neurons can be modified without tetanizing the associational pathways, provided that a tetanic input from the mossy terminals temporarily overlaps with the activity of the recurrent, associational fibers of the CA3 network.

At this point it is worthwhile to reiterate some of the physiological observations made on granule cells and pyramidal cells in the awake animal. As discussed above during exploratory activity the dentate hilar region provides tetanic output in the gamma band (40–100 Hz) to the CA3 network. Both granule cells and CA3 pyramidal cells discharge with a high probability on the positive phase of theta.[12,32] Therefore the temporal conjunction between the granule cell bursting and CA3 pyramidal neuronal cell discharges is exactly the same as that required for the modification of synaptic efficacy of the associational fibers in the above-discussed *in vitro* experiment. Specificity of the connections to be modified is ensured by the fact that only those pyramidal cells fire during exploratory behaviors which coherently determine the spatial position of the animal. Specificity may be aided further if entorhinal afferents and subgroups of granule cells selectively address the same CA3 pyramidal neurons.

At this point, three issues must be addressed. First is whether the synaptic modification during theta is sufficiently strong for holding memory traces for long time periods. Second, how will SPW-bursts affect the experience-induced altered neuronal network? Third, how does the memory trace get transferred from the hippocampus to the neocortex for permanent storage?

TWO-STAGE MODEL OF MEMORY-RELATED PLASTICITY IN THE HIPPOCAMPAL FORMATION

In the context of synaptic plasticity, a key issue is the degree of presynaptic convergence in a given time window in order to achieve large enough postsynaptic depolarization.[10] In the intact brain this can be approximated by the number of synchronously firing cells and the average number of action potentials emitted by the individual presynaptic neurons.

Several investigators have suggested that plastic changes of hippocampal synapses occur during exploration-associated theta activity.[44,65,66,70] As discussed above, at the termination of theta-related behaviors hippocampal SPW and associated high-frequency network oscillation of CA1 pyramidal cells replace the theta rhythm. SPWs are associated with the most synchronous population bursts of pyramidal neurons in the intact hippocampus. The problem therefore is why simultaneously bursting cells during SPWs do not induce random synaptic modifications and why SPW bursts do not attenuate or erase LTP-like changes brought about by theta bursts. Furthermore, LTP is not an all-or-none phenomenon and several stages of the LTP process with different biochemical machineries have been recognized during the past several years.[10] The logical progress of thought therefore is to hypothesize that synaptic plasticity *in vivo* also requires several stages.

We suggest that the behavior-dependent electrical changes in the hippocampus (theta and SPW-associated states) might subserve a two-stage process of information storage. In essence, the hypothesized routine is a two-step process: (1) explore and experience (on-line, theta) and (2) rest and consolidate (off-line, SPW). Granule cells are thus essential for "refreshing" the functional connections in the CA3 network during theta-associated behaviors. Viewed from this perspective both theta and SPW states are obligatory for normal memory trace formation (Figure 9).

We hypothesize that creation of the long-lasting form of memory trace begins at the termination of the exploratory (theta) state, with the onset of hippocampal SPW-bursts.[19] As discussed earlier, the initiator cells[60] of the self-generating population bursts are the very ones that were most strongly potentiated before the termination of the exploratory state.

We assume that recurrent collateral excitation in the CA3 region spreads in a hierarchical fashion: the most excitable cells fire first followed by less excitable ones, that is in the reversed order to that in which they were potentiated during exploration. As the population burst spreads, the maximal effect of the reverberating excitation will converge on the initiator cells and progressively less convergent excitation will occur on those neurons which were more weakly potentiated during exploration; again in the reversed order. These latter mechanisms ensure that only those neurons will be potentiated which carry information about the most recent events.

A subset of neurons in CA1, on which the initiator cells of the CA3 population burst converge, will be depolarized substantially more during the SPW-bursts than their neighbors. Their Schaffer synapses therefore will undergo LTP. These CA1 cells are the same neurons which discharged maximally during the exploratory stage. For example, at the termination of exploratory behavior a particular set of spatial units continues to discriminate the rat's position, but now firing of these cells will coincide with SPW-correlated population bursts. Due to the powerful depolarization of these spatial units, brought about by the population burst, their Schaffer synapses may undergo long-term potentiation.

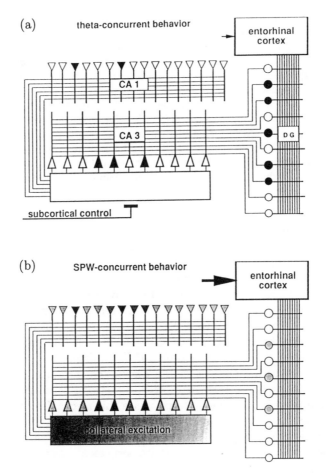

FIGURE 9 Two-stage model of memory storage. The static schemes represent activity in the hippocampal network just before the termination of exploratory activity or REM sleep (a) and SPW bursts (b). During theta-associated behavior the entorhinal input activates some selected CA3 and CA1 pyramidal cells directly (connections not shown) and/or via the granule cells (black circles). This activation will lead to the discharge of some pyramidal cells (black triangles). Some of these CA3 cells will receive concurrent activation from the perforant path, mossy fibers and their recurrent axon collaterals. Such a Hebbian conjunction is postulated to lead to transient potentiation of the synapses of the recurrent axon collaterals. (b) After the termination of the theta state, subcortical activation of inhibitory interneurons (not shown) is decreased, which leads to the emergence of CA3 population bursts and concurrent SPW in the CA1 region. The SPW-associated burst is initiated by the neurons with the highest excitability: these are the neurons that were potentiated last before the termination of the theta state (black triangles). During the SPW population event the excitation wave will spread (continued)

FIGURE 9   (continued) from the burst initiators to progressively less excitable ones, that is to those cells which were potentiated at progressively earlier times prior to the termination of the theta state (gray triangles). Neurons of the burst initiator group (i.e., information bearing cells) will be depolarized longest and strongest during the SPW event. Consequently, these neurons will further increase the probability of their joint discharge during subsequent SPW bursts. The Hebbian conjunction between presynaptic activity (from other burst-initiator partners) and the strong postsynaptic depolarization may trigger LTP in the synapses of the CA3 recurrent axons and in Schaffer collateral synapses on the most depolarized CA1 neurons. SPW-concurrent activation of CA1 pyramidal cells will provide a powerful excitatory output from the hippocampus to the entorhinal cortex. Such a mechanism is hypothesized to transfer the memory trace out of the hippocampus. (Reprinted with permission from Buzsáki.[19])

The above-outlined sequential potentiation mechanisms are assumed to ensure that discharge of a given set of entorhinal neurons during subsequent visits to the same part of the maze (recall) will reactivate the same subsets of neurons in CA3 and CA1. The ascending-descending hierarchy of neuronal firing during the SPW-associated burst therefore is precisely determined by the recent past of the neural network. The rules of burst initiation and reconvergent excitation, subserved by the anatomical-physiological organization of the CA3 region, ensure that the synchronized events carry biologically meaningful information. The model assigns an important role to the CA1 circuitry, as well. SPW bursts in the CA3 network will trigger a fast network oscillation in the CA1 region. The tetanizing output of the active CA1 pyramidal cells, in turn, will produce a strong depolarization in their retrohippocampal targets. As demonstrated above this mechanism will powerfully discharge deep-layer neurons of the entorhinal cortex and potentially exert an impact on other neocortical targets. Such a mechanism may serve to transfer the memory trace out from the hippocampus to its permanent site in the neocortex.

ACKNOWLEDGMENTS

This work was supported by NIH, the Human Frontier Science Program, and the Whitehall Foundation (G. B.), and ADRDA (J. J. C).

REFERENCES

1. Alonso, A., and R. R. Llinas. "Subthreshold Na$^+$-Dependent Theta-like Rhythmicity in Stellate Cells of Entorhinal Cortex Layer II." *Nature* **342** (1989): 175–177.
2. Amaral, D. G. "A Golgi Study of Cell Types in the Hilar Region of the Hippocampus in the Rat." *J. Comp. Neurol.* **182** (1978): 851–914.
3. Auerbach, L. "Nervenendigungen in den Centralorganen." *Neurol. Zentralbl.* **17** (1898): 445–454.
4. Baranyi, A., and O. Feher. "Synaptic Facilitation Requires Paired Activation of Convergent Pathways in the Neocortex." *Nature* **290** (1981): 413–415.
5. Barrionuevo, G., and T. H. Brown. "Associative Long-Term Potentiation in Hippocampal Slices." *Proc. Natl. Acad. Sci. USA* **80** (1983): 7347–7351.
6. Bland, B. H. "Physiology and Pharmacology of Hippocampal Formation Theta Rhythms." *Prog. Neurobiol.* **26** (1990): 1–54.
7. Bragin, A., G. Jandó, Z. Nádasdy, Z. Horvath, and G. Buzsáki. "The Dentate Spike: A New Network Pattern Reflecting Interneuronal Synchrony." *Soc. Neurosci. Abst.* **141(11)** (1992).
8. Bragin, A., G. Jandó, Z. Nádasdy, J. Hetke, K. Wise, and G. Buzsáki. "Gamma (40–100 Hz) Oscillation in the Hippocampus of the Behaving Rat." *J. Neurosci.* **15** (1995): 47–60.
9. Bliss, T. V. P., and T. Lømo. "Long-Lasting Potentiation of Synaptic Transmission in the Dentate Area of the Anaesthetized Rabbit Following Stimulation of the Perforant Path." *J. Physiology (London)* **232** (1973): 331–356.
10. Bliss, T. V. P., and G. L. Collingridge. "A Synaptic Model of Memory: Long-Term Potentiation in the Hippocampus." *Nature* **361** (1993): 31–39.
11. Buzsáki, G., and E. Eidelberg. "Direct Afferent Excitation and Long-Term Potentiation of Hippocampal Interneurons." *J. Neurophysiology* **48** (1982): 597–607.
12. Buzsáki, G., L. Leung, and C. H. Vanderwolf. "Cellular Bases of Hippocampal EEG in the Behaving Rat." *Brain Res. Rev.* **6** (1983): 139–171.
13. Buzsáki, G. "Feed-Forward Inhibition in the Hippocampal Formation." *Prog. Neurobiol.* **22** (1984): 131–153.
14. Buzsáki, G. "Hippocampal Sharp Waves: Their Origin and Significance." *Brain Res.* **398** (1986): 242–252.
15. Buzsáki, G., J. Czopf, I. Kondakor, and L. Kellenyi. "Laminar Distribution of Hippocampal Rhythmic Slow Activity (RSA) in the Behaving Rat: Current Source Density Analysis, Effects of Urethane and Atropine." *Brain Res.* **365** (1986): 125–137.
16. Buzsáki, G., H. L. Haas, and E. G. Anderson. "Long-Term Potentiation Induced by Physiologically Relevant Stimulus Patterns." *Brain Res.* **435** (1987): 331–333.

17. Buzsáki, G., T. G. Bickford, G. Ponomareff, L. J. Thal, R. J. Mandel, and F. H. Gage. "Nucleus Basalis and Thalamic Control of Neocortical Activity in the Freely Moving Rat." *J. Neuroscience* **8** (1988): 4007–4026.

18. Buzsáki, G., G. Ponomareff, F. Bayardo, T. Shaw, and F. H. Gage "Suppression and Induction of Epileptic Activity by Brain Grafts. " *Proc. Natl. Acad. Sci. USA* **85** (1988): 9327–9330.

19. Buzsáki, G. "A Two-Stage Model of Memory Trace Formation: A Role for 'Noisy' Brain States." *Neuroscience* **31** (1989): 551–570.

20. Buzsáki, G., G. L. Ponomareff, F. Bayardo, R. Ruiz, and F. H. Gage. "Neuronal Activity in the Subcortically Denervated Hippocampus: A Chronic Model for Epilepsy." *Neuroscience* **28** (1989): 527–538.

21. Buzsáki, G., Z. Horvath, R. Urioste, J. Hetke, and K. Wise. "High-Frequency Network Oscillation in the Hippocampus." *Science* **256** (1992): 1025–1027.

22. Charpak, S., D. Pare, and R. R. Llinás. "Entorhinal Cortex (EC) Generates 40-Hz Hippocampal Oscillations." *Soc. Neurosci. Abst.* **386.5** (1992).

23. Chattarji, S., P. K. Stanton, and T. J. Sejnowski. "Commissural Synapses, but not Mossy Fiber Synapses, in Hippocampal Field CA3 Exhibit Associative Long-Term Potentiation and Depression." *Brain Res.* **495** (1989): 145–150.

24. Christian, E. P., and F. E. Dudek. "Electrophysiological Evidence from Glutamate Microapplications for Local Excitatory Circuits in the CA1 Area of Rat Hippocampal Slices." *J. Neurophysiology* **59** (1988): 110–123.

25. Chrobak, J. J., R. Urioste, and G. Buzsáki. "Hippocampal-Retrohippocampal Interactions During Sharp Waves." *Soc. Neurosci. Abstr.* **141.13** (1992).

26. Chrobak, J. J., and G. Buzsáki. "Selective Activation of Deep Layer (V-VI)Retrohippocampal Cortical Neurons During Hippocampal Sharp Waves in the Behaving Net." *J. Neurosci.* **14** (1994): 6160–6170.

27. Churchland, P., and T. Sejnowski. *The Computational Brain.* Cambridge, MA: MIT Press, 1992.

28. Cole, A. E., and R. A. Nicoll. "Characterization of a Slow Cholinergic Postsynaptic Potential Recorded *in vitro* from Rat Hippocampoal Pyramidal Cells." *J. Physiology (London)* **352** (1984): 173–188.

29. Douglas, R. M. "Long-Lasting Synaptic Potentiation in the Dentate Gyrus Following Brief High Frequency Stimulation." *Brain Res.* **126** (1977): 361–365.

30. Douglas, R. M., and G. V. Goddard. "Long-Term Potentiation of the Perforant Path-Granule Cell Synapse in the Rat Hippocampus." *Brain Res.* **86** (1975): 205–215.

31. Eichenbaum, H., and T. Otto. "The Hippocampus—What Does It Do?" *Behav. Neural Biol.* **57** (1992): 2–36.

32. Fox, S. E., and J. B. Ranck, Jr. "Electrophysiological Characteristics of Hippocampal Complex-Spike Cells and Theta Cells." *Exp. Brain Res.* **41** (1981): 299–313.

33. Freund, T. F., and M. Antal. "GABA-Containing Neurons in the Septum Control Inhibitory Interneurons in the Hippocampus." *Nature* **336** (1988): 170–173.
34. Glickman, S. W., and B. B. Schiff. "A Biological Theory of Reinforcement." *Psychol. Rev.* **74** (1967): 81–105.
35. Gray, C. M. "Rhythmic Activity in Neuronal Systems: Insights into Integrative Function." In *1992 Lectures in Complex Systems*, edited by L. Nadel and D. Stein. SFI Studies in the Sciences of Complexity, Lect. Vol. V, 89–161. Reading, MA: Addison-Wesley, 1993.
36. Haas, H. L., and A. Konnerth "Histamine and Noradrenaline Decrease Calcium-Activated Potassium Conductance in Hippocampal Pyramidal Cells." *Nature (London)* **302** (1983): 432–434.
37. Hebb, D. O. *Organization of Behavior.* Wiley, New York, 1949.
38. Hull, C. L. *Principles of behavior.* New York: Appleton-Century-Crofts, 1943.
39. Ishizuka, N., J. Weber, and D. Amaral. "Organization of Intrahippocampal Projections Originating from CA3 Pyramidal Cells in the Rat." *J. Comp. Neurol.* **295** (1990): 580–623.
40. Jung, M. W., and B. L. McNaughton. "Spatial Selectivity of Unit Activity in the Hippocampal Granular Layer." *Hippocampus* **3** (1993): 165–182.
41. Kelso, S. R., A. H. Ganong, and T. H. Brown. "Hebbian Synapses in the Hippocampus." *Proc. Natl. Acad. Sci. (USA)* **83** (1993): 5326–5330.
42. Kohonen, T. *Self-Organization and Associative Memory.* Berlin: Springer-Verlag, 1984.
43. Konorski, J. *Conditioned Reflexes and Neuronal Organization.* Cambridge: Cambridge University Press, 1948.
44. Larson, J., and G. Lynch. "Induction of Synaptic Potentiation in the Hippocampus by Patterned Stimulation Involves Two Events." *Science* **232** (1986): 985–988.
45. Leung, L. S., and C. C. Yim. "Intrinsic Membrane Potential Oscillations in Hippocampal Neurons *in vitro*." *Brain Res.* **553** (1991): 261–274.
46. Leung, L. S. "Fast (beta) Rhythms in the Hippocampus: A Review." *Hippocampus* **2** (1992): 93–98.
47. Levy, W. B., and O. Steward. "Synapses as Associative Memory Elements in the Hippocampal Formation." *Brain Res.* **175** (1979): 233–245.
48. Li, X.-G., P. Somogyi, A. Ylinen, and G. Buzsáki. "The Hippocampal CA3 Network: An *in vivo* Intracellular Labeling Study." *J. Comp. Neurol.* **339** (1994): 181–208.
49. Llinás, R. R. "The Intrinsic Electrophysiological Properties of Mammalian Neurons: Insight into Central Nervous System." *Science* **242** (1988): 1654–1664.
50. Lorente de Nó, R. "Studies of the Structure of the Cerebral Cortex: II. Continuation of the Study of the Ammonic System. " *J. Psychol. Neurol.* **46** (1934): 113–177.

51. Lynch, G. *Synapses, Circuits, and the Beginnings of Memory.* Cambridge, MA: MIT Press, 1986.
52. Madison, D. V., and R. A. Nicoll. "Actions of Noradrenaline Recorded Intracellularly in Rat Hippocampal CA1 Pyramidal Neurons, *in vitro.*" *J. Physiology (London)* **321** (1986): 175–177.
53. Malinow, R., and J. P. Miller. "Postsynaptic Hyperpolarization During Conditioning Reversibly Blocks Induction of Long-Term Potentiation." *Nature (London)* **321** (1986): 175–177.
54. Marr, D. "Simple Memory: A Theory for Archicortex." *Phil. Trans. Roy. Soc. (London), Series B* **262** (1971): 23–81.
55. McCormick, D. A., and D. A. Prince. "Mechanisms of Action of Acetylcholine in the Guinea Pig Cerebral Cortex *in vitro.*" *J. Neurophysiology* **375** (1986): 169–194.
56. McNaughton, B. L., R. M. Douglas, and G. V. Goddard. "Synaptic Enhancement in Fascia Dentata: Cooperativity Among Coactive Afferents." *Brain Res.* **157** (1978): 277–293.
57. McNaughton, B. L., C. A. Barnes, and P. Andersen. "Synaptic Efficacy and EPSP Summation in Granule Cells of Rat Fascia Dentata Studied *in vitro.*" *J. Neurophysiology* **46** (1981): 952–966.
58. McNaughton, B. L., and R. G. M. Morris. "Hippocampal Synaptic Enhancement and Information Storage Within a Distributed Memory System." *Trends Neurosci.* **10** (1987): 408–415.
59. McNaughton, B. L., C. A. Barnes, J. Meltzer, and R. J. Sutherland. "Hippocampal Granule Cells are Necessary for Normal Spatial Learning but Not for Spatially-Selective Pyramidal Cell Discharge." *Exp. Brain Res.* **76** (1989): 485–496.
60. Miles, R., and R. K. S. Wong. "Single Neurons Can Initiate Synchronized Population Discharge in the Hippocampus." *Nature* **306** (1983): 371–373.
61. Miles, R., and R. K. S. Wong. "Excitatory Synaptic Interactions Between CA3 Neurons in the Guinea-Pig Hippocampus." *J. Physiology (London)* **373** (1986): 397–418.
62. Mitchell, S. J., and J. B. Ranck, Jr. "Generation of Theta Rhythm in Medial Entorhinal Cortex of Freely Moving Rats." *Brain Res.* **189** (1980): 49–66.
63. Mizumori, S. J. Y., B. L. McNaughton, C. A. Barnes, and K. B. Fox. "Preserved Spatial Coding in Hippocampal CA1 Pyramidal Cells During Reversible Suppression of CA3 Output: Evidence for Pattern Completion in Hippocampus." *J. Neuroscience* **9** (1989): 3915–3928.
64. O'Keefe, J., and L. Nadel. *The Hippocampus as a Cognitive Map.* Oxford: Clarendon, 1978.
65. Otto, T., H. Eichenbaum, S. I. Wiener, and C. G. Wible. "Learning-Related Patterns of CA1 Spike Trains Parallel Stimulation Parameters Optimal for Inducing Hippocampal Long-Term Potentiation." *Hippocampus* **1** (1991): 181–192.

66. Pavlides, C., Y. J. Greenstein, M. Grudman, and J. Winson. "Long-Term Potentiation in the Dentate Gyrus is Induced Preferentially on the Positive Phase of Theta Rhythm." *Brain Res.* **439** (1988): 383–387.
67. Quirk, G. J., R. U. Muller, J. L. Kubie, and J. B. Ranck, Jr. "The Positional Firing Properties of Medial Entorhinal Neurons: Description and Comparison with Hippocampal Place Cells." *J. Neuroscience* **12** (1992): 1945–1963.
68. Ramón y Cajal, S. *Textura del Systema Nervioso del Hombre y de los Vertebrados*, 3 vols. Madrid: Moya, 1889–1904.
69. Ranck, J. B., Jr. "Studies on Single Neurons in Dorsal Hippocampal Formation and Septum in Unrestrained Rats. I. Behavioral Correlates and Firing Repertoires." *Exp. Neurol.* **42** (1973): 461–531.
70. Rose, G., and T. V. Dunviddie. "Induction of Hippocampal Long-Term Potentiation Using Physiologically Patterned Stimulation." *Neurosci. Lett.* **69** (1986): 244–248.
71. Sastry, B. R., J. W. Goh, and A. Auyeung. "Associative Induction of Post-tetanic and Long-Term Potentiation in CA1 Neurons of Rat Hippocampus." *Science* **232** (1986): 988–990.
72. Schaffer, K. "Beitrag zur Histologie der Ammonshorn Formation." *Arch. Mikrosk. Anat.* **39** (1892): 611–632.
73. Sheffield, F. D., T. B. Roby, and B. A. Campbell. "Drive Reduction Versus Consummatory Behavior as Determinants of Reinforcement." *J. Comp. Physiol. Psychol.* **47** (1954): 349–368.
74. Sherrington, C. S. "The Central Nervous System." In *A Textbook of Physiology*, Pt. 3, edited by M. Foster. London: McMillan, 1897.
75. Skinner, B. F. *The Behavior of Organisms.* New York: Appleton-Century-Crofts, 1938.
76. Stewart, M., and S. E. Fox. "Do Septal Neurons Pace the Hippocampal Theta Rhythm?" *Trends Neurosci.* **13** (1990): 163–168.
77. Stumpf, C. "The Fast Component in the Electrical Activity of Rabbit's Hippocampus." *Electroencephal. Clin. Neurophysiol.* **18** (1985): 477–486.
78. Suzuki, S. S., and G. K. Smith. "Burst Characteristics of Hippocampal Complex Spike Cells in the Awake Rat." *Exp. Neurol.* **89** (1985): 90–95.
79. Suzuki, S. S., and G. K. Smith. "Spontaneous EEG Spikes in the Normal Hippocampus: I. Behavioral Correlates, Laminar Profiles and Bilateral Synchrony." *Electroencephal. Clin. Neurophysiol.* **67** (1987): 438–359.
80. Swanson, L. W., and C. Kohler. "Anatomical Evidence for Direct Projections from the Entorhinal Area to the Entire Cortical Mantle in the Rat." *J. Neuroscience* **6** (1986): 3010–3023.
81. Tamamaki, N., and Y. Nojyo. "Crossing Fiber Arrays in the Rat Hippocampus as Demonstrated by Three-Dimensional Reconstruction." *J. Comp. Neurol.* **303** (1991): 435–442.
82. Thompson, L. T., and P. J. Best. "Place Cell and Silent Cells in the Hippocampus of Freely-Behaving Rats." *J. Neuroscience* **9** (1989): 2832–2390.

83. Thomson, A. M., and S. Radpour. "Excitatory Connections Between CA1 Pyramidal Cells Revealed by Spike-Triggered Averaging in Slices of Rat Hippocampus are Partially NMDA Receptor Mediated." *Eur. J. Neurosci.* **3** (1991): 587–601.

84. Traub, R. D., R. Miles, and R. K. S. Wong. "Model of Rhythmic Population Oscillation in the Hippocampal Slice." *Science* **243** (1989): 1319–1325.

85. Treves, A., and E. T. Rolls. "What Determines the Capacity of Autoassociative Memories in the Brain?" *Network* **2** (1991): 371–397.

86. Vanderwolf, C. H. "Hippocampal Electrical Activity and Voluntary Movement in the Rat." *Electroencephal. Clin. Neurophysiol.* **26** (1969): 407–418.

87. Van Hoesen, G. W., and D. N. Pandya. "Some Connections of the Entorhinal (Area 28) and Perirhinal (Area 35) Cortices of the Rhesus Monkey. III. Efferent Connections." *Brain Res.* **95** (1975): 39–59.

88. Wigstrom, H., and B. Gustafsson. "On Long-Lasting Potentiation in the Hippocampus: A Proposed Mechanism for Its Dependence on Coincident Pre- and Postsynaptic Activity." *Acta Physiol. Scand.* **123** (1985): 519–522.

89. Ylinen, A., A. Sik, A. Bragin, Z. Nadasdy, G. Jando, I. Szabo, and G. Buzsáki. "Sharp Wave-Associated High-Frequency Oscillation (200 Hz) in the Intact Hippocampus: Network and Intracellular Mechanisms." *J. Neuroscience* **15** (1995): 30–46.

Jeff Shrager* and Mark H. Johnson**
*Department of Psychology, Carnegie-Mellon University, Pittsburgh, PA 15213
**MRC Cognitive Development Unit, 4 Taviton St., London, WC1H OBT

Waves of Growth in the Development of Cortical Function: A Computational Model

INTRODUCTION

The mammalian cortex is organized during development through a combination of endogenous and exogenous influences including genetic restructuring, subcortical influence, maturational timing, and the information structure of the organism's early environment. The goal of our work is to detail the way in which these influences lead to the particulars of the distribution of function and representation over the cortical sheet. In the present chapter we utilize a computational model of cortical development to explore the influence on cortical function of developmental timing.

Broadly speaking, the adult cerebral cortex can be divided into primary and secondary sensory and motor areas, and "association" areas wherein multiple signals from the sensory areas, and from other association areas, are integrated. Although signals are passed in many directions, subcortical signals (e.g., from the thalamus) largely feed into the primary sensory areas, which then largely feed forward to various secondary sensory areas, leading eventually into the morass of the parietal and frontal association areas. Pandya and Yeterian[15] suggest that the multimodal areas represent the most abstract domain-general information, and that the more domain-specific processing appears in the primary sensory areas. Indeed, each succeeding large-scale region of cortex can be thought of as processing increasing orders of invariants from the stimulus stream, and passing either the invariant information extracted from the stream, or the residual information once the invariant is extracted, forward to other regions of the brain. The image is that of a cascade of filters, processing and separating stimulus information in series, up toward the integration areas where it is combined, and eventually reaching the frontal association areas. Feedback from higher to lower systems may act to bias or tune this process (e.g., Mangun and Hillyard[12]). How does this structure arise?

A striking aspect of the development of the cerebral cortex is the initial over-production and subsequent loss of neural connections (synapses), resulting in its relatively sparsely connected final functional architecture.[17] In the macaque, our nearest primate model, the period of "exuberance" in synaptogenesis begins before birth and is in furious bloom at birth, reaching its peak in the first few postnatal weeks (Bourgeois[1] provides a concise review). This process is thought to be key in cortical ontogeny.

In some cases the patterns of synaptic loss in the cortex, or in thalamo-cortical connections, has been shown to be correlated with experience-dependent activity (Antonini,[22] this volume),[16,18] as may be the periods of cortical plasticity.[6] We hypothesize that the pruning process produces the observed hierarchical cortical structure by enabling each region of cortex to become attuned to pick up the simplest (lowest order, least abstract) regularities available to that region. By virtue of this process, the initially undifferentiated regions of cortex closest to the direct stimulation (the "earliest" regions) become atuned to the first order of information (i.e., the most apparent regularities) from the stimulus signal, in the process giving these early regions form and function. Once the early regions have taken shape and have developed some specific functioning, the next spatially adjacent regions of cortex—receiving their input from both subcortical afferents and from the re-cently formed cortical regions—will in turn become atunded to a slightly higher order of regularity (i.e., the next most apparent regularities, after the most apparent have been processed by earlier regions), and so on. This process could result in the particular modular structure and connectivity of the cortex.

An important component of this theory is the sequential nature of cortical development, from "earlier" to "later" regions. This can be conceived as a "wave of growth" that passes over the cortex with particular timing. A number of results suggest that there may be such dynamically differential plasticity in different regions of the cortex at different developmental times. First, note that the hypoth-esized cortical developmental trend accords with the specific-to-abstract structure observed by Pandya and Yeterian[15] (described above) in which the more specific representations can be found near the cortical periphery. There is also significant evidence for a dynamic trend such as the one described.

Indirect evidence for such a dynamic comes from Bourgeois,[1] who has demon-strated in the macaque that thinning of the synaptic array is not observable in the frontal regions until around the animal's puberty. More direct evidence comes from the PET observations of Chugani, Phelps, and Mazziotta,[2] and the experiments of

Harwerth, et al.[6] These studies suggest a developmental dynamic in which, generally speaking, the locus of maximum neural plasticity begins in the primary sensory and motor areas and moves toward the secondary and parietal association areas and finally to the frontal regions. Through analysis of the coherence of EEG waveforms in children between the ages of about one and seven years of age, Thatcher[20] was able to plot cortical "growth spurts" based upon the areas that are beginning to act together in terms of their electrical synchronization with one another. In the 1.5- to 3-year spurt there is a lengthening along the rostral-caudal dimension and a rotation from lateral to medial, which is repeated again at 5.5–6.5 years. He also observed a general rostral to caudal expansion of intracortical synchrony and a spurt of right frontal pole growth at age 5 yrs. Thatcher proposed that a wave of nerve growth factor proceeds, during the 2- to 4-year period, from the lateral cortical regions and rotates clockwise at a rate of about 1 cm/month until it runs the entire 24 cm rostral to caudal or lateral to medial length.

In this chapter we shall demonstrate, by way of a computational model of cortical development, how such a wave can accomplish the self-organization of a neural system.

MODELING THE DEVELOPMENT OF CORTICAL FUNCTION

Computational models have helped us to understand more about the possible processes underlying brain functions and their dynamics. A number of models deal with cortical ontogenetic organization. These models fall into the general class of systems in which activity leads a competitive network, which is initially wired randomly, to self-organize so that afferents with one sort of characteristic activity are differentiated from afferents with different characteristic activity.[3,7,9,10,13,14] The models of Kerszberg, Dehaene, and Changeux,[9] and of Grajski and Merzenich[5] are relatively accurate in terms of their modeling of the neural substrate, although they are organizationally and dimensionally much different than the actual brain. Notable among these is the model of ocular dominance column formation due to Miller et al.[13] A careful dynamical analysis carried out by Miller and his coworkers allows qualitative and quantitative predictions of column size and the time course of column appearance.

We take as our starting point a computer model of cortical development due to Kerszberg, Dehaene, and Changeux,[9] which we shall refer to as the KDC model. This program models the development of a functional architecture from an initially equipotent substrate that bears close resemblance to the known physiology of the cortex.

The KDC model differs from most others in two ways that are important to our goals. First, in the KDC model, as with some others, there is initial over-abundant dendritic arboration and later pruning of the arbor in accord with activity.[13,14]

However, the means of dendritic selection and elimination in the KDC model depends upon the activity-dependent transmission of a fixed resource of simulated "neuro-trophic factor" (TF) (cf. Montague, et al.[14]). A Hebbian association rule directs the transportation of TF from interneural space to synapses. Meanwhile, as time progresses, synapses that receive less TF eventually atrophy, whereas synapses that receive more TF eventually reach stability. Thus, the period of plasticity depends upon the transportation of TF, and may differ from one part of the network to another in accord with the activity-dependent diffusion of this factor.

Another important feature of the KDC model is that Kerszberg et al. not only described the targeting of afferents onto the cortex, but also were able to describe in fairly general terms the *local function* served by simulated neural units. These researchers employed a method of analysis by which they were able to assign one of the sixteen possible binary logic functions (and one "indeterminate" function) to each neuron in the network both before and after execution of the simulation. This enabled them to describe the progression from the mostly indeterminate functionality of the richly arborized early cortex, to a more specifically functioning, "post-development" cortex. Through this analysis Kerszberg et al. demonstrated that differential development of local functionality is produced in response to differential correlations of afferent stimulus—that is in response to differential information content of the stimulus stream, an exogenous influence.

In order to test our theory of the influence of a wave of growth on the development of cortical function we shall introduce into the KDC model a dynamic modulation of the TF-based plasticity of the cortical substrate—a "wave of plasticity"—that moves across the cortex at a fixed rate. We shall observe the influence of this manipulation on the development of function in the simulated cortical array. Our hypothesis is that such a wave will induce higher functional development later in the cortical material.

DETAILS OF THE KDC MODEL

The KDC model consists of three components: a 30-by-30 square array representing cortical material, which we shall call the "cortical array," and two one-bit afferent elements, which are referred to as A and B. The array is toroidal in the sense that the left and right edges are close to one another, as are the top and bottom edges. Each element of the array represents the body of a simulated neuron, and is referred to as a "unit." Units for links to one another, and may be either excitatory or inhibitory in the sense that they either excite or inhibit the units to which its output is delivered via the links. Each of the afferents (A or B) projects a number of excitatory and inhibitory links into the array, which connect to the excitatory and inhibitory cortical units. The model is driven synchronously in cycles of settling. Activation arriving from excitatory units, or from afferents, is summed, and activation arriving from inhibitory units, or from afferents, is subtracted from the total activation of a target unit on a particular cycle. In the present experiments, five such cycles, called "settling cycles," take place between each training phase. Thus, in a 500-cycle simulation, there will be 100 training phases—one after every five settling cycles. The value of each afferent is changed before each group of five settling cycles—that is, after each training phase. In the experiments reported here one of the afferents (A) is inverted on each change, so that it provides a cycling input as: 010101010.... The correlation between the values given the afferents is 0.5; that is, if afferent A is 1, there is a 50% chance that afferent B is also 1.

Training consists of moving trophic factor (TF) from pools associated with the cortical units to the incoming links according to a Hebbian association rule; deciding whether each link is stabilized, remains plastic, or is dead; and updating the firing thresholds of each cortical unit in accord with the stability of its efferent links. The resulting dynamic of the network is that links which lead to or are associated with appropriate cortical unit firings (i.e., nonfirings for inhibitory links, firings for excitatory links) are rewarded and eventually stabilize, and those which are not so associated eventually atrophy and die from lack of trophic factor. Since the network is initially randomly and heavily overwired with both afferent-to-cortex and intracortical connections, the eventual pattern of wiring, and functionality of the cortical units is determined primarily (in the original KDC model) by the statistical structure of the afferent stimulation, and by the targeting of the links from the afferents into the cortical array.

Functionality of cortical units in the KDC model may be determined at any point during a simulation run by trying out each possible combination of afferent values, allowing settling to take place, and then recording the resulting values of each cortical unit. Since there are two afferents (A and B), each of which can be set to either zero or one, each cortical unit can potentially respond in one of sixteen ways, representing the 16 logical function of two bits: always off, always on, on with A only, on with A & B only, on when A is on but not B, etc. The procedure just described is repeated a number of times, and units that do not consistently produce a single logical function from among the 16 are said to have an indeterminate function. Thus, there are 17 possible functions for each cortical unit: the 16 logical functions, and the indeterminate function.

It is important to note that the functionality of a block of cortical array, by virtue of its connectivity, is of far greater complexity than these 16 logical functions. For instance, units that never respond—i.e., which have the "False" function—are not necessarily disconnected. Instead, they may be connected in such a way that the signals from the afferents contradict one another. Combinations of functions, and their time-course dynamics, presumably results in extremely complex functionality of the brain that is not most easily nor most naturally described in boolean terms. However, it is incredibly difficult to determine this high-order functionality. Therefore, in the present analyses we will speak primarily of the general "order" of functionality in terms of the representation in the cortical array of zeroth-, first-, or second-order logical functions. The zeroth-order functions include "False" and

"True"; they take no account of the afferent input values. The first-order functions are "A," "B," "~A," and "~B," which rely only upon one or the other afferent value. The second-order functions are all others, which are some function of both A and B. This reflects the connectivity and afference upon one unit, but not upon or within a number of cortical units. Determining the contribution of more complex patterns of connectivity, as are found in the architectures of real brains, is a goal of our future work.

Kerszberg et al. demonstrated a number of basic results for their model. They determined parameters under which stability was achieved, demonstrating that the model was able to move from an architecture of mostly indeterminate functions, to one of mostly determinate functions. They also showed that the model was able to self-organize into a center-surround sort of functional architecture consisting of tightly grouped mutually excitatory sets of units, interconnected by fewer, mostly inhibitory longer connections. Those authors empirically explored some adjustments of the statistics of initial afference, demonstrating that the local functions associated with the cortical units are determined, as expected, largely in accord with afferent dominance, in terms of the frequency of one afferent versus the other targeting the cortical array, and stimulus correlations, in terms of the frequencies that afferent stimulus occurred together (versus occurring separately or neither taking place).

INTRODUCTION OF A TROPHIC FACTOR WAVE

We wish to explore the effect of dynamic plasticity, as described in the introduction, on the development of function in the KDC cortical model. We propose that such a "wave" of plasticity can produce the general topology of the cortical array, specifically the placement of association areas. We hypothesize that under certain regimes of wave propagation we may expect a tendency toward the development of higher-order functions in later parts of the cortical array. The reason for this will be explained presently.

The original Kerszberg et al. model had a uniform rule for TF transportation, dependent only upon synapse activity. In order to explore the effect of the "wave plasticity" theory we have introduced a dynamic gaussian *spatial modulation* of the rate of TF diffusion across the cortical array. This is done by multiplying the transmission of TF by the amplitude of the slowly moving gaussian wave at each point in the array. Suppose, for instance, that the TF modulation wave (hereafter simply referred to as the "wave") moves with a rate of 0.25 and has a peak value of 1.0. During the first training cycle a modulation vector is produced for the 30-row array that might be:

$$\{1.0, 0.86, 0.77, 0.66, 0.53, \ldots, 0.0, 0.0\} \, .$$

That is, TF transmission at location 1 of the array takes place normally whereas TF transmission at location 2 is reduced to 86% of what would have been moved, etc. On the next cycle, the wave moves to the right a small amount. Since in this example it takes four cycles for the wave to move one full row to the right, the above vector will read approximately as follows at training cycle 4 (real cycle 20 with 5 settling cycles between each training cycle):

$$\{0.86, 1.0, 0.86, 0.77, 0.66, \ldots, 0.0, 0.0\}$$

The progress of the wave thus modulates the transmission of trophic factor, leading to a dynamic plasticity in the cortical array; leftward rows are plastic early on, whereas they lose their plasticity early as well. The more rightward rows do not become plastic until later on, but are plastic toward the end of the run when most of the neurons are finally reaching asymptote in the stabilization and death process. Note that this manipulation effects only the amount of TF moved during training, not the total amount of TF in the array nor any other simulation parameter.

In certain regimes of this wave, we can expect to observe specific phenomena. First, we expect in general more synapse death because most synapses will receive proportionally less access to trophic factor during a simulation of the same length as those we have already seen. More interestingly, under certain regimes of wave propagation, we expect to observe a tendency toward the development of higher-order functions in the cortical array. The reason for this may be envisioned by considering two steps in the propagation of the wave from some leftward set of rows to the next set of rows to the right. Let us call these "LEFT" and "NEXT." LEFT, initially more plastic than NEXT, determines its function during receipt of input from A and B afferents, as was the case in the original KDC model. However, LEFT becomes fixated in its function relatively early, as the wave moves on to NEXT. Now, however, NEXT is receiving input that, in addition to the input coming from A and B afferents, includes the combined functions fixated by the earlier plasticity in LEFT. Thus, NEXT has, in effect, *three afferents*: A, B, and LEFT.

This account will depend upon a number of parameters of the model, but most especially the wave propagation rate. Therefore, we have explored two regimes of wave propagation. In experiment J the wave propagates at a rate of 0.25 rows per training cycle. This brings the wave across the array once over the entirety of the simulation run (generally about 500 to 550 total cycles, or about 100 training cycles). In experiment M we consider a wave propagation rate of three times that of the rate in experiment J. These will be contrasted with the results of the original KDC model, called here "experiment C." In all of these cases the correlation between A and B afferent activity is 0.5, as described above.

In order to observe the effects of wave propagation we will analyze the cortical array in terms of "slices." Each slice represents the density of functions that appear in the cortical array in a small number of rows—specifically, two rows in the cases that we shall see here, though this number was chosen arbitrarily. Adjacent slices

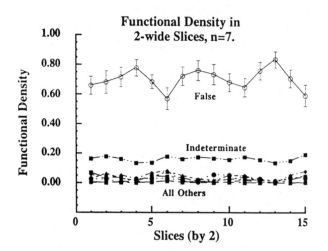

FIGURE 1 Slice analysis of the initial state of the array, $n = 7$. Functional density is computed in pairs of rows of the array. Since the entire array is 30 units wide, there are 15 two-row slices. None of the "All Others" functions are statistically different.

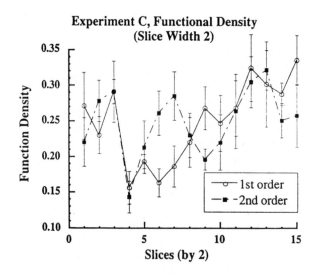

FIGURE 2 Percentage functional density in nonwave case (experiment C, $n = 5$). First-order functions are A, A, ~B, and ~B. Second-order functions are: B&~A, A&~B, A-xor-B, ~A&B, A&B, A=B, A≥B, A≤B, and AvB. The zeroth-order functions, True and False are not represented here. Most of the missing weight (to 100%) is represented by False. True and Indeterminate contribute essentially no weight. The depicted curves are not significantly different.

are compared with one another. This enables us to produce a plot of the dynamic effect of the wave on the array along the path of its progress. Figure 1 depicts the slice analysis applied to the initial state of the array, before the simulation takes place. There is no significant difference between any of the lines labeled "all others" in this figure.

Next we consider the slice analysis applied to the nonwave, post-training condition of study C, the baseline case with no TF wave. Figure 2 depicts this result. In accord with our prediction about the difference between production of high vs. low-order functions, we have divided the possible functions into "first-order" functions, which depend only upon one variable (A or B) and "second-order" functions, which depend both A and B afferent values. The first-order functions are A, A, B, and B. The second-order functions are: B& A, A& B, A-xor-B, [A&B], A&B, A=B, A≥B, A≤B, and AvB. The zeroth-order functions, True and False, are not represented in Figure 2; most of the missing weight (to 100%) is represented by False. The True and Indeterminate functions contribute very little weight.

Inspection of Figure 2 reveals a complex interplay in a fairly high-density range (about 25%) of the first-order and second-order functions. However, these curves are *not* significantly different, and therefore do not afford further analysis at present.

Now consider the slice analysis applied to experiment J, which has the exact same parameter structure as the baseline study (C) but in which a TF modulation wave which propagates at the rate of 0.25 rows per training cycle. The results of this manipulation are depicted in Figure 3. In contrast to the baseline analysis depicted in Figure 2, the first- and second-order function density curves appearing in Figure 3 *are* significantly different from one another, thus affording further analysis in order to assess our theoretical predictions. The density of second-order functions beyond the first slice is greater than the density of first-order functions. Also, with the exception of the tail of the graph, where most synapses are dying off from lack of trophic factor, our hypothesis predicts that these curves will stand in anticorrelation to one another because each subsequent region is taking on either a generally lower or generally higher functionality, displacing the other sort of functionality from the cortical units. Indeed, the first seven points are anticorrelated. A simple correlation on slices 1–7 has the small negative correlation of −.339. Since there is a dynamic of dying synapses lending a confusing overall curvature to this result, we can approximately co-vary that out by multiplying the density of False functions by each value here. This corrected correlation is much stronger in the predicted direction, at −.656 on these first seven nodes. (The influence of this confounding bend due to synapse death and the sense of co-varying according to the False function density may be seen more clearly in Figure 4.)

(It is important to note that although it is generally the case that some functions will always be anticorrelated with others since the total functional density is fixed in a zero-sum game, it is *not* the case that the density of *any* group of functions will be anticorrelated. Here we have *preselected* the specific groups of functions to compare, from the numerous ways in which the 15 functions (excluding the FALSE and indeterminate functions) can be subdivided. We have found support for our prediction in the comparison of the control case (C) with the present manipulation in this preselected functional grouping. Thus, this result yields strong support for our theoretical claim. Note, also, that until some method is available whereby we can analyze the complex functions of a cortical region, we can only measure two levels of complexity. In fact, it is possible that we have obtained the more general result but are unable to see the higher functions for lack of this analytic tool.)

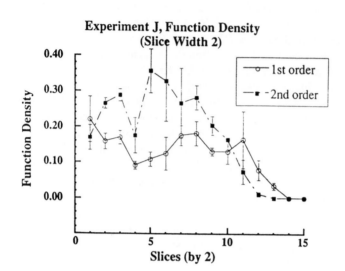

FIGURE 3 As Figure 2, but with TF wave (the "slow" wave, see below, $n = 3$). These curves differ at $t = -2.17$, $p = .048$, and the first seven points are anticorrelated. Simple correlation on items 1-7$= -.339$. Corrected correlation, by multiplying by False weights is $-.656$ on these first seven nodes.

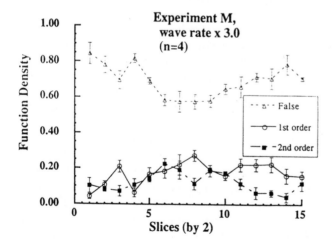

FIGURE 4 Experiment M, as Figure 3 but with the rate at which the wave progresses across the array multiplied by 3. The first- and second-order lines are different by a t-test at $t = 2.59$, $p = .02$, and have a corrected correlation of $-.413$. Note that the relative positions of the first- and second-order function are reversed between this figure and Figure 3.

Next we consider the latter experiment, M, in which the propagation rate of the wave has been tripled from the previous rate, depicted in Figure 4. Again, the first- and second-order functional density curves are significantly different, but this time the mean values are inverted, so that whereas in the slow-wave case the second-order functions were emphasized, in this fast-wave case it is the first-order functions which are emphasized. (The corrected anticorrelation is somewhat reduced to $-.413$). Note also that the absolute values of the second-order function density is much smaller than that of the former case (J, Figure 3). What appears to have happened here is that speeding up the wave (M) has had the effect of spreading out the higher-order functions over the array, as well as slightly increasing the total number of high-order (and indeterminate) functions relative to the slow-wave case (J).

DISCUSSION

The present study is a step toward an account of the way that the differential functional architecture of the cortex might arise in early development as an emergent result of the combination of organized stimulus and a neurotrophic dynamic. We have extended the results of Kerszberg et al. in order to explore the effects of "waves of growth" in neural trophic factor. We have also begun to approach the analysis of the functions produced in the cortical array in terms of the level of information that they represent, and to connect this analysis with timing manipulations by way of a logic of the development of the array.

There are a number of analytic and empirical directions in which we see this research moving. First, as mentioned above, we would like to be able to understand more complex functions than are represented by the simple functions analyzed by Kerszberg et al. and even beyond the higher- vs. lower-order analysis that we have introduced. In order to do this we need a method for the analysis of the connectivity left by the training process, because more complex functions will result from combinations of the simpler ones. Unfortunately, although cursory observations can be made of the patterns of connectivity left by the training process, we have yet to discover a rigorous means for such analysis. We would also like to document the dynamics of the training process towards a "microgenetic" account of the emergence of cortical function. At the moment, however, our simulation facilities are not fast enough to run studies in which the complete functional analysis is carried out on every training cycle.

Our next steps will be to move toward the manipulation of the information in a higher-dimensional stimulus space by utilizing stimuli which have greater information density along more dimensions, and in which the stimuli lie along those dimensions in organized ways. We also plan changes in the architecture of the model to bring it into better accord with the physical architecture of the primate cortex.

This should enable several bands of communication to develop between regions of the cortical array. These extensions will enable us to expand our computational account of the development of cortical function to true cortical representation, in which areas of the cortex not only take on higher functionality, but also come to represent relationships between points in the high-dimensional space of complex stimuli, such as those found in retinotopic maps of space in mammals and spatial maps of frequency in bats.[19][1] The cortical array would thus be taking on and spatially representing increasingly abstract levels of analysis of the stimulus space, as is, we suggest, the functional architecture of the human cortex.

The importance of the present theory with respect to the development of human cognition has not escaped our attention. One of the principle aspects of human development that distinguishes us from our nearest primate neighbors may be changes in the timing of development.[4] Among primates, the human brain remains relatively plastic until late in the post-natal period, whereas the brains of our closest relatives are more completely formed by birth.[1] Thus, humans have greater access to the complex experiences afforded by being out in the world during the most formative period of brain development. This may enable us to "tune in" to rapidly changing features of the environment that other animals, more constrained by evolutionary structuring of their brains, are unable to take account of. To the extent that these changes are reflected in similar timing changes in the hypothesized wave of cortical development, they may also lead to changes in the extraction of information from the stimulus environment during the early self-organization of the brain. (Gould[4] and Jerison[8] provide excellent discussions of these and other influences in the evolution of the brain.) Of course, along with this flexibility comes an extended period of immaturity, during which we are dependent upon our caretakers and our community for both support and training. Our theory therefore sees the coevolution of culture and cognition as a fundamental condition of human evolution.

ACKNOWLEDGMENTS

We thank Michel Kerszberg for providing the code for the KDC model, and for specific comments on a draft of this chapter. Others contributed significantly through discussion and advice, including J. Bourgeois, R. Gilmore, P. Welding and other members of the research communities of Carnegie Mellon University, the British

---

[1]Kohonen,[10] Jacobs and Jordan,[7] Durbin and Mitchison,[3] and Grajski and Merzenich[5] have all in some way addressed the problem of the creation of maps from a computational standpoint. Jacobs and Jordan, and Durbin and Mitchison have employed very abstract models that only produce very simple maps. The model of Grajski and Merzenich merely maps regions of subcortical activity into correlated cortical maps, though this is stimulus driven. Kohonen's model does, in fact, produce maps that are closely related to the actual stimulus information structure, but his method is not very analogous to the workings of the cortex.

Medical Research Council's Cognitive Development Unit, and the Institute Pasteur in Paris. We especially thank the editors of the present collection for their careful reading and comments.

REFERENCES

1. Antonini, A., M. P. Stryker, and B. Chapman. "Development and Plasticity of Cortical Columns and Their Thalamic Input." This volume.
2. Bourgeois, J. P. "Synaptogenesis in the Prefrontal Cortex of the Macaque." In *Developmental Neurocognition: Speech and Face Processing in the First Year of Life*, edited by B. de Boysson-Bardies, 31–39. The Netherlands: Kluwer, 1993.
3. Chugani, H. T., M. E. Phelps, and J. C. Mazziotta. "Positron Emission Tomography Study of Human Brain Functional Development." *Ann. Neurology* **22** (1987): 487–497.
4. Durbin, R., and G. Mitchison. "A Dimension Reduction Framework for Understanding Cortical Maps." *Nature* **343** (1990): 644–647.
5. Gould, S. J. *Ontogeny and Phylogeny.* Cambridge, MA: Belknap Press, 1977.
6. Grajski, K. A., and M. M. Merzenich. "Hebb-Type Dynamics is Sufficient to Account for the Inverse Magnification Rule in Cortical Somatotopy." *Neural Comp.* **2** (1990): 71–84.
7. Harwerth, R. S., E. L. I. Smith, G. C. Duncan, M. L. J. Crawford, and G. K. von Noorden. "Multiple Sensitive Periods in the Development of the Primate Visual System." *Science* **232** (1986): 235–238.
8. Jacobs, R. A., and M. Jordan. "Computational Consequences of a Bias Toward Short Connections." *J. Cog. Neurosci.* **4(4)** (1992): 323–336.
9. Jerison, H. J. *Evolution of the Brain and Intelligence.* New York: Academic Press, 1973.
10. Kerszberg, M., S. Dehaene, and J.-P. Changeux. "Stabilization of Complex Input-Output Functions in Neural Clusters Formed by Synapse Selection." *Neural Networks* **5** (1992): 403–413.
11. Kohonen, K. "The Self-Organizing Map." *Proceedings of the IEEE* **78(9)** (1990): 1464–1480.
12. Linsker, R. "Perceptual Neural Organization: Some Approaches Based on Network Models and Information Theory." *Ann. Rev. Neurosci.* (1990): 257–281.
13. Mangun, G. R., and S. A. Hillyard. "Modulations of Sensory-Evoked Brain Potentials Indicate Changes in Perceptual Processing During Visual-Spatial Priming." *J. Exp. Psychol.: Hum. Percep. & Perfor.* **17(4)** (1991): 1057–1074.

14. Miller, K. D., J. B. Keller, and M. P. Stryker. "Ocular Dominance Column Development: Analysis and Simulation." *Science* **245** (1989): 605–615.

15. Montague, P. R., J. A. Gally, and G. M. Edelman. "Spatial Signaling in the Development and Function of Neural Connections." *Cerebral Cortex* **1(2)** (1991): 199–220.

16. Pandya, D. N., and E. H. Yeterian. "Architecture and Connections of Cerebral Cortex: Implications for Brain Evolution and Function." In *Neurobiology of Higher Cognitive Functions*, edited by A. B. Scheibel and A. F. Weschler. New York: Coruilford Press, 1990.

17. Roe, A. W., S. L. Pallas, J.-O. Hahm, and M. Sur. "A Map of Visual Space Induced in Primary Auditory Cortex." *Science* **250** (1990): 818–820.

18. Stiles, J. "Plasticity and Development: Evidence from Children with Early Occurring Focal Brain Injury." This volume

19. Stryker, M. P., and W. A. Harris. "Binocular Impulse Blockade Prevents the Formation of Ocular Dominance Columns in Cat Visual Cortex." *J. Neurosci.* **6** (1986): 2117–2133.

20. Suga, N. "Cortical Computational Maps for Auditory Imaging." *Neural Networks* **3** (1990): 3-21.

21. Thatcher, R. W. "Cyclic Cortical Reorganization During Early Childhood." *Brain & Cog.* **20** (1992): 24–50.

22. Udin, S. B., and J. W. Fawcett. "Formation of Topographic Maps." *Ann. Rev. Neurosci.* (1988): 289–327.

Critical Periods in Brain Development

Antonella Antonini,† Michael P. Stryker,† and Barbara Chapman‡
†W.M. Keck Foundation Center for Integrative Neuroscience, Department of Physiology, University of California, San Francisco, CA 94143-0444
‡Center for Neuroscience, University of California at Davis, Davis, CA 95616

Development and Plasticity of Cortical Columns and Their Thalamic Input

INTRODUCTION

The visual cortex of mammals with frontal eyes presents a strikingly ordered and detailed multilevel, functional organization. One can consider the primary level of organization to be the topographic representation, whereby the visual field is systematically mapped onto the surface of the visual cortex. Superimposed on the topographical map are several columnar systems, defined anatomically and/or physiologically, which extend from the superficial to the deep layers of the cortex. The most studied of these systems, the ocular dominance system evenly subdivides the cortex into alternate columns in which neurons tend to be driven preferentially or exclusively by one or the other eye.[23,49] Orientation selectivity, by which neurons are selectively "tuned" for a specific orientation of the visual stimulus, is also organized in a columnar fashion, with sensitivity to a particular orientation changing gradually and progressively as one moves through the cortex from one column to the neighboring column in the tangential direction.[23] Finally, in some species, such as the ferret, neurons having receptive field centers specifically sensitive to bright or dark stimuli (on-center or off-center response characteristics) are also grouped in columns.[61]

Maturational Windows and Adult Cortical Plasticity, Eds. B. Julesz & I. Kovács,
SFI Studies in the Sciences of Complexity, Vol. XXIII, Addison-Wesley, 1995

How does this highly ordered organization of the visual cortex come about during development, and what is its potential for plastic modification? During early life, neuronal connections are much less specific. For example, the ocular dominance system is largely undetectable in cats before two weeks of age[4,34] and while some neurons are orientation-selective, visual responsiveness is poor.[23,53] During normal development, neuronal processes, recognized as activity- or use-dependent, remodel and refine these early cortical networks to achieve the functional specialization observed in the adult (see Fregnac and Imbert[18] and Stryker[56] for reviews). These activity-dependent processes appear to stabilize those synapses from converging pathways that activate a common target and reorganize neuronal circuits into precise columns with segregated stimulus response properties. During this "critical period," the remarkable plastic effects of environmental manipulations on cortical function may be ascribed to the powerful organizing role of neuronal activity, which is finely modulated by visual experience.

Is plasticity in the primary visual areas a phenomenon developmentally regulated and limited to the critical period, or can it be extended throughout adulthood? Generally, plasticity in the adult is considered in terms of the ability to adapt to a continuously changing sensory environment and is regarded as part of memory and cognitive processes that are supposedly elaborated in centers outside the primary geniculocortical pathway. However, there is now growing evidence indicating that some degree of plasticity even in the primary sensory areas, is still possible throughout life, allowing remarkable physiological reorganizations in response to injury.[20,39]

In the following pages, we briefly describe certain aspects of the structural and functional bases of the columnar systems, emphasizing how all columnar systems are dependent on the specific pattern of the major afferent input to the visual cortex. This pathway arises from the lateral geniculate nucleus (LGN) of the thalamus and terminates mainly in layer IV of the visual cortex. Next, we will review studies from our laboratory with particular emphasis on the regulatory role of neuronal activity on the structural plasticity of geniculocortical afferents under various environmental conditions. Finally, we will discuss current knowledge on the issue of the plasticity exhibited by the mature visual cortex and the possible pathways and cellular mechanisms involved in such plasticity.

THALAMOCORTICAL CONNECTIVITY AND THE COLUMNAR ORGANIZATION OF THE ADULT VISUAL CORTEX

In all species studied, the physiologically defined ocular dominance columns appear to have an anatomical basis in the specific pattern of thalamocortical innervation. Experiments based on transneuronal transport of substances injected into one eye, have shown that geniculocortical axonal terminals are indeed segregated in layer

IV in alternate domains, or "patches," according to their laminar origin in the lateral geniculate nucleus (LGN), and thus to the eye of origin.[1,25,27,49] Within these patches, neurons are either monocular, or, if binocular, they are preferentially activated through one eye. In general, eye preference is maintained throughout radial cortical columns from layer IV to the superficial layers II and III and finally to the deep layers V and VI. The clusterlike pattern of geniculocortical innervation has been confirmed in studies of the morphology of single geniculocortical fibers, labeled with horseradish peroxidase (HRP) from the white matter.[16,28,29] These studies have shown that in adult animals the terminal arborizations of geniculocortical axons are subdivided in distinct clusters separated by zones relatively free of collateral branches.

Zahs and Stryker[61] demonstrated that the ferret visual cortex contains a columnar system in which neurons are segregated on the basis of the type of response of their receptive field center (i.e., on- or off-center), and this organization is paralleled by the specific pattern of thalamocortical innervation. The activity of individual thalamocortical afferents could be recorded in animals in which cortical neuronal responses were silenced by superfusing the cortex with kainic acid. After this procedure, the majority of geniculocortical afferent activity was found to be spatially segregated into pure or predominantly on- or off-center responses and distributed within patches smaller than but similar to the ocular dominance patches of cortical neurons in layer IV.

Orientation selectivity also appears to have an anatomical basis in the specific pattern of thalamocortical innervation. Since geniculate neurons are not orientation selective, cortical orientation specificity must result from either a specific arrangement of the afferents or from local intracortical interactions. The initial functional model of orientation selectivity suggested an exclusive dependence on the pattern of geniculocortical innervation.[23] The model proposed that the transformation of nonoriented geniculocortical afferents into an oriented cortical response relies upon rules of strict topographic convergence. The receptive fields of cortical neurons receiving direct geniculate input (neurons classified as "simple") would be formed from the alignment of the centers of geniculate receptive fields.[41] A stimulus falling on the line of alignment of the geniculate receptive fields would produce a simultaneous activation of all these geniculocortical afferents and would thus produce an optimal response in the cortical neuron. This model has been tested by Chapman et al.[11] in the ferret visual cortex by comparing the orientation selectivity of neurons within a column to the array of receptive fields of geniculocortical afferents recorded in the same column. These afferent responses could be studied in isolation from responses of cortical origin by superfusing the cortex with muscimol, an agonist of the inhibitory neurotransmitter geniculocortical gamma aminobutyric acid (GABA), thus completely silencing cortical neurons. Consistent with the Hubel and Wiesel[23] model, this study demonstrated that the aggregate geniculate input is, in most cases, oriented and that the orientation matches the orientation of cortical cells in the column (see Figure 1). Other models of orientation selectivity call for local

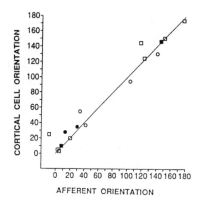

FIGURE 1   Relationship between the preferred orientation of the cortical neuron and the principal axis of geniculocortical afferent receptive fields arrays. The diagonal line ($x = y$) represents the predicted result if the orientation of the afferents matched perfectly with the orientation of the cortical neuron. From Chapman et al.[11]

mechanisms based on intracortical inhibitory interactions,[50] which might not only refine orientation selectivity within layer IV, the major geniculocortical recipient cortical layer, but also strongly act in layers outside layer IV.

In conclusion, it is striking how the diverse columnar systems in the mammalian visual cortex appear to utilize a common strategy for their basic structural-functional organization. This basic strategy consists of a distinct segregation of the afferents and the creation of functional modules. One can speculate that the realization of this modular type of processing represents the most economical mechanism for transferring thalamocortical information and creating the basis for efficient intracortical processing.

DEVELOPMENT OF THE COLUMNAR SYSTEM FOR ORIENTATION SELECTIVITY

In the cat and monkey, orientation selectivity in the visual cortex can be demonstrated as early as the first reliable responses can be electrophysiologically recorded.[4,7,23] Controversy still exists regarding the proportion of oriented neurons and their degree of selectivity. However, it is well established that, several weeks after birth, the representation of orientation selectivity in the visual cortex significantly increases and is distributed in all cortical layers. Is the process of maturation of orientation selectivity dependent on neuronal activity?

Chapman and Stryker[10] have studied this problem in the ferret, which allows postnatal study of the very initial stages of the development of orientation selectivity since gestation in this species is three weeks shorter than that in the cat. The natural development of orientation selectivity was studied in normal animals from postnatal day 20 (P20), corresponding to the day of birth in the cat, to adulthood. In order to determine whether the development of orientation-selective responses

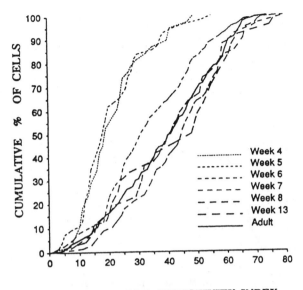

ORIENTATION SELECTIVITY INDEX

FIGURE 2 Cumulative percentage of cells at each degree of orientation selectivity (Orientation Selectivity Index-OSI). OSI was calculated from the orientation tuning histograms of cortical neurons to the presentation of moving light bars swept across the receptive field at different orientations (see Chapman and Stryker[10] for a detailed description of the method). OSI could vary from 0 (no orientation selectivity) to 100 (very tightly tuned for orientation). A value of OSI less than 25 indicates little or no evidence of orientation selectivity. The curves obtained at postnatal weeks 4 and 5 are significantly different from the curve obtained at week 6 ($p < 0.001$); and the week 6 curve is significantly different from the adult ($p < 0.009$). From Chapman and Stryker.[10]

was dependent on the presence of neuronal activity; the sodium channel blocker tetrodotoxin (TTX) was infused into the visual cortex causing a complete blockade of electrical activity, both in the afferent pathways and cortical circuits. The drug was delivered for approximately 25 days, starting at 4 weeks of age, by means of an osmotic minipump.

In Figure 2 we illustrate the changes of orientation selectivity during normal development. The first clear visual responses could be recorded during the fourth week of age when the vast majority of the cells appeared to be nonselective to orientation. Orientation selectivity begins to increase gradually at week 6, and by week 7 it is indistinguishable from that of the adult. TTX treatment, administered from the fourth to the seventh week, appears to completely prevent the development of orientation selectivity, freezing the visual cortex in an immature state (see Figure 3).

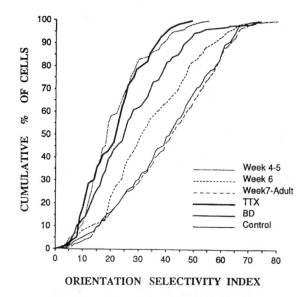

FIGURE 3 Comparison of orientation selectivity between normally reared animals, binocularly deprived animals and animals in which the visual cortex was silenced by infusion of TTX. Note that the distribution of orientation selectivity from the TTX-treated animals is indistinguishable from the distribution of normal animals at week 4. From Chapman and Stryker.[10]

Animals were also studied with a visual deprivation paradigm in which binocular lid suture was performed from eye-opening to postnatal week 8, or longer. This approach blocks patterned activity while maintaining spontaneous activity. Less severe developmental deficits in the maturation of orientation selectivity were noted than when all activity was blocked with TTX (Figure 3).

It should be noted that during normal development, a small number of cells did show finely tuned orientation responses even at P23 (fourth week of age). This may represent either a "pre-programmed" organizational disposition of the visual connections or the organizing effects of early postnatal activity. We cannot distinguish the relative importance of purely intracortical circuits from the specific arrays of geniculocortical afferents during development in establishing orientation selectivity (see Chapman et al.[11]).

DEVELOPMENT OF CORTICAL OCULAR DOMINANCE COLUMNS

While, in the adult, the geniculocortical terminals are characteristically arranged in alternate eye-specific bands, at early stages of development, the projections serving the two eyes are initially superimposed within layer IV. The columnar arrangement appears to develop by a process of progressive remodeling and segregation of terminals. The segregation process begins and has a time course typical of each species. Using autoradiographic techniques, LeVay, Stryker, and Shatz[35] demonstrated that this remodeling occurs entirely during the postnatal life in the cat. In kittens younger than two weeks of age, transneuronal labeling of the entire geniculocortical projection reveals a homogeneous distribution in layer IV with no hint of alternate bands. At this stage, the anatomical mixture of geniculate terminals renders the majority of neurons in layer IV equally responsive through both eyes. Initial evidence of segregation appears around the third postnatal week, and by the sixth week of age the adultlike pattern of ocular dominance domains is evident. The original interpretation of this experiment attributed the observed overlap between the two sets of afferents to the morphology of single geniculocortical fibers; that is, individual geniculocortical afferents, originally exuberant and overextended, would be compelled to share the same cortical territory. Progressive segregation would occur by removal of mispositioned branches from territories occupied predominantly by the other eye and restricting their terminals in the appropriate domains.

To test this hypothesis in the kitten, we[2] studied the morphology of single geniculocortical afferents between the third and the sixth postnatal week—the period in which segregation occurs. Single afferents were filled anterogradely by the Phaseolus lectin (PHA-L[19]) injected into the LGN of animals at four different ages (P19; P23; P30/31; and P39, where "P" is the postnatal day). The lectin was then visualized with standard immunohistochemical techniques and single axons terminating in the visual cortex were serially reconstructed in three dimensions. The geniculocortical arbors shown in Figures 4 and 5 at two different ages are representative of the morphological remodeling of axons during development. Axons at earlier ages show a very poorly ramified terminal arborization, extending homogeneously over a large expanse of area 17 (see Figure 4). Dramatic changes appear around the fourth week of age, when the terminal arborization becomes much richer, complex, and, for the first time, clearly subdivided into distinct patches (see Figure 5). The presence of clusters of terminals, a pattern characteristic of mature axons, would indicate that the segregation process is well advanced. The terminal-free zones between patches are presumably innervated by geniculocortical terminals serving the other eye. There is a tendency for arbors in older animals to be more restricted along the ventrodorsal axis than those in younger animals (see Figure 6). This tendency suggests that maturation of arbors entails the elimination of far-reaching branches.

P23

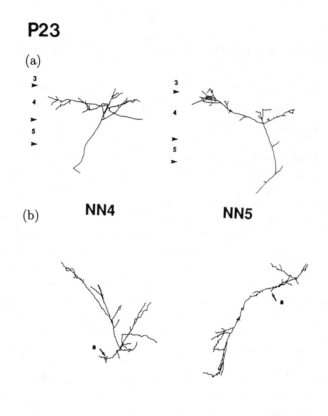

(a)

NN4   NN5

(b)

FIGURE 4 Computer reconstruction of PHA-L immunostained axonal arbors (NN4, NN5) in area 17 of a P23 kitten. In (a) we show the arbors as originally reconstructed in coronal view. Row B shows the same axons from a surface view, i.e., as viewed from the pia, after a 90° angle rotation along the dorsoventral axis. All axons are poorly branched and widely extended along layer IV. In (b), a indicates the main axonal trunk. Scale, 400μ. From Antonini and Stryker.[2]

Two other parameters were quantified in order to follow the developmental changes of geniculocortical arbors in normal animals. As a measure of growth, we considered the total length of the terminal arborization in layer IV (the summed length of all the branches) and, as a measure of complexity, the total number of branch points. In the normal group, older animals showed a small but significant increase in the total length (Figure 7(a)) and a dramatic increase in the number of branch points compared to younger animals (Figure 7(b)).

P30·31

(a)

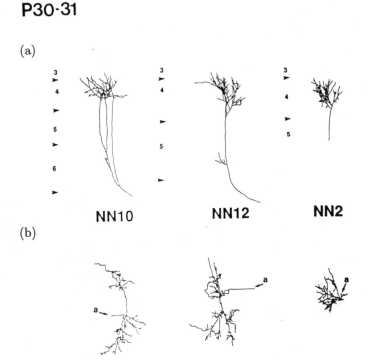

(b)

FIGURE 5   Axonal arbors (NN10, NN12, NN2) reconstructed from kittens at P30/31. Axons are shown in coronal view (a) and in surface view (b). Note that the terminal arborization of these axons is reduced in extension within layer IV compared to the arbors reconstructed at P23 (Figure 4). Also note the patches of terminals into which the terminal arborization of axons NN10 and NN12 are subdivided when viewed from the pial surface. In (b), a indicates the main axonal trunk. Scale, 400μ. From Antonini and Stryker.[2]

From these results we can summarize the characteristics of the remodeling processes of the afferents during normal development in the presence of activity in the visual pathway. Initially, the terminal arborization is formed by long, poorly ramified branches which sparsely innervate a wide expanse of layer IV. This pattern of innervation explains the spatial overlap of the two sets of afferents observed in transneuronal studies.[35] During development, remodeling of the arbors entails the elimination of the most far-reaching branches and a selective growth of collaterals at specific locations, resulting in the formation of patches. Thus, reoriented growth with a redistribution of terminals, and not a simple regression of preformed connections, characterize the remodeling processes.

The segregation process has come to be seen as the manifestation of activity-dependent competitive interactions between the two sets of afferents. The source of such competition appears to reside at the origin of the visual pathways and to arise from the asynchronous, uncorrelated activity between the ganglion cell

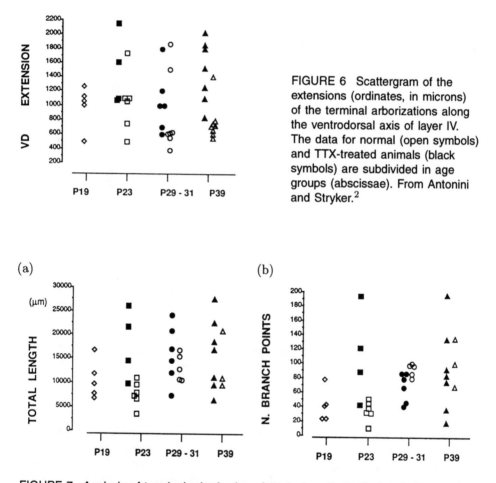

FIGURE 6   Scattergram of the extensions (ordinates, in microns) of the terminal arborizations along the ventrodorsal axis of layer IV. The data for normal (open symbols) and TTX-treated animals (black symbols) are subdivided in age groups (abscissae). From Antonini and Stryker.[2]

FIGURE 7   Analysis of terminal arborization of geniculocortical afferents in layer IV. (a) Scattergram of the total lengths (in microns) of the terminal arborizations. (b) Scattergram of the number of branch points. The data for normal (open symbols) and TTX-treated animals (black symbols) are subdivided in age groups (abscissae). From Antonini and Stryker.[2]

populations in the two retinae. The dependence of ocular dominance formation on retinal activity was unequivocally demonstrated by an experiment of Stryker and Harris.[54] In the kitten, if electrical activity within the optic nerves is abolished by intraocular injection of the sodium channel blocker tetrodotoxin (TTX) during the critical period, ocular dominance domains, as revealed by autoradiography, do not form. Concomitantly, most of cortical neurons in layer IV, normally dominated or driven exclusively by one eye, retain the binocularity typical of the juvenile cortex.

Stryker and Harris' interpretation of this study calls for a specific role of activity in the recognition process by which afferents serving the same eye are spatially combined, and become segregated from those serving the other eye. This hypothesis requires that activity *per se* would not interfere with growth and maturation processes. Another interpretation would suggest that activity could promote growth. In its absence, geniculocortical afferents would be frozen in a juvenile state and therefore remain unsegregated. Alternatively, the lack of activity could promote unselective neuronal growth resulting in overextended geniculocortical arbors. The failure of the ocular dominance formation in TTX-treated animals could therefore be explained by an overgrowth of the afferents which could mask or override the specific mechanisms of segregation. As a first step in testing these hypotheses, we studied the morphology of PHA-L-filled geniculocortical arbors in animals in which the afferent visual pathways were silenced bilaterally by repetitive intraocular injections of TTX. The study was carried out during the critical period, when normal segregation would have occurred.

A striking characteristic of arbors reconstructed from TTX-treated animals is the lack of an obvious age-dependent trend in morphological remodeling. Further, although very variable at all ages, these arbors generally demonstrate a larger ventrodorsal extension (Figure 6) and a normal or slightly greater rate of growth and complexity, as indicated by the total lengths and number of branch points (Figure 7(a,b)). These characteristics, of arbors developing in the absence of electrical activity, indicate that the lack of segregation observed in autoradiographic studies[54] is not due to the stabilization of the terminal arborizations in an immature, overlapped state. On the contrary, growth and elaboration of collateral branches appears to be a continuous process proceeding even in the absence of activity in the visual pathways. However, the evidence that arbors in TTX-treated group, at all ages, demonstrate an enormous variability in growth and complexity, suggests the importance of neural activity in organizing and coordinating growth among populations of geniculocortical afferents.

A second feature of arbors in TTX-treated kittens is their uniform distribution of terminals throughout layer IV. At an age at which *normal* geniculocortical afferents have already undergone segregation into distinct patches of terminals, afferents reconstructed from TTX-treated animals, although as dense and well developed as in normal animals, do not show any obvious clusterlike pattern in their arborization (compare Figures 5 and 8). Since these afferents show a normal growth rate, the arborization in layer IV is bound to contain random fluctuations in the density of terminals, mimicking the presence of clusters of a density similar to that of the distinct patches observed in normal kittens after P30.

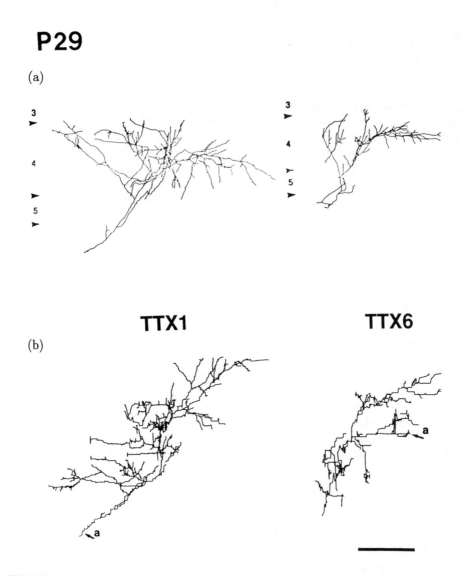

FIGURE 8   Axonal arbors (TTX1, TTX6) serially reconstructed from area 17 of a P29, TTX-treated kitten. Axons are shown in the coronal plane in (a), and in surface view in (b). The composite figure demonstrates the variability in morphology and ventrodorsal extent of the axonal arbors when viewed coronally, and the absence of a clear segregation into patches. In (b), a indicates the main axonal trunk. Scale, 400μ. From Antonini and Stryker.[2]

% DENSITY REDUCTION

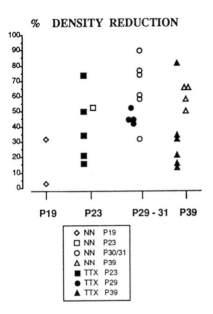

FIGURE 9 Percent decrease in density of the terminal arborization in the interpatch space relative to the density of the arborization measured at the border of the patch. The interpatch density measurement was taken at the midpoint between the borders of two patches of terminals. The density of the terminal arborization in layer IV was evaluated from the pial view of the arbor (see Methods in Antonini and Stryker's paper[2]). Data for normal (open symbols) and TTX-treated animals (black symbols) are subdivided in age groups (abscissa). From Antonini and Stryker.[2]

Is the presence of these clusters a sign of segregation? If segregation in eye-specific domains had occurred, then the region between clusters should be characterized by a low density, as this zone should be occupied by the afferents of the other eye. Alternatively, if segregation is incomplete, the density of the terminal arborization in the intercluster space should be comparable to the density at the border of the cluster. Density measurements in the regions surrounding the high-density clusters discloses a fundamental difference between arbors in normal and TTX-treated kittens (see Figure 9). In normal animals at and after P30, distinct, well-isolated clusters of terminals are present in large number. However, although many clusters are present in the TTX-treated group, the intercluster regions retain a high density of terminals indicating that well-sculpted patches are not common in animals in which the afferent activity has been silenced. The results in TTX-treated animals indicate that the lack of activity interferes specifically with the process of segregation. We hypothesize that this occurs by disrupting activity-dependent, competitive interactions among populations of geniculocortical afferents by which they are segregated in accordance to the eye of origin.

Originally proposed by Hebb,[21] and accommodated for a more modern perspective by Stent[52] and Changeux and Danchin,[9] the hypothesis of activity-dependent synaptic stabilization appears well suited for explaining both the developmental and plastic processes controlling eye dominance in the visual cortex. According to the Hebbian "rule," synaptic efficacy increases and synapses are stabilized when there is a temporal correlation between pre- and postsynaptic activity. The presence of correlated activity within one eye, either spontaneous or evoked,[37,38] and the absence of correlation between the two eyes would be used by the developing visual cortex to distinguish between the afferents serving the two eyes. Thus the presynaptic afferents serving one eye would aggregate because they would provide the most efficient input for activating the postsynaptic cortical cell. In contrast, the afferents serving the two eyes would become segregated due to the disjunctive effects of their uncorrelated activity. The conclusive evidence in support of this idea comes from an experiment by Stryker and Strickland[55] in which the activity in the two optic nerves was controlled by applying known patterns of electrical stimulation in TTX-treated animals. This experiment demonstrated that ocular-dominance columns, visualized autoradiographically, formed when the two optic nerves were stimulated asynchronously; but not when they were activated synchronously. It has also been confirmed that complete afferent segregation occurs in artificially strabismic animals where highly asynchronous activity exists between the two eyes.

PLASTICITY OF THE OCULAR DOMINANCE SYSTEM: EFFECTS OF MONOCULAR DEPRIVATION

The activity-dependent selective stabilization of synapses occurs not only during normal development but also during abnormal visual experience. The best-known example of experimental plasticity induced by an imbalance of activity between the two eyes is the alteration of cortical ocular dominance after unilateral lid suture. This experimental procedure, known as monocular deprivation, is particularly suitable for elucidating experience-dependent modifications of the visual cortex. Historically, this model was first used by Hubel and Wiesel[24,26] in their pioneering studies on cortical development to assert the dependence of cortical maturation upon activity in the afferent visual pathway. Since then, monocular deprivation has been used for studying the plastic capabilities of the visual cortex at different ages and thus for defining the time course of susceptibility to monocular deprivation, i.e., the critical period.

The physiological effects of monocular deprivation in animals deprived as neonates are manifested as a nearly complete disappearance of the neuronal responses through the deprived eye. Further, binocularly activated neurons, ordinarily found in normal animals, become rare, and the majority of neurons are dominated by the nondeprived eye. The period of susceptibility to monocular deprivation overlaps with the period when the major remodeling of geniculcortical projection occurs. In adult animals, binocular responses in the visual cortex are unaffected even after long periods of deprivation.[24,35] The anatomical correlates of the physiological effects of monocular deprivation are demonstrated in transneuronal transport experiments. In animals monocularly deprived for several months, from eye-opening to the end of the critical period, there is a striking reduction of the ocular domains pertaining to the deprived eye and an expansion of those of the nondeprived eye. In contrast, when monocular deprivation is performed in the adult, no changes in the cortical territories innervated by the deprived or nondeprived eye are observed.[35] In the adult, once a stable state has been reached, the pattern of geniculocortical innervation appears to be refractory to experience-dependent modifications.

Interestingly, the physiological changes induced by monocular deprivation during the critical period are clearly detectable even after two or three days. It has been suggested that in short-term monocular deprivation, the connections from the deprived eye become functionally subliminal due to functional suppression and/or to physiological down-regulation of the efficacy of existing synapses from the deprived eye. Supporting this hypothesis are studies in which acute suppression of

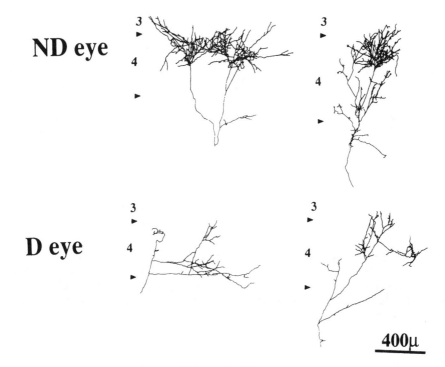

FIGURE 10 Coronal view of PHA-L immunostained geniculocortical arbors reconstructed in kittens in which one eye had been occluded for more than four weeks. The terminal arborization of the deprived (D) eye in layer IV shows a dramatic pruning in branches and a general reduction in complexity as compared to the nondeprived (ND) eye. From Antonini and Stryker.[3] Copyright ©1993 AAAS; reprinted by permission.

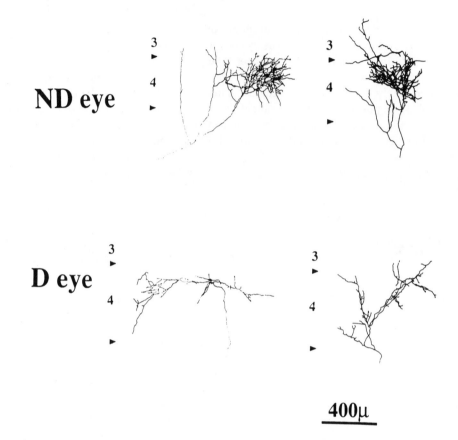

FIGURE 11   Coronal view of PHA-L immunostained geniculocortical arbors reconstructed in kittens in which one eye had been occluded for seven days. Note that the remodeling of the arbor of the deprived (D) eye is comparable to that observed in long-term deprivation (Figure 10). From Antonini and Stryker.[3] Copyright ©1993 AAAS; reprinted by permission.

input from the experienced eye, by enucleation or anesthesia of the optic nerve, appears to reveal this subliminal functional input.[8,15,42] In this view, the anatomical changes induced by a brief period of deprivation, would be too subtle to be detectable in the light microscope. However, the recovery in acute experimental conditions is never complete and depends critically on the duration of eye closure, suggesting that, although some connections from the deprived eye may be genuinely suppressed and can be restored to function, others are abnormal and permanently disrupted.

Our approach to the study of the mechanisms underlying short- and long-term monocular deprivation, was to reconstruct single axons in kittens monocularly deprived from eye-opening to P40, at which time the animals were sacrificed (long-term monocularly deprived group), and from kittens deprived for only 6 or 7 days (short-term monocularly deprived group) prior to sacrifice at P40.[3] We expected to see a remodeling of axons in the long-term group, in agreement with the autoradiographic data, but not in the short-term group where modifications were thought to be too small to be detected in axonal reconstructions.

In close correlation with the physiological observations, we saw a dramatic remodeling of the axons serving the deprived eye in both short- and long-term deprivation (see Figures 10 and 11). To quantify these observations, we measured and compared in both groups the total length of the terminal arborization and the number of branch points. Following both short- and long-term deprivation, both parameters were significantly smaller in the deprived eye arbors (see Figure 12). After short-term deprivation, the Total Length of arbors for the deprived eye, was also significantly reduced compared to axons reconstructed in normal animals at P30/31; an age close to that when the deprivation was initiated. This finding demonstrates

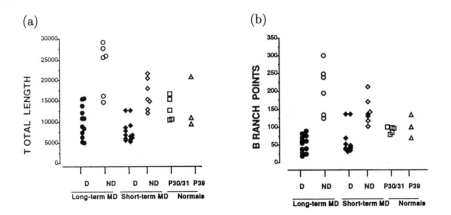

FIGURE 12   Analysis of terminal arborization of geniculocortical afferents in layer IV. (a) Scattergram of the total lengths of the terminal arborizations of geniculocortical axons serving the deprived (D) eye (filled symbols) and nondeprived (ND) eye (open symbols), in long- and short-term monocularly deprived animals (circles and diamonds, respectively). For comparison, data from normal animals at P30/31 (open squares) and at P39 (open triangles) are also plotted. (b) Scattergram of the number of branch points. Symbols as for (a). From Antonini and Stryker.[3] Copyright ©1993 AAAS; reprinted by permission.

that short-term MD does not merely "freeze" arbors in the state they were when the deprivation started but induces an effective elimination of axonal branches. Interestingly, arbors serving the nondeprived eye were not significantly richer than arbors reconstructed in normal animals. A possible overgrowth of the nondeprived arbors is instead suggested by the transneuronal transport experiments in long-term deprived animals. Our finding thus indicates that constructive processes leading to an overgrowth of branches, if present, require a longer period to be fully expressed, whereas destructive processes leading to branch elimination are very rapid.

While geniculocortical arbors serving the deprived eye appear to be affected in the same manner both in short- and long-term deprived animals, the plastic potentiality of the visual cortex in the two experimental conditions is certainly different. The effects of long-term monocular deprivation are not reversible by visual experience if the eye occlusion extends after the critical period. If the deprived eye is opened before the end of the critical period, some degree of recovery is still possible. However, in these cases, the recovered responses through the originally deprived eye show abnormal properties and the receptive fields of the newly formed binocular neurons have mismatched response characteristics. In contrast, if the animal is allowed normal vision following a brief episode of monocular deprivation, the deprived eye is still able to recapture the cortex in a complete and meaningful manner. In this case, the recovered responses are congruent with those of the originally experienced eye. It has been proposed that, in short- but not in long-term monocular deprivation, geniculocortical circuits have been "primed" or specified by their previous normal visual experience, and are therefore able to reestablish precise functional connections providing complete functional recovery once the eye is exposed to normal visual experience.[43] The mechanisms for such "priming" is unknown, but our results suggest that this mechanism allows for the regrowth of connections from the deprived eye according to a preexisting model of anatomical connections. Alternatively, we can speculate that, after short-term monocular deprivation, the recovered precise functionality of the deprived eye depends on an increase in the efficacy of synaptic sites on the remaining axonal branches.

THE CRITICAL PERIOD

The remarkably rapid functional modifications of visual cortical neurons after monocular deprivation are temporally limited to the critical period. In the cat, susceptibility to the effects of monocular deprivation begins shortly after birth, peaks around the fifth or sixth week of age, then declines gradually over the next few months. This decline of sensitivity is supported by the observation that longer periods of monocular deprivation are required to produce the same cortical effects.[45] Finally, in the adult, capture of cortical responses by the experienced eye are no longer observed even after extensive periods of monocular deprivation.[24,35]

To what extent is the physiological cortical plasticity dependent on the degree of maturation of geniculocortical projections? There is now convincing evidence that the time course of the critical period is different for neurons located in or outside layer IV.[14] The binocularity of neurons in layer IV becomes unaffected by monocular deprivation after the sixth postnatal week which is temporally coincident with the segregation of geniculocortical afferents. In contrast, within the extragranular layers (the layers outside layer IV), the critical period appears to decline slowly between the sixth week and one year of age.

In addition, dark rearing experiments, in which the time course of the critical period had been altered, confirm that different mechanisms are involved during the critical period for the maturation of layer IV and the extragranular layers. Cynader and Mitchell[12] and Mower et al.[44] raised kittens in total darkness beyond the critical period and then allowed a period of monocular experience. They determined that monocular deprivation did not affect binocularity of neurons within layer IV, suggesting that the critical period for afferent segregation and ocular dominance plasticity is restricted to early life. In contrast, in the extragranular layers, there was a significant shift in the ocular dominance in favor of the open eye. This suggests that in the extragranular layers, the critical period is far less age-dependent and can be influenced by prior visual experience. Thus the extragranular layers maintain plasticity for a significantly longer period than required for the geniculocortical afferents to establish a stable pattern of segregation within layer IV. Therefore, it appears that the mechanism controlling ocular dominance in layer IV primarily involves geniculocortical afferents, while ocular dominance in the extragranular layers appears to be predominantly influenced by intracortical circuits.

There is evidence indicating that both noradrenergic and cholinergic pathways may be involved in the mechanism for plasticity.[32,51] In addition, specific glutamate receptors (N-methyl-D-aspartate-receptors, NMDA receptors) have been suggested to be critically associated with plasticity, as they are involved in the activity-dependentfox potentiation of synapses.[5] It is of interest that NMDA receptors in layer IV are more abundant and provide a greater contribution to visual responses during the period of afferent segregation.[6,58] Later in development and in adulthood, NMDA receptors are activated by the visual input in layers II and III, but no longer in layer IV. It should be noted that the interpretation of an instructive role of these transmitter pathways in experience-dependent modification of cortical responses is controversial in that their manipulation interferes with the functional state of the cortex and is bound to alter plasticity by nonspecific mechanisms. For further discussion the reader is directed to reviews by Fox and Daw,[17] and Fregnac and Imbert.[18]

PLASTICITY IN THE ADULT

There is growing evidence of activity-dependent plasticity in the visual cortex of the adult. For example, in the adult monkey, monocular enucleation or blockade of optic nerve activity by intraocular injection of TTX results in a profound and rapid alteration in the expression of neurotransmitter phenotypes in the deprived ocular dominance columns, indicating that the neuronal component of layer IV is still capable of activity-dependent plasticity.[30] Similarly, monocular deprivation in the adult, although ineffective in producing a physiological alteration in ocular dominance, induces modifications in the expression of cytochrome oxidase in the visual cortex.[59] These biochemical changes may appear subtle in comparison to the striking plastic effects during the critical period. However, the observation that the same plastic response, such as the light-induced expression of immediate-early genes, is induced more strongly and extensively during development than in adulthood,[60] suggests that the major difference in plasticity at the two different ages may reside not in the nature, but in the degree of the functional and/or anatomical alterations.

Another attractive hypothesis is that similar functional changes underlie cortical plasticity in both infant and adults. In the infant, however, this functional plasticity induces rapid changes in structure. From this new structural base, further plasticity, first functional then structural can follow. Over many cycles of plasticity, inputs could be enhanced many times or lost entirely. According to this hypothesis, only the first half cycle of functional plasticity would take place in adults.

Recent experiments by several groups[20,22,31] have demonstrated that in the mature brain the visual cortex is able to undergo dynamic alterations of cortical topography and receptive field size. These experiments are similar to those in the somatosensory system where plastic reorganization in the adult had previously been demonstrated.[1][39,40] In a study by Gilbert and Wiesel,[20] focal lesions were placed in corresponding loci in both retinae and cortical topography was studied at various times after the intervention. As expected, immediately after the lesion, visual cortical neurons with receptive fields located within the lesioned area were initially unresponsive to visual stimulation. However, even at this early stage, neurons located close to the lesion boundaries showed a large increase of receptive field size, most likely attributable to a functional reorganization of neuronal circuitry, such as release of inhibitory interactions, rather than to morphological changes.[33] Long-term changes were more dramatic. Over time the "silenced" cortex underwent a striking topographic reorganization and developed a representation of a different part of the retina. Receptive fields located near the margins of the silenced area expanded in size and "filled" the silenced area so that the representation of the part of the retina surrounding the lesion had developed an enlarged cortical representation. After several months recovery, the remapping of the cortical topography involved as much as 6–10 mm of cortical territory.

---

[1]See also Ramachandran[47]; Pons[46]; Taub[57]; Merzenich and Jenkins[40]; this volume.)

Where might this reorganization occur in the visual pathway? Electrophysiological recordings indicated the persistence of a silent area within the geniculate. As such, the reorganization must have an intracortical basis. We have previously noted that the ability of geniculocortical connectivity to undergo changes in response to manipulation of the environment is lost early in life. Gilbert and Wiesel[20] suggest that the existing long-range horizontal connections in layers II and III provide the anatomical basis for the cortical reorganization after retinal lesions, as they spread for distances comparable to the expanse of the topographic reorganization. Originally these connections appear to be subthreshold and inefficient, and the need for long-term recovery for the complete "filling in" phenomenon suggests that an increase of the synaptic efficacy of the preexisting horizontal connections, or additional sprouting in the preexisting neuronal framework must have occurred (Taub,[57] this volume).[46] Indeed, axonal sprouting in the functionally reorganized visual cortex has been demonstrated,[13] indicating that the potential for an activity-dependent plasticity in these long-range horizontal corticocortical connections, observed in kittens' early in development,[36] is still present in the mature animal.

CONCLUSION

The visual pathway provides a model for studying the organization and development of sensory systems. A thorough understanding of its mechanisms of plasticity should provide insights into the issues and opportunities for the recovery of function. In particular, with greater understanding of the cellular events underlying the plasticity responsible for normal development in the infant, we now have an opportunity to understand where such plasticity fails following injury in adults and how to restart it to facilitate recovery.

ACKNOWLEDGMENTS

The research reported in this chapter was supported by Grants NIH EY09768 and EY02874.

REFERENCES

1. Anderson, P.A., J. Olivarria, and R. C. Van Sluyters. "The Overall Pattern of Ocular Dominance Bands in Cat Visual Cortex." *J. Neurosci.* **8** (1988): 2183–2200.

2. Antonini, A., and M. P. Stryker. "Development of Individual Geniculocortical Arbors in Cat Striate Cortex and Effects of Binocular Impulse Blockade." *J. Neurosci.* **13** (1993): 3549–3573.

3. Antonini, A., and M. P. Stryker. "Rapid Remodeling of Axonal Arbors in Visual Cortex." *Science* **260** (1993): 1819–1821.

4. Blakemore, C., and R. van Sluyters. "Reversal of the Physiological Effects of Monocular Deprivation in Kittens: Further Evidence for a Sensitive Period." *J. Physiol. (Lond.)* **237** (1974): 195–216.

5. Bliss, T. V. P., and M. A. Lynch. "Long-Term Potentiation of Synaptic Transmission in the Hippocampus: Properties and Mechanisms." In *Long-Term Potentiation: From Biophysics to Behavior*, edited by P. W. Landfeld and S. A. Deadwyler, 3–72. New York: Alan R. Liss, 1988.

6. Bode-Greuel, K. M., and W. Singer. "The Development of N-methyl-D-aspartate Receptors in Cat Visual Cortex." *Dev. Brain Res.* **46** (1991): 197–204.

7. Buisseret, P., and M. Imbert. "Visual Cortical Cells: Their Developmental Properties in Normal and Dark Reared Kittens." *J. Physiol. (Lond.)* **255** (1976): 511–525.

8. Burchfiel, J. L., and F. H. Duffy. "Role of Intracortical Inhibition in Deprivation Amblyopia: Reversal by Microiontophoretic Bicuculline." *Brain Res.* **206** (1981): 479–484.

9. Changeux, J., and A. Danchin. "Selective Stabilization of Developing Synapses as a Mechanism for the Specification of Neuronal Networks." *Nature* **264** (1976): 705–711.

10. Chapman, B., and M. P. Stryker. "Development of Orientation Selectivity in Ferret Visual Cortex and Effects of Deprivation." *J. Neurosci.* **13** (1993): 5251–5262.

11. Chapman, B., K. R. Zahs, and M. P. Stryker. "Relation of Cortical Cell Orientation Selectivity to Alignment of Receptive Fields of the Geniculocortical Afferents that Arborize Within a Single Orientation Column in Ferret Visual Cortex." *J. Neurosci.* **11** (1991): 1347–1358.

12. Cynader, M., and D. E. Mitchell. "Prolonged Sensitivity to Monocular Deprivation in Dark-Reared Cats." *J. Neurophysiol.* **43** (1980): 1026–1040.

13. Darian-Smith, C., and C. Gilbert. "Axonal Sprouting Accompanies Functional Reorganization in Adult Cat Striate Cortex." *Nature* **368** (1994): 737–740.

14. Daw, N. W., K. Fox, H. Sato, and D. Czepita. "Critical Period for Monocular Deprivation in the Cat Visual Cortex." *J. Neurophysiol.* **67** (1992): 197–202.

15. Duffy, F. H., S. R. Snodgrass, J. L. Burchfield, and J. L. Conway. "Bicuculine Reversal of Deprivation Amblyopia in the Cat." *Nature* **260** (1976): 256–257.

16. Ferster, D., and S. M. LeVay. "The Axonal Arborizations of Lateral Geniculate Neurons in the Striate Cortex of the Cat." *J. Comp. Neurol.* **182** (1978): 923–944.

17. Fox, K., and N. W. Daw. "Do NMDA Receptors Have a Critical Function in Visual Cortical Plasticity?" *TINS* **16** (1993): 116–122.
18. Fregnac, Y., and M. Imbert. "Development of Neuronal Selectivity in Primary Visual Cortex of Cat." *Physiol. Rev.* **64** (1984): 325–434.
19. Gerfen, C. R., and P. E. Sawchenko. "An Anterograde Neuroanatomical Tracing Method that Shows the Detailed Morphology of Neurons, Their Axons and Terminals: Immunohistochemical Localization of an Axonally Transported Plant Lectin, Phaseolus Vulgaris Leucoagglutinin (PHA-L)." *Brain Res.* **290** (1984): 219–238.
20. Gilbert, C. D., and T. N. Wiesel. "Receptive Field Dynamics in Adult Primary Visual Cortex." *Nature* **356** (1992): 150–152.
21. Hebb, D. O. *Organization of Behaviour*. New York: John Wiley & Son, 1949.
22. Heinen, S. J., and A. A. Skavenski. "Recovery of Visual Responses in Foveal V1 Neurons Following Bilateral Foveal Lesions in Adult Monkey." *Exp. Brain Res.* **83** (1991): 670–674.
23. Hubel, D. H., and T. N. Wiesel. "Receptive Fields, Binocular Interaction and Functional Architecture in the Cat's Visual Cortex." *J. Physiol. (Lond.)* **160** (1962): 106–154.
24. Hubel, D. H., and T. N. Wiesel. "The Period of Susceptibility of the Physiological Effects of Unilateral Eye Closure in Kittens." *J. Physiol. (Lond.)* **206** (1970): 419–436.
25. Hubel, D. H., and T. N. Wiesel. "Laminar and Columnar Distribution of Geniculocortical Fibers in the Macaque Monkey." *J. Comp. Neurol.* **146** (1972): 421–450.
26. Hubel, D. H., and T. N. Wiesel. "Functional Architecture of the Macaque Monkey Visual Cortex." *Proc. R. Soc. B.* **198** (1977): 1–59.
27. Hubel, D. H., T. N. Wiesel, and S. LeVay. "Plasticity of Ocular Dominance Columns in Monkey Striate Cortex." *Philos. Trans. R. Soc. Lond. B* **278** (1977): 377–409.
28. Humphrey, A. L., M. Sur, D. J. Uhlrich, and S. M. Sherman. "Projection Patterns of Individual X- and Y-Cell Axons from the Lateral Geniculate Nucleus to Cortical Area 17 in the Cat." *J. Comp. Neurol.* **233** (1985): 159–189.
29. Humphrey, A. L., M. Sur, D. J. Uhlrich, and S. M. Sherman. "Termination Patterns of X- and Y-Cell Axons in the Visual Cortex of the Cat: Projections to Area 18, to the 17/18 Border Region, and to Both Areas 17 and 18." *J. Comp. Neurol.* **233** (1985): 190–212.
30. Jones, E. G. "The Role of Afferent Activity in the Maintenance of Primate Neocortical Function." *J. Exp. Biol.* **153** (1990): 155–176.
31. Kaas, J. H., L. A. Krubitzer, Y. M. Chino, A. L. Langston, E. H. Polley, and N. Blair. "Reorganization of Retinotopic Cortical Maps in Adult Mammals After Lesions of the Retina." *Science* **248** (1990): 229–231.
32. Kasamatsu, T., and J. D. Pettigrew. "Depletion of Catecholamines: Failure of Ocular Dominance Shift After Monocular Occlusion in Kittens." *Science* **194** (1976): 206–109.

33. Katz, E., J. D. Victor, and K. P. Purpura. "Dymanic Changes in Cortical Responses Following Removal and Restoration of Nearby Visual Inputs." This volume

34. LeVay, S. M., M. P. Stryker, and C. J. Shatz. "Ocular Dominance Columns and Their Development in Layer IV of the Cat's Visual Cortex. A Quantitative Study." *J. Comp. Neurol.* **179** (1978): 559–576.

35. LeVay, S. M., T. N. Wiesel, and D. H. Hubel. "The Development of Ocular Dominance Columns in Normal and Visually Deprived Monkeys." *J. Comp. Neurol.* **191** (1980): 1–51.

36. Lowel, S., and W. Singer. "Selection of Intrinsic Horizontal Connections in the Visual Cortex by Correlated Neuronal Activity." *Science* **255** (1992): 209–212.

37. Mastronarde, D. N. "Correlated Firing of Cat Retinal Ganglion Cells. I. Spontaneously Active Inputs to X- and Y-Cells." *J. Neurophysiol.* **49** (1983): 303–324.

38. Mastronarde, D. N. "Correlated Firing of Cat Retinal Ganglion Cells. II. Response of X- and Y-Cells to Single Quantal Response." *J. Neurophysiol.* **49** (1983):325–345.

39. Merzenich, M. M., G. H. Recanzone, W. M. Jenkins, and K. A. Grajski. "Adaptive Mechanisms in Cortical Networks Underlying Cortical Contributions to Learning and Nondeclarative Memory." In *The Brain.* Cold Spring Harbor Symposia on Quantitative Biology, Vol. 55, 873–887. New York: Cold Spring Harbor, 1990.

40. Merzenich, M. M., and W. M. Jenkins. "Cortical Plasticity, Learning and Learning Dysfunction." This volume.

41. Miller, K. D. "A Model for the Development of Simple Cell Receptive Fields and the Ordered Arrangement of Orientation Columns Through Activity Dependent Competition Between On- and Off-Center Onput." *J. Neurosci.* **14** (1994): 409–441.

42. Mioche, L., and W. Singer. "Chronic Recordings from Single Sites of Kitten Striate Cortex During Experience-Dependent Modifications of Receptive-Field Properties." *J. Neurophysiol.* **62** (1989): 185–197.

43. Movshon, J. A. "Reversal of the Physiological Effects of Monocular Deprivation in the Kitten's Visual Cortex." *J. Physiol. (Lond.)* **261** (1976): 125–174.

44. Mower, G. M., C. J. Caplan, W. G. Christen, and F. H. Duffy. "Dark Rearing Prolongs Physiological but not Anatomical Plasticity of the Cat Visual Cortex." *J. Comp. Neurol.* **235** (1985): 448–466.

45. Olson, C. R., and R. D. Freeman. "Profile of the Sensitive Period for Monocular Deprivation in Kittens." *Exp. Brain Res.* **39** (1980): 17–21.

46. Pons, T. P. "The Plastic Brain of Adult Primates." This volume.

47. Ranachandran, V. S. "Plasticity in the Adult Human Brain: Is There Reason for Optimism?" This volume.

48. Shatz, C., S. H. Lindstrom, and T. N. Wiesel. "The Distribution of Afferents Representing the Right and Left Eyes in the Cat's Visual Cortex." *Brain Res.* **131** (1977): 103–116.
49. Shatz, C. J., and M. P. Stryker. "Ocular Dominance in Layer IV of the Cat's Visual Cortex and Effects of Monocular Deprivation." *J. Physiol. (Lond.)* **281** (1978): 267–283.
50. Sillito, A. M. "The Contribution of Inhibitory Mechanisms to the Receptive Field Properties of Neurones of the Striate Cortex of the Cat." *J. Physiol (Lond.)* **250** (1975): 305–329.
51. Singer, W. "Evidence for a Central Control of Developmental Plasticity in the Striate Cortex of Kittens." In *Developmental Biology of Vision*, edited by E. D. Freeman, Vol. 27, 135–147. New York: Plenum, 1979.
52. Stent, G. S. "A Physiological Mechanism for Hebb's Postulate of Learning." *Proc. Natl. Acad. Sci. USA* **70** (1973): 997–1001.
53. Stryker, M. P. "The Role of Early Experience in the Development and Maintenance of Orientation Selectivity in the Cat's Visual Cortex." *Neurosci. Res. Bull.* **15** (1977): 454–463.
54. Stryker, M. P., and W. A. Harris. "Binocular Impulse Blockade Prevents the Formation of Ocular Dominance Columns in Cat Visual Cortex." *J. Neurosci.* **6** (1986): 2117–2133.
55. Stryker, M. P., and S. L. Strickland. "Physiological Segregation of Ocular Dominance Columns Depends on the Pattern of Afferent Electrical Activity." *Invest. Ophthalmol. Vis. Sci. (suppl)* **25** (1984): 278.
56. Stryker, M. P. "Activity-Dependent Reorganization of Afferents in the Developing Mammalian Visual System." In *Development of the Visual System*, edited by D. N. Lam and C. Shatz. Cambridge, MA: MIT Press, 1991.
57. Taub, E., and J. E. Cargo. "Increasing Behavioral Plasticity Following Central Nervous System Damage in Monkeys and Man: A MEthod with Potential Application Human Developmental Motor Disability." This volume.
58. Tsumoto, T., K. Hagihara, H. Sato, and Y. Hata. "NMDA Receptors in the Visual Cortex of Young Kittens are More Effective than Those of Adult Cats." *Nature* **327** (1987): 513–514.
59. Wong-Reley, M., and E. W. Carroll. "Effect of Impulse Blockade on Cytochrome Oxidase Activity in Monkey Visual System." *Nature* **307** (1984): 572.
60. Worley, P. F., A. J. Cole, T. H. Murphy, B. A. Christy, Y. Nakabeppu, and J. M. Baraban. "Synaptic Regulation of Immediate-Early Genes in Brain." In *The Brain.* Cold Spring Harbor Symposia on Quantitative Biology, Vol. 55, 213–223. New York: Cold Spring Harbor, 1990.
61. Zahs, K. R., and M. P. Stryker. "Segregation of On and Off Afferents to Ferret Visual Cortex." *J. Neurophysiol.* **59** (1988): 1410–1429.

Maree J. Webster,*† Jocelyne Bachevalier,*‡ and Leslie G. Ungerleider*
*Laboratory of Neuropsychology, National Institute of Mental Health, Building 49, Room 1B80, Bethesda, MD 20892
‡Present address: University of Texas Medical School, Department of Neurobiology and Anatomy, 6431 Fannin, Room 7176, Houston, TX 77225
†Correspondence to Dr. Maree J. Webster, Laboratory of Neuropsychology, NIMH, Building 49, Room 1B80, Bethesda, MD 20892, 301- 496-5625, ext. 226 (voice), 301-402-0046 (fax), mwebster@ln.nimh.nih.gov

Development and Plasticity of Visual Memory Circuits

This research was funded by the U.S. Government, therefore it is not copyrightable.

The ability to see an object and remember having seen it before, even after a single brief exposure, is termed recognition memory. This is an explicit form of memory retrieval, involving the conscious recall of a prior experience. Recognition memory is to be distinguished from implicit memory retrieval, which is manifest without conscious recall (e.g., Jeo et al.,[14] this volume). In primates, the cortical pathway for recognition memory of visually presented objects consists of projections from primary visual cortex to multiple visual areas in prestriate cortex, which, in turn, project to areas TEO and TE, located in the posterior and anterior parts, respectively, of the inferior temporal cortex (for reviews, see Desimone and Ungerleider,[8] Felleman and Van Essen,[9] Maunsell and Newsome,[17] Ungerleider,[30] Van Essen et al.,[32] and Weller[36]). Visual information received by area TE is then transmitted to limbic structures within the medial temporal lobe, including the amygdala, hippocampus, and rhinal cortex. Area TE projects directly to both the amygdala and perirhinal cortex and indirectly to the hippocampus via perirhinal and entorhinal cortex[1,2,12,13,15,26,29,33,34] (see Figure 1). Conscious recognition of an object can

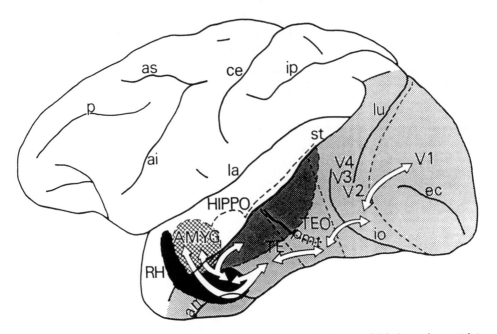

FIGURE 1 Flow of visual information from primary visual area (V1) through prestriate cortical areas (V2, V3, and V4) to inferior temporal areas TEO and TE, and from TE into the limbic structures (rhinal cortex [RH], amygdala [AMYG], and hippocampus [HIPPO]). Sulcal abbreviations: ai, inferior arcuate; amt, anterior middle temporal; as, superior arcuate; ce, central; ec, external calcarine; io, inferior occipital; ip, intraparietal; la, lateral; lu, lunate; p, principal; pmt, posterior middle temporal; st, superior temporal. Reproduced from Ungerleider and Murray.[31]

only occur through the interaction of the visual pathway and the limbic system. Disrupting this interaction, for example by removal of area TE or by combined damage to the limbic structures, results in a severe impairment of recognition memory.[20,21]

In the course of studying the development of recognition memory, we have found that limbic system damage in infancy, like that in adulthood, causes severe impairment in recognition memory. By contrast, while damage to area TE in adulthood also leads to a severe impairment, the same damage in infancy leads to sparing of memory function. Indeed, monkeys with TE lesions in infancy demonstrate almost normal recognition memory when tested both as infants[6] and later as adults.[4] Therefore, the sparing of memory function appears to be permanent. Thus, the question arises: How does the visual cortical pathway interact with the limbic structures after neonatal removal of area TE? In this paper we describe several anatomical and behavioral studies undertaken to answer this question. The results of these investigations have revealed, first, that normal infant monkeys possess transient corticolimbic projections which retract during development.[34] Second, neonatal lesions of area TE induce the maintenance of these transient projections as well as the sprouting of additional ones.[35] Finally, visual cortical areas not normally involved in recognition memory may become involved if area TE is removed early in life.

BEHAVIORAL ASSESSMENT OF RECOGNITION MEMORY: DELAYED NONMATCHING-TO-SAMPLE

To test recognition memory for visually presented objects, we use the delayed nonmatching-to-sample (DNMS) task.[19] Each trial consists of an acquisition phase, in which the monkey is presented with a baited sample object over a central foodwell, followed 10 seconds later by a test phase. In the test phase, the sample object, now unbaited, is paired with a baited novel object, each of which is presented over a lateral foodwell. The monkey's task in the test phase is to select the novel object to get its food reward. Thirty seconds later another set of trials is administered in the same way, but with a new pair of objects, the novel object appearing over the right or left foodwell in a pseudo-random order. Testing continues in this manner at the rate of 20 trials per day, each with a new pair of objects, until the animal reaches a criterion of 90 correct responses in 100 consecutive trials.

Following a two-week rest period, the monkey is retrained to criterion on DNMS and then given a performance test in which, first, the delay between acquisition and test is increased in stages from the original 10 seconds to 30 seconds, 60 seconds, and finally 120 seconds, each given for a block of 100 trials distributed over five sessions; and then, the number, or list length, of sample objects presented successively in acquisition before pairing each with a novel object in the test phase is increased in stages from the original single object to 3, 5, and finally 10 objects, each presented for a block of 150 trials distributed over five sessions.

In Figure 2 we show the performance of monkeys tested on the DNMS task averaged across all delays and list lengths. The mean performance score for normal adult monkeys is 96%, whereas monkeys with bilateral TE removal in adulthood are significantly impaired with a mean score of 71% (also see Mishkin et al.[19,21]). No doubt the ability of these monkeys to perform above chance indicates that the lesion had not totally disconnected the limbic system from its visual input. Like normal adult monkeys, normal infant monkeys, tested at ten months of age, perform well on the task, obtaining a mean performance score of 91%. Monkeys with bilateral TE removal in the first two weeks of life and tested at ten months of age perform nearly as well, obtaining a score of 84%.[6] Moreover, this sparing of function appears

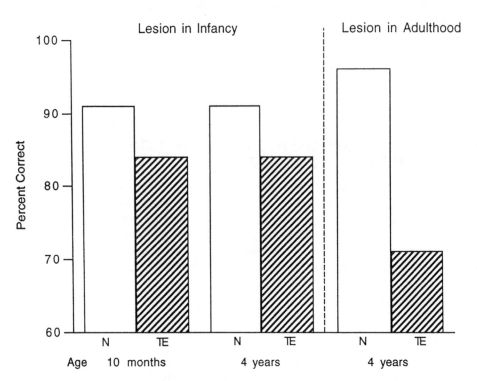

VISUAL RECOGNITION PERFORMANCE TEST

FIGURE 2 Mean scores on the recognition performance test (averaged across delays and list lengths) of normal monkeys (N) and monkeys with TE lesions (TE) in infancy or in adulthood.

to be permanent in that monkeys with TE removed in infancy continue to perform well even when tested at four years of age.[4]

TRANSIENT CORTICO-LIMBIC CONNECTIONS IN INFANT MONKEYS

Because recognition memory depends on the interaction of the visual cortical pathway with the limbic structures, we began our anatomical studies by examining how this interaction could occur in the absence of area TE. As a first step, we compared the projections of area TEO in normal infant monkeys to those in normal adults.[34] Based on previous reports of exuberant projections in the brains of newborn animals,[11] we hypothesized that TEO in infants might also show such exuberant projections, and one possible target would be the limbic system.

To test this possibility, area TEO was injected with tritiated amino-acids ($^3H - AA$) or wheat germ agglutinin conjugated to horseradish peroxidase (WGA-HRP) in 1-week-old and 3- to 4-year-old rhesus monkeys. The injection sites were of comparable size and location, thus allowing us to compare infant and adult cases. Although many of the connections were similar, several striking differences between infants and adults were noted. First, TEO projects to the lateral basal nucleus of the amygdala in infants but not in adults. As shown in Figure 3, injections of area TEO in adult monkeys produced retrogradely labeled cells in the lateral basal nucleus

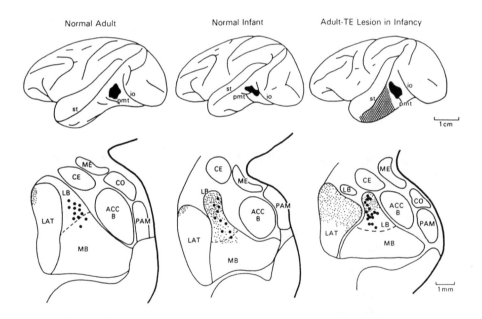

FIGURE 3 Location of area TEO injection sites in normal adult and normal infant monkeys and in adult monkeys with bilateral lesions of area TE in infancy. Injection sites are shown in black on the lateral views of the hemispheres. The hatched region represents the extent of the lesion on the lateral surface of the hemisphere. The distribution of retrogradely labeled cells (large dots) and anterogradely labeled terminals (small dots) are shown on coronal sections through the amygdala. Abbreviations of amygdala nuclei: ACC B, accessory basal; CE, central; CO, cortical; LAT, lateral; LB, lateral basal; ME, medial; MB, medial basal; PAM, periamygdaloid. For sulcal abbreviations, see Figure 1. Figure adapted from Webster et al.[34,35]

(LB) of the amygdala but no anterogradely labeled terminals, supporting previous reports that LB projects to area TEO but this projection is not reciprocal.[2,12,13] In infant monkeys, by contrast, injections of area TEO produced both retrogradely labeled cells and anterogradely labeled terminals in LB. This projection from area TEO to LB in the infant must be transient since it does not exist in the adult. In both infants and adults, we found a small patch of anterogradely labeled terminals in the dorsal part of the lateral nucleus (L) of the amygdala (Figure 3).

The second difference between infants and adults is that TEO projects to parahippocampal area TF in infants but not in adults (Figure 4). In adult monkeys, injections of area TEO produced retrogradely labeled cells but not anterogradely labeled terminals in area TF. In infant monkeys, by contrast, both cells and terminals in area TF were observed. Like the projection from TEO to LB of the amygdala, the projection from TEO to TF in the infant must be transient since it does not exist in the adult.

It therefore appears that there exist in the infant but not in the adult several pathways, other than the one through area TE, whereby visual information can reach the limbic structures. First, there is a direct projection from area TEC to the amygdata. And second, there is an indirect projection from area TEO to the hippocampus and rhinal cortex via area TF. Either or both of the projections in infant monkeys could sustain their spared memory function, following TE removal.

ANATOMICAL REORGANIZATION AFTER AREA TE LESIONS

Given the presence of projections from TEO to both the amygdala and area TF in infant monkeys, we hypothesized that a lesion of area TE early in development might lead to the maintenance of these normally transient projections and thereby account, at least in part, for the sparing of visual recognition memory. To test this possibility, we compared the connections of area TEO in adult monkeys that had received TE lesions in infancy to the connections of area TEO in adult monkeys that had received TE lesions in adulthood.[35]

As shown in Figure 3, injections of area TEO in adult monkeys that sustained lesions of TE in infancy produced both retrogradely labeled cells and anterogradely labeled terminals in LB of the amygdala. Thus, the normally transient projection from area TEO to LB had been maintained as a result of the early TE lesion. In addition, anterogradely labeled terminals were found throughout L, indicating that the normally limited projection from area TEO to the dorsal part of L had expanded to invade the terminal space normally occupied by terminals from TE. That is, the axons projecting from area TEO to L had sprouted additional arbors to terminate in the deafferented portion of L. Injections of area TEO in monkeys that sustained lesions of TE in adulthood produced retrogradely labeled cells in LB This

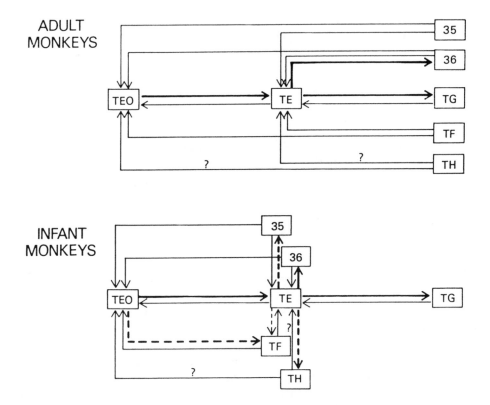

FIGURE 4 Summary diagram illustrating the feedforward and feedback projections in adult and infant monkeys based on laminar patterns of connections following injections of retrograde and anterograde tracers in areas TEO and TE. Heavy solid lines indicate feedforward projections, i.e., those originating in layers III and/or terminating mainly in layer IV. Thin solid lines indicate feedback projections, i.e., those projections originating mainly in layer V/VI and/or terminating outside layer IV. Broken lines denote transient projections that are present in infants but not in adults. Question marks indicate those projections that originate from both layer III and V/VI and thus may turn out to be of the intermediate type rather than feedback. As one progresses from left to right in the figure, there is a progression from lower-order to higher-order areas; areas within a column are at the same hierarchical level. Thus, in the adult, areas 35, 36, TG, TF, and TH are higher order than area TE, whereas in the infant, areas 35, 36, TF, and TH are at the same hierarchical level as area TE. The adult pattern is achieved by the removal of transient projections from area TEO to area TF, from area TE to areas 35, TF and TH, and from area TE to layer I of area 36. Reproduced from Webster et al.[34]; reprinted by permission.

and a small patch of anterogradely labeled terminals in the dorsal part of L. pattern of labeling was exactly the same as that found in normal adult monkeys, indicating that no reorganization of TEO-amygdalar connections had resulted from the adult lesion. Unlike the normally transient projection from TEO to LB of the amygdala, the one from TEO to TF was not maintained as a result of early TE removal.

PLASTICITY OF VISUAL ASSOCIATION CORTEX: BEHAVIORAL STUDIES

To determine if the maintenance and sprouting of projections from area TEO to the amygdala could play a role in the permanent preservation of visual memory ability in monkeys that had received bilateral removal of area TE in infancy, we severed this connection by removing area TEO bilaterally in four such monkeys when they reached adulthood. As shown in Figure 5, their performance, unexpectedly, did not decline after this lesion. The mean performance score on DNMS for monkeys with lesions of area TE in infancy was 85%, compared to 84.5% after the additional TEO lesion in adulthood. This finding suggests that the projections from area TEO, either to the amygdala or elsewhere, are not critical for the sparing of memory function. As will be described below, however, TEO does appear to contribute to such sparing.

In the next series of experiments, we investigated whether visual association areas that are not normally important for visual recognition memory become important if area TE is removed in infancy. The most likely candidates are those cortical areas that are known both to receive visual information and to project to medial temporal-lobe structures. These areas include: (1) the superior temporal polysensory (STP) area, located on the upper bank of the superior temporal sulcus adjacent to area TE; (2) area PG in the inferior parietal cortex; and (3) area TF, located in the posterior parahippocampal gyrus. Because all of these areas could conceivably have contributed to the spared visual recognition memory after early TE damage, we prepared a group of monkeys with neonatal TE removal who, at two years of age, were given additional, combined lesions of areas STP, PG, TF, and TEO. A second group of monkeys with neonatal TE removal was given, at two years of age, combined lesions of STP, PG, and TF, but not TEO. As shown in Figure 5, this latter group was not impaired following the additional lesion. Their mean score on the performance test was 81%, whereas the group with the additional lesion that included area TEO was significantly impaired with a mean score of 68%. This score is not significantly different from the mean score of 71% obtained by monkeys that received lesions of area TE in adulthood. Moreover, combined lesions of areas STP, PG, TF, and TEO in adults that were previously normal produced only a relatively mild impairment (mean score of 81%) when compared to their performance prior to the lesion, supporting the idea that these areas are not normally critical in adult-hood for recognition memory. Thus, the results suggest that, during infancy, visual

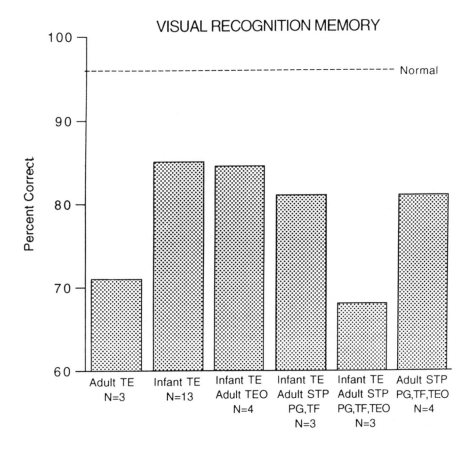

FIGURE 5   Mean scores on the recognition performance test, averaged across delays and list lengths, for six groups of monkeys. The groups include monkeys with lesions of area TE in adulthood, monkeys with lesions of area TE in infancy, monkeys with lesions of area TE in adi;tjppd plus an additional lesion of area TEO in adulthood, monkeys with lesions of area TE in infancy plus an additional lesion of areas STP, PG, and TF in adulthood, monkeys with a lesion of area TE in infancy plus an additional lesion of areas STP, PG, TF, and TEO in infancy, and finally normal monkeys with a combined lesion of areas STP, PG, TF, and TEO in adulthood. The dashed line represents the mean performance of normal adult monkeys.

memory functions are widely distributed throughout many visual association areas, but that, with further maturation, the function gradually becomes more localized to area TE. As a result of early damage to area TE, however, it appears that visual recognition memory processes remain widely distributed throughout the visual cortical areas, all of which, consequently, contribute to the resultant sparing of visual memory function.

FURTHER EVIDENCE FOR CORTICAL IMMATURITY

There is additional evidence indicating that association areas of cortex, such as area TE, are immature at birth and may therefore possess the capacity for functional plasticity. First, not only do transient projections exist in infancy which are eliminated during development, but even for many of those projections that are retained the laminar distribution of their terminals are initially widespread and only later become pruned to achieve the adultlike pattern. One example is that whereas area TE in adults projects to layer I in perirhinal areas 35 and 36, in infants the projection is to layers I and IV. Further evidence of cortical immaturity in infants is provided by our studies showing that there is an areal-specific laminar pattern in the distribution of both cholinergic and opiatergic receptors in sensory association cortex in adult monkeys, but these receptors are evenly distributed across all layers of association cortex in infants.[3,25] Finally, metabolic mapping studies have shown that adultlike levels of glucose utilization in visual association cortex develop gradually, and within area TE are not reached until about six months of age.[5] Together, this evidence points to the relative immaturity of association cortex in neonates and its potential for reorganization.

THE ROLE OF THE RHINAL CORTEX

Early investigations into the neural substrate underlying recognition memory in adult monkeys found that combined lesions of the amygdala and hippocampus produced a profound impairment in recognition memory ability.[19,20,37] However, this finding was complicated by the fact that these lesions almost always involved additional damage to the adjacent rhinal cortex, including both the entorhinal (Brodmann area 28) and perirhinal (Brodmann areas 35 and 36) areas. Moreover, removal of the amygdala invariably also damaged the perirhinal afferents that ascend adjacent to the lateral aspect of the amygdala.[23] Thus, it was at least possible that some or all of the recognition memory impairment produced by combined lesions of the amygdala and hippocampus was due to the involvement of the rhinal cortex.

Recent behavioral studies have evaluated the contribution of rhinal cortex to recognition memory. These studies have found, first, that removal of the rhinal cortex alone is sufficient to produce severe recognition memory impairments,[18,22] and second, that neurochemical lesions of the amygdala and hippocampus alone (which completely spare the rhinal cortex) leave recognition memory intact.[24] Thus, the neural substrate for visual recognition memory appears to depend on visual inputs from area TE to rhinal cortex rather than to either the amygdala or hippocampus, at least for short delay intervals. Future studies of sparing of memory function should investigate whether inputs to the rhinal cortex from visual association areas become reorganized as a result of a neonatal TE lesion.

CONCLUSION

The studies described here reveal a high degree of plasticity in the postnatal primate brain as a result of early brain damage. We have described the survival of transient TEO-amygdalar connections in response to an a neonatal TE lesion as well as the sprouting of additional TEO-amygdalar projections in response to this lesion. Although TEO-amygdalar rewiring may not be relevant to the sparing of visual memory, it nonetheless suggests the potential for a remarkable degree of reorganization in the postnatal period.

In addition to this anatomical rewiring, we have found that visual areas not normally involved in recognition memory become involved after an early lesion of area TE. This finding indicates that many areas of the cortex, perhaps by virtue of their diffuse anatomical connections, have the potential for multiple functions early in development, but that with maturation the functions gradually become localized within specific areas. An early brain lesion may cause a function to remain widely distributed and thereby account for the preservation of function that is often observed after early brain damage (e.g., see Bates,[7] Goldman-Rakic et al.,[10] Kolb and Whishaw,[16] Stiles and Thal,[27] and Stiles,[28] this volume).

ACKNOWLEDGMENTS

We thank Mortimer Mishkin for his generous support during all phases of this work.

REFERENCES

1. Aggleton, J. P., M. J. Burton, and R. E. Passingham. "Cortical and Subcortical Afferents to the Amygdala of the Rhesus Monkey (*Macaca mulatta*)." *Brain Res.* **190** (1980): 347–368.
2. Amaral, D. G., and J. L. Price. "Amygdalo-Cortical Projections in the Monkey (*Macaca fascicularis*)." *J. Comp. Neurol.* **230** (1984): 465–496.
3. Bachevalier, J., L. G. Ungerleider, J. B. O'Neill, and D. P. Friedman. "Regional Distribution of (^{3})Naloxone Binding in the Brain of a Newborn Rhesus Monkey." *Develop. Brain Res.* **25** (1986): 302–308.
4. Bachevalier, J., and M. Mishkin. "Long-Term Effects of Neonatal Temporal, Cortical and Limbic Lesions on Habit and Memory Formation in Rhesus Monkeys." *Soc. Neurosci. Abst.* **14** (1988): 4.
5. Bachevalier, J., C. Hagger, and M. Mishkin. "Functional Maturation of the Occipitotemporal Pathway in Infant Rhesus Monkeys." In *Brain Work and Mental Activity, Alfred Benzon Symposium 31*, edited by N. A. Lassen, D. H. Ingvar, M. E. Raichle, and L. Friberg, 231–240. Copenhagen: Munksgaard, 1991.
6. Bachevalier, J., and M. Mishkin. "Effects of Selective Neonatal Temporal Lobe Lesions on Visual Recognition Memory in Rhesus Monkeys." *J. Neurosci.* **14** (1994): 2128–2139.
7. Bates, E. "Language Development." *Curr. Opin. Neurobiol.* **2** (1992): 180–185.
8. Desimone, R., and L. G. Ungerleider. "Neural Mechanisms of Visual Processing in Monkeys." In *Handbook of Neuropsychology*, edited by F. Boller and J. Grafman, 267–299. Amsterdam: Elsevier, 1989.
9. Fellman, D. J., and D. C. Van Essen. "Distributed Hierarchical Processing in the Primate Cerebral Cortex." *Cerebral Cortex* **1** (1991): 1–47.
10. Goldman-Rakic, P. S., A. Isseroff, M. L. Schwartz, and N. M. Bugbee. "The Neurobiology of Cognitive Development." In *Handbook of Cognitive Development: Biology and Infancy Development*, edited by P. Mussen, 281–344. New York: John Wiley, 1983.
11. Innocenti, G. M. "The Development of Projections from Cerebral Cortex." In *Progress in Sensory Physiology*, Vol. 12, D. Ottoson, 65–114. Berlin: Springer-Verlag, 1991.
12. Iwai, E., and M. Yukie. "Amygdalofugal and Amygdalopetal Connections with Modality-Specific Visual Cortical Areas in Macaques (*Macaca fuscata, M. mulatta*, and *M. fascicularis*)." *J. Comp. Neurol.* **261** (1987): 362–387.
13. Iwai, E., M. Yukie, H. Suyama, and S. Shirakawa. "Amygdala Connections with Middle and Inferior Temporal Gyri of the Monkey." *Neurosci. Lett.* **83** (1987): 25–29.

14. Jeo, R. M., Y. Yonebayashi, and J. M. Allman. "Perceptual Memory of Cognitively Defined Contours: A Rapid, Robust and Long-Lasting Form of Memory." This volume.

15. Jones, E. G., and T. P. S. Powell. "An Anatomical Study of the Converging Sensory Pathways Within the Cerebral Cortex of the Monkey." *Brain* **93** (1970): 793–820.

16. Kolb, B., and I. Q. Whishaw. "Plasticity in the Neocortex: Mechanisms Underlying Recovery From Early Brain Damage." *Progress in Neurobiology* . **32** (1989): 235–276.

17. Maunsell, J. H. R., and W. T. Newsome. "Visual Processing in Monkey Extrastriate Cortex." *Ann. Rev. Neurosci.* **10** (1987): 363–401.

18. Meunier, M., J. Bachevalier, M. Mishkin, and E. A. Murray. "Effects on Visual Recognition of Combined and Separate Ablations of the Entorhinal and Perirhinal Cortex in Rhesus Monkeys." *J. Neurosci.* **13** (1993): 5418–5432.

19. Mishkin, M. "A Memory System in the Monkey." *Phil. Trans. Roy. Soc. London B.* **298** (1982): 85–95.

20. Mishkin, M., B. J. Spiegler, R. C. Saunders, and B. L. Malamut. "An Animal Model of Global Amnesia." In *Alzheimer's Disease: A Report of Progress*, edited by S. Corkin, K. L. Davis, J. H. Growdin, E. Usdin, and R. J. Wurtman, 235–247. New York: Raven Press, 1982.

21. Mishkin, M., and R. R. Phillips. "A Corticolimbic Memory Path Revealed Through Its Disconnection." In *Brain Circuits and Functions of the Mind: Essays in Honor of Roger W. Sperry*, edited by C. Trevarthen, 196–210. Cambridge: Cambridge University Press, 1990.

22. Mishkin, M., and E. A. Murray. "Stimulus Recognition." *Curr. Opin. Neurobiol.* **4** (1994): 200–206.

23. Murray, E. A. "Medial Temporal Lobe Structures Contributing to Recognition Memory: The Amygdaloid Complex Versus the Rhinal Cortex." In *The Amygdala: Neurobiologic Aspects of Emotion, Memory, and Mental Dysfunction*, edited by J. P. Aggleton, 453–470. New York: Wiley-Liss, 1992.

24. O'Boyle, V. J., E. A. Murray, and M. Mishkin. "Effects of Excitotoxic Amygdala-Hippocampal Lesions on Visual Recognition in Rhesus Monkeys." *Soc. Neurosci. Abst.* **19** (1993): 438.

25. O'Neill, J. B., D. P. Freidman, J. Bachevalier, and L. G. Ungerleider. "Distribution of Muscarinic Receptors in the Brain of a Newborn Rhesus Monkey." *Soc. Neurosci. Abstr.* **12** (1986): 809.

26. Seltzer, B., and D. N. Pandya. "Some Cortical Projections to the Parahippocampal Area in the Rhesus Monkey." *Exp. Neurol.* **50** (1976): 146–160.

27. Stiles, J., and D. Thal. "Linguistic and Spatial Cognitive Development Following Early Focal Brain Injury: Patterns of Deficit and Recovery." In *Brain Development and Cognition: A Reader*, edited by M. Johnson, 643–665. Oxford: Blackwell, 1993.

28. Stiles, J. "Plasticity and Development: Evidence from Children with Early Occurring Focal Brain Injury." This volume.

29. Turner, B. H., M. Mishkin, and M. Knapp. "Organization of the Amygdalopetal Projections from Modality-Specific Cortical Association Areas in the Monkey." *J. Comp. Neurol.* **191** (1980): 515–543.

30. Ungerleider, L. G. "The Corticocortical Pathways for Object Recognition and Spatial Perception." In *Pattern Recognition Mechanisms,* edited by C. Chagas, R. Gattass, and C. G. Gross, 21–37. Vatican City: Pontifical Academy of Sciences, 1985.

31. Ungerleider, L. G., and E. A. Murray. "Primates, Visual Perception and Memory in Nonhuman." In *Encyclopedia of Learning and Memory,* edited by L. R. Squire, 537–541. New York: Macmillan Publishing Co., 1992.

32. Van Essen, D. C., D. J. Felleman, E. A. DeYoe, J. Olavarria, and J. J. Knierim. "Modular and Hierarchical Organization of Extrastriate Visual Cortex in the Macaque Monkey." *Cold Spring Harbor Symp. Quant. Biol.* **55** (1991): 679–696.

33. Van Hoesen, G. W., and D. Pandya. "Some Connections of the Entorhinal (Area 28) and Perirhinal (Area 35) Cortices of the Rhesus Monkey. I. Temporal Lobe Afferents." *Brain Res.* **95** (1975): 1–24.

34. Webster, M. J., L. G. Ungerleider, and J. Bachevalier. "Connections of Inferior Temporal Areas TE and TEO With Medial Temporal-Lobe Structures in Infant and Adult Monkeys." *J. Neurosci.* **11** (1991): 1095–1116.

35. Webster, M. J., L. G. Ungerleider, and J. Bachevalier. "Lesions of Inferior Temporal Area TE in Infant Monkeys Alter Cortico-Amygdalar Projections." *NeuroReport* **2** (1991): 769–772.

36. Weller, R. E. "Two Cortical Visual Systems in Old World and New World Primates." In *Progress in Brain Research,* Vol. 75, edited by T. P. Hicks and G. Benedek, 293–306. Amsterdam: Elsevier Press, 1988.

37. Zola-Morgan, S., and L. R. Squire. "Complementary Approaches to the Study of Memory: Human Amnesia and Animal Models." In *Memory Systems of the Brain: Animal and Human Cognitive Processes,* edited by N. W. Weinberger, J. L. McGaugh, and G. Lynch, 463–477. New York: Guilford Press, 1985.

Masakazu Konishi
Division of Biology 216-76, California Institute of Technology, Pasadena, CA 91125

A Sensitive Period for Birdsong Learning

Many animals produce sounds for communication, but few of them must and can learn their acoustic signals. Human beings and birds are the only animals that can imitate complex vocal signals. Cetaceans (whales and dolphins) and bats may also be vocal learners, although their ability to learn their complex vocal signals has not been experimentally shown. Evidence for vocal learning includes the failure to develop normal voice in the absence of a natural or tape-recorded teacher and the ability to copy the whole or aspects of an appropriate tutor model. Among avian species, parrots, songbirds, and some hummingbirds are the only groups that meet these criteria for vocal mimicry. Other birds such as doves and chickens do not copy any sound.[10,19]

Male birds use song to both repel rivals in territorial disputes and attract mates. A song consists of brief sounds with silent intervals between them. Many birds sing songs lasting less than 2 seconds, while some birds sing for minutes. The smallest component of a song is the note which appears as a single dark marking on a soundspectrograph. A song may contain many different notes. Two or three notes may be grouped together to form a syllable. Several syllables of the same note composition are usually repeated in a song. Syllables of the same or different types may be grouped together to form a phrase. A song may be composed of one or more phrases. Songs do not develop suddenly but gradually under the influence of testosterone. Young birds produce soft rambling utterances which are not clearly organized into stable notes, syllables, and phrases. This phase of song development is called the subsong stage. In the next phase, called the plastic song stage, the organization of a song becomes clearly recognizable except that its syllables are still not completely fixed. When all the properties of a song become unchangeable, the song is said to be crystallized. Such a song is also called a full song.

Birds learn many features of their songs from their parents or other adults. Song learning has been well known to bird fanciers for centuries. For example, Japanese afficionados developed elaborate criteria and terms for the judgment of the aesthetic qualities of birdsong for singing competitions and strove to produce better singers by various methods among which the most important was the tutoring of young birds with prize-winning singers.[9] These songstars earned high tuitions for their owners by serving as teachers. Some people cheated by hiding young birds in their kimono, while they pretended to admire songsters. The Japanese knew which species of birds learn song and which do not. For example, they were aware that they could not improve the quality of crowing in the Japanese quail by tutoring. The most impressive knowledge possessed by these birds fanciers is about the process of song learning. Young birds do not sing after their tutor but only memorize his song during an early impressionable period. The singing of a memorized song occurs as birds become sexually mature several months after they heard the song. These people knew not only the existence of an impressionable period but also its differences between species. For example, young Japanese yellow buntings (*Emberiza sulphurata*) must hear a tutor between 7–21 days after birth, whereas skylarks (*Alauda arvensis*) can modifiy their songs by listening to a tutor even at one year of age. The Japanese bush warbler (*Settia diphone*) which is one of the most favorite songsters is usually tutored three times during the first year, and in this case too, the bird has already begun to sing during the last tutoring session in January. The duration of tutoring was also known for some species. For example, 80 to 100 days for Siberian meadow buntings (*Emberiza cioides*), 50 days for skylarks, and 7 days or even 3 days for Japanese robins (*Erithacus akahige*).

Despite this wealth of knowledge, the scientific study of song learning did not start until the 1950s in Europe. The introduction of tape recorders and the sound-spectrograph marks the beginning of the modern study of birdsong learning. These instruments allow the investigator to record, analyze, and select and present desired tutor songs with precise timing and volume for defined periods. The new sound equipment also made it possible to compare tutors' and pupils' songs objectively. Thorpe was the first to take full advantage of this technology in his now classical study of song development in Chaffinches (*Fringilla coelebus*).[23,24] This study led him to the introduction of three important ideas that have guided birdsong research ever since. He noted some resemblance between song learning and imprinting in which an animal's early experience irreversibly biases its preference for social and sexual partners in adulthood. He used this similarity to put forth the concept of a critical period of song learning. Thorpe wrote:

"whatever song or songs an individual Chaffinch has learnt by the time it is about thirteen months old, they remain its song or songs for the rest of its life. The learning-period is cut short abruptly in June or July of its first adult year and under no circumstances normally encountered does it apparently ever learn anything more. This restriction of learning to a period in the early life, a period which is brought to an abrupt close by internal factors not yet understood, but presumably hormonal in nature, recalls a similar restriction of learning-ability to a particular type of object and to a sharply defined sensitive period which has been called imprinting."
—Thorpe,[25] pp. 80–81

The first 13 months in a Chaffinch's life is hardly an "early" period, because it amounts to about one fifth of his life span in the wild. But Thorpe also recognized an early period in which exposure to a normal species song affects the later development of song in Chaffinches. Young birds caught and placed in acoustic isolation in September developed more normal songs than birds raised in isolation from a few days of age. In another experiment, he found that autumn-caught young did not learn artificially modified Chaffinch songs such as a song played backward, whereas hand-reared birds learned them. Thorpe deduced two additional characteristics of song learning from these observations: exposure to a tutor song before the onset of singing can influence the subsequent development of song, and early exposure to conspecific (own species) song prevents birds from learning alien songs. Furthermore, his Chaffinches preferred the song of their own species as a tutor model to alien songs. He used this observation to propose the concept of a blueprint or an innate predisposition to learn conspecific song.

Many subsequent studies of song learning dealt with the critical period and selectivity of song learning.[11,12,14,22] In later years, however, some pointed out the need to change the term "critical period" for "sensitive period or phase," because birds do not begin and cease to learn song as abruptly as the original term indicates.[8] All agree, however, that birds go through a period of hightened readiness to learn conspecific song. For example, when Marler and Peters[15] tape-tutored young swamp sparrows (*Melospiza georgiana*) to different sets of songs every two weeks from 14 to 300 days of age, 60% of the songs copied by the birds were the ones they had heard between 14 and 50 days of age and 40% of those heard after this period. Also, some of the birds learned songs when they were several months of age.

What determines the end of the sensitive phase is largely unknown. It does not appear to be strictly age-dependent. When a Chaffinch is castrated before the first singing season, it does not sing. Such a bird can learn a new tutor song, when it receives a testosterone implant in the second year when the learning of new songs does not normally take place.[16] Thus, the readiness to learn song does not depend on age, but this experiment does not show what closes it. Testosterone induces singing and song crystallization. As Thorpe found, song crystallization marks the end of Chaffinches' readiness to learn song. So, it may be either song crystallization or the high level of testosterone itself that shuts off the readiness to learn song. No serious attempt has been made to discriminate between these two possibilities, because the hormone inevitably causes song crystallization.

Thorpe's work also suggested that the nature of auditory experience itself affects a bird's readiness to learn song. Several recent studies confirm this view. In the Zebra finch, the readiness to learn song normally lasts from 25–35 to 60–80 days of age.[7,5] Zebra finches that are exposed to conspecific songs during this period sing normal songs and are refractory to further tutoring. If young birds are removed from their parents and raised in acoustic isolation from 35 days of age, they usually develop abnormal songs. These birds remain capable of learning a normal song at 120 days of age, if they are exposed to a tutor.[5] Similarly, when young Zebra finches are reared in a family without a father, they develop songs composed of sounds resembling the mother's call notes. If these birds are allowed to hear a male Zebra finch from 65 days of age, they modify or abandon their abnormal songs and learn the normal song of the tutor.[6]

There are other factors that affect both the sensitive phase and selectivity of song learning. All of the Zebra finch experiments mentioned above used live tutors. Tape-tutoring has been the main method in other species. In some species, the results of tape-tutoring differ from those of live tutoring.

For example, young white-crowned sparrows (*Zonotrichia leucophrys*) learn from tapes only conspecific songs presented during the period between 14 and 50 days of age.[14] On the other hand, white-crowned sparrows learn not only conspecific songs but also the song of song sparrows (*Melospiza melodia*) after 50 days of age when the birds are exposed to a live tutor.[3,21] Similarly, young marsh wrens (*Cistothorus palsustris*) do not ordinarily learn from tapes in the first spring, but they learn readily from live tutors.[13] Different species appear to respond differently to tape- and live tutoring. Marler and Peters[15] compared the effects of tape- and live tutoring in swamp sparrows. The results show that a majority of the birds learned more of the song types heard between 14 and 50 days of age than those outside that period irrespective of the method of tutoring.

The sensitive period of song learning can be prolonged by manipulations such as mentioned above, but it does not appear to be extended indefinitely.

White-crowned sparrows do not learn new songs even from live tutors after about 100 days of age.[21] Little can be said about other species, because few studies covered periods after the first singing season. There are, however, so-called open learners such as canaries which continue to be able to modify song annually after the first year.[20,26] Whether or not this ability lasts indefinitely is not known. Whatever neural differences that distinguish open learners from closed learners would be interesting to investigate. Seasonal changes and the appearance of new neurons in the brain areas for the control of song in canaries are thought to be related to the birds' ability to modify song every year.[17,18] But there is no direct evidence that links these neural events to song renewal.

Seasonal changes in song nuclei also occur in birds which do not change song annually.[1,4] Conversely, seasonal singers may not show any obvious change in their song system.[2] Nevertheless, the role of new neurons in song plasticity deserves further investigation.

REFERENCES

1. Arai, O., I. Taniguchi, and N. Saito. "Correlation Between the Size of Song Control Nuclei and Plumage Color Change in Orange Bishop Birds." *Neurosci. Lett.* **98** (1989): 144–148.
2. Baker, M. C., S. W. Bottjer, and A. P. Arnold. "Sexual Dimorphism and Lack of Seasonal Changes in Vocal Control Regions of the White-Crowned Sparrow Brain." *Brain Res.* **295** (1984): 85–89.
3. Baptista, L. F., and L. Petrinovich. "Social Interaction, Sensitive Phases and the Song Template Hypothesis in the White-Crowned Sparrow." *Anim. Behav.* **32** (1984): 172–181.
4. Brenowitz, E. A., S. B. Nall, J. C. Wingfield, and D. E. Kroodsma. "Seasonal-Changes in Avian Song Nuclei Without Seasonal Changes in Song Repertoire." *J. Neurosci.* **11** (1991): 1367–1374.
5. Eales, L. A. "Song Learning in Zebra Finches: Some Effects of Song Model Availability on What is Learnt and When." *Anim. Behav.* **33** (1985): 1293–1300.
6. Eales, L. A. "Song Learning in Female-Raised Zebra Finches; Another Look at the Sensitive Phase." *Anim. Behav.* **35** (1978): 1356–1365.
7. Immelmann, K. "Song Development and in the Zebra Finch and Other Estrildid Finches." In *Bird Vocalizations*, edited by R. A. Hinde, 61–74. London and New York: Cambridge University Press, 1969.
8. Immelmann, K., and S. J. Suomi. "Sensitive Phases in Development." In *Behavioral Development: The Bielefeld Interdisciplinary Project*, edited by K. Immelmann, G. W. Barlow, L. Petrinovich, and M. Main, 395–431. London and New York: Cambridge University Press, 1981.
9. Kawamura, T. *Science of Birdsong*. Tokyo, Chuokoronsha, 1974.
10. Konishi, M. "The Role of Auditory Feedback in the Control of Vocal Behavior in Domestic Fowl." *Z. J. Tierphychol.* **20** (1963): 349–367.
11. Konishi, M. "Birdsong: From Behavior to Neuron." *Ann. Rev. Neurosci.* **8** (1985): 125–170.
12. Kroodsma, D. E, and E. H. Miller. *Acoustic Communication in Birds, Vol. 2, Song Learning and Its Consequences*. New York and London: Academic Press, 1982.
13. Kroodsma, D. E., and Pickert. "Sensitive Phases for Song Learning—Effects of Social Interaction and Individual Variation." *Anim. Behav.* **32** (1984): 389–394.

14. Marler, P. "A Comparative Approach to Vocal Learning: Song Development in White-Crowned Sparrows." *J. Comp. Physiol. Psychol.* **71** (1970): 1–25.

15. Marler, P. and S. Peters. "Sensitive Periods for Song Acquisition from Tape Recordings and Live Tutors in the Swamp Sparrow, *Melospiza georgiana.*" *Ethology* **77** (1988): 76–84.

16. Nottebohm, F. "The 'Critical Period' for Song Learning." *Ibis* **111** (1969): 93–107. 1969.

17. Nottebohm, F. "Birdsong as a Model in Which to Study Brain Related to Learning." *Condor* **86** (1984): 227–236.

18. Nettebohm, F. "Neuronal Replacement in Adulthood." *Ann. NY Acad. Sci.* **457** (1985): 143–161.

19. Nottebohm, F., and M. E. Nottebohm. "Vocalizations and Breeding Behavior in Surgically Deafened Ring Doves (*Streptopelia risoria*)." *Anim. Behav.* **19** (1971): 313–327.

20. Nottebohm, F., and M. E. Nottebohm. "Relationship Between Song Repertoire and Age in the Canary, *Serinus canaria.*" *Z. Tierpscychol.* **46** (1978): 298–305.

21. Petrinovich, L., and L. Baptista. "Song Development in the White-Crowned Sparrow: Modification of Learned Song." *Anim. Behav.* **35** (1987): 961–974.

22. Slater, P. J. B. "Bird Song Learning: Theme and Variations." In *Perspective in Ornithology*, edited by A. H. Brush and G. A. Clark, Jr., 475–499. New York and London: Cambridge University Press, 1983.

23. Thorpe, W. H. "The Process of Song Learning in the Chaffinch as Studied by Means of the Sound Spectrograph." *Nature* **173** (1954): 465.

24. Thorpe, W. H. "The Learning of Song Patterns by Birds, with Especial Reference to the Song of the Chaffinch *Fringilla coelebs.*" *Ibis* **100** (1958): 535–570.

25. Thorpe, W. H. *Birdsong.* New York and London: Cambridge University Press, 1961.

26. Waser, M. S., and P. Marler. "Song Learning in Canaries." *J. Comp. Physiol. Psychol.* **91** (1977): 1–7.

Plasticity of the Adult Brain

Avi Karni†‡* and Dov Sagi‡
†Laboratory of Neuropsychology, N.I.M.H., N.I.H., Building 9, 1N107, Bethesda, MD 20892
‡Neurobiology, Brain Research, Weizmann Institute of Science, Rehovot 76100, Israel
*To whom correspondence should be addressed

A Memory System in the Adult Visual Cortex

INTRODUCTION

This review addresses several aspects of human learning and memory as related to basic visual processing. It is an attempt to suggest a tentative, specific context for some of the basic questions raised by the phenomenon of perceptual learning, i.e., the finding that genuine and long-lasting changes are induced by experience (practice) in adult visual processing. Our main conjecture is that certain types of memories—perceptual skills of the type evolving through texture discrimination learning is our paradigm—are mediated by discrete, experience-dependent changes in the specific sensory system involved in the performance of the task. We suggest there is a reasonable case to be made for the hypothesis that all levels of visual processing, including the primary visual cortex, could under specific retinal input and task-defined conditions, undergo long-term, experience-dependent changes (functional plasticity). Furthermore, there is evidence indicating the possibility that the locus of these changes is determined by the double constraint of retinal input (selectivity; differential activation by the specific stimulus) and task demands (relevancy). Thus the conjecture is that the acquisition (learning) and retention (memory) of visual skills would occur at the earliest level within the visual processing stream where the minimally sufficient neuronal computing capability (expressed either as single-unit response properties, or as the product of a local neuronal assembly) is available for representing stimulus parameters that are the relevant input for the performance of a specific task (The Minimal Level Hypothesis). Adult perceptual learning is contingent on the functional architecture of the sensory system but, at the same time, modifies it.

Until recently, it was commonly believed that the functional properties of neurons within early sensory processing areas, as well as the circuitry of the sensory cortex, are fixed in adulthood. However, in parallel to psychophysical evidence in humans,[1,2,3,4,5,6,7] there is an accumulating body of electrophysiological evidence suggesting that even at the earliest stages of sensory processing, neuronal properties are subject to experience-dependent plasticity in the adult brain.[8,9,10,11,12] Although much of the work concerning adult cortical plasticity has been done in sensory modalities other than vision, the main focus of this review is the conjectured correspondence between perceptual (visual skill) learning and functional (developmental, as well as adult) cortical plasticity. This conjecture has provided several strong constraints and new testable predictions on the nature of the neural substrates underlying some types of human learning.

The observation that prompted our experiments was the finding that adult observers practicing in a simple visual discrimination task (in which optimal stimuli for "automatic," preattentive texture segregation were presented[13,14,15,16,17]) showed remarkable day-to-day improvements. Psychophysical data and computational models have previously suggested that the performance of this task is determined by low-level, stimulus-dependent visual processing stages.[18,15,19,20] Therefore the finding that adult observers show large gains in the performance of such a basic task of form vision was unexpected. One would have expected that during the course of normal development, indeed as a result of everyday experience, this task would be perfected to the limit. However, this result suggested a possible probe, by way of psychophysical measurements, into the nature and extent of the modifications induced by practice in the adult visual system. Potentially, we were posed to look at not only what changes with repeated sensory experience (practice), but rather at where and when these changes occur within the adult brain.

To investigate these questions we restated a general problem: what are the neural mechanisms mediating the acquisition and retention of improved performance as a function of practice—in terms that could provide psychophysical constraints for the functional characterization of neuronal assemblies undergoing practice-related changes. A cornerstone of perceptual learning research in recent years, has been the notion that a dependence of the learning process on specific stimulus parameters should provide these constraints.[1,2,3,4,5,6,7] For example, if the learning effect can be shown to be retinotopically local, i.e., it would not transfer (or generalize) from a trained to an untrained part of the visual-field, it must presumably involve changes in an early, low-level processing stage where the retinotopic organization of the visual input is still retained. Similarly, a high degree of monocularity (i.e., learning that would not transfer from a trained to an untrained eye) would suggest that learning affected a level within the visual system where cells preferentially respond to input from one retina (monocular cells). This is because information about the eye of origin of the signal is not retained in mid- and high-level visual processing area.[21] These considerations suggested the following general design for our psychophysical experiments: we recorded the course of learning, using a specific stimulus configuration, until performance has asymptoted. Then, the specificity (dependence) of the learning process for basic attributes of the sensory experience was probed by measuring the effects, on performance, of discrete manipulations of the stimuli's physical parameters. Finally, this procedure was extended to provide a closer look at the time course of learning and the effects of task demands (extra-retinal constraints on learning).

MAGNITUDE AND SPECIFICITY OF THE LEARNING PROCESS

The psychophysical paradigm is quite simple. (Detailed description of stimulus parameters and testing procedure are to be found elsewhere.[4,22]) Examples of a stimulus and a masking pattern are shown in Figure 1(a). In these studies, observers were required to identify the shape of a small target texture composed of three high-contrast line-elements differing only in their orientation from a background texture made of identical elements. The target shape was defined by the geometrical arrangement of the target elements. For each observer, element orientation and target location (within a restricted part of the visual field) were kept unchanged throughout training. A very brief presentation time (10 ms)—so no eye movement could displace the projection of the stimulus on the retina—was employed to ensure that the target consistently appeared in a specific retinal location, and fixation was enforced by a concurrent letter discrimination task presented at the center of the display. Performance was measured as the mean correct response for increasingly shorter time intervals between the briefly presented stimulus and a patterned mask (stimulus-to-onset-asynchrony, SOA). As the SOA sets the limit on stimulus availability, it is a measure of the time the visual system requires to obtain a workable precept (representation) of the sensory input (sensory processing time) independent of motor response times. (On the biological significance of such a measure of human performance, see Merzenich and Jenkins[23] and Tallal[24] in this volume).

The main effect of practice was a leftward shift of the performance curves which indicate genuine increases in the visual system's sensitivity on consecutive sessions spaced 1–3 days apart (Figure 1(b)). Thus these increments in performance reflect perceptual learning retained from session to the next. The learning effect is quite large: Where perception completely fails on the initial session, observers can perform > 90% correct discrimination on the following day (Figure 1(b)). In terms of SOA, the visual system's sensitivity was more than doubled by the time performance asymptoted.

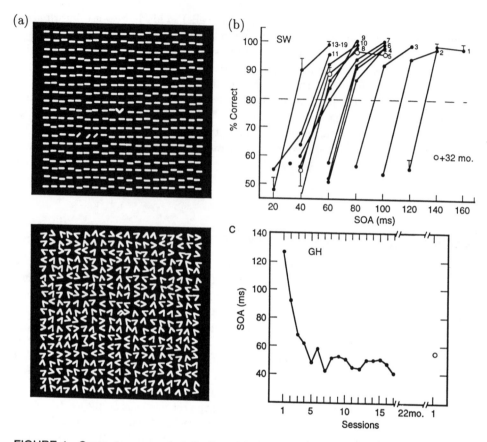

FIGURE 1 Computer-generated displays (a). (top) A test stimulus with a small target texture (three diagonal bars) embedded within a background of horizontal elements. Display size was 14° by 14° of visual angle viewed from a distance of 110 cm, with an array of 19-by-19 slightly jittered line segments (subtending 0.42° × 0.03° each, with a luminance of 35 cd/m² and spaced 0.70° apart). A small rotated letter (either T or L) at the center of display served as the fixation target. The target texture's position was varied randomly from trial to trial but always within a specific display quadrant and within 2.5°–5° of visual angle from center of display. (bottom) Mask pattern made of randomly oriented V-shaped micropatterns and at the center, a compound micropattern of superimposed T and L. (b) Psychometric curves for performance on consecutive daily sessions (spaced 1–2 days apart) for observer SW (□), and on a probe session 32 months later (o) (she had no psychophysical experience with visual textures in the interval). Results indicate persistent day-to-day improvements and almost no forgetting on a timescale of years. Each data point represents the mean percent correct responses (± sd) from three to five consecutive blocks (150–250 trials) for a specific SOA. The initial performance curve is on the right; as learning occurs, (continued)

FIGURE 1 (continued) the curves are displaced to the left (shorter processing times needed for task performance) indicating improved sensitivity. The left-most curve represents asymptotic performance. (−−−), 80% correct (threshold) performance. (c) Learning curve for observer GH. SOA required for threshold discrimination on consecutive daily sessions (□), and for a probe session 22 months later (o). Each point refers to a single session, interpolated from the respective psychometric curve. The large learning effect has not decayed in the interval (where no psychophysical testing or training was done). [Reprinted, with permission, from Karni and Sagi.[22]]

This large improvement was found to be highly specific for some simple physical attributes of the retinal input.[4] (a) It is very local in a retinotopic sense. Indeed, displacing the target by just 3° of visual angle from a previously trained visual-field locality, necessitated retraining. (b) It is specific for the background elements' orientation. Thus, new independent learning is required when the background elements' orientation were flipped to the orthogonal or rotated by 45°. Surprisingly, learning was not specific for the target elements' orientation. However, learning was restricted to the target textures location; i.e., repeated exposure to background elements per se was not enough to induce texture discrimination learning. This apparent paradox can be resolved by assuming that learning occurs only where texture gradients, relative to a specific background, are available as essential input.[25] Finally, (c) learning is monocular. The effects of practice show little transfer from a trained to an untrained eye.

WHERE PRACTICE MAKES PERFECT

The above results indicate that a substantial part of the texture discrimination learning effect is subserved by retinal-input-dependent changes at a level within the visual system where monocularity, and the retinotopic organization of the visual input, are still retained and different orientations are processed independently. Furthermore, an orientation-gradient dependent mechanism may be implicated.

The most parsimonious, yet biologically plausible, interpretation of these results is that texture discrimination learning involves experience-dependent local plasticity within primary visual cortex (Area 17). This tentative localization is in agreement with the fine-grained retinotopy of the learning effect. However, it is the significant monocularity of the learning effect that implicates changes occurring at or before area 17 as a locus of learning. Only at these early stages of visual processing one finds neurons that preferentially respond to input from one retina and are thus committed to processing information from a specific eye. Orientation-selective neurons which would still have disparate monocular inputs, and thus satisfy all the above constraints, are found, in primates, only in V1,[26,21] which corresponds to area 17 in the human brain.

Though by no means conclusive, a strictly reductionistic interpretation of these results is possible. The learning effect may be accounted for by Hebbian activity-dependent synaptic changes (functional plasticity).[4,25] Consider the interaction between (a) first-level ("presynaptic") orientation-selective, monocular cells and (b) second-level ("postsynaptic") gradient-sensitive, binocular cells. These second-level cells would respond to simultaneous activity generated in disparate first-level cells responding to stimuli presented within a specific (but quite large) retinotopic neighborhood. Both these types of cells have been described in primate V1.[27] At, and only at, retinal locations presented with texture borders, a concurrent, correlated activation of both first-level and second-level cells will occur, leading to enhanced synaptic connections with repeated stimulus presentation. Other mechanisms that could, presumably, subserve texture discrimination learning in early visual processing stages, such as the improvement of background orientation long-range horizontal connections are discussed by Karni[25] and Karni and Sagi.[4] Yet again, Hebbian rules of correlated-activity-dependent synaptic modification could support experience-dependent changes at this level (see Polat and Sagi[28,29] and Katz, Victor, and Purpura[30] in this volume.) Of course, single-synapse plasticity as the neuronal implementation of a human memory phenomenon is simplistic. However the basic idea of experience-dependent modification of local, discrete, neuronal response properties as the locus of human learning, is defensible. More than 40 years ago, Mishkin and Forgays, investigating the retinotopy of word recognition, have suggested a very similar idea as the Hebbian interpretation for the development of visual-field-specific reading skills.[31] More recently, several examples of stimulus specific perceptual learning, in nonhuman primates, have suggested functional plasticity in primary somatosensory[32,9] and auditory[10,12] cortex. The resemblance of the monkey data to the human learning data, is striking.

WHAT IMPROVES?

Two testable predictions of this functional localization of the learning process to improved local representation of gradient-defined contours can be made. One, a low-level orientation-gradient computing mechanism is involved in the learning process (undergoes an experience-dependent shift in processing efficiency). If so, a reasonable expectation would be that practicing texture discrimination will concurrently improve texture-gradient-defined target detection, and possibly vice versa. A second prediction would be that learning should transfer across the target's global shape. For example, once the appropriate sensory input parameters are used any global shape, defined by a texture gradient boundary, should be better represented after learning has occurred.

LEARNING A VISUAL SKILL

Both these predictions were borne out by our results.[33,25] Our results show that performance undergoes a remarkable improvement for both texture target discrimination and texture target detection. This outcome is independent of which of these two tasks was used in training. As different (higher) levels of computational complexity are needed to solve a discrimination, as compared to a detection task (using the very same stimulus), our results suggest the localization of the learning effect into a common processing stage which both these functions utilize. A good candidate would be a local gradient detection mechanism. The output of such a mechanism would be the explicit representation of the location of texture gradients, i.e., the boundaries of texture objects.

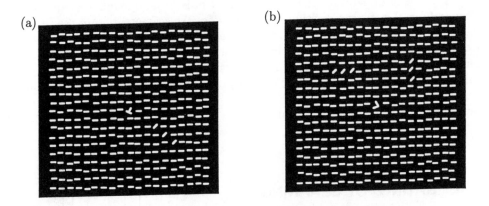

FIGURE 2   Modified stimulus arrays. Display parameters were set as in Figure 1 with two discrete modifications. (a) The target's shape (configuration as defined by the three diagonal elements) was changed to randomly alternate between left and right oblique. Note that the observer's task was to discriminate the target's global shape (left leaning/right leaning), rather than the target texture's elements' orientation (which for some observers were switched too so as not to change the target's width between the two conditions). (b) In this modification of the original stimulus, two physically identical target textures were presented—to the corresponding quadrants of the two hemifields. Each target's shape was alternated randomly, and independently, between horizontal and vertical. Two sets of experiments were run. In the first, observers were instructed to report the shape (orientation) of the target appearing to the left (others to the right) of fixation point with the relevant target (location) unchanged until performance has asymptoted. In the second set of experiments observers were required to compare both targets and report whether the two were the same shape (both horizontal or both vertical) or different (orthogonal to each other). The time course and magnitude of the learning in these two sets of experiments were not significantly different.

There is also complete transfer of the performance gain acquired by training in the discrimination of one pair of target shapes as defined by the three target element configuration (horizontal vs. vertical bars) to a new configuration (left oblique vs. right oblique bars) (Figure 2(a)) and even to more complex shapes such as letters.[34] Again, because the target's global shape is physically defined by the texture gradients, an improved mechanism of local gradient representation would improve both shape discriminations equally well. Thus, while texture discrimination learning is dependent on, and very specific for, simple (low level) attributes of the retinal input, it is not specific for higher level attributes of the input such as global shape. Observers can learn "how to" discriminate target shapes irrespective of "what" these target shapes are. This dissociation is a hallmark of procedural ("habit," skill) learning.[35,36]

One concern in pursuing the possibility that functional changes in the primary visual cortex are the locus of texture discrimination learning, is whether area 17 has a role in orientation-gradient-dependent object/background segmentation. How early in the stream of visual processing does the segmentation of the retinal input by way of gradient defined contours occur? Two recent studies of human subjects, one an evoked potentials study,[37] the other a functional magnetic resonance imaging study,[38] have documented a specific (in the latter study, retinotopically local) orientation-gradient-dependent (evoked) response in the human primary visual cortex. This is in agreement with the primate data,[27] and indirectly supports our interpretation of the psychophysical data.

THE "GATING" OF LEARNING

A second question concerns the minimal necessary conditions that must be satisfied for adult perceptual learning to occur. Is repetitive, consistent, retinal exposure to an appropriate visual stimulus all that's required to induce experience-dependent changes in the adult brain? It would be surprising, if large and long-term changes in basic visual circuitry were "allowed" without some manner of nonvisual control. Moreover, pursuing the analogy between perceptual learning and functional plasticity, one would expect some extra-retinal control mechanism to "gate" functional plasticity—i.e., control the adaptive state of cortical neurons. Such mechanisms play a decisive role during developmental plasticity,[39,40,41] and presumably account for the fact that only behaviorally relevant neuronal plasticity occurs in the adult brain.[11]

To test this proposal, a modified stimulus was devised (Figure 2(b)). Our results show that for observers consistently presented with two targets of which only one is relevant for task performance, learning occurs only for the task-related target.[42,25] Although the two targets are physically identical, learning occurs independently for each target as determined by the target's relevance for task performance. However, when both targets are relevant (e.g., in a comparison, same/different, task), learning occurs for both in parallel.

Several mechanisms could underlie this nonretinal-input-determined selectivity of the learning process. For example, plasticity in mammalian visual cortex was shown to be dependent on motor and ocular activity, arousal, thalamic inputs and tonic effects of neuromodulators.[39,40,43,41,11] Our results would suggest a much more specific, selective mechanism. Nonetheless, it is possible that the fine specificity and selectivity of the learning effect is due to retinal-input-dependent local neuronal activation while the gating mechanisms are relatively "coarse." In a study of auditory conditioning, a convergence of specific auditory input and task-dependent ACh release has been suggested to underlie the modification of auditory information processing by experience.[12] Behavior-dependent modulation of single unit responses have been shown at several levels of visual processing.[44,45]

Independent of the neuronal implementation, our results suggest that learning is gated by extra-retinal, task-dependent inputs. It is the combination of the specific sensory (retinal) input and the task demands may provide sufficient constraints to determine the evolution of perceptual learning and control the loci of experience-dependent plasticity. Two recent studies suggest that task demands may designate the relevant physical aspects of the stimulus and therefore determine which neurons are relevant for performance and learning.[1,7] Learning may occur only in those neuronal assemblies that are activated by the stimulus and are, at the same time, task relevant.

LATER BUT (ALMOST) FOREVER (TWO MECHANISMS OF MEMORY)

The time course of texture discrimination learning provides more compelling, although indirect, support for the reductionistic interpretation of perceptual learning.[22] In a recent study, we have uncovered two stages, possibly two processes, in the acquisition of improved perception. The first, involves fast, within session, improvement which can be affected by a limited number of trials on a time scale of a few minutes, but only if high-quality sensory input is provided. It consistently occurs only early in the very first practice session of naive observers and both its time-course and stimulus specificity profile are similar to those reported in previous paradigms of human perceptual learning.[3,5,6] However, our results show that while the fast learning effect quickly saturates, there seems to follow a slower, time-consuming stage of learning which has not been described before (but has been recently shown to occur in several other perceptual learning paradigms[22]; see also Polat and Sagi[29] in this volume). This stage underlies the emergence of a large performance gain several hours after, but not during or shortly following the practice session (latent learning phase).

Finally, once asymptotic performance was reached for a specific stimulus configuration, there is almost no forgetting. In Figure 1(b) we depict the discrimination performance of S.W. on consecutive daily sessions during September–October 1989, and her performance on a probe session 32 months later, with no training in the interval. Almost three years later most of her performance gain is retained. This is also the case for G.H., after an interval of 22 months (Figure 1(b)).

Although the relationship between fast and slow learning is unclear, they may involve different levels (stages) of visual processing. This is suggested by the finding of different stimulus specificities for the two tasks. Only the slow, latent phase-dependent, learning—but not the fast phase improvement—is monocular and its spatial specificity is much narrower. On the other hand, only fast learning seems to be specific for target element orientation. These results imply that fast learning is mediated by later stages of visual processing. Fast learning is a process critically dependent on high-quality sensory input and may reflect the setting up of task-specific routines for solving the perceptual problem[24,46] (for example, through a process of "adaptive filtering" which could occur at all relevant levels of processing[44,45,8,5]). It probably involves top-down processes, presumably selecting the optimal sensory units for the performance of the task. Slow learning, however, reflects an ongoing long-term, perhaps structural, modification of basic perceptual modules; it may be implemented through the strengthening (and presumably weakening[28,29]) of links between sensory neurons (those which respond differentially to the critical stimulus parameters) as a function of stimulus-dependent correlated activity. While the nature of the task determines which aspects of a stimulus are critical for the performance of the task, it is the interaction of the sensory input and the functional architecture of the sensory system which determines the minimal level at which these critical stimulus parameters are differentially represented in terms of neuronal responses. The Minimal Level Hypothesis predicts that at this level experience-dependent plasticity, subserving (slow) skill learning, will occur.

The main result uncovered by following the time course of texture discrimination learning was a latent phase of several hours duration in the evolution of superior performance, i.e., a latent phase in human learning. We have suggested the term "consolidation" for the process, presumably initiated during the practice session, which underlies the improvement of perceptual sensitivity several hours after visual experience was terminated, and results in very long-term retention. In this we follow use of the term in developmental plasticity studies; investigating developmental plasticity in the cat, several studies have documented the progression of input-dependent selectivity commitment of visual neurons hours after the termination of the visual stimulation.[47,48] More recently, Heggelund et al. have shown, using a pharmacological paradigm, that visual cortex plasticity is a progressive, continuous process that terminates after about 22 hours.[40] Finally, several behavioral paradigms of mammalian memory consolidation have shown a latent phase of several hours duration before the long-term retention of a specific skill.[49,32] There is, therefore, reasonable ground to conjecture that slow learning reflects a functional property of basic neuronal mechanisms of learning and memory storage within the sensory (visual as well as other modalities) cortex itself. These mechanisms, subserving developmental and maturational plasticity, may have been preserved in the adult cortex, and may underlie adult perceptual skill learning.

Recently, evidence pointing to a possible role for acetylcholine in the consolidation of perceptual skill learning was provided by investigating the relationship between sleep and texture discrimination learning.[50] Unlike the awake state, normal sleep is parsed into discrete stages—each characterized by distinct electrophysiological and neurochemical events.[51] Of these, REM stage is strongly associated with cholinergic activity.[51,52] Experiments involving selective sleep stage deprivation showed, first, that performance has improved after a normal night's sleep. Second, REM sleep deprivation effectively abolished any performance gain during the sleep interval, while non-REM, stage 3 and 4 sleep deprivation resulted in significant improvement, comparable to that found after an undisturbed night. Finally, REM sleep deprivation was shown not to have any detrimental effects on performance when a previously well-practiced stimulus configuration was presented, as a control. On the other hand, there was a small but significant detrimental effect of stage 3–4 sleep deprivation on the previously learned (control) task. This dissociation suggests that REM deprivation affected the consolidation of the recent perceptual experience, but not perceptual performance by itself, making it unlikely that the effects we observed were nonspecific consequences of disturbed sleep. This deleterious effect of post-training REM deprivation on the consolidation of skill memory suggests the possibility that the evolution of the activity-dependent neural changes into an enduring and efficient memory trace, are acetylcholine dependent. One such mechanism, by which a cholinergic input may play a critical role in memory consolidation at the cellular level, has been proposed by Bear and Singer[53]; see also Juliano et al.[43] and Metherate and Weinberger.[8]

A MEMORY SYSTEM FOR SKILL LEARNING

Though going beyond the data, there is a reasonable case to be made for the reductionistic interpretation of the constraints provided by the texture discrimination learning studies, as well as other paradigms of perceptual learning. For example, that a high degree of plasticity has been preserved in the adult visual cortex. This plasticity may underlie the long-term storage of procedural knowledge. One context perceptual learning can be viewed in, is the classical procedural ("how to") vs. declarative ("what"), or the "habit" vs. memory, dichotomies.[35,36] These dichotomies have been suggested to account for the dissociation of memories and skills in brain-damaged patients and lesioned primates. They postulate that the retention of experience entails two widely differing processes. A more cognitive, and flexible, cortico-limbic-dependent system, and a second system which is independent not only of cortico-limbic processing but also of recognition and perhaps some other types of associative memory.[35] This second, perhaps more primitive, system of learning is a slow learning system. Its effects are best documented within a time frame of hours and days, and it is very specific for many parameters of experience that we don't usually recognize in the normal everyday business of learning.[22,54,35] However, assuming that "where the brain does it—it's remembered," and assuming a limited repertoire of neuronal mechanisms that mediate memory functions throughout the mammalian cortex, there is a case to be made for the possibility that not only other types of human skill learning (e.g., motor skill learning[54]) but perhaps the formation of some types of long-term associative memory, should show the same organizational principles.

REFERENCES

1. Ahissar, M., and S. Hochstein. "Attentional Control of Early Perceptual Learning." *Proc. Natl. Acad. Sci. USA* **90** (1993): 5718–5722.
2. Ball, K., and R. Sekuler. "Direction-Specific Improvement in Motion Discrimination." *Vision Res.* **27** (1987): 953–965.
3. Bear, M. F., and W. Singer. "Modulation of Visual Cortical Plasticity by Acetylcholine and Noradrenaline." *Nature* **320** (1986): 172–176.
4. Beck, J., ed. "Textural Segmentation." In *Organization and Representation in Perception*, 285–317. Hillsdale, NJ: Erlbaum, 1982.
5. Buissert, P., E. Gary-Bobo, and M. Imbert. "Ocular Motility and Recovery of Orientation Properties of Visual Cortical Neurons in Dark-Reared Kittens." *Nature* **272** (1978): 816–817.
6. Desimone, R., L. Chelazzi, E. K. Miller, and J. Duncan. "Neuronal Mechanisms of Visual Attention." In *Linking Psychophysics, Neuropsychology and Computational Vision*, edited by T. Papathomas. Cambridge, MA: MIT Press, 1994 (in press).
7. Fiorentini, A., and N. Berardi. "Learning in Grating Waveform Discrimination: Specificity for Orientation and Spatial Frequency." *Vision Res.* **21** (1982): 1149–1158.
8. Fregnac, Y., D. Shulz, S. Thorpe, and E. Bienenstock. "Cellular Analog of Visual Cortical Plasticity." *Nature* **333** (1988): 367–370.
9. Gilbert, C. D. "Rapid Dynamic Changes in Adult Cerebral Cortex." *Curr. Opin. Neurobiol.* **3** (1993): 100–103.
10. Heggelund, P., K. Imamura, and T. Kasamatsu. "Reduced Binocularity in the Noradrenaline-Infused Striate Cortex of Acutely Anesthetized and Paralyzed, Otherwise Normal Cats." *Exp. Brain Res.* **68** (1987): 593–605.
11. Hobson, J. A. "Sleep and Dreaming." *J. Neuroscience* **10** (1990): 371–382.
12. Hubel, D. "Exploration of Primary Visual Cortex." *Nature* **299** (1982): 515–524.

13. Jasper, H. H., and J. Tessier. "Acetylcholine Liberation from Cerebral Cortex During Paradoxical (REM) Sleep." *Science* **174** (1970): 601–602.

14. Julesz, B. "Towards an Axiomatic Theory of Preattentive Vision." In *Dynamic Aspects of Neocortical Function*, edited by G. M. Edelman, W. E. Gall, and W. M. Cowan, 585–612. New York: John Wiley & Sons, 1984.

15. Julesz, B. "Texton Gradients: The Texton Theory Revisited." *Biol. Cybernetics* **54** (1986): 464–469.

16. Julesz, B. "Early Vision is Bottom Up, Except for Focal Attention." *Cold Spring Harbor Symp. Quant. Biol.* **55** (1990): 973–978.

17. Juliano, S. L., W. Ma, and D. Eslin. "Cholinergic Depletion Prevents Expansion of Topographic Maps in Somatosensory Cortex." *Proc. Natl. Acad. Sci. USA* **88** (1991): 780–784.

18. Karni, A., and D. Sagi. "Texture Discrimination Learning is Specific for Spatial Location and Background Orientation." *Invest. Ophtal. & Vis. Sci. (Suppl.)* **31** (1990): 562.

19. Karni, A., and D. Sagi. "Human Texture Discrimination Learning: Evidence for Low-Level Neuronal Plasticity in Adults." *Perception* **19** (1990): A13.

20. Karni, A., and D. Sagi. "Where Practice Makes Perfect in Texture Discrimination: Evidence for Primary Visual Cortex Plasticity." *Proc. Natl. Acad. Sci. USA* **88** (1991): 4966–4970.

21. Karni, A. "What, Where and When—Making Memories of Visual Textures." Ph.D. Thesis, Weizmann Institute of Science, Rehovot, 1992.

22. Karni, A., and D. Sagi. "The Time Course of Learning a Visual Skill." *Nature* **362** (1993): 250–252.

23. Karni, A., L. G. Ungeleider, J. Haxby, P. Jezzard, L. Pannier, C. A. Cuenod, R. Turner, and D. Lebihan. "Stimulus Dependent MRI Signals Evoked by Oriented Line-Element Textures in Human Visual Cortex." *Neurosci. Abstr.* **19** (1993): 1501.

24. Karni, A., G. Meyer, P. Jezzard, M. Adams, R. Turner, and L. G. Ungerleider. "The Acquisition and Retention of a Motor Skill: A Functional MRI Study of Long-Term Primary Motor Cortex Plasticity." *Neurosci. Abst.* **20** (1994): 1291.

25. Karni, A,. D. Tanne, B. S. Rubenstein, J. J. M. Askenasy, and D. Sagi. "Dependence on REM Sleep of Overnight Improvement of a Perceptual Skill." *Science* **265** (1994): 679–682.

26. Karni, A., Braun, and D. Sagi. Unpublished results.

27. Katz, E., J. D. Victor, and K. Purpura. "Dynamic Changes in Cortical Responses Following Removal and Restoration of Nearby Visual Inputs." This volume.

28. Lamme, A. F., B. W. van Dijk, and H. Spekreijse. "Organization of Texture Segregation Processing in Primate Visual Cortex." *Vis. Neurosci.* **10** (1993): 781–790.

29. Marr, D. *Vision*, 49–86. San Francisco: W. H. Freeman, 1982. . Matthies, H. "In Search of a Cellular Mechanism of Learning." *Progress Neurobiol.* **32** (1989): 277–349.

30. McGaugh, J. L. "Time-Dependent Processes in Memory Storage." *Science* **153** (1966): 1351–1358.

31. Merzenich, M. M., and K. Sameshima. "Cortical Plasticity and Memory." *Curr. Opin. Neurobiol.* **3** (1993): 187–196.

32. Merzenich, M. M., and W. M. Jenkins. "Cortical Plasticity, Learning, and Learning Dysfunction." This volume.

33. Metherate, R., and N. M. Weinberger. "Cholinergic Modulation of Responses to Single Tones Produces Tone-Specific Receptive-Field Alteration in Cat Auditory Cortex." *Synapse* **6** (1990): 133–145.

34. Mishkin, M., and D. G. Forgays. "Word Recognition as a Function of Retinal Locus." *J. Exp. Psychol.* **43** (1952): 43–48.

35. Mishkin, M., B. Malamut, and J. Bachevalier. "Memories and Habits: Two Neuronal Systems." In *The Neurobiology of Learning and Memory*, edited by G. Lynch, J. L. McGaugh, and N. M. Weinberger, 64–88. New York: Guilford Press, 1988.

36. Nothdurft, H. C. "Orientation Sensitivity and Texture Segmentation in Patterns with Different Line Orientation." *Vision Res.* **25** (1985): 551–560.

37. Peck, C. K., and C. Blakemore. "Modification of Single Neurons in the Kitten Visual Cortex After Brief Periods of Monocular Visual Experience." *Exp. Brain Res.* **22** (1975): 57–68.

38. Poggio, T., M. Fahle, and S. Edelman. "Fast Perceptual Learning in Visual Hyperacuity." *Science* **256** (1992): 1018–1021.

39. Polat, U., and D. Sagi. "Spatial Interactions in Human Vision: From Near to Far via Experience Dependent Cascades of Connections." *Proc. Natl. Acad. Sci. USA* **91** (1994): 1206–1209.

40. Polat, U., and D. Sagi. "Plasticity of Special Interactions in Early Vision." This volume.

41. Ramachandran, V. S., and O. Braddick. "Orientation-Specific Learning in Stereopsis." *Perception* **2** (1973): 371–376.

42. Recanzone, G. H., M. M. Merzenich, and C. E. Schreiner. "Changes in the Distributed Temporal Response Properties of S1 Cortical Neurons Reflect Improvements in Performance on a Temporally Based Tactile Discrimination Task." *J. Neurophysiol.* **67** (1992): 1071–1091.

43. Recanzone, G. H., C. E. Schreiner, and M. M. Merzenich. "Plasticity in the Frequency Presentation of Primary Auditory Cortex Following Discrimination Training in Adult Owl Monkeys." *J. Neuroscience* **13** (1993): 87–103.

44. Rubenstein, B. S., and D. Sagi. "Spatial Variability as a Limiting Factor in Texture Discrimination Tasks: Implications for Performance Asymmetries." *J. Opt. Soc. Am. A* **7** (1990): 1632–1643.

45. Sagi, D., and B. Julesz. "'Where' and 'What' in Vision." *Science* **228** (1985): 1214–1219.

46. Shiu, L.-P., and H. Pashler. "Improvement in Line Orientation Discrimination is Retinally Local but Dependent on Cognitive Set." *Percept. Psychophys.* **52** (1992): 582–588.
47. Singer, W. "Central Core Control of Developmental Plasticity in Kitten Visual Cortex: Diencephalic Lesions." *Exp. Brain Res.* **47** (1982): 209–222.
48. Singer, W., F. Tretter, and U. Yinon. "Evidence for Long-Term Functional Plasticity in the Visual Cortex of Adult Cats." *J. Physiology* **324** (1982): 239–248.
49. Squire, L. R. "Mechanisms of Memory." *Science* **232** (1986): 1612–1619.
50. Tallal, P. "Development and Disorders of Speech and Language: Implications for Neural and Behavioral Plasticity." This volume.
51. Ullman, S. "Visual Routines." *Cognition* **18** (1984): 97–159.
52. Van Essen, D. C., E. A. DeYoe, J. F. Olavarria, J. J. Knierim, J. M. Fox, D. Sagi, and B. Julesz. "Neural Responses to Static and Moving Texture Patterns in Visual Cortex of the Macaque Monkey." In *Neural Mechanisms of Visual Perception,*, edited by D. M. K. Lam and C. Gilbert, 49–67. Texas: Portfolio, 1989.
53. Weinberger, N. M., J. H. Ashe, R. Metherate, T. M. McKenna, D. M. Diamond, and J. Bakin. "Retuning Auditory Cortex by Learning: A Preliminary Model of Receptive Field Plasticity." *Concepts Neurosci.* **1** (1990): 91–132.
54. Zeki, S. "Functional Specialization in the Visual Cortex of the Rhesus Monkey." *Nature* **274** (1978): 423–428.

Uri Polat and Dov Sagi
Department of Neurobiology, Brain Research, The Weizmann Institute of Science, Rehovot 76100, Israel

Plasticity of Spatial Interactions in Early Vision

1. INTRODUCTION

When a person is asked to perform a visual (or any other sensory) discrimination task it is often the case that he or she improves with practice, even on very simple tasks. This improvement occurs without any reinforcement and does not seem to involve conscious effort, but rather it seems to be controlled by some inherent subconscious process. During the last decade perceptual learning was shown to be involved in a variety of visual tasks: Stereoscopic vision,[25,31] gratings detection,[5,8] hyper-acuity,[23,30] phase discrimination,[8] motion detection,[2] texture discrimination (Karni and Sagi, this volume),[1,13,14] search,[38] and pattern discrimination.[24] Some of these studies showed specificity of learning for location in the visual field[2,8,14,24,25,30] (what was learned at one retinal location could not be used when stimulus was presented at another location), for orientation,[1,2,8,14,20,30,31] spatial frequency,[8] and direction of motion.[2] Though in most of these experiments learning was found to transfer across eyes (what was learned with one eye only could be used with the other eye), some studies showed only partial transfer[2] or absence of transfer,[14] thus supporting a low-level anatomical site for the learning to take place. In some cases learning was found to persist for a few weeks,[2,8] or even for years[15] without further practice. A new wave of studies provide more insight into the processes involved in perceptual learning. In particular, texture segmentation,[1,14,15,16,17] lateral masking,[29] and hyperacuity[7,30,40] are being studied providing interesting results. These experiments demonstrate again the specificity of learning for stimulus features. However, learning was found to be also specific for non-stimulus variables, such as the task used for training,[1,16] implying higher level controls over learning. The existence of two types of learning, fast (binocular) and slow (monocular), was demonstrated,[15] indicating learning at different levels of processing.[16] The slow phase was found to require a consolidation period[15] of about six hours, which, when during sleep time, was found to depend on the integrity of REM sleep stage.[17]

While all these studies show improvement of performance with time, and provide hints for the possible anatomical localization of the sensory modifications

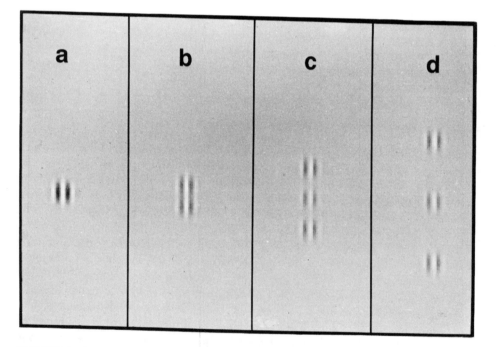

FIGURE 1 Stimuli configurations demonstrating some target to mask distances used in the present experiments. Distance (center to center as illustrated on the right) equals (a) 0λ, (b) 1.5λ, (c) 3λ, and (d) 6λ. Observers task is to detect the central patch, however, here target contrast (central patch) is somewhat enhanced for demonstration purpose.

involved, there is no clear idea as for the type of modifications and mechanisms involved. Recently, we have shown, using a lateral masking paradigm,[27,28] that perceptual learning involves increased range of interactions in early vision.[29] In these studies observers were trained to detect a Gabor signal (see Figure 1) in the presence of two flanking high contrast but otherwise similar signals (masks). Target detection was found initially to improve by the presence of masks at a short distance only,[27] implying short-range interactions. Practice had the effect of a continuous increase of interaction range, in a way that long-range interactions could not be established before medium-range interactions were becoming effective. It was suggested that long-range interactions are produced by chains of local interactions. In this chapter we show that this type of learning is highly specific. Learning was found to be specific for eye, spatial frequency and retinal location (to within a neighborhood of half a degree). Thus, our results demonstrates that an early level of visual processing, which is dominated by local processes,[35] can be modified, even at adulthood, to detect long-range correlations.

2. METHODS

Observers were trained to detect a Gabor target flanked by two high contrast Gabor masks,[27,28,29] with the distance varied during the course of the experiments (Figure 1). Stimuli were displayed as graylevel modulation on a Hitachi HM-3619A color monitor, using an Adage 3000 raster display system. The video format was 56 Hz noninterlaced, with 512×512 pixels occupying a $9.6^0 \times 9.6^0$ area. The mean display luminance was 50 cd/m^2 in an otherwise dark environment. A two-alternative temporal forced-choice paradigm was used. Each trial consisted of two stimuli presented sequentially, only one of which had a target. Before each trial, a small fixation cross was presented at the center of the screen. When ready, the observers pushed a key to activate the trial sequence . This sequence consisted of a no-stimulus (i.e., uniform grey) interval (500 msec), a stimulus presentation (90 msec), a no-stimulus interval (1000 msec), and a second stimulus presentation (90 msec). The observer's task was to determined which of the stimuli contained the target. Auditory feedback, by means of a keyboard bell, was given on observers' error immediately following the response. A staircase method[28] was used to determine the contrast threshold. The observers' vision in both eyes was normal, with stimuli viewed from a distance of 180 cm.

3. RESULTS

3.1 INCREASING THE INTERACTION RANGE

Observers were trained with stimuli having different target to mask separations (samples can be seen in Figure 1). The range of distances used during each daily session was 0 to 12λ, and this was repeated few times per week, for a few weeks. The results show a slow increase in interaction range by up to a factor of two for different signal wavelengths: 0.075^0, 0.15^0 (Figure 2), and 0.3^0.[29] Assuming that receptive field size is two times its optimal wavelength[27] then the foveal filter integrates now inputs from far more than six times its receptive field size. A larger range of

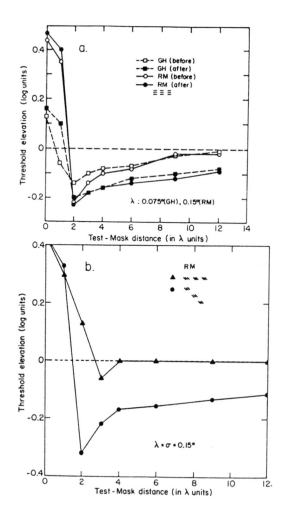

FIGURE 2 Dependence of target threshold on target-to-mask distance. Threshold elevation is computed relative to that of an isolated target. (a) Data is presented for horizontal target and masks arranged along the horizontal meridian, before (empty symbols) and after thirty sessions of practice (filled symbols), for two observers on two different λ's. (b) Data is presented for diagonal target and masks arranged along the horizontal (▲) or diagonal (■) meridian. The same number of sessions, λ and σ as presented for observer RM in (a). Note that extensive practice on the noncollinear configuration resulted no change of enhancement range, indicating dependence of learning on already existing connections. (From Polat and Sagi[29]; reprinted by permission of the authors.)

interactions, up to distances of 20λ, were observed when more extensive practice included these far distances.

3.2 EVIDENCE FOR A CONSOLIDATION PERIOD

Karni and Sagi[15,16] showed that texture discrimination learning involves a latent period in which the effect of practice is being consolidated. Measurements showed that improvement in performance can be seen only when two practice sessions are separated by 6 to 10 hours.[15] We have made similar measurements for lateral masking learning and present here results of repeated measurements of enhancement at a distance of 6λ. Enhancement is computed as the logarithm of the ratio between thresholds of the masked target and the unmasked (isolated) target. We found that enhancement gain is 0, 0.01, −0.01, 0.14, and 0.09 for inter-session times of 1, 2, 6, 8, and 24 hours respectively (data samples taken from three observers).

3.3 THE CRITICALITY OF INTERMEDIATE CONNECTIONS

In all training sessions observers were presented with a variety of separations (0, 1, 2, 3, 4, 6, 9, 12λ). We have shown before[29] that, although the main effect of learning is an increased sensitivity for large distances, practicing on large distances (4–12λ) alone does not produce any learning effect. We have suggested that the increased range of interactions is obtained by chaining together local interactions. Practice has the effect of improving local connections, thus allowing for multiple transmission across several links (synapses).

Here, the necessity of intermediate connections in generating long-range interactions is being confirmed by using a sparse sampling of target to mask distances within each session. We divided the set of training into two subsets; The first included distances of 0, 2, 4, and 9λ and the second set included the 1, 3, 6, and 12λ. No learning effect was found when observers practiced on each of the two subsets separately (see Figure 3). On the contrary, here, practice had the effect of reducing enhancement at locations where previously exist. This effect can be attributed to weakening of local interactions. We suggest[29] that the efficacy of interactions between two units can be reduced by repetitive activation of one of them while the other unit is not active. Only when both units are active, their connections efficacy improves (Hebbian learning). These results provide further support to the idea that long-range interactions cannot be obtained, unless intermediate connections are established first.

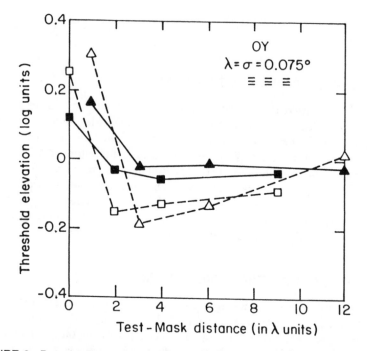

FIGURE 3 Data from experiments were an observer was trained on two sets of distances; the first included distances of 0, 2, 4, and 9λ (△ before, and ▲ after practice) and the second included distances of 1, 3, 6, and 12λ (□ before, and ■ after practice). The observer practiced the two sets on the same days, but with one hour separating between them.

INTEROCULAR TRANSFER

We trained observers with one eye covered (monocular viewing), until an increase in the range of interactions was observed. When testing the untrained eye we found no increase in the interaction range (Figure 4(a–b)). This effect of no interocular transfer suggests a low-level anatomical loci for the learning effect to take place.[14] To account for these results it is sufficient to assume that the synapses being modified receive input from monocular cells, thus it is possible that the post-synaptic side is binocular. However, dichoptic viewing experiments, where the target was presented to one eye while the two flanking masks to the other eye, support a monocular site (post-synaptic) for the spatial interactions to take place. These experiments show no interactions between target and masks.

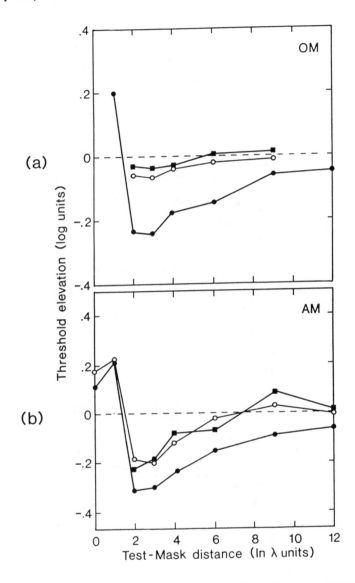

FIGURE 4   No interocular transfer of the learning effect. Range of interactions before (empty symbols) and after (filled symbols) practice. (a) Right eye before (○) and after (●) practice; Left eye tested after practice of Right eye (■). (b) Same as (a) but training with the Left eye (○, ●) and then a test of the Right eye (■). (continued)

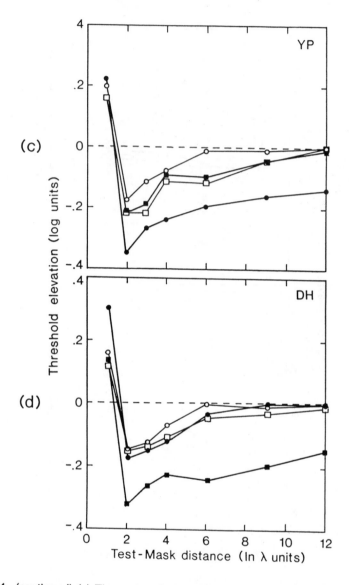

FIGURE 4 (continued) (c) The range of both eyes tested before (○,□) and after (●,■) practicing of only one eye (R), indicating that the enhancement range of the untrained eye (L) is unaffected by practicing the other eye. (d) Same as (c) but practicing the Left eye.

3.4 SPATIAL FREQUENCY SPECIFICITY

Training with Gabor signals of one spatial frequency ($\lambda = 0.075^0$) and testing with a second spatial frequency ($\lambda = 0.3^0$) showed no transfer of interaction range (Figure 5(a)). A similar result was found when first training with lower spatial frequency ($\lambda = 0.3^0$) and then testing with the higher one ($\lambda = 0.075^0$) (Figure 5(b)).

3.5 RETINAL LOCATION

Few indications for retinotopic specificity were found: (1) When training with horizontal collinear configuration and testing with diagonal collinear configuration, retraining was needed to establish the effect of learning. This effect can also be attributed to orientation specificity. (2) Threshold measurements performed at a distance of 2λ (0.15^0) distal to the largest practiced distance revealed no enhancement. However, an extension of the practice range up to this distance did show an effect of facilitation. Note that the magnitude of the spatial specificity is correlated with receptive field size, i.e., about 2λ.

---

4. DISCUSSION

Lateral masking experiments provide a very efficient and promising tool for exploring the architecture of early vision and plasticity. We believe that this paradigm is useful for exploring detailed connectivity of early visual processes and their dynamics. The basic results presented here are: (1) Thresholds are affected by target to mask distance (D): threshold increases for $D < 2\lambda$ and decreases for $2\lambda > D < 6\lambda$. (2) The range of enhancement can be increased up to at least 20λ with practice, when the observers are trained on all distances within one session. (3) The practice effect is specific for eye, orientation, spatial frequency and location.

The results obtained support an early visual system, composed of many spatial filters, each of which is selective for a limited range of orientations, spatial frequency and retinal locations.[35] Neighboring filters interact,[27] but mostly when they share the same orientations and spatial-frequency.[27] The longer range facilitatory interactions (see Figure 2) were observed so far only for collinear configurations, that is for cases where all interacting units are oriented along the line between them. Weaker interactions were observed for cases where local orientation is orthogonal to the connecting line.[28] Thus, these interactions can be used for line segmentations and for grouping, maybe serving the Gestalt rule of good continuation (Kovács and Julesz,[19] this volume).[18] The short-range effects ($0–2\lambda$) seen in Figure 2 may reflect a balance between different types of interactions. For this range one has to consider the direct effect of the masks on the target filter, an effect that depend on receptive field size and can produce both suppression and facilitation, depending on mask contrast and target to mask distance. Recent experiments, covering a wider range of stimulus parameters, suggest

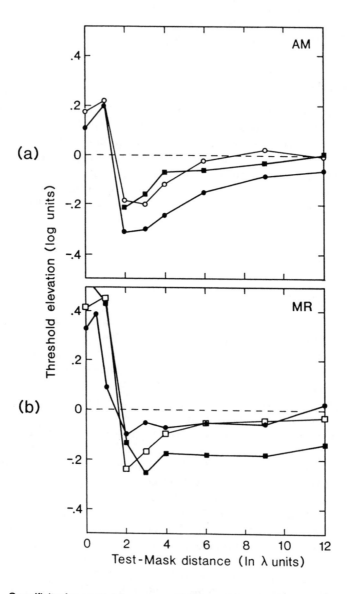

FIGURE 5 Specificity for spatial frequency. Training with one spatial frequency ($\circ, \bullet \lambda = \sigma = 0.075^0$) (a) or ($\square, \blacksquare \lambda = \sigma = 0.3^0$) (b), and testing with the other. Before ($\circ\square$) and $\bullet$ after ($\bullet\blacksquare$) practice.

that short-range interactions are dominated by nonlinear inhibitory connections.[45]

The main issue explored here is the stability of lateral interactions. The data indicate instability of interactions. Though the types of connectivity modifications taking place during long periods of practice are not understood yet, it seems that the main effect is an increase in interaction range. In some experimental conditions we observe a weakening of interactions (Figure 3; also see Polat and Sagi[29]). Within the context of a network having short-range inhibitory connections and longer range excitatory connections, one has to consider modifiability of all interactions involved. Here we consider a model assuming plasticity of excitatory connections only,[29] though recent results,[45] showing disappearance of the suppression zone ($D < 2\lambda$) with practice, support also modifiability of inhibitory connections. We suggest that the increase of enhancement range reflects an increased range of interactions via a cascade of filters which are locally connected. Learning involves increasing efficacy of existing excitatory connections where connections are not distributed randomly but are arranged along the filter preferred orientation and orthogonal to it. Efficacy of connections increases only if both filters involved are being activated within a certain time window (of a few minutes). Efficacy decreases if only one filter is activated. These rules of learning are equivalent to Hebbian rules but with synchrony defined on a slower time scale.

Thus, in experimental conditions where all filters are being activated by external stimuli, all local connections improve their efficacy. However, when only a partial set of stimuli (masks) are presented, there is a reduction in efficacy of connections between activated filters and their nonactivated neighbors. This reduced efficacy reduces the chain's ability to transmit signals between filters across multiple connections, causing a loss of efficacy across all connections between mask activated sites and target activated sites. This scenario accounts for the phenomenon shown in Figure 3.

We believe that the laws of learning emerging from this study are applicable to human learning in general, and are not limited to perceptual learning or to procedural learning. The perceptual learning paradigm seems to provide a well-defined context to understanding the dynamics of learning, as we have a reasonably good understanding of brain processes operating on the sensory input. The high degree of specificity of visual learning for different image attributes indicates plasticity at sensory cortical areas as area V1. So far, only area V1 is known to contain cells which are highly local, orientation selective and monocular.[44] Also, recent electrophysiological studies show plasticity in a variety sensory cortical areas,[21,22] such as visual,[4,9,11,12,26,37] auditory,[6,34,39,41] and somato-sensory.[32,33] However, it is possible that, since multiple levels of processing are involved in a perceptual task, learning occurs at different processing levels. Of particular interest here is the distinction between "attentive" or selective processes and "nonattentive"[3] processes. It is possible that in some cases attention is being used to filter out from the stimulus the relevant information for the task, and learning may reflect an improved selection or filtering.[10] Indeed, recent studies show task dependent learning,[1,16,36] however, monocular learning is difficult to reconcile with the 'attention' hypothesis since attentive process cannot make a selection based on eye of origin information.[42] According to recent findings,[15] perceptual learning on a given task involves both types of learning, an initial phase of fast (within session) learning (binocular and probably task dependent), followed by a slower phase (monocular) requiring a few hours of consolidation In some of the earlier learning experiments showing interocular transfer learning was found on the faster time scale,[8,30] while experiments showing slower learning showed less interocular transfer.[2] The data presented here also indicate monocular and slow learning.

5. CONCLUSION

Psychophysical and electrophysiological studies provide evidence for plasticity of primary sensory areas. Perceptual learnings seems to provide an excellent behavioral paradigm for exploring human learning, especially when coupled with current understanding of human vision. Perceptual learning seems to have two major components: fast (few hundreds of trials) and slow (days). The fast component seems to affect higher levels of processing (above the site of binocular integration) and probably involves top-down processes, improving the link between task dependent units and sensory units while selecting optimal sensory units for the task. Once these links become efficient, the task becomes "automatic" (nonattentive) and performance is then limited by sensory architecture only. The slow component seems to follow the fast one and involves low-level processes (monocular) within primary sensory areas. At this stage, links between sensory units are strengthened or weakened according to their activity correlations, thus establishing new associations and dissociations. First-order associations (via one link) are limited to direct connections, but higher order associations are possible by establishing chains of associations. Thus, while we are limited by system architecture in what we can perceive as direct associations, it is possible to perceive more complex percepts (or concepts) by indirect associations. Fast learning probably takes place on-line, when the stimulus is still effective or immediately after, but slow learning and the consolidation of associations seem to be performed off-line, for hours after stimulus presentation while the observer is not aware of the problem being solved. Though consolidation of associations may take place during day time, it seems that it also depends on processes that are active during REM (dream) sleep.

ACKNOWLEDGMENT

The authors acknowledge and thank Avi Karni who was instrumental in initiating this research venture. This research was supported by the Basic Research Foundation, administered by the Israel Academy of Science and Humanities.

REFERENCES

1. Ahissar, M., and S. Hochstein. "Attentional Control of Early Perceptual Learning." *Proc. Natl. Acad. Sci. USA* **90** (1993): 5718–5722.
2. Ball, K., and R. Sekuler. "Direction-Specific Improvement in Motion Discrimination." *Vision Res.* **27** (1987): 953–965.
3. Braun, J., and D. Sagi. "Vision Outside the Focus of Attention." *Percept. Psychophys.* **48** (1990): 45–58.
4. Chino, Y. M., J. H. Kaas, E. L. Smith, A. A. L. Langston, and H. Cheng. "Rapid Reorganization of Cortical Maps in Adult Cats Following Restricted Deafferentation in Retina." *Vision Res.* **32** (1992): 789–796.
5. De Valois, K. K. "Spatial Frequency Adaptation Can Enhance Contrast Sensitivity." *Vision Res.* **17** (1977): 1057–1065.
6. Edeline, J.-M., and N. M. Weinberger. "Receptive Field Plasticity in the Auditory Cortex During Frequency Discrimination Training: Selective Retuning Independent of Task Difficulty." *Behav. Neurosci.* **107** (1993): 82–103.
7. Fahle, M., and S. Edelman. "Long-Term Learning in Vernier Acuity: Effects of Stimulus Orientation, Range and of Feedback." *Vision Res.* **33** (1993): 397–412.
8. Fiorentini, A., and N. Berardi. "Learning in Grating Waveform Discrimination: Specificity for Orientation and Spatial Frequency." *Vision Res.* **21** (1982): 1149–1158.
9. Fregnac, Y., D. Shulz, S. Thorpe, and E. Bienenstock. "Cellular Analogs of Visual Cortical Epigenesis. I. Plasticity of Orientation Selectivity." *J. Neurosci.* **12** (1992): 1280–1300.
10. Gibson, E. J. *Principles of Perceptual Learning and Development.* New York: Appleton-Century-Crofts, 1969.
11. Gilbert, C. D., and T. N. Wiesel. "Receptive Field Dynamics in Adult Primary Visual Cortex." *Nature* **356** (1992): 150–152.
12. Gilbert, C. D. "Rapid Dynamic Changes in Adult Cerebral Cortex." *Curr. Opin. Neurobiol.* **3** (1993): 100–103.
13. Gurnsey, R., and R. A. Browse. "Micropattern Properties and Presentation Condition Influencing Visual Texture Discrimination." *Percept. Psychophys.* **41** (1987): 239–252.

14. Karni, A., and D. Sagi. "Where Practice Makes Perfect in Texture Discrimination: Evidence for Primary Visual Cortex Plasticity." *Proc. Natl. Acad. Sci. USA* **88** (1991): 4966–4970.

15. Karni, A. and D. Sagi. "The Time Course of Learning a Visual Skill." *Nature* **365** (1993): 250–252.

16. Karni, A., and D. Sagi. "A Memory System in the Adult Visual Cortex." This volume.

17. Karni, A., D. Tanne, B. S. Rubenstein, J. J. M. Askenasy, and D. Sagi. "Dependence on REM Sleep of Overnight Improvement of a Perceptual Skill." *Science* **265** (1994): 679–682.

18. Kovács, I., and B. Julesz. "A Closed Curve is Much More than an Incomplete One: Effect of Closure in Figure-Ground Segmentation." *Proc. Natl. Acad. Sci. USA* **90** (1993): 7495–7497.

19. Kovács, I., and B. Julesz. "Long-Range Spatial Interactions of Early Vision Revealed by Psychophysically Measured Sensitivity Maps." This volume.

20. Mayer, M. J. "Practice Improves Adults' Sensitivity to Diagonals." *Vision Res.* **23** (1983): 547–550.

21. Merzenich, M. M., and K. Sameshima. "Cortical Plasticity and Memory." *Curr. Opin. Neurobiol.* **3** (1993): 187–196.

22. Merzenich, M. M., C. Schreiner, W. Jenkins, and X. Wang. "Neural Mechanisms Underlying Temporal Integration, Segmentation and Input Sequence Representation: Some Implications for the Origin of Learning Disabilities." *Ann. NY Acad. Sci.* **682** (1993): 1–22.

23. McKee, S. P., and G. Westheimer. "Improvement in Vernier Acuity with Practice." *Percept. Psychophys.* **24** (1978): 258–262.

24. Nazir, T. A., and J. K. O'Regan. "Some Results on Translation Invariance in the Human Visual System." *Spatial Vision 5* (1990): 81–100.

25. O'Toole, A. J., and D. J. Kersten. "Learning to See Random-Dot Stereograms." *Perception* **21** (1992): 227–243.

26. Pettet, M. W., and C. D. Gilbert. "Dynamic Changes in Receptive Field Size in Cat Primary Visual Cortex." *Proc. Natl. Acad. Sci. USA* **89** (1992): 8366–8370.

27. Polat, U., and D. Sagi. "Lateral Interactions Between Spatial Channels: Suppression and Facilitation Revealed by Lateral Masking Experiments." *Vision Res.* **33** (1993): 993–997.

28. Polat, U., and D. Sagi. "The Architecture of Perceptual Spatial Interactions." *Vision Res.* **34** (1994): 73–78.

29. Polat, U., and D. Sagi. "Spatial Interactions in Human Vision: From Near to Far Via Experience Dependent Cascades of Connections." *Proc. Natl. Acad. Sci. USA* **91** (1994): 1206-1209.

30. Poggio, T., M. Fahle, and S. Edelman. "Fast Perceptual Learning in Visual Hyperacuity." *Science* **256** (1992): 1018–1021.

31. Ramachandran, V. S., and O. Braddick. "Orientation-Specific Learning in Stereopsis." *Perception* **2** (1973): 371–376.

32. Recanzone, G. H., W. M. Jenkins, G. H. Hradek, and M. M. Merzenich. "Progressive Improvement in Discriminative Abilities in Adult Owl Monkeys Performing a Tactile Frequency Discrimination Task." *J. Neurophysiology* **67** (1992): 1015–1030.
33. Recanzone, G. H., M. M. Merzenich, and C. E. Schreiner. "Changes in the Distributed Temporal Response Properties of SI Cortical Neurons Reflect Improvements in Performance on a Temporally Based Tactile Discrimination Task." *J. Neurophysiology* **67** (1992): 1071–1091.
34. Recanzone, G. H., C. E. Schreiner, and M. M. Merzenich. "Plasticity in the Frequency Presentation of Primary Auditory Cortex Following Discrimination Training in Adult Owl Monkeys." *J. Neuroscience* **13** (1993): 87–103.
35. Rubenstein, B. S., and D. Sagi. "Spatial Variability as a Limiting Factor in Texture Discrimination Tasks: Implications for Performance Asymmetries." *J. Opt. Soc. Am. A* **7** (1990): 1632–1643.
36. Shiu, L.-P., and H. Pashler. "Improvement in Line Orientation Discrimination is Retinally Local But Dependent on Cognitive Set." *Percept. Psychophys.* **52** (1992): 582–588.
37. Shulz, D., and Y. Fregnac. "Cellular Analogs of Visual Cortical Epigenesis. II. Plasticity of Binocular Integration." *J. Neuroscience* **12** (1992): 1301–1318.
38. Steinman, S. B. "Serial and Parallel Search in Pattern Vision?" *Perception* **16** (1993): 389–398.
39. Weinberger, N. M. "Learning-Induced Changes of Auditory Receptive Fields." *Curr. Opin. Neurobiol.* **3** (1993): 570–577.
40. Weiss, Y., S. Edelman, and M. Fahle. "Models of Perceptual Learning in Vernier Hyperacuity." *Neural Comp.* **5** (1993): 695–718.
41. Weinberger, N. M., R. Javid, and B. Lepan. "Long-Term Retention of Learning-Induced Receptive Field Plasticity in The Auditory Cortex." *Proc. Natl. Acad. Sci. USA* **90** (1993): 2394–2398.
42. Wolfe, J. M., and S. L. Franzel. "Binocularity and Visual Search." *Percept. Psychophys.* **44** (1988): 81–93.
43. Wolford, G., F. Marchack, and H. Hughes. "Practice Effects in Backward Masking." *J. Exp. Psychol. HPP* **14** (1988): 101–112.
44. Zeki, S. "Functional Specialization in the Visual Cortex of the Rhesus Monkey." *Nature (London)* **274** (1978): 423–428.
45. Zenger, B., and D. Sagi. "Isolating Excitatory and Inhibitory Non-Linear Spatial Interactions." *Perception* **23** (1994): 2.

Ilona Kovács and Bela Julesz
Laboratory of Vision Research, Rutgers University, Busch Campus-Psych Bldg., Piscataway, NJ 08854

Long-Range Spatial Interactions of Early Vision Revealed by Psychophysically Measured Sensitivity Maps

INTRODUCTION

Learning on any chosen scale of time is produced by interactions among neural elements. Local spatial interactions of early vision are discussed in this volume with respect to their plasticity in adults (Polat and Sagi[12]). In the present chapter, we will look at these interactions as they are related to the global structure of visual stimuli. Our attempt is to see how these interactions tie distributed neural responses into assemblies that reflect external stimulus structure. We introduce a human psychophysical method that allows us to measure the effect of perceptual organization on the activity pattern of local visual detectors.[10] We map luminance contrast sensitivity for a small target within globally defined shapes, where target locations are distributed over the whole region enclosed by a contour. We find that local contrast sensitivity is affected by the presence of the contour even for far distances between the contour and the target, and that locations of maximal sensitivity change within the maps are determined by global shape properties. Our data indicate that long-range interactions of early vision result in "skeletons" of visual shapes. A skeletal representation of objects offers a structurally simplified shape description that can be used for higher level operations and for coding into memory. We suggest that a skeletal representation is naturally obtained by long-range interactions in a retinotopic neural projection.

METHOD: SENSITIVITY MAPS

We measured differential contrast thresholds for a Gabor target that was always presented on the same central location (in the center of fixation). The target was surrounded by a dense background field of randomly positioned and oriented Gabor signals and by a contour, embedded in the background.[9,10] The distance between the contour and the target was varied in these experiments (Figure 1). Stimuli were presented as grey-level modulation on a Mitsubishi color monitor, controlled by a Silicon Graphics Iris Indigo XZ 4000 machine. The display had a mean luminance of 32 cd/m^2. The patterns were viewed from a distance of 90 cm, and each pattern subtended $16° \times 16°$ of visual angle. The orientation of the target and the embedded contour was randomized across trials, while the orientation of the target was always parallel to the closest segment of the contour. Contrast increment thresholds for the target were measured as a function of target-contour distance in a two-alternative temporal forced-choice procedure. One trial consisted of two successive presentations of 170-msec stimulus frames (interframe interval was 500 msec), with the target presented either in the first or second frame. Contrast thresholds were estimated by a staircase procedure. To determine the effect of a circular contour on the sensitivity for the target as a function of contour-target separation, we used at least eight different measuring sites with one target period (λ) resolution along one radial direction, both for internal and external target positions. We computed the relative change in sensitivity as compared to the sensitivity for an isolated probe. For ellipses, more complete sensitivity maps were obtained with additional measuring sites: measurements were made with a resolution of one target period (λ) in one quadrant of the ellipse. Data from 52 measuring sites were reflected symmetrically to the other quadrants to generate the map. Inhomogeneity factors, such as visual field anisotropies, were first averaged out by presenting the enclosing boundary at random positions around fixation. Finally, the complete map was generated from the corrected radial values. A total of six human observers participated in the experiments.

(a) 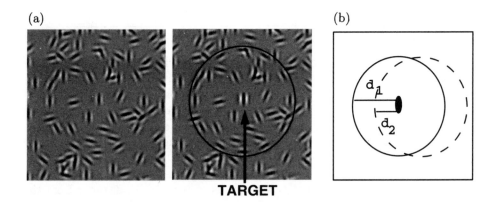 (b)

TARGET

FIGURE 1   (a) Stimuli for the contrast sensitivity measurements. Two sequential frames of one trial (only a small central portion of the stimulus frames is shown). Among the randomly positioned and oriented segments, there is an embedded circle (the continuous black circle helps the reader to find the contour). The two frames are equivalent except for the contrast of the central element, which is higher in the second frame. The observers' task was to indicate which frame contained the high-conrast target. (b) Target-contour distance (d_1, d_2 on the figure) was varied. The target was presented on the same central location (in the center of fixation), and the circle was moved closer or farther from it. Contrast thresholds were measured as a function of target-contour distance (with a sampling of 1 target period (λ)).

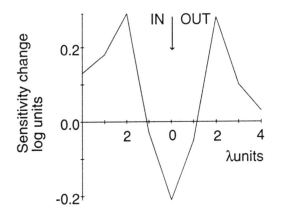

FIGURE 2   Contrast sensitivity change for a target in the vicinity of a circular contour. Target-contour distance is expressed in Gabor wavelength units ($\lambda = 0.18°$; results are shown only up to 4λ target-contour distance; at 0λ distance, contour and target overlapped; the center of the circle was at 8λ distance). Sensitivity enhancement peaked at 2λ both inside and outside of the circle. Averaged results of three observers.

SHORT-RANGE INTERACTIONS

Sensitivity change effects along the contour show similarities to detection threshold variations in the paradigm of lateral masking.[12,13,14] In contrast threshold measurements for a central Gabor target flanked by two Gabor signals, the maximal spatial range of interaction (without the long-term effects of practice) was found to be 5–6λ in a colinear configuration,[12,13] and it was only 2–3λ when the three Gabor signals were orthogonal to the virtual line connecting them.[14] The latter applies to our configuration considering that the target was always parallel to the nearest contour segment. As Figure 2 shows, we found reduced sensitivity between 0-1λ, and enhancement beyond that with peaks at $0.36° = 2\lambda$ distance from the perimeter. Note that the facilitatory effect occurs symmetrically on both sides of the contour. The agreement between our data and those obtained in lateral masking experiments suggests that the completed contours in our experiment play the same role as the contrast defined maskers in lateral masking, and that threshold changes in both paradigms reflect similar nonlinear interactions in the short spatial range.

LONG-RANGE INTERACTIONS ARE SPECIFIC FOR THE "INSIDE"

In the complete sensitivity map (Figure 3, and Reference Kovács and Julesz[9]) we found a second enhancement peak inside of a circle. The striking sensitivity enhancement at the center, where contrast sensitivity for the target increased by a factor > 2, was at $1.44° = 8\lambda$ distance from the perimeter. This is a result of interactions spreading much further than the known psychophysically measured local interactions (2-3λ in a parallel arrangement[14]). Outside of the circle, sensitivity change was down to zero at 4λ. The interior specific long-range effect suggests that "inside" and "outside" regions are distinguished at the level where the measured variations in contrast sensitivity occur. Results anologous to our observations were reported in the primary visual cortex of the macaque monkey, where a strong asymmetry was found in the cells' responses depending on whether the receptive field was positioned inside or outside of a figure.[11,15] These neuronal correlates of figure-ground segregation suggest an early cortical locus for our long-range, interior specific interactions.

LONG-RANGE INTERACTIONS ARE DETERMINED BY SHAPE

To test how long-range interactions are affected by the shape of the contour, we performed measurements on ellipses.[10] Figure 4(b) shows the sensitivity map of an ellipse (aspect ratio = 1.2). There was no enhancement in the center, and two displaced peaks arose along the major axis (at $0.36° = 2\lambda$ distance from the center). The long-range interactions seem to be affected by the global shape of the contour (a single peak for a circle, two displaced peaks for an ellipse).

The relative peak locations were independent of the absolute size of the ellipse (within a range of 2° to 4° diameter[10]), indicating that the peak locations do not depend on fixed visual angles or tissue separations in the visual cortex.

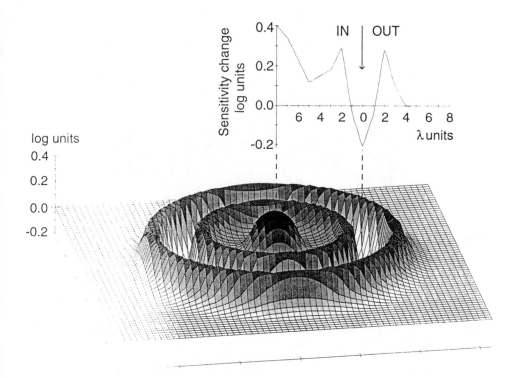

FIGURE 3 Complete sensitivity map of a circle. The circle as a whole induced *enhanced sensitivity at its center* (dark shading/peak of trough). At 2λ distance from the contour, both inside and outside, there were rings of enhanced sensitivity. On the circular contour (arrow at 0λ), sensitivity was decreased (light shading/depth of trough). Outside of the contour sensitivity change was down to zero at 4λ.

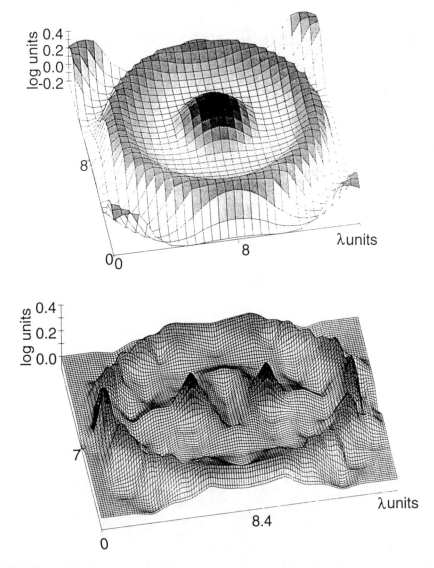

FIGURE 4   Sensitivity maps within enclosing contours. (a) Sensitivity change within a circle (the central part of Figure 3 is replotted here). (b) Sensitivity change within an ellipse (aspect ratio = 1.2). Note that the center shows no change in sensitivity, while two peaks can be localized 2λ away from the center.

THE RULE OF EQUIDISTANCE

Long-range interactions generate a single sensitivity peak at the only equidistant location within a circle.

We have shown that the peak locations within an ellipse are also on quasi-equidistant locations.[10] Inside of an ellipse there is no location that is equidistant from all of the boundary points. However, there are singularities that are approximately equidistant from a large proportion of the boundary. Figure 5(a) illustrates one possible way to estimate these equidistant locations: at every internal point, a "D-function" is defined as the percentage of boundary points that are equidistant within a tolerance of 1% of the boundary length. The maxima in this space are displaced from the center along the major axis. To test whether the D-function can

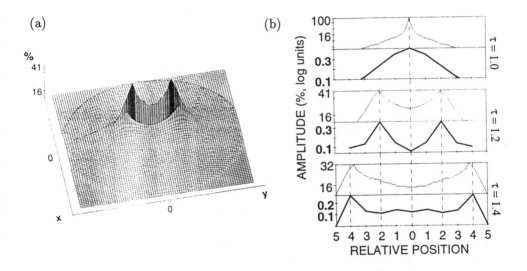

FIGURE 5   Peaks of contrast sensitivity can be predicted by the D-function. (a) D-function (within an ellipse of 1.2 aspect ratio). x and y are spatial positions. The two maxima sign those locations which are equidistant from the largest portion of the boundary. (b) Equidistant points predicted by the D-function (thin lines) for a circle (aspect ratio: $\tau = 1.0$) and two ellipses ($\tau = 1.2$ and $\tau = 1.4$), and corresponding contrast sensitivity data (thick lines). Abscissa: locations along the major axes (the center of the conic sections is at 0). Ordinate: percentage of equidistant points on log scale (thin lines) and amplitude of sensitivity change in log units (thick lines). The conformity between the data and the computed equidistant points is very strong. Data are means of three observers for each conic sections. (The D-function was computed by the DAVID visualization software, Fluid Sciences Inc., 1992.)

predict maxima in the ellipse sensitivity maps, we repeated the measurements for an ellipse with 1.4 aspect ratio. Figure 5(b) shows the predicted singularities and the measured maxima for conic sections of 1.0 (circle), 1.2 and 1.4 (ellipses) aspect ratios. Note that the D-function predicts sensitivity maxima for all the three conic sections.

GRASSFIRE

The D-function is strongly related to the growth geometry introduced by Blum[1,2,4] that describes shapes with their "skeletons" (or medial axis transform). An important outcome of our experiments is the indication of a medial axis-based shape representation in human visual processing.

As opposed to conventional boundary tracing, an axis-based shape description is derived in a direction orthogonal to the boundary, where the "skeleton" (medial axis or "stick-figure") of a shape is made explicit. One way to describe the medial-axis transformation is by analogy to how a grassfire would traverse from the object's boundary into the object's interior. At the last moments when the "grass" burns down, the original shape collapses into a skeleton that consists of quench points naturally equidistant from the boundary. *The central peaks in the sensitvity maps we report correspond to the major quench points* of the simple, smooth boundaries we used. It is known that small perturbations of more complex boundaries may change the skeleton dramatically. To overcome this difficulty, and still provide both the appropriate details and the general form of an object, it has been suggested that the representation should be obtained at various resolutions of different spatial scales.[3,5,7,8] With this extension, the representation provides a shape descriptor that is based on local analysis, that can define constituent components without using *ad hoc* primitives, and that seems to be an optimal way for coding in memory and to form associations. Amorphous biological forms can be categorized in a translation and rotation invariant manner since it does not bring in an external coordinate system. The only requirement is a retinotopic projection of the visual world, where close points of the pattern stay close and far apart points stay far apart.

Although our data are not yet conclusive with respect to the implementation of the grassfire, an interesting property of the transformation is that the equidistance metric can be substituted for by the temporal progression of waves. If one assumes a constant velocity activity propagation at right angles from the contour and exchanges spatial distance for time, the skeleton can be defined by the singularities where the waves arrive at the same time; i.e., equi-temporally. The equi-temporality constraint suggests that spatially separated neural events are linked through those units in a cell assembly where spreading activity from a large number of units arrive simultaneously, in temporal synchrony. As neurobiology will start to reveal propagation velocities of corresponding cortical areas, it will be possible to map our findings from the spatial domain into temporal propagation of neural activity across an extensive medium. Recent findings already provide parameters of a massive cortical activity spread in macaque monkey V1 with the method of real-time optical imaging.[6]

CONCLUSION

We introduced a psychophysical method which allowed us to visualize the interaction pattern of a large number of local detectors (addressing the level of the primary visual cortex) as they are affected by perceptual organization. We mapped luminance contrast sensitivity for a target in the context of globally defined shapes. Local contrast sensitivity was affected by the presence of the contour at far distances within the contour, and the locations of maximal sensitivity enhancement were determined by global shape properties. The results indicate the presence of an axis-based shape representation in the human visual system, which seems to be made explicit at a relatively low level of processing.

The emerging hypothesis is that visual encoding of biological shape is mediated by an "inverse growth" process that transforms a spatially distributed stimulus into it's core (the inverse of natural growth that develops from the core). The transform has the capacity to provide a continuous dialog between memory and stimulus[4] in the early visual system. The hypothesis, more extensively developed and tested, may lead to a better understanding of our capacity for fast categorization of visual stimuli. It also offers interesting perspectives for more general theories of brain function, considering that the formation of "shape" goes beyond vision and underlies our capability to generate (or ruin) coherent patterns in any domain.

ACKNOWLEDGMENT

Preparation of this chapter was supported by the cooperative efforts of NSF and OTKA within the U.S.–Hungarian Science and Technology Joint Fund (JF-360).

REFERENCES

1. Blum, H. J. "A New Model of Global Brain Function." *Pers. Biol. Med.* **10** (1967): 381–407.

2. Blum, H. J. "A Transformation for Extracting New Descriptors of Shape." In *Symposium on Models for the Perception of Speech and Visual Form*, edited by W. Wathen-Dunn, 362–380. Cambridge, MA: MIT Press, 1967.

3. Blum, H. J. "Biological Shape and Visual Science (Part I)." *J. Theor. Biol.* **38** (1973): 205–287.

4. Blum, H. J., and R. N. Nagel. "Shape Description Using Weighted Symmetric Axis Features." *Pattern Recognition* **10** (1978): 167–180.

5. Burbeck, C. A., and S. M Pizer. "Object Representation by Cores." *Invest. Opth. Vis. Sci.* **35** (1994): 1626.

6. Grinvald, A., E. E. Lieke, R. D. Frostig, and R. Hildesheim. "Cortical Point-Spread Function and Long-Range Lateral Interactions Revealed by Real-Time Optical Imaging of Macaque Monkey Primary Visual Cortex." *J. Neurosci.* **14(5)** (1994): 2545–2568.

7. Kimia, B. B., A. R. Tannenbaum, and S. W. Zucker. "Shapes, Shocks, and Deformations I: The Components of Two-Dimensional Shape and the Reaction-Diffusion Space." *Int. J. Comp. Vis.* (1994): in press.

8. Koenderink, J. J., and A. J. van Doorn. "Dynamic Shape." *Biol. Cyber.* **53** (1986): 383–396.

9. Kovács, I., and B. Julesz. "A Closed Curve is Much More Than an Incomplete One: Effect of Closure in Figure-Ground Segmentation." *Proc. Natl. Acad. Sci. USA* **90** (1993): 7495–7497.

10. Kovács, I., and B. Julesz. "Perceptual Sensitivity Maps within Globally Defined Visual Shapes." *Nature (London)* **370** (1994): 644–646.

11. Lamme, V. A. F. "Neuronal Correlates of Figure-Ground Segregation in Primary Visual Cortex." *Invest. Opth. Vis. Sci.* **35** (1994): 1489.

12. Polat, V., and D. Sagi. "Plasticity of Spatial Interactions in Early Vision." This volume.

13. Polat, U., and D. Sagi. "Lateral Interactions Between Spatial Channels: Suppression and Facilitation Revealed by Lateral Masking Experiments." *Vision Res.* **33** (1993): 993–997.

14. Polat, U., and D. Sagi. "The Architecture of Perceptual Spatial Interactions." *Vision Res.* **34** (1994): 73–78.

15. Zipser, K., T. S. Lee, V. A. F. Lamme, and P. H. Schiller. "Invariance of Figure-Ground Segregation Mechanimsms in V1 for Depth, Orientation, Luminance, and Chrominance Cues." *Invest. Opth. Vis. Sci.* **35** (1994): 1973.

Richard M. Jeo, Yuka Yonebayashi, and John M. Allman
Caltech, Division of Biology 216-76, Pasadena, CA 91125

Perceptual Memory of Cognitively Defined Contours: A Rapid, Robust, and Long-Lasting Form of Memory

Many aspects of perceptual memory, such as the memory of cognitively defined contours, are difficult to measure objectively. To this end, we have developed stimuli made up of random polygon arrays, with an embedded figure made up of a subset of the polygons (see Figure 1). The contours of the embedded figure are initially hard to see, until the figure is cued in some manner, for example, by movement or closure. We tested both human and owl monkey subjects, and found that once subjects "learn to see" the embedded figure, it is readily seen again. This memory is robust and long-lasting. Additionally, this memory is not rotation invariant, that is, rotating the entire stimulus degrades both accuracy and reaction time. We hypothesize that this type of learning takes place in visual cortex, and that there are neurons that will respond differently to the same polygon array before and after cueing the cognitive contour. Our paradigm has the advantage that a monkey can easily learn a novel stimulus within the length of time that we can record from a neuron. We plan to record single and multi-unit activity in the owl monkey's visual cortex, before, during, and after learning these cognitively defined figures.

Maturational Windows and Adult Cortical Plasticity, Eds. B. Julesz & I. Kovács,
SFI Studies in the Sciences of Complexity, Vol. XXIII, Addison-Wesley, 1995   **137**

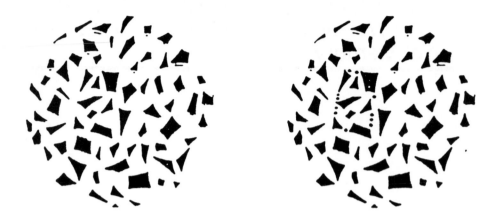

FIGURE 1 Sample stimulus pattern to test visual perceptual memory. A rectangular figure is embedded in the random polygon array. The figure is not obvious until it is cued (by closure in this example), shown on the right. The subject's task is to report the orientation of the embedded figure before and after cueing. The stimulus was generated by cutting up small slips of black paper and sprinkling them on a white background. The image was then captured as a computer bitmap, using a CCD camera and a frame grabber. We can generate an unlimited number of novel stimuli with this method.

INTRODUCTION

COGNITIVE CONTOURS

Viewed from an ecological perspective, the main task of the visual cortex is to extract behaviorally meaningful patterns from noisy and ambiguous images of the natural world. Because of the inherent ambiguity of natural images, multiple and conflicting interpretations may be possible. The task of the visual cortex is to select the most appropriate interpretation quickly and reliably. This task must often be performed on the basis of incomplete information. This function requires a kind of perceptual learning which, we hypothesize, occurs in the visual cortex.

A classic example is represented in Figure 2 taken from the Mooney series. Most subjects initially find it very difficult to see the greyhound embedded in the noisy background. Without cueing, most subjects eventually detect the dog's nose or trunk and the perceptual solution seems to spatially propagate to other parts of the dog's anatomy in the process of segregating the figure of the dog from the noisy background. The spatial propagation within feature space may involve an underlying propagation within a neocortical map.[4] Once the dog has been discerned, it is quickly seen again if the figure is reexamined months or years later.

FIGURE 2   Greyhound embedded in a noisy environment. Copyright © C. M. Mooney[15]; reprinted by permission of the author.

These striking, but highly qualitative perceptual learning phenomena are difficult to study objectively. We have developed a method to study this putative learning function of visual cortex through the use of cognitively defined contours, which are the borders of patterns embedded in a noisy background. We create stimuli that are made up of randomly arranged polygons, with an embedded rectangle composed of a subset of the polygons.

The embedded figure is not obvious to the observer until it is cued in some manner, such as by closure (Figure 1) or motion. These patterns are difficult to see until revealed by special cues such as the brief movement of the embedded pattern with respect to the background of polygons. Our perceptual experience with these cognitive contours is that, once they have been revealed, they are very readily seen again and that this capacity persists for months or years for a particular stimulus pattern.

THE PERCEPTUAL MEMORY SYSTEM

The learning of cognitive contours is similar to a type of long-term learning described by Warrington and Weiskrantz[25] in amnesiac patients. These patients, who

FIGURE 3   Sample item from the incomplete-pictures task of Gollin.[8] Reprinted from Milner, Corkin, and Teuber[14] by permission.

had severe deficits in their capacity to remember recent events, showed a remarkable ability to identify visual patterns when they viewed fragmented residues of whole patterns. For example, in Figure 3, amnesiac patients who had previously viewed these images retained the ability to identify the airplane on the basis of the fragmented images in sets 1 and 2.

The amnesiac patient, HM, whose medial temporal lobe including hippocampus had been surgically removed bilaterally, showed retention of his capacity to identify fragmented images in these tests.[14]

This capacity has been termed "priming" and has been postulated to be performed by a "perceptual representation system" thought to reside in extrastriate visual cortex.[24] Retention due to priming is long lasting with no decay after 1 week[11,16] and some retention after 3 months.[25]

Recently, PET studies have revealed that priming with visual images produces reduced blood flow upon retesting in a region of right occipital extrastriate visual cortex in human subjects.[23] This result suggests that priming facilitates the neural mechanism for perceiving images. Consequently, less energy is expended and presumably the perceived image is represented with a higher signal-to-noise ratio in the neural populations involved. Access to priming memory is hyperspecific in that it depends, among other things, on the exact geometrical configuration of the priming stimulus.[24] Hyperspecificity of access suggests that priming memory may be stored within the visuotopically mapped cortical visual areas.

These experiments are an extension into the temporal domain of the exploration of the nonclassical responses of visual cortical neurons.

Although neglected until fairly recently, a large number of studies of visual neurons indicated that the true receptive fields for most neurons extended well beyond the classical receptive fields as mapped by conventional stimuli against a featureless background.[2,3,6]

These results indicated that visual neurons often responded in very specific ways to stimuli presented outside their classical, defined receptive fields, which offered a potential mechanism for the local-global integration of visual information.

Recently these results have been extended to "illusory contours" that were implied by stimuli that were entirely beyond the classical receptive field for neurons in the second visual area.[17] A similar "interpolation" of stimuli presented outside the classical receptive field has even been found in V1.[7]

The perceptual memory system is distinct from other forms such as declarative memory or habituation.[24] The neural mechanisms underlying the memory for cognitive contours are probably different from those for delayed-matching-to-sample[5,13,10] and stimulus familiarity[9] that have been studied in area V4 and inferotemporal cortex.

The functional properties of visual cortical neurons have been viewed as very highly specialized filters set to detect different aspects of visual stimuli such as the direction of motion, binocular disparity, orientation, or color. We suggest that in addition to these classical features of visual cortical neurons, there is the capacity to respond selectively to patterns on the basis of prior experience. In other words, we hypothesize that the visual cortex can "learn to see" ambiguous patterns embedded in a noisy background. The neural mechanisms of learning may be mediated by changes in functional connectivity. Ahissar and colleagues[1] measured functional connectivity *in vivo* by calculating spike cross-correlation between two or more neurons. They found that changes in functional connectivity are dependent on changes in firing correlation, but only for behaviorally relevant stimuli. Merzenich[12] has also observed changes during the learning of tactile discriminations in the synchrony of neural activity in somatosensory cortex. We plan to determine whether the spike cross-correlation between neurons changes during learning to see embedded figures.

We further suggest that these perceptual learning capacities may be localized in a manner analogous to the evident perceptual specializations present in the various areas. For example, perceptual learning related to differential motion might be preferentially related to area MT. To test this idea we will use different types of cues (differential motion, closure, shading and stereoscopic depth) to determine whether the nature of the cue might affect the site of storage within the visual cortical areas.

METHODS

WHY OWL MONKEYS?

Studies of the visual cortex have never been done in awake-behaving owl monkeys. The development of this preparation offers several major advantages for the study of the neural mechanisms of perception.

1. The organization of the cortical visual areas have been mapped in the owl monkey.[20,21,22]
2. The visual cortex is relatively smooth. Areas DL and MT, and many other cortical visual areas are located on the exposed, smooth dorsolateral surface of the brain. This allows us to easily find and sample these extrastriate visual areas. Much of the comparable visual cortex lies deeply buried in the convoluted brain of macaque monkeys, and visual areas are more difficult to localize.

3. The accessibility of extrastriate visual cortex facilitates possible future experiments. Specific portions of the visual field map in particular areas could be temporarily deactivated by local injections of drugs blocking neural activity. Additionally, the owl monkey's smooth visual cortex is particularly well suited for optical recording.

We have developed new training procedures and built equipment specially adapted for owl monkey training and electrophysiology. Owl monkeys do not respond well to standard procedures used for training macaque monkeys. Owl monkeys, and all other new world monkeys, cannot sit comfortably in training chairs designed for macaque monkeys because they lack ischial callosities. We designed a special training apparatus consisting of a lexan alcove with two keys that attaches to the cage in which the monkey lives. This alcove is designed to accommodate the owl monkey's natural squatting posture. The monkey learns to enter the alcove and report discrimination of various images by pressing one of the two keys for a fruit juice reward.

PSYCHOPHYSICAL METHODS

In order to measure perceptual learning and memory, we tested the capacity of both monkeys and humans to detect these figures embedded in noise. The embedded figures were either horizontal or vertical in orientation. The subjects task was to report the orientation in a forced-choice paradigm, by pressing right key for horizontal and the left for vertical figures.

In a typical experiment, blocks of 10 to 30 novel stimuli were presented in pseudo-random order. For the initial block, each stimulus was presented without any cue for the embedded figure, and the subject was to respond to the novel stimulus. After the subject responded, we immediately activated the cue for the embedded rectangle. Owl monkeys were allowed to respond to the cued figure, while human subjects only viewed the cued stimulus. For the next block of presentations, the stimuli were cued only for incorrect responses. For the owl monkeys, a final block was added, during which the stimuli were presented without any cues, to prevent the monkey from simply waiting for the cues before making a judgment.

As a control condition, to ensure that the subjects are performing the figure detection and not simply memorizing the entire figure, we measured the effects of rotating elements in the surround with rotating elements forming the contour boundary in the embedded figure. If the subject is responding to the embedded figure and not simply memorizing the entire array, changing elements forming the boundary of the embedded figure should disrupt performance more than changing surround elements (see Figure 7).

INITIAL RESULTS
OWL MONKEYS AS BEHAVIORAL SUBJECTS

Owl monkeys have been used extensively as subjects for motor, auditory and somatosensory tasks.[18,19] Not surprisingly, we found that owl monkeys are easily trained to perform visual discrimination tasks, and are very good psychophysical subjects—we have trained two owl monkeys to successfully perform this task. Both monkeys that we trained performed this task very well; one monkey learned over 100 different stimulus patterns. The monkeys work daily and performs up to 1500 trials, in two to three hours of steady work.

PSYCHOPHYSICS

We hope to record neural activity while the monkey is in the process of learning new stimuli. The time that it takes for the monkey or a human subject to learn a new stimulus varies from one cued presentation for easy figures, to many viewings of the stimulus for more difficult ones. Reaction time and its standard deviation both decrease as the stimuli are learned (see Figure 4). The monkey can learn novel stimulus patterns in a single training session, within the approximate time that we can record from a single neuron. Data from the first 50 trials of learning a new pattern is shown in Figure 5.

The memory is very long lasting. After several weeks without exposure to the same stimuli, there is no decrease in accuracy. There is an initial increase in reaction time followed by a return to previous performance levels (Figure 4). We tested subjects up to six months after the initial learning and found that the memory of learned figures was still intact.

We also found that performance is not rotation invariant for both owl monkey and human subjects. Rotating the entire polygon array, or displaying the array as a mirror image degrades both accuracy and reaction time. Typical human performance is shown in Figure 6.

Results after rotating elements in the embedded figure within Figure 7. Rotating elements in the embedded figure significantly disrupts learning. Rotating elements in the surround had no significant effects.

CONCLUSIONS

We have demonstrated that owl monkeys can be easily and successfully trained as psychophysical subjects. This will allow us to exploit the major advantages of

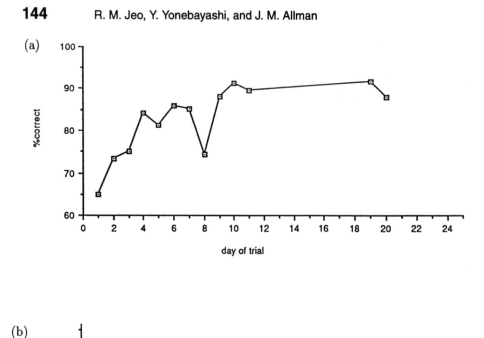

(a)

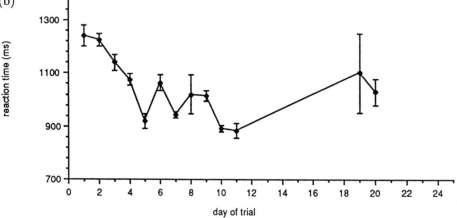

(b)

FIGURE 4 Typical owl monkey performance for ten new stimuli. Top: Performance goes from chance levels (54 percent, Day 1 .w/ cue) to 76 percent (Day 1 after cue), and stays at steady levels, even after a 13-day break (Day 5–Day 18). Bottom: Reaction time and standard deviation. Reaction time improves slightly from Day 1 to Day 5. Standard deviation of reaction time also decreases from Day 1 to Day 5. After a 13-day break, there is an initial increase in the standard deviation of the reaction time, followed by a return to previous performance levels.

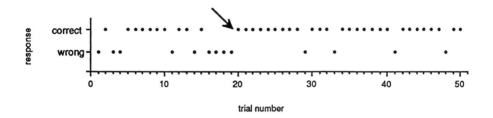

FIGURE 5   Monkey's performance for learning a new stimulus pattern on a trial by trial basis. Trial numbers 1–20 were cued and trial numbers 21–50 were presented without cues. This pattern was pseudorandomly interleaved with a group of 30 stimulus patterns. The elapsed time for the 50 trials was about 45 minutes (516 total trials within this time).

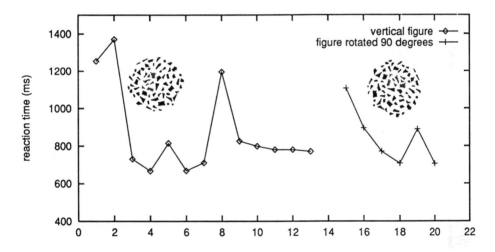

FIGURE 6   Typical human performance, measured by reaction time, when then entire stimulus is rotated by 90 degrees. Trials 1–13 show an improvement in reaction time, which stabilizes around 800 ms. Trials 15–20 show an initial increase in reaction time after the entire figure is rotated by 90 degrees.

the owl monkey preparation, the visuotopic maps of many visual areas on the smooth dorsolateral cortical surface. We have developed unique stimuli to test the phenomenon of perceptual memory, through the use of cognitive contours. The monkey can learn new stimuli within the time that we can record from single neurons. This learning is robust and long-lasting. Additionally, we can easily and quickly

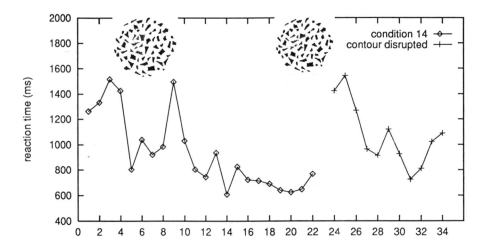

FIGURE 7   Control experiment where the contours of the embedded figure are disrupted. Polygons that make up the contours of the embedded figure are rotated by 90 degrees. These stimuli were interleaved with other learned stimuli. Trials 1–22 show typical reaction time improvement. Rotating the polygons in the embedded figure increases the subjects reaction time, reflected in trials 24–34.

generate an unlimited number of new stimuli and can tailor the contours of the embedded figure to the receptive field of each cell. We are now preparing to do single and multi-unit electrophysiology while the monkey is performing the perceptual memory discrimination task. We will also continue to study the phenomenon psychophysically using human subjects.

ACKNOWLEDGMENTS

Supported by grants from McDonnell Pew Program in Cognitive Neuroscience and NSF(IBN 9309393). Thanks to Miriam Rusch for animal care, Dr. Janet Baer for veterinary care, and to Atiya Hakeem, Allan Dobbins, David Rosenbluth, Tina Joe, and Giesla Sandoval for technical assistance.

REFERENCES

1. Ahissar, E., E. Vaadia, M. Ahissar, H. Bergman, A. Arieli, and M. Ableles. "Dependence of Cortical Plasticity on Correlated Activity of Single Neurons and on Behavioral Context." *Science* **257** (1992): 1412–1415.
2. Allman, J., F. Miezin, and E. McGuinness. "Stimulus Specific Responses from Beyond the Classical Receptive Field: Neurophysiological Mechanisms for Local-Global Comparisons in Visual Neuron." *Ann. Rev. Neurosci.* **8** (1985): 407–430.
3. Allman, J., F. Miezin, and E. McGuinness. "Direction and Velocity-Specific Responses from Beyond the Classical Receptive Field in the Middle Temporal Visual Area (MT)." *Perception* **14** (1985): 105–126.
4. Allman, J. "The Origin of the Neocortex." *Sem. Neurosci.* **2** (1992): 257–262.
5. Desimone, R. "The Physiology of Memory: Recordings of Things Past." *Science* **258** (1992): 245–246.
6. Desimone, R., S. Shein, J. Moran, and L. G. Ungerleider. "Contour, Color and Shape Analysis Beyond Striate Cortex." *Vision Res.* **25** (1985): 441–452.
7. Fiorani, M., R. Gattass, M. Rosa, and C. Rocha-Miranda. "Changes in Receptive Field Size of Single Cells in Primate V1 as a Correlate of Perceptual Completion" *Soc. Neurosci. Abstracts* **16** (1990): 1219.
8. Gollin, E. "Development Studies of Visual Recognition of Incomplete Objects." *Percep. & Motor Skills* **11** (1960): 289–298.
9. Li, L., E. K. Miller, and R. Desimone. "Representation of Stimulus Familiarity in Anterior Inferior Temporal Cortex" *J. Neuroscience* submitted.
10. Maunsell, J. R., G. Sclar, T. A. Nealey, and D. D. DePriest. "Extraretinal Representations in Area V4 in Macaque Monkey." *Visual Neurosci.* **7** (1991): 561–573.
11. McAndrews, M., E. Glisky, and D. Schacter. "When Priming Persists: Long-Lasting Implicit Memory for a Single Episode in Amnesiac Patients." *Neuropsychologia* **25** (1987): 497–506.
12. Merzenich, M. Personal communication, 1993.
13. Miller, E. K., L. Li, and R. Desimone. "Activity of Neurons in Anterior Inferior Temporal Cortex During a Short-Term Memory Task." *J. Neuroscience* (1993): in press.
14. Milner, B., S. Corkin, and H-L. Teuber. "Further Analysis of the Hippocampal Amnesiac Syndrome: A 14-Year Follow-Up Study of H.M." *Neuropsychologia* **6** (1968): 215–234.
15. Mooney, C. M. "Closure Test." Unpublished manuscript, McGill University, Montreal, no date.
16. Musen, G., and A. Treisman. "Implicit and Explicit Memory for Visual Patterns." *J. Exper. Psychol.: Learning, Memory & Cognition* **16** (1990): 127–137.

17. Peterhans, E., and R. Von der Heydt. "Mechanisms of Contour Perception in Monkey Visual Cortex. I. Contours Bridging Gaps." *J. Neuroscience* **9** (1989): 1749–1763.

18. Recanzone, G. H., M. M. Merzenich, and C. E. Schreiner. "Changes in the Distributed Temporal Response Properties of SI Cortical Neurons Reflect Improvements in Performance on a Temporally Based Tactile Discrimination Task." *J. Neurophysiology* **67** (1992): 1071–1091.

19. Recanzone, G. H., C. E. Schreiner, and M. M. Merzenich. "Plasticity in the Frequency Representation of Primary Auditory Cortex Following Discrimination-Training in Adult Owl Monkeys." *J. Neuroscience* **13** (1993): 87–103.

20. Sereno, M., and J. Allman. "Cortical Visual Areas in Mammals." In *The Neural Basis of Visual Function*, edited by A. Levinthal, 160–172. London: Macmillan, 1990.

21. Sereno, M., C. T. MacDonald, and J. M. Allman. "Analysis of Retinotopic Maps in Extrastriate Cortex." *Cerebral Cortex* **4** (1994): 601–620.

22. Sereno, M. I., C. T. McDonald, and J. M. Allman. "Retinotopic Organization of Extrastriate Cortex in the Owl Monkey—Dorsal and Lateral Areas." *Cerebral Cortex* (1994): in press.

23. Squire, L., J. Ojemann, F. Miezin, S. Petersen, T. Videen, and M. Raichle. "Activation of the Hippocampus in Normal Humans: A Functional Anatomical Study of Human Memory." *Proc. Natl. Acad. Sci. USA* **89** (1991): 1837–1841.

24. Tulving, E., and D. Schacter. "Priming and Human Memory Systems." *Science* **247** (1990): 301–306.

25. Warrington, E., and Weiskrantz. "New Method of Testing Long-Term Retention with Special Reference to Amnesiac Patients." *Nature* **217** (1968): 972–974.

Ephraim Katz,† Jonathan D. Victor, and Keith P. Purpura
Department of Neurology and Neuroscience, Cornell University Medical College, 1300 York Avenue, New York, NY 10021
†voice: (212) 746-6520; fax: (212) 746-8532; e-mail: ephraim@med.cornell.edu

Dynamic Changes in Cortical Responses Following Removal and Restoration of Nearby Visual Inputs

INTRODUCTION

PLASTICITY: SENSORY MANIPULATION DURING DEVELOPMENT MANIFESTED IN THE ADULT

The mature central nervous system in general, and the visual system in particular, is affected by sensory input during development. Plasticity in the CNS was first established by comparing the nervous systems of adults whose sensory experience was altered during development with those of normals. For example, poor visual learning in congenitally blind humans who gained sight as adults[65] and the profound effects of early sensory deprivation observed in mature dark-reared chimpanzees[47] demonstrated the dependence of the development of normal CNS on sensory input. This dependence of adequate development of various aspects of adult behavior on early manipulation of sensory input served as one of the building blocks of Hebb's neuropsychological theory of behavior.[15,16]

These early studies relied on differences among groups rather then direct evidence of change within individual subjects. Within-subject demonstration of plasticity awaited the pioneering studies of Wiesel and Hubel on the effects of monocular deprivation in the cat.[19,68,69,70,71] They demonstrated behavioral (placing reflex), morphological, and physiological abnormalities consequent to visual deprivation.

The vast literature on monocular deprivation in kittens, reviewed extensively by Sherman and Spear[58] indicates that manipulation of visual experience from birth through the end of the critical period(s) alters the morphology and functional physiology at every level (retina, lateral geniculate nucleus, superior colliculus, cortex) of the adult visual system. Similar findings were later also reported in primates.[1,20,63,64] These studies introduced the notion of plasticity in the visual system in the context of functional and/or morphological changes, *induced during development*, before maturation, usually within a critical period, and lasting into adulthood. These changes were due to removal or alteration of sensory input.

EFFECTS OF SENSORY REMOVAL IN THE ADULT

Recent studies have shown that permanent removal of sensory input in the mature adult induces reorganization of the recipient auditory[48] and motor[11,51,50] cortical areas as well as the thalamic VPL (ventral posterior lateral) nucleus,[12,32] spinal cord[10,32] and the dorsal column nuclei.[32] Cortical plasticity in the adult has been reported in the somatosensory system[24,33] and in the visual system.[14,22] In both systems, receptive fields of cortical neurons within the thalamorecipient sensory area reorganize to cover input areas adjacent to the void (i.e., missing digit or scotoma) created by the permanent removal of sensory input. Moreover, the changes in the visual system have been linked to changes in axonal sprouting.[8]

The literature on receptive field reorganization in the sensory and motor systems has been reviewed by Kaas.[23] In this review the author suggests that "Small alterations are compatible with synaptic and other modifications within previously existing structural frameworks, whereas larger modifications may imply the sprouting of new connections." This view risks overlooking the important possibility that larger alterations in response properties may be due to the intrinsically dynamic nature of normal, cortical responses to normal sensory stimulation. As we demonstrate here, cortical responses to visual stimuli undergo significant changes within one minute of removal and subsequent restoration of luminance modulated inputs. Thus we would like to suggest that time rather then size (small or large) should serve as the criteria for deeming response changes as due to *plasticity per se* (e.g., sprouting of new connections) or dynamic characteristics (within previously existing structural frameworks). Indeed, several studies have demonstrated cortical changes which occur either immediately[5] or within 45 minutes[51] following lesions or other sensory manipulations such as behavioral tasks.[21] Simulation peripheral to the receptive field under study, has also been demonstrated to alter the cortical response.[13] Such changes in the receptive field, large as they are, could not be attributed to new major morphological changes. These rapid changes indicate that the CNS is not only plastic but is also dynamic, and its response properties are modified rapidly by the removal of sensory input. Furthermore, examination of cortical responses following rapid removal and restoration of sensory input can be most informative in estimating the dynamic capabilities of the CNS.

In this chapter we present a study of the time course of cortical responses in the adult cat and monkey within the span of minutes to hours following focal removal and restoration of visual input. In the somatosensory system, precision injections of local anesthetic can be used to selectively remove sensory input from focal regions on the skin.[40] Sensory input from the injected skin is eventually restored when the anesthetic effect dissipates. Analogously, appropriately designed visual stimuli can be used to apply, remove, and restore visual input with precise temporal and spatial control.

METHODS

GENERAL

Local field potentials (LFP's) were recorded from four cats and four monkeys. All animals were anaesthetized and paralyzed throughout the recording session. The monkeys were also used for another study which provides further details on general preparation of animals for recording.[62]

Adequate anesthesia was maintained throughout the recording session by continuous infusion of sufentanil (monkeys, 1–3 mg/kg/hr) or bolus infusions of urethane once every 24 hours (cats, 200 mg/kg every 12 hrs). Eye movement were minimized by paralysis maintained by infusion of gallamine triethiodide, and in cats also by cervical sympathectomy.[49] Clear contact lenses and periodic irrigations with Ringer's kept the corneas in good optical condition. Pupils were dilated by topical application of 1% atropine sulfate. In cats the nictitating membrane was retracted by topical application of 10% phenylephrine hydrochloride. Blood pressure, heart rate, EKG, EEG were monitored to assess level of anesthesia. Oxygen saturation, expired CO_2 and rectal temperature were kept at physiological levels.

VISUAL STIMULATION

The optic disk, area centralis (cats) or the foveal pit (monkeys), were projected on a tangent screen via a modified fundus camera. All animals were refracted by slit retinoscopy and corrected for 114 cm by standard trail lenses, and 3-mm artificial pupils were centered in front of both eyes.

Visual stimuli were generated by a Milkman[35] stimulator controlled by a minicomputer (PDP 11/93) and displayed on a Conrac 7351 monitor with mean luminance of 97 cd/m^2 and frame rate of 135 Hz. The same mini-computer also collected the data at twice the frame rate.

In order to map the "receptive field" of the local field potentials we used m-sequence stimuli (see Victor et al.[62] for further details) consisting of a sequence of patterns in which the luminance in each of multiple regions (249 in this study) is modulated time by a pseudo-random binary sequence (m-sequence) derived from a shift register.[59,60] The properties of the binary sequence guarantee that the luminance modulation in each of the spatial regions is linearly independent of modulations in all the other regions. That property, in turn, allows identifications of the spatial regions that contribute input to the cortical responses by cross-correlation of the response with the binary sequence. This procedure yields "first-order kernels" (here denoted K1) which are essentially the impulse response to luminance stimulation in each region.

In addition, certain nonlinear components of the response can be identified by the m-sequence technique, by combining responses to the standard stimulus described above, and the same stimulus repeated with inverted contrast. These nonlinear components include a "second-order first off-diagonal slice" associated with each stimulus region. The "second-order first off-diagonal slice" (here denoted K2), is essentially the response to temporal luminance contrast in that region, independent of the polarity of that luminance change.

In this study we used an order-12 binary m-sequence, which consist of a sequence of 4095 (2^{12}-1) distinct spatial patterns. Each member of the stimulus sequence was presented for 14.8 msec. At least 6 repeats of each m-sequence (3 standard and 3 inverse repeats) were presented in each experimental condition. In each run (standard or inverse repeat) the stimulus was displayed for 2 sec. before data collection began. At the end of each run (60 sec. of data collection) the CRT returned to mean luminance for about 30 sec during which data were transferred from the computer's memory to its hard disk.

There were two classes of m-sequence stimuli: baseline and test (Figure 1). In the *baseline* condition all 249 regions were modulated. In the *test* condition one or more regions were held fixed at mean luminance, except for one experiment, in which part of the screen was covered by a simple occluder. Baseline and test stimuli were administered by one of two protocols: blocked or interleaved. In the *block* protocol each pair of standard m-sequence and inverse-repeat were presented a few times (typically 6 to 8) in a block of one condition (either baseline or test) followed by a similar block of the second condition. In the *interleaved* protocol a single run of the baseline condition was followed by a single run of the test condition and then the inverse-repeats would be presented in the same order. Typically, there were more then one test condition alternating with an equal number of baseline conditions.

DATA ACQUISITION AND ANALYSIS

Local field potentials (LFP's) were recorded with a multi-contact electrode provided by Dr. Charles Schroeder of the Albert Einstein College of Medicine in New York.[52] The electrode was inserted at an orientation judged to be perpendicular to the cortical surface of areas 17 and 18 in the cat and V1 in the monkey. The recording

(a)   (b)

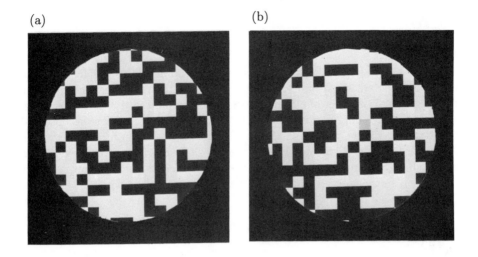

FIGURE 1 Examples of the m-sequence visual stimuli. (a) Example of a baseline stimulus in which luminance was modulated in all spatial regions. (b) Example of a test stimulus in which luminance modulation was removed from one region by setting it equal to the background illumination.

contact points, spaced 150 μm (with the exception of the most distal site which was 1000 μm from its nearest neighbor), spanned the depth of cortex. In the monkey the distal recording sites occasionally penetrated the underfold of area V2. The recording contact points have impedances ranging 40–100 KΩ.

Recorded signals were fed to a unity-gain FET preamplifier, and differential signals from nearest-neighbor recording sites were amplified 10,000 times, filtered (1–100 Hz), and fed into the same computer that controlled the visual stimulator for storage and analysis. A recording site was selected, from among the 15 available differential pairs, on the basis of a prominent response to monocular stimulation. Demarcation of the recording site was achieved by passing current (5 μA for 5 sec) from the contact point at the end of the experiment. See Figure 3(c) in Victor et al.,[62] for example. The animal was sacrificed, desanguinated, and perfused. The brain was recovered, sectioned (40 μ) and alternate slices were stained by Nissl and cytochrome oxidase.[18]

The time course of K1 responses and K2 responses to baseline and test stimuli, were extracted as described above. A time period containing the peak of the response in all relevant regions was defined, and the average response amplitude in this period was calculated. These values were used to plot response amplitude as a function of spatial location. Paired t-test statistics were used to compare average response amplitude to baseline stimuli and test stimuli.

RESULTS

THE CORTICAL RESPONSE TO INPUT REMOVAL AND RESTORATION

Our study was aimed at evaluating cortical responses following spatially localized removal of modulated visual input and after its restoration. In all cases removal of luminance modulation from one spatial region caused increased amplitudes of responses to luminance modulation in one or more adjacent regions. This was observed both in "first-order" (K1) responses (Figure 2) and "second-order first off-diagonal" (K2) responses (Figure 3) recorded in cat area 17 and area 18 and monkey V1 and V2. These changes in response amplitude were not accompanied by changes in the time course. We now proceed to analyze these changes in more detail.

CORTICAL RESPONSES DURING CENTRALLY LOCATED PARTIAL OCCLUSION

In the first cat, we recorded from area 18 with the CRT placed at 61 cm. In this configuration, a relatively large number of spatial regions, subtending in total approximately $8° \times 8°$, contributed to the cortical response (Figure 4(a)). Following a short run to ascertain that the central portion of the CRT contained the spatial regions serving as input to the cortical response, an opaque card measuring approximately $4.7° \times 5.6°$ was placed to occlude the center of the display. Visual stimulation continued in the test (occluded) condition for 210 min. At the end of that period the occluder was removed and stimulation resumed for another 210 min. The data (Figure 4) show average response amplitude during the first 15 min of each condition. Comparison of the two plots reveal that when visual stimulation was removed from several regions, amplitude of responses to stimulation in nearby regions increased. Analysis of the first 30 min of each condition[27] showed the same effect as did analysis of the entire 210 min. In some of the regions adjacent to the occluder, the enhanced response was higher then any of the responses prior to occlusion. Because the occluder produced a region of lower mean luminance that of the modulated adjacent regions, it is possible that the observed enhancement was simply a manifestation of a decrease in lateral inhibitory influences flowing from the occluded regions or an increased effective Weber contrast. These explanations were ruled out in subsequent experiments.

REMOVAL OF INPUT FROM A SMALL SPATIAL REGION AFFECTS CORTICAL RESPONSES

In the rest of the experiments luminance modulation was removed from one or more regions by replacing the light-dark luminance modulation with the mean luminance, rather than with a physical occluder. This allowed us to interleave baseline

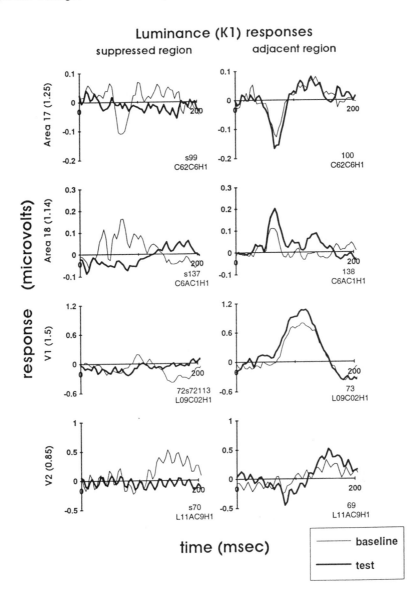

Luminance (K1) responses

suppressed region   adjacent region

time (msec)

baseline
test

FIGURE 2 "First-order" (K1) baseline (thin line) and test (solid line) responses in cat area 17, area 18 and monkey V1 and V2. The left column demonstrates the size of the response in the suppressed region during baseline and test luminance modulation condition. The right column demonstrates the enhanced response in the adjacent region during test condition. (Animals C6/2, C6/A, M9, M11.) The length of the square spatial regions is indicated in parenthesis.

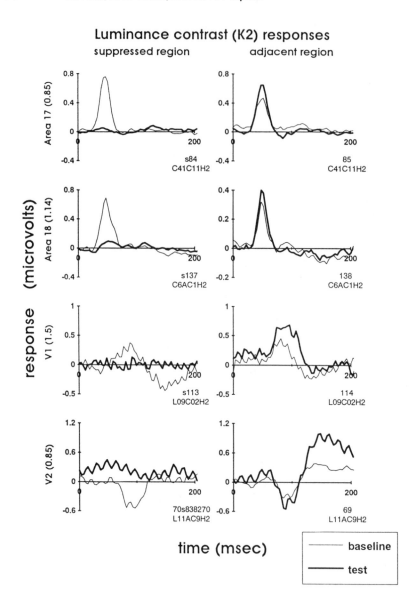

FIGURE 3   "Second-order off diagonal" (K2) baseline and test responses in cat area 17, area 18 and monkey V1 and V2. Data presented as in Figure 2. (Animals C4/1, C6/A, M9, M11.)

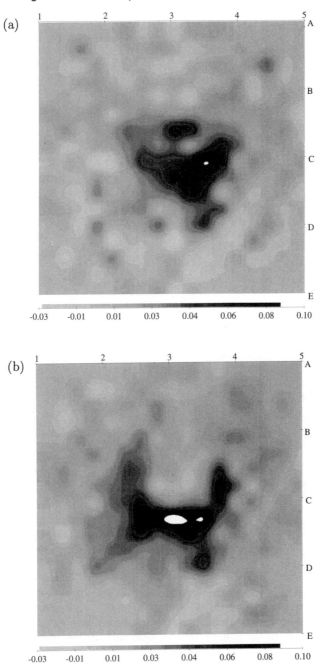

FIGURE 4 Comparisons of K2 responses elicited in cat area 18 by baseline stimulation (a), and a test condition (b) in which the central portion of the CRT was occluded. Average response amplitude in μV (gray scale) during a time slice of 74–100 msec from stimulus onset is plotted against vertical (Y-axis) and horizontal (X-axis) locations on the CRT. Animal C3.

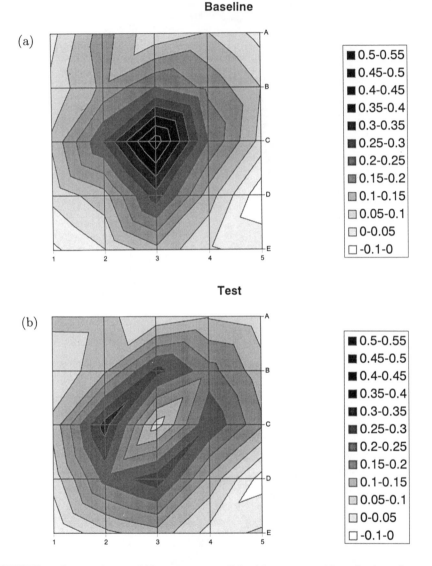

FIGURE 5   Comparisons of K2 responses elicited in cat area 18 under baseline
(a) and test condition. Each spatial region measured 1.14° × 1.14°. Responses are
averaged across interleaved runs of each condition during a time slice of 44–55.5 msec
from stimulus onset. Intersections of coordinates represent centers of square spatial
regions on the CRT.

and test conditions, and to probe the dynamics of the response enhancement. In
the experiment illustrated in Figure 5, luminance modulation was eliminated only

from one spatial region, measuring $1.14° \times 1.14°$, in the test condition. Averaged K2 responses recorded from area 18 during 90 minutes of interleaved baseline (A) and test (B) stimulation are shown in Figure 5 in contour plots. The differences between the two graphs indicate that removal of luminance modulation from a relatively small spatial region (centered at the intersection of coordinates 3C), raised responses from the regions surrounding it (e.g., 2C, 2D, 4C). Moreover, this change occurred within one minute of input removal and reversed with input restoration within the same time. The peak response, in region 3C, to baseline stimulation was $0.46 \mu V$. We were interested to examine whether despite the removal of luminance modulation input from region 3C, in the test condition, the sum of response amplitude from all nine regions (2B, 3B 4B, 2C, 3C, 4C, 2D, 3D, 4D) would be the same. In this experiment the sum of responses were $1.97 \mu V$ in the baseline condition and $1.96 \mu V$ in the test condition. Further examination revealed that while contribution to the cortical response from two of the surrounding regions (4B and 4D) were the same under baseline and test condition, the remaining six regions showed an average increase of 35%. This increased response in the test condition exactly balanced the loss of $0.46 \mu V$ response from the suppressed central region.

REVERSIBILITY OF CHANGES IN CORTICAL RESPONSES FOLLOWING 1 MINUTE AND 45 MINUTES OF INPUT REMOVAL

In Figure 6 we compared the change in response elicited by one minute runs to the change in the response elicited by longer blocks of each condition. Baseline stimuli were interleaved with two types of test stimuli: one in which luminance modulation in region 97 was suppressed and one in which modulation in the adjacent region 84 was suppressed. These stimuli were presented in two ways: 45-minute blocks (Figure 6(a)) and 1-minute interleaved runs (Figure 6(b)). In either case elimination of stimulation in one region led to increase of responses in the adjacent region. The striking similarity of the responses in blocked and interleaved modes indicates that any changes in cortical responses over the 45 min were fully developed within the first minute. Furthermore, when sensory input is restored to baseline, irrespective of the test condition, cortical responses return to the baseline level as well, and this change also occurs within one minute. Analogous experiments in monkey V1 and V2 led to similar conclusions.

ANALYSIS

In order to quantify the results from all the experiments in which luminance modulation was suppressed in a single spatial region, two indexes were calculated: the "ratio index" and the "difference index" (see Table 1). The ratio index was derived by dividing the response amplitude to test stimuli by the response amplitude to baseline stimuli. Ratio index values larger than 1 indicates that the contribution of luminance modulation in a given region is higher in the test condition than in the baseline condition. The difference index was defined as the difference between the response amplitude in test and baseline condition divided by the baseline response associated with the region from which luminance modulation was removed in test stimulation. This normalization was designed to remove differences in overall response size across recording sites. A difference index larger than zero indicates that the response is higher in the test condition than in the baseline condition.

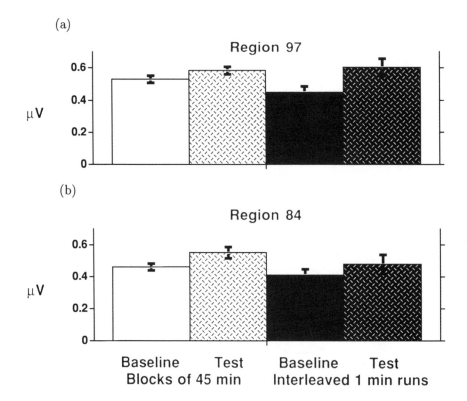

FIGURE 6   Comparison between K2 baseline responses (solid) and test responses (cross-hatch) obtained with 45-minute blocks of stimulation (light) and 1 min of interleaved stimulation (dark) for spatial regions 97 (a) and 84 (b). Regions 97 and 84 are adjacent and in the alternating test conditions either region 84 was suppressed (cross-hatch in (a)) or 97 was suppressed (cross-hatch in (b)). The enhancement of responses from regions adjacent to the suppressed region were similar in "blocked" and "interleaved" conditions. Both experiments lasted 180 min and region size was 1.3° × 1.3°. Error bars represent 1 standard deviation of the measurement noise. Area 17, animal C4/1.

SPATIALLY SPECIFIC INTEROCULAR INTERACTIONS

Unilateral reversible removal of somatosensory input, thought to be relevant only to the contralateral hemisphere, has been demonstrated to affect cortical responses in both hemispheres.[6] Our final goal in this study was to examine whether the effect of visual input removal would transfer between eyes. In Figure 7 we show the time course of responses from a recording site in monkey V1 to binocular stimulation under baseline condition. Six separate regions were found to contribute to the cortical response (a). Responses to baseline monocular stimulation of the left eye (b) and the right eye (c) indicated that four spatial regions contributed to the response from each eye. The two central regions (82 and 83) provided input to this region via both eyes.

These initial observations served as the basis for establishing evidence of interocular transfer (Figure 8). Four test stimuli were constructed. In three of the test stimuli (a, b, c) input was removed from a single region (83, 70, 82). In the fourth (d) input was removed from all three regions. Baseline stimuli were interleaved with test stimuli in the sequence depicted schematically in Figure 8(e). The baseline time course on each of the four graphs ((a)–(d)) is the average of the

TABLE 1 Summary of the data set of all the experiments in which luminance modulation input was removed from a single spatial region. Indices were calculated as described in the text for 'first-order' (K1, or luminance responses) and 'second-order first off diagonal' (K2, or temporal luminance contrast responses) for each cortical site studied, and averaged across all experiments.

	CAT		MONKEY	
	Area 17	Area 18	V1	V2
Number of records				
K1 responses	3^a	1	12^b	4
K2 responses	7	1	12	4
Spatial region length (deg)				
Average	0.97	1.14	1.01	0.85
Range	0.84-1.25	1.14	0.70-1.50	0.85
Ration index				
K1 responses	1.45	1.07	1.31	1.29
K2 responses	1.27	1.31	1.28	1.15
Difference index				
K1 responses	0.63	0.08	0.24	0.14
K2 responses	0.06	0.10	0.11	0.08

[a]In four experiments, only K2 responses were presented.
[b]In four experiments, in one animal, electrode position could not be confirmed by histology.

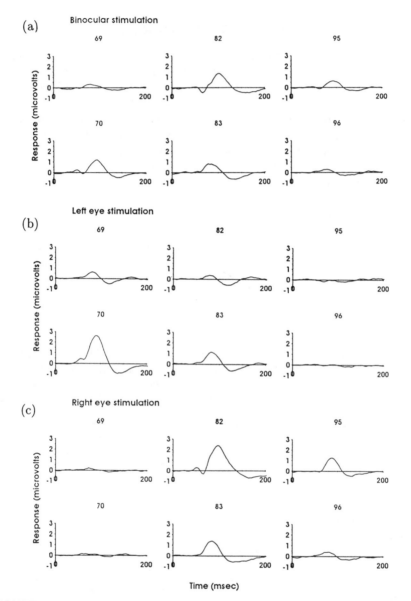

FIGURE 7 Interoccular interactions I: responses to binocular baseline stimulation (a), left eye only (b) and right eye only (c). Input from spatial regions 69 and 70 reaches recording site exclusively via the left eye, while input from spatial regions 95 and 96 reaches the recording site exclusively via the right eye. Luminance modulation in spatial regions 82 and 83 contribute to the cortical response binocularly. K1 responses recorded in infra granular monkey V1. Animal M11. Region size 0.85° ×0.85°.

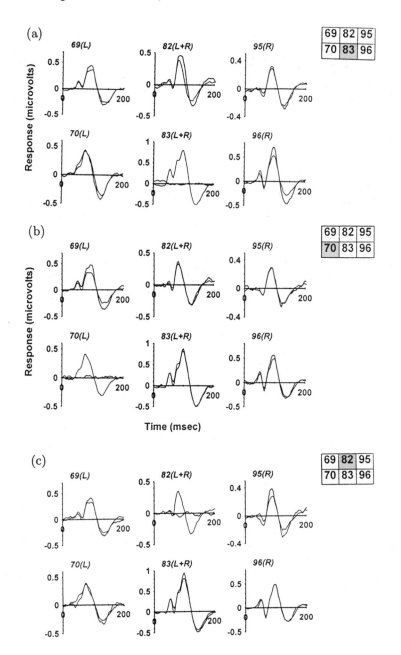

FIGURE 8 Interoccular interactions II: An interleaved sequence of baseline and four types of test stimuli was presented binocularly in a standard run followed by an inverted repeat 16 times. When input was removed from three spatial regions (during test stimulation) responses from the three remaining active regions were (continued)

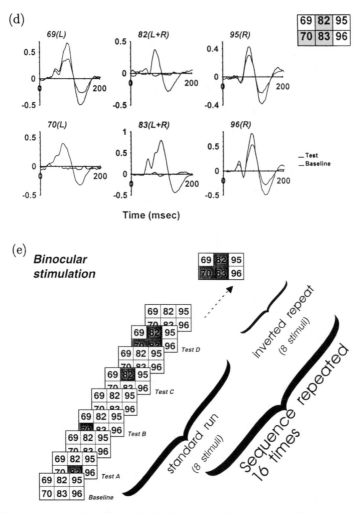

FIGURE 8 (continued) increased (d). Removal of input from either binocular regions (a and c) caused increase in contribution to the cortical response to luminance modulation in the active binocular region as well as in the nearby monocular regions. Removal of input from the monocularly driven region 70 (b) caused an increase in response amplitude not only in the adjacent region sharing the same eye but also in region 96 that serves the other eye exclusively. K1 responses in infra granular monkey V1. Size of spatial regions is as in Figure 7. Schematic representation of experimental protocol in (e). Animal M11.

responses to the two baseline trials flanking the particular test trial. The data indicate that removing input from all three regions at the same time resulted in the expected increase of responses contributed by the three remaining active regions (d). Removal of input from either of the spatial regions 83 (a) or 82 (c) that stimulate both eyes (binocular regions) resulted in increased contributions to the cortical response from the remaining active binocular region as well as from the surrounding monocular spatial regions. Removal of input from the monocular region 70 (b), which contributes to the cortical response only through the left eye, produced the expected increases from nearby-region 69 driven by the same eye. However, the crucial observation is that this input removal has also caused an increase in the response from a monocular region (96) that contributes to the response only via the right eye. Region 96 is not adjacent to the suppressed region (70) in either eye, but its cortical representation via the right eye is adjacent to the cortical representation of region 70 via the left eye (Figure 7). The increment in the response from region 96 when input from region 70 is removed demonstrates spatially specific interocular transfer. This interocular transfer places the origin of this phenomenon in the visual cortex rather than the retina.

DISCUSSION
SUMMARY OF RESULTS

Local field potentials (LFP's) were recorded from cat areas 17 and 18 and monkey areas V1 and V2. Removal and restoration of luminance modulation was achieved via stimulation with patterns derived from m-sequences. The removal of luminance modulation from a spatial region within the "receptive field" of a cortical neural population leads to increased contributions to the cortical response from nearby regions of space. When input is removed from a single spatial region, response enhancement in the eight surrounding spatial regions is typically 25% (see ratio index values in Table 1). This change occurs within less than 1 min of luminance modulation input removal. When the luminance modulation input is restored to baseline conditions, the responses return to baseline within 1 min. Changes in response amplitude are not accompanied by changes in time course. Spatially specific interocular transfer indicates that these response changes are cortical in origin.

DYNAMICS VS. PLASTICITY

While our results could be considered to be a manifestation of plasticity in the adult cortex, we would be very cautious about the use of this term in relation to our observations. A strict definition of plasticity in the adult is the capacity for sensory and/or pharmacological manipulations to induce permanent (or long-term) changes stemming from mechanisms not present in the naive animal. Thus, plasticity in the adult does not include phenomena like light adaptation and "...gain in discriminative ability in the first 300 to 500 trials of a particular task configuration...."[72] This definition does include habituation of the time constant of the vestibulo-ocular reflex[7,26]—which has been known for a long time but was never labeled as manifestation of plasticity in the adult. The changes in cortical responses that we report occur within one minute and are readily reversible. The spatially specific interoccular interactions, and the lack of response changes in LGN,[14] indicate that the response changes observed by us, as well as those observed immediately following a localized scotoma,[14] should therefore be considered as manifestations of the dynamic nature of the normally functioning visual cortex, rather than plasticity.

It remains to be seen whether there are indeed two distinct classes of response changes following the removal of sensory input. On the one hand, there are response changes which can be observed immediately after sensory manipulation. These readily reversible changes result probably from a gain control mechanism. They may be related to the psychophysically observed long-range interactions (Kovács and Julesz,[29] this volume).[28] On the other hand, there are cortical reorganizations which can be observed as long as 12 years after input removal.[42] Perceptual manifestations of such long-term reorganizations have been also observed[44] (Ramachandran et al.,[43] this volume). It is unclear to what extent these phenomena are distinct. Rather, it is possible that prolonged exposure of the adult to altered sensory input produce long lasting changes (Merzenich and Jenkins,[34] this volume) through mechanisms of the type suggested recently by Barlow.[2] The answer may lie in studies of learning-induced long-term cognitive changes (Polat and Sagi,[41] Merzenich and Jenkins,[34] this volume)[45,67] and studies of morphological changes following input removal.[8]

GAIN CONTROL MECHANISMS IN THE NORMAL VISUAL SYSTEM

One aspect of the dynamic nature of the receptive fields of cortical neurons is the phenomenon of gain control or response normalization. Gain control mechanisms may serve both to limit saturation of neural responses and to allow nonlinear feature extractors to operate over a range of contrasts. Several kinds of processes, all of which can be considered gain controls, are present in the visual system. Since these mechanisms have properties that account for cortical response changes due to variations in sensory input,[37,38,4,46] we review them here. Of note, these mechanisms are present in the naive adult animal prior to the removal of sensory input, and have been demonstrated in kittens as well.[53]

Contrast gain control[55] or contrast normalization[17] is the name given to the observation that visual neurons' response amplitude and dynamics are modulated by the amount of contrast present in nearby regions of space and in recent time.[56] In the retina, a contrast gain control sharpens the temporal frequency tuning of ganglion cells responses based on contrast within the receptive field, even if the contrast is presented in the surround in a manner which by itself does not elicit a response. This retinal gain control operates within 100 msec.[54,57] These properties of the retinal contrast gain control motivated our last experiment, in which we demonstrated interocular transfer, which implies a cortical origin for the lateral interactions we observed.

In cortex, there appear to be several mechanisms which fall under the general category of a gain control. Blakemore and Campbell[3] showed that the human cortical visual evoked potential (VEP) elicited by a near-threshold grating was reduced following a 30-sec adaptation to a high contrast grating. This correlated with psychophysical subjective threshold elevation, and presumably had a relatively sluggish time course lasting at least many seconds. More recently, Victor and Conte[61] showed that VEP measures of responses to markedly suprathreshold gratings also demonstrated the effects of a contrast gain control, but this adaptation occurred within 700 msec of changes in contrast.

There have been several studies of contrast adaptation at the cellular level in the anaesthetized animal. Movshon and Lennie[36] used conditions analogous to those of Blakemore and Campbell, and demonstrated that there was a lower response to drifting gratings following a high-contrast adapting stimulus, and this response returned to preadaptive level within 12 minutes after adaptation has ended. Ohzawa and colleagues[37,38] developed a technique for assessing the contrast-response function across a range of states of contrast adaptation. Neurons in striate cortex were adapted for 80 sec with an optimal grating of a particular contrast. Subsequently, five stimuli spanning one octave about the adapting contrast were interleaved randomly for a 4 sec presentation each. Responses to the test stimuli decreased as the contrast level of the adapting stimulus increased. From these studies, it appeared that the neural measure of contrast was based on the classical receptive field; the gain control was no stronger when gratings covered a much wider area ($30° \times 22°$). The absence of this phenomenon in LGN neurons indicated that this contrast gain control mechanism originates in cortex. The average time constant of the cortical contrast gain control (i.e., the time to achieve a new state of adaptation) was 6 sec.

Bonds[4] showed that contrast gain control mechanisms are important in cortical visual processing, even at contrast levels that are well below the saturation level of cat striate neurons (0.035–0.56). Furthermore, by using an ordered sequence of contrasts rather than a random one, his data demonstrated that gain control mechanisms can produce hysteresis. This was evident even if the preceding high contrast stimulus was presented only for 50 msec. Again, analogous contrast-dependent effects were not seen in LGN.

Temporal properties of gain control mechanisms were studied by Dean et al.[73] They recorded responses of single neurons in cat striate cortex to optimal stationary gratings whose contrast was modulated sinusoidally at 1.25, 7.75 Hz and the sum of both sinusoids. Dean et al.[73] showed that under high-contrast conditions (the sum condition), the response to the high-temporal frequency component relative to that of the low-temporal frequency component was higher. Reid et al.[46] used an eight-sinusoid approach to show that the main dynamical effect of increased contrast was a decrease in the effective integration time of simple and complex cells. Thus, the effect of increased contrast on neurons of cat striate cortex is not only to increase threshold, but also must change dynamics.

Our findings fall into the general category of a contrast gain control. Overall response size is increased in the absence of nearby stimulation, and the magnitude of the effect that we observe is precisely that which is expected from a mechanism which would preserve response size despite reduced area of stimulation. Furthermore, this change is rapid and reversible. However, there is at least one significant difference between our results and the single-unit studies reviewed above: we find no change in dynamics associated with increasing contrast, unlike the more rapid dynamics seen at higher contrasts in single-neuron studies it is unclear what mechanisms generate this difference. Perhaps this difference is merely a consequence of the difference between single-unit activity and field potential activity. Nevertheless, one important difference is that our stimuli were not designed to be optimal for a single neuron under study, but rather to provide a general measure of cortical responsiveness.

CONCLUSION

The neural substrate for a cortical contrast gain control and its lateral spread, is still unknown. However, it is likely that any rapid changes observed immediately following modification of sensory input are due to existing synaptic connections,[31,66] rather than plasticity *per se*. It has been postulated that long-term reorganization of visual cortical responses (i.e., plasticity per se) following scotomas is mediated by the horizontal connections[14] which traverse the visual cortex parallel to the surface and form functional connections along the way.[30] We postulate that these connections, independent of any role that they may have in plasticity, form the basis of spatial lateral interactions[39,25,28,29] and the gain control mechanism we observe. This gain control mechanism, although it may have a superficial resemblance to plasticity, is fundamentally a manifestation of a dynamic cortex rapidly adjusting its response properties according to varied stimulus conditions.

ACKNOWLEDGMENTS

We thank A. Canel and M. Conte for technical assistaance, Dr. C. Aoki for assistance with histology, and Dr. C. Schroeder for providing the multicontact electrode.

This work was supported by The Revson foundation, National Eye Institute Grant EY-9314, The McDonnell-Pew Foundation, and the Hirschl Trust.

REFERENCES

1. Baker, F. H., P. Grigg, and G. K. von Noorden. "Effects of Visual Deprivation and Strabismus on the Response of Neurons in the Visual Cortex of the Monkey, Including Studies on the Striate and Prestriate Cortex in the Normal Animal." *Brain Res.* **66** (1974): 185–208.
2. Barlow, H. B. "A Theory About the Functional Role and Synaptic Mechanism of Visual After-Effects." In *Vision Coding and Efficiency*, edited by C. Blakemore, 363–375. Cambridge: Cambridge University Press, 1990.
3. Blakemore, C., and F. W. Campbell. "On the Existence of Neurons in the Human Visual System Selectively Sensitive to the Orientation and Size of Retinal Images." *J. Physiology* **203** (1969): 237–260.
4. Bonds, A. B. "Temporal Dynamics of Contrast Gain in Single Cells of the Cat Striate Cortex." *Visual Neurosci.* **6** (1991): 239–255.
5. Calford, M. B., and R. Tweedale. "Immediate and Chronic Changes in Responses of Somatosensory Cortex in Adult Flying-Fox After Digit Amputation." *Nature* **332** (1988): 446–448.
6. Calford, M. B., and R. Tweedale. "Interhemispheric Transfer of Plasticity in the Cerebral Cortex." *Science* **249** (1990): 805–807.
7. Cohen, H., B. Cohen, T. Raphan, and W. Waespe. "Habituation and Adaptation of the Vestibular Reflex: A Model of Differential Control by the Vestibulocerebellum." *Exp. Brain Res.* **90** (1992): 526–538.
8. Darian-Smith, C., and C. D. Gilbert. "Axonal Sprouting Accompanies Functional Reorganization in Adult Cat Striate Cortex." *Nature* **368** (1994): 737–740.
9. Dean, A. F., D. J. Tolhurst, and N. S. Walker. "Non-linear Temporal Summation by Simple Cells in Cat Striate Cortex Demonstrated by Failure of Superposition." *Exp. Brain Res.* **45** (1982): 456–458.
10. Devor, M., and P. D. Wall. "Reorganization of Spinal Cord Sensory Map After Peripheral Nerve Injury." *Nature* **276** (1978): 75–76.
11. Donoghue, J. P., S. Suner, and J. N. Sanes. "Dynamic Organization of Primary Motor Cortex Output to Target Muscles in Adult Rats II. Rapid Reorganization Following Motor Nerve Lesion." *Exp. Brain Res.* **79** (1990): 492–503.
12. Garraghty, P. E., and J. H. Kaas. "Functional Reorganization in Adult Monkey Thalamus After Peripheral Nerve Injury." *NeuroReport* **2** (1991): 747–750.
13. Gilbert, C. D., and T. N. Wiesel. "The Influence of Contextual Stimuli on the Orientation Selectivity of Cells in Primary Visual Cortex of the Cat." *Vision Research* **30** (1990): 1689–1701.
14. Gilbert, C. D., and T. N. Wiesel. "Receptive Field Dynamics in Adult Primary Visual Cortex." *Nature* **356** (1992): 150–152.
15. Hebb, D. O. *Organization of Behavior.* New York: John Wiley & Sons, 1949.

16. Hebb, D. O. "A Neuropsychological Theory." In *Psychology: A Study of Science*, edited by S. Koch, Vol. 1, 622–643. New York: McGraw-Hill, 1959.

17. Heeger, D. J. "Normalization of Cell Responses in Cat Striate Cortex." *Visual Neurosci.* **9** (1992): 181–197.

18. Hevner, R. F., and M. T. T. Wong-Riley. "Regulation of Cytochrome Oxidase Protein Levels by Functional Activity in the Macaque Monkey Visual System." *J. Neuroscience* **10** (1990): 1331–1340.

19. Hubel, D. H., and T. N. Wiesel. "Receptive Fields of Cells in Striate Cortex of Very Young, Visually Inexperienced Kittens." *J. Neurophysiology* **26** (1963): 994–1002.

20. Hubel, D. H., T. N. Wiesel, and S. Le Vay. "Plasticity of Ocular Dominance Columns in Monkey Striate Cortex." *Phil. Trans. R. Soc. Lond. B* **278** (1977): 377–409.

21. Jenkins, W. M., M. M. Merzenich, M. T. Ochs, T. Allard, and E. Guic-Robles. "Functional Reorganization of Primary Somatosensory Cortex in Adult Owl Monkeys After Behaviorally Controlled Tactile Stimulation." *J. Neurophysiology* **63** (1990): 82–104.

22. Kaas, J. H., L. A. Krubitzer, Y. M. Chino, A. L. Langston, E. H. Polley, and N. Blair. "Reorganization of Retinotopic Cortical Maps in Adult Mammals After Lesions of the Retina." *Science* **248** (1990): 229–231.

23. Kaas, J. H. "Plasticity of Sensory and Motor Maps in Adult Mammals." *Ann. Rev. Neurosci.* **14** (1991): 137–167.

24. Kaas, J. H., M. M. Merzenich, and H. P. Killackey. "The Reorganization of Somatosensory Cortex Following Peripheral Nerve Damage in Adult and Developing Mammals." *Ann. Rev. Neurosci.* **6** (1983): 325–356.

25. Kapadia, M. K., C. D. Gilbert, and G. Westheimer. "A Quantitative Measure of Short-Term Cortical Plasticity in Human Vision." *J. Neurosci.* **14** (1994): 451–457.

26. Katz, E., V. J. DeJong, J. A. Buttner-Ennever, and B. Cohen. "Effects of Midline Medullary Lesions on Velocity Storage and the Vestibulo-Ocular Reflex." *Exp. Brain Res.* **87** (1991): 505–520.

27. Katz, E., and J. D. Victor. "Lateral Interactions in Visual Cortex." *Soc. Neuroscience* **19** (1993): 425 (abstract).

28. Kovács, I., and B. Julesz. "Perceptual Sensitivity Maps Within Globally Defined Visual Shapes." *Nature* **370** (1994): 644–646.

29. Kovács, I., and B. Julesz. "Long-range Spatial Interactions of Early Vision Revealed by Psychophysiclaly Measured Sensitivity Maps." This volume.

30. McGuire, B. A., C. D. Gilbert, P. K. Rivlin, and T. N. Wiesel. "Targets of Horizontal Connections in Macaque Primary Visual Cortex." *J. Compar. Neurology* **305** (1991): 370–392.

31. Merrill, E. G., and P. D. Wall. "Factors Forming the Edge of a Receptive Field: The Presence of Relatively Ineffective Afferent Terminals." *J. Physiology* **226** (1972): 825–846.

32. Merrill, E. G., and P. D. Wall. "Plasticity of Connection in the Adult Nervous System." In *Neuronal Plasticity*, edited by C. W. Cotman, 97–111. New York: Raven Press, 1978.
33. Merzenich, M. M., R. J. Nelson, M. P. Stryker, M. S. Cynader, A. Schoppmann, and J. M. Zook. "Somatosensory Cortical Map Changes Following Digit Amputation in Adult Monkey." *J. Compar. Neurology* **224** (1984): 591–605.
34. Merzenich, M. M., and W. M. Jenkins. "Cortical Plasticity, Learning, and Learning Dysfunction." This volume.
35. Milkman, N., G. Schick, M. Rossetto, F. Ratliff, R. M. Shapley, and J. D. Victor. "A Two-Dimensional Computer-Controlled Visual Stimulator." *Beh. Res. Meth. & Intrum.* **12** (1980): 283–292.
36. Movshon, J. A., and P. Lennie. "Pattern-Selective Adaptation in Visual Cortical Neurons." *Nature* **278** (1979): 850–852.
37. Ohzawa, I., G. Sclar, and R. D. Freeman. "Contrast Gain Control in the Cat Visual Cortex." *Nature* **298** (1982): 266–268.
38. Ohzawa, I., G. Sclar, and R. D. Freeman. "Contrast Gain Control in the Cat's Visual System." *J. Neurophysiology* **54** (1985): 651–667.
39. Pettet, M. W., and C. D. Gilbert. "Dynamic Changes in Receptive-Field Size in Cat Primary Visual Cortex." *Proc. Natl. Acad. Sci. USA* **89** (1992): 8366–8370.
40. Pettit, M. J., and H. D. Schwark. "Receptive Field Reorganization in Dorsal Column Nuclei During Temporary Denervation." *Science* **262** (1993): 2054–2056.
41. Polat, U., and D. Sagi. "Plasticity of Spatial Interactions in Early Vision." This volume.
42. Pons, T. P., P. E. Garraghty, A. K. Ommaya, J. H. Kaas, E. Taub, and M. Mishkin. "Massive Cortical Reorganization After Sensory Deafferentation in Adult Macaques." *Science* **252** (1991): 1857–1860.
43. Ramachandran, V. S. "Plasticity in the Adult Human Brain: Is There Reason for Optimism?." This volume.
44. Ramachandran, V. S., D. Rogers-Ramachandran, and M. Stewart. "Perceptual Correlates of Massive Cortical Reorganization." *Science* **258** (1992): 1159–1160.
45. Recanzone, G. H., C. E. Schreiner, and M. M. Merzenich. "Plasticity in the Frequency Representation of Primary Auditory Cortex Following Discrimination in Training in Adult Owl Monkeys." *J. Neuroscience* **13** (1993): 87–103.
46. Reid, R. C., J. D. Victor, and R. M. Shapley. "Broadband Temporal Stimuli Decrease the Integration Time of Neurons in Cat Striate Cortex." *Visual Neurosci.* **9** (1992): 39–45.
47. Riesen, A. H. "The Development of Visual Perception in Man and Chimpanzee." *Science* **106** (1947): 107–108.

48. Robertson, D., and D. R. F. Irvine. "Plasticity of Frequency Organization in Auditory Cortex of Guinea Pigs with Partial Unilateral Deafness." *J. Compar. Neurology* **282** (1989): 456–471.

49. Rodieck, R. W., J. d. Pettigrew, P. O. Bishop, and T. Nikara. "Residual Eye Movements in Receptive-Field Studies of Paralysed Cats." *Vision Research* **7** (1967): 107–110.

50. Sanes, J. N., S. Suner, and J. P. Donoghue. "Dynamic Organization of Primary Motor Cortex Output to Target Muscles in Adult Rats I. Long-Term Patterns of Reorganization Following Motor or Mixed Peripheral Nerve Lesions." *Exp. Brain Res.* **79** (1990): 479–491.

51. Sanes, J. N., S. Suner, J. F. Lando, and J. P. Donoghue. "Rapid Reorganization of Adult Rat Motor Cortex Somatic Representation Patterns After Motor Nerve Injury." *Proc. Natl. Acad. Sci. USA* **85** (1988): 2003–2007.

52. Schroeder, C. E., C. E. Tenke, S. J. Givre, J. C. Arezzo, and H. G. J. Vaughan. "Striate Cortical Contribution to the Surface-Recorded Pattern-Reversal VEP in the Alert Monkey." *Vision Research* **31** (1991): 1143–1157.

53. Sclar, G., I. Ohzawa, and R. D. Freeman. "Contrast Gain Control in the Kitten's Visual System." *J. Neurophysiology* **54** (1985): 668–675.

54. Shapley, R. M., and J. D. Victor. "The Effect of Contrast on the Transfer Properties of Cat Retinal Ganglion Cells." *J. Physiology* **285** (1978): 275–298.

55. Shapley, R. M., and J. D. Victor. "The Contrast Gain Control of Cat Retina." *Vision Res.* **19** (1979): 431–434.

56. Shapley, R. M., and J. D. Victor. "Nonlinear Spatial Summation and the Contrast Gain Control of Cat Retinal Ganglion Cells." *J. Physiology* **290** (1979): 141–161.

57. Shapley, R. M., and J. D. Victor. "How the Contrast Gain Control Modifies the Frequency Responses of Cat Ganglion Cells." *J. Physiology* **318** (1981): 161–179.

58. Sherman, S. M., and P. D. Spear. "Organization of Visual Pathways in Normal and Visually Deprived Cats." *Physiol. Rev.* **62** (1982): 738–855.

59. Sutter, E. E. "A Practical Nonstochastic Approach to Nonlinear Time-Domain Analysis." In *Advanced Methods of Physiological System Modeling*, edited by V. Z. Marmarelis, 303–315. Los Angeles: Biomedical Simulation Resource, University of Southern California, 1987.

60. Sutter, E. E. "The Fast m-Transform: A Fast Computation of Cross Correlations with Binary m-Sequences." *SIAM J. Comput.* **20** (1991): 686–694.

61. Victor, J. D., and M. M. Conte. "Dynamics of the Human Gain Control, as Assessed by Visual Evoked Potentials." *Invest. Ophthal. & Visual Sci. Suppl.* **35** (1994): 1439 (abstract).

62. Victor, J. D., K. P. Purpura, E. Katz, and B. Mao. "Population Encoding of Spatial Frequency, Orientation, and Color in Macaque V1." *J. Neurophysiology* **72** (1994): 2151-2166.

63. Vital-Durand, F., L. J. Garey, and C. Blakemore. "Monocular and Binocular Deprivation in the Monkey: Morphological Effects and Reversibility." *Brain Res.* **158** (1978): 45–64.
64. von Noorden, G. K., and B. R. Middleditch. "Histology of the Monkey Lateral Geniculate Nucleus After Unilateral Lid Closure and Experimental Strabismus: Further Observations." *Invest. Ophthal. & Visual Sci.* **14** (1975): 674–683.
65. von Senden, M. *Raum-und gestaltauffassung bbei operierten blind-geborenen vor und nach del operation.* Free Press-Leipszip: J. Barth, 1960. English translation under the title: *Space and Sight.* Glencoe, IL: Free Press, 1960.
66. Wall, P. D. "The Presence of Ineffective Synapses and the Circumstances Which Unmask Them." *Phil. Trans. R. Soc. London B* **278** (1977): 361–372.
67. Weinberger, N. M., R. Javid, and B. Lepan. "Long-Term Retention of Learning-Induced Receptive-Field Plasticity in the Auditory Cortex." *Proc. Natl. Acad. Sci. USA* **90** (1993): 2394–2398.
68. Wiesel, T. N., and D. H. Hubel. "Effects of Visual Deprivation on Morphology and Physiology of Cells in the Lateral Geniculate Body." *J. Neurophysiology* **26** (1963): 978–993.
69. Wiesel, T. N., and D. H. Hubel. "Single-Cell Responses in Striate Cortex of Kittens Deprived of Vision in One Eye." *J. Neurophysiology* **26** (1963): 1003–1017.
70. Wiesel, T. N., and D. H. Hubel. "Comparison of the Effect of Unilateral and Bilateral Eye Closure on Cortical Unit Responses in Kittens." *J. Neurophysiology* **28** (1965): 1029–1040.
71. Wiesel, T. N., and D. H. Hubel. "Extent of Recovery from the Effects of Visual Deprivation in Kittens." *J. Neurophysiology* **28** (1965): 1060–1072.
72. Zohary, E., S. Celebrini, K. H. Britten, and W. T. Newsome. "Neuronal Plasticity that Underlies Improvement in Perceptual Performance." *Science* **263** (1994): 1289–1292.

Tim P. Pons
Department of Neurosurgery, Bowman Gray School of Medicine, Medical Center Blvd.,
Winston-Salem, NC 27157-1029; (910)716-9712; fax (910)716-3065;
e-mail: tpons@isnet.is.wfu.edu

Abstract: Lesion-Induced Cortical Plasticity

Since the work of Hubel and Wiesel in the 1960s, a tenet in the neuroscience's has been the concept of a "critical period," a window of opportunity early in development of mammals, after which the brain is thought to be hardwired and incapable of making new connections or major alterations in cortical sensory representations. This tenet underwent serious challenge during the 1980s, from experiments by Merzenich and Kaas and their colleagues which demonstrated that postcentral somatosensory cortex is capable of undergoing limited (1.5–2.0 mm^2) reorganization in adult animals after manipulations of peripheral nerves. An unexpected result of our electrophysiological work was the finding that SII undergoes major functional reorganization after total (but not any subtotal) removal of the hand representations in postcentral cortex.[6,7]

Although the affected region in SII is initially unresponsive, within several weeks the foot representation in the adjacent portions of SII has expanded to fully occupy the initially deactivated cortical zone, across a distance of five or more millimeters of cortex. These reorganizational changes are far more extensive than those previously reported by Merzenich, Kaas, and others, following various manipulations of peripheral nerves.

There are, however, at least three differences between our study and earlier ones that could have accounted for the difference in results.

First, only a portion of the hand was denervated in the earlier studies whereas we removed the entire hand representation in postcentral cortex. Second, the previous studies examined reorganizational changes in "primary," i.e., postcentral, somatosensory cortex, whereas we examined them in a later part of the processing pathway, i.e., in SII. Third, the earlier studies used manipulations of the peripheral nervous system only, whereas we examined the effects of manipulating the central nervous system.

CORTICAL PLASTICITY AFTER PERIPHERAL DEAFFERENTATION

In order to examine the first variable listed above (extent of denervation), while keeping the others constant, we cut and tied all three nerves normally innervating the hand and, six to eight weeks later, recorded from both primary (postcentral strip) and nonprimary (SII) cortex.[9] We found that although cortex normally devoted to the postcentral hand representations did become responsive to somatic stimulation of both the arm and face, the stimulation thresholds for eliciting a neuronal response were abnormally high, and much of the affected region still remained unresponsive. Moreover, sites in the expected location of the SII hand representation almost never responded to somatic stimulation. The few sites that did respond had receptive field locations restricted to the forearm, and response thresholds were virtually identical to those in the reorganized portion of the postcentral strip.

Although the finding that some sites in postcentral "hand" cortex had receptive fields on the face was unexpected, the reorganization was not nearly as great as that seen in SII after removal of the postcentral hand representation. This suggests that changes occurring early in an ascending system are simply relayed to the next processing station along "hard wired" connections, imposing constraints on the changes that can occur at this next level. Conversely, central manipulations, such as ablation of the postcentral hand representations, directly remove axonal terminals on cells in the next processing station, opening up a relatively large synaptic space for inputs from other sources. We therefore tested whether a central manipulation at the closest possible point to the peripheral nervous system would result in more extensive reorganization than the peripheral manipulations had.

PLASTICITY IN THE POSTCENTRAL STRIP FOLLOWING LONG-STANDING DORSAL RHIZOTOMIES

A dorsal rhizotomy is a procedure in which sensory nerve roots are severed after they exit the dorsal root ganglion just before entering the spinal cord, and is thus a central nervous system manipulation. Such a procedure denervates ascending sensory information to the brainstem, thalamus, and cortex. Thus the cortical sensory maps that normally receive input from the affected subcortical regions might be expected on the basis of traditional views simply to remain deactivated, i.e., unresponsive to somatic stimulation. To test if this was so, we recorded electrophysiological responses from the postcentral cortex of four monkeys that had undergone unilateral or bilateral dorsal rhizotomies of the nerve segments representing the upper limb.[9] The results indicated that this entire upper limb representation had become completely reorganized, all of the tissue now responding to stimulation of the contralateral chin and jaw. These dramatic findings extend the previously presumed upper limit for cortical reorganization by an order of magnitude from about 1–2 mm^2 to 1.5–2.0 cm^2, or 1/3 of the postcentral strip, and they raise the possibility that the upper limit may be even greater. Further, because this degree of reorganization greatly exceeds the cortical arborization zones of single axons from the thalamus,[1,11] no currently accepted mechanism is adequate to explain the magnitude of the reorganization.

REFERENCES

1. Garraghty, P. E., T. P. Pons, M. Sur, and J. H. Kaas. "The Arbors of Axons Terminating in Middle Cortical Layers of Somatosensory Area 3b in Owl Monkeys." *Somatosensory Res.* **6** (1989): 401–411.
2. Pons, T. P., P. E. Garraghty, C. G. Cusick, and J. H. Kaas. "The Somatotopic Organization of Area 2 in Macaque Monkeys." *J. Comp. Neurol.* **241** (1985): 445–466.
3. Pons, T. P., J. T. Wall, C. G. Cusick, P. E. Garraghty, and J. H. Kaas. "Consistent Features of the Representation of the Hand in Area 3b in Macaque Monkeys." *Somatosensory Res.* **4** (1987): 309–332.
4. Pons, T. P., P. E. Garraghty, D. P. Friedman, and M. Mishkin. "Physiological Evidence for Serial Processing in the Somatosensory System." *Science* **237** (1987): 417–420.
5. Pons, T. P., P. E. Garraghty, and M. Mishkin. "Lesion-Induced Plasticity in the Second Somatosensory Cortex of Adult Macaques." *Proc. Natl. Acad. Sci.* **85** (1988): 5279–5281.
6. Pons, T. P., P. E. Garraghty, and M. Mishkin. "Plasticity in Nonprimary Somatosensory Cortex of Adult Macaques." In *Post Lesion Neural Plasticity*, edited by H. Flohr, 511–517. Berlin: Springer-Verlag, 1988.
7. Pons, T. P. "A Cortical Pathway Important for Tactual Object Recognition in Macaques." In *Information Processing in the Somatosensory System*, edited by O. Franzen and J. Westman, Vol. 57, 233–244, Wenner-Gren International Symposium Series. Basingstoke, England: Macmillan, 1991.
8. Pons, T. P., P. E. Garraghty, A. K. Ommaya, J. H. Kaas, E. Taub, and M. Mishkin. "Massive Cortical Reorganization After Sensory Deafferentation in Adult Macaques." *Science* **252** (1991): 1857–1860.

9. Pons, T. P. "Perceptual Correlates of Massive Reorganization, a Response." *Science* **13** (1992): 1159–1160.

10. Pons, T. P., P. E. Garraghty, and M. Mishkin. "Serial and Parallel Processing in Somatosensory Cortex of Rhesus Monkeys." *J. Neurophysiology* **68** (1992): 518–527.

11. Pons, T. P. "Cortical Reorganization and Deafferentation in Adult Macaques. Technical Response." *Science* **265** (1994): 546–547.

V. S. Ramachandran, M.D.
Brain and Perception Laboratory, Center for Research on Brain and Cognition, 0109, University of California, San Diego, 9500 Gilman Drive, La Jolla, CA 92093-0109; Tel: (619)534-6240, Fax: (619)534-7190

Plasticity in the Adult Human Brain: Is There Reason for Optimism?

INTRODUCTION

In this article I would like to consider one of the most fascinating syndromes in clinical medicine—phantom limbs. Despite over a century of research, there has been an unfortunate tendency within the medical profession to regard this phenomenon as an enigmatic clinical curiosity. My goal, in this essay, will be to bring this illusion into the arena of modern neuroscience and to point out that it illustrates certain general principles concerning the functional organization of the normal human brain.

When I began my career as a medical student nearly 15 years ago, I was taught that no new neural connections can be formed in the adult mammalian brain. Once connections have been laid down in fetal life, or in early infancy, it was assumed that they hardly change later in life. It is this stability of connections in the adult brain, in fact, that is often used to explain why there is usually very little functional recovery after damage to the nervous system and why neurological diseases are so notoriously difficult to treat. In this article I will present some evidence that suggests that we may need to radically revise these views.

It is known that a complete somatotopic map of the entire body surface exists in the somatosensory cortex of primates.[14] In a series of pioneering experiments,

Merzenich et al.[15] amputated the middle finger of adult primates and found that within two months the area in the cortex corresponding to this digit starts to respond to touch stimuli delivered to the adjacent digits; i.e., this area is "taken over" by sensory input from adjacent digits. If more than one finger was amputated, however, there was no "take over" beyond about 1 mm of cortex. Merzenich et al. concluded from this that the expansion is probably mediated by arborizations of thalamo-cortical axons that typically do not extend beyond 1 mm.

This figure—1 mm—was often cited as the fixed upper limit of reorganization of sensory pathways in adult animals.[3] A remarkable experiment performed by Pons et al.,[17] however, suggests that this view might be incorrect. They found that after long-term (12 years) deafferentation of one upper limb, the cortical area originally corresponding to the hand gets taken over by sensory input from the face. The cells in the "hand area" now start responding to stimuli applied to the lower face region! Since this patch of cortex is over 1 cm in width, we may conclude that sensory reorganization can occur over at least this distance—an order of magnitude greater than the original 1-mm "limit."

PERCEPTUAL CORRELATES OF PLASTICITY IN HUMANS

Despite the wealth of physiological experiments demonstrating striking plasticity in the primary sensory areas of primates, there has been almost no attempt to directly look for the behavioral consequences of this reorganization in humans. Pons et al.'s[17] observation, for example, makes the curious prediction that if one were to touch a monkey's face after long-term deafferentation, the monkey should experience the sensations as arising from the *hand* as well as from the face. To test this prediction, we recently studied the localization of sensations in several adult human subjects who had undergone amputation of an upper limb. Two of these (VQ and WK) have been described in detail elsewhere.[18,19,20] In this essay, I will just briefly summarize our findings for these two patients and will also describe some preliminary results from three new patients (FA), (DS), and (LC).

PATIENT VQ

Patient VQ was an intelligent alert 17-year-old whose left arm was amputated 6 cm above the elbow about 4 weeks prior to our testing him. He experienced a vivid phantom hand that was "telescoped"; i.e., it felt like it was attached just a few centimeters below his stump and pronated. We studied localization of touch (and light pressure) in this patient using a Q-tip that was brushed at various randomly selected points on his skin surface. His eyes were shut during the entire procedure and he was simply asked to describe any sensations that he felt and to report the perceived location of these sensations. Using this procedure, we found that even stimuli applied to points remote from the amputation line were often systematically mislocalized to the phantom arm. Furthermore, *the distribution of these points was not random.*[19] There appeared to be two clusters of points with one cluster being represented on the lower part of the face ipsilateral to the amputation. There was a systematic one-to-one mapping between specific regions on the face and individual digits (e.g., from the cheek to the thumb, from the philtrum to the index finger and from the chin to the fifth finger or "pinkie"). Typically, the patient reported that he simultaneously felt the Q-tip touching his face and a "tingling" sensation in an individual digit. By repeatedly brushing the Q-tip on his face we were even able to plot "receptive fields" (or "reference fields") for individual digits of the (phantom) left hand on his face surface. The margins of these fields were remarkably sharp and stable over successive trials. Stimuli applied to other parts of the body such as the tongue, neck, shoulders, trunk, and axilla were never mislocalized to the phantom hand and no referred sensations were ever felt in the other (normal) hand. There was, however, one specific point on the contralateral cheek that always elicited a tingling sensation in the phantom elbow.

The second cluster of points that evoked referred sensations was found about 7 cm above the amputation line. Again there was a systematic one-to-one mapping with the thumb being represented medially on the anterior surface of the arm and the pinkie laterally, as if to mimic the pronated position of the phantom hand.

We repeated the whole procedure again after one week and found a very similar distribution of points. We concluded, therefore, that these one-to-one correspondences are stable over time—at least over the one-week period that separated our two testing sessions (but see below).

PATIENT WK

In testing the second patient (WK) we found a very similar pattern of results although there were some interesting differences as well. This patient had a right "forequarter" disarticulation; i.e., his entire right arm and right scapula were removed. We tested him exactly one year after amputation.

We had WK close his eyes and firmly rubbed the skin of his right lower jaw and cheek with one of our fingers or the tip of a ball-point pen. A representation of the entire phantom arm was found on the ipsilateral face with the hand being represented on the anterior lower jaw, the elbow on the angle of the jaw, and the shoulder on the temporamandibular joint. Again, as in patient VQ, there appeared to be a precise and stable point-to-point correspondence between points on the lower jaw and individual digits.

A second cluster of reference fields representing the hand was found just below the axilla. Since this region is close to the line of amputation, it may be analogous to the cluster of points we found on VQ's upper arm. In this region even a Q-tip was effective in eliciting referred sensations in the thumb, forefinger, pinkie, or palm. And lastly, there was also a third cluster of points near the right nipple and the arrangement of these points also showed some hint of topography. Thus it would appear that there is a tendency towards the spontaneous emergence of multiple somatotopically organized maps even in regions remote from the line of amputation. The exact mechanism by which such maps are formed remains an interesting question for future research.

We tried to relate these perceptual effects to the "remapping" experiments of Pons et al. We suggested, for example, that the reason we see two "clusters" of points—one on the lower face region and a second set near or around the amputation line—is because the map of the hand on the sensory homunculus is flanked on one side by the face and the other side by the upper arm (Figure 1). If the sensory input from the face and from the upper arm were to "invade" the territory of the hand, one would expect precisely this sort of clustering of points.

This view represents a specific hypothesis about the origin of referred sensations after amputation or nerve injury and we shall refer to it as the "remapping hypothesis."[18,20] The hypothesis also makes several new predictions that can be easily tested. For example, after trigeminal ganglion section one would expect sensations from the hand to be "referred" to the face. Also, after lower limb amputation, two clusters of points should be seen—one immediately proximal to the stump and one on the genitals—and there is some evidence that this is indeed true.[2,20] Our

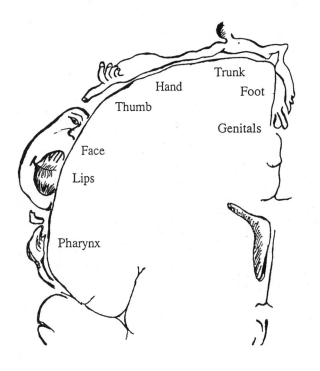

FIGURE 1 The Penfield "homunculus." Notice that the sensory hand area is flanked below by the face and above by the upper arm and shoulder—the two regions where we usually find reference fields in arm amputees. Also, note that the area representing the genitals is just below the foot representation. It has not escaped our notice that this might explain the frequent occurrence of certain foot fetishes even among normal individuals.

findings suggest, therefore, that far from being a mere clinical curiosity, phantom limbs might provide a valuable opportunity for exploring neural plasticity in the adult human brain. Even if the remapping hypothesis turns out to be wrong in detail, if it leads to new questions and new lines of enquiry, it will have adequately served its purpose.

It is especially noteworthy that the topographically organized map on patient VA's face and the modality-specific referral of temperature was seen just four weeks after amputation. We suggested, therefore, that the remapping may be based, at least in part, on "unmasking" or strengthening pre-existing connections rather than on sprouting new ones (Wall[23] was the first to demonstrate "unmasking" physiologically in animals). This view also receives some support from the recent observation that referred sensations are seen in "phantom breasts" as early as five days after radical mastectomy.[1]

Based on the preliminary observations that we made on patients VA and WK, we also raised several additional questions.[18] For example, would referred sensations be seen following anesthetic block of the brachial plexus? Would the map on the face be seen in all patients? How similar are the maps across patients? And lastly, how stable are the maps if the same patient is tested again on month or a year after the initial testing? We have now studied several additional patients and the results might help answer at least some of these questions.

SUBJECTS

Including VA and WK, we studied a total of eleven patients—ten after amputation and one after a brachial plexus avulsion. Of these eleven patients, the referral of sensation from the face to the phantom was seen in four of the amputees and in the single patient with the brachial avulsion. The second "cluster" of points proximal to the amputation, however, was seen in eight of the eleven amputees.

It is not clear why some patients do not experience referral of sensations from the face to the phantom but one possibility is that they eventually learn to ignore the anomalous sensations through compensatory changes at some subsequent state in processing. (See below under "intersubject variability.") Consistent with this view we have seen at least one patient in whom we clearly observed "remapping" using magnetoencephalography (MEG) but the patient did *not* refer sensations from the face to the phantom. We may conclude, therefore, that although remapping may be necessary for the emergence of referred sensation, it is certainly not sufficient.

TESTING PROCEDURE

The following testing protocol was used on each patient. First, a complete neurological examination was conducted. (All nine patients were found to be neurologically intact, except patient DS who had Horner's syndrome: left-eye partial ptosis and meiosis.) After that the patient sat on a stool with his eyes shut and he was simply asked to describe the nature and location of tactile sensations that he experienced while the examiner touched various randomly selected parts of his body (including face) with a Q-tip. If more than one sensation was experienced, he was asked to describe both of them—pointing to the corresponding locations on the examiner's body, if necessary. After this crude mapping had been carried out, we attempted to obtain more detailed maps by concentrating on those skin regions that systematically yielded referred sensations in the phantom limb. The Q-tip was brushed repeatedly over these regions in order to plot "reference fields"—patches of skin surface that yielded precisely localized sensations that were confined to a small region of the phantom.[19,20] Sometimes, we found that a Q-tip was completely ineffective and we had to resort to using deep pressure (e.g., repeated rubbing over the periostium of the mandible) applied with the eraser end of a pencil to elicit referred sensations in the phantom. This was true on patient WK's face,[19] for example. Referral of temperature was tested by using a using a Q-tip that was dipped in ice cold water (0°C) or in water that had been heated in a microwave until it was just tolerably hot.

The margins of the reference fields were demarcated using a felt pen and photographed (whenever practical, the entire sensation was also videotaped for subsequent analysis). To determine the stability of the referred sensation, we repeated the experiments following identical procedures on consecutive weeks (or, sometimes, on consecutive days).

PATIENT FA

Mr. FA's right arm was crushed on a fishing boat in 1982 and was amputated about 8 cm below the elbow. He experienced a very vivid "telescoped" phantom hand. He could, however, voluntarily extend his hand so that it acquired a subjectively normal length and indeed could even attempt to grasp objects, fend off blows, or break a fall with his phantom.

FA was one of the subjects we examined who did not *initially* have a map on his face. As in the other patients, however, he had points near the amputation line that elicited referred sensations. There were, in fact, *two* distinct somatotopic representations on the arm (Figure 2). Stimuli-applied points in between these two maps did not produce referred sensations even though the skin was normal. We also repeated the testing twice, at weekly intervals and although the two maps proximal to the stump were found again, no map was found on the face.

Later, patient FA also participated as a subject in an MEG (magnetoencephalogy) recording experiment.[26,27,28] Magnetic fields evoked on the surface of his brain were recorded using a SQUID machine during tactile stimulation. This enabled us to demonstrate a striking reorganization of the somatosensory "homunculus" in the hemisphere contralateral to the amputation. Intriguingly, the patient also reported that shortly after his MEG recording sessions had begun, he had started to

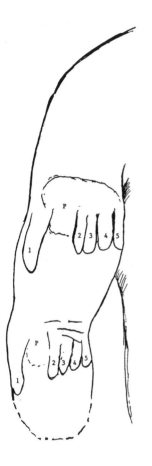

FIGURE 2 Somatotopic maps of referred sensations in patient FA. By repeatedly brushing a Q-tip on the skin, we plotted the margins of "reference fields" (analogous to receptive fields). Notice that there are two distinct maps—one close to the line of amputation and a second one 6 cms above the elbow crease. The maps are almost identical except for the absence of fingertips in the upper map: 1=thumb; 2=index finger; 3=middle finger; 4=right finger; 5=pinkie. These reference fields usually elicited sensation in the *glabrous* portions of these digits. The dorsal surface of the hand (D) was represented on the dorsolateral part of the upper arm lateral to the palm (P) and thumb (2) representations. No referred sensations in the phantom could be elicited by stimulating the skin region in between these two maps.

notice sensations being referred from his face to his phantom limb (see below under "Long-term changes in maps").

PATIENT DS

Patient DS had a brachial avulsion following a motorcycle accident in 1985 and a year after the accident, he had his arm amputated. He experienced a vivid phantom that felt "paralyzed"—as though his brain had learned the paralysis that preceded the amputation. In other words, if he tried to move his phantom voluntarily, he could not do so, even if he put in considerable effort of will. ("It feels like it is frozen in concrete" was the expression he used.) This was true whether or not he simultaneously made mirror symmetric movements with the other hand (see below). He maintained, also, that the phantom arm had always been of normal length; i.e., it had never been "telescoped" and he had never experienced even the slightest flicker of movement in it during the last ten years since the amputation.

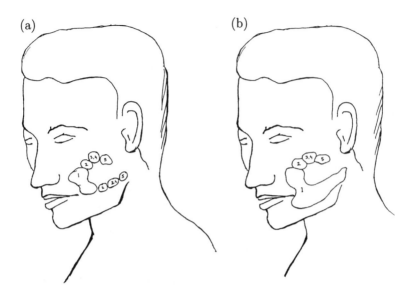

FIGURE 3 Distribution of reference fields in patient DS. Notice the prominent representation of the thumb and the roughly topographic arrangement of digits 1, 2, 3, 4, and 5 on the face. This pattern was nearly identical 24 hours later but after six months the representations of some of the digits had changed noticeably. This may occur as a result of sensory input and spontaneous activity from the face (and stump) continuously remodeling neural connections in S1. If this interpretation is correct, then phantom limbs might provide a valuable "preparation" for studying the manner in which sensory maps emerge and change in the adult nervous system.

We mapped the distribution of areas yielding referred sensations ("reference fields") in this patient extensively on three separate occasions, the first two separated by 24 hours and the third one after six months (Figure 3(a)). Notice the topographic arrangement of digits on the zygomatic arch. Curiously, there was also a second "map" of sorts on the mandible. (Stimulating the buccal region in between the two maps elicited diffuse tingling on the palm.) The reference fields on the zygoma usually corresponded to the distal interphalangeal joint and the one on the mandible to the base of the digit.

The map remained stable during the first two testing sessions but after six months, the thumb region appeared to have "expanded" to stretch across the entire mandible (Figure 3(b)). One wonders whether such changes occur as a result of changing patterns of sensory input (and spontaneous activity) from the face and from the stump. If so, would stimulating a specific region of the map (e.g., the index finger reference field) for a few days to increase the size of that reference field? As expected, a second map was found in the region of the deltoid muscle and this, too, was topographically organized. Unlike the face map, however, it remained stable across all three testing sessions.

Intriguingly, when the Q-tip was *moved* continuously from the angle of the mandible to the symphysis menti, the referred sensation (RS) also felt like "it was moving from the ball of the thumb to the tip in an arclike motion." Also, if a *short* excursion was made on the jaw, the excursion on the hand was correspondingly short. These experiments were repeated several times with identical results.

MODALITY-SPECIFIC EFFECTS

The neural pathways that mediate the sensations of pain, warmth, and cold are quite different from those that carry information about touch.[9,10,11] Does remapping occur separately in each of these pathways? When we placed a drop of warm water on VQ's face, he felt the warm water on his face, of course, but remarkably he reported (without any prompting) that his phantom hand also felt distinctly warm. And when the water accidentally trickled down his face, he exclaimed, with surprise, that he could actually feel the water trickling down his phantom arm! We have also seen this effect in a patient who had an avulsion of the brachial plexus; he was even able to use his normal hand to trace out the exact path of the illusory trickle along his paralyzed arm as a drop of cold water flowed down his face. Finally, in patient DS, a vibrator placed on the jaw evoked "vibration" in the phantom hand.

Both modality specificity and topography have been noticed previously on the *stump*[4,8] but these were ascribed (incorrectly in my view) to either stump reinnervation or to the fact that the phantom hand was "telescoped" or superimposed on the stump so that "the location of referred sensations in the phantom hand in phenomenal space corresponds to that of the stimulus in physical space."[4] The topography and modality specificity of sensations referred from the *face* that we have observed obviously cannot be explained in this manner and we consider the remapping hypothesis to be the most parsimonious explanation.

Next, we tried applying a drop of hot (or cold) water on different parts of patient DS's face and found that the heat or cold was usually referred to individual fingers so that there was a sort of crude map of referred temperature that was roughly superimposed on the touch map. (For example, warm water on the thumb reference field on the face evoked warmth in the thumb alone. Interestingly, "hot" on the face was always felt as *warm* on the face rather than hot; i.e., there was some attenuation of intensity.) To make sure that these effects were not simply due to simultaneous activation of touch receptors, we also tried touching the thumb reference field on the face with warm water while simultaneously applying tepid water to the pinkie region of the map. The patient then reported that he could feel the touch in both digits—as expected—but that the warmth was felt *only* in the thumb. Reversing the stimulation the face produced a corresponding reversal in the phantom. If these preliminary results are confirmed, they would imply that there are independent modality-specific "reference fields" for touch, heat, and cold on the face and that these reference fields are usually in approximate spatial registration.

If this effect is confirmed in additional patients, it raises an important question about modality-specific coding in the nervous system. For if there are indeed separate brain areas for touch, warmth, and cold, then why is the remapping identical for all three areas and yet different across patients? Is it conceivable that there is some cross talk between modalities that constrains the remapping process and preserves spatial registration?

"LEARNED" PARALYSIS OF PHANTOM LIMBS

Most patients who have lost a limb experience very compelling phantom arm or leg which they can "move" voluntarily. We noticed, however, that if the patient had a pre-existing *paralysis* of the arm caused by a peripheral nerve lesion (e.g., a brachial plexus avulsion or infiltration by carcinoma), then he usually complained that he could not *voluntarily* move the phantom—it felt "paralyzed" and usually occupied, learned paralysis of— the same position that the paralyzed arm[19,20] had before amputation (e.g., neither patient DS nor patient WK could move his phantom voluntarily, whereas FA and VQ had no difficulty). It was almost as though during the months preceding the amputation, the patient has *learned that the limb was paralyzed*; i.e., every time he tried to move his limb, there was both visual feedback and proprioceptive feedback from the limb muscles informing him that the limb was not following the command. Perhaps these contradictory signals somehow get "wired" into the brain so that there was a permanent memory trace of the paralysis left in place.

A similar mismatch between command signals and feedback may account for the apparent "paralysis" that was observed in the silver spring monkeys. Ed Taub[22] has noted that these monkeys seemed paralyzed—their arms appeared limp and lifeless even though only the sensory neurons had been cut (by a dorsal rhizotomy). Despite the fact that the entire motor system was intact, the animals could not use the system to generate movement in the arms.

RELEVANCE TO STROKE REHABILITATION: THE VIRTUAL REALITY BOX

But if the phantom is paralyzed because the patient's brain has *learned* that it is paralyzed, then would it be possible to "unlearn" the paralysis? One way to achieve this might be to encourage the patient to simply perform a mirror symmetric movement with his *other* normal hand since this might *facilitate* the corresponding neural circuits in equivalent locations in the other hemisphere. A second method might be to use a "virtual reality box" to trick the patient into thinking that his phantom was moving.[21] A mirror was placed vertically on a table in front of patient DS in the sagittal plane and he was asked to view the reflection of his *normal* hand in the mirror in order to create the illusion that he now had two hands. When he then attempted to execute mirror symmetric movement with both his hands, he "saw" his phantom come to life and move as if it was obeying his commands. A few seconds later he exclaimed, with considerable surprise, "Mind-boggling. My arm is plugged in again; it's as if I am back in the past. All these years I have often *tried* to move my phantom several times a day without success, but now I can actually *feel* I'm moving my arm, doctor. It no longer feels like it's lying lifeless in a sling." I then removed the mirror and verified that, as before, he could no longer feel his phantom moving even if he closed his eyes and tried mirror symmetric movements. ("It feels frozen again," he said.) Patient DS also tried moving his index finger and thumb *alone* while looking in the mirror but, this time, the phantom thumb and index finger *remained paralyzed*—they were *not* revived. This is an important observation for it rules out the possibility that the previous result was simply a confabulation in response to unusual task demands.

The concept of "learned paralysis" may have important implications for rehabilitation from stroke. Hemiplegia usually arises from permanent, irreversible neural damage caused by stroke, but is it conceivable that at least some of the paralysis is learned? For example, even if there is some recovery—as a result of ""—the patient may not use his arm because his brain has learned during the acute stages that his limb is paralyzed. If so, then the "mirror therapy" described above may eventually prove useful in accelerating recovery of function in at least a subset of stroke victims.

We asked Mr. DS to take the box home with him to practice moving his hands every day. After 20 ten-minute sessions of therapy distributed over a three-week period, he noticed something quite remarkable and drew our attention to it without our prompting him. He claimed that his arm was now considerably shorter than it used to be, so that his hand and fingers were dangling from the stump near the upper arm—something he had never experienced during the ten years that had elapsed since the amputation. He seemed quite intrigued by the effect since he was unaware of the clinical phenomenon of "telescoping." The telescoping was apparently permanent since it had been almost two weeks since he had stopped the mirror therapy. (It remains to be seen, of course, whether the arm will spontaneously revert to its normal length after a few months.)

Finally, patient DS added that even though his hand was telescoped, he was actually able to flex or extend all his fingers simultaneously, although not individually. (And he could now do this whether or not he used the box and even without moving the other hand.) He seems rather pleased with this since he said he had never been able to generate even the slightest flicker of movement in his phantom during the last ten years. Also, he pointed out that whereas previously he used to experience excruciating pain in his phantom elbow, the pain was gone now since his elbow had vanished as a result of the telescoping. Obviously these results need to be replicated on additional patients. One would like to know especially whether there is anything special about the box or whether the telescoping was simply induced by the patient continuously paying attention to his phantom arm. (This seems unlikely since the patient's attention had already been on the arm for long periods as a result of his pain.) If the results hold up, however, they would imply that one can use virtual reality to produce a virtual amputation of a virtual elbow in order to eliminate virtual pain.

We have no simple explanation of why experience with the box should lead to telescoping of the phantom. One possibility is that the profound intersensory conflict produced by the virtual reality device leads to a complete shutdown and inhibition of the phantom limb in the parietal lobes in a manner analogous to the denial of limb ownership (somatoparaphrenic delusions) seen in parietal lobe syndrome. However, since the fingers and hand are over-represented in the sensory cortex, they might be more resistant to this inhibition than the rest of the limb. The net outcome would be a deletion of the limb without a deletion of the hand and this might lead to telescoping as a default percept.

Whatever its ultimate interpretation, however, this finding is the first report of a permanent telescoping of the phantom being induced by brief doses of a relatively simple procedure. It serves to remind us, once again, of the enormous lability of neural connections in the adult brain.

A NEW TREATMENT FOR PHANTOM LIMG PAIN?

After amputation of an upper limb many patients also experience a "clenching spasm" of the hand. The clenchin gcan be excruciatingly painful—occur several times a week and last for an hour or me each time. One such patient was Mr. R. T. whose left arm had been amputated above the elbow 6 months prior to our testing him. He found that he could relieve the pain by unclenching the hand with intense voluntary effort but the procedure usually ttook half an hour. When looking in the virtual reality box, however, he could immediately unclench ihs Phantom hand by watching the mirror reflection of his normal hand being unclenched simultaneously and this produced instant and dramatic relief from the pain! He repeated the procedure on four consecutive days—with identical results.

It would be difficult to explain these results in terms of current concepts in neuroscience. We suggest that when commands are sent to the hand from the motor cortex, these are normally damped by error feedback from proprioception. In the absence of the arm, such damping is not possible—so that the motor output is amplified even further—thereby flooding the system and being experienced as pain. What the virtual reality does is to provide an extraneous visual feedback signal to damp the mor output, so that the pain is abolished. These ideas can be tested directly by using modern imaging techniques such as fMRI and PET.

PATIENT LC: THE ROLE OF THE CORPUS CALLOSUM

LC was a 23-year-old patient who fell off a train and lost his left arm 19 days prior to our testing him. After verifying first that he was neurologically intact, we blind-folded him and applied sensory stimuli to various parts of his body. Like some of our other patients, he referred sensations from his lower ipsilateral face to his phantom fingers but there were no clearly defined "reference fields"—possibly because not enough time had elapsed after the amputation. An especially intriguing effect was observed, however, when we applied stimuli to the normal hand. For example, when his right index finger was scraped with a knee hammer, he experienced his phan-tom index finger also being "scraped." When we held his pinkie or index finger and passively dipped it into a glass of hot or ice-cold water, he felt the corresponding finger on the phantom also "dipping into water" although, curiously, the warmth or cold was felt only in the right hand—it was not referred to the phantom. This rules out confabulation for if the patient were confabulating, why should he refer only the "dipping" sensation and not the temperature? We conclude therefore that we are dealing with a genuine sensory phenomenon. No referral of sensations occurred from any other part of the body and the effects remained stable across two succes-sive testing sessions separated by 24 hours. (The patient could not be followed up subsequently since he left the country.)

We suggest that the phenomenon arises from activation of preexisting transcal-losal connections. There is physiological evidence suggesting that even in normal individuals touching a finger on (say) the right hand activates not only the fin-ger area of the left hemisphere but also the mirror-symmetric location in the right hemisphere.[3] This input is ordinarily subliminal—i.e., too weak to activate the neu-rons in area 3b that get a much stronger input from the left hand. After amputation of the left hand, however, this weak input from the right hand gradually takes over these neurons and becomes strong enough to activate them, thereby leading to re-ferred sensations. This would be analogous to shifts in ocular dominance observed in young monkeys after monocular deprivation.[24] This interpretation is different from "unmasking," of course, but it implies a *strengthening* of pre-existing connections rather than a sprouting of new axons across the corpus callosum!

STABILITY OF MAPS OVER TIME

In patients WK, VQ, and FA the overall features of the map were remarkably stable with repeated testing across weekly intervals (for four weeks). In patient FA, however, we made a very intriguing observation that suggests that the fine details of the map may be dynamically maintained. Mr. FA's phantom hand usually occupied a position halfway between pronation and supination. Out of curiosity, we asked him to voluntarily pronate his phantom hand all the way and remapped the points on the upper arm while his hand was still pronated. To our astonishment, we found that the entire map had shifted systematically leftward by about 1 cm as if to partially follow the pronation.[20] Also, when he returned the phantom to its resting position, the map also shifted rightward and returned to its original location. If a constant stimulus such as a small drop of water was placed on (say) the pinkie region of the map, he reported that he very distinctly felt the drop of water moving from the pinkie to the ring finger when he pronated his phantom. But if the drop was hot, only the "drop" moved but the warmth remained confined to the original digit! (A similar effect occurred if he simply clenched and unclenched his phantom fingers; the drop jumped from the finger to the palm but the warmth remained confined to the finger.)

These observations suggest that either the map in S1 itself or its subsequent "readout" can be profoundly modified by reafference signals from motor commands sent to the hand.

LONG-TERM CHANGES IN MAPS OF REFERRED SENSATIONS

As noted earlier, in patient FA, during the first three testing sessions there were no reference fields on the face at all. Yet when we repeatedly prodded his face for obtaining MEG recordings,[26,27,28] he reported, with some surprise, that he had started to notice some sensations in his phantom hand. These referred sensations were more noticeable the following day when he was shaving, than during the actual MEG recording session. It was as though the repeated mechanical stimulation had somehow revived dormant connections that had always been there. (Alternately, the sensations might have emerged spontaneously even without the prodding. This needs to be explored in additional patients.) Interestingly such sensations were now evoked for *both* sides of the face, although less reliably from the contralateral side than the ipsilateral side. The contralateral effects may be based on callosal connections[3,20] as noted above. The reference fields were clearly defined on the ipsilateral face, especially for digits one and two but there was no discernible topography. Such long-term changes in the map on the face have also been recently reported by Halligan, Marshall, Wade, et al.[7] who studied their patient on two successive occasions separated by a year.

The short-term and long-term changes may be based on very different mechanisms, but whatever the explanation might be, they are sure to have important implications for our understanding of brain function. They provide the first *behavioral* evidence for the views of Merzenich, Kaas, Wall, Nelson, Sur, and Felleman[14] and Edelman[5] that even in the adult brain, neural connections are being modified continuously in the sensory pathways.

INTERSUBJECT VARIABILITY

Of the eleven patients we have seen so far, the "map" on the face was seen in five. The second cluster of points near the line of amputation, on the other hand, was seen in eight patients.

Why do the maps vary so much and why do many patients not have a cluster of points on the face? There are at least six possibilities that are not mutually exclusive. First, the brain maps themselves might vary slightly from patient to patient, and this, in turn, might constrain the degree of remapping. Second, the remapping may occur at multiple stages (e.g., thalamus vs cortex) and adjacency of body parts might be different at different stages. Third, some patients may eventually learn to ignore the referred sensations from the face by using visual feedback. Fourth, even without visual feedback the plasticity exhibited by the afferent pathways may be propagated further along the pathways to perception,[25] so that the input gets correctly interpreted as originating from the face alone. Fifth, the aberrant connections that are formed may get deleted by the same genetic mechanism that causes their elimination in the embryo. And sixth, if the patient uses the stump constantly the skin corresponding to it may regain the territory that was initially lost to the face.[20]

It was our impression, also, that patients who referred sensations from the face to the phantom either had a preexisting long-standing pathology in that arm (e.g., a brachial avulsion, infiltration by carcinoma, etc.) *or* were seen soon (e.g., 4–6 weeks) after a traumatic amputation. Patients who were seen several years after a "clean" nontraumatic amputation (with no preexisting neural pathology) tended not to have a map on the face. Clearly, additional experiments are needed to see if this distinction holds up.

PHYSIOLOGICAL REMAPPING IS NOT SUFFICIENT TO GUARANTEE PERCEPTUAL MISLOCALIZATION

In at least one patient (CB) we saw clear evidence of remapping in the somatosensory areas using MEG (magnetoencephalograph) but the patient *did not* mislocalize sensations from the face to the phantom limb. This provides evidence for the third or fourth hypothesis discussed in the previous section; i.e., the patient's brain must be "correcting" for the remapping at some subsequent stage in processing. It remains to be seen whether this correction can occur spontaneously or whether it requires visual feedback, but in either case it raises important theoretical questions about how the brain assigns "local-sign" to a sensory stimulus.

NONSPECIFIC EFFECTS

In addition to the clearly defined "reference fields" described so far, we found that nonspecific sensations could also occasionally be evoked in the phantom limbs of some patients. Regarding these nonspecific sensations: (1) They tended to be *diffuse* and usually less intense. (2) They were usually highly *variable* in their occurrence and distribution; e.g., stimulating the same point would evoke sensations in very different locations in the phantom on different trials. (3) The distribution of the points that evoked these sensations was usually quite random; i.e., there was no clearly discernible clustering on the lower jaw and around the amputation line.

The mechanisms underlying these nonspecific effects is obscure but they may have more in common with diffuse "arousal" than with the remapping phenomena that we have considered so far. Some support for the arousal interpretation comes from the recent physiological work of Leclere, Dykes, and Avendano[12] who found *two* classes of novel responses in the deafferented hand area of the cortex (S1) of cats: (1) cells with clearly defined receptive fields, on the face, and (2) a second class of responses that could be obtained by touching almost any part of the animal: i.e., there was no clearly defined receptive field. Dykes et al. suggest that these responses are not "truly sensory in character" and that they may be mediated by brainstem arousal mechanisms.

DISCUSSION: THE REMAPPING HYPOTHESIS

After one hundred years of meticulous neurology, it would have been quite remarkable if no one had noticed referred sensation in phantom limbs and indeed such effects have been reported several times.[4,16] In a classic monograph published in 1951, Cronholm[4] noted clearly that points remote from the stump could sometimes evoke sensations in the phantom. What these researchers did not recognize, however, was that there was something *special* about the face or that there was a specific *pattern* of distribution of points yielding referred sensations—one set of points on the ipsilateral lower face and one on the upper arm. Nor did they suggest that this clustering of points can be explained in terms of Penfield's map—an explanation that we refer to as the "remapping hypothesis." Notice, especially, that this hypothesis *dissociates proximity in the brain from proximity on the body surface.*

As a note of caution, we would add, however, that although many of our observations are compatible with the remapping hypothesis, not all of them are. The complete absence of a map on the face in many patients and the variability in the distribution of reference fields from patient to patient is especially troublesome. One reason for the variability might be that the remapping occurs simultaneously at multiple levels (e.g., dorsal column nuclei, thalamus, cortex) within the system—a proposition that can be tested by combining behavioral studies with modern imaging techniques such as PET, functional MRI, and Magnetoencephalography (MEG).[27,28]

Yet, despite these reservations, the one important conclusion that does emerge clearly from our experiments (together with the elegant recent work of Melzack[13] and of Halligan et al.[1,2,6,7]) is that we must give up the notion that the human brain is composed of a fixed set of anatomical connections specified largely by the genome. Our results suggest, instead, that even the adult brain is a dynamic biological system in which new connections as being created and deleted all the time partly in response to novel sensory inputs and partly as a result of self-organizing principles. Everyone recognizes, of course, that *some* changes must be possible even in the adult brain for, otherwise, you could not account for phenomenon such as learning and memory. What our results imply, however, is that even the basic circuitry or "hardware" in the brain—such as the sensory maps—can be altered with surprising rapidity. No one would have suspected, for example, that the famous "Penfield homunculus," which every medical student learns about, can be reorganized over a distance of 2 cm in less than four weeks or that Phantom limb pain can be cured by simply using a mirror. And remarkably, the remapping, at least in some cases, is precise and orderly, for if it wasn't, one could not account for the emergence of a topographically organized, modality-specific reference fields on the face or for the referral of complex sensations such as "trickle" from the face to the phantom. It is unclear, at present, how one could harness this latent ability of the brain to accelerate recovery from brain injury, but if our view of the brain is correct, then there is at least reason for optimism.

ACKNOWLEDGMENTS

We thank F. H. C. Crick, J. Bogen, P. Churchland, V. Mountcastle, L. Franz, A. P. 0. Sacks, J. Smythes, T. Sejnowski, P. J. Halligan, J. Marshall, A. Damasio, T. Sejnowski, D. Rogers-Ramachandran, and J. Ramachandran for stimulating discussions and the NIMH for support.

REFERENCES

1. Aglioti, S., F. Cortese, and C. Franchini. "Phantom Breasts as a Perceptual Correlate of Neural Plasticity." *NeuroReport* **5** (1994): 473–476.
2. Aglioti, S., A. Bonazzi, and F. Cortese. "Phantom Lower Limb as a Perceptual Marker for Neural Plasticity in the Mature Human Brain." *Proc. Roy. Soc. Lond.* (1994): in press.
3. Calford, M. B., and R. Tweedale. "Interhemispheric Transfer of Plasticity in the Cerebral Cortex." *Science* **249** (1990): 805–807.
4. Cronholm, B. "Phantom Limbs in Amputees. A Study of Changes in the Inntegration of Centripetal Impulses with Special Reference to Referred Sensations." *Acta Psychiatr. Neurol. Scand. Suppl.* **72** (1951): 1–310.
5. Edelman, G. M. *The Remembered Present.* New York: Basic Books, 1989.
6. Halligan, P., J. Marshall, D. T. Wade, et al. *NeuroReport* **4** (1993): 233–236.
7. Halligan, P., J. Marshall, D. T. Wade, et al. *NeuroReport* (1994): in press.

8. James, W. "The Consciousness of Lost Limbs." *Proc. Amer. Soc. Psych. Res.* **1** (1887): 249–258.

9. Kenshalo, D. R., H. Hensel, I. P. Graziade, and H. Fruhstorfer. In *Oral-Facial Sensory and Motor Mechanisms*, edited by R. Dubner and Y. Kawamura, 23–45. New York: Appleton-Crofts, 1971.

10. Kreisman, N. R., and I. D. Zimmerman. "Cortical Unit Responses to Temperature Stimulation of the Skin." *Brain Res.* **25** (1971): 184–187.

11. Landgren, S. "Thalamic Neurons Responding to Cooling of the Cat's Tongue." *Acta Physiol. Scand.* **48** (1960): 255–267.

12. Leclere, S., R. Dykes, and C. Avendano. "Evolution of Cortical Responsiveness to Peripheral Nerve Transection." *J. Comp. Neurol.* (1994): in press.

13. Melzack R. "Phantom Limbs." *Sci. Am.* **266** (1992): 90–96.

14. Merzenich, M. M., J. H. Kaas, J. T. Wall, R. J. Nelson, M. Sur, and D. Felleman. "Topographic Reorganization of Somatosensory Cortical Areas 3b and 1 in Adult Monkeys Following Restricted Deafferentation." *Neuroscience* **8** (1983): 33–55.

15. Merzenich, M. M., R. Nelson, M. S. Stryker, M. Cynader, A. Schoppmann, and J. M. Zook. *J. Comp. Neurol.* **224** (1984): 591–605.

16. Mitchell, S. W. "Phantom Limbs." *Lippincott's Magazine of Pop. Lit. & Sci.* **8** (1871): 563–569.

17. Pons, T. P., E. Preston, A. K. Garraghty, et al. "Massive Cortical Reorganization after Sensory Deafferentation in Adult Macaques." *Science* **252** (1991): 1857–1860.

18. Ramachandran, V. S., D. Rogers-Ramachandran, and M. Stewart. "Perceptual Correlates of Massive Cortical Reorganization." *Science* **258** (1992): 1159–1160.

19. Ramachandran, V. S., M. Stewart, and D. C. Rogers-Ramachandran. "Perceptual Correlates of Masssive Cortical Reorganization." *NeuroReport* **3** (1992): 583–586.

20. Ramachandran, V. S. "Behavioral and MEG Correlates of Neural Plasticity in the Adult Human Brain." *Proc. Natl. Acad. Sci. USA* **90** (1993): 10413–10420.

21. Ramachandran, V. S. *Soc. Neurosci. Abstr.* (1994).

22. Taub, E. and J. E. Cargo. "Increasing Behavvioral Plasticity Following Central Nervous System Damage in Monkeys and Man: A Method with Potential Application to Human Development Motor Disability." This Volume

23. Wall, P. "The Presence of Inaffective Synapses and the Circumstances which Unmask Them." *Phil. Trans. Roy. Soc. Lond. B* **278** (1971): 361–372.

24. Wiesel, T. N., and D. H. Hubel. "Single-Cell Responses in Stratiate Cortex of Kittens Deprived of Vision in one Eye." *J. Neurophysiol.* **28** (1965): 1029–1040.

25. Weiss, P. *Principles of Development.* New York: Holt, 1939.

26. Yang, T., C. Gallen, V. S. Ramachandran, S. Cobb, and F. Bloom. *Soc. Neurosci. Abstr.* **19** (1993): 162.

27. Yang, T., C. Gallen, V. S. Ramachandran, B. Schwartz, F. Bloom, and S. Cobb. "Sensory Maps in the Human Brain." *Nature* **368** (1994): 592–493.
28. Yang, T., C. Gallen, V. S. Ramachandran, et al. "Noninvasive Dectection of Cerebral Plasticity in Adult Human Somatosensory Cortex." *NeuroReport* **5** (1994): 701–704.

Developmental Disabilities and Plasticity: Is There a Reason for Optimism?

Edward Taub† and Jean E. Crago‡

†Department of Psychology, University of Alabama at Birmingham, 415 Campbell Hall, University Station, Birmingham, AL 35294

‡Department of Physical Therapy, University of Alabama at Birmingham, Spain Rehabilitation Center, University Station, Birmingham, AL 35294

Increasing Behavioral Plasticity Following Central Nervous System Damage in Monkeys and Man: A Method with Potential Application to Human Developmental Motor Disability

In the course of basic research on the role of somatic sensation in movement and learning, my coworkers and I found that it was possible to induce a monkey, with an upper extremity rendered useless by unilateral deafferentation to employ that limb extensively; one of two general techniques to be described below were used. More recently, my laboratory and other investigators have been able to apply the same approach in humans for the remediation of serious motor deficits in chronic stroke and traumatic brain injury patients. One of the two main objectives of this chapter will be to explore the possible relationship between the behavioral plasticity we have been able to induce following central nervous system damage in monkeys and man, and the exciting new discoveries relating to cortical plasticity that several contributors to this volume have made. The second aim will be to introduce data indicating that the maturational window for one complex type of movement, thumb-forefinger prehension, is much longer than has generally been assumed and, in addition, that the method for inducing behavioral plasticity described in this article is effective for bringing into existence thumb-forefinger prehension in animals in whom it fails to develop. It will be suggested that this approach may have applicability to the rehabilitation of developmental disabilities in motor categories other than prehension and that this applicability may extend to the human case. If the hypothesis proves to be correct, there would then be some reason for adopting a tentatively positive answer to one aspect of the question posed by the title of the symposium on which this volume is based: "Maturational Windows and Cortical Plasticity in Human Development: Is There Reason for an Optimistic View?"

THE REHABILITATION OF MOVEMENT FOLLOWING DEAFFERENTATION IN MONKEYS

The spinal nerves emerge from the spinal cord in two roots. The dorsal root is sensory. Thus, by severing all of the dorsal roots innervating a limb one can eliminate all sensation from that limb involved in the support of ongoing behavior sequences, while leaving the motor innervation intact over the ventral root. When a single forelimb is deafferented in a monkey, the animal stops making use of it in the free situation.[7,9,13,39] However, it was found to be possible to induce a monkey to use the deafferented limb by two general types of behavioral techniques.

One technique involved restriction of movement of the intact upper extremity through the use of a device that left the deafferented limb free.[8,26] Use of the deafferented limb would usually begin within an hour after the restriction device had been secured, often for postural support while the animal was in a sitting position. Within several hours the limb could typically be used, though somewhat clumsily, for a wide variety of activities, including ambulation, climbing, and thumb-forefinger prehension of small objects. When the animals were left in the intact limb restriction device for a period of time, typically one week (though for one animal it was a period as short as three days), the use of the deafferented limb persisted after the device was removed with no apparent diminution of range or quality of movement. Moreover, use of the limb was permanent, being observed for the remainder of the animals' lives, which in one case was over four years.[27,28,29] In this fashion a useless limb was converted into a limb that could be used extensively.

A second method for overcoming the inability to use a single deafferented limb was found to be the application of procedures for training that limb. In initial work, conditioned response techniques were employed for enabling the animals to make a variety of movements with the deafferented limb, including phasic forelimb flexion,[7,8,31,32] grasp,[34] sustained forelimb flexion[27,28] and compensation for progressively increasing loads on the arm.[27,28,42,43] However, transfer never occurred between the experimental and life situations.[27,28] The movements that were trained in the conditioning chamber were never observed to be performed in the colony environment.

The conditioned response paradigm is, of course, just one type of training technique. An even more effective training method for inducing recovery of motor function was found to be shaping, in which a desired motor or behavioral objective is approached in small steps, by successive approximations.[12,17,23,24,25] With shaping techniques, the animals not only learned to employ a single deafferented limb in the training situation, but its use transferred to the life situation as well. This was in contrast to the case for conditioned response training. Shaping appeared to provide a bridge from the training situation, enabling extensive movement in the animal's normal environment. The behaviors shaped included: (1) pointing at visual targets,[35] (2) prehension in juveniles deafferented on day of birth[37] and prenatally[38] who had never exhibited any prehension previously. In both cases, shaping permitted an almost complete reversal of the motor disability, which progressed from total absence of the target behavior to very good (though not normal) performance.

THE EXTENDED MATURATIONAL WINDOW FOR PREHENSION IN MONKEYS

In most of the research described above, the subjects were adolescent monkeys with considerable motor experience prior to deafferentation. It was found that these animals could use their deafferented limbs to perform an extensive repertoire of behavior. The question still remained, however, whether somatic sensation is necessary early in life for the ontogenetic development of normal patterns of coordination. To investigate this question, monkey infants were subjected to bilateral forelimb deafferentation on the first day of life, within hours after birth.[37] Ambulation, climbing, and reaching toward objects developed spontaneously in all four infants and were as good at 3 months of age as in monkeys deafferented in adolescence. However, grasp, individual finger use, and accurate hand-eye coordination did not appear spontaneously. In the immediate postoperative period, there was a profound motor impairment but this rapidly disappeared. Various age-characteristic movements and postures emerged only approximately 1.8 weeks later in the deafferented infants than in intact infants, except for the just noted movements of the distal musculature.

In pursuing the question of the role of somatic sensation in the ontogenetic development of behavior, deafferentation was carried out even earlier than the day of birth. Monkey fetuses were exteriorized at the end of the second trimester of pregnancy, placed in a temperature-controlled saline bath, subjected to forelimb deafferentation, and then replaced *in utero* for the completion of embryonic development.[38] When the spinal cord was protected with a vertebral prosthesis, which substituted for the portions of the vertebrae removed during surgery, forelimb function was found to be similar in all respects to the results of deafferentation carried out on the day of birth. An additional monkey fetus was deafferented two-fifths of the way through gestation. The behavioral results for this animal were similar in all respects to those of animals deafferented two-thirds of the way through gestation.

It was mentioned above that grasp of objects between thumb and forefinger, individual finger use, and accurate eye-hand coordination did not develop spontaneously in animals deafferented prenatally or on the day of birth. With animals deafferented in adolescence, we had previously been able to behaviorally shape accurate visually directed pointing when this type of behavior was virtually nonexistent before training. Given that success, an attempt was made to use the same type of shaping approach to improve manual dexterity in monkeys deafferented on day of birth or prenatally. The first subjects were two infants that had shown a transient capacity for loose and poorly executed four-finger grasp (the second to fifth digits acting in unison without participation of the thumb) when 3 months old. Within two weeks after its appearance, even this rudimentary capacity had disappeared. At 4 months the infants were subjected to a gradual shaping procedure. Training was carried out on the preferred hand with the subject seated in a restraining chair, and the nonpreferred hand was tied down to prevent it from interfering with the procedure. Apple cubes of various sizes, and later raisins, served both as target objects and as reinforcement for desired performance at five graded training stages representing successively closer approximations to the target terminal behavior. The performance requirements at the various stages and the time spent at each stage by one animal are reported elsewhere.[38] After 31 half-hour sessions (15-1/2 hours of training) 70% of the subject's attempts involved the typical rhesus monkey prehension posture of the fingers, with the thumb being brought against the radial side of the index finger at the junction of the middle and distal phalanges. Training was continued for an additional 9 sessions, but no further improvement occurred.

Two infants had been left untrained. One expired at the age of 7 months; it had never developed thumb-forefinger prehension. The other had still not developed this behavior at 15 months, at which time a training program similar to that described above was initiated. Within 30 half-hour sessions, it progressed from a complete inability to secure objects with the fingers to thumb-forefinger prehension as good as that of animals trained at 4 months of age. This finding indicates that if there is a critical period in rhesus monkeys for the development of this category of movement, it has not ended by the 15th month after birth (the equivalent of 4 years of age in humans).

THE MECHANISM

In order to understand these data one must examine the case of adolescent and infant monkeys separately. In adolescence, substantial neurological injury usually leads to a shock-like phenomenon, whether at the level of the spinal cord (spinal shock) or brain (diaschisis or cortical shock). With regard to deafferentation, the elimination of somatosensory input results initially in a reduction within the spinal cord in the background level of excitation that maintains neurons in a subliminal state of readiness to respond. This effect is most marked in the deafferented segments of the spinal cord, where the depressed condition of motoneurons greatly elevates the threshold for incoming excitation necessary to produce movement. The early postsurgical spinal shock may also be partly due to active inhibitory processes. As time elapses following deafferentation, recovery processes that are at present incompletely understood, raise the background level of excitability of motoneurons so that movements can once again, at least potentially, be expressed. The period of spinal shock in adolescent monkeys lasts from two to six months following forelimb deafferentation.[28]

Thus, immediately after operation, the monkeys cannot use a deafferented limb; recovery from spinal shock requires considerable time. An animal with one deafferented limb tries to use that extremity in the early postoperative period, but it cannot. As a result of repeated unsuccessful attempts to use the limb, a strong tendency develops to not try to use it. This tendency persists, growing stronger with time and prolonged nonuse of the extremity, and consequently the monkeys never determine that several months after operation, the limb has become potentially useful. Moreover, the animals get along reasonably well in the laboratory environment using just three limbs.

When the movements of the intact limb are restricted several months after unilateral deafferentation, the situation changes dramatically. The animal either uses the deafferented limb or it cannot feed itself, locomote or carry out a large portion of its normal activities of daily life with any degree of efficiency. This new constraint on behavior increases the motivation to use the limb and induces the monkey to do so.

The conditioned response and shaping situations described above also involve placing major constraints on the animals' behavior. In the conditioning chamber, if the monkeys do not perform the required response, they either receive electric shock or do not receive food pellets or liquid when hungry or thirsty, respectively. Similarly, during shaping, hunger and the need to make an improved movement place a new requirement on behavior. The animals can not "get along" in either situation using just the intact forelimb, as they can in the colony environment.

Thus, the movement restriction, conditioned response, and shaping situations share a common feature; each involves a constraint-induced facilitation (CIF) of impaired improvement. This would appear to be the mechanism responsible in each case for enabling the remediation of motor ability.

In the case of monkeys deafferented on day of birth or prenatally, cortical or spinal shock would not be importantly involved in the genesis of the observed motor deficits, as in the case of animals deafferented in adolescence. In very young animals nervous system shock phenomena disappear quickly. Indeed, in the prenatally deafferented infants, surgical intervention had taken place a full two months before birth so that spinal shock could be expected to have dissipated entirely, or very nearly so, by the time extrauterine life and experimental observation began. Therefore, the failure of prehension and accurate hand-eye coordination to develop would not be due to the presence of nervous system shock, but would instead presumably be due to the absence of an educative contribution from somatic sensation in the ontogenetic development of these animals. Though the origin of their special deficit in manual dexterity would be different than the complete nonuse occurring in unilaterally deafferented adolescent monkeys, the mechanism for remediating the deficit is nevertheless the same: constraint-induced facilitation.

IMPROVING THE REHABILITATION OF MOVEMENT IN CHRONIC STROKE PATIENTS

If this analysis was correct, and given the general nature of the mechanism, it was reasoned that constraint-induced facilitation might be an appropriate approach for the rehabilitation of motor impairments due to other types of injury to the nervous system. For example, stroke in humans often leaves patients with an apparently permanent loss of function in an upper extremity, though the limb is not paralyzed. In addition, the motor deficit is preponderantly unilateral. These factors are similar to the situation after unilateral forelimb deafferentation in monkeys. It, therefore, seemed reasonable to formulate a formal protocol for simply transferring the techniques used for converting a useless limb to one that could be used extensively from unilaterally deafferented monkeys to human patients who had experienced a stroke.[29]

Preliminary application to human chronic stroke patients of one of the early conditioned response paradigms developed in primate deafferentation research had actually taken place previously and some success had been reported.[3,4] Subsequently, Wolf and coworkers took the limb restriction portion of the published protocol (but not the training component) and applied it to chronic stroke and traumatic brain injury patients, with resulting improvement in function.[16,41] This stimulated the next research effort by Taub et al.,[36] which made some modifications in the research design of Wolf and coworkers and added the training aspect of the suggested protocol[29] to the treatment of patients.

The subjects were chronic stroke patients who had experienced cerebrovascular accidents from 1 to 18 years earlier. Patients with this degree of chronicity, according to the traditional belief of the field, have presumably reached a plateau in their motor recovery and will not exhibit any further improvement for the rest of their lives. The focal criterion for inclusion in the study was the ability to extend at least 20 degrees at the wrist and 10 degrees at the fingers. Approximately 20–25% of the chronic stroke population with motor deficit are capable of meeting or exceeding this requirement,[40] and are therefore presumably optimally amenable to the treatment approach to be described.

Persons who met the study's inclusion criteria were assigned by a random process to either an experimental group or an attention-comparison group. For the experimental group, the unaffected limb was secured in a resting hand splint and then placed in a sling; the affected arm was left free. The subjects agreed to wear the movement constraint device for approximately 90% of waking hours for 12 days. On each of the 8 weekdays during this period, patients spent seven hours at the rehabilitation center and were given a variety of tasks to be carried out by the paretic upper extremity for six hours. No explicit training of any kind (including shaping) was given; the subjects simply practiced the tasks repeatedly. The purpose was primarily to provide experience in use of the affected limb. The procedures given to the comparison group were designed to focus attention on the involved extremity.[36]

Two laboratory tests of motor function[10,41] were administered to experimental and comparison subjects just before and immediately after their two-week intervention period. To summarize the findings, there were significant changes in the motor ability of the subjects whose uninvolved extremity was constrained and these changes were large. In contrast, the performance of the comparison group subjects was not significantly changed at their postintervention testing on any of the parameters measured.

A third instrument, the Motor Activity Log, provided information about motor function in the life situation and therefore addressed the critical issue of transfer from the experimental situation to the activities of daily life. The comparison subjects did not improve on this instrument reliably in relation to the year preceding their entry into the project. In contrast, the movement restriction subjects improved almost two and one-half rating steps out of six. There was virtually no overlap in the records of the two groups during treatment or during the followup period. Moreover, the treatment gains of the experimental subjects were fully maintained two years after the completion of the two weeks of treatment. Thus, the improvement was long term. New activities included: brushing teeth, combing hair, picking up a glass of water and drinking, eating with a fork or spoon, and writing, among others. There was a mean increase of 97.1% in the number of activities on the Motor Activity Log that the patients could carry out one month after restraint compared to the period before treatment. In the most dramatic case, motor improvement was sufficiently great as to permit part time clerical employment. One of this subject's main tasks was answering the phone with the unaffected hand and writing messages with the affected hand. She was thereby able to relieve a self-reported depressed state because she previously "had nothing to do except spend most of my days staring at the four walls of my apartment."

In current research[33] we have completed work with three additional chronic stroke patients given motor constraint of the unimpaired arm and, in addition, given shaping programs focused on improving the motor deficits that were greatest in each individual case. The results indicate that shaping further enhances the motor recovery induced by the constraint procedures we had previously used.

BEHAVIORAL PLASTICITY AND CORTICAL PLASTICITY

Three chapters in this volume by Merzenich and Jenkins, Pons, and Ramachandran discuss significant discoveries by their authors indicating that the adult monkey and (possibly) adult human central nervous system is capable of much greater plastic reorganization after sustaining damage than had previously been thought possible. The question is asked repeatedly whether this neuronal plasticity is related to the recovery of behavioral function after nervous system damage and, if so, whether it can be made use of to improve functional recovery. A set of techniques is described above that can produce substantial improvement in the recovery of movement after two types of damage to the nervous system. At the beginning of this chapter it was stated that one of its two goals was to explore the possible relationship between the recent discoveries concerning neuronal plasticity and the behavioral plasticity observed in connection with constraint-induced facilitation of impaired movement in our experiments. First, it would be of value to summarize the neuronal plasticity results of greatest relevance for this discussion.

NEURONAL PLASTICITY IN MONKEYS

Merzenich and his colleagues[11] reported plastic reorganization of the primary somatosensory cortex subsequent to the amputation of individual digits in adult monkeys. The representation of neighboring intact digits "invaded" the cortical space that was formerly occupied by the representation of the amputated portions of the hand. In a recent study in adult macaque monkeys, Pons and coworkers[20] reported massive reorganization of primary somatosensory cortex subsequent to sensory deafferentation. In the primary somatosensory cortex that had been deprived of inputs by deafferentation, the region that would normally be the arm area anomalously responded to tactile stimulation of the face. Moreover, there was an exact topographical isomorphism between specific facial locations of tactile stimulation and evoked responses in the (deafferented) cortical area normally representing the digits. Whereas the reorganization reported by Merzenich et al. spanned a distance of 1–2 mm, Pons et al. observed plastic changes in the cortical map that were approximately an order of magnitude greater (up to 14 mm).

SENSORY CHANGES AFTER AMPUTATION IN MAN

In human upper extremity amputees, Ramachandran,[21] this volume; Ramachandran et al.[22] reported that sensory stimuli applied to specific regions on the skin of the face or amputation stump could evoke, in an apparent parallel to the Pons et al. results, well-localized sensations in the phantoms of some amputated limbs that bore a constant topographical relationship to facial and amputation stump sites of stimulation. They referred to this phenomenon as "remapping" of the amputated limb and they and others[6,19] were of the opinion that it might be the perceptual correlate of a reorganization of the primary sensory cortex in human amputees similar to the reorganization observed in the animal studies of Merzenich et al.[11] and, especially, Pons,[18] this volume; Pons et al.[20] This is a conceptually attractive possibility both because of the parallelism in the perceptual and electrophysiological data and because it would represent the first demonstration of a relationship between cortical plasticity and post-injury functional changes. However, this proposal involves two linked hypotheses that require empirical evaluation: (1) cortical reorganization of the somatosensory map takes place in humans following upper extremity amputation (with its attendant section of major peripheral nerves) and, (2) this cortical reorganization is responsible for the remapping. Before the proposal can be accepted, both hypotheses must be shown to be correct.

MOTOR IMPROVEMENT AFTER CONSTRAINT-INDUCED FACILITATION

With respect to developing a basic understanding of the functional significance of neuronal plasticity in the adult nervous system, identification of its sensory or perceptual correlates is as important as identification of its motor correlates. However, from the practical point of view of rehabilitation medicine, the remediation of motor deficits is the major consideration for enabling individuals to establish functional independence. Stroke usually involves mixed sensory, motor and integrative effects, while somatosensory deafferentation is a sensory lesion. However, complete limb deafferentation always, and stroke often results in serious motor deficits and it is for this type of loss that constraint-induced facilitation techniques have been shown to produce improvement. To ascertain the nature of this plasticity with respect to motor function, two questions appear particularly salient. (Because the data on neuronal plasticity that are currently available come from experiments relating to somatosensory deafferentation or the somatosensory aspect of either peripheral nerve section or other interventions,[5] it would simplify matters to limit the discussion to behavioral plasticity after somatosensory deafferentation. However, all of the important considerations in this discussion apply equally to the case of motor improvement after stroke.)

First, one might ask what the mechanism(s) is that is responsible for the recovery of behavioral function in monkeys following unilateral somatosensory deafferentation in monkeys that is produced by training and movement restriction of the intact arm. The answer can be discussed in terms of two general types of processes. (1) Neuronal plasticity—the specific mechanism producing neuronal plasticity might be one or more of those discussed in the conference upon which this volume is based. (2) Behavioral plasticity—this might involve constraint-induced facilitation of impaired movement, as described above. It is important to recognize that these two types of mechanism come from two domains, nervous system function and behavior, that coexist, mutually interact, and indeed can often be resolved into one another experimentally. They are not mutually exclusive.

In terms of the current state of our knowledge, the mechanism(s) that could be responsible for behavioral recovery after deafferentation can be outlined as follows:

I. Neuronal plasticity

   A. Sprouting—cortical, subcortical and/or spinal (the formation of new synapses resulting from the growth of collateral neural processes from intact axons located near a region that has lost input because of nervous system damage; one source of input and synaptic activation is thereby replaced by another, e.g., Darlan-Smith and Gilbert[1]).

   B. Unmasking—cortical, (the activation of existing but previously unused connections, e.g., Gilbert and Wiesel[2]), subcortical and/or spinal.

   C. Merzenich-type synaptic remodeling,[11] increasing the synaptic density within the dendritic arborization of existing neurons that have fields overlapping into the region deprived of its usual input.

II. Behavioral plasticity

    A. Constraint—induced facilitation of impaired movement

    1. Initial period of nonuse

    a. Period of spinal shock—extremity cannot be used

    b. Tendency to not use extremity becomes stronger with repetition

    2. Restraint of unaffected extremity and/or training overcomes nonuse of extremity

    B. Other (?)

For the purposes of the present discussion, the most significant issue is the nature of the interaction between neuronal and behavioral plasticity. One possibility is that the two processes are complementary. First, constraint-induced facilitation could give rise to one or more of the plastic neuronal changes listed. Conversely, the behavioral change could be predicated on a prior neuronal change. Another possibility is that the observed motor improvement associated with constraint-induced facilitation might have no relation to the specific mechanisms of neuronal plasticity that are listed. This is, the data indicate that both neuronal and behavioral changes occur after somatosensory deafferentation, but the specific neural changes listed above might be independent of the observed behavioral changes. A resolution of these issues awaits further experimentation.

The second important question referred to above, relating to the nature of the behavioral plasticity recorded in our experiments, involves the finding by Pons and coworkers[20] that the deafferented zone (former arm area) in the somatosensory cortex of deafferented monkeys becomes responsive to sensory input resulting from tactile stimulation of the lower jaw. Placing to one side for the moment the issue discussed above of the specific nature of the neuronal mechanism responsible for this reorganization of the cortical somatosensory map, one might ask whether the Pons et al. phenomenon plays a role in the behavioral phenomena that occur following somatosensory deafferentation. This question is rendered particularly relevant by virtue of the fact that the monkeys studied by Pons and coworkers were deafferented 12 years earlier in my laboratory by exactly the same surgical technique as that employed with the monkeys in whom constraint-induced facilitation was discovered; their care and behavioral treatment were also the same.

The first possibility is that the cortical reorganization found by Pons et al. might be a major factor in *preventing* monkeys with unilateral deafferentation from recovering function in their single affected limb. Constraint-induced facilitation, then, would have the effect of overcoming this influence. The main consideration mitigating against this explanation is the fact, not discussed in this chapter until now, that monkeys with deafferentation of both forelimbs do not exhibit a permanent nonuse of those extremities.[8,27,28] There is an initial period of nonuse, presumably related to the presence of spinal shock, but this is followed by a spontaneous and gradual recovery of function that is usually complete within 6-12 months. After spontaneous recovery, movement is clumsy (as a result of the absence of somatic sensation), but it is extensive; the limb can be used in ambulation, climbing, thumb-finger prehension, and even individual finger use. One of the animals in the Pons et al. study[20] had received a bilateral forelimb deafferentation, and the electrophysiological results for this animal were the same as for animals receiving unilateral deafferentation. This finding indicates that cortical reorganization follows bilateral forelimb deafferentation; however, it does not inhibit the spontaneous recovery of function that occurs in these animals. Thus, it is not clear why it should do so in unilaterally deafferented animals, as this hypothesis requires.

The second possibility is essentially the opposite of the first. The suggestion would be that cortical reorganization *permits* recovery of behavioral function to take place or aids in this process, but is masked in unilaterally deafferented monkeys by the inhibitory process described above in the subsection entitled "The Mechanism." Constraint-induced facilitation overcomes this inhibitory process and thereby permits the expression of the latent motor capacity. Behavioral capacity is not masked in bilaterally deafferented animals because the inability to use either forelimb in the spinal shock period renders the animals virtually helpless. As opposed to the unilateral case, where the use of the intact forelimb gives the animals considerable functional independence, the seriously incapacitated bilateral animals retain a strong motivation to employ the deafferented limbs. The bilateral animals thus keep attempting to use their forelimbs, even after repeated lack of success, so that as motor function gradually and progressively returns, it is rapidly made use of. In light of this explanation, what might the specific role of the cortical reorganization observed by Pons et al. be in the recovery of behavioral function in deafferented animals? What is it specifically about the corital reorganization that permits behavioral recovery to take place? One suggestion is that the neuronal plasticity serves to either cause or facilitate the recovery from spinal shock. More generally, neuronal plasticity may also lead to recovery from shock after other types of nervous system damage. This may not be its only role, but it may be one of them.

The third possibility is that there is no relation between cortical reorganization and behavioral recovery following somatosensory deafferentation. As above, the resolution of these issues awaits additional experimental work.

THE POSSIBILITY OF A NEW APPROACH TO REHABILITATION OF MOVEMENT IN DEVELOPMENTALLY DISABLED HUMAN INFANTS AND CHILDREN

Are maturational windows closed for remediating physical handicaps in children? Research reported above indicates that for young monkeys given forelimb deafferentation on day of birth or prenatally, the maturational window for rehabilitating one complex type of movement, thumb-forefinger prehension, had not closed by the early to middle portion of the post-infant, juvenile period. If this work has relevance to the human case, it would suggest that there may be a great deal more behavioral plasticity in some developmentally disabled children than was previously thought to be the case, and that this behavioral plasticity could be used as the basis for the rehabilitation of some motor handicaps that would otherwise persist throughout life.

It has been found that motor status does not improve any more in developmentally disabled children given well-executed traditional physical therapy than in either untreated or attention-placebo-treated control subjects. Very substantial sums are spent on traditional physical therapy for the developmentally disabled each year, largely because society feels that these children should not be abandoned. However, there is little evidence that this expenditure does very much good. The development of effective new techniques for the rehabilitation of motor impairment has been identified as one of the greatest unmet needs of developmentally disabled children in multiple statewide Needs Assessment Surveys. The new techniques developed in this laboratory involving constraint-induced facilitation may offer promise for reducing a portion of these incapacitating motor deficits. The conditions that may be amenable to this approach include perinatal stroke and perinatal anoxial damage when the deficit is primarily unilateral. The effects of both conditions are often classified under the catchall term of cerebral palsy. In all, approximately 29% of all cerebral palsy cases involve hemiparesis.[14,15] Clinicians often note in these children an ability to initiate movement with the affected limb, but a strong tendency not to use it. Other conditions that often produce unilateral motor deficit are: brachial plexus injury (Erb's palsy) that sometimes occurs during the birth process, often during difficult breech or forceps delivery; traumatic brain injury as the result of car collision, falls and other types of accidents.

Some children who have suffered perinatal stroke and the other injuries mentioned should be as amenable to improvement with the application of constraint-induced facilitation techniques as adults. Moreover, these techniques continue to be effective even if begun years after the focal event in adults. Thus, it is possible that these techniques may also be effective well into childhood or even adolescence for individuals who have developmental disabilities as a result of perinatal nervous system injury.

ACKNOWLEDGMENTS

The research with human stroke patients was supported in part by grants from the Biomedical Research Support Grant Program, National Institutes of Health (SO7RR07178, Bethesda, MD), and the Center for Aging, University of Alabama at Birmingham. We thank Samuel L. Stover, M.D., Director, and Hugh S. Gainer, Administrator, Spain Rehabilitation Center, University of Alabama at Birmingham for their help in implementing this work.

REFERENCES

1. Darlan-Smith, C., and C. D. Gilbert. "Axonal Sprouting Accompanies Functional Reorganization in Adult Cat Striate Cortex." *Nature* **368** (1994): 737–740.
2. Gilbert, C. D., and T. N. Wiesel. *J. Neurosci.* **3** (1983): 1116–1133.
3. Halberstam, J. L., H. H. Zaretsky, B. S. Brucker, and A. Guttman. "Avoidance Conditioning of Motor Responses in Elderly Brain-Damaged Patients." *Archives of Phys. Med. & Rehab.* **52** (1971): 318–328.
4. Ince, L. P. "Escape and Avoidance Conditioning of Response in the Plegic Arm of Stroke Patients: A Preliminary Study." *Psychonomic Sci.* **16** (1969): 49–50.
5. Jenkins, W. M., M. M. Merzenich, M. T. Ochs, T. Allard, andE. Guic-Robles. "Functional Reorganization of Primary Somatosensory Cortex in Adult Owl Monkeys after Behaviorally Controlled Tactile Stimulation." *J. Neurophysiol.* **63** (1990): 82–104.
6. Katz, J. "Psychophysiological Contributions to Phantom Limbs." *Canadian J. Psych.* **37** (1992): 282–298.
7. Knapp, H. D., E. Taub, and A. J. Berman. "Effects of Deafferentation on a Conditioned Avoidance Response." *Science* **128** (1958): 842–843.
8. Knapp, H. D., E. Taub, and A. J. Berman. "Movements in Monkeys with Deafferented Forelimbs." *Exper. Neurol.* **7** (1963): 305–315.
9. Lassek, A. M. "Inactivation of Voluntary Motor Function Following Rhizotomy." *J. Neuropath. & Exper. Neurol.* **3** (1953): 83–87.
10. McCulloch, K., E. W. Cook, III, W. C. Fleming, T. A. Novack, C. S. Nepomuceno, and E. Taub. "A Reliable Test of Upper Extremity ADL Function." *Archives of Phys. Med. & Rehab.* **59** (1988): 755.
11. Merzenich, M. M., R. J. Nelson, M. P. Stryker, M. S. Cynader, A. Shoppmann, and J. M. Zook. "Somatosensory Cortical Map Changes Following Digit Amputation in Adult Monkeys." *J. Comp. Neurol.* **224** (1984): 591–605.
12. Morgan, W. G. "The Shaping Game: A Teaching Technique." *Behav. Therapy* **5** (1974): 271–272.
13. Mott, P. W., and C. S. Sherrington. "Experiments upon the Influence of Sensory Nerves upon Movement and Nutrition of the Limbs." *Proc. Roy. Soc. of London* **57** (1895): 481–488.
14. Niswander, K. R., and M. Gordon. "The Collaborative Perinatal Project." In *The Women and Their Pregnancies. Department of Health, Education and Welfare Publication Number* 73–379. 1972.
15. Nelson, K. B., and J. H. Ellenburg. "Epidemiology of Cerebral Palsy." In *Advances in Neurology*, Vol. 19. New York: Raven Press, 1978.

16. Ostendorf, C. G., and S. L. Wolf. "Effect of Forced Use of the Upper Extremity of a Hemiplegic Patient on Changes in Function." *J. Am. Phys. Therapy Assoc.* **61** (1981): 1022–1028.

17. Panyan, M. V. *How to Use Shaping.* Lawrence, KS: H & H Enterprises, 1980.

18. Pons, T. P. "Abstract: Lesion-Induced Cortical Plasticity." This volume.

19. Pons, T. P. "Response to Ramachandran, Rogers-Ramachandran and Stewart." *Science* **258** (1992): 1160.

20. Pons, T. P., P. E. Garraghty, A. K. Ommaya, J. H. Kaas, E. Taub, and M. M. Mishkin. "Massive Cortical Reorganization after Sensory Deafferentation in Adult Macaques." *Science* **252** (1991): 1857–1860.

21. Ramachandran, V. S. "Plasticity in the Adult Human Brain: Is There Reason for Optimism?" This volume.

22. Ramachandran, V. S., D. Rogers-Ramachandran, and M. Stewart. "Perceptual Correlates of Massive Cortical Reorganization." *Science* **258** (1992): 1159–1160.

23. Risley, T. R., and D. M. Baer. "Operant Behavior Modification: The Deliberate Development of Behavior." In *Review of Child Development Research*, Vol. III, Development and Social Action, edited by M. Caldwell, and H. N. Riccuiti. Chicago: University of Chicago Press, 1973.

24. Skinner, B. F. *The Behavior of Organisms.* New York: Appleton-Century-Crofts, 1938.

25. Skinner, B. F. *The Technology of Teaching.* New York: Appleton-Century-Crofts, 1968.

26. Stein, B. M., and M. W. Carpenter. "Effects of Dorsal Rhizotomy upon Subthalamic Dyskinesia in the Monkey." *Archives of Neurology* **13** (1965): 567–583.

27. Taub, E. "Motor Behavior following Deafferentation in the Developing and Motorically Mature Monkey." In *Neural Control of Locomotion*, edited by R. Herman, S. Grillner, H. J. Ralston, P. S. G. Stein, and D. Stuart, 675–705. New York: Plenum Press, 1976.

28. Taub, E. "Movement in Nonhuman Primates Deprived of Somatosensory Feedback" In *Exercise and Sports Sciences Reviews*, Vol. 4, 335–374. Santa Barbara: Journal Publishing Affiliates, 1977.

29. Taub, E. "Somatosensory Deafferentation Research with Monkeys: Implications for Rehabilitation Medicine" In *Behavioral Psychology in Rehabilitation Medicine: Clinical Applications*, edited by L. P. Ince, 371–401. New York: Williams & Wilkins, 1980.

30. Taub, E. "A New Approach to Treatment in Physical Medicine." In *Clinical Applied Psychophysiology*, edited by J. G. Carlson, A. R. Seifert, and N. Birbaumer, 185–220. New York: Plenum Press.

31. Taub, E., R. Bacon, and A. J. Berman. "The Acquisition of a Trace-Conditioned Avoidance Response after Deafferentation of the Responding Limb." *J. Comp. & Physiol. Psychol.* **58** (1965): 275–279.

32. Taub, E., and A. J. Berman. "Avoidance Conditioning in the Absence of Relevant Proprioceptive and Exteroceptive Feedback." *J. Comp. & Physiol. Psychol.* **56** (1963): 1012–1016.
33. Taub, E., J. Crago, L. D. Burgio, T. E. Groomes, E. W. Cook, III, S. C. Deluca, and N. E. Miller. "An Operant Approach to Rehabilitation Medicine." *J. Exper. Anal. Behav.* **61** (1994): 281–293.
34. Taub, E., S. J. Ellman, and A. J. Berman. "Deafferentation in Monkeys: Effect on Conditioned Grasp Response." *Science* **151** (1966): 593–594.
35. Taub, E., I. A. Goldberg, and P. E. Taub. "Deafferentation in Monkeys: Pointing at a Target Without Visual Feedback." *Exper. Neurol.* **46** (1975): 178–186.
36. Taub, E., N. E. Miller, T. A. Novack, E. W. Cook, III, W. D. Fleming, C. S. Nepomuceno, J. S. Connell, and J. E. Crago. "Technique to Improve Chronic Motor Deficit after Stroke." *Archives of Phys. Med. & Rehab.* **74** (1993): 347–354.
37. Taub, E., P. N. Perrella, and G. Barro. "Behavioral Development Following Forelimb Deafferentation on Day of Birth in Monkeys With and Without Binding." *Science* **181** (1973): 959–960.
38. Taub, E., P. N. Perrella, E. A. Miller, and G. Barro. "Diminution of Early Environmental Control through Perinatal and Prenatal Somatosensory Deafferentation." *Biol. Psychiatry* **10** (1975): 609–626.
39. Twitchell, T. E. "Sensory Factors in Purposive Movement." *J. Neurophysiol.* **17** (1954): 239–254.
40. Wolf, S. L., and S. A. Binder-Macloud. "Electromyographic Biofeedback Applications to the Hemiplegic Patient: Changes in Upper Extremity Neuromuscular and Functional Status." *J. Am. Phys. Therapy Assoc.* **63** (1983): 1393–1403.
41. Wolf, S. L., D. E. Lecraw, L. A. Barton, and B. B. Jann. "Forced Use of Hemiplegic Upper Extremities to Reverse the Effect of Learned Nonuse among Chronic Stroke and Head-Injured Patients." *Exper. Neurol.* **104** (1989): 125–132.
42. Wylie, R. M., and C. F. Tyner. "Weight-Lifting by Normal and Deafferented Monkeys: Evidence for Compensatory Changes in Ongoing Movements." *Brain Res.* **219** (1981): 172–177.
43. Wylie, R. M., and C. F. Tyner. "Performance of a Weight-Lifting Task by Normal and Deafferented Monkeys." *Behav. Neurosci.* **108** (1989): 273–282.

Joan Stiles
University of California, San Diego

Plasticity and Development: Evidence from Children with Early Occurring Focal Brain Injury

The term plasticity has been applied to processes operative at many levels of the neural and cognitive systems, from metabolic activity, to the workings of cell assemblies, to behavior. Separate lines of evidence for the plasticity of neural systems come from a range of clinical and basic science disciplines. It could be argued that it is problematic to use a common term to describe the patterns of flexibility observed at these very different levels of the neural system. Plasticity in each case may well refer to quite disparate functions. However, there are commonalties in the usage of the term plasticity which suggest that the joint consideration of data from these very different levels of inquiry may be quite profitable. Work on the neural mechanisms of learning have demonstrated that very rapid changes in patterns of neural connectivity are associated with change in behavior (see Jeo et al.,[39] this volume). Animal and human studies of brain development have shown that massive overproduction and subsequent loss of neurons and synapses is a basic feature of brain development.[15,32,36,70] Recent studies of adult humans (see Ramachandran,[72]) and animals (see Merznick and Jenkins,[51] this volume) have shown that even established neural systems have the capacity for reorganization and change. Developmental clinical neuropsychology has long-reported evidence for behavioral resiliency following early focal brain injury in children. Recent animal models of early injury to specific brain systems support and extend this view (see Webster et al.,[96] this volume). Taken together, these lines of evidence suggest that plasticity is an ubiquitous property of neural and cognitive systems.

In each of the cases sited above, the term plasticity is used to refer to a process, that is, to some dynamic feature of the system which brings about change at a structural or functional level. This change is generally adaptive in that plastic systems marshall or recruit new or different resources. In addition, plastic change is not haphazard. A principle of system organization underlies descriptions of plasticity even under nonoptimal conditions. This organization reflects both structural features of the system and the system's response to its environment or local context.

This chapter will focus on the construct of plasticity as it has been used in the literature from developmental clinical neuropsychology. Research in this field has long established children's resilience to behavioral and cognitive deficit in the wake of early neurological insult.[40,47,82] The common explanation for this finding is that the developing system is "plastic" in that it can respond to effects of early injury in a way that the adult system cannot. This chapter will argue that the specific application of the construct within clinical neuropsychology is limited and does not take account of recent data from studies of brain development, and of plasticity in adult neural systems (see also Almli and Finger,[3] for recent arguments). Data from these three areas, that is developmental neuropsychology, brain development and reorganization in adult brains, are mutually informative, and conjointly offer an alternative view on the nature and course of development following early brain injury. Based on the convergence evidence from these three fields of study, it will be argued that plasticity is a fundamental property of functioning neural and cognitive systems. It is not, as has been at least implicitly suggested within various subdisciplines, a system response to pathological insult, nor is it a property unique to development. Rather, plasticity is a basic feature of neural and cognitive operation which is most apparent under the catastrophic conditions of insult or during the early stages of system organization and development.

PERSPECTIVES ON PLASTICITY: DEVELOPMENTAL NEUROPSYCHOLOGY, BRAIN DEVELOPMENT, AND REORGANIZATION IN ADULTS

Within the field of developmental clinical neuropsychology, traditional views of cognitive and linguistic development following early focal brain injury have been quite optimistic. The available behavioral data suggested that the brain is sufficiently plastic early in development to compensate for insult. Recovery from pre- or perinatal injury has been considered to be essentially complete. However, with later occurring injuries the neurological capacity for functional recovery decreases. This decrease is accompanied by a concomitant decline in the prognosis for behavioral recovery.

Evidence for this pattern of functional recovery comes from a number of sources. Two very influential investigators were Margaret Kennard and Eric Lenneberg. In the 1930s Kennard reported the results of a series of experimental studies with monkeys examining the effects of early brain injury on motor system development. In an influential paper published in 1936, Kennard reported two case studies focused on motor development in infant monkeys lesioned in the perinatal period. In one case a left hemispherectomy was performed at ten days of age, in the other left motor and premotor areas were ablated. In reporting the results of the hemispherectomy case Kennard noted, "The immediate recovery after the operation was surprising. Within 24 hours the animal walked about, using all four extremities, with only a slight lag in those of the right side...it disappeared gradually during the second month of life. . . . The animal then developed at the normal rate and showed no motor deficit" (p. 142). Similar results were reported for the case of lesions to specific motor areas. The dramatic recovery, or more appropriately development, of motor skills in the absence of cortical regions usually responsible for their mediation, provided strong evidence for functional and neural plasticity in the developing brain.

The work of Eric Lenneberg has also been instrumental in shaping the clinical neuropsychological view of early brain plasticity. In 1967 Lenneberg published a book entitled *The Biological Foundations of Language.* In that book he reviewed a large body of data on language development in children with either early focal brain injury, or hemispherectomy resulting from intractable seizure conditions of early developmental onset. Based upon these data Lenneberg, too, concluded that the capacity for functional recovery is excellent when injury occurs early in life, and that later occurring injury produces progressively poorer outcomes:

> Between the ages of three and the early teens the possibility for primary language acquisition continues to be good, the individual appears to be most sensitive to stimuli at this time and to preserve some innate flexibility for the organization of brain function to carry out the complex integration of subprocesses necessary for the smooth elaboration of speech and language. After puberty, the ability for self-organization and adjustment to the physiological demands of verbal behavior quickly declines. The brain behaves as if it has become set in its ways and primary basic language skills not acquired by that time, except for articulation, usually remain deficit for life (1967, p. 158).

Although strong views of neural plasticity such as Lenneberg's have been debated particularly in recent years[22,24,25,27,38,48,84,88,92,97] (also see later discussion in this chapter of longitudinal data from children with early brain injury), the idea that the developing brain has an essentially unlimited capacity for reorganization and recovery has remained influential within the clinical community. Indeed, there is a large body of empirical data showing that the effects of early injury are markedly attenuated relative to those of injury occurring later in life.[4,5,6,21,22,25,80,83,87,88]

However, attempts to explain why the timing of injury should have such dramatically different effects on behavioral outcome have been limited. Most accounts have suggested that some kind of ancillary system is marshalled, at least for a brief period early in development, in response to pathological insult. The operation of these ancillary systems accounts for the observations of early behavioral plasticity.

A variety of possible ancillary systems have been described in the neuropsychological literature. The principles of "equipotentiality and mass action," most clearly articulated by Lashley,[46] assert that it is the mass of tissue removed and not the tissue location that is critical to outcome. This account assumes that, at least in the initial stages of development, systems are diffusely organized and functionally underspecified. "Sparing of function" refers to a compensatory mechanism whereby new neurophysiological and behavioral processes are recruited to serve the function normally carried out by the damaged brain area. The notion of "sparing" is often closely associated with the "crowding hypothesis" which asserts that a neural system can reorganize or alter its mode of operation in order to replace functions usually mediated by another. The most commonly sited example of sparing and crowding comes from studies of language functioning following early unilateral brain injury. There are many well-documented examples of right-hemisphere mediated language function in patients with early left hemisphere injury.[54,82] The crowding hypothesis suggests that language moves into right brain areas homologous to the normal left hemisphere language sites, displacing spatial functions assumed to be carried out normally by these brain regions. "Functional redundancy" assumes that, early in development, redundant, secondary systems are available to take over functioning in cases where the primary system is lost. In the normal course of development, these secondary systems are gradually recruited into alternative roles, and thus lose their capacity to serve as back-up systems.

These accounts of plasticity all evoke the idea of compensation in one form or another. There is the sense that plasticity serves a kind of failsafe, or civil defense, function. In each account, plasticity is described as a kind of reactive function designed to guard against the effects of neural assault early in development. Along with the "civil defense" metaphor comes a second set of assumptions concerned with functional priority. Embodied in the accounts of right hemisphere crowding effects or preferential sparing of language is the idea that in the wake of neurological insult, the neural system will give preference to language functions. Indeed, there is an abundance of data documenting change in neural mediation of cognitive and linguistic functions, and those findings often include evidence of normal or near normal language functioning. These findings are not in question. However, the description that this shift in mediation comes about via preferential sparing of one function and crowding out of another is problematic. Such an account would almost literally have language packing its lexicon in one suitcase and its grammar in another, and taking off across the corpus callosum to take up residence in the homologous right-hemisphere-brain regions. Once there, in the true fashion of a carpetbagger, it not only moves in but it also takes over the local government, as evidenced by the well-documented decline in what have been considered to be more traditional right hemisphere mediated activities. However, this account does not address the question of why language is preferentially spared. What is the evolutionary pressure to select language over other systems such as visual spatial processing or motor functioning? Why would preference in the elaborate civil defense network be given to language when other functions may be arguably more central to the survival of the organism?

These kinds of accounts of plasticity present unlikely scenarios. Indeed going back to investigators like Kennard, we find early speculation in her published writings that the kinds of plasticity observed following early injury may not represent a system response to insult. Kennard[40] suggested instead that a more basic, developmental process may account for the kinds of functional change observed in the early lesioned animals. Her ideas were speculative, given her limited database. But she postulated that perhaps it is the inherent plasticity of developing systems that could account for the superior outcomes encountered following brain injury.

Subsequent animal studies of brain development support Kennard's early speculations about the nature of plasticity of developing neural systems. Hubel and Wiesel's[35] seminal studies on development of ocular dominance columns highlighted the importance of both specific input and timing of experience on the development of conventional patterns of cortical organization. Recent literature on the role of subtractive events in brain development demonstrate the dynamic nature of change in the neural substrate. The now extensive literature on naturally occurring cell death,[16,26,32,36,37,62,63,65,66] indicates that from 20–80% of neurons in different cortical regions are lost in the course of development. Much of this loss occurs relatively late in the prenatal and in the postnatal period, following the expression of many cell characteristics including the projection of cell processes and formation of synapses. Analogous patterns of initial exuberance and subsequent loss have been reported for synaptic connections.[13,14,15,36,70,71] This massive synapse loss and cell death appears to be governed by competitive processes.[14] Availability of neurotrophic agents[69] stimulation of afferents projecting to target sites[64] and stimulation emanating from the target zone[62] have all been implicated as contributors to the competitive processes. Some of the activity critical to the competitive shaping of the neural system is endogenous,[34] but much of the input comes from sources remote from the core system or external to the organism.[66] Cowan[15] has suggested that one of the primary functions of synapse loss is to achieve population matching, that is, the optimization of patterns of connectivity within the neural system.

Work from a number of sources suggests that optimal patterns of brain organization are not necessarily fixed, but indeed depend on the configuration and functioning of patterns of connectivity in local regions of the brain. Studies of cross-modal plasticity[28,29,89,90] have shown that if early visual relay sites are eliminated, retinal axons will project to nonvisual targets. For example, Sur et al.[89] ablated the visual cortex and superior colliculus, and deafferented the major input pathways to the medial geniculate nucleus in one-day old ferrets. He thus eliminated two major visual relays, and reduced input to a major auditory relay. The retinal projections in these animals invaded the MGN, thus establishing a visual input pathway to auditory cortex via MGN. Electrophysiological recordings from these animals showed that the auditory cortex responded to visual input. In an important related series of studies, Neville[55,56,57,58,59,60] has recorded electrophysiological responses to visual input over traditional auditory areas of the brains of congenitally deaf adult human subjects.

Tissue transplantation work has shown, at least for very young animals, neurons from different regions of neocortex can survive and adapt to conditions in cortical regions other than the one to which they initially migrated. For example,[61] transplanted sections of sensorimotor and visual cortex from the brain of a late fetal rat into the opposite sites in the brain of a newborn rat. They found that the cells not only survived the transplant, they began to take on characteristics of cells in the host environment. Projections from layer V of the transplanted visual cortex extended permanent axons to the spinal cord, a subcortical target for sensorimotor neurons. Sensorimotor tissue transplanted into visual cortex initially extended axons to the spinal cord, but these connections were subsequently lost. However, these cells also extended axons to the superior colliculus, a subcortical visual target, which were retained. Transplanted tissue in both areas established callosal and thalamic projections typical of their host environment.

Recent studies of adult animals have shown that this flexibility in the organization of neural systems is not limited to the early phases of development (see chapters by Merznick and Jenkins[51] and Pons,[68] this volume). Studies examining the reorganization of cortical maps in motor and somatosensory cortex, and in thalamus have demonstrated that the capacity of the neural system for plastic adaptation is not lost. However, the range over which reorganization can occur in adults may be more limited than that observed in the developing nervous system. Recent work by Ramachandran[72] suggests that neural plasticity is a property of the adult human brain as well.

COGNITIVE AND LINGUISTIC DEVELOPMENT IN CHILDREN WITH EARLY FOCAL BRAIN INJURY

According to traditional accounts in developmental neuropsychology, the behavioral consequences of early focal brain injury are minimal. Children appear to be quite resilient, in comparison with adults. They recover, or more precisely acquire, cognitive functioning following injury to the brain that would leave adults permanently impaired.[2,11,12,31,33,43,47,49,73] However, in the past few years, retrospective studies of adults and older children whose injuries occurred early in life have used somewhat more detailed measures and found evidence of specific cognitive deficits within the general pattern of recovery.[17,20,22,25,41,42,80,81,93,94,97,98] The profiles of deficit in the population are generally described as subtle, or mild, compared with impairment observed among adults with similar injury. The retrospective studies suggested that it might be possible to identify cognitive deficits in young children with focal brain injury. Recent prospective studies of young children with congenital or early acquired focal brain lesions support this view.

The central issues underlying the study of children with early focal brain injury focus on identification of early deficit and documentation of developmental patterns. These studies seek to determine: (1) whether specific deficits are evident early in development, (2) whether the association between pattern of behavioral deficit and site of brain injury among children are comparable to the patterns of association observed among adult patients with injury to comparable brain areas, (3) whether there is evidence of persistent behavioral deficit over time, or significant recovery of function, and (4) whether patterns of behavioral deficit change over time?

The data presented in the remainder of this section provides a brief overview of recent studies of spatial and linguistic development in a group of children who have been tested as part of a large prospective study of behavioral development following early focal brain injury. This is a multi-site project based primarily in San Diego and New York. The data from this project document deficits very early in both spatial and linguistic development. This suggests that even very early the maturing brain is not equipotential for all functions. On the other hand, the observed patterns of deficit tend to be less severe and they do not always follow the right/left and anterior/posterior profiles familiar in the literature on focal brain injury in adults.

DESCRIPTION OF SUBJECTS

The children in this population were identified as having had localized brain injury occurring before the end of the first 6-months of life. Focal brain injury is a comparatively rare disorder in young children. The most common cause of localized injury in young children is stroke. In all cases, the site and extent of neural involvement was documented using either CT scan or MRI. Children were excluded from the population if their medical history or imaging study indicated evidence of multiple lesions, disorders with potential of more global damage such as congenital viral infection, maternal drug or alcohol abuse, bacterial meningitis, encephalitis, severe anoxia, or chronic lesions such as tumor or arteriovenus malformation. Within the population children were classified by site of lesion, which included whether their lesion was on the left or right side of the brain, and which cortical lobe or lobes were involved. The children in this population typically do well on most standard behavioral indices. They do not manifest gross cognitive deficits. They score within the normal range on standardized IQ measures and usually attend school in mainstream classrooms.

SPATIAL COGNITIVE DEVELOPMENT

The studies of spatial cognitive development in children with focal brain injury have focused on spatial analytic functioning, which is an important basic spatial ability that is known to be differentially affected by localized right or left posterior brain damage in adults.[79] Spatial analysis is defined as the ability both to segment a pattern into a set of constituent parts, and to integrate those parts into a coherent whole. Studies of adults[7,18,19,30,44,45,50,67,77,78,91,95] have shown that injury to left posterior brain regions results in difficulty defining the parts of a spatial array, while injury to right posterior brain regions results in difficulty with the configural aspects of spatial pattern analysis.

Studies of children with right or left posterior injury have shown that they have patterns of deficit similar to those observed in adults. However, the deficits are less severe among children than adults, and children appear to overcome their deficits more readily. In the early preschool period, children with both right and left posterior brain injury are impaired in spontaneous and structured block play tasks, but the profiles of impairment differ by side of injury. At about 3 years of age, children with left posterior injury produce simplified constructions using very elementary combinatorial relations.[87] The constructions include simple stacks and lines which are typical of the constructions produced by 2 year old normal children. The children with left posterior injury improve over time, reaching ceiling level of performance, but much later than their normal peers.[85] The profile of behavior on these tasks is best described as delayed. The children eventually master the task and the sequence of development mirrors that of normal children, however the time course is protracted. Whereas normal children master these simple block construction tasks by about 3.5 years, the children with left hemisphere injury do not reach ceiling levels until about 5 years. The profiles of development for children with right hemisphere injury is quite different. At about 3-years, they produce simplified constructions consisting mainly of stacks and lines. However, as the children develop and begin to produce more complex constructions, the type of construction diverges markedly from normal. By about 4 years, the children very systematically produce heaps or piles of blocks which lack structure and organization. Their use of combinatorial relations becomes more complex, but the constructions lack coherence. Like the children with left hemisphere injury, the children with right hemisphere injury eventually achieve ceiling performance on these tasks, but the developmental profile is clearly deviant and mastery is very late, about 5.5 to 6 years.

One important question that arises from the data on these early spatial tasks is whether the improvement observed on the block construction tasks reflects a generalized improvement in spatial skills or whether improvement is more limited. The preschool period is a time of rapid change, and these children are developing a wide range of cognitive and linguistic skills. Children may be able to marshall this growing repertoire of skills to master the simple block construction task, but on more challenging tasks, tasks appropriate for older children, a persistent, underlying deficit in spatial analytic functioning may be apparent. Indeed, data from several tasks suggest that this is the case.

In one task, 5- to 6-year-old children were asked to reproduce from memory a series of hierarchical forms. Hierarchical forms consist of a set of small letters or geometric shapes arranged to form a larger letter or shape. Work by Delis, Robertson, and Efron[19] with adult stroke patients has shown that patients with left posterior injury have difficulty reproducing the small letters in such a task. They produce the larger letter, but fail to include the small forms. By contrast patients with right posterior injury, produce the small letters but fail to arrange them in the configuration of the larger letter. Work by Stiles, Dukette, and Nass[86] has shown that between about 5 and 6-years of age, the children with early injury show a similar pattern. Children with left posterior injury fail to produce the small letters showing a deficit as least as marked as adults on this task; children with right posterior injury, while not as impaired as their adult counterparts, use construction strategies that indicate difficulty with the global configuration. By about 7 years of age most children show marked improvement on this task. They are able to retain information about both levels of the pattern hierarchy and to reproduce them following a delay. Evidence of improvement among the children on this task is particularly important , because it is a task for which adult patients do not show improvement. The children's improvement on this task is accompanied, once again, by evidence of persistent deficit on another, more challenging task. Preliminary data from a study using the Rey-Osterrieth Complex Figure show that at 7 to 8 years of age the children with focal brain injury are impaired in their ability to copy the form compared to normal children.[1]

The data from this series of spatial tasks suggest that early focal brain injury results in well-defined deficits of spatial analytic functioning. The association between site of injury and profile of behavioral impairment is similar to that reported for adult patients. Further, the deficits appear to persist over time. Tasks which are challenging for the children at different points in development provide age-specific indices of impairment. Although the specific tasks that are sensitive to deficit are not the same across development, the profile of impairment across tasks is consistent over time. It should also be noted that this changing metric of impairment flags an important difference between the child and adult populations. Children show a consistent pattern of improvement on individual measures of spatial analytic ability. At each point in development, measures that present a challenge (that is, a challenge for both normal children and children with focal brain injury) also provide an index of deficit. Over time, and with development, the children's performance on individual tasks consistently improves. The children are able to compensate for their deficits in ways that adults apparently cannot. It is this capacity to compensate for deficit that defines the concept of mild or subtle impairment in the child population. Children's performance on tasks during the period when they are most challenging cannot be described as mildly impaired. The heaps of blocks produced by children with right hemisphere injury do not constitute a subtle impairment of spatial integrative ability. The initial performance of children with left hemisphere injury on the hierarchical forms task is identical to that of adult patients, reflecting a comparable level of deficit. What is different about the children is that, on a task by task basis, their performance improves. Over time, they are able to compensate in ways that adults cannot. It is in that sense that children's deficits are milder than those of adults.

LANGUAGE DEVELOPMENT

Studies of the very earliest phases of language development in children with focal brain injury have provided a very different profile of development than that observed in the studies of spatial analytic development. Virtually every child in the population was delayed in the early stages of language acquisition.[48,92] That is, regardless of where the child's injury occurred, the course of language acquisition was affected. This finding was unexpected and stands in sharp contrast to the profile of linguistic functioning following focal injury in adult patients. In the vast majority of adults, language is mediated by regions of the left frontal and temporal lobes of the brain. Injury to left posterior brain regions typically results in a receptive form of aphasia in which comprehension is compromised, while productive language remains relatively intact. By contrast injury to more anterior brain areas results in the reverse profile, where productive language is affected while comprehension is relatively spared.

Studies from a number of laboratories examining the effects of early and later acquired focal brain injury are consistent in suggesting that the effects of early injury are less pronounced than those of later injury,[4,20,23,75,76,94] and that associations between profile of impairment and site or size of lesion are less consistent than among adult patients.[8,9] Most of these studies examine children beyond the first phases of language acquisition, at a point when children had already acquired most of the critical features of the language. The studies presented in this section focus on the very earliest phases of language acquisition. They focus on development in the first years of life, when children are engaged in the process of mastering the basics of language.

Marchman, Miller, and Bates[48] reported the results of a longitudinal study of five children: two with left posterior injury, two with left anterior injury, and one with right anterior injury. The children were studied between 10 and 22 months of age and compared with 10 normal controls. All of the children with focal brain injury were delayed in all aspects of communicative development. An analysis of their very early phonological production, that is, their babbling, showed that even though the children vocalized as much as controls, both the form and content of the babbling was deviant. The children did show improvement over time. However, that improvement was not uniform across children. The children with left posterior injury showed the longest delays.

Thal, Marchmanet et al.[92] examined a group of 18 children, focusing on the acquisition of first words and early grammar. They reported that all of the children in their sample were delayed in expressive language regardless of lesion site. However, different patterns were associated with injury to different sites. Children with left hemisphere injury showed near normal comprehension and delayed production; while children with right hemisphere injury were either delayed in both comprehension and production, or showed greater impairment for comprehension. Once again, at this slightly later period in language acquisition, the profile of delay regardless of lesion site was evident.

The group of children with left posterior injury provide more specific information about the mapping of deficit to lesion site. Recall that adults with left posterior injury typically present with a receptive form of aphasia, specifically they show preserved production and impaired comprehension. The children in the subgroup with left posterior lesions showed the opposite profile, that is they showed marked delays in expressive language at all phases of development, with relatively preserved comprehension. Specifically, Marchman et al.[48] found evidence for pronounced delays in phonological development, and Thal et al.[92] showed evidence for delay in the first stages in word production (but not comprehension). A preliminary study from a different sample of older children with left posterior injury suggests that these children are also delayed in the early phases of expressive grammar. In short, damage to left posterior brain regions may be associated generally with delays in expressive language, thus presenting a very different profile from that of adults. Bates, Thal, and Janowsky[10] have suggested that these findings may reflect developmental changes in cortical specialization for language, including changes in lateralization and changes along the anterior/posterior axis.

Finally, available evidence on language functioning in the school-age period, suggests that children with focal brain injury show a remarkable degree of recovery. Evidence from a number of laboratories indicate that by about 7 years of age linguistic deficits in this population are subtle and involve fairly complex aspects of grammar and discourse.[74,75,76]

Studies of language acquisition following early focal brain injury present a very different profile from that of spatial cognitive functioning. While specific and well-defined impairment of linguistic functioning is evident at least early in development, the association between deficit and site of injury do not conform well to patterns observed among adult patients. Injury to widely dispersed regions of the brain appear to affect language acquisition. Injury to traditionally described left hemisphere language areas, does not produce the classical patterns of adult aphasia. There are also indications that children show considerable improvement with development, and typically achieve highly functional levels of language by the early school-age period.

PLASTICITY AND DEVELOPMENT AFTER EARLY BRAIN INJURY

These longitudinal studies of the effects of early focal brain injury on subsequent linguistic and cognitive functioning present a very different view than those offered in the traditional literature on neuropsychological development. Across domains children showed evidence of initial, but subtle, deficit. However, both the extent to which deficits persist and the consistency with which the mapping of functional deficit to site of injury correspond to patterns observed in adults varies by domain. These data do not present a uniform pattern which can be easily described by any of the traditional models such as sparing, crowding, or redundancy.

In the early stages of language acquisition, language is not spared. Indeed it appears to be affected by lesions to widely distributed brain regions. Mills, Coffey, and Neville's[52,53] data on the distribution of electrophysiological responses of young children to linguistic input suggests why this may be so. In the earliest phases of normal language development when children are acquiring their first words, widely distributed regions of the brain participate in language processing. Patterns of activation are bilateral and involve both anterior and posterior brain regions. This widely distributed pattern of activation may reflect the fact that the task of processing linguistic input during the initial stages of language acquisition is different from the task of processing language once linguistic skills develop. Given these data, it is not surprising to find that young children with pre- or perinatal brain injury have difficulty acquiring language—regardless of where in the brain their lesion occurs. If processing language is initially a resource-intensive neural function, then injury to many brain regions could result in delayed acquisition. Mills, Coffey and Neville's[52,53] data also show that when normal children become more efficient users of their language, the distribution of brain electrical activity becomes focused on traditional left hemisphere language areas. One interpretation of these data is that as children become efficient processors of language, they require fewer neural resources and language processing becomes centered in those regions best suited to processing linguistic information. If this is the case, then it is not surprising to find either that most children with focal brain injury eventually achieve a highly functional level of linguistic ability, or that nontraditional brain regions eventually mediate language. If language processing is initially widely distributed with an optimal neural processing region only gradually acquired, then perhaps there are multiple solutions to the problem of neural mediation of language.

Data from spatial-analytic processing present a very different profile. Children do show evidence of subtle, persistent deficit following early brain injury, and the mapping of site of injury to functional deficit is consistent with those observed among adults. These data suggest that the neural system for processing spatial information is much more highly specified than is the system for processing language. Thus, there are domain specific, or information specific, differences on the extent to which the neural system can respond flexibly to early insult. The demand for processing spatial information is phylogenetically much older than the demand for processing linguistic information, and the neural substrate may be much more constrained. Thus there is less capacity to achieve an "alternative solution" to the problem of processing spatial-analytic information. It should be noted, however, that the effects of early injury on spatial processing are markedly attenuated relative to those of later injury, suggesting some capacity for reorganization and functional compensation within the more constrained spatial system. Finally, addressing the traditional neuropsychological views, the compromise of spatial abilities following left hemisphere injury does not require evocation of a crowding hypothesis. There is ample data showing that the left hemisphere participates in critical aspects of spatial analytic processing, thus injury to the left hemisphere could, itself, account for impairment in spatial processing. Thus, while there may well be a differential distribution of attenuated resources, the usual model of language crowding out space is unwarranted.

A major difference between the current view and that of traditional developmental neuropsychology is the focus on process. Traditional accounts treat cognitive and linguistic functioning as though they are objects which reside within specifically defined brain loci. These loci are treated as centers for mediating particular functions. Thus language is localized to language-specific centers in the brain. By this account, early brain plasticity is viewed as the capacity, early in development, for a behavioral object, like language, to move from the normal language center to some other neural location in the event of some catastrophe. If language is instead viewed as a process operating on specific types of information, and the neural substrate as a highly organized but flexible mediator of information processing then a fundamentally different view of plasticity after early brain injury follows. This view takes account both the central role of plasticity in normal brain development, and the now quite large body of data showing that neural systems retain at least limited capacity for reorganization into adulthood.

In conclusion, the current account of development following early brain injury diverges from traditional explanations. It is proposed that the developmental profiles of children with pre- or perinatal brain injury reflect the perturbation of a normally operating system. An account of the differences observed in the behaviors of adults and children following injury, does not require the postulation of specialized, early, transient systems. Children do not show resiliency because of any ancillary or back-up modification system. Functional systems are not redundant, spared, or crowded out. In normal development, cognitive and linguistic systems develop through the interaction of a highly organized but flexible neural substrate and input. Both the neural substrate and the cognitive system are modified by the processes involved in this functional interaction. A property of the normally developing neural system is flexibility and adaptability. There is abundant evidence from the literature on neural development that the brain organization is profoundly affected by input to the system. Indeed, the normal mature patterns of organization requires specific kinds of input. The capacity to adapt is attenuated with the development of the system, but it is becoming increasingly clear that the *potential* for neural reorganization is not lost. Rather, the progressive commitment of neural resources, which is a fundamental property of development, limits the range of the system's capacity to adapt.

Early focal brain injury perturbs the normal operation of the system. Injury reduces neural processing capacity, but it does so in specific and well-defined ways. Individual structures and regions of cortex are lost; those structures and regions had specialized functional properties. The loss of such specialized structures results in a nonoptimal neural system, but early in development it is one that is sufficiently uncommitted in its organization allowing it to retain a significant degree of processing flexibility. Processes, such as language, which are initially widely distributed in their functioning are at first affected by the perturbation of the system regardless of where it occurs, but by virtue of their functional distribution they are more flexible, have more degrees of freedom in the ways in which development can proceed, and thus show considerable improvement. Spatial analytic processing is much more highly constrained in its initial neural specification; that is, it is more reliant on specific neural systems. Injury to those systems results in deficits which resemble the patterns found in adults, because the system does not have the capacity at any point in development to adapt to an alternative mode of processing. The attenuation of deficit observed with spatial analysis may reflect a much more limited and more localized capacity for reorganization.

In summary, functional plasticity is, itself, an important basic process. It is not a reserve system which is recruited in the wake of insult. It plays a central role in the development of neural systems, but it is neither a transient function, nor one that is unique to developing organisms. With development, neural systems stabilize and optimal patterns of functioning are achieved. Stabilization reduces, but does not eliminate, the capacity of the system to adapt. As the system stabilizes, plasticity becomes a less prominent feature of neural functioning, but it is not absent from the adult system. This is a very different view of plasticity than that offered by traditional neuropsychological accounts. It is an important revision of the definition of early functional plasticity. It is a view that not only takes account of the data from children with early occurring brain injury, but is also consistent with recent data on early brain development, and plasticity in adult organisms.

REFERENCES

1. Akshoomof, N. A., and J. Stiles. "Effects of Early Focal Brain Injury on the Ability to Copy a Complex Figure." Poster to be presented at Cognitive Neuroscience Society Inaugural Meeting, San Francisco, March 27-29, 1994.
2. Alajouanine, T., and F. Lhermitte. "Acquired Aphasia in Children." *Brain* **88** (1965): 553–562.
3. Almli, C., and S. Finger. *Early Brain Damage*. New York: Academic, 1984.

4. Aram, D. M. "Language Sequelae of Unilateral Brain Lesions in Children." In *Language Communication and the Brain*, edited by F. Plum, 171–197. New York: Raven Press, 1988.

5. Aram, D. M., B. L. Ekelman, D. F. Rose, and H. A. Whitaker. "Verbal and Cognitive Sequelae Following Unilateral Lesions Acquired in Early Childhood." *J. Clin. & Exper. Neuropsychol.* **7(1)** (1985): 55–78.

6. Aram, D. M., S. C. Meyers, and B. L. Ekelman. "Fluency of Conversational Speech in Children with Unilateral Brain Lesions." *Brain & Lang.* **38(1)** (1990): 105–121.

7. Arena, R., and G. Gainotti. "Constructional Apraxia and Visuoperceptive Disabilities in Relation to Laterality of Cerebral Lesions." *Cortex* **14** (1978): 475–483.

8. Basso, A., A. Bracchini, E. Capitani, M. Laiacona, and M. Zanobio. "Age and Evolution of Language Area Functions: A Study on Adult Stroke Patients." *Cortex* **23** (1987): 475–483.

9. Basso, A., A. Lecours, S. Moraschini, and M. Vanier. "Anatomoclinical Correlations of the Aphasias as Defined Through Computerized Tomography: Exceptions." *Brain & Lang.* **26** (1985): 201–229.

10. Bates, E., D. Thal, and J. Janowsy. "Symbols and Syntax: A Darwinian Approach to Language Development." In *Biological and Behavioral Determinants of Language Development*, edited by N. Krasnegor, D. M. Rumbaugh, R. L. Schiefelbusch, and M. Studdert-Kennedy. Hillsdale, NJ: Lawrence Erlbaum Assoc, 1992.

11. Brown, J. W., and J. Jaffe. "Hypothesis on Cerebral Dominance." *Neuropsychologia* **13(1)** (1975): 107–110.

12. Carlson, J., C. Netley, E. Hendrick, and J. Pritchard. "A Reexamination of Intellectual Abilities in Hemidecorticated Patients." *Trans. Am. Neurol. Assoc.* **93** (1968): 198–201.

13. Changeux, J.-P., and S. Dehaene. "Neuronal Models of Cognitive Functions. Special Issue: Neurobiology of Cognition." *Cognition* **33(1-2)** (1989): 63–109.

14. Changeux, J. P., and A. Danchin. "Selective Stabilization of Developing Synapses as a Mechanism for the Specification of Neuronal Networks." *Nature* **264** (1976): 705–712.

15. Cowan, W. M., J. W. Fawcett, and D. M. O'Leary. "Regressive Events in Neurogenesis." *Science* **225** (1984): 1258–1265.

16. Cowan, W. M., and E. Wenger. "Cell Loss in the Trochlear Nucleus of the Chick During Normal Development and After Radical Extirpation of the Optic Cesicle." *J. Exper. Zool.* **164** (1967): 265–280.

17. Day, P. S., and H. K. Ulatowska. "Perceptual, Cognitive, and Linguistic Development After Early Hemispherectomy: Two Case Studies." *Brain & Lang.* **7** (1979): 17–33.

18. Delis, D. C., M. G. Kiefner, and A. J. Fridlund. "Visuospatial Dysfunction Following Unilateral Brain Damage: Dissociations in Hierarchical Hemispatial Analysis." *J. Clin. & Exper. Neuropsychol.* **10(4)** (1988): 421–431.

19. Delis, D. C., L. C. Robertson, and R. Efron. "Hemispheric Specialization of Memory for Visual Hierarchical Stimuli." *Neuropsychologia* **24(2)** (1986): 205–214.

20. Dennis, M. "Capacity and Strategy for Syntactic Comprehension After Left or Right Hemidecortication." *Brain & Lang.* **10** (1980): 287–317.

21. Dennis, M. *Language and The Young Damaged Brain.* American Psychological Association, Washington, DC, 1988.

22. Dennis, M., and B. Kohn. "Comprehension of Syntax in Infantile Hemiplegics After Cerebral Hemidecortication." *Brain & Lang.* **2** (1975): 472–482.

23. Dennis, M., M. Lovett, and C. Wiegel-Crump. "Written Language Acquisition After Left or Right Hemidecortication in Infancy." *Brain & Lang.* **12** (1981): 54–91.

24. Dennis, M., and H. Whitaker. "Hemispheric Equipotentiality and Language Acquisition." In *Language Development and Neurological Theory*, edited by S. J. Segalowitz and F. A. Gruber, 93–106. New York: Academic, 1977.

25. Dennis, M., and H. A. Whitaker. "Language Acquisition Following Hemidecortication: Linguistic Superiority of The Left Over the Right Hemisphere." *Brain & Lang.* **3** (1976): 404–433.

26. Finlay, B. L., and S. L. Pallas. "Control of Cell Number in the Developing Mammalian Visual System." *Prog. Neurobiol.* **32** (1989): 207–234.

27. Fletcher, J. M. "Afterword: Behavior-Brain Relationships in Children." In *Atypical Cognitive Deficits in Developmental Disorders: Implications for Brain Function*, edited by S. H. Broman and J. Grafman, 297–326. Hillsdale, NJ: Lawrence Erlbaum Associates, 1993.

28. Frost, D. O. "Anomalous Visual Connections to Somatosensory and Auditory Systems Following Brain Lesions in Early Life." *Dev. Brain Res.* **3(4)** (1982): 627–635.

29. Frost, D. O. "Axonal Growth and Target Selection During Development: Retinal Projections to the Ventrobasal Complex and Other 'Nonvisual' Structures in Neonatal Syrian Hamsters." *J. Comp. Neurol.* **230** (1984): 576–592.

30. Gainotti, G., and C. Tiacci. "Patterns of Drawing Disability in Right and Left Hemispheric Patients." *Neuropsychologia* **8** (1970): 379–384.

31. Gott, P. S. "Cognitive Abilities Following Right and Left Hemispherectomy." *Cortex* **9** (1973): 266–274.

32. Hamburger, V., and R. Levi-Montalcini. "Proliferation, Differentiation and Degeneration in the Spinal Ganglia of the Chick Embryo Under Normal and Experimental Conditions." *J. Exper. Zool.* **162** (1949): 133–160.

33. Hammill, D., and O. C. Irwin. "I.Q. Differences of Right and Left Spastic Hemiplegic Children." *Percep. & Motor Skills* **22** (1966): 193–194.

34. Harris, W. A. "Neural Activity and Development." *Annl. Rev. Physiol.* **43** (1981): 689–710.

35. Hubel, D. H., and T. N. Wiesel. "Cortical and Callosal Connections Concerned with the Vertical Meridian of Visual Fields in the Cat." *J. Neurophysiol.* **30(6)** (1967): 1561–1573.

36. Huttenlocher, P. R. "Morphometric Study of Human Cerebral Cortex Development." *Neuropsychologia* **28(6)** (1990): 517–527.
37. Huttenlocher, P. R. "Morphometric Study of Human Cerebral Cortex Development." In *Brain Development and Cognition*, edited by M. H. Johnson, 112–124. Cambridge, MA: Blackwell, 1993.
38. Isaacson, R. L. "The Myth of Recovery From Early Brain Damage." In *Aberrant Development in Infancy*, edited by N. G. Ellis, 1–26. New York: Wiley, 1975.
39. Jeo, R. M., Y. Yonebayashi, and J. M. Allman. "Perceptual Memory of Cognitively Defined Contours: A Rapid Robust and Long-Lasting Form of Memory." This volume.
40. Kennard, M. "Age and Other Factors in Motor Recovery From Precentral Lesions in Monkeys." *Am. J. Physiol.* **115** (1936): 138–146.
41. Kohn, B. "Right Hemisphere Speech Representation and Comprehension of Syntax After Left Cerebral Injury." *Brain & Lang.* **9** (1980): 350–361.
42. Kohn, B., and M. Dennis. "Selective Impairments of Visuospatial Abilities in Infantile Hemiplegics After Right Cerebral Hemidecortication." *Neuropsychologia* **12** (1974): 505–512.
43. Krashen, S. "Lateralization, Language Learning, and The Critical Period: Some New Evidence." *Language learning* **23(1)** (1973): 63–74.
44. Lamb, M. R., L. C. Robertson, and R. T. Knight. "Attention and Interference in the Processing of Global and Local Information: Effects of Unilateral Temporal-Parietal Junction Lesions." *Neuropsychologia* **27(4)** (1989): 471–483.
45. Lamb, M. R., L. C. Robertson, and R. T. Knight. "Component Mechanisms Underlying the Processing of Hierarchically Organized Patterns: Inferences from Patients with Unilateral Cortical Lesions." *J. Exper. Psychol.: Learning, Memory, & Cog.* **16** (1990): 471–483.
46. Lashley, K. S. *Central Mechanisms in Behavior.* New York: Wiley, 1951.
47. Lenneberg, E. H. *Biological Foundations of Language.* New York: Wiley, 1967.
48. Marchman, V. A., R. Miller, and E. A. Bates. "Babble and First Words in Children with Focal Brain Injury." *Applied Psycholinguistics* **12(1)** (1991): 1–22.
49. McFie, J. "Effects of Hemispherectomy on Intellectual Function." *J. Neurology, Neurosurgery, and Psychiatry* **24** (1961): 240–249.
50. McFie, J., and O. L. Zangwill. "Visual-Constructive Disabilities Associated with Lesions of the Left Cerebral Hemisphere." *Brain* **83** (1960): 243–260.
51. Merznich, M. M., and W. M. Jenkins. "Cortical Plasticity, Learning, and Learning Dysfunction." This volume.
52. Mills, D. L., S. A. Coffey, and H. J. Neville. "Variability in Cerebral Organization During Primary Language Acquisition." In *Human Behavior and the Developing Brain*, edited by G. Dawson and K. Fischer. New York: Guilford Publishers, 1993.

53. Mills, D. L., S. A. Coffey-Corina, and H. J. Neville. "Language Acquisition and Cerebral Specialization in 20-Month-Old Infants." *J. Cog. Neurosci.* **5(3)** (1993): 317–334.
54. Milner, B. "Interhemispheric Differences in the Localization of Psychological Processes in Man." *Brit. Med. Bull.* **27(3)** (1971): 272–277.
55. Neville, H., M. Kutas, and A. Schmidt. "Event-Related Potential Studies of Cerebral Specialization During Reading: I. Studies of Normal Adults Adults." *Brain & Lang.* **16** (1982): 300–315.
56. Neville, H., M. Kutas, and A. Schmidt. "Event-Related Potential Studies of Cerebral Specialization During Reading: II. Studies of Congenitally Deaf Adults." *Brain & Lang.* **16** (1982): 316–337.
57. Neville, H., and D. Lawson. "Attention to Central and Peripheral Visual Space in a Movement Detection Task: An Event Related Potential and Behavior Study. I. Normal Hearing Adults." *Brain Resh.* **405** (1987): 253–267.
58. Neville, H., and D. Lawson. "Attention to Central and Peripheral Visual Space in a Movement Detection Task: An Event Related Potential and Behavior Study. II. Congenitally Deaf Adults." *Brain Resh.* **405** (1987): 268–283.
59. Neville, H., and D. Lawson. "Attention to Central and Peripheral Visual Space in a Movement Detection Task: III. Separate Effects of Auditory Deprivation and Acquisition of a Visual Language." *Brain Resh.* **405** (1987): 284–294.
60. Neville, H., A. Schmidt, and M. Kutas. "Altered Visual-Evoked Potentials in Congenitally Deaf Adults." *Brain Resh.* **266** (1983): 127–132.
61. O'Leary, D. D. M., and B. B. Stanfield. "Selective Elimination of Axons Extended by Developing Cortical Neurons is Dependent on Regional Locale: Experiments Utilizing Fetal Cortical Transplants." *J. Neurosci.* **9** (1989): 2230–2246.
62. Oppenheim, R. W. "Neuronal Cell Death and Some Related Regressive Phenomena During Neurogenesis: A Selective, Historical Review and Progress Report." In *Studies in Developmental Neurobiology, Essays in honor of Viktor Hamburger*, edited by W. M. Cowan 74–133. New York: Oxford University Press, 1981.
63. Oppenheim, R. W. "Naturally Occurring Cell Death During Neural Development." *Trends in Neurosci.* **8** (1985): 487–493.
64. Oppenheim, R. W. "Muscle Activity and Motoneuron Death in the Spinal Cord of the Chick Embryo." In *Selective Neuronal Death*, edited by G. Bock and M. O'Connor, 96–112. New York: Wiley, 1987.
65. Oppenheim, R. W. "The Neurotrophic Theory and Naturally Occurring Moto-neuron Death." *Trends in Neurosci.* **12** (1989): 252–255.
66. Oppenheim, R. W. "Cell Death During Development of the Neurosystem." *Ann. Rev. Neurosci.* **14** (1991): 453–501.

67. Piercy, M., H. Hecaen, and J. Ajuriaguerra. "Constructional Apraxia Associated with Unilateral Cerebral Lesions: Left and Right Sided Cases Compared." *Brain* **83** (1960): 225–242.

68. Pons "Abstract: Lesion-Induced Cortical Plasticity." This volume.

69. Purves, D. *Body and Brain, A Trophic Theory of Neural Connections.* Cambridge, MA: Harvard, 1988.

70. Rakic, P. *Plasticity of Cortical Development.* Cambridge, MA: MIT Press, 1991.

71. Rakic, P., and K. P. Riley. "Regulation of Axon Number in Primate Optic Nerve by Prenatal Binocular Competition." *Nature* **305(5930)** (1983): 135–137.

72. Ramachandran, V. S. "Plasticity in the Adult Human Brain: Is There Reason for Optimism?." This volume.

73. Reed, J. C., and R. M. Reitan. "Verbal and Performance Differences Among Brain-Injured Children with Lateralized Motor Deficits." *Neuropsychologia* **9** (1971): 401–407.

74. Reilly, J. S., E. A. Bates, and V. A. Marchman. "Grammar and Narrative Discourse in Children with Focal Brain Injury." In preparation.

75. Riva, D., and L. Cazzaniga. "Late Effects of Unilateral Brain Lesions Sustained Before and After Age One." *Neuropsychologia* **24(3)** (1986): 423–428.

76. Riva, D., L. Cazzaniga, C. Pantaleoni, N. Milani, and E. Fedrizzi. *J. Ped. Neurosci.* **2** (1987): 239–250.

77. Robertson, L. C., and D. C. Delis. "'Part-Whole' Processing in Unilateral Brain Damaged Patients: Dysfunction of Hierarchical Organization." *Neuropsychologia* **24(3)** (1986): 363–370.

78. Robertson, L. C., and M. R. Lamb. "The Role of Perceptual Reference Frames in Visual Field Asymmetries." *Neuropsychologia* **26(1)** (1988): 172–181.

79. Robertson, L. C., and M. R. Lamb. "Neuropsychological Contributions to Theories of Part/Whole Organization." *Cog. Psychol.* **23** (1991): 299–330.

80. Rudel, R. G., and H. L. Teuber. "Spatial Orientation in Normal Children and in Children with Early Brain Damage." *Neuropsychologia* **9** (1971): 401–407.

81. Rudel, R. G., H. L. Teuber, and T. Twitchell. "Levels of Impairment of Sensorimotor Function in Children with Early Brain Damage." *Neuropsychologia* **12** (1974): 95–108.

82. Satz, P., E. Strauss, and H. Whitaker. "The Ontogeny of Hemispheric Specialization: Some Old Hypotheses Revisited." *Brain & Lang.* **38(4)** (1990): 596–614.

83. Smith, A. "Early and Long-Term Recovery from Brain-Damage in Children and Adults: Evolution of Concepts of Localization, Plasticity, and Recovery." In *Early Brain Damage*, edited by C. R. Almli, and S. Finger, 299–324. New York: Academic, 1984.

84. St. James-Roberts, I. "Neurological Plasticity, Recovery from Brain Insult, and Child Development." In *Advances in Child Development and Behavior*, edited by H. W. Reese, 253–319. New York: Academic, 1979.

85. Stern, C., and J. Stiles. "The Effects of Pre and Perinatal Stroke on Spatial Cognitive Development." Poster to be presented at IXth Biennial International Society on Infant Studies Meeting, Paris, June 2-5, 1994.

86. Stiles, J., D. Dukette, and R. Nass. "Selective Deficits of Visuo-Spatial Processing in Children with Early Right or Left Early Rght or Left Posterior Focal Brain Injury." Paper presented at The Child Neurology Society Conference, New Orleans: October, 1992.

87. Stiles, J., and R. Nass. "Spatial Grouping Activity in Young Children with Congenital Right or Left Hemisphere Brain Injury." *Brain & Cog.* **15(2)** (1991): 201–222.

88. Stiles, J., and D. Thal. "Linguistic and Spatial Cognitive Development Following Early Focal Brain Injury: Patterns of Deficit and Recovery." In *Brain Development and Cognition*, edited by M. Johnson, 643–664. Cambridge, MA: Blackwell, 1993.

89. Sur, M., P. E. Garraghty, and A. W. Roe. "Experimentally Induced Visual Projections into Auditory Thalamus and Cortex." *Science* **242** (1988): 1437–1441.

90. Sur, M., S. L. Pallas, and A. W. Roe. "Cross-Modal Plasticity in Cortical Development: Differentiation and Specification of Sensory Neocortex." *Trends in Neurosci.* **13** (1990): 227–233.

91. Swindell, C. S., A. L. Holland, D. Fromm, and J. B. Greenhouse. "Characteristics of Recovery of Drawing Ability in Left and Right Brain-Damaged Patients." *Brain & Cog.* **7** (1988): 16–30.

92. Thal, D. J., V. A. Marchman, J. Stiles, D. Aram, D. Trauner, R. Nass, and E. Bates. "Early Lexical Development in Children with Focal Brain Injury." *Brain & Lang.* **40(4)** (1991): 491–527.

93. Vargha-Khadem, F., A. O'Gorman, and G. Watters. "Aphasia in Children with 'prenatal' Versus Postnatal Left Hemisphere Lesions: A Clinical and CT Scan Study." Presented at 11th meeting of the International Neuropsychological Society, Mexico City, 1983.

94. Vargha-Khadem, F., A. O'Gorman, and G. Watters. "Aphasia and Handedness in Relation to Hemispheric Sides, Age at Injury, and Severity of Cerebral Lesion During Childhood." *Brain* **108** (1985): 667–696.

95. Wasserstein, J., R. Zappulla, J. Rosen, and L. A. O. Gerstman. "In Search of Closure: Subjective Contour Illusions, Gestalt Completion Test, and Implications." *Brain & Cog.* **6(1)** (1987): 1–14.

96. Webster, M. J., J. Bachevalier, and L. G. Ungerleider. "Development and Plasticity of Visual Memory Circuits." This volume.

97. Woods, B., and S. Carey. "Language Deficits After Apparent Clinical Recovery From Childhood Aphasia." *Ann. Neurol.* **6** (1979): 405–409.

98. Woods, B. T. "The Restricted Effects of Right-HemispHere Lesions After Age One: Wechsler Test Data." *Neuropsychologia* **18(1)** (1980): 65–70.

Paula Tallal
Rutgers—The State University of New Jersey, 197 University Avenue, Newark, NJ 07102

Development and Disorders of Speech and Language: Implications for Neural and Behavioral Plasticity

How is speech processed? More specifically, how is it that the developing nervous system comes to recognize the acoustic parameters that represent the phonological units of language, and how are these represented in the brain? One approach to studying speech perception is to investigate how it develops. A particularly fruitful approach, which has provided a unique "window" into the neurobiological processes underlying speech perception, has been the study of children who are failing to develop language normally.

To set the scene, we must keep in mind that most investigators who work on language have tended to think that language is particularly recalcitrant to a neuroscience approach. There has been an implicit assumption that language is processed differently in the nervous system than other sensory and cognitive events, that it is innate, uniquely human, and that it has its own unique neural modules and/or processes.[3,4] Based on this strong assumption, it would follow that studying the basic physiology underlying sensory information processing, at the level we have been discussing in this volume, will tell us very little about language as a rule-governed, linguistic system, or even how language is processed and represented in the brain.

Our laboratory has taken a very different approach from this predominant perspective. We conceptualize higher cognitive processes, including language, from an information processing perspective. We begin first by questioning how more basic

Maturational Windows and Adult Cortical Plasticity, Eds. B. Julesz & I. Kovács,
SFI Studies in the Sciences of Complexity, Vol. XXIII, Addison-Wesley, 1995   **239**

sensory information travels through the nervous system, and then how this information is subsequently represented as speech and language. From birth the infant is exposed to the sounds of its envioronment, including the voices of others as well as its own vocal output. The speech signal is rarely explicitly segmented into its component sounds (phonemes), but rather occurs as a fluent, rapidly changing acoustic stream. However, the infant does not begin by mimicing this continuous, fluent acoustic signal or even whole, discrete words. Rather, the baby begins by segmenting out and reiteratively producing individual steady-state vowels and consonant-vowel (cv) syllables, as any proud ma-ma or da-da can tell you. The baby, in its crib often can be heard "practicing" the production of these sounds in its early cooing, and subsequent repetitive production of rhythmic syllables (/ba-ba-ba-ba..., da-da-da-da/). Interestingly, deaf babies begin the cooing process, but without sufficient auditory input/feedback fail to progress to the production of speech babble. Thus, if the child cannot process the essential components of complex sounds (intensity, duration, frequency) appropriately in the initial stages, we can hypothesize that the child will have a significant problem setting up distinct neural representations of each phoneme and, as such, in learning words and complex grammar. The deaf child, deprived of sign language, is ample proof of the importance basic processing of the acoustic signal plays in all subsequent stages of speech and language development. Thus, if we are interested in understanding the neural substrates that subserve language development, one approach may come from the detailed study of central auditory and memory and motor processes that might be prerequisites to developing speech and language functions. If we are ultimately interested in the developmental progression leading to language learning, we might learn a great deal by investigating children who are having difficulty acquiring language and observing how the level of fundamental perceptual cognitive and motor functions that might be considered necessary and/or sufficient for "building" a functional oral language system.

Epidemiological studies estimate that between 5 to 10% of the population of preschool age children have a developmental language disability. When you rule out all other deficits, such as hearing loss and mental retardation, about 3 to 5% of children have what has come to be referred to a "specific language impairment" (LI). Our research studies have focused on this latter group. The subjects of our investigations comprise a highly selected group of children who are normal in every respect, except for their speech and language development. These children have normal non-verbal intelligence, hearing, and emotional development. They have not been diagnosed as being hyperactive. They have normal oral peripheral function and they have no frank neurological damage (e.g., seizures, hemiplegia, etc.). Despite their otherwise normal development, these children are characterized by severely delayed onset and progression of language milestones. Most of them are impaired in receptive as well as expressive language abilities.

The children in the studies I will report here were between 5 and 9 years old when tested. Group size varied from our first series of studies, in which there were

12 language impaired (LI) and 12 matched controls, to our most recent series of studies which included 100 LIs and 60 matched controls.

As our interests have always been to relate higher cortical functions, specifically speech and language, to neural substrates, we have relied heavily on data derived from animal studies we have focused specifically on studies of central auditory processing. Based on the studies of Dewson and Cowey,[2] in which they had operantly trained monkeys to respond to increasingly complex auditory information, Tallal and Piercy[8,9,10] adapted a novel research paradigm that could be used with young, language impaired as well as nonimpaired children. This paradigm included a hierarchical series of operant tasks that could assess the basic subskills necessary for more complex acoustic analysis. This began with the initial detection of a sensory event, and proceeded to assess the association of that event with a specific motor response, discrimination between events, sequencing and serially recalling a series of events and the ability to process sensory information at various rates. Initially, we focused on the physical components of sound: intensity, duration (or time cues), and frequency cues. Using this hierarchical paradigm we investigated whether children with developmental language problems could respond appropriately on all of the subskills we posed were necessary to organize the complex acoustic events involved in speech perception. The results from a very large series of studies using this paradigm to assess the auditory processing abilities of LI children demonstrated that language-impaired (LI) children are completely normal in all respects in their ability to respond correctly on all aspects of this hierarchical series of tasks, with one exception. They need orders of magnitude more time between successive events than do normally developing children to perform *any* of the subskills.[8,9]

Figure 1 shows the percent-correct performance for responding to two 75-msec duration tones (100 Hz and 300 Hz) presented sequentially. The important variable, appears to be the interstimulus interval in msec between stimuli. The interstimulus interval (ISI) is the intervals between the offset of the first signal and the onset of the second signal. What we see in Figure 1 is that the LI children are not significantly different from controls in their ability to listen to two tones and press two panels on a response box to indicate either (a) the order in which the tones were presented, or (b) whether they were same or different, provided they have a relatively long ISI (over 300 msec). However, when we decreased the interval between the end of the first signal and the beginning of the second signal, the LI children's performance dropped to chance. Normally developing children (age 6 years and above) needed only 8 msec between two 75-msec duration tones to respond at 75% correct or above. Language-impaired children, on the other hand, needed over 150 msec. ISI to respond at the same level of accuracy.

Two aspects of these data are very important. First, we see a step function for the LI children. That is, we do not observe a steady, linear decrement in performance. Rather, the LI children demonstrate more of an all or none kind of processing. They can either process the individual tones, and then can do all

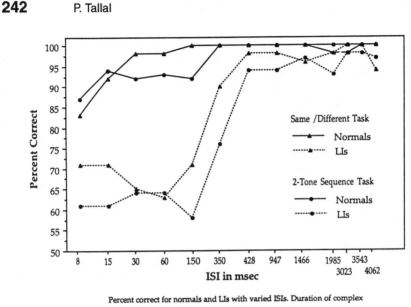

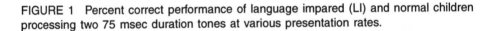

Percent correct for normals and LIs with varied ISIs. Duration of complex
tones = 75 msec (tone 1 = 100 Hz, tone 2 = 300 Hz).

FIGURE 1   Percent correct performance of language impared (LI) and normal children
processing two 75 msec duration tones at various presentation rates.

of the subsequent higher-level functions (sequence, recall, etc.) with that information or they are unable to process the tones, and hence can not discriminate,
sequence or recall them. The second important aspect to these data is that the LI
children need *orders of magnitude* more processing time on these tasks as compared
to the control children to perform even the easiest, most basic processes.

Performance does not appear to be related to attention *per se*, as the stimuli
were presented randomly so the children did not know when they were going to
be presented with a longer interval or a shorter interval. If the problem was lack
of attention, or even motivation, then we would expect that the LI children would
make random errors that would result in a flat function on this task. That is not at
all what the data show. Rather, the LI children show selective errors on the more
rapidly presented stimuli while maintaining near perfect performance on the same
stimuli, when presented with longer intervals.

Importantly, the LI children have just as much difficulty discriminating between
signals (that is indicating whether they are the same or different) at very rapid rates
of presentation, as they do sequencing them. So it's not a sequencing problem,
per se, although LI's certainly do have severe sequencing difficulties. Rather, the
problem occurs at an even more basic level—they do not have enough time to
integrate two or more rapidly presented acoustic signals that subsequently have to
be discriminated, sequenced, or remembered.

These results with nonverbal acoustic signals led us to pose specific questions about the nature of speech perception and production deficits in LI children. For example, how would difficulty in processing information within tens of msec effect speech perception and production? Many of the most important acoustic differences between speech sounds, that are absolutely critical for making discriminations between them, occur within this time window. Thus, we hypothesized that LI children would have most difficulty discriminating between those speech sounds that differed only by temporal or frequency changes that occurred within this time range, but would be unimpaired in discriminating speech contrasts that relied on longer duration acoustic cues. We undertook a large series of studies in which we used computer-generated speech sounds that differed only in brief temporal cues, frequency cues, or amplitude cues.[10,14] Using these stimuli, which allowed us to control the acoustic spectra of speech, we investigated the speech discrimination abilities of LI children.

The results demonstrated that LI children are significantly impaired in discriminating between any speech sounds that incorporate *very brief acoustic cues* that are followed quickly in time (within tens of msec) by other acoustic cues (for a complete review of this work see Tallal et al.[15]). An example is the contrast pair /ba/ vs /da/. As seen in Figure 2, the vast majority of the acoustic signal in both of these syllables is the same vowel /a/. The only discriminable portion of the acoustic spectra occurs at the onset of the syllables. Thus, in order to discriminate /ba/ from /da/, one has to track the rapidly changing frequencies called "formant transitions" that occurs within about 40 msec at the onset of each syllable. What we found is that language impaired children are unable to discriminate between speech sounds like these, that incorporated brief or rapidly changing acoustic cues, but are able to discriminate between other syllable contrasts if they do *not* require rapid temporal integration.

We subsequently investigated what would happen if we gave the LI children more time within the difficult syllables to track transient cues. We used a speech synthesizing computer to extend the durations over which the critical time components occurred within these speech syllables. We demonstrated remarkable improvement in LI children's ability to discriminate between speech sounds by extending the temporal components of the acoustic wave form to durations outside of the time window which seems to be closed to them.[11] A similar pattern was found in studies of *speech production*. Spectrographic analyses of LI children's speech output showed that these children's motor control of the temporal cues within their speech was vastly overextended in duration, leading to perceived distortion of the speech signal to the listener.[12,13]

These data suggest that the processing time window may be opened wider for LI children, through the use of computer manipulation of the acoustic waveform of speech.[1,11] Specifically, we have demonstrated that remarkable improvement can be achieved in LI children's ability to discriminate speech syllables, that are differentiated only by brief temporal cues, when the duration of these cues are extended through computer manipulation. This finding at the syllable level suggests that extending the brief temporal components within ongoing speech may lead to improved receptive language abilities for LI children. We are currently conducting studies in collaboration with Merzenich and colleagues[5] to determine the therapeutic validity of using temporally modified fluent speech as well as direct temporal interaction training, to improve speech and language skills with LI children (see Merzenich and Jenkins[5] this volume). Preliminary results are extremely encouraging.

The work presented in this volume by Julesz and Kovács (introduction) as well as by Karni and Sagi, and Polat and Sagi[7] demonstrated the remarkable plasticity that can be achieved in altering basic psychophysical thresholds through direct training or experience. Interestingly, these authors claim that certain types of perceptual learning occur through chains of interactions among neural elements, and that learning in these cases is a slow, step-by-step learning, moving from basic to more complex processing. This seems to be of particular relevance to issues that may pertain to temporal processing remediation for LI individuals. The research presented in this volume by Merzenich and Jenkins[5] shows, further, that direct sensory experience (training) is reflected by physiological plasticity altering cortical representation at the cellular level in the nervous system. Finally, the dramatic demonstration of recovery of motor function through forced use of the impaired limb in the Silver Springs monkeys, reported here by Taub,[16] raises further hope that basic sensory/motor deficits, such as temporal processing thresholds may be modifiable with training.

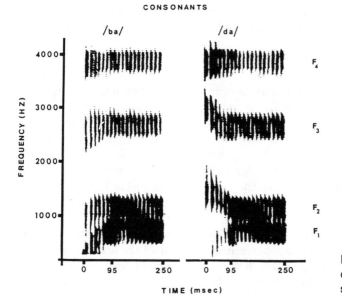

FIGURE 2 Spectograms of computer generated speech syllables.

We have recently begun developing novel, and hopefully more effective, therapies for LI individuals that are based on remediating their temporal processing deficit *per se*. Collaborative studies with Merzenich's laboratory are currently underway. Our preliminary studies suggest that the temporal processing deficits of LI children can be significantly modified through direct training. Further, these early studies demonstrate that improved temporal integration abilities result in markedly improved speech perception and language comprehension abilities for these children as well.[6] We are actively purssuing the clinical implications of these exciting new research results.

We have demonstrated that some developmental phonological problems which characterize many language and reading impaired (dyslexic) children may result from a more primary deficit in rapid temporal integration. This may have important implications for issues of plasticity (i.e., remediation). We are now in a position to address issues pertaining to plasticity for language functions from a novel perspective. The data presented at this conference, taken together with our findings of significant temporal sensory/motor deficits in LI children, suggest that there may be reason for real optimism in developing novel strategies for remediating the speech and language deficits of LI children, by either modifying their temporal thresholds and/or providing them with an acoustic signal (computer extended speech) which better matches the temporal processing capabilities of their nervous system.

REFERENCES

1. Alexander, D. "Increasing the Rate of Auditory Processing in Language-Delayed Children." Unpublished Ph.D. Thesis, University of Calgary, Canada, 1979.
2. Dewson, J. H., and A. Cowey. "Discrimination of Auditory Sequences by Monkeys." *Nature* **222** (1969): 695–697.
3. Fodor, J. *Modularity of Mind.* Cambridge, MA: MIT Press, 1983.
4. Liberman, A. M. "Speech Perception, Time is Not What it Seems." In *Temporal Information Processing in the Nervous System*, edited by P. Tallal, A. Galaburda, R. Llinas, and C. von Euler, Vol. 682, 264–271. New York Academy of Sciences, 1993.
5. Merzenich, M. M., W. M. Jenkins. "Cortical Plasticity, Learning, and Learning Dysfunction." This volume.
6. Miller, S. L., W. M. Jenkins, M. M. Merzenich, and P. Tallal. "Modification of Auditory Temporal Processing Threshold's in Language Impaired Children." Paper presented at the Second Annual Meating of the Cognitive Neuroscience Society, 1995.
7. Polat, U., and D. Sagi. "Plasticity of Spatial Interactions in Early Vision." This volume.

8. Tallal, P., and M. Piercy. "Defects of Non-verbal Auditory Perception in Children with Developmental Aphasia." *Nature* **241** (1973): 468–469.

9. Tallal, P., and M. Piercy. "Developmental Aphasia: Impaired Rate of Non-Verbal Processing as a Function of Sensory Modality." *Neuropsychologia* **11** (1973): 389–398.

10. Tallal, P., and M. Piercy. "Developmental Aphasia: Rate of Auditory Processing and Selective Impairment of Consonant Perception." *Neuropsychologia* **12** (1974): 83–93.

11. Tallal, P., and M. Piercy. "Developmental Aphasia: The Perception of Brief Vowels and Extended Stop Consonants." *Neuropsychologia* **13** (1975): 69–74.

12. Tallal, P., R. E. Stark, and B. Curtiss. "Relation Between Speech Perception and Speech Production Impairment in Children with Developmental Dysphasia." *Brain & Lang.* **3** (1976): 305–317.

13. Stark, R. E., and P. Tallal. "Analysis of Stop Consonant Production Errors in Developmentally Dysphasic Children." *J. Acoust. Soc. Am.* **66** (1979): 1703–1712.

14. Tallal, P., and R. E. Stark. "Speech Acoustic-Cue Discrimination Abilities of Normally Developing and Language-Impaired Children." *J. Acoust. Soc. Am.* **69** (1981): 568–574.

15. Tallal, P., S. Miller, and R. Fitch. "Neurobiological Basis of Speech: A Case for the Preeminence of Temporal Processing." In *Temporal Information Processing in the Nervous System: Special Reference to Dyslexia and Dysphasis Annals of the New York Academy of Sciences*, Vol. 682, 27–47, 1993.

16. Taub, E., and J. E. Cargo. "Increasing Behavioral Plasticity Following Central Nervous System Damage in Monkeys and Man: A Method with Potential Application to Human Developmental Motor Disability." This volume.

Michael M. Merzenich and William M. Jenkins
W. M. Keck Center for Integrative Neurosciences, HSE-828, University of California at San Francisco, San Francisco, CA 94143-0732

Cortical Plasticity, Learning, and Learning Dysfunction

INTRODUCTION

The objective of this review is to briefly summarize how recent studies of the neural bases of learning might relate to the perceptual performance characteristics of the language-based "learning-disabled" child. We shall begin by summarizing some relevant aspects of the representational plasticity in the brain that underlies skill learning. The implications of these recent findings for our understanding of the neurological nature of—and possible origins of—language-based learning disabilities will be considered. General strategies for the possible remediation of learning disabilities will then be briefly discussed from the specific point of view of the brain mechanisms underlying learning.

Maturational Windows and Adult Cortical Plasticity, Eds. B. Julesz & I. Kovács,
SFI Studies in the Sciences of Complexity, Vol. XXIII, Addison-Wesley, 1995   **247**

CORTICAL PLASTICITY AND LEARNING: SOME BASIC PRINCIPLES

1. CORTICAL PLASTICITY IN LEARNING; BASIC PHENOMENOLOGY

Studies conducted principally over the past two decades have produced an increasingly clear understanding of the basic neural processes in the cerebral cortex that underlie its contributions to learning. Understanding these processes is a prerequisite for understanding how their normal function or dysfunction might relate to and account for "learning disability." Changes induced in cortical neuronal responses in parallel with learning have been the subject of many experiments. A large number of these studies have employed Pavlovian associative conditioning procedures[70] to track alterations in neuronal responses from the cerebral cortex that parallel behaviorally demonstrated learning and extinction.[57,103,104,112] Such experiments have shown that when animals are trained to associate a sensory stimulus with an aversive stimulus, for example, a noise or tone with a puff of air to the anterior face, the neuronal "representations" of both of those stimuli rapidly change in the cortex, in a number of respects: (a) Neurons become more sensitive to, and (b) more selective for these specific inputs.[4,12,15,19,60,109,111,113] (c) Far more neurons represent these now-behaviorally-important stimuli selectively after conditioning than before.[4,12,15,19,60,109] (d) Distributed neurons representing behaviorally important inputs come to be more strongly positively interconnected.[1] (e) Changes are recorded in a number of cortical areas that are engaged by any behaviorally important stimulus.[12,57,60,103,104] (f) Changes are roughly reversed to the pre-training situation if the conditioning is "extinguished" by a period of non-associated stimulation.[4,12,15,111,103,104,112]

It might be noted that in the Pavlovian conditioning paradigm, behavioral conditioning is signaled by the animal responding in a way that demonstrates that the "conditioned" and "unconditioned" stimuli—in this case, the sound stimulus and the air puff to the face—have been associated, for example, by the animal moving upon presentation of the sound as if to avoid the expected, aversive air puff. The motor cortical activities accounting for these "conditioned responses" have also been assessed in some of these preparations. They also change rapidly and specifically, in parallel with this "classical conditioning."[22,109,110,111,113]

What is the magnitude of such induced change in the cerebral cortex? The responses of neurons over broad sectors of a number of cortical areas are induced to change in any such experiment, often after only a limited training period. The dimensions of the region of change in these areas depend upon the nature of conditioned and unconditioned stimuli. For example, a noise stimulus very widely excites auditory cortical areas to change, while a tonal stimulus induces more specific changes over a more limited cortical zone. In either event, the response selectivities and sensitivities of tens of thousands or hundreds of thousands or more neurons are altered by such simple behavioral conditioning, in each participating cortical area. Extrapolated across sensory and motor "systems" that are engaged to change by Pavlovian conditioning, significant changes are expressed for even this simple behavior for the specific responses of many hundreds of thousands or millions of neurons. These changes in the effectivenesses with which neurons are excited by these behaviorally important stimuli endure for as long as conditioning can be demonstrated, that is, for periods of up to at least many weeks.[105]

More recently, we have conducted a series of "instrumental" or "operant" conditioning studies in which young adult monkeys have been trained to detect, discriminate, recognize, or categorize acoustic or tactual stimuli, while assessing the changes in the brain induced by the training that might account for the monkey's perceptual learning.[38,39,53,54,55,77,78,79] In operant conditioning in this form, the animal is rewarded immediately after the fact for each correct performance trial, and very mildly punished with a behavioral "time out" for performance misses. We have also trained monkeys in simple motor skills, with the objective of again defining how neuronal response changes might account for skill acquisition.[53,54,55,62]

These experiments along with the studies of others[2,45,44,63,64,67,68,91] have again shown that the representations of behaviorally important stimuli are exaggerated in the cortices of trained individuals as a consequence of several weeks to months of such training. Training-induced changes are similar to those recorded in associative conditioning in a number of respects, i.e.: (a) Cortical neurons can develop a modestly heightened sensitivity to behaviorally important training stimuli.[78] (b) Very large cortical neuronal populations emerge. (c) These populations are highly selective for just those stimuli that are applied in behavioral training.[2,38,39,44,53,54,55,63,64,77,78] (d) Behaviorally important stimuli come to be represented by more synchronously responding cortical neuronal populations,[39,78,91,115] presumably manifesting a strengthening of positive cortical network interconnections for neuronal populations representing specific training signal inputs. (e) Again, such changes are induced at a number of cortical levels.[44,57,60,77]

The same mechanisms appear to operate for motor skill learning. When a monkey employs specific sensory inputs to guide a motor skill, e.g., a reach to retrieve small food objects, major changes in the representations of the skin surfaces or visual or auditory cues or target stimulanda are generated in sensory and premotor areas,[2,32,53,54,55,63,62,68,91,115] and there is a substantial enlargement of the motor cortical zone from which the learned movement can be selectively evoked.

Again, if we consider changes induced across all system levels in a monkey learning a new perceptual or motor skill, induced changes are massive, and involve enduring changes in the effectivenesses of behaviorally important inputs involving millions of cortical neurons.[21,57,60]

Thus, as the brain of a child develops new perceptual and motor skills, it is achieved by a process that dramatically remodels distributed brain responses. We now know that this functional self-organization is achieved by the brain actually changing its local wiring patterns. The brain after learning is a different one than the brain before learning. How, we might begin to wonder, is the brain of a learning disabled child different in these learning operations from that of a normal child? The problem might lie with a defect in the learning machinery that renders it permanently defective in its change operations. Or the problem might arise from the learning history of the child. Our ultimate objective in this report is to discuss the relative merits of these two general possibilities.

2. CORTICAL PLASTICITY IN LEARNING: SOME ASPECTS OF UNDERLYING MECHANISMS

To relate the dramatic self-organizing processes of the human forebrain that operate in learning to the phenomenology of learning dysfunction, it is important to understand more about the processes that actually underlie it. More complete reviews of cortical change mechanisms are available. Here, we focus on aspects of changes that are especially relevant for understanding the phenomenological expressions of human speech and language-based learning disabilities.

(A) THE BASIC CHANGE PROCESS IN LEARNING IS COINCIDENT INPUT-BASED. In 1949, Donald Hebb formally recognized the power of coincident input synaptic effectiveness change mechanisms for creating selective representations of behaviorally important stimuli in the brain, and speculated about particular mechanisms that might underlie such input co-selection.[37] The Hebbian Principle: Behaviorally important inputs that excite neurons simultaneously in time (in an appropriate behavioral learning context) are mutually strengthened.

For example, consider an infant in the presence of a speaking mother with a brain that cannot yet interpret her oral utterances. The combinations of sounds and associated visual cues that are received nearly simultaneously in time and the contexts in which the infant hears and sees them, arrive together and engage a significant subset of the 70 or 80 functional areas of its cerebral cortex. There, enabled by cognitive inputs (e.g., triggered by many forms of positive response—rewards—from the mother) that signal that changes should be recorded, multiple cortical areas are induced to change on the basis of which specific inputs, moment by moment in time, engage each small sector of the cortical machine. *Inputs that arrive together in time at any given locus* achieve a new prominence—*are "co-selected"*—i.e., now together selectively change their input effectivenesses to thereafter excite engaged neurons in a phoneme-specific/word-specific/word-in-context-specific/prosodic feature-specific, etc. way.

Many neuroscientists have conducted many hundreds of studies designed to test Hebb's hypothesis. His principle of coincident-input strengthening has been repeatedly confirmed, albeit with identification of cellular and molecular mechanisms of origin that Hebb could not have conceived of in 1949, and that elaborate his general learning principle in great detail.

(B) CORTICAL REMODELING IN LEARNING INVOLVES PROCESSES THAT HAVE A RELATIVELY SHORT INTEGRATIVE TIME CONSTANT. For these change mechanisms, you might ask: "What do you mean by 'simultaneous' or 'coincident'? What, for the brain, is a 'moment' in time?" Mutual input strengthening cannot occur over too long a time epoch. In that case, there could be no basis for creating the refined response selectivity required to distinguish one external object or event from another. The phonetic distinctions crucial for establishing separated, phonologically based representations of the mother's speech elements would be inappropriately integrated over time, and phonological representations could not be established.

At the same time, coincident input co-selection cannot be limited to too short a time epoch. In that case, inputs that arrive from an external object or event could not be adequately and reliably combined to represent their object/event-specific combinatorial features. The crucial features of inputs that mark consonant transients in our mother's speech, for example, would not be adequately represented combinatorially. In actual fact, *the cortical machine operates to integrate information in time chunks ranging from tens of milliseconds to tenths of seconds in duration.* Inputs that arrive together, in every cortical area engaged by behaviorally important tasks, are co-selected—integrated—location by location, if they arrive at the cortical machine with this degree of temporal correspondence.

(C) CORTICAL PLASTICITY MECHANISMS ARE COMPETITIVE. If a monkey or human practices a task involving particular sensory inputs and resulting in particular movements, those inputs and movements are exaggerated in their representation during skill acquisition. That exaggeration can only occur at the expense of other, formerly effective movements. That is another way of saying that every human individual is a behavioral specialist, driven by the evolution of their learned behaviors to create an operationally unique brain that excels at many endeavors but is less proficient at others. These differences reflect individual differences in our behavioral progressions and practice schedules that result in—and come from—differences in competition-induced representational change in our forebrain.

What is the scale of this competition? The brain of a child that develops American Sign Language as its first language is clearly massively specialized for its representation, with large areas dominated by inputs from peripheral vision that would otherwise be dominated by acoustic speech and language inputs.[65] The brain of an adult amputee very rapidly changes its representations of the body surface and of limb movements, to completely occupy the several square centimeter cortical zone of the missing limbs with skin and movement representations from the amputation stump and proximal limb muscles.[56,72,74] The brain areas of a nursing mother rapidly change to exaggerate and elaborate the representations of the ventral body surface and breast skin.[116] The brain representations of our exemplary child will rapidly change with the applications of hundreds, then thousands, then hundreds of thousands, then millions of phonetic element inputs delivered in a rich variety of contextual conditions and from many speakers, in the generation of highly reliable, speaker-invariant, experiential-language-specific phonetic representational constructs. These are a few among many experimentally argued examples of brain self-organization that have revealed to us that *competitive representational translocations and substitutions occur on a major scale, throughout life.* That should hardly be surprising, given our lifelong capacities for behavioral change driven by our idiosyncratic experiences and training.

(D) COINCIDENT INPUT CO-SELECTION IS ENABLED BY, AND LIMITED BY (i) THE SOURCES OF, AND (ii) THE OVERLAPS IN DISTRIBUTIONS OF INPUTS PROJECTING TO EACH CORTICAL AREA. Those input sources and spreads are specific for each of the roughly 70 or 80 or more functional areas of the human cerebral cortex.[25] They differ especially dramatically as a function of cortical system "level." As a consequence of these area-specific differences, each cortical field engaged by behaviorally important inputs generates field-specific representational constructs.[57,60] At lower system levels like the primary auditory (A1), visual (V1), and somatosensory (area 3b in SI) cortical zones, anatomically topographic input projections and their circumscribed projection overlaps limit combinations, and create and conserve relatively complete and robust representations of abstracted stimulus "primitives." By contrast, at "high" system levels, neurons receive inputs from very many sources that are widely dispersed in a virtually all-to-all anatomical projection schema. There, complex object- or event-specific combinations of abstracted features of real-world stimuli are accomplished—but remember that they are set up by coincident input co-selection mechanisms that are in operation all across engaged representational systems.

(E) THE CORTEX PROCESSES INFORMATION IN SPATIAL AND TEMPORAL "CHUNKS." Temporal integration and temporal segmentation ("time chunking") are also subject to plastic change in learning. Most cortical physiologists study the representations of discrete, transient stimuli. In reality, the cortex is almost always engaged by continuous input streams. Many psychophysicists but few neurophysiologists have studied how the brain processes information in those streams. Studies indicate that the brain represents fundamental features of stimuli within separate, parallel, spectral/spatial, and to some extent feature-selective input channels, and that it *creates its descriptions of stimulus features by temporally "chunking" the input.* Considered in simplest terms, inputs that arrive at the cortical machine within a time chunk are integrated, while inputs arriving at wider time separations are representationally *segregated.*[13,16,31,58] At least in hearing, there appears to be a spatially arrayed and channel-specific treatment of this temporal chunking.[82,83,114]

If we reflect back on the basic time constants governing cortical input co-selection, behaviorally manifested time chunking may simply reflect the time constants of cortical integration mechanisms. It is certainly in the correct time domain, i.e., tens to several hundreds of milliseconds.

The basic temporal chunking of the cortical machine has been investigated by scientists who have engaged animal physiological and human psychophysical and physiological models with simple input sequences. Physiological studies indicate that any transient input engages cortical pyramidal cells to pass through excitatory-inhibitory cycles that endure for several tens to hundreds of milliseconds. Strongly engaged sectors of cortical networks cannot be very effectively excited by a second stimulus until a period of time passes—not shorter, as a rule, than 15 to more than 300 or 400 or more milliseconds.[61,80,82,83,114] These physiological cycle times correspond roughly to cortical "integration times" as they are estimated perceptually. We can think of the cortical machine in this respect as being designed to read out its integrated resultants every 30 or 50 or 100 or 150 or 200 milliseconds, when it recovers its excitability and a response is again effectively evocable in a new input "moment."

There are a number of lines of evidence that indicate that this basic "chunk time" or "integration time," whatever its neurological origins, can be shortened by behavioral training. In psychophysical studies, investigators have shown that the basic perceptual integration time—e.g., the minimal durations of detectable or recognizable stimuli—can be reduced severalfold by training a subject in a signal detection, signal discrimination, modulation-fusion, backward masking, or time order judgment behavioral task (Karni and Sagi,[41] this volume).[5,6,33,42,43]

Interestingly, no human studies have yet investigated the obvious possibility that the basic temporal processing time might also be *degraded* by appropriate behavioral practice. On the other hand, our studies show that it clearly degrades in the absence of behavioral practice, and a growing body of evidence indicates that it can be *actively* degraded in learning. Studies now underway in our laboratory are designed to directly elaborate these important issues.

(F) CORTICAL PLASTICITY STUDIES INDICATE THAT THERE ARE AT LEAST THREE POSSIBLE CONTRIBUTORY SOURCES OF TEMPORAL CHUNKING, AND TO BEHAVIORALLY INDUCED CHANGES IN TIME CHUNKING. *First*, as a behaviorally important stimulus engages a cortical sector, it drives changes in input effectivenesses not just in extrinsically delivered inputs, but for interconnections within the cortical network itself.[1,14,39,57,60,75,76,78,100,101] As a consequence, as complex stimuli repeatedly engage a cortical network zone in behavior, neurons that selectively represent parts or all of crucial stimulus features for each moment in time come to be more and more strongly positively *interconnected*, again by operation of a Hebbian synapse strengthening rule operating within the cortical net. There are several important consequences of this strengthened interneuronal coupling of distributed neuron populations that concurrently and selectively represent complex features of behaviorally important inputs.[14,16,39,60,78,100,101]

i. Neurons begin to respond more and more alike, because they operate progressively more strongly as a syncitium in their mutual swapping of specific behaviorally important input combinations.

ii. More concurrently responding neurons hypothetically "bind" distributed response events into an external object- or event-specific distributed neuron assembly.

iii. The more powerfully coherent these distributed responses become over time, the more salient they are for encoding the specific stimulus moment, and the more powerful they are for inducing changes at "higher" system levels that are driven to change by the operation of the same coincident-input co-selection mechanisms.

iv. Finally, with neurons discharging progressively more synchronously to each event in time, individual stimulus events are represented not only more saliently, but also more *discretely* in time.

Thus, if we track the representation of behaviorally important stimuli reconstructed all across a cortical area they engage through a period of training-based improvements in time order judgment behavior, in the naive case they excite neurons with a proportionally high level of distributed temporal response dispersion. With training, the numbers of neurons responding to these stimuli progressively increases—but paradoxically, temporal dispersions of neuronal discharges in distributed populations are greatly reduced, apparently because of progressively strengthened, positive network cross-coupling. That is another way of saying that successive temporal stimuli are progressively more sharply time-marked, more discretely separated in their individual representation, in time. With practice, the monkey (and presumably our child) can now detect and discriminate and recognize finer differences in temporal order in the input stream because individual stream events are now represented more discretely and saliently in time.

Second, we have constructed cortical network models that emphasize an obvious feature of cortical nets operating on the basis of coincident input co-strengthening: The cortical machine creates selective representations of different temporal input sequences by virtue of its fixed excitatory and inhibitory processes.[7,8] In other words, within the limits of several hundred milliseconds of time, if a local region of a cortical network is delivered inputs like a consonant-vowel stimulus or a temporal order judgment stimulus pair in a given time sequence, a subpopulation of network neurons will be automatically engaged to respond selectively *to that* (or within the limits of several hundred milliseconds, to any other) *specific temporal sequence.* Again, we believe that Hebbian-based plasticity mechanisms in the cortex have the capacity to selectively strengthen the representations of these relevant-sequence-specific neurons.

Third, the cortex has built-in "extrinsic" and "intrinsic oscillators" that are engaged by transient inputs, and that modulate cortical network excitability.[11,52,80,86] Base oscillation periods appear to range from a few tens of milliseconds up to more than a hundred milliseconds; i.e., they are in the right time frame to contribute to temporal chunking of the input stream. The base periods of these "neural oscillators" are increased by membrane depolarization,[86] which is a function of the strengths of behaviorally important inputs. Hypothetically, a behaviorally engaged cortical sector will develop more strongly correlated activation of these neurons, which should depolarize them, thereby increasing their base oscillation frequency and contributing to faster input stream chunking.

It would appear likely that all three of these main effects contribute to the striking plasticity of temporal processing that has been recorded in animal and human behavioral experiments.

(G) LEARNING CAN GENERATE BOTH "POSITIVE" AND "NEGATIVE" REPRESENTATIONAL CHANGES. When we engage our nervous systems in a learning exercise, we change representations both positively and negatively, in at least three respect. First, the forms of applied stimuli can generate changes that result in more, or *less* spatially or temporally refined representational constructs. For example, if our child exercises its auditory cortical zones with its mother's temporally and spectrally refined inputs, that will result in the creation of cortical representations that progressively devolve in their neural representational form to represent these stimuli in more and more detail. On the other hand, if those training stimuli are spectrally and temporally diffused—muffled, for example, because our child has the misfortune to have its ears filled with fluid and bacteria while it struggles to understand its mother's speech—representational constructs generated in the cortex can have *degraded* representational detail.

Second, weak or consistently meaningless stimuli can actually generate negative, connectional-*weakening* changes in the cortex.[1,10,18,20,57,59] This "unlearning" appears to be as much an active, synapse-modifying process as is learning itself. In the case of our now (alas) hearing-defective child, it could hypothetically contribute powerfully and enduringly to the generation of a poor, incomplete—and ultimately for language operations inadequate—representation of the phonological features of aural speech and language.

Third, as noted above, cortical plasticity processes are competitive. If our hypothetical child had earlier learned American Sign Language as its first language, as described above, ASL would have competitively occupied language areas normally dominated by aural inputs, and without (probably even with) heavy training, thereby competitively limit the establishment of hearing-based speech constructs across these same forebrain zones.

(H) CORTICAL REPRESENTATIONAL CHANGE IS MODULATED AS A FUNCTION OF BEHAVIORAL STATE. Cortical representational changes are driven in the cerebral cortex in an animal performing an important (attended, rewarded) behavior. Little or no enduring change is generated when stimuli are delivered with the monkey not attending to or responding to them.[1,78,79]

(I) THE CEREBRAL CORTEX IS A "LEARNING MACHINE." CHANGES REPRESENTING LEARNED BEHAVIORS FADE WHEN AN OVERLEARNED BEHAVIOR BECOMES "AUTO-MATIC." Finally, it might be noted that when practiced behaviors become more automatic, they generate change in the cortex to a proportionally lesser degree, and that with high automaticity, learning-based changes fade in the cortex.[36,35,57,59,60,66,69] In this respect, the cortex can be viewed as a learning machine that creates a kind of homeostatic representation of learned behaviors. That is:

i.   Positive changes are induced in the cortex during attended learning, with the generation of progressively more salient, more temporally synchronized distributed neuronal representations of all of the important spectral and temporal events in the behavior.

ii. The progressively spectrotemporally-more-predictable behavior is driven to stereotypy. In stereotyped form, it provides a much more statistically reliable and neurologically powerful source of "teaching signals" for higher cortical levels and for extracortical structures.

iii. Changes fade in the cortex when a well-learned stereotyped behavior does not have to be held in memory for its performance or is performed automatically—without attention—presumably because the crucial enabling modulatory inputs that signal the cognitive importances of inputs and response events in the behavior are no longer present.

iv. If the behavior fails or degrades when it is performed without attention, the cortex can be reengaged to again contribute to its reestablishment or re-refinement, by reattention.

v.   Automatic behaviors provide a reliable platform for the full engagement of the cortical machine for higher-level and more elaborated behaviors.

IMPLICATIONS OF CORTICAL PLASTICITY MECHANISMS FOR THE ORIGINS OF LEARNING DISABILITIES

1. DYSPHASIA AND DYSLEXIA PHENOMENOLOGY

There is a complicated history of study of the perceptual capabilities of dyslexics and dysphasics. Here, we focus on several simple aspects of the behavioral phenomenology of language-based learning disabled (LD) children that appear to be plausibly related to cortical learning mechanisms.

(A) LANGUAGE-BASED LEARNING DISABLED CHILDREN HAVE ABNORMAL TEMPO-
RAL INTEGRATION AND TEMPORAL SEGMENTATION CAPABILITIES. Perhaps the
best documented fundamental "deficiency" in learning disabled (LD) individuals
is in their processing of temporally sequenced inputs. At least a large percentage
of dysphasic and dyslexic children have adequate time order judgment, backward
masking and modulated input-fusion (e.g., flicker fusion) capabilities for relatively
long-duration stimulus elements presented in sequence, but break down in their
stimulus segmentation and stimulus event recognition at higher stimulus input
stream rates, and with shorter-duration stimulus element events (Tallal,[92] this
volume).[3,24,85,93,94,95,99,107,108] While this deficit is commonly interpreted to be
a failure of the neural mechanisms that account for stimulus element segmentation, it presumably also reflects the fact that the integrative processes in their
forebrains—what the learning machinery interprets as "simultaneous" or as stimulus "moments"—would appear to have longer durations than apply for normal
children. In this respect, it is interesting to note that limited observations indicate that LD children appear to have nearly normal capabilities for reconstructing
speech element combinations when successive fast elements fall within different
frequency channels, but cannot recognize or separate equally fast input sequences
when successive elements fall largely within the same channel.[117]

   That suggests that the deficiency lies with an abnormal operation of the fundamental integration/segmentation process itself, and not with the forebrain's abilities
to deal with sequenced inputs or to recognize fast elements, *per se.*

   The exact nature of the temporal processing deficit is still incompletely defined.
While we and others are now working to resolve remaining uncertainties, what is
unequivocally demonstrated in numerous neuropsychological studies in LD children
is that at least a large proportion of them inappropriately integrate and segment
fast incoming acoustic stream information.

(B) LD CHILDREN MAY ALSO HAVE ABNORMAL SPATIAL (SPECTRAL) LOCALIZATION
AND INTEGRATION BEHAVIORS. Several classes of studies indicate that dyslexic
children have a wider or less stable field of view than do normal children. That is
suggested, for example, by their eye movement behaviors in vision, in which the
eyes can be relatively stable for viewing long orthographic strings.[23,48] Abnormal
spectral/spatial processing is also indicated by studies that demonstrated a poorer
ability for locating visual stimuli,[88,102] and in studies that indicate that there is a
relatively wide visual spatial domain over which "lateral masking" effects can be
generated in simple psychophysical studies.[9,30,89] Parametrically controlled studies
of this class have not yet been conducted in the auditory sphere.

   These scattered, limited findings are consistent with neurophysiological evidence that indicates that there may be a consistent link between normal and defective temporal segmentation and spectral/spatial integration in the cerebral cortex.[84]
In general, slower temporal chunking might be expected to arise in a system that

treats inputs with broader input filters because they deliver inputs into the system that consistently have greater temporal dispersion. This aspect of the basic psychophysics of LD children should be more completely investigated.

(C) THESE DEFICIENCIES OPERATING IN THE AUDITORY FOREBRAIN ARE PROBABLY THE MAIN CAUSE OF THE CREATION OF A WEAK PHONOLOGICAL REPRESENTATION OF SPEECH. There is now wide agreement that LD children including dyslexics, through their early childhood history, develop an inadequate representation of the phonological features of speech.[34,71,81,87,95] This poor language-element reference base contributes substantially to reading acquisition difficulties. At the same time, it should be emphasized that in parallel with this deficient speech element representation, abnormal temporal processing of fast element input rates in the speech input stream must be a continuing and persistent problem for speech reception and production in these special children.

(D) THE ABNORMAL TEMPORAL AND SPATIAL PERFORMANCE LIMITATIONS IN LEARNING DISABLED CHILDREN APPEAR TO BE EXPRESSED FOREBRAIN-WIDE. One fascinating aspect of the temporal processing deficit that marks the LD condition is that it appears to be expressed forebrain wide. That is, simple temporal segmentation measures expressed in stimulus modulation or time order judgment behaviors appear to be defective in these children in the somesthetic, auditory, and visual cortical systems[51,87,96,117]—and movement (speech production) representations also appear to be roughly equivalently temporally defective.[50,90] This last fact is potentially important for the development and persistence of temporal processing inadequacies in speech reception, because roughly half of the speech that the LD child hears—its very own, and of course its most invariant, learned model of "acoustically correct" speech—is consistently temporally sluggish.

2. HOW MIGHT LEARNING/PLASTICITY MECHANISMS RELATE TO OR ACCOUNT FOR THESE MULTIMODAL "ABNORMALITIES" IN TEMPORAL AND POSSIBLY SPATIAL/SPECTRAL INPUT PROCESSING THAT MARK THE LD CONDITION?

There are at least three main classes of explanation that might account for these abnormal psychophysical performance capabilities in a LD child. First, the child might have inherited learning machinery that permanently limits its temporal integration/segmentation capacities. Second, the child might have created temporally defective speech representations through the operation of normal learning mechanisms processing defective aural (or visual) inputs. Third, the child might have developed temporally limited speech feature representations through normal learning, by its use of a particular learning strategy that has resulted in a persistent, slower-than-normal time chunking.

It might be noted that the child might also have developed inadequate phonological representations because of a history of experiential deprivation, or of early language-cortex competition. On the other hand, the first of these special cases would almost certainly result in manifold learning and cognitive and psychophysical deficiencies. Physiological models of this condition indicate that all aspects of the creation of learned constructs are degraded in this scenario. Severe deprivation will also interplay with the latter scenario, which can have complex consequences in neurobehavioral development that are beyond the scope of this review.

What does our understanding of learning mechanisms in the brain inform us about these main LD origin scenarios?

(A) SCENARIO I. LEARNING DISABILITIES ARE DUE TO INHERITED, DEFECTIVE LEARNING MACHINERY. The fundamental biochemical and cellular mechanisms underlying learning are the subject of intensive and extensive investigation that is beyond our purview. Suffice it to say that a number of key molecular elements and processes in the learning process have been identified, and the consequences of manipulating or eliminating a growing number of them has been investigated by the use of pharmacological blockers and genetic "knockout" preparations. While a number of proteins and peptides have been shown to participate in the learning processes of the brain, *none* have yet been shown to play a critical role in temporal feature representation that could account, in their absence or dysfunction, for generating specific temporal processing deficits. However, this work is still very incomplete, and temporal processing-specific effects due to genetic mutations may ultimately be recorded. Moreover, it should be pointed out that despite its potential importance for understanding the possible origins of LDs, few cellular or molecular neurobiologists studying these issues actually investigate how molecular processes in neurons or local neuron circuits might relate to the integration and segmentation of temporally sequenced inputs.

At this point, there is little compelling evidence for the inheritance of any specific molecular deficit as a primary cause of the LD condition. While LDs that occur in children with normal nonverbal intelligence may run in families,[49,97,98] the causes of such LDs have not yet been demonstrated to lie with any specific gene or protein—indeed, have not yet been linked to any defect in the learning machinery of the brain itself.

A second class of explanation for the inheritance of LDs has come from evidence that there may be physical differences in the brains of LD children, for example, selectively affecting magnocellular parts of their visual and auditory systems,[28,29] or possibly manifested by differences in auditory cortical zones[17,27,40,46,47] or in other anomalous anatomical and functional features expressed more widely across the forebrain.[26,28,40] These explanations have the important virtue that they plausibly involve forebrain projection axes in at least the visual system that account for its fastest temporal processing. In the visual system of dyslexics, the magno-cellular retinal/central visual projection axis that accounts for the highest temporal resolution in vision appears to be morphologically and functionally defective. There is growing evidence for biochemical differences between this projection axis and the second great "system" (the "parvocellular system") which constitutes a basis for possibly selective, genetically based system dysfunction. On the other hand, the system deemed to be morphological normal in the auditory domain in these children is a fast transmission system; and the morphological changes in auditory and visual systems are not great, and could well represent *effects* of predominantly slow temporal processing, rather than their cause. The same effect/cause relationship might also apply for the failure of the auditory cortices in the LD child to develop normal morphological—or temporal processing—hemispheric asymmetry.[17,40,46,47,97,99] Moreover, functional degradation of aspects of cerebral dominance for speech can arise in non-LD subjects (e.g., in schizophrenics),[73,106] indicating that at least some aspects of the emergent, abnormally symmetric processing recorded in dyslexics might be acquired by experience, rather than inherited.

It should be noted in these respects that there is a long history of study of morphological change induced by system disuse or proportional inactivity that could account for the physical brain effects recorded in this functional disability.

It might be noted that our child acquiring speech and language beginning on its mother's lap who has inherited a flawed learning system will have deficiencies that undoubtedly represent a complex, compound product of the essential deficits resulting from the flaw and of the complex, multiple-level speech/language learning in the nervous system that carries this genetic flaw.

(B) SCENARIO 2. LEARNING DISABILITIES ARISE FROM A BRAIN THAT DEVELOPS ITS SPEECH/LANGUAGE CONSTRUCTS FROM A HISTORICAL PLATFORM OF DEFECTIVE AURAL (OR VISUAL) INPUTS. Consider a second plausible scenario for the origins of childhood LDs. During the period of development of speech reception and production, our child has chronic middle ear infections. As a consequence, its hearing is consistently muffled. The speech of its mother is weakly modulated, and statistically unreliable. Its own babble, and later its organized utterances, are heard weakly, and with statistical uncertainties that would not normally occur. While it struggles to develop hearing-based speech constructs, visual and gestural inputs are proportionally more important than for a normal child.

On the basis of what we now understand about the nature of learning mechanisms in the brain, there can be expected to be two main consequences of this early experiential history. *First,* behaviorally important inputs for this child will be marked by substantially greater-than-normal temporal dispersion. This muffled, weakly modulated and statistically unreliable speech will be inherently less powerful for generating reliable phonological constructs in its hearing nervous system. Moreover, with greater input dispersion, temporal integration must occur over longer time periods to generate reliable outputs. By these two causes, slow time chunking that applies for the very young infant cannot be very substantially further refined. *Second*, the child's own speech is an unreliable acoustic input source, with far less power contributed to the development of its phonological representations. Moreover, the child's own speech is most clearly understood when it matches the time characteristics of its developing reception apparatus. Operating synergistically normally, here speech reception and speech production plasticity operate synergistically to meet the requirements of a persistent, slow-time-chunking processing of the input stream.

As the condition of muffled hearing persists, the child receives thousands, tens of thousands, hundreds of thousands, millions of speech inputs, which in their degraded delivery into the hearing nervous system create a treatment of speech reception that is optimally adapted to the child's own limited hearing and clumsy speech. However, at some point in the life of our child, the middle ear infections are overcome and more normal hearing restored. The child's own speech and its reception of externally received speech is now mismatched with its auditory forebrain's formerly optimal processing mode, because the temporal chunking that is most reliable for representing muffled speech is scarcely adequate for representing the now-normal acoustic input stream.

At this point, the child's forebrain has created an experientially based trap, an exaggerated version of what commonly confronts a high school or college student who has undertaken the learning of a foreign language. In the foreign language class, deliberately produced and spoken speech has been well understood. The language has been mastered, *but not in fast time.* Many distinctions in the speech stream that were clear to the language student when learned when the input stream was slow are undetected with the normal metre of speech generated by a native speaker.

For our child, the consequences of defective hearing will be more severe, for four reasons. First, the temporal processing deficit is more severe. Second, half of the speech that the child hears, its own, is statistically powerful, temporally defective, and (unlike the foreign language student) the only speech that it has in its motoric repertoire. Third, by virtue of its extensive temporally defective speech-based hearing practice, the child has learned to chunk acoustic information for all of its other auditory reception operations as a rule. Fourth, to align its motor outputs and visual and other sensory inputs with its receptive processing in audition across a developmental period of life, the child has apparently imposed the slow temporal chunking generated initially from its auditory system on signal processing operations that apply forebrain wide. Reversal of this defective temporal processing is no longer limited to the speech domain alone, but now involves heavily practiced, multimodal and multilevel changes that are deeply embedded all across our child's forebrain.

The result: A poor phonological representation generated for externally received speech; defectively produced speech, which contributes to the maintenance of defective speech reception; and defective forebrain-wide temporal chunking that shall ultimately have cognitive consequences that extend far beyond the operations of speech and language—all now resident in the forebrain in a massive and deeply embedded form.

It might be pointed out that this scenario may not be strictly dependent upon early defective hearing. It could conceivably also arise from infant limitations in vision or movement. In that case, the sluggish temporal processing arising in those systems could be imposed on the hearing nervous system, just as the opposite would apply from an early hearing loss scenario. The same ultimate result would be recorded: Temporally defective speech reception and speech production would be optimum for a system struggling to maintain coordinated temporal treatment of visual imagery and speaking faces, and aurally received speech, but inadequate for creating strong phonological constructs of external speech reception streaming into the system in its real-time metre.

(C) SCENARIO 3. LEARNING DISABILITIES ARISE AS A PRODUCT OF NORMAL LANGUAGE LEARNING. It seems highly likely to us that Scenario 2 does occur. Early school age children identified as learning disabled frequently have a clear history of middle ear infections, and when the temporal processing of such children has been documented, they have been found to be indistinguishable from LD children in which the disabilities has originated from idiopathic causes. It is also highly likely that some of the genetic determinants of LD actually apply to preconditions for eye control or hearing through early childhood that predispose children to LD origin.

At the same time, we would also like to emphasize that the development of defective temporal processing in these children does not necessarily require that any abnormal learning operations were ever in play in our child. To the contrary, the powerful self-organizing mechanisms of the human neocortex almost certainly operate to produce the most salient information possible from the input stream, in a brain that provides continual feedback modulating positive change on the basis of the value or estimated correctness of its perceptual and motoric products. For many LD children, there is no obvious source of defective inputs. Could it be possible that temporal processing deficits could arise in a completely normal individual, without any assist from defective hearing or vision?

Let us imagine that our child on its mother's lap adapted a different listening or seeing strategy than applies for the majority of infant humans. As it is developing controlled eye movements, it adopts a strategy of wider-than-normal viewing, or less sharply filtered hearing than do other children. We might imagine that this strategy could be developed as a learned habit, rewarded in the developing nervous system, plausibly because our child has greater primitive powers of signal integration in very early life than would otherwise be the case. Wide field viewing or hearing means that inputs are received with statistically greater than normal temporal dispersions. In such a scenario, our hypothetical, perfectly normal child prefers and intensively practices wide-field complex viewing and listening—which, alas, is maladapted for speech reception and speech production acquisition. As a consequence of its early training, our child has not refined its temporal processing in the visual or hearing domain, and its self-organizing exercises have imposed slow temporal chunking forebrain wide. The production of mutually reinforcing sluggish speech and slow temporal processing in speech reception results.

ON THE BASIS OF WHAT WE UNDERSTAND ABOUT BRAIN PLASTICITY IN LEARNING, AND GIVEN THESE ORIGIN SCENARIOS, WHAT APPROACHES COULD WE ADOPT FOR REMEDIATING LDs IN CHILDREN?

If we inherit genetic defects that account for LDs, the prospect for correcting this condition may ultimately depend upon a "gene replacement therapy" designed to correct the molecular/structural defect that is at fault. That does not mean, however, that we cannot employ the normal, powerful learning mechanisms of the brain to potentially significantly remediate this condition. At the heart of designing that remediation strategy is our gaining a more complete understanding of the perceptual operational deficiencies of the learning machinery, and of the root cause(s) of these deficiencies and how their existence might affect learning optima.

If we commonly acquire LDs by normal learning mechanisms operating on either defective inputs, or operating aberrantly on normal inputs, then the learning machinery can be expected to be substantially or completely intact. Parts of sensory systems may have atrophied due to their limited functional engagement; but there is a long history of forebrain studies that point to a strong potential for reversing such atrophy. However, given an experiential history that has very strongly embedded defective temporal processing widely across the forebrain, how can we hope to reverse it?

We believe that there are two obvious strategies that could be pursued. First, a major task is to strengthen our LD child's phonological constructs. We are trying to achieve that by providing LD children with processed speech inputs that, even for their defective brain machinery, are (a) more salient and temporally prolonged, and thereby more intelligible, and (b) temporally modified to provide more synchronous—for the coincidence-input based cortical learning machinery more powerful—teaching inputs for creating a stronger phonological representation with the cortical learning machinery. In collaboration with Dr. Paula Tallal and colleagues (at Rutgers University, Newark), we are conducting studies in which we are trying to intensively train children to make temporal order distinctions in training exercises, and in which children are exercised intensively with running speech processed to increase its salience and learning power. Our objective is to determine if we can significantly remediate and possibly ultimately overcome the fundamental temporal processing deficit that marks the LD condition in these children.

Second, because defective temporal processing in these children is commonly expressed forebrain wide, we are also working to develop multisensory/motor training strategies, in an attempt to sharpen temporal processing in coordinated, integrated speech reception/speech production and speech/nonspeech behaviors.

One or both of these approaches should contribute to at least the partial remediation of this condition whatever its true origins, because these are strategies by which the consequences of learning-based improvements in temporal chunking can be optimized with respect to the specific requirements of the brain's learning machinery. On the basis of our growing understanding of the principles of learning mechanisms in the brain, and from information gained from specific models of the origins and remediation of LDs, it may ultimately be possible for a large percentage of the LD population to substantially overcome this common human disability.

ACKNOWLEDGMENTS

This work was supported by NIH Grant NS-10414, the Dana Foundation, Hearing Research, Inc., and the Coleman Fund.

REFERENCES

1. Ahissar, E., E. Vaadia, M. Ahissar, H. Bergman, A. Arieli, and M. Abeles. "Dependence of Cortical Plasticity on Correlated Activity of Single Neurons and on Behavioral Context." *Science* **257** (1992): 1412–1415.
2. Aizawa, H., M. Inase, H. Mushiake, K. Shima, and J. Tanji. "Reorganization of Activity in the Supplementary Motor Area Associated with Motor Learning and Functional Recovery." *Exp. Brain Res.* **84** (1991): 778–671.
3. Anderson, K. C., C. P. Brown, and P. Tallal. "Developmental Language Disorders: Evidence for a Basic Processing Deficit." *Curr. Opin. Neurol. Neurosurg.* **6** (1993): 93–106.
4. Aou, S. J., C. D. Woody, and D. Birt. "Change in the Activity of Units of the Cat Motor Cortex After Rapid Conditioning and Extinction of a Compound Eye Blink Movement." *J. Neurosci.* **12** (1992): 549–559.
5. Ball, K., and R. Sekuler. "A Specific and Enduring Improvement in Visual Motion Discrimination." *Science* **218** (1982): 697–698.
6. Ball, K., and R. Sekuler. "Direction-Specific Improvement in Motion Discrimination." *Vision Res.* **27** (1987): 953–965.
7. Buonomano, D., and M. Merzenich. "A Cortical Neural Network Model of Temporal Information Processing." *Neurosci. Abstr.* **19** (1993): 1609.
8. Buonomano, D., and M. Merzenich. (1994) [need reference]
9. Carmean, S. L., and R. A. Regeth. "Optimum Level of Visual Contrast Sensitivity for Reading Comprehension." *Percept. Motor Skills* **71** (1990): 755–762.
10. Clothiaux, E. E., M. F. Bear, and L. N. Cooper. "Synaptic Plasticity in Visual Cortex: Comparison of Theory with Experimental." *J. Neurophysiol.* **77** (1992): 1785–1804.
11. Connors, B. W., and M. J. Gutnick. "Intrinsic Firing Patterns of Diverse Neocortical Neurons." *Trends Neurosci.* **13** (1990): 99–104.
12. Diamond, D. M., and N. M. Weinberger. "Classical Conditioning Rapidly Induces Specific Changes in Frequency Receptive Fields of Single Neurons in Secondary and Ventral Extosylvian Auditory Cortical Fields." *Brain Res.* **3672** (1986): 357–360.
13. diLollo, V. "Temporal Integration in Visual Memory." *J. Exp. Psychol.* **109** (1980): 75–97.
14. Dinse, H., G. H. Recanzone, and M. M. Merzenich. "Alterations in Correlated Activity Parallel ICMS-Induced Representational Plasticity." *NeuroReport* **5** (1993): 173–176.
15. Disterhoft, J. F., and D. K. Stuart. "Trial Sequence of Changed Unit Activity in Auditory System of Alert Rat During Conditioned Response Acquisition and Extinction." *J. Neurophysiol.* **39** (1976): 266–281.
16. Dixon, P., and V. diLollo. "Beyond Visible Persistence: An Alternative Account of Temporal Integration and Segregation in Visual Processing." *Cog. Psychol.* **26** (1994): 33–63.

17. Duara, R., A. Kushch, K. Gross-Glenn, W. W. Barker, B. Jallad, S. Pascal, D. A. Loewenstein, J. Shendon, M. Rabin, and B. Levin. "Neuronanbatomic Differences Between Dyslexic and Normal Readers on Magnetic Resonance Imaging Scans." *Arch. Neurol.* **48** (1992): 410–416.
18. Dudek, S. M., and M. E. Bear. "Bidirectional Long-Term Modification of Synaptic Effectiveness in the Adult and Immature Hipposcampus." *J. Neurosci.* **143** (1993): 2910–2918.
19. Edeline, J. M., P. Pham, and N. M. Weinberger. "Rapid Development of Learning-Induced Receptive Field Plasticity in the Auditory Cortex." *Behav. Neurosci.* **107** (1993): 5329–5551.
20. Edeline, J. M., and N. M. Weinberger. "Receptive Field Plasticity in the Auditory Cortex During Frequency Discrimination Training: Selective Retuning Independent of Task Difficulty." *Behav. Neurosci.* **107** (1993): 82–103.
21. Edelman, G. M. *Neuronal Darwinism: The Theory of Neuronal Group Selection.* New York: Basic Books, 1987.
22. Engel, Jr., J., and C. D. Woody. "Effects of Character and Significance of Stimulus on Unit Activity at Coronal-Pericruciate Cortex of Cat During Performance of Conditioned Motor Response." *J. Neurophysiol.* **35** (1972): 220–229.
23. Evans, B. J., and N. Drasdo. "Review of Opthalmic Factors in Dyslexia." *Opthal. Physiol. Optics* **10** (1990): 123–132.
24. Farmer, M. E., and R. Klein. "Auditory and Visual Temporal Processing in Dyslexic and Normal Readers." *Ann. NY Acad. Sci.* **682** (1993): 339–341.
25. Felleman, D. J., and D. C. Van Essen. "Distributed Hierarchical Processing in the Primate Cerebral Cortex." *Cerebral Cortex* (1992): 1–47.
26. Flynn, J. M., W. Deering, M. Goldstein, and M. H. Rahbar. "Electrophysiological Correlates of Dyslexic Subtypes." *J. Learn Dis.* **25** (1992): 133–141.
27. Galaburda, A. M., G. F. Sherman, G. D. Rosen, F. Aboitiz, and N. Geschwind. "Developmental Dyslexia: Four Consecutive Patients with Cortical Anomalies." *Ann. Neurol.* **18** (1985): 222–233.
28. Galaburda, A. M. "Neuranatomic Basis of Developmental Dyslexia." *Neurol. Clinics* **11** (1993): 161–173.
29. Galaburda, A., and M. Livingstone. "Evidence for a Magnocellular Defect in Developmental Dyslexia." *Ann. NY Acad. Sci.* **682** (1993): 70–82.
30. Geiger, G., J. Y. Lettvin, and M. Fahle. "Dyslexic Children Learn a New Visual Strategy for Reading: A Controlled Experiment." *Vision Res.* **34** (1994): 1223–1233.
31. Gerken, G. M., V. K. Bhat, and M. Hutchinson-Clutter. "Auditory Temporal Integration and the Power Function Model." *J. Acoust. Soc. Amer.* **88** (1990): 767–778.
32. Germain, L., and Y. Lamarre. "Neuronal Activity in the Motor and Premotor Cortices Before and After Learning the Associations Between Auditory Stimuli and Motor Responses." *Brain Res.* **611** (1993): 175–179.

33. Gibson, E. J. *Principles of Perceptual Learning.* New York: Appleton-Century-Crofts, 1969.
34. Goswami, U. "Phonological Skills and Learning to Read." *Ann. NY Acad. Sci.* **682** (1993): 296–311.
35. Grafton, S. T., J. C. Mazziotta, S. Presty, K. J. Friston, R. S. Frackowiak, and M. E. Phelps. "Functional Anatomy of Human Procedural Learning Determined with Regional Cerebral Blood Flow and PET." *J. Neurosci.* **12** (1992): 2542–2548.
36. Haier, R. J., B. V. Siegel, E. MacLachlan, E. Soderling, S. Lotenberg, and M. S. Buchsbaum. "Regional Glucose Metabolic Changes After Learning a Complex Visuospatial/Motor Task: A Positron Emission Tomographic Study." *Brain Res.* **570** (1992): 134–143.
37. Hebb, D. O. *The Organization of Behavior: A Neuropsychological Theory.* New York: Wiley, 1949.
38. Jenkins, W. M., M. M. Merzenich, M. T. Ochs, T. Allard, and R. E. Guic. "Functional Reorganization of Primary Somatosensory Cortex in Adult Owl Monkeys After Behaviorally Controlled Tactile Stimulation." *J. Neurophysiol.* **63** (1990): 82–104.
39. Jenkins, W. M., R. Beitel, C. Xerri, B. Peterson, X. Wang, and M. M. Merzenich. "Behavioral Measurements of Vibrotactile Frequency Response and Temporal Response Properties of Neurons in S1 Cortex of Trained Owl Monkeys: Threshold Shifts and Duration Effects." *Neurosci. Abstr.* **19** (1993): 162.
40. Jernigan, T. L., J. R. Hesselink, E. Sowell, and P. A. Tallal. "Cerebral Structure on Magnetic Resonance Imaging in Language and Learning-Impaired Children." *Arch. Neurol.* **48** (1991): 539–545.
41. Karni, A., and D. Sagi. "A Memory System in the Adult Visual Cortex." This volume.
42. Karni, A., and D. Sagi. "Where Practice Makes Perfect in Texture Discrimination—Evidence for Primary Visual Cortex Plasticity." *Proc. Natl. Acad. Sci. USA* **88**: 4966–4970.
43. Karni, A., and D. Sagi. "The Time Course of Learning a Visual Skill." *Nature* **365** (1993): 250–252.
44. Kobatake, E., K. Tanaka, G. Wang, and Y. Tamori. "Effects of Adult Learning on the Stimulus Selectivity of Cells in the Inferotemporal Cortex." *Neurosci. Abstr.* **19** (1992): 975.
45. Kossut, M. "Plasticity of the Barrel Cortex Neurons." *Prog. Neurobiol.* **39** (1992): 389–422.
46. Kusch, A., K. Gross-Glenn, B. Jallad, H. Lubs, H. Rabin, E. Feldman, and R. Duara. "Temporal Lobe Surface Area Measurements on MRI in Normal and Dyslexic Readers." *Neuropsychologia* **31** (1993): 811–821.
47. Larson, J. P., T. Hoien, I. Lundberg, and H. Odegaard. "MRI Evaluation of the Size and Symmetry of the Planum Temporale in Adolescents with Developmental Dyslexia." *Brain & Language* **39** (1990): 289–301.

48. Lennerstrand, G., and J. Ygge. "Dyslexia; Opthalmological Aspects." *Acta Opthal.* **70** (1992): 3–13.

49. Lewis, B. A., N. J. Cox, and P. J. Bayard. "Segregation Analysis of Speech and Language Disorders." *Behav. Genetics* **23** (1993): 291–297.

50. Lovegrove, W. J., R. P. Garzia, and S. R. Nicholson. "Experimental Evidence for a Transient System Deficit in Specific Reading Disability." *J. Amer. Optom. Assoc.* **61** (1990): 137–146.

51. Lovegrove, W. "Weakness in the Transient Visual System: A Causal Factor in Dyslexia?" *Ann. NY Acad. Sci.* **682** (1993): 57–69.

52. McCormick, D. A. "Neurotransmitter Actions in the Thalamus and Cerebral Cortex and Their Role in Neuromodulation of Thalamocortical Activity." *Prog. Neurobiol.* **39** (1992): 337–388.

53. Merzenich, M. M., G. H. Recanzone, W. M. Jenkins, T. Allard, and R. J. Nudo. "Cortical Representational Plasticity." In *Neurobiology of Neocortex*, edited by P. Rakic and W. Singer. New York: Wiley, 1988.

54. Merzenich, M. M., G. M. Recanzone, and W. M. Jenkins. "How the Brain Functionally Rewires Itself." In *Natural and Artificial Parallel Computations*, edited by M. Arbib and J. A. Robinson. New York: MIT Press, 1990.

55. Merzenich, M. M., G. M. Recanzone, W. M. Jenkins, and K. A. Grajski. "Adaptive Mechanisms in Cortical Networks Underlying Cortical Contributions to Learning and Nondeclarative Memory." *Cold Spring Harbor Symp. Quant. Biol.* **55** (1990): 873–887.

56. Merzenich, M. M., and W. M. Jenkins. "Reorganization of Cortical Representations of the Hand Following Alterations of Skin Inputs Induced by Nerve Injury, Skin Island Transfers, and Experience." *J. Hand Ther.* **8** (1993): 898–104.

57. Merzenich, M. M., and K. Samashima. "Cortical Plasticity and Memory." *Current Opin. Neurobiol.* **3** (1993): 187–196.

58. Merzenich, M. M., C. S. Schreiner, W. M. Jenkins, and X. Wang. "Neural Mechanisms Underlying Temporal Integration, Segmentation, and Input Sequence Representation: Some Implications for the Origin of Learning Disabilities." *Ann. NY Acad. Sci.* **682** (1993): 1–22.

59. Merzenich, M. M., and C. DeCharms. "Neural Representations, Experience and Change." In *Mind and Brain*, edited by R. Llinas and P. Churchland. Cambridge, MA: MIT Press, in press.

60. Merzenich, M. M., and W. M. Jenkins. "Cortical Representation of Learned Behaviors." In *Memory Concepts*, edited by P. Anderson, O. Hvalby, O. Paulsen, and B. Hokfelt. Amsterdam: Elsevier, 1994.

61. Merzenich, M. M., C. DeCharms, and K. Sameshima. Unpublished observations.

62. Milliken, G. W., R. J. Nudo, R. Grenda, W. M. Jenkins, and M. M. Merzenich. "Expansion of Distal Forelimb Representations in Primary Motor Cortex of Adult Squirrel Monkeys Following Motor Training." *Neurosci. Abstr.* **18** (1992): 506.

63. Mitz, A. R., M. Godschalk, and S. P. Wise. "Learning-Dependent Neuronal Activity in the Premotor Cortex: Activity During the Acquisition of Conditional Motor Associations." *J. Neurosci.* **11** (1991): 1855–1872.

64. Miyashita, Y. "Inferior Temporal Cortex: Where Visual Perception Meets Memory." *Ann. Rev. Neurosci.* **16** (1993): 245–263.

65. Neville, H. J. "Intermodal Competition and Compensation in Development. Evidence from Studies of the Visual System in Congenitally Deaf Adults." *Ann. NY Acad. Sci.* **608** (1990): 71–91.

66. Nudo, R., W. M. Jenkins, and M. M. Merzenich. Unpublished findings.

67. Pascual-Leone, A., and F. Torres. "Plasticity of the Sensorimotor Cortex Representation of the Reading Finger in Braille Readers." *Brain* **116** (1993): 39–52.

68. Pascual-Leone, A., A. Cammarota, E. M. Wassermann, J. P. Brasil-Neto, L. G. Cohen, and M. Hallett. "Modulation of Motor Cortical Outputs to the Reading Hand of Braille Readers." *Ann. Neurol.* **34** (1993): 33–37.

69. Pascual-Leone, A., J. Grafman, and M. Hallett. "Modulation of Cortical Motor Output Maps During Development of Implicit and Explicit Knowledge." *Science* **263** (1994): 1287–1289.

70. Pavlov, I. P. *Conditioned Reflexes. An Investigation of the Physiological Activity of the Cerebral Cortex.* London: Oxford University Press, 1927.

71. Pennington, B. G., G. C. Van Orden, S. D. Smith, P. A. Green, and M. M. Haith. "Phonological Processing Skills and Deficits in Adult Dyslexics." *Child Devel.* **61** (1990): 1753–1778.

72. Pons, T. P., P. E. Garraghty, A. K. Ommaya, J. H. Kaas, E. Taub, and M. Mishkin. "Massive Cortical Reorganization After Sensory Deafferentation in Adult Macaques." *Science* **252** (1991): 1857–1860.

73. Ragland, J. D., T. E. Goldberg, B. E. Wexler, J. M. Gold, E. F. Torrey, and D. R. Weinberger. "Dischotic Listening in Monozygotic Twins Discordant and Concordant for Schizophrenia." *Schizophren. Res.* **7** (1992): 177–183.

74. Ramachandran, V. S. "Behavioral and Magnetoencephalographic Correlates of Plasticity in the Adult Human Brain." *Proc. Natl. Acad. Sci. USA* **90** (1993): 10413–10420.

75. Recanzone, G. H., and M. M. Merzenich. "Alterations of the Functional Organization of Primary Somatosensory Cortex Following Intracortical Microstimulation or Behavioral Training." In *Memory: Organization and Locus of Change*, edited by L. R. Squire, N. M. Weinberger, G. Lynch, and J. L. McGaugh. New York: Oxford University Press, 1991.

76. Recanzone, G. H., M. M. Merzenich, and H. R. Dinse. "Expansion of the Cortical Representation of a Specific Skin Field in Primary Somatosensory Cortex by Intracortical Microstimulation." *Cerebral Cortex* **2** (1992): 181–196.

77. Recanzone, G. H., M. M. Merzenich, and W. M. Jenkins. "Frequency Discrimination Training Engaging a Restricted Skin Surface Results in an Emergence

of a Cutaneous Response Zone in Cortical Area 3a." *J. Neurophysiol.* **67**: 1057–1070.

78. Recanzone, G. H., M. M. Merzenich, and C. E. Schreiner. "Changes in the Distributed Temporal Response Properties of S1 Cortical Neurons Reflect Improvements in Performance on a Temporally Based Tactile Discrimination Task." *J. Neurophysiol.* **67**: 1071–1091.

79. Recanzone, G. H., C. E. Schreiner, and M. M. Merzenich. "Plasticity in the Frequency Representation of Primary Auditory Cortex Following Discrimination Training in Adult Owl Monkeys." *J. Neurosci.* **13** (1993): 87–103.

80. Sameshima, K., and M. M. Merzenich. "Intrinsic Oscillator Contributions to Response Properties of SI Cortical Neurons." *Neurosci. Abstr.* **19** (1993): 1565.

81. Sawyer, D. J. "Language Abilities, Reading Acquisition, and Developmental Dyslexia: A Discussion of Hypothetical and Observed Relationships." *J. Learn. Disabilities* **25** (1993): 82–95.

82. Schreiner, C. E., and G. Langner. "Coding of Temporal Patterns in the Central Auditory Nervous System." In *Auditory Function*, edited by G. M. Edelman, W. E. Gall, and W. M. Cowan. New York: Wiley, 1988.

83. Schreiner, C. E., and J. V. Urbas. "Representation of Amplitude Modulation in the Auditory Cortex of Cat. II. Comparison Between Cortical Fields." *Hearing Res.* **32** (1988): 49–64.

84. Schreiner, C. Unpublished observations.

85. Shapiro, K. L., N. Ogden, and F. Lindblad. "Temporal Processing in Dyslexia." *J. Learn. Disabilities* **23** (1990): 99–107.

86. Silva, L. R., Y. Amitai, and B. W. Connors. "Intrinsic Oscillations of Neocortex Generated by Layer 5 Pyramidal Neurons." *Science* **251** (1991): 432–435.

87. Slaghuis, W. L., W. J. Lovegrove, and J. A. Davidson. "Visual and Language Processing Deficits are Concurrent in Dyslexia." *Cortex* **29** (1993): 601–615.

88. Solman, R. T., and J. G. May. "Spatial Localization Discrepancies: A Visual Deficiency in Poor Readers." *Amer. J. Psychol.* **103** (1990): 243–263.

89. Solman, R. T., S. J. Dain, and S. L. Keech. "Color-Mediated Contrast Sensitivity in Disabled Readers." *Optometry Vis. Sci.* **68** (1991): 331–337.

90. Stark, R. E., and P. Tallal. "Analysis of Stop Consonant Production Errors in Developmentally Dysphasic Children." *J. Acoust. Soc. Amer.* **66** (1979): 1703–1712.

91. Suner, S., D. Gutman, G. Gaas, J. N. Sanes, and J. P. Donoghue. "Reorganization of Monkey Motor Cortex Related to Motor Cortex Related to Motor Skill Learning." *Neurosci. Abstr.* **19** (1993): 775.

92. Tallal, P. "Development and Disorders of Speech and Language: Implications for Neural and Behavioral Plasticity." This volume.

93. Tallal, P., and M. Piercy. "Developmental Aphasia: Impaired Rate of Nonverbal Processing as a Function of Sensory Modality." *Neuropsychologia* **11** (1973): 389–398.

94. Tallal, P., and M. Piercy. "Developmental Aphasia: Rate of Auditory Processing and Selective Impairment of Consonant Perception." *Neurpsychologia* **12** (1974): 83–93.

95. Tallal, P. "Auditory Temporal Perception, Phonics and Reading Disabilities in Children." *Brain & Language* **9** (1980): 182–198.

96. Tallal, P., R. Stark, C. Kallman, and D. Mellits. "A Reexamination of Some Nonverbal Perceptual Abilities of Language-Impaired and Normal Children as a Function of Age and Sensory Modality." *J. Speech Hear. Res.* **24** (1981): 351–357.

97. Tallal, P., R. E. Stark, and E. D. Mellits. "Identification of Language-Impaired Children on the Basis of Rapid Perception and Production Skills." *Brain Language* **25** (1985): 314–322.

98. Tallal, P., J. Townsend, S. Curtiss, and B. Wulfech. "Phenotypic Profiles of Language-Impaired Children Based on Genetic/Family History." *Brain & Language* **41** (1991): 81–95.

99. Tallal, P., S. Miller, and R. H. Fitch. "Neurobiological Basis of Speech: A Case for the Pre-eminence of Temporal Processing." *Ann. NY Acad. Sci.* **682** (1993): 27–47.

100. Wang, X., R. Beitel, C. E. Schreiner, and M. M. Merzenich. "Representations of Natural and Synthetic Vocalizations in the Primary Auditory Cortex of an Adult Monkey." *Neurosci. Abstr.* **19** (1993): 1422.

101. Wang, X., M. M. Merzenich, and C. Schreiner. "Differential Representations of Behaviorally Important Vocalizations by Distributed Neuronal Populations in the Primary Auditory Cortex of the Marmoset Monkey." *Nature* (1994): submitted.

102. Warrington, E. K., L. Cipolotti, and J. McNeil. "Attentional Dyslexia: A Single Case Study." *Neuropsychologia* **31** (1993): 871–885.

103. Weinberger, N. M., J. H. Ashe, R. Metherate, T. M. McKenna, D. M. Diamond, and J. Bakin. "Retuning Auditory Cortex by Learning: A Preliminary Model of Receptive Field Plasticity." *Concepts Neurosci.* **1** (1990): 91–122.

104. Weinberger, N. M. "Learning-Induced Changes of Auditory Receptive Fields." *Curr. Opin. Neurobiol.* **3** (1993): 570–577.

105. Weinberger, N. M., R. Javid, and B. Lepan. "Long-Term Retention of Learning-Induced Receptive-Field Plasticity in the Auditory Cortex." *Proc. Natl. Acad. Sci. USA* **980** (1993): 2394–2398.

106. Wexler, B. E., E. L. Giller, Jr., and S. Southwick. "Cerebral Laterality, Symptoms, and Diagnosis in Psychotic Patients." *Biol. Psychiat.* **29** (1991): 103–116.

107. Williams, M. C., and K. Lecluyse. "Perceptual Consequences of a Temporal Processing Deficit in Reading Disabled Children." *J. Amer. Optom. Assoc.* **61** (1990): 111–121.

108. Woolf, P. H. "Impaired Temporal Resolution in Developmental Dyslexia." *Ann. NY Acad. Sci.* **682** (1993): 87–103.

109. Woody, C. D., and J. Engel. "Changes in Unit Activity and Thresholds to Electrical Microstimulation at Coronal-Pericruciate Cortex of Cat with Classical Conditioning of Different Facial Movements." *J. Neurophysiol.* **36** (1972): 230–252.

110. Woody, C. D., and P. Black-Cleworth. "Differences in Excitability of Cortical Neurons as a Function of Motor Projection in Conditioned Cats." *J. Neurophysiol.* **36** (1973): 1104–1116.

111. Woody, C. D., J. D. Knispel, T. J. Crow, and P. A. Black-Cleworth. "Activity and Excitability to Electrical Current of Cortical Auditory Receptive Neurons of Awake Cats as Affected by Stimulus Association." *J. Neurophysiol.* **39** (1976): 1045–1061.

112. Woody, C. D. "Understanding the Cellular Basis of Memory and Learning." *Ann. Rev. Psychol.* **327** (1986): 433.

113. Woody, C. D., E. Gruen, and D. Birt. "Changes in Membrane Currents During Pavlovian Conditioning of Single Cortical Neurons." *Brain Res.* **539** (1991): 76–84.

114. Wright, B. A., and H. Dai. "Detection of Unexpected Tones with Short and Long Durations." *J. Acoust. Soc. Amer.* **95** (1994): 931–938.

115. Xerri, C., W. M. Jenkins, B. Peterson, S. Santucci, and M. M. Merzenich. "Acquisition of Digital Dexterity and Parallel Remodeling in Area 3b Representations in Adult Owl and Squirrel Monkeys." *Neurosci. Abstr.* **19** (1993): 1570.

116. Xerri, C., J. M. Stern, and M. M. Merzenich. "Alterations of the Cortical Representation of the Rat Ventrum Induced by Nursing Behavior." *J. Neurosci.* **14** (1994): 1710–1721.

Index

ILLINOIS CENTRAL COLLEGE
PN1657.S3
STACKS
Public domain;

A12900 252841

W9-ADK-060

A12900 252841

PN
1657   SCHECHNER
.S3   Public domain

39326

WITHDRAWN

Illinois Central College
Learning Resource Center

Public Domain

Public Domain

Essays on the Theatre

by

Richard Schechner

Illinois Central College
Learning Resource Center

THE BOBBS-MERRILL COMPANY
Indianapolis and New York

39326

PN
1657
.S3

This book was developed from essays which appeared in TDR, which I edit, and in periodicals, books, and newspapers over the last six years. I would like to thank the editors and publishers of these books and journals for permitting me to collect my work at this time.

"Exit Thirties, Enter Sixties" was originally published as a preface to Fawcett/Premier's *Stanislavski and America*, edited by Erika Munk, copyright 1967 by Richard Schechner. "In Warm Blood" is copyright 1968 by the *Educational Theatre Journal*. "There's Lots of Time in Godot" is copyright 1966 by *Modern Drama*. "Megan Terry: The Playwright as Wrighter" was first published by Simon & Schuster as a preface to her *Viet Rock and Other Plays*, Simon & Schuster, copyright 1966 by Megan Terry. "Pornography and the New Expression" is copyright 1966 by *The Atlantic Monthly*. The essay "Happenings" was developed from two pieces, one with the same title which appeared in TDR in 1965 and another, "Is It What's Happening, Baby?" copyright 1966 by *The New York Times*. "Negotiations with Environment" is copyright 1968 by *Tri-Quarterly*, "Public Events for the Radical Theatre" is copyright 1967 by *The Village Voice*, Inc., and reprinted with their permission, and "The Politics of Ecstasy" is copyright 1968 by the *New York Free Press*. "Approaches" was developed from "Theatre Criticism," copyright 1965 by TDR, and "Approaches to Theory / Criticism," copyright 1965 by TDR. "Ford, Rockefeller, and Theatre" is copyright 1964 by TDR, and "Six Axioms for Environmental Theatre" is copyright 1968 by TDR.

Excerpts from "The Theatre of Revolt," copyright 1962, 1963, 1964 by Robert Brustein, are reprinted with the permission of Atlantic-Little, Brown and Company.

The Bobbs-Merrill Company, Inc.
A Subsidiary of Howard W. Sams & Co., Inc.
Publishers / Indianapolis • Kansas City • New York

Copyright © 1969 by Richard Schechner
All rights reserved
Library of Congress catalog card number 68-29296
Manufactured in the United States of America
First printing 1969

Prefatory Note

All of the essays included here have been revised somewhat, and a few extensively. "Approaches" is a combination of two pieces, "Theatre Criticism" and "Approaches to Theory / Criticism." "In Warm Blood" was written before I became involved in *Dionysus in 69*, The Performance Group version of *The Bacchae*. The essay does not reflect what I learned about Euripides by directing him. "Happenings" is a combination and revision of a brief piece by the same name and another, "Is It What's Happening, Baby?" "The Politics of Ecstasy" has been rewritten three times.

It is impossible to list all of the people who, over the past ten years, have helped me write this book. There are students and teachers, writers and actors, demonstrators and sergeants, lovers and friends. Among the many who have helped shape my experience I would like publicly to thank my parents, Selma and Sheridan Schechner, and Franklin Adams, Helen Brown, Paul Epstein, Paul Gray, Theodore Hoffman, Donald and Louise Kaplan, Michael Kirby, Monroe Lippman, Philip McCoy, Ethelyn Orso, Judith Reed, Donna Surla, and Arthur Wagner.

And to give special thanks to Sue Conley, Kelly Morris, and Erika Munk for their careful reading of my all-too-messy manuscript —and their important suggestions for clarification and elaboration.

Finally, an inexpressible gratitude to Joan MacIntosh, who loved me when I was most unlovable because she knew how much I loved my work.

New York City
May 1968

To
The Performance Group
and
The New Orleans Group

Table of Contents

Public Domain

Exit Thirties, Enter Sixties

1965

When, in May 1963, Paul Gray (who first had the idea), Theodore Hoffman, and I met to plan *TDR*'s Stanislavski issues,[1] we thought of them as guidelines to future theatre practice. By the time our research, interviewing, writing, and editing were completed fifteen months later, we found that we had compiled a history of the American theatre's most important epoch. This accidental achievement fell to us because the era we investigated had passed away even while we were examining it.

Many of the men who made this era—Lee Strasberg, Elia Kazan, Robert Lewis, Paul Mann, Harold Clurman, and others—are still active in our theatre, and will be for some time. But they represent an aesthetic that is no longer representative. Their impress, so important and formative, is fading as another generation assumes leadership. Our theatre is undergoing basic revaluation.

The process began in the fifties and its most visible presence was the regional professional theatre characterized and led by Herbert Blau and Jules Irving in San Francisco, Zelda and Tom Fichandler in Washington, Nina Vance in Houston, Paul Baker in Dallas, and, more recently, Tyrone Guthrie, Oliver Rea, and Peter Zeisler

---

[1] Tulane Drama Review (*now* The Drama Review, *both hereafter referred to as* TDR), *Vol. IX, Nos. 1 and 2.*

in Minneapolis and Stuart Vaughan in Seattle. Within the last two years this movement has proliferated and cities like Hartford, New Haven, Baltimore, Oklahoma City, Los Angeles, Atlanta, Milwaukee—to name just a few—now have "resident, professional theatres." Much can be said in criticism of these theatres, but their very existence indicates a decentralization of our theatre.[2]

So much has happened during the last year that 1964–'65 is marked for long memory. Kazan and Robert Whitehead were booted out of Lincoln Center and replaced by Blau and Irving; two anthologies of new American playwrights were published; Joseph Chaikin's Open Theatre presented fortnightly "other directed" improvisations and plays at the Sheridan Square Playhouse; the Barr-Wilder-Albee producing unit sponsored for the second year continuous programs of new plays; America's leading novelist, Saul Bellow, and poet, Robert Lowell, both turned playwright—for the time being at least; Robert W. Corrigan and Hoffman developed plans for the comprehensive NYU School of the Arts; William Ball's American Conservatory Theatre was created to link professional training and performance; the Arena Stage announced a training program; the new play laboratory at the University of Minnesota, after a rough beginning, seemed to enter a more productive phase. The American theatre had never seen such concentrated *new* activity.

Blau and Irving are not schooled in the Group Theatre-Actor's Studio tradition. They are aware of it, perhaps indebted to it, but they are not part of it. This same combination of awareness and dissociation marks the other new activity. And when Blau and Irving came to the Lincoln Center Repertory Theatre, the New York Establishment, by hiring them, gave *de facto* recognition to the regional professional theatre, marking it as the most productive sector of our national theatre. It was not simply the old list, but

---

[2] *All this has changed rapidly. People have moved around—and out of—the regional theatre. And the regional theatre itself—from a 1968 perspective—seems creaky, middle class, and anything but the hopeful prospect so many thought it to be.*

the ideas which that list characterized that were exhausted. Why else reach to San Francisco for the directors and actors of a theatre that had failed financially and install them at Lincoln Center? (That installation obviously did not work out. For one thing, the San Francisco Workshop's actors were not very good, and second, Blau was a helter-skelter director. But what the Workshop had was a determined vision and commitment. This vision and commitment was compromised at Lincoln Center. Blau and Irving tried to make it in New York, keeping just enough San Francisco in their style to dissatisfy both their company and their critics. Had they gone all the way with their original vision, the heart of their project would have remained intact. Blau quit in 1967 when it became obvious that the institutional pressures of Lincoln Center were too much for any artist to bear. Irving has converted the theatre into a conventional upper-middle-class pastime. He will probably succeed where Blau failed. But succeed in doing what?)

Far to the south of New York the Free Southern Theater is the first large-scale enterprise since the thirties which sees theatre as part of the social, economic, and political community. As such, FST aesthetics are formed in dialogue between a revolutionary South and a set of honored theatrical standards. A popular theatre that charges no admission, the FST tours the towns of the Black Belt performing plays which range from *In White America* to *Waiting for Godot*. Although there are similarities between the FST and the Group, the differences are more educative. Influenced by both regional theatre and regional politics, the FST is aimed away from New York; it has accepted the most radical alternative to box-office theatre: no tickets at all. Its orientation is toward "participatory democracy." Its acting, directing, and repertory are actively anti-Strasberg and pro-Brecht. The difficulties the FST has had measure the complexity of its goals.[3]

It is of course difficult to separate cause and effect in a process

---

[3] See *Thomas C. Dent, Richard Schechner and Gilbert Moses (eds.),* The Free Southern Theater by The Free Southern Theater (*New York: Bobbs-Merrill, 1969*), *especially the Documents and Letters section.*

still active. The best one can do is offer the data. In addition to the things already listed there are others, less immediately dislocating but just as far-reaching. The National Theatre School of Canada began in 1963 to graduate actors whose training—though using many Stanislavski techniques—is not beholden to Strasberg and the Method. Most important, the Montreal school is the only one on our continent to offer complete professional training outside of a university. The New York "trade schools" upon which so much of our talent has depended have always been inadequate. Strasberg has said:

> There is no real training today for the actor, in the Studio or any-where else. The actor there comes in contact with a certain directed stimulus, but there is no consecutive and systematic adherence to a routine as a result of which the actor can become skillful and able easily to accomplish the kind of thing that craft or technique make it possible for him to do.

In other words, New York training attends to the "inner technique" but not voice, speech, and body work. And university training—where it has been at all professional (at less than a half-dozen schools)—is hobbled by administrative red tape, incompetent and/or squabbling faculties, and non-directive leadership. Under the pressures of the regional theatres (which need talent and have standards) some universities have begun the agonizing job of re-structuring their programs. Happenings, theatre games, inter-media, and other theatrical activities are flourishing in and out of New York. These provide beneficial confrontations between theatre people and painters, dancers, sculptors, and musicians; in addition they are broadening our conceptions of what theatre is and ought to be.

Thus the pattern of theatre experience offered by the Group in the thirties and rigidly maintained by former Group members and their students in the forties and fifties is yielding to a more diverse set of experiences. It becomes less and less easy to set up dichotomies such as Broadway versus off-Broadway, regional versus New York, commodity versus art, script versus improvisation, art versus politics, or even theatre versus non-theatre.

TWO KINDS OF PLAYING

Strasberg, in an interview ("Working with Live Material"),[4] spoke of affective memory and in so doing offered a definition of acting.

> Affective memory is a basic element of the actor's reality. Vakhtangov emphasized that in acting we never use literal emotion. You've heard actors say, "Hit me, hit me—if you won't hit me, I won't get it." Well, that's not acting. Sure, if I hit you, you're going to fall down. What's the acting in that? The whole point is that I *seem* to hit you, and yet the way in which I hit you is so believable, and is so filled with all the tension and reality of the hitting, that you fall down and you are hurt, and I haven't touched you. That's acting.

Strasberg goes on to explain that the "actor's emotions on the stage should never be really real. It always should be only *remembered* emotion. . . . Remembered emotion is something that the actor can create and repeat; without that the thing is hectic." Kazan has said that the director's job is "to convert psychology into behavior," which is an epigrammatic paraphrase of what Strasberg is talking about. Between them we have the idea of acting as developed in the Group and taught at the Studio—that is, the kind of acting which has dominated the American stage for thirty years. Let us put aside sterile arguments about naturalism versus realism, prose versus poetry, and instead, see what kind of demands this acting makes.

The actor is asked to re-create the circumstances, either real or imaginary, in which an emotion was or is to be felt. It promises him that the re-felt emotion will be "controllable," usable in a play. By accurately remembering the place, people, time of day, talk, etc.—the "given circumstances"—the actor will experience again the emotion concomitant with these circumstances. If the re-creation is "imaginary," that is, taken from a play, the actor either chooses a parallel situation from his own life or works directly from the play, believing "as if" the circumstances were "real." (The objection here is that the mind is not easy to fool: "as if" is simple to write but

---

[4] TDR, IX, No. 1, 117–135.

difficult to believe.) Sometimes these parallels are far-fetched. Robert Lewis, speaking of the emotions which accompany killing, said, "You do know *something* about killing—have you not at one time or other been so tortured by a mosquito that in a fine rage you . . . squashed the bloody life out of the pest?" Of course; but is Othello's murder of Desdemona merely an enlargement of his killing a mosquito or, indeed, of the slaughter he manages during battle? In fact, the inherent danger of affective memory is that the emotions called for by a play will *often* be those for which only a far-fetched and qualitatively inaccurate parallel can be found in the direct experience of the actor's life. However, this serious objection is not the principal one. And the goal of affective memory is admirable: to represent "real," "true," or "sincere" emotion on stage.

The notion and technique of affective memory can be traced to the nineteenth-century French psychologist Theodule Ribot and from him to Stanislavski, who called the operation "emotional memory." It was introduced to America by Richard Boleslavski in lectures to the American Laboratory Theatre in 1925; later it formed a chapter of Boleslavski's widely read *Acting: The First Six Lessons*. Boleslavski called it "memory of emotion"; it has also been called "emotional recall." By whatever name, the process is the same. To a generation schooled in Pavlov, as Strasberg claims to be, affective memory is an example of a conditioned response. Strasberg is explicit about the kind of reality affective memory offers the actor.

> We know from psychology that emotions have a conditioning factor. That's how we're trained, not from Freud but from Pavlov. [. . .] By singling out certain conditioning factors, you can arouse certain results. We go through the whole thing every night—I think of the place I was in, and what I wore, and how it felt on my body, and where I was hot and where I was cold, and the light in the room, and I try to see the light, and so on, and I hear a voice, and I try to hear that voice, and see somebody and try to touch that person, touch and try to remember that touch, and so on, and try to hear what was said, try to hear what I answered, and so on. As I do that the emotion is relived. [. . .] After a couple of years, when the actor has done the affective memory thing a number of times, you find a new conditioning has been set up. As soon as the actor starts to

think about it, it turns up like that. Even at the beginning, by the way, at the Group Theatre, we took the famous minute for preparation, and literally, it took no more than a minute.

In other words the actor, over a span of years, builds in himself a card file of emotions the cues to which he keeps consciously before him. Of course this way of acting tends to eliminate the authenticity and particularity of what each scene presents. In the language of another day, affective memory leads directly to stock acting. And when I asked Strasberg about another obvious difficulty—that the actor is often in two realities, the one in the play and the one relived from his life, Strasberg replied:

> This duality always must exist in the actor. [. . .] The actor works on various levels of his being all the time. He remembers his cues. [. . .] In his mind it's all laid out, and yet, the less it can appear laid out—that is what we call the illusion of the first time.

The answer is acceptable. The difficulty lies elsewhere.

The most interesting thing about affective memory—or any conditioned response—is that it duplicates the felt reality of the first time. The dog who salivates when the bell is rung undergoes a set of physiological changes that are exactly those he had when given a piece of meat. This reality is both the strength and weakness of affective memory for the theatre. The weakness is not, as we might expect, in the possible lack of control (for training has the double purpose of arousing and controlling the responses), but in the very "sincerity" of the response. It is wrong to call a feeling aroused by affective memory an "illusion"; physiologically it is exactly what it was the first time, only now it is an effect without its original cause. Thus the actor when recalling a sad event feels sad, when recalling a happy one he feels happy, and so forth. But how can this be a disadvantage? Isn't this exactly what affective memory is supposed to do?

Conditioned response is not new to the techniques of art. William Wordsworth in his "Preface to the *Lyrical Ballads*" (1800) describes it rather exactly:

> I have said that poetry is the spontaneous overflow of powerful feelings; it takes its origin from emotion recollected in tranquility: the

emotion is contemplated till, by a species of reaction, the tranquility disappears, and an emotion, kindred to that which was before the subject of contemplation, is gradually produced, and does itself actually exist in the mind. In this mood successful composition generally begins, and in a mood similar to this it is carried on [. . .].

But Wordsworth makes an important qualification:

[. . .] the emotion, of whatever kind, and in whatever degree, from various causes, is qualified by various pleasures, so that in describing any passion whatsoever, which are voluntarily described, the mind will, upon the whole, be in a state of enjoyment [. . .]. The poet ought to profit from [Nature's lesson] and ought especially to take care, that, whatever passions he communicates to his Reader, those passions [. . .] should always be accompanied with an over-balance of pleasure.

It is this "overbalance of pleasure" which is missing from many contemporary performances. It is missing because the use of affective memory does not admit of anything but a duplication of the original response. However, Wordsworth's solution—the use of Romantic, lyric forms—is not viable for our day. Is there another way?

Child play is generally unsentimental, deeply felt, and pleasurable both to the child and to those who watch him. Furthermore, one can safely say that no human emotion is alien to child play. And yet affective memory—both theoretically and practically—cannot be operating here because the child has no possible storehouse of real experience out of which to shape his acted-out emotions. Neither is imitation—the way the child learns the actions he plays with—the only source of the feelings which accompany those actions. When, for example, two children play cowboys and Indians, one is shot and dies, usually undergoing great "agony." But this agony is pleasurable, both to the child and to anyone watching. This is because the child is testing and toying with his emotional apparatus. In a sense he is doing the opposite of affective memory which is a re-living; the child is pre-living, anticipating a set of emotions he may later, as an adult, find use for. The actor using affective memory is paying back old debts; the child is storing up resources. Although the psychological explanation of the child's pleasure source would be too complicated to present here, it depends on three mechanisms. First, the child is experimenting with events that he has not directly experienced and he derives pleasure from the mimetic nature of his activity. Secondly, the child is testing (or, if you will, "rehearsing") his psychic apparatus and there is simple joy in finding out what the emotions are that are available to him. Thirdly, in such mimicry and testing the child builds up more psychic energy than he can discharge on an "unreal" situation and his pleasure is directly proportional to this surplus energy. This is one reason why children enjoy intense games of make-believe which involve them in incredibly complicated and often painful or morbid situations.

J. Huizinga in *Homo Ludens* defines play as activity embodying "formal characteristics [. . .] a joyful mood [. . .] and the consciousness, however latent, of only pretending." Such a definition—and it seems accurate—might include Method acting. But child play is nearer to the center of what Huizinga is talking about, and in the mechanics of child play we may find a more proper model for stage acting than that offered us by affective memory. No one denies that Method acting, bringing with it all the original hurt or joy of an experience, is startling and moving, calling up sympathetic harmonies from the audience. But is it the kind of acting best suited to the wide repertory of world theatre, or even the emerging repertory of our own theatre?

EARLY VERSUS LATE STANISLAVSKI

As Gray's "Critical Chronology"[5] clearly shows, Stanislavski's ideas evolved, while the American theatre took its shape from what Stanislavski was doing in the First Studio. The Russian Revolution and its aftermath sent several waves of immigrants to America, including Boleslavski, Michael Chekhov, Maria Ouspenskaya, Vera Soloviova, and others. During the twenties these Russians created the first successful systematic actor-training programs in American

---

[5] *TDR*, *IX*, *No. 2, 21–60.*

theatre history. All these people studied with Stanislavski at the First Studio (1911–1916) and the techniques they brought with them were heavily dependent upon affective memory. Strasberg and Clurman, both of whom studied with Boleslavski and Ouspenskaya in the twenties, absorbed this work. And when the Group translated new material from the Russian in the thirties, the ideas were immediately adapted into a framework already conditioned to the First Studio. What has been taught at the Actor's Studio since its beginning in 1947 is almost identical to what Stanislavski was teaching during the teens of this century.

But Stanislavski himself continued to work until his death in 1938. Both his methods and his overview of acting changed. He moved from a method based on the inner technique (affective memory and its derivatives) to one based on the "logic of physical action." This work is more mimetic and more closely allied to the mechanics of child play than the exercises of the First Studio. The argument persists whether Stanislavski merely modified and transcended his early work or whether he abandoned its theoretical bases altogether. The argument is sterile because Bertolt Brecht intervened to urge a complete revaluation of acting.

BRECHT AND THE CHILD AT PLAY

From his earliest days to his last, interrupted only by the *lehrstücke* years, Brecht maintained that theatre's job was to entertain (or, as Wordsworth would say, to give the audience an "overbalance of pleasure"). Brecht's clearest statement of this is in his *Short Organum*. "From the first it has been the theatre's business to entertain people, as it also has of all the other arts. It is this business which gives it its particular dignity; it needs no other passport than fun, but this it has got to have." And the system of acting which Brecht painstakingly grew over the years was intended mainly to preserve the theatre's fun. If this seems like an untenable conclusion, I shall not press it here, but urge the reader to look at *Brecht on Theatre* again. This much is clear: Brecht could not do what he wanted to do with actors trained in the "old" way; and it seems that he was distrustful of Stanislavski-trained actors as well. Certainly, Brecht's politics would have tempted him to accept Stanislavski, and this he never did. The most Brecht would concede is that actors should "identify" with their roles at a certain point in rehearsal before going on to the work of "social criticism" which separates Brechtian acting from other kinds. In reviewing Stanislavski's work, Brecht had the most respect for the late theories.

> Stanislavski's "method of physical action" is most likely his greatest contribution to a new theatre. [. . .] This method is not difficult for us of the Berliner Ensemble. B. always asks that at the first rehearsals the actor show the plot, the event, the business, convinced that feeling and mood will eventually take care of themselves.[6]

In other words, Brecht relied on mimetics. But what about child play?

There is no direct statement of Brecht's that I know of that compares his kind of acting to child play. But a striking similarity exists in Brecht's admonition to his actors that they are never to forget (during performance) that they are acting—or, as Huizinga has it in another context, "the consciousness, however latent, of only pretending." Furthermore, Ensemble rehearsal techniques, based on close observation and experimentation rather than introspection, seem very like football or baseball practice. Brecht may have modeled his plays on life, but his rehearsals were modeled on games. Brecht's theory, his practice at the Ensemble, and his plays all suggest a consciousness which is at once totally "involved" in an activity and "removed" from it at the same time. This kind of consciousness is not at all abstruse: it is the everyday experience of athletes and their audiences. And the skill and pleasures of sportsmen are, according to several authorities, nothing other than the continuation of child play in adult modes.

Early in his career (1926) Brecht wrote:

> When people in sporting establishments buy their tickets they know exactly what is going to take place; and that is exactly what does take place once they are in their seats: viz. highly trained persons

---

[6] *Bertolt Brecht, "Notes on Stanislavski," TDR, IX, No. 2, 160.*

developing their peculiar powers in the way most suited to them, with the greatest sense of responsibility yet in such a way as to make one feel that they are doing it primarily for their own fun. *Against that the traditional theatre is nowadays quite lacking in character.* There seems to be nothing to stop the theatre having its own form of "sport."[7]

This conviction stayed with Brecht throughout his career and I think it is at the bottom of many of his techniques, if not his theories. But Brecht is not talking about all sporting events—only those in which the athletes "make one feel that they are doing it primarily for their own fun." Only those, that is, in which the "overbalance of pleasure" so typical of child play remains. Many sports and most acting are no longer any fun either for performer or spectator.

And here things begin to come together. Much more could be written on the relationship between child play, sport, theatre, and ritual. Each is a mimetic form, and as the series progresses the operation becomes more "serious." Sport and theatre—comprising the middle terms—must share both in play's light mood (and, if you will, its "alienation") and ritual's trance. But when theatre, or acting, becomes too serious it destroys its own essential base: play. Brecht understood this and tried to incorporate it into his aesthetic. The American Method teachers and directors, on the other hand, in hoping to make something *more* out of acting have, instead, made something *else* out of it. But is it for nothing that a drama is called a "play" and the actor's art "playing"?

---

[7] *Brecht,* Brecht On Theatre, *ed. and tr. by John Willett (New York: Hill and Wang, 1964), p. 6.*

Ford, Rockefeller, and Theatre

1965

—*And we?*
—*I beg your pardon?*
—*Where do we come in?*
—*Come in? On our hands and knees.*

SAMUEL BECKETT, PLAYWRIGHT

*If a painting after all means more
than an object for economic
speculation, what does it mean?*

W. MCNEIL LOWRY,
VICE-PRESIDENT, FORD FOUNDATION

1968 note: The statistics here are dated. I have not followed closely either the patterns of foundation spending or the development of the regional theatre. However, I think the essay does point out some structures which still operate both within the foundations and throughout the regional theatre.

What has happened since 1965? Foundation support for theatre has declined in both absolute and relative terms. There are several reasons for this. The Vietnam war has cut heavily into cultural appropriations. The federal government has gone back on its promises to help the cities, and foundations have tried—though not successfully—to fill some of the gaps, necessarily curtailing efforts in other directions. Also, foundations have always wanted to plant "seed money" and then move on. This means they will initially support some theatres—but foundations are wary of "continuing support," although it must by now be clear to all that the theatre can exist in this country only with substantial and continuing subsidy. The reasons that foundations shy away from continuing support are as tied to public relations as to anything else. If foundations got deeply involved in a number of continuing projects, they could not seek new projects. They would not "look ahead," "probe new areas"—their monies would be tied down.

They would no longer be the "pioneers" they feel the public expects them to be.

Some of the foundations' fondest hopes—Ford's Theatre Communications Group, the playwriting programs of both major foundations—have not matured.[1] The alienation of regional theatre artists from their audiences and, more recently, from their boards of directors has become a general and open crisis. A rash of firings and resignations marked the last two seasons.[2] No theatre has developed an ensemble—a stable group of artists working on a stable set of artistic problems. Washington's Arena Stage has come close, and a careful study of that theatre's history and policies is called for. Generally, productions in the regional theatre are worse than dull—they are irrelevant. These years have been crisis years for America. But rarely in our regional theatre have our cultural, social or political crises been reflected, let alone probed. The old charges that have so long been launched against Broadway can be effectively used against the regional theatre. In our day we have seen demonstrated the thesis that the "classics" can be as bourgeois, soporific, and mind-blunting as anything Neil Simon can dish out.

In the early sixties, many looked beyond New York with what proved to be utopian hopes. We look there now with nostalgia and dismay, sometimes with disgust. But we should not be surprised. A society like ours cannot be expected to foster a relevant "majority art." In its management and in the ultimate location of power the regional theatre was always designed to be a reflection of majority tastes. And why should we believe that people who support the Vietnam war, who ignore the conditions of the ghettos, who put down the questions of the young should sponsor anything significant in the arts? The people who control the regional theatre (not

---

[1] For what happened, see Theodore Hoffman, "A Hard Times Letter to TCG," TDR, XII, No. 2, 21–27. For a survey of playwriting programs, see Robert Pasolli, "The New Playwrights' Scene of the Sixties," TDR, XIII, No. 1, 150–162.

[2] For an analysis of the attitudes of those who construct regional theatres and sit on their boards, see Alvin H. Reiss, "Who Builds Theatres and Why," TDR, XII, No. 3, 75–92. See also Dugald MacArthur, "Art in Arkansas," same issue, 37–39.

so much the actors and directors who work in it, though they share the blame) do not wish to be disturbed. When threatened, they may move a bit, but only to find a more comfortable slumbering place. I wish that soon we can say of them: Rest in Peace.

THE FORD FOUNDATION

The Ford Foundation is big business. Between 1956 and 1964 Ford appropriated more than $1.3 billion. Its total assets exceed $2.8 billion and 1964 income was $147 million. Appropriations during the past three years have run nearly $100 million ahead of income each year. Ford assets are primarily Ford Motor stock ($2.4 billion), U.S. Government securities, real estate, and diversified stock in more than seventy corporations, both domestic and foreign. If this portfolio suggests that the Ford Foundation can hardly be a friend to the Establishment's enemies, it does not mean that the Foundation is reactionary or unsophisticated. On the contrary, its actions seem more or less motivated by its proclaimed goal, "the advancement of human welfare." It is the style of the Ford Foundation's pursuit of its objective that troubles me.

Ford Foundation policy—carefully worked out by the trustees —has been summarized in a pamphlet the Foundation issued in 1962, *The Ford Foundation in the 1960's.*

> Since 1950 great social, political, and scientific changes have altered the framework within which the Foundation works towards its fundamental objective—the advancement of human welfare. Since then, too, the Foundation has become the largest private philanthropy and has gained extensive experience in the course of making grants totalling more than $1.5 billion. [. . .] The crisis in the world today requires that democracy do more than restate its principles and ideals; they must be translated into action. We must take affirmative action toward the elimination of the basic causes of war, the advancement of democracy on a broad front, and the strengthening of its institutions and processes. [. . .] The Foundation, therefore, must be concerned with society as a whole [. . .] it must be prepared to act globally.

Having said this, the trustees, in a chauvinistic flush, "recognize, however, that one of the most effective ways to contribute to world peace and the peaceful solution of international disputes is through the invigoration and enrichment of American society." This preamble reveals assumptions which run through the entire operation. The Foundation is autonomous—"it" does this and that, "it" has "gained extensive experience." It views democracy as a *thing* that can be "advanced on a broad front." The Foundation is aware of and impressed by its own bigness. The trustees are not modest, nor should they be: the first step toward wise control of power is the recognition that one has it. The Ford Foundation program operates in five areas: (1) education, (2) international affairs, (3) public and economic affairs, (4) overseas development, and (5) the arts and sciences.

> The Foundation [. . .] has flexibility, speed of action, and the ability to pioneer and be highly selective. It can make significant contributions even in fields where other institutions have the decisive role. The quality of American education, for example, depends on a variety of public and private agencies and institutions and, basically, on the commitment of citizens at the local level. Yet the Foundation can help clarify educational goals, assist in overcoming fundamental shortcomings, and support efforts toward major new approaches in educational practices and processes.

In theatre—regional professional theatre at least—the Ford Foundation has become the "decisive institution," because before Foundation aid began these theatres hardly existed at all. The trustees have specified their policies and there is no reason to suppose that policies which hold generally will not be applied locally to theatre.

> The Foundation should exercise discrimination and selectivity and give its funds largely for significant activity not likely to be supported by others.

> The Foundation should single out and support ideas, people, and institutions whose outstanding performance in vital fields can serve as models.

> It should seek out, sustain, and amplify excellence and, where necessary, create new centers of excellence.

[. . .]

It should work through appropriate institutions wherever they may be found, throughout society and throughout the world.

The Foundation should help to increase the vigor of private institutions and private initiative in areas of critical concern to society.

[. . .]

It should not support a given recipient indefinitely.

In wanting both to "give its funds . . . for significant activity not likely to be supported by others" and feeling that it should "not support a given recipient indefinitely," the Foundation has assigned to those individuals and institutions it aids the difficult task of generating local interest and finances. It makes of theatre (and the other arts) an *industry* which, in times of "depression," needs only "pump-priming" until the usual "laws" of supply and demand can healthily assert themselves. The regional theatre's response has been to seek a subscription audience among that sector of the population *currently* most willing to pay for tickets. An example is Washington's Arena Stage, where a survey showed that more than 70 per cent of the audience earned over $10,000 a year. And what the Foundation means by "appropriate institutions wherever they may be found, throughout society and throughout the world" can be understood only after a careful survey of who got money.

During the years 1956–1964 the Ford Foundation gave a little more than $12.3 million to theatre. The arts and humanities together got $55.4 million. Theatre, therefore, represented 22 per cent of the Ford Foundation interest in the arts and humanities and .9 per cent of its *total* interest. Not a great proportion, but enough to stimulate the regional theatre to its most active decade. According to Ford Foundation annual reports the theatre grants were:

Lincoln Center, New York (not limited to theatre)	$2,500,000
Alley Theatre, Houston	2,262,000
Mummers' Theatre, Oklahoma City	1,250,000
Arena Stage, Washington, D.C.	990,000
American Shakespeare Festival, Stratford, Conn.	699,800
Theatre Group, UCLA, Los Angeles	500,000

Actor's Workshop, San Francisco	353,000
Tyrone Guthrie Theatre, Minneapolis	337,000
Actors Studio Theatre, New York	250,000
American Place Theatre, New York	225,000
Cleveland Play House	160,000
Phoenix Theatre, New York	120,000
Fred Miller Theatre, Milwaukee	100,000
Stratford Shakespearean Festival, Canada	60,000
Goodman Theatre, Chicago	10,000
Oregon Shakespeare Festival	7,500
Theatre of the Golden Hind, Berkeley, California	2,500
	$9,826,800

Not counted in these figures (or in the $12.3 million total) is a 1965 grant of $5 million to the Kennedy Center in Washington; but this performing arts center is not yet performing, so I shall leave it out of my considerations. The remainder of the $12.3 million has gone for projects such as the Theatre Communications Group, administrative internships, playwrights' and directors' programs, support of the Shakespeare quadricentennial celebration, the "ideal theatres" exhibit, and travel grants for critics and editors. These important—though tangential—programs will be discussed later.

One is perhaps surprised to find on the list four New York theatres receiving a total of $3.1 million. Lincoln Center is the most heavily endowed performing arts project in the world and, until Herbert Blau and Jules Irving took over the Repertory Theatre, it presented a special case for the Ford Foundation. The aid to the American Place Theatre should be classified as part of the playwrights' program; the Actors Studio Theatre is not a resident professional theatre but a Broadway producing unit; aid to the Phoenix began and ended in 1960. Thus, despite statistics, Ford Foundation theatre work has been directed—and increasingly so—toward regional theatre. But these theatres are not all equal and they have not been rewarded according to quality. Several theatres which responsible critics have thought worthy of help have not gotten anything. None of the grants met total needs and few of the theatres have become financially self-sufficient, either at the box office or through local donations. One can then ask: what was the criterion for giving? The clearest answer comes from W. McNeil Lowry, a Ford Foundation vice-president, still operationally head of its program in the arts and humanities, and the most important source of Ford Foundation theatre policy.

On December 10, 1962—exactly two months after Ford announced its $6.1 million bonanza for nine theatres—Lowry spoke on "The Arts and Philanthropy" at Brandeis University. There he discussed the "five motives" for art in our society: status, social, economic, educational, and professional. "Only the professional motive can justify what we do," Lowry concluded. "Our acceptance of the artist and the arts on their own terms." Well and good. But what are these terms as Lowry sees them?

> At its most basic level, art is not about money, or facilities, or social acceptance; it is about the surge of artistic drive and moral determination. It is about the individual professional artist or artistic director. And philanthropy, in the arts at least, is professionally motivated only when it accepts the artist and the arts on their own terms, and learns from the artist himself *at least* to recognize the atmosphere in which the artistic process is carried out. What is that atmosphere? None of us can describe it to the complete satisfaction of anyone else, but [. . .] it derives importantly from the drive or fanaticism or whatever of the person who has made his choice, and will often have to eschew anything else—money, the elite identification of a university degree, even health—to develop the latent talent he hopes he has. It comes also from the pride of doing for oneself, of making ends meet, of giving society what it will pay for even if what it pays is inadequate to sustain a normal life, of working in the midst of a fraternity that will show the same fanaticisms and abnegations. It comes from the endless time, time, time spent on doing one thing, only one thing, and then starting all over again. It comes, finally, from the acceptance of such distortion as a way of life, a way of life, you will note, that is in some ways completely antithetical to the ideal objective of a liberal and humane education. Some of the most professional, the most talented, and the most mature artists I have met lack either the time or the capacity to sort out a decent personal life from the endless hours of their artistic concentration. Only a rare heredity or early environment and not, I am afraid, a very good education, has given some of these artists a humanity that separates them from the very talented bums in their midst.

This quaint nineteenth-century definition of the bohemian who is "called" to his art (giving up everything for it), translated into the cool but somewhat jealous rhetoric of the educated administrator, boils down to the contention that the artist is alienated from society. Lowry is correct in his observation but wrong to imply that this alienation is the motor of the artist's creativity. How would Lowry support the assertion that the artist wants to give "society what it will pay for even if what it pays is inadequate to sustain a normal life" without making out of the artist an unprofitable industry? This industrious, pay-as-you-go view is incorrect. The artist wishes to express what he sees and feels and pay is extraneous. It is a measure of our misunderstanding that the artist's disdain for economics has led to his brutal exploitation rather than to his adequate support. Lowry brings this exploitation into the formula and makes it a most important part of the artist's life: a measure, in fact, of his devotion to his art. But surely starvation and comfort are both irrelevant to art.

Lowry describes a pattern which, in his own words, makes the artist accept "distortion as a way of life." Rather than seek the source of this distortion elsewhere, Lowry seems satisfied with accepting it as an inseparable component of the artistic personality itself: an unchanging historical fact. But might not the distortion spring from the unnatural relationship between artist and society? Is it not possible to conceive (and work for) conditions in which the artist would not be alienated from his community? The question is, of course: who is to compromise, artist or community? Such questions of basic reconstruction are not discussed by Lowry. Because the Ford Foundation has helped establish theatre institutions of a certain kind, one can conclude that Lowry sees no need for society to be reconstructed; neither does he want the artist to change. He insists, rather, that the artist be accepted on "his own terms." The whole thing comes a cropper because there are contradictions between artist and institution.

On October 10, 1962, in the Ford Foundation announcement of the $6.1 million grants, Lowry is quoted:

> Given the situation prevailing in commercial theatre and television, the emergence of permanent companies over the past decade has

become the chief hope for the advancement of serious American drama. The resident theatre is fast becoming a major outlet for the professional dramatist, director, and actor, and the most important avenue for the development of younger theatre artists and technicians. It is fortunate also that these trends in theatre are matched by a new awareness of theatre as an important cultural resource by community leaders.

The Ford Foundation Annual Reports also speak of the kind of theatre institution Lowry would like to see established:

> The over-all aim of the program is to help the participating theatres ultimately sustain themselves through box office receipts. (1962)

> The resident theatre movement is growing rapidly, partly under the stimulus of Foundation programs. [. . .] The ability of non-profit theatres to attain artistic and economic continuity as permanent institutions still remains to be demonstrated. (1964)[3]

Individually Lowry asks for acceptance of the artist on his own terms; *ex cathedra* he speaks of "cultural resource," break-even budgets, and "permanent institutions." Both the person and the Foundation administrator are speaking sincerely, but they are not talking to each other. What Lowry fails to analyze is the *impossible relationship* he urges between artist and institution. The alienated artist cannot live unalienated in institutions which reflect society's present values. So we change the values of the institutions, creating islands. These islands cannot hope for break-even budgets based on community support. Finally, we must support these island institutions until the values of the large community are reconstructed or are sufficiently diverse. Those theatres that wish to play for the students, the poor, or in very small houses need permanent support. However, support for islands or permanent support is against Ford Foundation policy. If one asks why the policy is that way, the answer, though difficult to document, is obvious: the Foundation is neither the sponsor of revolutions nor a patron of the arts. It

---

[3] For *a statistical demonstration of the uncertainty of that growth, see William J. Baumol and William G. Bowen,* Performing Arts: The Economic Dilemma *(New York: Twentieth Century Fund, 1966).*

supplies, rather, non-repayable venture capital to *businesses* which in turn produce art. The theatre business, for its part, demonstrates its "artistic and economic continuity" by retaining a resident Equity company, performing a non-Broadway repertory, and generating local box office and donated support. It all would work quite well, except that the theatres are forced to seek a one-class—middle-class— audience, and then the work suffers or seems disconnected from the audience, or both.

The history of the San Francisco Actor's Workshop supports my theory. That theatre was an island, in both its aesthetic and its political assertions. Its community did not support it with money or capacity attendance, and *for these reasons* Ford Foundation help was proportionately stinting. How else can one explain $2.2 million for Houston, $1.25 million for Oklahoma City, and only $353,000 for San Francisco? Certainly artistic boldness and international reputation were more the properties of the Workshop than of the Alley and Mummers. The Workshop folded—or at least is now forced to begin again—and its directors, with many of the company (the island institution moved), went to the already financially guaranteed Lincoln Center.

In addition to direct theatre aid for actors and construction, Ford has sponsored directors, playwrights, designers, and architects, administrators, critics, and editors: a complete theatrical survey, excluding only professional training. It is not easy to estimate the success of these projects, for which more than $1.3 million has been appropriated. Certainly the administrative internships (not limited to theatres) have helped train needed personnel and contributed to the stabilization of some theatres. It is good to have critics and editors shake off provincialism through travel, though one regrets some of the nonentities who were selected.

The most dubious, expensive ($981,000), and changed of these programs is the playwrights'. The changes show the admirable flexibility of the Ford Foundation, a demonstration in self-education that some theatres could well emulate. The playwrights' program has had three phases. First the Foundation helped some writers get their work done. Next a group of poets and fiction writers were packed off to "a close working relationship with a theatre or opera house in the United States or Europe in order that they might test their interest in writing in the dramatic form." It seems as if the poets and fiction writers weren't much interested in the dramatic form. The artificial grafts did not take because they were artificial. Playwrights assigned to theatres complained that their work was not performed and that they were ignored by both the administrative and artistic theatre people. The theatre people, for their part, complained that the writers didn't know anything about the theatre and refused to learn. The predictable outcome was that the writer went home to write and the sought-after "working relationship" rarely materialized.

The third phase of the program—$225,000 to the American Place Theatre and $325,000 for "a variety of arrangements to encourage the association of playwrights with leading professional theatres"—is most promising. Theatres are now permitted to find real ways of engaging the playwright: hiring him to write a specific script for production, keeping him around during rehearsals and for revisions (even when the play isn't a commissioned work)—any situation that fits a particular theatre and writer. The initiative both in choosing the writer and in defining his relationship to the theatre is entirely left up to the theatre and the writer. The American Place Theatre solves some of the problems involved in asking non-theatre writers to compose for the theatre. It will do only new works; although it cannot provide long-term immersion in theatre craft, it can offer the novelist or poet a place for full productions, readings, works-in-progress, or one-act plays. The writer is not bucking an already established repertory or a company not particularly interested in experimenting with new work. The American Place Theatre has already produced Robert Lowell's masterful *The Old Glory*, itself worth the $225,000 nut. But if, under these new and reasonable stimulations, American playwriting does not begin to flourish, we must look for other hindrances to creative work: the artist-institution-society hang-up which, I feel, operates more menacingly against the writer than against the actor or director.

Aside from money going directly to theatres, the most important Ford Foundation program has been the Theatre Communications Group, established in 1961 "to improve cooperation among professional, community, and university theatres." Since then TCG has evolved new objectives which it quietly pursues among resident theatres. In 1964, TCG incorporated itself as "an autonomous, non-profit organization which will no longer work within a membership structure but concentrate its facilities on particular resident professional theatres seeking TCG assistance." Translated this means that TCG was no longer interested in a rapprochement between the community, university, and regional professional theatre; nor did it wish to be tied specifically to all the theatres and individuals who helped found it. Ostensibly the 1964 declaration meant independence from the Ford Foundation. But in practice this was not so. The TCG admirably reflects Lowry's policies, and executes them well.

TCG's most valuable functions are its auditions and its visitation program. Through auditions many recent graduates of theatre schools find employment in the regional theatre. Through the visitation program directors, administrators, designers, and actors can observe the work at theatres other than their own. Largely because of TCG sponsorship (both real and as a model), there is great mobility within the regional theatre. Of course, this has both its good and its bad consequences. Theatres find it difficult to keep actors and directors; at the same time, salaries have risen somewhat above subsistence.

In October 1961, when TCG was barely seven months old, Lowry spoke in New Orleans on "The University and the Creative Arts."

The best equipped theatres in the United States are [. . .] maintained by universities [. . .] in the catalogue are course sequences not only in theatre history or dramatic literature but in acting, directing, technical direction, costuming, even in theatre management. And the university, through its accreditation to grant degrees . . . competes with the few remaining independent drama schools for the student who thinks he wants to make the theatre a career. . . . The young actor normally is led to believe that there is nothing in the American theatre *between* academic theatre and Broadway . . . and he leaves the university to beat a path to New

York or Los Angeles, where he joins hundreds of other young actors who have been similarly indoctrinated. The fact that he still has not had a professional apprenticeship [. . .] is ignored.

[. . .]

The university has largely taken over the functions of professional training in the arts but in the main has sacrificed professional standards in doing so. The absence of discrimination has proceeded partly from the strong popularizing currents already at work in the society outside the campuses, and partly from the university's original objective, the liberal education of numerous individuals drawn from an affluent democracy.

[. . .]

The trend is irreversible. The future of professional training in the arts depends, first, upon a radical shift in the university atmosphere surrounding students considered potential artists, and, second, upon the provision of postgraduate opportunities for professional apprenticeship removed from an academic environment.

[. . .]

The requisite shift in the university environment for the arts will be achieved only under great difficulties, if at all. Opportunities exist for new forms of cooperation between the university and professional institutions in the arts, provided the university will regard the arts as important and give financial support to the cooperative mechanisms that must be established.

It was here that Lowry described the artist—later self-quoted in the Brandeis speech and cited earlier in this essay. Obviously, if society has been unable to accommodate the artist, the university, with few exceptions, has proven even more hostile. Clark Kerr's multiversity in California is a closed model of the larger community, and only a revolution like the one at Berkeley can challenge such power. Even then, for how long and with what lasting effect?

Theodore Hoffman (TCG's first chairman) took up Lowry's invitation to debate in the October 1963 *Educational Theatre Journal*. He claimed that the university theatre ducks Lowry's challenge "by buying half-trained students (at commercial rates) for allegedly professional (and certainly commercial) companies. [. . .] The same mentality that provides 'multipurpose' theatre and 'creative' Ph.D.'s is perfectly capable of jazzing up amateur theatre to masquerade as professional." In short, Hoffman rejected university training and protested the propaganda that makes it *sound* so good. And as Hoffman went, so went TCG, prodded by its active professional members. TCG, beginning as a tool for cooperation between "professional, community, and university theatres" became a viable all-professional organization. Its only contact with the universities is the auditions it sponsors, which bring students and theatre directors together. And when TCG dropped its membership to become a service organization, it functioned more than before as a federating body. This paradox is easy to understand. TCG's first Executive Secretary, Michael Mabry, maintained close touch with the leaders of the resident theatre movement. Mabry did not label these as a group, but those theatres most willing to use TCG programs constituted an identifiable group. Whether or not it was so designed, a "chain of theatres" came into being. The split between university and professional theatre steadily widened, as the theatres improved their programs, while the schools did little to meet professional needs or standards.

The thrust of Ford Foundation aid has been to bring the artist and the institution together, each on their own (and often contradictory) terms. TCG does precisely this. The objective is commendable enough but, as I have suggested, there are difficulties of the most basic kind.

THE ROCKEFELLER FOUNDATION

If the Ford Foundation program in theatre can be closely identified with Lowry, no one person sets Rockefeller Foundation theatre policy. The Rockefeller Foundation's projects are both more cooperatively worked out by the Foundation staff and less consistent in their overall objectives. Kenneth Brown, author of *The Brig* and formerly with the Living Theatre, has received a Rockefeller grant and so has the University of Minnesota. Furthermore, the Rockefeller Foundation's theatre program is just now taking shape. Criticism, therefore, is both difficult and tentative.

Most of what has been said about general Ford Foundation policy applies as well to the Rockefeller Foundation; the figures are different, and smaller, but the two giant philanthropies are colleagues. Rockefeller assets, held in a diversified investment program, were valued at more than $720 million at the end of 1963. Rockefeller interests are comparable to Ford's, but with less of a "global strategy" ring. It lists "total war" and "the impact of unrestrained population increase" as the two most urgent world problems. On the domestic scene, the Rockefeller Foundation is concerned with "equal opportunity" (Negro rights), university development, and cultural development. Norman Lloyd, former dean of the Oberlin College Conservatory of Music, has been named head of the Rockefeller Foundation arts program, in which the Foundation promises "expanded efforts." In 1964, grants to the arts totaled $1.5 million—lowest of the "major interests"; the highest, conquest of hunger, got $7 million. There will be an accelerating commitment to the arts during the next several years.

Having outlined all this, it will perhaps surprise many to know that the Rockefeller Foundation gave $17.4 million to the performing arts between 1956 and 1964. The figures are deceptive, because $15 million went to Lincoln Center and $1 million to the Kennedy Center. In the Rockefeller Foundation President's Review for 1964, the Foundation's hopes for theatre are outlined.

> During the past ten years the professional theatre has taken root in a number of large cities throughout the country. This is in part because commercial pressures in New York [. . .] have forced playwrights, directors, and actors to look elsewhere for serious performance opportunities, and also because other communities are showing their willingness to support resident companies. The decentralization of theatre [. . .] is of fundamental interest to the Foundation, whose concern is not with commercial productions but with the training of competent professionals—not only playwrights and actors, but also directors, designers, and other craftsmen.

Although it would be wrong to suggest that Ford and Rockefeller are competing, their theatre programs rarely overlap and the thrust of Rockefeller aid has been in directions which Ford has either ignored or renounced. Lowry is explicit about his disappointment in university theatre, while the Rockefeller Foundation takes a constructive view.

> The Foundation takes the position that collaboration between professional groups and universities strong in theatre can be mutually rewarding, and can enrich the life of their communities: the Foundation is convinced that a serious effort should be made to break down the barriers between professional and educational theatre.

But rhetoric, even bolstered by cash, will find these barriers hard to breach, for to do so would mean the complete reconstruction of university theatre: new faculties, changed administrative attitudes, academically unconventional programs, non-liberal-arts-oriented students.

One of the first efforts of the Rockefeller Foundation in this direction raised questions which, if nothing else, should educate the Foundation to the tasks it has set itself. In 1963, $75,395 was granted to the University of Minnesota for a playwrights' program. Arthur Ballet of the University's theatre department administered the program, which is continuing under a second grant. These seem to be the only clear facts in a picture otherwise confused by charges, counter-charges, assertions, and denials. In the *Educational Theatre Journal* for May 1965, Ballet describes the program as follows:

> Our project has determined to concentrate its facilities on playwrights, who perhaps hold the key to opening the vistas of American theatre. [. . .] We plan to invite several selected playwrights to avail themselves of a facility tailor-made for them to help them solve their problems of creativity and experimentation. [. . .] Once the playwrights are selected, we choose an appropriate director and cast to serve as the playwrights' working laboratory. [. . .] The playwright comes to the project with his dramaturgical or theatrical problem, the facility being placed at his disposal, and an adequate working period allowed wherein the problem can be examined, tested, rejected, or incorporated, and evaluated by the playwright. [. . .] The laboratory is at the disposal of the writer and could conceivably even bring an entire play *up to the point* of full production —to the point, let us say, where in New York the show would be ready to go out-of-town for its tryout. [. . .] Production *per se* would not be the goal of the laboratory or this project. Similarly, public

performances of the play will not be the goal of the work; we assume the writer, as well as his cast and director, can learn much about the creative project at hand short of performance and production. In short, the project is *not* in any sense an out-of-town try-out of a new play.

Ballet is so insistent about the fact that the play is not to be produced because last year (before his insistence was so definite) two playwrights "misunderstood" him. Terrence McNally and Arthur Kopit were brought to Minneapolis with a New York cast, and the facility of the Guthrie Theatre was hired as a "laboratory." The playwrights thought their plays were going to be produced. Then questions arose about McNally's *And Things That Go Bump in the Night*, a play with homosexual themes and characters. University officials feared public reaction. (What must they have felt about the title of Kopit's Play, *The Day the Whores Came Out to Play Tennis?*) Public performances of the play were shelved and Ballet—caught between the professionals and the academics—converted the situation into a "laboratory," where the playwright would be given "a theatre, a cast, a director, and, if he wishes, an invited group of viewers." Ballet justified this position on the basis that University "commitment has been to a playwright rather than a play, its production, performance, or 'try-out' in the commercial sense." In a letter to me, Ballet said: "The playwrights wanted performance and production and the project never envisioned either performance or production *per se*." In an earlier letter, Ballet said: "There was *never* any intention of having a public production or performance. The issue finally settled down that they would not or could not accept these terms." Kopit left for New York charging the University with "censorship in its most invidious form." McNally stayed and his play was performed for an invited audience. Ballet told me that "well over 1,000 viewers" saw McNally's play. This during four performances in a theatre that seats 1,200 and after many who called for tickets were told that they were unavailable. In other words, there were *too many* people present to constitute an "invited audience," and *not enough* to test the play against a public. Whatever rationalizations Ballet may offer in his article after the fact (he *never* mentions the incident directly, but simply repeats again and again the nonperformance nature of the program), the playwrights clearly understood something else, and one of them chose to leave the program. One may legitimately ask what the difference is between "performance" and "performance *per se*" and if the project never envisioned performance why retain a 1,200 seat theatre? How does one commit oneself to a playwright and not his play? The double-talk is the language of compromise and bad faith.[4]

Other Rockefeller Foundation moves in the direction of strengthening relationships between professional and university theatres include substantial grants to Stanford, Yale, and New York Universities. Totaling in the millions of dollars, these monies helped establish the Stanford Repertory Company and the NYU School of the Arts. At Yale, the money helped Dean Robert Brustein set up the Yale Repertory and further his plans for close on-campus cooperation between professional theatre people and professionally oriented students.

Each of these three programs is interesting; they are not identical but probe in related directions. At Stanford, a $300,000 grant was made to:

> assist the Stanford administration and the Department of Speech and Drama to act on their conviction that the role of a professional company on campus is not only to insist on excellence of production, but also to become an integral part of the teaching faculty. The senior members of this professional theatre company, who will be selected primarily on artistic grounds without regard to academic credentials, will concentrate to begin with on the intensive training of some twenty carefully selected students—would-be actors, direc-

---

[4] *In more recent years the Office of Aid to Dramatic Research program has settled down. Although Rochelle Owens complained (and rightly) that her play, Futz, was badly produced and misrepresented to its audience, many playwrights have found the Minnesota project valuable simply because they have had a chance to see their work done. Writers who have been produced include Megan Terry, Sam Shepard, and other off-off Broadway notables. The drawback is that the plays are frequently done out of their milieu by directors and performers who are not receptive to the new work. The OADR made a good forward step when it engaged Minneapolis' Firehouse Theatre to work in the program. That theatre is avant-garde and truly sympathetic to new writing and production techniques.*

tors, and designers holding a BA or its equivalent—who must also take courses in academic areas associated with a major field in theatre arts. Teaching will be conducted in a direct, personal way and steadily associated with practice in the preparation and rehearsal of plays. The full professional company will at the same time give regular performances on the Stanford campus, emphasizing new approaches in directing, acting, and design.

But points raised by Lowry and Hoffman are not answered. No simple "presence" will change basic structure. The test at Stanford is whether or not the university administration will be flexible enough to admit the theatre on its own terms—will the university encourage an island that, by its very being (if artistically constituted), challenges the school to change it ways? The Yale relationship is similar, except that Yale has a strong and ongoing professional school which will make the accommodation between professional and university staff that much easier. NYU has no professional performance operation. The Rockefeller grant went solely toward the establishment of a training program for actors, directors, and a few playwrights, designers, and administrators. The NYU program was largely designed by Hoffman. The real question to be addressed to all programs situated on campus—whether new or refurbished—is whether universities can sponsor innovation. It is ironic that campuses have fostered several scientific revolutions while remaining stubborn tories in the arts. There is scant hint that the pattern is changing.

During the spring of 1965 the Rockefeller Foundation made two strong moves to encourage training within the resident theatres. Again, because these programs are not yet operating and because, structurally at least, they promise a great deal, there is no basis for criticism, just an opportunity to outline their intentions. A grant of $106,500 was made to the Arena Stage for a three-year training program for the company which will include forty-week sessions in voice and speech, acting technique, movement, and specialties. In addition there will be a six-week summer workshop in 1966, to be repeated if the experience proves valuable. Last summer (1964) Rockefeller funded a workshop at the Seattle Repertory. A grant of $77,900 was made to the Guthrie Theatre for a special program in voice and speech directly by Kristine Linklater. She will select a limited number of potential voice and speech teachers and work with them in New York and in Minneapolis. They will not only get classroom training but also a direct theatre experience at the Guthrie and with Ball's American Conservatory Theatre. If successful, the program would begin to build a needed reservoir of trained voice and speech teachers.

The major Rockefeller Foundation probes, therefore, have oscillated between university and professional orientations. They are united in their concentration on training. The Rockefeller Foundation has shown an ability as well to deal locally with small but important requests. Playwrights have received writing grants, and total individual support averages $20,000 a year in widely varying stipends. Grants have supported the (dubious) work at the Institute for Advanced Studies of Theatre Art and the somewhat more fruitful sweats of the Actors Studio Playwrights' Unit. The Seattle Repertory, Milwaukee Repertory, Dallas Theatre Center, Pittsburgh Playhouse, and Stratford, Connecticut, Shakespeare Festival have received amounts of up to $50,000 during the past several years. One hundred thousand dollars was given to the Arena Stage toward the construction of its theatre. And *TDR*, in several grants, has received $83,000 to support special issues, distribution to ANTA members, and editorial and reviewer travel.

There is no definitive pattern yet to Rockefeller Foundation aid. There may be none. However, the Foundation, once educated to the real difficulties of professional-university cooperation, may more actively encourage basic changes in university structure. Without such changes the "cooperation" will be a paper victory, or a total defeat for the artists.

AESTHETICS, DOLLARS, POLITICS, AND MADNESS

Unearned income of all kinds—foundation, business, and individual donations—probably totaled more than $50 million during the past ten years. The two giant foundations alone gave $35 million. Tax relief, though a negative figure, is substantial. But the most important negative dollar, from both the economic and human point of view, is the low pay. The artist and administrator are here given ample opportunity to demonstrate their loyalty to the resident theatre idea. With the exceptions of Lincoln Center, the Seattle Repertory, and Guthrie, none of the regional theatres now performing would exist without the initial (and frequently continuing) sacrifices of their personnel. (As Lowry noted, the entrepreneur spirit lives actively in the artist.) Other than construction costs, foundation aid has done little more than neutralize this negative income. Few actors, even with subsidy, earn more than $200 a week for forty weeks: $8,000 a year before taxes, hardly a king's ransom. And most earn shamefully less. Exploitation, donation, and tax relief comprise major sectors of resident theatre income. The box office dollar is only part of the budget scheme. The commercial theatre, on the other hand, has only two factors: exploitation and box office.

However, through a policy which demands at least the promise of black budgets, the foundations (primarily Ford) have made certain that the box office maintains its hold over resident theatre. By examining the strategy which is assumed here—one which allies the foundations with the audience and then insures a special kind of audience—we may more clearly understand the unrelieved alienation of theatre artists and the potential shambles threatening our theatre. I use the word "assume" advisedly. The strategy I am about to describe is built into the most well-meaning project because despite all protestations to the contrary theatre is an industry which is asked to conform to the "usual" business practices. Both the foundations and those who have received grants absolutely deny any interference. But the question is one not of "interference" but of "pattern."

Most foundation grants depend upon a careful analysis of a theatre's subscription audience and community dollar support. The first is measured in numbers and the second in cash. But subscription audiences are reduced to cash as well, since what counts is how many people buy season tickets, not how many come to the theatre. Community support usually comes from a few rich individuals, corporations, and local foundations. Many may give, but a few donate the bulk of the money, and in a matching funds scheme it is the money that counts.[5] When the combined income (either real or promised) from subscriptions and community support is large enough, foundation aid is easy to get. All this, of course, if professional standards are maintained. Community support itself depends upon the subscription audience—a theatre must achieve a certain (though variable) level of "popularity" and "stability" before it becomes the darling of philanthropists and chambers of commerce. In the case of the Seattle Repertory and Guthrie, subscription campaigns and community mobilization coincided—both before the theatres were producing plays. This "total effort" may be the new way of starting resident theatres, thus eliminating the slow and painful process of individual sacrifice. But the logical relationship between subscriptions, community support, and foundation aid remains the same. The "total effort" idea eliminates the possibility for the organic development of local talents, as Blau and Irving grew in San Francisco, Zelda Fichandler in Washington, and Nina Vance in Houston. A big name is prerequisite for the blind buying of a theatre.

What is a subscription program? It is selling a season ticket to a lot of people. The cost of these tickets, though reasonable, ranges from $8 to $25, depending upon how many plays are to be produced, what night of the week the patron wishes to attend the theatre, and what seat he buys. Subscription audiences range as high as 21,295 and comprise at many theatres a very substantial part of the nightly audience. TCG offers a specialist in subscription campaigns to assist theatres in programming their efforts. At Guthrie a computerized audience analysis, now automated on tape, helps determine which neighborhoods to canvass and how. This successful system is bound to be imitated. Every theatre wants to pinpoint that "2 per cent" of the population who will pay to go to the theatre. The inescapable result is a middle-class audience—and a not very representative one at that.

---

[5] *Local businessmen are eager to pay for construction. Then they back off program support. Everyone wants a brick-and-mortar monument, no one wants to feed actors. For a study of the dynamics of "Community Mobilization" see Reiss's "Who Builds Theatres and Why," TDR, XII, No. 3, 75–92.*

An alliance is thus formed between the foundation and the audience, and the theatre is willingly caught between. Without responding to the direct needs of its audience the theatre cannot hope to build subscriptions, and without these there will be no substantial foundation help. But the theatre has neither the time nor the money to finance large-scale educational programs which would bring a multi-class audience to the theatre. Neither can it offer large blocks of tickets at give-away prices to attract the poor or the students. The theatre follows the path of least resistance to its audience and even programs its campaigns to reinforce old patterns of theatre attendance.

The first aesthetic consequence of the audience-foundation alliance is a program of classic plays, the favorites being Shakespeare, Molière, Chekhov, Shaw, Miller, and Williams. Little truly adventurous drama has been done by resident theatres—even within the scope of the writers they have chosen. The "regular" plays of the "great writers" please the audience most. And when new foreign or American writers are given a hearing, for the most part they are done in "experimental" or "laboratory" productions, which means that the administrators seek a limited or "other" audience for these plays. The difficult plays of Euripides, Ibsen, Shakespeare, Strindberg, O'Casey, and a dozen other acknowledged masters are rarely attempted. There is a dreary sameness of repertory, which indicates a coincident sameness among the audiences: this is the real evidence supporting the charge of a "chain of theatres."

The second aesthetic consequence, hand in hand with the first, is that productions have a museum quality. One is pleased but not excited, kept awake but not stimulated. The charlatanism of Broadway is replaced by an equally sham "great plays" program which at best familiarizes its audience with theatre literature of the sort they have most likely read in high school and college. I use the word "literature" with conscious opprobrium. The bookish stolidity of the resident theatre is perhaps an expected and necessary reaction to the mindless foppery of Broadway, from which many of the directors and actors have fled. But it is none the better for this and it probably springs from sources other than artistic revulsion. Only in San Francisco, and, more recently, in a production at Arena Stage, did I see notable exceptions to this pattern. But the Workshop was an island unable to afford talent meted to its aspirations and its productions suffered, while the Arena is stifled by an audience so homogeneous that its excellent productions simply slide by.

Indeed audiences want the "great plays," and the lobby talk (which offers little comfort) is that "this is as good as New York, even better." No David Merrick is more responsive to audience wishes than a producer who knows that his livelihood depends upon subscriptions. And if his audience is homogeneous he doesn't even have the opportunity to play the taste of one sector off against another. There is little active commitment to leading the audience, challenging it, and even, from time to time, attacking it. When there are attacks, these can be shrugged off by an audience which is secure in its monolithicity. At best, one or two plays a season are "sneaked in" that may disturb the subscribers, but even if the texts are upsetting, the productions themselves often neutralize the plays. The resident theatres, then, become accurate reflections of their communities. Everyone seems happy. The theatres flourish, the foundation annual reports gloat over the speed with which the "quality, content, and moral fiber" of American society is being improved, and the audiences take great civic pride in participating in cultural uplift. With very little effort everything is accommodated. Even actors are congratulated for at last having families and settling down.

But relatively few settle down. No ensembles are formed. Productions keep the same quality from year to year. Significant new plays do not come. Off-Broadway, for all its ills, incompetence, and Broadway-mimicking, still provides more excitement. In short, the artist is now alienated *within* his institution rather than outside it. Often where the productions are truly well done—as at Guthrie, Arena, Alley—there is a strange dissociation, as if they had been done "elsewhere" by "others." The Guthrie best illustrates this. Sir Tyrone came from England, his actors from New York, and his theatre from the tireless efforts of those who wished to "raise the cultural level" of the Twin Cities. A hidden but deep colonial burden rests on these theatres. The institution which is the theatre joins the foundation-audience alliance and becomes the property of the class which underwrites both foundation and theatre institution. The actors, not part of this alliance, perform in a vacuum. Their alienation may not be so sharp as it is where no institution administers basic comforts, but the dissociation is real and reflected in performances that are *for* but not *with* an audience. At theatres I have visited during the past three years, actors and directors were generally dissatisfied without being able to pinpoint the source of their unrest. But the source is not difficult to find. One need only look outside the theatre to the communities. The dreary list of correct criticisms need not be repeated here. A people that lives in the kind of houses we build, eats the food we eat, travels on the highways we lay down, cannot be saved by being reassured. No proliferation of museums, of whatever quality and kind, can offer the necessary set of challenges. A resident theatre that has systematically retreated into the middle class is doomed to a monotony equivalent to a Kansas highway. Those in our theatre who are artists now feel doubly cut off: they accepted Herbert Blau's call and went West only to find there that the institutions that were to be *theirs* simply *contained* them. And the pay isn't good enough to buy them into the values they oppose.

Two theatres that have tried to buck this pattern have had scant luck with foundations. The Living Theatre is now in exile and the Free Southern Theater is still touring the deep South with top salaries pegged at $35 per week. John O'Neal, general manager of the FST, says, "Money is not the only currency. Bodies in action are also currency." He wonders, even if the FST were able, whether the theatre should pay its actors more than their audience earns. Resident theatre actors get less than their audience and are squeezed out from the top. The other theatre that went against the grain, the San Francisco Workshop, transplanted itself to New York and devastation.

Only a multi-class audience can save our theatre. The move away from the proscenium is one which encourages the audience to watch each other as well as the stage. But if the audience is homogeneous then the aesthetic excitement of multi-focus is destroyed and the presence of others in the auditorium becomes a distraction rather than a part of the theatre experience. When I sat in the Arena Stage watching Millard Lampell's bitter and funny *Hard Travelin'* (written on commission from Arena), I thought how the excellent production had been wasted because everyone in the audience was so much alike. Here was a play which offered comparisons between the thirties and the sixties, the Depression and the Poverty Program. It satirized, shocked, blatantly outlined the contradictions of America's self-image, but the diverse life on the stage was denied by the oneness of the audience. They liked the play (itself a strange irony) that so sharply attacked their basic values because none of the poor—who were at the center of Lampell's work—were there in the audience. As for the poor who were not there, they missed another chance at self-identification which the theatre alone can give. From the actors' and director's point of view, it was not necessary to reach out to a diverse audience (as the Elizabethans and Greeks had to do) but to play isolated on a stage that invited community. Finally, it is the aesthetic values of a play that are enlivened by a multi-class audience. Yet even if a manager wished to take the leap and seek such an audience, he would find little encouragement among the foundations, who steadfastly insist on break-even budgets. Who then is to *subsidize the audience?* Subsidize it so that campaigns for audiences may be organized in communities that do not now attend the theatre either because they have no money or they lack interest, or both? Who will clearly recognize that bringing such a diverse audience into the theatre will substantially change the bases of both productions and play selection? How can the theatre provide an unalienated environment for its artists?

Permanent deficit spending is publicly offensive to the foundations for the same reason that the national debt disturbs Senator Dirksen (who, by the way, in the thirties, helped kill the Federal Theatre): it is not in the American tradition "to run a business that way." But the foundations have themselves undertaken vast deficit spending. Ford Foundation appropriations during the past three years outran income by nearly $100 million each year, and Rockefeller Foundation appropriations were nearly $40 million ahead of income. Most resident theatres are already financed (*de facto* if not *de jure*) through permanent deficit; donations and foundation aid are not gravy, but meat. Thus traditional objections to subsidy are met by contrary practice, although these subsidies have not yet been applied directly to the audience. Little real attempt is being made at bringing a multi-class audience to the theatre. Such mobilization would mean more than offering very cheap tickets. It would involve theatres in an extensive public education program, neighborhood touring, and, eventually, basic revaluation of their repertory and production methods. Not only the community but the artists would benefit by such revaluation. It would change the resident theatre from a middle-class institution to one more in touch with the dissenting parts of our population. No complicated argument is needed to show that most significant American art has long been in agreement with these dissenters. But the step from theatre subsidy to audience subsidy is an extremely difficult one simply because of the other changes it entails. It would also mean public acknowledgment of the absolute necessity for permanent and substantial subsidy, and for most Americans accepting subsidy is one thing—proclaiming it is heresy.

Even if both theatres and foundations proclaimed the heresy, would they be able to go through with the program? Is it not true that if we have been dissatisfied with theatre in this country we shall find no hope in aligning ourselves—in whatever way—with the very powers that have made American mainstream culture what it is (not)? Is there not a powerful argument to be made for the assertion that doing a beautiful thing in 1965 is revolutionary? Is art so out of joint with society that its only stance—for the time being—is revolution? I do not mean insurrection, but the presentation of plays which through their texts and/or productions challenge, disturb, and attack an audience intellectually while (hopefully) pleasing it aesthetically. The work of Peter Brook and Peter Hall in England would offer an approximate model. If a middle-class audience is unacceptable and a multi-class audience unobtainable, what choice has the artist but to set up for himself island institutions which at least put him in harmony with his own work? The American tendency to which the theatre might become opposed is one that alternates between reassurance (what Lyndon Johnson calls "consensus") and impossible solutions to insupportable situations. So

Leroi Jones asks for a black-white slaughter (while teaching at the New School and Columbia) which compensates for his own accommodations and permits his *white* audience to justify their bigotry ("If they hate us, why can't we hate them?"). All this while urging a program so brutal that it would be madness to follow it. But Jones and Johnson counsel the same thing. The demand for an impossible action is a mode of reassurance.

Does all this mean that we reject foundation aid? Or that we abandon the resident theatre movement? Frankly, I do not know but I should hope not, if only because what we now have is better than what we had ten years ago. I am convinced the only way to disrupt the foundation-audience alliance is openly and consciously to challenge it. This may mean there will be no more money next year (exactly what happened in San Francisco). Or, if enough theatres take this position and hold it, it may break foundation policy. Certainly, in theory at least, we all recognize that "culture" is not the "property" of any class—either to be kept or distributed exclusively. Perhaps the foundations recognize that their corporate job will have been well done when philanthropy as they now conceive it no longer exists.

A less satisfactory alternative to a multi-class theatre involves a three-part process. First the theatre artist *and* his institutions recognize that middle-class values as they have evolved in our society are "too easy," or, if you will, corrupt. Next, the theatre institutions are constituted as islands expressing radical democratic values which, in our century at least, have been the sources of America's best plays and productions. Finally, after (and if) the society is reconstructed on the basis of these values (or on a multi-value system, which is even better), the theatre operates in harmony with the society or with that sector of it with which it sympathizes. To wish to be in harmony now is to surrender to values which, beyond their political nastiness, have sponsored bad art.

Multi-class or anti-middle-class, these are the long range goals. They may of course be combined. Frankly, I think that foundations are more likely to take the long view than theatres—but my hopes aren't high in either case. Both are now locked into an alliance which involves our society at deeper levels than theatrical production. The federal government is the only "institution" large enough to promote a revolution without extensive bloodshed; the promulgation of that revolution depends upon whether or not the middle class is willing to surrender its prerogatives (and, in so doing, make possible those basic changes in taste that are the aesthetic counterparts of that larger movement). Current experience shows that government, too, is locked into the alliance. The persistent and enormous pressure for adaption—for "consensus"—is backed by interlocking institutions so powerful that a careful analysis drives me up the wall. And the mainstream of the culture to which we are being adapted has provided few objects of enduring aesthetic worth.

The forecast is not pleasant. But the fight is not over. The theatre cannot, even if it wished, abstract itself from this struggle: to remain neutral is to support the more powerful side. If, finally, the choice is between alienation and surrender, the theatre artist is in a bad way. If he surrenders, his life may be pleasant, but his art will be ephemeral. If he remains alienated (within his institution or outside it), his art may be significant but only as sporadic testimony. Theatre which depends first of all on the ensemble cannot do its best when neither the theatre's institutions nor the society welcomes the artist's work, and the theatre institution's life is determined by the relationship it has with its audience. There is only one way out: those "island theatre institutions," some multiclass, some expressing radical democratic values, some both. The steady retreat of the resident theatre has almost closed the circle. The rest is catastrophe.

Approaches

Work-in-Progress

1965-1966, 1968

1.

The function and the vocabulary of criticism and theory are important, difficult problems. Important because theatre deserves what other disciplines have, a consistent, intelligent, effective, and reciprocal exchange between theorists and practitioners—an exchange so close, in fact, that many painters, musicians, and dancers can claim both theory and practice as their own. The critic's function is to analyze, the practitioner's function is to do, and the theoretician forges the middle link between analysis and action. In the modern theatre, many people have tried to forge this link. Artaud, Craig, Appia, Stanislavski, Brecht, Grotowski are all notable theoreticians. Their exploratory work was done in "laboratories" or "studios," and they attempted to test their ideas against practice and deduce systems from experience. The American theatre has generally been unreceptive to such work, though it has been eager to accept European conclusions. Our most noteworthy practitioners have not been dedicated theoreticians; and our theoreticians have not engaged in extended and systematic practical work. Because we have had little effective interaction between theory and practice, our critics are academic and our practitioners unimaginative. The separation between the two is so pronounced that theatre exists in an atmosphere of mutual contempt. Most critics feel that it is enough to be "familiar" with theatre productions, and most practitioners think it is enough to proclaim loftily about "art." Few people act as if theatre were a process and as such susceptible to the kind of systematic experimentation that Stanislavski and Brecht practiced for so many years.

The situation is ironic. Critics have claimed "dramatic literature" as theirs and practitioners have claimed "production." Between the two little real dialogue takes place. And both criticism and theatre production are the poorer. The names of the great theoreticians are handed around and treasured. But the example of their work is largely ignored. The function of this essay is to examine where criticism is today, to suggest what the critic's role might be, and to offer certain theoretical approaches. If the theoreticians have left us a coherent legacy, it is simply this: the art of the theatre cannot advance unless and until those who write about theatre do it and those who do it can articulate how and what they have done.

2.

In the December 1964 *Evergreen Review*, Susan Sontag raised a hue and cry against interpretive criticism. "Interpretation is a radical strategy for conserving an old text [. . .] by revamping it. [. . .] The modern style of interpretation excavates and as it excavates, destroys; it digs 'behind' the text, to find a sub-text which is the true one." In today's theatre, interpretation is also a way of imposing a form and extracting a meaning from difficult texts which are not ready-made reflections of everyday life, or for imposing meaning on theatrical experiences for which no text exists. A field day for critics who wish to display how much they "got out of" Beckett, Genet, Ionesco, Pinter. Happenings and environmental theatre have been interpreted at the expense of being experienced. The habit of theatre interpretation is a carry over from the practice of interpreting literature. But as theatre reasserts itself and proves its claim of independence from literature, a criticism will be forced into existence, which, as Artaud argued, assumes that theatre has its own language—and that this language is spatial, active, transformational. Such a criticism will have to be structural.[1]

Sontag suggests, without thoroughly expounding, a criticism which makes "works of art—and, by analogy, our own experience—more, rather than less, real to us. The function of criticism should be to show *how it is,* even *that it is what it is,* rather than to show *what it means.*" Sontag's argument is not new. In his essay, "The Function of Criticism," T. S. Eliot warned in 1923 that "Interpretation [. . .] is only legitimate when it is not interpretation at all, but merely putting the reader in possession of facts which he would otherwise have missed." Implied here, of course, is the often cited, difficult to pin-point, and seldom honored distinction between fact and opinion. Fact, as it applies to theatre, is the play, its performance, and its audience—and, now that theatre is loosening its relationship to texts and to a fixed stage—the social setting, the author's or scenarist's intentions, the sources of the work and its production, and the variations among performances. Opinion is the critic's reaction (not description or analysis) to any of these.

The question of interpretation in theatre is peculiarly complex because theatre has both an oral and a written tradition. In literature or painting the artwork remains fixed. Each age sees in it something new or different but this is because the times have changed. Theatre has texts which remain fixed, but productions constitute an oral tradition in which conventions are continually changing. Common language makes this distinction clear. We "see" a painting or "read" a book and no one can paint someone else's painting or write someone else's book. But we "go to" a play and the performers "do" that play for us. Each "doing" of a play is an interpretation, a recasting of the written tradition in the ongoing terms of the oral tradition. In seeing a Rembrandt, the viewer is

---

[1] *There are plenty of examples of structural criticism. The best are Kenneth Burke's* A Grammar of Motives *and portions of Francis Fergusson's* The Idea of a Theatre. *Strictly speaking these are not fully articulated theatre criticism. The techniques and the underlying assumptions of structuralism have been most thoroughly explored by the French anthropologists-linguists-sociologists, notably Claude Lévi-Strauss and Lucien Goldmann.*

confronted by an object from another time and he must himself mediate the differences between Rembrandt's time and his own. In going to a play, even a very old play by Sophocles, the spectator witnesses an already mediated event; the first confrontation takes place during rehearsals and by the time of performance the play exists more "now" than it does, say, in Athens in the fifth century B.C.

Because theatre is "done," productions which radically interpret a text are not only plausible but inevitable. But to whom does this task of interpretation belong? Experience shows that except in rare cases the only people who understand the oral tradition are those who work in crafting it. Most critics who try to "interpret" plays fall into the trap of applying one portion of the written tradition to another. The written tradition is hemmed in by a grammar that asks for consistency and sequence. Oral tradition is more liberal, functioning along associative and even contradictory lines. In writing criticism, I can only say that sexuality, power, and farce are simultaneously present in Ionesco's *The Lesson*. In directing the play I can explore these things simultaneously, with subtlety, and infuse the performance with nuances that cannot be communicated by the written word.

The only kind of written interpretation that has theatrical value is one that throws all caution away. After all, the function of interpretation is not to be "just," but to trace your own madness in the shape of the text you are studying. This is precisely what Jan Kott does in *Shakespeare Our Contemporary*, and why that book has proven to be the starting point of so many performances. The interpretive critic cannot have it two ways. He cannot stand above his text and still fit it to his own predispositions.

And because most critics have shown themselves unable or unwilling to pursue and expose their madness, I, with Eliot, prefer from criticism the humblest fact rather than the most scintillating opinion. Generally, the interpretive critic's impulse is to reduce images to statements, to distort the overall shape of the artwork into its effect on him. The interpretive critic's weakness is precisely his strength. He goes on about a play and avoids going into it. He becomes the most cunning member of the audience, refining what he thinks they ought to feel into hardened opinion. Criticism then becomes a tug-of-war between the critic and the director and performers. The critic is not required to put his ideas to the practical test. As for the audience, they remain either ignorant or opinionated.

Most of America's best critics reject interpretation and aspire instead toward thematic criticism, a genre established here in 1946 when Eric Bentley published *The Playwright as Thinker*. The thematic critic must first do the work of the structural critic and then marry that to whatever relevant knowledge he draws from auxiliary facts. In practice, of course, few critics are pure in their approach. Martin Esslin leans strongly toward interpretation but writes considerable amounts of thematic and structural criticism. The pitfall of thematic criticism is vanity. The critic substitutes his creativity for the playwright's. In his foreword to *The Theatre of Revolt*, Robert Brustein sets forth the methodology of thematic criticism.

> The purposes of this book are threefold: to examine the development of a single consuming idea or attitude in eight modern playwrights; to analyze the work of these writers in depth; and to suggest an approach to the modern drama as a whole. The undertaking is ambitious, and, no doubt, smacks of presumption. How can eight men adequately represent such a large and complicated manifestation as modern dramatic literature? How indeed can one attitude or idea suitably encompass the variety of work in these eight alone? To justify my claim, I hope to demonstrate, during the course of this study, that the theme of revolt is sufficiently general and inclusive to merit this unusual emphasis: it is the current which runs through the majority of modern plays. Similarly, I hope to show how a playwright's handling of these themes determines his approach to character, plot, diction, and style. If I can persuade the reader he will then be able to see, I hope, how this method can be fruitfully applied to many playwrights not directly considered in these pages.[2]

Like the lady in the song, the thematic critic needs a gimmick. What Brustein offers as a "method" is really a set of related insights sup-

---

[2] *Robert Brustein,* The Theatre of Revolt *(Boston: Little, Brown, 1964), p. vii.*

porting a central theme. The theme is the gimmick. Brustein is a brilliant man and he develops his theme with impressive erudition. He delivers what he promises, and one goes away from *The Theatre of Revolt* almost convinced that Brecht and Chekhov were equally men of the revolution. That result is surely more interesting than most interpretations, but only a little less perilous. Instead of facing each writer and each play directly, Brustein interposes (and too often imposes) the theme—always "this theme." His chapter on Chekhov begins:

> Since Anton Chekhov is the gentlest, the subtlest, and often the most dispassionate of all the great modern dramatists, it is open to argument whether he properly belongs in this discussion at all. I believe that his title as a rebel playwright [who awarded this title?] can be effectually—if only partially—established. [. . .] Certainly, the surface of Chekhov's art is not promising evidence of his rebellious inclinations. [. . .] On the other hand, the Chekhovian surface is deceptive, and for all its thickness and texture, it is not inpenetrable. Beneath lie depths of theatricality, moral fervor, and revolt [. . .] beneath this surface is a satiric, admonitory moralist, shaping, selecting, and even judging in much the same way as the other rebel dramatists. [. . .] Chekhov, in short, "observes, chooses, guesses, combines" for a special purpose—not to remedy the particular evils but to represent them accurately—and it is through this representation that he exercises, indirectly, the moral function of his art.[3]

But of what great playwright can this not be said? It is equally true of Aeschylus, Shakespeare, Molière, and Racine. I suppose Brustein would not quarrel with the observation that "all significant drama is theatre of revolt." That would be thematic inclusiveness in the grand style and would indeed convert his insights into a method. But unfortunately the assertion is not provable except as a platitude. And the peril is that Brustein's theme submerges the naked originality of Chekhov in the "current which runs through the majority of modern writers." A good half of Brustein's chapter on Chekhov is devoted to proving the thesis of revolt. Such devotion deserves the

---

[3] Ibid., *pp. 137, 147.*

reprimand which Northrup Frye administered to all dogmatic critics.

> It would be easy to compile a long list of such determinisms in criticism, all of them, whether Marxist, Thomist, liberal-humanist, neo-Classical, Freudian, or existentialist, substituting a critical attitude for criticism, all proposing not to find a conceptual framework for criticism within literature [in our case, theatre] but to attach criticism to one of a miscellany of frameworks outside it. The axioms and postulates of criticism, however, have to grow out of the art it deals with. [. . .] It is clear that the absence of systematic criticism has created a power vacuum, and all the neighboring disciplines have moved in.[4]

3.

Aristotle was the first theatre critic. His *Poetics* is a descriptive, structural study of the Greek theatre. It is neither interpretive nor thematic. His judgments refer to what worked and what didn't work on the Greek stage of his day (about one hundred years after the great age of tragedy). The *Poetics* reflects a mode of thought Aristotle explored more fully in his other works. That mode can most succinctly be described as "organic." Aristotle deeply believed in causal chains, in the ordered development of nature. He felt that the best art was the one which was internally consistent. His criticism of Euripides must be seen in that light. But Aristotle does not simply "prefer" Sophocles' "inevitability" over Euripides' "happenstance." He is explicit about his premises and exact in his descriptions. It is very easy to separate fact from opinion in the *Poetics* and where Aristotle offers an opinion it is only after relating the facts.[5] Euripides is "melodramatic" because his plots were such-and-such. Melodrama is "bad" because things don't happen that

---

[4] *Northrup Frye*, Anatomy of Criticism (*Princeton: Princeton University Press, 1957*), *p. 6. I am only too aware that my own devotion to techniques of structural anthropology may put me directly in Frye's line of fire.*

[5] *Of course, Aristotle's facts are conditioned by his cultural situation. His thought is entirely consistent, and his premises clear. More than that we cannot ask.*

way in life, or if they do, such events do not follow the "logic of organic development."[6] The *Poetics* has been influential throughout most of Western theatre history because it centers on aspects of theatre which time and historical relativity are least likely to corrode. Again Frye:

> Aristotle seems to me to approach poetry as a biologist would approach a system of organisms, picking out its genera and species, formulating the broad laws of literary experience, and in short writing as though he believed that there is a totally intelligible structure of knowledge attainable about poetry which is not poetry itself, or the experience of it, but poetics.[7]

Aristotle's work was closely tied to the theatre he observed, and his aesthetics were viable in his own day. Only later did his descriptive aesthetic become prescriptive, frozen into "rules" by Renaissance and neoclassical critics. When used more flexibly, Aristotle retains his relevance. Fergusson observes:

> Did the Moscow Art Theatre people get their basic technical concept from Aristotle's *Poetics?* Or was it by mere chance that they used the same word [action] that Aristotle used, as the basis of *his* theory of art? [. . .] The *Poetics* certainly makes more sense if one reads it after a long immersion in Boley's [Richard Boleslavski] and Madame's [Maria Ouspenskaya] practical lore of action. [. . .] Conversely, the Moscow technique makes more sense when cultivated in the light of Aristotle's doctrine of action.[8]

Stanislavski's later work—"the method of physical action"—converges in many ways with Brecht's work. Brecht rails frequently

---

[6] *Our understanding of life process is different these days. Aristotle's relevance can be questioned on the basis of its deepest assumptions about order, consistency, coherence, and completion. These assumptions were not his own invention, but were shared by many Greek thinkers of his time.*

[7] *Frye, op. cit., p. 14.*

[8] *Francis Fergusson, "The Notion of Action," TDR, IX, No. 1, 86. Fergusson is one of the critics/theoreticians who, at least early in his career, combined writing and doing. He studied with Boleslavski and Ouspenskaya, was director of the Bennington College theatre. It is no accident that his rich interpretation of Aristotle in* The Idea of a Theater *is continually of use to both theoreticians and practitioners.*

enough against Aristotle, but his disagreement is not with the central premise of Aristotle's aesthetic. Aristotle, Stanislavski, and Brecht agree that the *event*—the action—is the soul of theatre. Brecht saw and explored the possibilities of disjunctive and contradictory action, but he never lost sight of the central position of a related set of gestures which express, both harmoniously and through contradiction, the situation of the character. While Stanislavski concentrated on the world of the characters, Brecht enlarged his focus to include the characters, the performers as such, the theatrical mechanism, and the audience. But however he enlarged the range of his attention, his thought remained consistent with Aristotle's essential premises.

These premises, understood in their widest applications, are not inconsistent with today's avant-garde. Aside from some pure neo-Dada, all theatrical activity—from Allan Kaprow's Happenings to Peter Brook's Shakespeare or *Marat/Sade*—functions from the logic of events. If one concentrates on the events, there is little danger that the play—or any performance—will dissolve in a flood of secondary matters. It is here that the distinction between theatre and literature is most clear. A written event, no matter how lucid and image-laden, is always a description. The "real events" of literature are grammar, rhetoric, verbal imagery, and so on. The "real events" of theatre are performers performing. A literary critic can speak only metaphorically about "real things happening." A theatre critic can speak of little else.

The modern theatre critic, as I see him, takes as his major job the examination of a play's structure. His goal is descriptive—to outline the various events and the interaction between them. If he works from texts, he should understand that the text is a "pre-text" for action. Modest as this task may seem, it is immensely complicated. A play isn't this way or that way, but many ways. All dramatic structure—even something as tightly put together as Racine's *Phèdre*—is "open-structured." That is, it is designed for performance and includes in its very conception room for the performers to "interpret," in other words, to find a variety of solutions to any given textual situation. Discovering underlying structures is like mapping one set of routes through complicated territory. The structural critic opens new territories—places that cannot be thoroughly explored by criticism. Only through many productions can the spatial and simultaneous structures which have been mapped be probed, thoroughly and subtly. A structural analysis of a text centers on the actions stated or implied in the text, and the relationships among the characters. Thus the structural critic who cannot carry his research through a production will not be able to write meaningfully about theatre. And a director who does not understand structure will be scarcely able to shape an artwork.

There are, obviously, two sets of problems here. The first deals with the text. The second deals with performance, and includes the mechanics of the theatre and the audience. The two sets of problems overlap, but they are not identical. In mapping structures discovered in the text, the critic prepares the way for production. During production, and in the training that precedes production, the performance problems—interrelations between actors, the relationship between the stage and the auditorium, the possibility of shared space between performers and audience—are explored. While these problems impinge upon the structural analysis of a text, a text can be analyzed without considering these problems in detail. However, the more the critic knows about the mechanics of the theatre, the better he is able to evaluate the possibilities of a text and the less likely he is to be sidetracked.

The structural critic's work is to mediate between the play and those who produce it—not between the play and its audience. His work is rewarded by better productions, not by more enlightened audiences.[9] Structural criticism is more technical and detailed and therefore less popular than interpretive or thematic criticism. Far-

---

[9] *Someone will remind me that I have spoken in favor of "facts"—why then the preposterous myth that practitioners read criticism and audiences do not? I bow to the objection that I am indulging my own wishes. There is this to add: if criticism were structural, practitioners might choose to read it because it would contain information relevant to their work. Structural criticism does not intrude itself willy-nilly between an audience and a production, whereas most interpretive and thematic criticism is appropriate only after a play has been seen. The playgoer can then measure his own opinions against the critic's and, with the help of the critic, situate the play within its cultural frame. To so locate a work before seeing it is to cheat theatre of its immediacy.*

ther on in "The Function of Criticism," Eliot says some things about those who discuss poetry that can be said about theatre critics.

> To the member of the Browning Study Circle, the discussion of poets about poetry may seem arid, technical, and limited. It is merely that the practitioners have clarified and reduced to a state of fact all the feelings that the member can enjoy only in the most nebulous form; the dry technique implies, for those who have mastered it, all that the member thrills to; only that has been made into something precise, tractable, under control. That, at all events, is one reason for the value of the practitioner's criticism—he is dealing with his facts, and he can help us to do the same.

The structural critic's factual questions are very simple. Why does this scene follow that one? Why does this character say or do that now? How many actions, and of what kind, are occurring simultaneously? What decisions have the characters made, when, and why? What is the infrastructure—the action, in Fergusson's sense—of the scene, of the play? Precisely what transformations take place, when, in what situations, and why? Answering these questions will give the critic or director enough information to begin work on an interpretation or production. The structural critic's work, when properly and thoroughly done, is lengthy and detailed. He uses what tools are available to him, including schematic and conceptual models. Although he may find himself working with texts alone, he is aware that the text is not the play but the conceptual model from which many productions may flow.

The peculiar burden of theatre criticism is tied to the confrontation between written and oral traditions. In theatre there is no original artwork. There is the text and there are the productions. It is fruitless to argue which is the artwork. Given a great production of a great text—say Peter Hall's *Henry* V—one cannot easily divide the credit and responsibility among Shakespeare, Hall, and the actors. The artwork is the confrontation between all involved. In Hall's *Henry* V, the rather routine scene in which the French ambassador asks Henry to surrender is converted into a moment of high art and truth. Hall had some soldiers hold down and muffle a wounded English soldier so that Henry's rejection of the French demand would not be marred by the screams of the suffering man. Henry was able to deliver his disdainful and heroic lines amid a stunning, and expensive, silence. The wounded soldier died. The scene became agonizingly ironic—in keeping with a production which converted *Henry V* from a jingoistic expression of English valor into an anti-war, anti-hero play. Many of Shakespeare's lines— both plain and famously heroic (the St. Crispin's Day speech, for example)—were undercut and transformed into telling mockery. To whom does the credit belong? It was still Shakespeare's play, his lines, his scenes. But it was Hall's direction, Ian Holm's superb acting, the entire ensemble of the Royal Shakespeare Company that made *this* production what it was. Jerzy Grotowski's "confrontations" with classic texts[10] provide even more radical examples. For the theatre critic simply to ignore these particulars is foolish. But he is hard pressed to include them in his discussion if he writes before he has seen the play. Therefore, there is no alternative for the theatre critic but to relinquish his precious authority. He can speak only of artworks-in-process. A performance occurring as he writes, halfway around the world, may alter the very nature of the artwork he is so confidently expounding.

What then ought to be the relationship between text, production, and critic? Obviously he should see and study as many performances as he can. He should be, if at all possible, a practitioner himself. If he is one, his written work will be systematic speculations and explorations based on his practical work, feeding back into it. If his thoughts, imagination, creativity, and experience are of an exceptional order, he may become a major theoretician as Brecht and Stanislavski were. If his gifts are more modest, he may make contributions about the nature of the theatrical event and the structure of texts, as Fergusson has done. Still more modestly, it will be enough if he understands that theatre is the concurrence of simultaneous events. He will come finally to know that his criticism—

---

[10] *I discuss Grotowski's work in several essays in this book, most notably "Six Axioms for Environmental Theatre." Writing by and about Grotowski has appeared in TDR, VIII, No. 4, 120–133; IX, No. 3, 60–65; XI, No. 3, 153–189; and XIII, No. 1, 29–45.*

like all artistic work in the theatre—is partial. When complete it is incomplete, once written it belongs to the practitioners. This is no license for either despair or irresponsibility. The critic is no worse off than directors, actors, designers, or playwrights.

4.

Structural criticism frequently lacks the literary elegance of interpretive or thematic criticism. But it has its own special elegance: a rigorous attention to its subject. Again, ideally, it should be written by practitioners—as reports of their work or preparations for work. If these reports are systematic, and if the practitioner-writer is gifted, structural criticism is theory. Much valuable theoretical work has been done during the past seventy years. The theories are still rudimentary, and too often highly sophisticated problems have been treated at the expense of more basic ones. But each of this century's great theoreticians—Stanislavski, Brecht, Artaud, and Grotowski—has tried to develop systematic approaches to the basic components of theatre: audience, performers, text, space. None of them has treated these components as independent; they have tried to make systematic sense out of them and develop vocabularies indigenous to them. Stanislavski was most concerned with character and the relationship between performers and text; Artaud with the relationship between performers and space. Brecht gave his large mind to all four components, but was most interested in audience, performers, and text. Grotowski's theories are still in the early stages of their formation. But, like Brecht, his interests are inclusive. Moreover, he has taken Artaud's suggestions about space—"the theatre is a concrete physical place which asks to be filled, and to be given its own concrete language to speak"[11]—and tested them in a variety of situations.[12]

---

[11] *Antonin Artaud*, The Theatre and Its Double *(New York: Grove Press, 1958), p. 37.*
[12] *For accounts of some of Grotowski's ideas, including writing by him and interviews with him, see* Teatr·Laboratorium, Institut de Recherches sur le jeu de l'acteur *(Wrøclaw, Poland: n.d.). The booklet, prepared by Grotowski and his staff, is in French and may be obtained by writing directly to the Institut,*

Whatever contributions I can make to these studies in this essay will be limited.[13] I want the license to go off in various directions, sketching and outlining approaches to the overall problems of theatrical structure and organization. My speculations will touch on relationships between nonliterate and our own theatre, elements of game theory, comparisons between play, games and sports, theatre, and ritual. What follows is a groundwork on which some kinds of structural criticism could be built—a modest contribution to theory.[14]

5.

But, whether one deplores or rejoices in the fact, there are still zones in which savage thought, like savage species, is relatively protected. This is the case of art, to which our civilization accords the status of a national park with all the advantages and inconveniences attending so artificial a formula [. . .][15]

One of the oldest saws of criticism is the distinction between

---

Rynek Ratusz 27, Wrøclaw. Also, Towards the Poor Theatre (*Holsteboro, Denmark: Odin Teatrets Forlag, 1968*). This book, in English, edited by a Grotowski disciple, Eugenio Barba, contains texts by Grotowski and interviews with him—including descriptions of exercises and mises-en-scènes. See fn. 10 for other Grotowski references.

[13] *"Six Axioms for Environmental Theatre" and "Negotiations with Environment"—both included in this book—deal directly with the problems of space, audience, and text.*

[14] *At the risk of redundancy, I wish to make absolutely clear my distinction between "critic" and "theoretician." The theoretician must be a practitioner. It is in production that he develops and tests his theories. The structural critic may be a practitioner, but his main job is understanding the shapes of a text and its productions and the transactions within them.*

[15] *Claude Lévi-Strauss,* The Savage Mind (*Chicago: University of Chicago Press, 1966*), p. 219. It would be difficult to assess the impact of the French anthropologist, Lévi-Strauss. He has affected the disciplines of linguistics, social anthropology (specifically ethnology, comparative studies, myth theory), and history. He has been important to contemporary literary criticism. Some of his work is available in English, most notably The Savage Mind *and* Structural Anthropology (*New York: Basic Books, 1963*)—the former is a study of classificatory systems among nonliterate cultures and the latter an important collection of essays on subjects as wide-ranging as linguistics, kinship theory, shamanism, myth, and nonliterate iconography.

form and content. Form is an abstract system which contains or conveys the content. Form exists on a different, higher "level" than content. It is separate from and independent of the phenomena it contains. The metaphors emanating from this ancient dichotomy are endless. On a simplistic level: new wine (= content) in old bottles (= form). The bottle is not drinkable. But without it the wine spills and is lost. The bottle exists before we fill it and it will exist after we empty it. If our new wine is explosive, it will burst our old bottle and we must come up with a new form: a bottle better suited to our vintage.

Lévi-Strauss and other proponents of structuralism[16] assert that structure is the arrangement of and relationships among actions, objects, discourses (or whatever is being examined). Structure, unlike form, is concrete. It can be of phonemes and morphemes (linguistics), "bits" (information theory), kinship groups (ethnology), thoughts, affects, and behavior (psychology), dialogue (drama), scenes, actors, audience, space (theatre)—or anything else. Structuralism is comprehensive because it is a methodology, not a subject. Its adherents think it is *the* method for "The Sciences of Man"—the analysis of culture in all its manifestations. Whether or not structure is inherent in the universe is moot. It is certainly inherent (say the structuralists) in the human mind. Its simplest and most compelling expression is man's passion for classification, his need to develop taxonomies for his environment, social organization, and behavior.

The distinction between structuralism and formal analysis is not a quibbling one. Formal analysis tends to make phenomena lie still, elevating them to an existence where they can be considered in peace, quiet, and immutability. The turbulent complexity of human action is denied. Structural analysis, on the other hand, is always

---

[16] *Structuralism is largely a French movement in anthropology, psychiatry, linguistics, literary criticism, and philosophy. A good introduction to it in English is* Yale French Studies, *double issue, Nos. 36–37 (October 1966). Aside from Lévi-Strauss, among the more important structuralists are Lucien Goldmann, Roland Barthes, and Jacques Lacan. A reasonably comprehensive, if somewhat carping, article on structuralism is Peter Caws'* "What Is Structuralism?" Partisan Review, *Winter 1968, pp. 75–91.*

partial and unfailingly concrete. It admits of no final repository of cultural categories. It seeks "laws" of transformation which are endlessly variable—laws which can be reduced to simple systems but which yield innumerable concrete circumstances. Every structural analysis must begin and end with a set of these circumstances. Every phenomenon (or set of circumstances and actions) is assumed to have many simultaneous structures. None of these arrangements is any "better" or "higher" than the others. These structures may, and most often do, interpenetrate. For example, a spoken sentence can be analyzed (at least) as a phonemic, morphemic, or grammatical utterance. The structure of the sentence will vary, depending upon which perspective you select. But in each instance, a concrete set of relationships is under scrutiny.

For theatre, the consequences of the structural method are great. Theatre, like music and dance, is extraordinarily difficult to analyze because it is performed. Each instance is but another possible representation and variation of an infinite series. What Lévi-Strauss said of music and myth applies as well to theatre.

> It is clear now in what way music resembles myth; myth, too, overcomes the antinomy of historical elapsed time; it has also overcome the limitations of permanent structure. [. . .] Music and mythology confront man with virtual objects whose shadow alone is real; they offer conscious approximations—a musical score and a myth can be nothing else—of the ineluctably unconscious truths which are consecutive to them.[17]

Or, to use two of Lévi-Strauss' favorite words, performance is both diachronic and synchronic: a concrete occurrence at a certain place and time and a recapitulation (or denial) of the score or script and its history of performances and variations. Even to begin the concrete analysis of such complex phenomena is to encounter problems of the most intractable kind.

One could begin by accepting Lévi-Strauss' assertion that art is a special preserve of "savage thought" within modern cultures.

---

[17] *Lévi-Strauss*, "*Overture to* le Cru et le cuit," Yale French Studies, *double issue, Nos. 36–37, pp. 41–65.*

What, precisely, might this mean? And what are its specific consequences for the study of theatre?

Savage thought—as Lévi-Strauss understands it—is characterized "both by a consuming symbolic ambition such as humanity has never again seen rivaled, and by scrupulous attention directed entirely towards the concrete, and finally by the implicit conviction that these two attitudes are but one [. . .]"[18] This is a difficult paradox: symbolic = concrete. It goes against our preconception of the symbolic and the concrete as opposing terms. But what, other than a fusion of the two, is "the life of Hamlet" or the involved Greek myths which issue forth in extraordinary selective detail in *The Oresteia, Oedipus,* or *The Bacchae?* Even more modern, more dissociated figures—Borkman, the weird characters and actions of Strindberg's *Ghost Sonata,* the frail and convincingly "whole" people of *The Three Sisters,* the fragmentary, even mad anti-characters of Ionesco—seem to suit an "implicit conviction" that the symbolic and the concrete are one.

Perhaps we are on the verge of resolving one of aesthetics' most perplexing dilemmas. Put in its simplest form we—as "civilized" and technologically sophisticated people—cannot truly appreciate the way nonliterate people live. We cannot comfortably climb into their huts, do without electricity, antibiotics, plumbing: the technological paraphernalia that seems so aptly to define—in the largest sense—our way of life. We cannot be transported to Papua, the drylands of Australia, or the central African jungle and enjoy ourselves. However, we can take home a totem, a mask, a piece of carving. We can listen to "primitive" music; watch with admiration the long dances, the protracted cycle plays and festivals. The contradiction between our way of life and theirs vanishes when art is the mediator. We can even hear in Euripides' chorus from *The Bacchae* echoes of rhythms and customs hundreds, perhaps thousands, of years more ancient than the Athens of the fifth century B.C.:

---

[18] The Savage Mind, *p. 220.*

> When shall I dance once more
> with bare feet the all-night dances,
> tossing my head for joy
> in the damp air, in the dew,
> as a running fawn might frisk
> for the green joy of the wide fields,
> free from the fear of the hunt,
> free from the circling beaters
> and the nets of woven mesh
> and the hunters hallooing on
> their yelping packs? And then, hard pressed,
> she sprints with the quickness of wind,
> bounding over the marsh, leaping
> to frisk, leaping for joy,
> gleeful with the green of the leaves,
> to dance for joy in the forest,
> to dance where the darkness is deepest,
>   where no man is.[19]

How much is this like the molimo dances of the BaMbuti, who "roam the [African] forest at will, in small isolated bands or hunting groups"?[20]

> The molimo was often referred to as the "animal of the forest," and the women were supposed to believe that it really was an animal, and that to see it would bring death. [. . .] The animal sounds it produced were certainly realistic, but I wondered what the women thought when it sang. What kind of animal was it that one moment could make such threatening sounds, and the

---

[19] The Bacchae, tr. *William Arrowsmith, in* Euripides V *(Chicago: University of Chicago Press, 1959), ll. 863–878. The translation is accurate, but even if it were not—even if it were a modern version of what Euripides wrote—my point would be valid. The jump would then be that much longer, from the twentieth century back to what "savage" time?*

[20] *Colin M. Turnbull,* The Forest People *(New York: Simon & Schuster/ Clarion Books, 1968), p. 14. Turnbull's book is one of the best ethnographic studies for theatre people. Not only does he describe in detail a number of ceremonies, but he has a true love for the BaMbuti, a sense of their humor and humanity.*

next instant sing more beautifully than anything else in the whole forest?[21]

The art of nonliterate peoples is at the center of our own experience. It "speaks" to us; we can "understand" it. We may not know the totemic or magic function of the mask we are looking at; we may not know the connection between tribal history and the dance we are seeing—but we feel the impact of the art nonetheless. Competing and unequal technologies do not long coexist. But no cultural difference can make art seem absolutely "different" to us. Thus the dilemma: why the arts, but not the technologies?

The answer: because our art, like theirs, is "savage." Technology is progressive, cumulative, additive. It develops by abandoning old ways, finding new solutions to constant problems. Once electricity becomes available, lighting by other methods survives only to preserve certain special moods. The function of technology is constant: to control and adapt the environment to man's needs. Until perfect controls are found, which is unlikely, technology will continue to evolve.[22]

The function of art is not so easy to discern. It is tied to social structure and experience. It attempts to make connections between phenomena—connections that are both logical and paralogical, linear and associative, diachronic and synchronic. Art does not find "better" ways. When we go to the palace at Knossos and see the flush toilet built for the Minoan queen, we marvel at the ingenuity of Minoan technology and know that American Standard builds better

---

[21] Ibid., p. 82. The molimo is a long tube, traditionally of bamboo or similar natural material, that is played like a trumpet/flute. An interesting side note on the technology-art paradox. The molimo that Turnbull observed was made of an old metal pipe. The BaMbuti told him that it made approximately the same sound as the traditional instrument, and it didn't decay as natural wood did. At least with this fragment of modern technology, the BaMbuti were able to accommodate themselves. As they assured Turnbull, it is the sound not the substance of the molimo that counts. See pp. 73–81.

[22] Cultures have "lost" their technologies. But in a strict sense they haven't —cultures have been so totally disrupted they have ceased to exist and new, less technologically sophisticated cultures replace the old. Available technology is the one irresistible cultural component. Turn on a light next to your lightless neighbor, and, sooner or later, he will want a light too.

flush toilets. But when we look at the Minoan wall paintings, we know that nothing we have done is any better. There is room in technology for only one "best" solution to each problem. There is room in art for innumerable representations. Finally, we come back to Lévi-Strauss' somewhat opaque definition. Art is both symbolic and concrete. It has nowhere to go. It cannot develop. Each instance of it, regardless of its cultural matrix, can be terrible or sublime. And we do not know which by any description—only the experience of seeing or participating can validate an artwork. Every artwork is a first try; each school or tradition a set of first tries.

Each artwork is a first try because there is nothing another artist can do for you to guarantee your artistic success. There is no surefire method of artistic construction. There are skills that can be learned, but these techniques—unlike the skills of technology—guarantee nothing. The artistic creative process remains a mystery. Lévi-Strauss on music:

> Music raises a much more difficult problem [than myth] because we are thoroughly ignorant of the mental conditions behind musical creation. In other words, we do not know what the difference is between a small number of minds which secrete music and those, vastly more numerous, where no such phenomenon occurs even though such minds show musical sensitivity. The difference is so clear and manifests itself with such precocity that we suspect it implies properties of a special nature which are doubtless to be found at the deepest levels. But that music is a language by whose means messages are elaborated, that such messages can be understood by the many but sent out only by the few, and that it alone among all the languages unites the contradictory character of being at once intelligible and untranslatable—these facts make the creator of music a being like the gods and make music itself the supreme mystery of human knowledge. All other branches of knowledge stumble into it, it holds the key to their progress.[23]

Freud, among others, tried to probe the mysteries of artistic creation and was forced to lay down his arms before them.[24] The artwork is

---

[23] *"Overture to* le Cru et le cuit," *p. 64.*
[24] *See, for example, the papers of Freud collected in* On Creativity and the Unconscious *(New York: Harper & Row, 1958).*

visible, it is possible to analyze it into its elemental structures and to know the artist's state of mind during creation. But when artists try to describe "inspirations," the descriptions are as mystifying as the process they attempt to unveil.

Something "happens" within the artist that concretizes a set of impulses, observations, and intuitions. He is able to translate these into specific arrangements that surpass, without abandoning, the details that combine to make the artwork. But the problem of artistic creativity is different from, and more opaque than, the problem of artistic structure. For the time being, we must settle for discussions of the artworks themselves, not the processes that bring them into being.

I have made no distinction between "primitive" ritual and sophisticated art. We all know that in nonliterate societies there is no "art for art's sake." It is only within our own and some similar cultures that the artist works for himself. However, this apparent difference between ritual and art will not hold up from a structural point of view. There is, of course, a functional difference between ritual art and art for art's sake. But with nothing more than a direct experience of the artwork, one cannot discern which objects or performances serve a ritual and which some other function.[25] Into what category would one assign Michelangelo's church paintings? Picasso's *Guernica?* Shakespeare's *Macbeth?* Arthur Miller's *Death of a Salesman?* Functions are complicated and rich networks. Structures are difficult but more tractable. Homologies can be identified. Furthermore, the preponderance of ethnographic data indicates that the strict distinction we assume between the sacred and the profane is not distinct at all—in our culture or in any other. For example, women are forbidden to participate or even see the molimo cere-

---

25 *One of the qualities of a technological instrument—a hammer, a clock, an arrow—is that its structure usually reveals its function. This is not true of aesthetic or ritual objects. In structure, we cannot tell the difference between a "ritual" knife and a "common" knife. Unless we know something about the cultural matrix of the thing in question, structure alone will not tell us what a painting, mask, piece of music, or dance is used for (if anything other than for itself). This is not denying that aesthetic things have functions. They certainly do. But these functions are often separate from their structures.*

mony of the BaMbuti.[26] But they watch anyway, and make critical comments about the dancing and singing of the men. The men are supposed to be spirits during the ceremony, and the women are supposed to die if they spy—but they spy, and they taunt, and they indulge in name calling. The performance is sacred, but it is a sacred game, not a nonliterate version of our own heavy-handed sanctimony.[27]

Lévi-Strauss suggests that myth is constructed both diachronically and synchronically. The problem of myth is difficult, and it is not unlike the problem of performance.

> Mythology confronts the student with a situation which at first sight appears contradictory. On the one hand it would seem that in the course of a myth anything is likely to happen. There is no logic, no continuity. Any characteristic can be attributed to any subject; every conceivable relation can be found. With myth, everything becomes possible. But on the other hand, this apparent arbitrariness is belied by the astounding similarity between myths collected in widely different regions. Therefore, the problem: if the content of a myth is contingent, how are we going to explain the fact that myths throughout the world are so similar?[28]

The problem of performance is homologous to that of myth. We have the original text; it is not immutable; it can lead to contradictory performances. The dialogue varies because the director wishes it to, the actors are unable to memorize the lines as written, so much time has elapsed between the time of writing and the time of performance that changes in the language are necessary to make it intelligible, a text is translated for foreign performance. The scenic organization is at once more and less flexible than the text. Theatres

---

26 *See Turnbull, op. cit., pp. 73–93.*

27 *This notion of the sacred game (Gilbert Murray's sacer ludus, which he theorizes is the ultimate source of Greek tragedy) is present in many, if not most, nonliterate societies. See, for example, C. W. M. Hart and Arnold R. Pilling,* The Tiwi of North Australia *(New York: Holt, Rinehart & Winston, 1966), pp. 80ff., and many passages in F. E. Williams,* The Drama of the Orokolo *(Oxford: Oxford University Press, 1940). I shall elaborate on the sacred game when I discuss specific correlations and differences between nonliterate and Western performances.*

28 *Lévi-Strauss, "The Structural Study of Myth," in* Structural Anthropology, *p. 208.*

come in different sizes and shapes, blocking varies from production to production and even from performance to performance. And yet there is a consistency within the scenic structure—a solidity there that transcends language changes or particular staging configurations. This consistency Stanislavski called the "action," and it is to be found at the heart of every scene. Every performance comes up against this "action" and must contend with it—either by acquiescence or denial.

It is this scenic organization which is both diachronic and synchronic: moving ahead in both actual and symbolic time, it repeats and amplifies "bundles of relations" that recur throughout the performance. It has both an ongoing, linear existence and a timeless, simultaneous existence. The action proceeds, yet it is always "there," changing only within a system of transformations that may not be present in the text at all—therefore, Stanislavski's crucial coinage: "subtext." Stanislavski has offered us one view of this structure of action. Lévi-Strauss offers another: "What gives the myth an operational value is that the specific pattern described is timeless; it explains the present and the past as well as the future."[29] This scenic organization is independent of the literary quality of the play. It is part of the events—a set of circumstances every bit as concrete as the dialogue.

> Myth is the part of language where the formula *traduttore, traditore* reaches its lowest truth value. [. . .] Whatever our ignorance of the language and the culture of the people where it originated, a myth is still felt as a myth by any reader anywhere in the world. Its substance does not lie in its style, its original music, or its syntax, but in the *story* which it tells.[30]

How much this is like Aristotle, who calls the "perfect plot" one which is "so constructed that, even without the aid of the eye, he who hears the tale told will thrill with horror and melt to pity at what takes place."[31] In other words, like myth, theatrical action

---

[29] Ibid., *p. 209.*
[30] Ibid., *p. 210.*
[31] The Poetics, *tr. Francis Fergusson (New York: Hill and Wang, 1961),* *p. 78.*

depends upon scenic organization. Lévi-Strauss goes on to show that the "constituent units of a myth are not the isolated relations but *bundles of such relations,* and it is only as bundles that these relations can be put to use and combined so as to produce a meaning."[32] These bundles are structured synchronically.

Written play-texts have the appearance of diachronic structure which is inherent in the nature of written discourse where one thing follows another. Performances, however, are both diachronic and synchronic. Othello's jealousy is something that "develops" during the performance (i.e., diachronically). But for the actor playing the role, Othello's jealousy was "there" from the first rehearsal, somehow awaiting him at a specific time and place. For the audience, a balance is struck between the unfolding action (a system of surprises) and the virtual destiny of the action (a system of certainties). The tension between these two systems gives the performance its texture—its "reality" and its "irony."

A synchronic analysis of a text-into-performance will yield anchor points and recurrent actions and relationships that are nodes of meaning and action. We discover that theatrical structure is not a steady increase, climax, and denouement, but an uneven series of gathering tensions, nodes where decisions are made within conflict situations. This discontinuous, often bumpy structure makes full use of simultaneity: a brief moment on stage may resolve a number of conflicts or incorporate a swift set of important, consequential decisions. Other, long stretches are relatively quiet.

6.

Nodes (Lévi-Strauss' "bundles of relations") where various and contradictory conflicts, motives, and actions join; a moment, or quick succession of moments, of intense confrontation and decision; consequences streaming from these decisions in different and not always harmonious directions; between nodes a bumpy, sometimes indirect ride where irrelevant material often occupies our attention;

---

[32] *Lévi-Strauss, "The Structural Study of Myth," in* Structural Anthropology, *p. 211.*

39326

a textual surface that is apparently out of touch with subtextual moves and counter-moves—this is the overall structure of a scene. A turbulent and unsteady alternation and altercation in which the grace and consistency of language is disturbed by the ambivalence of action.

Literary criticism applied to theatre is inadequate. Literary criticism works too easily on the verbal surface of scenes, accepting as "fact" only what the text can verify. This denies what every performer knows: the accidental insights he shares with his character and which turn out to be more important than the "studies" he has made; his uneasy steps into the virtual past and future of a play (recapitulated during rehearsals, where through action the performer must attempt to recollect and project his own virtual past and future); the uneasy confusions which lie at the heart of every decision, no matter how clearly enunciated or wholly "believed." Scenic structure in performance is neither determinate nor indeterminate—but somewhere between. Language has a grammar which is logical and linear, throwing off from that core rich and associative meanings. Action has no comparable grammatical core, no systemized set of relationships that hold up in every circumstance. The structure of action is not smooth and confident. Each moment it condenses out of the situation to make a new nexus of meaning. Transformations can be sudden, unclear, and paralogical. Any theory of scenic structure must start from these contradictory details of action.

Take even a straightforward scene—the agon between Oedipus and Teiresias (ll. 300–461).[33] Oedipus wants information which Teiresias withholds because to give it would further enrage Oedipus and thereby endanger Teiresias. Knowing Oedipus' reputation for rage, Teiresias answers his questions with riddles. But Oedipus drives him on with accusations and threats. Fearing for his own safety, Teiresias says, "You are the land's pollution" (l. 350), and then, "you are the murderer of the king / whose murderer you seek" (l. 362), and, finally, "This day will show your birth and will destroy

---

[33] All quotations from Oedipus are from David Grene's translation in Sophocles I (Chicago: University of Chicago Press, 1954).

you" (l. 438). Teiresias recapitulates these revelations in detail and adds to them a parting prophecy of doom (ll. 449–461). Oedipus, in turn, accuses Teiresias of conspiracy, murder, and treason. He even hints, gangland style, that he will take care of Teiresias: "once gone, you will not trouble me again" (l. 446).

But underneath this apparently simple scene of conflict—of accusation, counter-accusation, and revelation—there are other currents. To trace one: it would appear from the surface of the scene that Teiresias has all the information and Oedipus has none. But is this true?

Could Oedipus be unaware of his own name? Oedipus equals "swollen-foot." Is he unaware of the scars on his ankles? We find out later in the play that Oedipus has always been very aware of his name and his scars.

> OEDIPUS. What ailed me when you took me in your arms?
> MESSENGER. In that your ankles should be witnesses.
> OEDIPUS. Why do you speak of that old pain?
> MESSENGER.   I loosed you;
>   the tendons of your feet were pierced and fettered,—
> OEDIPUS. My swaddling clothes brought me a rare disgrace.
> MESSENGER. So that from this you're called your present name.
> OEDIPUS. Was this my father's doing or my mother's?
>   For God's sake, tell me.
> MESSENGER. I don't know.

ll. 1031–1038

The question of whether it was Oedipus' father or mother—and the urgency with which Oedipus asks it—is a detail not to be overlooked. For at this moment in the play, Oedipus does not (consciously) know *who* his parents are. He does know, by now, that Polybus was not his father, but it is not until well into the scene with the Herdsman that Oedipus discovers conclusively that he is Laius' son. Clearly, however, there is another kind of recollection gathering within Oedipus, one much more concrete than universal guilt, one based on specific evidence and associations.

Let us return to the question of the name, "swollen-foot." Given this unusual name and the awareness of its unfortunate source, would Oedipus have been struck by the name of the king he replaced? Laius equals "left-sided" or "lame-on-the-left." And what would Oedipus' associations be when he found out that Laius' father was named Labdacus (= "lame")? These are three unusual, concretely descriptive names. The older pair are joined by a father-son relationship. Oedipus continues the line—of course he is not aware of that. But could he be unaware of the coincidence—particularly if this coincidence is corroborated by other evidence?

Oedipus is very concerned about who gave the child away. The Herdsman answers the question the Messenger was unable to answer:

> HERDSMAN. The child was called his [Laius'] child; but
> she [Jocasta] within,
> your wife would tell you best how all this was.
> OEDIPUS. *She* gave it to you?
> HERDSMAN. Yes, she did, my lord.
>
> ll. 1170–1173

Oedipus is more struck with the fact that Jocasta gave the child to the Herdsman than that he is the son of Laius. Why? If Jocasta gave the child to the Herdsman, then she without a doubt knew of the wounded ankles. Is it likely that she would ever forget those special wounds, so unmistakable and consequential that Oedipus was named after them? Would Jocasta have desisted through all the years of their marriage to ask Oedipus how he got his strange name? Could she have seen those unique scars and not questioned him about them? Of course she could have remained silent, but what would that indicate? A lack of interest?

What was Jocasta thinking when, shortly after the death of Laius, a man appeared who looked like a young Laius (ll. 743–744), marked with scars to match her abandoned son's wounds? Would Jocasta have been unaware of her abandoned son's age? Would she have never asked Oedipus his? Why then, if these things never crossed her mind, did she send the Herdsman so far from Thebes immediately after the murder of Laius and the appearance of Oedipus (ll. 759–763)? Jocasta wanted children. She could have no more with Laius because of his fear of the oracle. When Laius was killed, and a replacement appeared, Jocasta lost no time in bearing four children. And if Jocasta knew who Oedipus was, could she keep it a perfect secret, never revealing it subtly, unintentionally, in any of the countless and intimate gestures between man and wife, mother and son?

Let us now return to the scene between Oedipus and Teiresias. All the information and associations I have suggested were available to Oedipus over the years between Laius' death and the scene with Teiresias. What effect would this material, perhaps subliminally remembered, have on Oedipus when he is faced with the need to stop the plague by finding the murderer of Laius? And what turbulence is stirred by Teiresias' accusation? Oedipus' open reaction is enraged denial and counter-charge. But underneath these, a complicated set of awarenesses seem to be crowding into articulation; circumstances that tie Oedipus ever closer to Jocasta, Thebes, the house of Labdacus. Surely the apparently straightforward conflict between Teiresias and Oedipus draws along with it a large system of unassimilated and highly suggestive material. This material does not center on the murder of Laius, but on Oedipus' identity and his relationship to Jocasta.

There is one powerful textual hint in the scene. Oedipus has cursed Teiresias, ordered him to go, and called him a fool. Teiresias replies:

> TEIRESIAS. I am a fool then, as it seems to you—
>   but to the parents who have bred you, wise.
> OEDIPUS. What parents? Stop! Who are they of all the world?
>   ll. 435–437

So early in the play Oedipus must surely still think himself the son of Polybus. His question indicates that some part of him is not sure. These three lines, it seems to me, point toward the heart of the scene's complicated action structure.

This structure cannot be probed further without rehearsal. The hidden currents and cross-currents of the Oedipus-Teiresias encounter are not unique to that scene or play. Nor have these difficult relationships been unexplored by performers and critics. But how are we to chart these currents, to keep track of their swiftly changing direction, their deep plunges, and sudden variations in intensity? When we deal directly with theatre, we come face-to-face with an art that is a simulation of life processes. No analysis can hope to chart with any completeness all the transactions and transformations in a scene. And even if it could, the resulting analysis would be too complicated to be of much use. In fact, the analytic process in theatre is the rehearsal. There a group can concentrate for many hours on the concrete scenic structures, working them out as they must be worked out: in relation to a specific group of individuals whose job it is to confront, trace, select, and organize some (but only some) of the actions clearly indicated, associated, or suggested by the text. The rehearsal framework can be very open, the associations in harmony with or opposed to the intentions of the author. Theatre can be an almost ritualistic replication of a text or it can be a game with many possibilities or it can approach the free-style of play. Each of these, and the innumerable intermediary terms, can combine in a single performance. That's what gives theatre its special qualities, and makes it so difficult to write about.

7.

Theatre is special. But it isn't unique. The external structure of theatre is in many ways homologous to play, games and sports, and ritual. On the surface, it would seem that distinctions between these are easy to make. But even a little thought reveals overlaps, coincidences, confusions and—what is more difficult—movement among these activities. They are transformational and not permanent structures. They change from culture to culture and within cultures. In some cultures, and during some historical periods, the middle terms—games, sports, and theatre—are identical. The analysis I am about to sketch is an ethnocentric one.

Spectator sports—football and baseball, for example—have always been theatrical. TV has accented this tendency to "stage" rather than "play" sports. Sheer ability diminishes in importance as showmanship increases: the winning ways (both in skill and personality) of a superstar, the dramatic stroke at the right moment, the "image" of the whole team. Vince Lombardi is a theatre director as well as a football coach; the New York Mets are popular for reasons which go beyond their skills as baseball players.

Particularly now, when the outer fabric of society is in shreds, theatre is steadily incorporating ritual. Many new theatre groups work toward a kind of participation and audience involvement that touches religious rather than histrionic sensibilities.

> Grotowski often speaks of "theatrical magic." What he means is that an actor worthy of the name must be able to perform physical and vocal feats absolutely beyond the ability of the spectator. He is a sorcerer who enthralls the spectator. [. . .] He must force the spectator outside of himself and make him part of the dramatic action—an action which is no longer narrowly limited by the stage and which necessitates a new rapport between actors and spectators united in the creation of a theatrical world. [. . .] In the Theatre Laboratory, the spectators are made to face the most secret, the most carefully hidden part of themselves. Brutally thrown into the world of myths, they must identify with them and judge them at the same time. They must evaluate them in the light of the life of twentieth-century men. Many experience the revelation as a blasphemy.[34]

There is a continuum, and along it a shift appears to be taking place toward the right:

$$play \rightarrow games\ and\ sports \rightarrow theatre \rightarrow ritual$$

Unlike the color spectrum, this continuum is not regular. Generally each structure blends into the next, but, in particular instances, structures cannibalize elements from anywhere along the line. Furthermore, play and ritual are very much alike and transform the continuum into a spiral with ritual amplifying—at a new level of intensity and meaning—the structures of play.

Several qualities are shared by all the activities: (1) a special ordering of time, (2) a special value attached to objects used in the activity, (3) nonproductivity, (4) rules. As we move right on the

---

[34] *Eugenio Barba and Ludwik Flaszen, "A Theatre of Magic and Sacrilege," TDR, IX, No. 3, 173–174. See also Lévi-Strauss' analysis of magic in "The Sorcerer and His Magic," in* Structural Anthropology, *pp. 167–185.*

PERFORMANCE CHART

Qualities	Play	Games	Sports	Theatre	Ritual
Special ordering of time	Usually	Yes	Yes	Yes	Yes
Special value for objects	Yes	Yes	Yes	Yes	Yes
Nonproductive	Yes	Yes	Yes	Yes	Yes
Rules	Inner	Frame	Frame	Frame	Outer
Special Place	No	Often	Yes	Usually	Usually
Appeal to other	No	Often	Yes	Yes	Yes
Audience	Not necessarily	Not necessarily	Usually	Yes	Usually
Self-Assertive	Yes	Not totally	Not totally	Not totally	No
Self-Transcendent	No	Not totally	Not totally	Not totally	Yes
Completed	Not necessarily	Yes	Yes	Yes	Yes
Performed by Group	Not necessarily	Usually	Usually	Usually	Usually
Symbolic reality	Often	No	No	Yes	Often
Scripted	No	No	No	Yes	Usually

Note: *Happenings and related activities are not included as theatre in this chart. Happenings would not necessarily have an audience, they would not necessarily be scripted, there would be no necessary symbolic reality. Formally, they would be very close to play.*

73

continuum, space is more formally acknowledged. In many rituals, space is holy.[35]

Other qualities—such as the presence of an audience, an appeal to the other, whether or not the player is self-assertive or self-transcendent[36]—are treated differently by different activities. The similarities and differences in these qualities are summarized in the Performance Chart.

Time

Time is special in these activities because it is subject to innumerable variations. The major varieties of performance time are:

1. Event time. The activity has a set form and all steps within that form must be completed no matter how long (or short) the elapsed clock time.

   Examples: Baseball, racing. Rituals in which a response or a "state" is sought, such as rain dances, cures effected by shamans, or revival meetings. A theatrical performance, taken as a whole.

2. Set time. An arbitrary time pattern is imposed on the events— they begin and end at a certain moment or a set span of time is fixed for their performance. Here, frequently, there is a "race against the clock."

   Examples: Football, basketball (in which overtimes allow for the game to be completed). Games structured on "how many"

---

[35] *The varieties of holy space is itself a subject for a book. There seems to be a system of opposites. Either the space is preserved from antiquity or obliterated immediately after the rite is completed. Examples: shrines and holy places vs. the hogan built for the sand-painting cure of the Navaho or the Succoth built for the harvest celebration of the Jews. Either the space is architecturally enshrined or it is defined simply by the placement of the ritual implements (the mosque vs. the prayer rug laid simply to face Mecca). Either the rite is oriented toward whatever directions the culture feels are important or it is circular and "directionless." Either it is closely tied to nature—such as holy rocks, glens, and so on—or it is out of nature altogether—such as heaven or hell. I do not think that this emphasis of spatial organization is accidental, nor is it unrelated to a simliar emphasis in athletics and theatre.*

[36] *The terms are Arthur Koestler's. See "Some Aspects of the Creative Process," in* Control of the Mind, *ed. Seymour M. Farber and Roger H. L. Wilson (New York: McGraw-Hill, 1961), pp. 188–208.*

74

or "how much" you can do in N time. Task-oriented happenings such as Ann Halprin's *Esposizione*.[37] Religious observances that go from "the beginning" to dusk or which begin at dawn, and so on.

3. Symbolic time. The span of the activity represents another (longer or shorter) duration of clock time.

Examples: Theatre. Rituals of enactment. Make-believe children's play.

Boxing, certainly one of the most direct, brutal, and theatrical of sports, is an interesting combination of event and set time. The length of the fight and the duration of each round is set time. But a knockout can end the fight at any moment and convert it into event time. Furthermore, a knockdown is measured by the ten-count and is set time.

Theatre uses symbolic time. But recently the other kinds of time have been used too. Allan Kaprow's *Self-Service*[38] has a very loose time structure. Events are spread out over most of a summer, and one can do them during any weekend of the summer. This pattern fits none of my categories. It is a rough combination of event and set time. Many happenings deliberately avoid—or even destroy—symbolic time. Perhaps this is so because the cultural activities associated with symbolic time seem archaic and are frequently inauthentic. To rebel against symbolic time is to question at a very deep level traditional Western aesthetics.

The first scene of Genet's *The Maids* combines event and set time. Step by step the maids act out the ritualized routine that is supposed to lead to the murder of Claire/Madame by Solange/Claire. Just before the murder is to take place, the alarm clock goes off, ending the scene. Claire complains, "It's over already. And you didn't get to the end." Solange answers, "The same thing happens every time. And it's all your fault, you're never ready. I can't finish you off." The ritual of dressing, fawning, taunting, and murder is event time. It is cut off, incomplete, by the alarm clock

---

[37] *See "Yvonne Rainer Interviews Ann Halprin," TDR, X, No. 2, 150–155.*
[38] *For the scenario of* Self-Service *see TDR, XII, No. 3, 160–164.*

which is set time. The tragi-farce tone of this scene stems directly from the contrast between these two time patterns.

For reasons that are well enough known, modern drama has been deprived of much of its traditional material—individuated heroes involved in stories which focus conflicts. This material is the source of traditional dramatic structure. And until the twentieth century most drama was structured dialectically and organically— protagonist vs. antagonist leads to a resolution all within the context of a "believable" chain of events. Once this material became dysfunctional, drama sought among its secondary elements for structural units that could give it coherence. Time was one of the most important of these secondary elements. Time, which is traditionally a simple strategy in drama, became—in some instances (*No Exit*, *Waiting for Godot*)—the subject and center of the drama.

Symbolic time has the qualities of "normal" clock time. It is "symbolic" because the hours onstage are different in correspondence and duration from the "real" hours registered on the clock backstage. Symbolic time can be shortened, lengthened, or inverted. The permutations of event and set time are more complicated. These can be distorted, transformed, turned back on themselves—all without disturbing the congruence between the elapsed stage and clock times.

Time in modern drama is usually either circular or bracketed. Circular time is a series of events, one necessarily following the other, contained in a single unit that necessarily repeats itself. This is the logic of electric circuitry, not narrative. It is also the logic of day-night-day or the seasons. More important, this logic is not causal. Day follows night (or vice versa) but day does not cause night, nor winter spring. Ionesco's *The Lesson* is a play which is structured on the basis of circular event time. The pupil enters, the professor greets her, they add, she is successful, they subtract, she fails, she can multiply but cannot divide, he becomes agitated and begins lecturing her on "philology," she gets a toothache, wishes to go but cannot find the energy to move, he teaches her how to pronounce "knife," she hurts all over, he rapes and kills her, her corpse is disposed of (along with thirty-nine others), a new student rings the bell—"Good morning, miss! You are the new pupil? You have come for the lesson? The Professor is expecting you."

There are associative links between these events, and a definite pattern discernible within them. But they are not causally determined. The comic sense of *The Lesson* depends upon an audience's knowing that the sequence of events is the "opposite" of caused. Just as day follows night, so it follows that . . . "arithmetic leads to philology and philology to crime."

If the structure of *The Lesson* is circular, its time texture is event time. Like a shaman, the professor must work himself up to philology and from there to murder. Each section of the play takes on the ritualized quality that comes from the compulsive nature of the professor's personality. The pupil is the willing and entranced sacrificial victim.

Bracketed time is very like circular time except that the events within a set do not necessarily follow one another in the same order, nor are the same events necessarily repeated each time. Any day is an example of bracketed time. About twelve hours after dawn it will be dark again. Actions occur within the bracket dawn-dark but they have no necessary relation to each other. The bracket itself gives these events the appearance of relatedness. In *Waiting for Godot*, Gogo and Didi come to an appointed place each evening at dusk to wait for Godot—or for night to fall. Within the bracket dusk-dark they are free to do whatever they like—"to give the impression" that they exist, as Gogo says. The action of *Godot* consists in Gogo and Didi's inventing games to pass the time—they are struggling toward the terminus of their bracket. The specific things that Gogo and Didi do are variations of event time. Pozzo and Lucky have a different time pattern—one more recognizably "organic." Pozzo and Lucky have "careers." In the second act, Pozzo is near the end of his career, and his rage comes directly from the conflict between his ever-shortening sense of time and Gogo's and Didi's sense of event time:

> Have you not done tormenting me with your accursed time! It's abominable! When! When! One day, is that not enough for you, one day he went dumb, one day I went blind, one day we'll go deaf, one day we were born, one day we shall die, the same day, the same second, is that not enough for you?

It is neither enough nor too much nor too little for them. Gogo and Didi do not measure time—they cannot calibrate it. They live entirely in a world of event time governed by set time (the dusk-dark bracket). In their world night falls suddenly, without warning: an announcement that Godot is not coming. They want time to pass—but they are not clear about what this means—and once it does pass and night falls, "they do not move." Time for them passes unevenly, depending upon whether or not they are distracted by their games, routines, habits, and memories. Time for them comes in bursts or lingers, clustered around events and the lack of events. The unusual time structure of *Godot* brings to mind George Kubler's suggestion that "organic structure" is not properly descriptive of art.

> Perhaps a system of metaphors drawn from the physical sciences would have clothed the situation of art more adequately than the prevailing biological metaphors: especially if we are dealing in art with some kind of energy: with impulses, generating centers, and relay points; with increments and losses in transit; with resistance and transformers in the circuit. In short, the language of electrodynamics might have suited us better than the language of botany. [. . .][39]

The idea of nodes is applicable here. It applies to *Godot*, and even better to the structure of happenings and environmental theatre. A complicated circuitry capable of instant transformations and swift shifts of matrices (for example, from character to time to dramatic events to technical effects to random selectivity).

The traditional or organic metaphor is Greek in origin. Aristotle was not only a biologist—he applied biological models to art. Susanne Langer has made a modern application of this old idea.

> Tragic drama is so designed that the protagonist grows mentally, emotionally, or morally, by the demand of the action, which he himself initiated, to the complete exhaustion of his powers, the limit of his possible development. He spends himself in the course of one dramatic action. This is, of course, a tremendous foreshortening of life; instead of undergoing the physical, psychical, many-sided, long process of an actual biography, the tragic hero lives and

---

[39] *George Kubler*, The Shape of Time *(New Haven: Yale University Press. 1962), pp. 8–9.*

matures in some particular respect; his entire being is concentrated in one aim, one passion, one conflict and ultimate defeat. For this reason the prime agent of tragedy is heroic; his character, the unfolding situation, the scene, even though ostensibly familiar and humble, are all exaggerated, charged with more feeling than comparable actualities would possess. [. . .][40]

Miss Langer is accurately describing the situation of traditional drama. A drama of heroes, resolutions, and closed structures that have beginnings, middles, and ends—a structure of "life-career" in which through foreshortening, intensification, and exaggeration the life crises of consciousness and action are exposed and confronted. This dialectical, triangular model of dramatic action has the double quality of completeness and focus. It suits very well much of Western drama from the Greeks through the nineteenth century.

Contemporary drama and theatre, however, are not so well described by the organic or career model. It is misleading if applied to *Godot, Endgame, The Bald Soprano, The Lesson, The Maids, The Blacks, The Screens, Marat/Sade*, many farces, and dozens of modern plays. It cannot describe happenings or environmental theatre. Much of modern drama—many farces, happenings, and environmental theatre—is structured from "life-rhythms."[41]

Life-rhythms are generally circular and are a function of event or set time: hunger-eating-hunger, breathing-in breathing-out breathing-in, day-night-day, the seasons, the phases of the moon, and so on. If these rhythms are not integrated into a career system— if they become something in themselves, or if they are the basis of a dramatic structure—a form develops that has neither beginning, middle, nor end. One completed rhythm is a cycle—but the cycle ends only to begin again. Important events are associated with phases of the cycle, but are not necessarily caused by the cycle. The cycle itself is linked through association, not causality in the strict

---

[40] *Susanne Langer,* Feeling and Form *(New York: Charles Scribner's Sons, 1953), p. 357.*

[41] *This is not altogether a historical observation.* Mother Courage, The Price, Who's Afraid of Virginia Woolf?—*to name just a few—are structured on careers, while* The Bacchae *is in many ways closer to* The Maids *than to* Sophocles' Electra.

sense. The human organism responding directly to these rhythms is entirely dependent on them. These rhythms are a function of time—and in modern theatre, frequently enough, time replaces destiny. When there are no careers, the passing of time "makes things happen." Of course, this is illusory. Time measures the span in which things happen, no more. The paradox at the heart of much contemporary drama is that man is both entirely free and entirely trapped (most clearly demonstrated in *No Exit*—where there is no exit from time but no limitations on what may be done during that endless expanse).

A theatre built on life-rhythms has an open form of increasing tension, explosive release, and a return to the original situation.

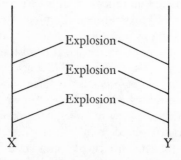

X and Y are the forces or characters in conflict. Although the tensions have been released through an explosive discharge of energy, the situation is not resolved, but returned either to its original configuration or a more intensified amplification of that configuration. Often these rhythms are set within the context of a game, and in many contemporary plays rules replace plots. A single game or a series of related games, usually of a rhythmic-explosive kind, is played. Instead of an action's being completed, permutations of a given set are explored. The story yields to the game as the matrix of the theatrical situation. Thus we have the game of "killing Madame" in *The Maids*, the game of "waiting for Godot," the game of "the lesson," and so on. These games are controlled more by event and set time than by symbolic time.

In happenings and environmental theatre the games are played not only among the characters but between the performers and the audience and between the whole set of circumstances that is the performance and those who watch or participate in it. In a multi-focus performance, the audience is encouraged to structure the events as they wish—there is no "best" and "worst" seat because the game has no single, all-encompassing, and immutable structure. In traditional staging there are good and bad seats. This comes from single-focus—if you sit in the eighth row center you will see, as the director and performers wish you to see, what's going on. If you are in the second balcony or far to the left or right, you get a distorted image of what you are "supposed" to see. But in environmental theatre—where there is no single focus—the spectator is encouraged to shift his position, to change his perspective. The performance itself moves throughout the whole space—parts of it expansive and inclusive and parts contracted and exclusive.[42]

Objects

Not much can be said about the quality of special value for objects except that it exists and needs more study. In everyday life, objects are valued for their uses (tools), their scarcity and beauty (jewels, precious metals, artworks as objects), their bartering power (money, exchange goods), or age (antiques, artworks as objects, relics). In play, games and sports, theatre, and ritual objects—except for ritual implements and religious relics[43]—have a market value much below the value assigned to them within the activity. You can buy a football cheaply, but try to take one away from the Green Bay Packers on fourth down. Or lose a child's favorite toy and try to buy him a new one. Or take away an actor's favorite prop. Balls, pucks, bats, goblets, crucifixes, costumes, and props all absorb the significance of the activity of which they are a part. Often, as in sports or ritual, these objects are the focus of the conflict or cere-

---

[42] See "Six Axioms for Environmental Theatre," pp. 157–180 of this book.

[43] Gold, silver, and precious jewels adorn many rituals, and relics have a magical and immeasurable value. But the market value of these things—were they offered without reference to their religious, historical, or ritual associations —would be far below the value assigned to them as "holy things." Priceless paintings still bring a price—but could the Vatican auction off its relics? In the days when relics were sold, the fraud was that people thought they were purchasing "priceless" things, while the priests knew the objects for their "real" worth. In between was profit. The practice continues.

mony. Sometimes, as in theatre, they help create the symbolic reality.

From the standpoint of strict practicality it is silly to put so much energy into moving a ball ten yards or to think that a costume and some props can make a king out of an actor. In fact, the value within activity is an inversion of the values of productive work.[44] This inversion is a key feature of play, games and sports, theatre, and ritual.

Nonproductivity

What J. Huizinga and Roger Caillois said about play applies to all performance activities:

> Summing up the formal characteristics of play, we might call it a free activity standing quite consciously outside "ordinary" life as being "not serious," but at the same time absorbing the player intensely and utterly.[45]

> A characteristic of play, in fact, is that it creates no wealth or goods.[46]

But how can this be? On every side we see professional sports and theatre (not to mention the church) enmeshed in business, making profits and paying salaries. Money is spent on admissions, wages, facilities, and promotion; it is earned from tickets, concessions, TV,

---

[44] Burton Melnick, in an unpublished study applying elements of my theories to specific plays, notes that "productive work is almost never presented in theatre. Even in plays like John Gabriel Borkman or The Cherry Orchard, where the productive mentality is an important theme, we never see the producer actually working. [. . .] When theatre imitates, it usually imitates some kind of performance (with the exception of play). This is natural enough, because ritual, sports, and many kinds of games are structured in order to appeal to an audience. Productive work is not." Furthermore (I would add), productive work is antithetical to performance (except of course where the work is performing), for reasons which I hope will soon be clear. It is interesting to note that in plays where productive work is represented—as in The Adding Machine—it is stylized and transformed into something other than work. The movies have no such problem—but that's another, and complicated, story. See also Melnick's "Theatre and Performance," TDR, XI, No. 4, 92-98.

[45] J. Huizinga, Homo Ludens (New York: Roy Publishers, 1950), p. 13.

[46] Roger Caillois, Man, Play, and Games (New York: The Free Press of Glencoe, 1961), p. 21.

donations, and so on. It changes hands through betting. Side industries—such as endorsements and the manufacture of clothing and sports equipment—flourish. And, as more leisure time becomes available, there will be an increase in these investments. Only children's play seems "pure"—and even here toy manufacturers and stores make a huge profit. Are we then to believe, as Huizinga did, that modern play is "decadent" because it has entered so fully into the economic arrangements of society? The issue can be unraveled only by examining certain structural elements of these activities.

In productive work the economic arrangements determine the structure of the activity. A man with little money can run a small automotive shop. A large corporation will run an assembly line. The process of the small shop will be structurally and qualitatively different from that of the assembly line. In those sectors of our economy where both small and large manufacture continues—furniture, for example—the method of work, the means of assembly, and even the product are different in the two operations. It is not simply a case of "increased efficiency" or the production of more objects. The operation takes its shape from its size. However, the difference between sandlot and major league baseball is one of quality, not structure. The same rules apply to both games—although these rules may be applied more loosely to sandlot ball. The San Francisco Giants may have better players than the Sixth Street Eagles—but the Giants can't have more players on the field. When rules are changed, they are generally changed all the way down the line. No matter how much is spent, bet, or in some way tied to play, games and sports, theatre, and ritual, their specific structures remain constant. When money does corrupt the structure—as when a game is fixed or a star hired simply for his box office appeal—we can indeed agree with Huizinga that the activity shows signs of decadence.[47]

---

[47] *How much corruption has occurred in modern, industrial society could only be determined by a detailed study of the evolution of rules and conventions. Doubtlessly, much "decadence" has entered into these ideally "free" activities. However, rules defend against a general invasion, and a certain amount of structural decadence has always been there. Can we say for sure that the Olympics were never fixed, or that a Choregus was never chosen for his purse rather than his ability?*

Economic arrangements affect the players, their bosses, the audience, the bettors or parishioners—everyone—while the activity itself remains largely unaffected. The money, services, and goods generated *by* and *for* these activities are not part *of* them. The quality of equipment has something to do with the quality of play, but is not—as in manufacturing—the determining factor. In games and sports, theatre, and ritual (play is a separate case) the rules are designed not only to tell the players how to play but to protect the activity from outside encroachment. If you are going to find a better way to play football or perform the mass, for example, either you have to change the rules for everyone (as Vatican II did) or you must devise strategies within the acknowledged rules (as hundreds of successful priests and quarterbacks have done). The activities themselves are conservative in the most basic way.

Rules

Rules are formulated and they persist because play, games and sports, theatre, and ritual are something apart from everyday life.[48] A special world is established where men can make the rules, rearrange time, assign an arbitrary value to objects, and work for pleasure or for gods' sake. This special world is not gratuitous—it is a vital component of human life. No society has done without it. It is "special" only when contrasted to productive work. In psychoanalytic terms, the world of these activities is the pleasure principle institutionalized.[49] Freud believed that art was the productive sublimation of the conflict between the pleasure and the reality principles—between the demand for gratification and the need for work. No human being is whole without both. Freud identified art with play; indeed, individuated art may be as Freud tentatively described

---

[48] *Even in non-industrial societies, where the means of production are not technologically sophisticated, play, games and sports, theatre, and ritual are set apart from the regular workday. Often these performance activities are thought to be necessary for production: a ritual must be performed or the crops won't grow, etc. But this link is not a confusion between the two kinds of activities, but an acknowledgment that both kinds are necessary for life.*

[49] *In play and individual fantasy this world has not been institutionalized but remains the private privilege of each. It is in fantasy that we break the rules—even the rules of sports, etc.—and get away with it.*

it. But these performance activities are something different. All but one (theatre) are not art. And the individual must conform to rules he didn't make in all but one (play). The structures themselves—the generative rules—are separate from "real life." These activities are the social counterparts to individual fantasy. Their social function is to stand apart from productive work, both idealizing it and criticizing it—why can't *all* life be a game? There are, therefore, continual analogues between productive life and these activities. Each is, in some way, a metaphorical enactment of abstracted experience.

Perhaps this will be clearer if we consider briefly where most of these activities generally take place. Arenas, stadiums, churches, holy places, and theatres are structures which are frequently non-self-supporting: donations and subsidies keep them economically viable. They are generally situated in population centers where real-estate comes high. In any event, since they are for the public, they must be accessible. Much of this space is fallow for long periods of time, coming to life only during a game, a service, or a performance. Unlike office or industrial space, these performance spaces are used rhythmically and intensively, not regularly. A ball park may be used almost every day during the season, but only during several hours of the day. An industrial plant, however, is used eight, sixteen, or even twenty-four hours a day.[50] The space is organized so that a large group can watch a small group—and become aware of itself at the same time. These arrangements foster "celebration" and "ceremony." In Erving Goffman's words, there is "an expressive rejuvenation and reaffirmation of the moral values of the community" in spaces where "reality is being performed."[51] Certainly, more than elsewhere, these places reinforce solidarity: one "has" a reli-

---

[50] I *speculate that there are three major life activities: play, games and sports, theatre, and ritual; productive work; and home life. Each has its unique way of dealing with space, time, and behavior. The three interact and frequently blend and conflict. But at the heart of each is a specific set of structures and activities that are irreducibly unique.*

[51] *Erving Goffman,* The Presentation of Self in Everyday Life *(New York: Anchor Books, 1959), pp. 35–36. I am quoting Goffman out of context. He means that any place where something is done that "highlights the official values of the society"—such as a party, or "where the practitioner meets his*

gion, "roots for" a team, and "goes to" the theatre for essentially the same reasons.[52]

Referring to the Performance Chart (see p. 73), we see that theatre has more in common with games and sports than with play or ritual. However, certain key elements of happenings and environmental theatre relate more to play than to anything else. This is a strong indication of a real break between traditional and "new" theatre. Furthermore, play is obviously the ontogenetic (not phylogenetic) source of the other activities.[53] The break between

---

client"—such as a doctor's office, a ball park, or a theatre—is a celebratory space. Goffman thinks that performance is a "quality" of living that can be "applied" to almost any situation. This is true enough, and transactional analysis (as it is used in psychology and sociology) develops consequences from this observation. However, I mean something more limited by performance. In the large Goffman sense performance may characterize the mode of any activity; in the smaller sense performance is part of the structure of many kinds of play, games and sports, theatre, and ritual. It is true that some activities legitimately called play, games and sports, theatre, and ritual would not be included in my smaller definition of performance. My definition is further complicated by the fact that game theory applies to performance and non-performance activities equally. However, in trying to manage the relationships between a general theory and its specific applications to a limited range of activities, it seems best to center my definition of performance around certain acknowledged qualities of theatre—the most stable being the audience. Even where the audience does not exist—as in certain happenings and in some nonliterate theatre—its function persists: part of the performing group watches what the other part is doing. The parts are interchangeable. Thus, performance I might (reluctantly) define as an activity done by an individual or a group largely for the pleasure of another individual and group; and this activity involves an overt doing and showing (not a mental calculation or the passing of a love note, for example).

[52] Going to the theatre is less a solidarity function than the other activities. People go generally because the mimetic event is empathic and the social event brings them close to their friends. However, there is no denying that both these solidarity functions of theatre-going have declined if compared to fifth-century B.C. Athens or Elizabethan England. At one time theatre-going was a civic event; later it became a social event (in which theatre-goers were segregated according to class). Presently it is little more than a simple pastime. That is why the audience for theatre is so small—there are cheaper and more efficient pastimes.

[53] The relationship between child play and adult fantasy needs more exploration. Adults also play, and the relation between adult play and work is a subject that has not, I believe, been given sufficient attention. I define play as an activity in which the participant makes up his own rules. A game has generally acknowledged rules. Therefore, many of the activities which transactional analysts call games I call play.

games and sports and theatre on the one hand, and play and ritual on the other, is indicated by the different quality and use of the rules which govern these activities. Thus, the five activities can be rather neatly subdivided into three groups. Play is "free activity" in which one makes one's own rules. Ritual is strictly programmed, expressing the individual's submission to forces "larger" or at least "other" than himself. Ritual epitomizes a transcendent reality principle—the agreement to obey rules that are given.[54] Games, sports, and theatre mediate between the extremes of play and ritual. These center terms express social behavior. Of course, the three groupings are a continuum; but differences in degree become differences in kind.

SELF-ASSERTIVE "I":	SOCIAL "WE":	SELF-TRANS-CENDENT "OTHER":
play	games sports theatre	ritual
rules established by player	"Do" [free choice] "Don't do"	rules given by authority
pleasure principle, Eros, id, private world	balance between pleasure and reality principles, accommodation with world, ego	reality principle, parental, Thanatos, superego

Games, sports, and theatre are the middle terms, balancing and in some way combining play and ritual. The balance of games, sports,

---

[54] *Eric Berne in* Games People Play *(New York: Grove Press, 1964), pp. 36ff., defines ritual in an operative way: "[. . .] a ritual is a stereotyped series of simple complementary transactions programmed by external social forces. [. . .] The form of a ritual is parentally determined by tradition. [. . .] Some formal rituals of special historical or anthropological interests have two phases: 1) a phase in which transactions are carried on under rigid parental strictures, 2) a phase of parental license in which the child is allowed more or less complete transactional freedom, resulting in an orgy." This fits neatly my speculation that ritual and play are identical in some ways.*

and theatre is a tension: a dynamic elasticity incorporating the self-assertive quality of play and the self-transcendent quality of ritual. In games, sports, and theatre the rules are frames. Some rules say what must be done and others what must not be done. Between these frames there is freedom (from the rules), and the better the player the more effectively will he be able to devise strategies to exploit the room left to him between "do" and "don't do." For the actor, the frames around his "free activity" are numerous. The largest frame is the physical stage on which he is to perform. Then there are the conventions of the day, the play itself, the instructions of his director. Finally, the actor is free to explore—along with his fellow actors—the role he is assigned to perform.

The fact that theatre has more in common with sports and games than with ritual or play should prompt the application of mathematical and transactional game analysis to performance. Some work along these lines has begun.[55] There is more to it than the "theatre games" performed by Second City and taught in some theatre schools. These are fine exercises, but they barely touch what game theory is about—"a method for the study of decision making in situations of conflict."[56] Or what transactional analysis—a kind of game theory without mathematics—takes as its subject: the relations that go either smoothly or are "crossed" beneath the surfaces of usual discourse.

Theatre is like games and sports. But recently it has also begun to adapt structures from play and ritual. The traditional structure of theatre has been transformed and we can identify a new model. Comparing it to the traditional:

---

[55] See Arthur Wagner's "Transactional Analysis and Acting," TDR, XI, No. 4, 81–88; and my essay, "In Warm Blood"; pp. 93–107 of this book.

[56] From Martin Shubik, Game Theory and Related Approaches to Social Behavior (New York: John Wiley and Sons, 1964). This book, and many others, came to my attention because of "Game Theory and Theatre: A Handlist," prepared by Philip McCoy. The "Handlist" is unpublished but, I assume, it is available from McCoy who teaches theatre at the University of California at Santa Barbara. McCoy has done extensive and extremely helpful research in game theory and its relation to theatre. If ever someone is to write a definitive study of these deep and potentially fruitful relationships, it will be McCoy.

TRADITIONAL	OPEN
life-careers	life-rhythms
stories	games, rules
plot	rhythm, pattern, transformation
characters	characteristics
sequential time	circular, bracketed, event, and set time
action	activity
connections	jumps
resolution	circularity, indeterminate
dialectic	no synthesis
single-focus	multi-focus
flow	explosions
acting the events	becoming the events
time makes changes	time is a cue
causal	random

Probably no single play or performance has all the characteristics of its model. And the elements of one structure can be combined with the elements of the other. Chekhov is particularly interesting because his late plays appear traditional when, after analysis and performance, they reveal themselves to be open structured. In *The Three Sisters* the situation at the end of the play seems to resolve the conflicts present at the beginning—the loves of Masha for Vershinin and of Irene for Tusenbach; the fact that the sisters will not go to Moscow. But a closer look reveals that these were transparent conflicts. A strong triangular form evaporates during the play and is replaced by an open form. That open form is the "ghost" of the play, operating quietly within the action. Later it is progressively revealed, becoming the visible structure, while the triangular form becomes the "ghost," apparently resolving the conflict, while actually changing very little.

In *The Three Sisters* the conflict is between "going to Moscow" (or, having a meaningful love relationship) and "lives wasted by time." The sisters know that if they don't "go to Moscow"—do something meaningful with their lives—they will shrivel into old age. Vershinin arrives and brings the crisis to a head by seeming to present a new example amid old memories. But soon it becomes clear that the soldiers are living meaningless lives too. Irene wishes to break the pattern by leaving town with Tusenbach (who will resign from the army). The other sisters make no real plans. Masha and Vershinin are involved in a hopeless affair. Natasha systematically takes over the house—the scene of the struggle between Moscow and the Provinces—and, at the end of the play, the sisters (except Irene, who plans to leave "tomorrow") have moved from the house.[57]

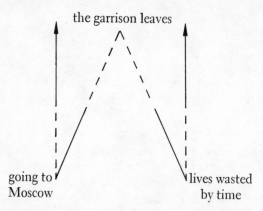

Irene's plans end with Solyony's bullet. Possibly she will still go away—we don't know. Clearly the play shows the garrison "passing through" the town. (A favorite image of Chekhov's: a reasonably stable situation violated by someone or a group "passing through," apparent turbulence, and an affective situation at the end not much changed from that of the beginning.) It is this sense of "passing

---

[57] *This movement from the house is brilliantly reflected in Chekhov's settings. Act I: The drawing and ball rooms, filled with the sisters and their friends. Natasha enters, is ridiculed, and goes off into a corner where Andrey comforts her. Act II: The same setting, but with Natasha in control. Masha and Irene meet their lovers quietly, in corners and semi-darkness. The party is called off by Natasha, who needs only to whisper to Chebutykin that Bobik isn't sleeping well. During all of Act II, the three sisters are not once on stage together. Act III: Set in the bedroom now shared by Olga and Irene. Isolated here, the sisters are unable to control Natasha, who treats Anfisa miserably. The fire leads to the invasion of the house by the town. Of course, Natasha is a local, not a Muscovite. Act IV: Set in the garden outside the house. Olga has moved to the school. Irene is planning to leave. Andrey pushes the baby carriage.*

through" that characterizes *The Three Sisters*. When all is done, nothing has been done. The death and parting that seem to resolve everything merely clarify a situation that was there from the start.

The excitement of the garrison's presence, the two romances, even the fire—briefly hide the sisters' real situation: like Gogo and Didi they are in their appointed place, between the brackets of youth and old age, doing what they can to relieve their boredom through fantasy and fitful action. The explosive qualities of many Chekhovian speeches (in this play, and others) is the discharge of energy at the climax of a game. Chekhov's characters have no true careers. They are victimized by the routines—the rhythms—of their lives. It is this hopeless routinization, combined with the desperate wanting for career, that gives his plays their rare mixture of naturalness, humor, and despair.

8.

Structuralism is an analytic method which works from concrete instances. It makes no separation between form and content. The structure is the arrangement of the content—and these arrangements may be multiple and simultaneous within a single artwork. They may include language, movement, subtextual action, ideas: there is no definable limit. Nor is there a "best" structure. There are many structures. One can look into an artwork to find its internal system or to find its relationship to external systems. Ultimately, the structure of theatre takes one into the theatre—to work out the problems during rehearsal and performance.

Structuralism seeks connections among apparently disparate elements, tracing links between social systems and art, nonliterate and Western cultures. It can be applied directly to the four anchors of performance: space, audience, performers, text (or scenario). Structuralism is apt for theatre because it works out systems of transformation, transaction, and interaction: the scenic language of performance.

In Warm Blood:
The Bacchae

1967

1.

A boy, Pentheus, is killed. By his own mother. Not only murdered, but mangled, cannibalized. The ecstatic (*ex stasis*: standing outside oneself) mother innocently dances with the severed head of her man-son, not recognizing him. "I struck him first [. . .] the whelp of a wild mountain lion. [. . .] Look, look at the prize I bring." She shows her son's head to her neighbors. Was ever a mother so delirious? "Happy was the hunting. [. . .] See, the whelp is young and tender. Beneath the soft mane of its hair, the down is blooming on the cheeks." Her own boy's head, joyously caressed, danced with, celebrated (as some demonic priest might celebrate the mass with a real sacrifice). The men of the town look on, horrified. Agave (this mother) does not know her son, knowing him already too well.

Even more terrible to this strait-laced town—it could be some place in Kansas where violence comes like the spring tornadoes, and subsides as astonishingly—are Agave's friends: for all the women of the town dance with her, share her celebration, her delirium, her lethal glee. Yet none of the women remembers anything. Only the men—seeing the trophy danced in on a stick, the neck strands still sticky—know the atrocity of the murder. Agave's father, old Cadmus, realizes that "this god of our own blood destroyed us all, every one." The god *of* their blood, *in* their blood. But no one can give an explanation for what has happened. All is grief, silence. Not the silence of crime, but the stillness of innocence.

Certain evidence is assembled. The corpse of the boy is pieced together, collected from the grassy hillside where the women had rent it leg by leg, arm by arm. Bloody chunks are brought back to the main street, where the men lay out the body parts, uncertain of whether they should sew them back together before burial. Cadmus speaks (all quotations are from the Arrowsmith translation):

> This was Pentheus
> whose body, after long and weary searchings
> I painfully assembled from Cithaeron's glens
> where it lay, scattered in shreds, dismembered
> throughout the forest, no two pieces
> in a single place.

The schoolmaster remembers Osiris, similarly torn; and Acteon (a member of this same cursed family) ripped by dogs. The history of dismemberment is old and common. But this is scant comfort.

Further evidence indicates orgies, night rituals of love-making raised toward infinite intensities. There is talk of sodomy, naked dancing, and suckling of young animals. Then sudden terror, shrieking, and wild female teeth biting what they had just nourished. All the women of the town are implicated in this madness, this utter unleashing of repression. The secret cannot be kept. The town is burdened with heavy shame. Families drift away, names are changed. The earth reclaims the streets.

2.

There is another boy, the cousin of the murdered one. This second boy arrives in town a few days before the murder. He is a stranger to the town, although he had been born there. His background is unclear. He is a bastard, his mother (Agave's sister Semele) claims to have been impregnated by God, to have been driven to total ecstasy by the very sight and touch of him who impregnated her. She is mocked as insane. And soon she is dead—killed by her madness.

This second boy, Semele's son, Dionysus, is blond and lovely. The townsfolk are short and brown, hard-working people, church-going people. The blond cousin is light-skinned, lanky, soft-talking, bemused. His hands are smooth, and his hips move with a dancer's grace. When he speaks the women grow moist. But the blond cousin is not really interested in the women. He is polymorphous perverse, the eternally ungratified, unquenchably pleasure-seeking young man of great sensual possibility. And he is bored.

This boredom, this hint of irony in everything he says and does, evokes the hatred of the men. Dionysus is the very opposite of all they have become.

MEN OF THEBES	DIONYSUS
Dark	Blond
Homefolk	Wanderer
Hard-working	Never works
Heterosexual	Polymorphous perverse
Clumsy	Graceful
Pleasure later	Everything now
"Women stay home"	"Women come with me"
Repressive	Expressive

He is not of their stock or kind. They want him to go. Not only does he stay—he makes preposterous demands. Softly he asks the town to honor him, to recognize him as the great prophet of a new god—a god of mysteries and love. The men arrest him, charge him with vagrancy and incitement to riot, and jail him. But the blond cousin slips through the jailhouse bars and the jail burns down. The men of the town fear him, and some talk of lynching. Pentheus, with all the certainty of adolescence, especially hates his blond cousin.

"Where do you come from?" Pentheus asks Dionysus. "My country is Lydia." (The East with its warmth, its flesh, its perfume, its dancing.) But, for all his hate, Pentheus cannot leave Dionysus alone, cannot stop "wrestling" with him. They are of the same generation, and some fateful attraction brings them ever closer. The night of Pentheus' murder, Dionysus persuades him to dress as a woman and come to the hillside to watch the orgies. "Would you like to see their revels on the mountain?" Dionysus asks. "I would pay a great sum to see that sight," Pentheus replies. Later, dressed in his costume, excited beyond speech, Pentheus leaves with Dionysus, who says:

> A great ordeal awaits you. But you are worthy
> of your fate. I shall lead you safely there;
> someone else shall bring you back.

3.

What Dionysus brings to Thebes is confusion. Thebes is a sophisticated city. The "division of labor" which Durkheim first identified with civilization is far advanced in Thebes. The men have their tasks, the women theirs; the government is highly organized and centralized; political and religious power have been separated, each with its own claims, traditions, and spokesmen. When Dionysus arrives he embodies the antithesis of all this. He is, after all, his own prophet: the Dionysus who pretends he is not Dionysus the better to represent Dionysus. Such is the first, and basic, confusion.

> I am Dionysus, the son of Zeus,
> come back to Thebes, this land where I was born.
>
> [. . .]
>
> And here I stand, a god incognito,
> disguised as a man.

And he does not arrive alone, but leading a wild band of his Asian women.

The wisest, oldest, most traditional heads of Thebes—Cadmus, the ex-king, and Teiresias, the revered prophet—wish to placate the blond cousin, to integrate him into their system. Their strategy, as opposed to Pentheus', is profound pagan humanism: there is room enough in the pantheon of Thebes for many gods, many rituals. If Thebes is structured on division of labor, authority, responsibility—then surely it can accommodate new gods.

> CADMUS. Insofar as we are able, Teiresias, we must
> do honor to this god, for he was born
> my daughter's son, who has been revealed to men,
> the god, Dionysus.
>
> [. . .]

TEIRESIAS. We do not trifle with divinity.
No, we are the heirs of customs and traditions
hallowed by age and handed down to us
by our fathers.

In fact, the Thebes that Dionysus returns to is a unique community—at least in the history of drama. There is no seething trouble, no long unsolved crime or overhanging curse. Dionysus in the prologue says he is "dishonored" in Thebes. But all except Pentheus are willing to give him his honor, no matter how dubious his claim might seem. Cadmus, the old king, gave up his throne to Pentheus and Pentheus, unlike Lear's daughters, respects Cadmus. There is no "original" trouble in the Thebes of *The Bacchae*, none like the plague that disrupts Oedipus' Thebes and sets off the search for Laius' murderer. Nor is the legitimate king absent, as in Aeschylus' *Agamemnon*. There is no war of succession, as in *Colonus* or *Seven Against Thebes*. Pentheus' Thebes is simply susceptible—to what, we are not quite certain. But it is this underlying and irreducible susceptibility—the very fragility of human social and political organization—that is probed, brought to the surface, and exploited during *The Bacchae*. The "traditions" themselves—whatever they happen to be—are called into question by Dionysus. His "order" is the disorder that topples order, just as his earthquake shakes Pentheus' palace. Dionysus is natural disorder, human chaos, the original stuff civilization struggles against to survive.

The blond cousin is not satisfied with "customs and traditions hallowed by age." He wishes no orderly place in the pantheon, but to *replace* the pantheon. He wants nothing less than to return Thebes to primitive homogeneity. Dionysus' genius is to reduce civilization to its undifferentiated origins. We do not know whether men ever lived in communities in which there was no separation of vital functions. Probably not, because even non-human primate cultures seem to show family structure and division of labor. But the human infant first experiences the world as an undifferentiated environment. Thus it is ontogenetic rather than phylogenetic primitivism which Dionysus brings to Thebes. The pleasure sources he taps are the more powerful for being a part of the direct experience of every human. The blond cousin is unslakable infantile lust.

What is this confusion he brings to Thebes? First he drives the women to the hillside, entirely disrupting family life. Next he confronts the political authorities, mocking their procedures, destroying their jail, taunting their king. He claims, and then demonstrates that women are stronger than men, lust stronger than law, pleasure seeking better than work, night better than day, oneness better than plurality.

Everything is fused into One. The primal emotion contains in undifferentiated form all other emotions. Love, suckling, dancing, anger, rage, terror, explosive sexual violence are all combined—and the Dionysian ecstasy transcends them all. The confusion in Thebes is a fusion of all feelings: on Cithaeron there is only one affect. The confusion Pentheus feels when Dionysus offers to take him to Cithaeron to watch the orgy is the confusion of a child who wishes more than anything to see his parents make love—but who dreads that sight. Overwhelmed—quite literally flooded—by sexual excitement, Pentheus goes to Cithaeron, transformed inwardly by his own irresistible prurience and transformed outwardly by the transvestite robe and wig of the Bacchantes. The boy is led to a scene of primal emotion. At last he can see the forbidden games from his vantage atop the phallic fir tree. Pentheus watches and his excitement surpasses his ability to act. If *Oedipus* taps the fears and desires Freud spoke of, *The Bacchae* taps another, related, and equally compelling set of fears and desires. For every child wishes to penetrate those mysteries his parents enact. To see them, and not to see them; to participate by watching—to "find out" what it is all about.

Pentheus is exposed, humiliated, tortured, killed, dismembered. The primal emotion is the affective energy released by interrupting the primal scene. Such utter destruction as follows—the dismemberment—is the physical fact of *The Bacchae* and the psychic fact of this kind of infantile trauma. These chthonic undertows course through *The Bacchae*. But Dionysus' "mysteries" are not so mysterious after all. They are described twice in the text. They are metaphors of other, more common, mysteries. But these rituals, transferred from domestic privacy to public places, threaten the state. Pentheus' most basic confusion is that between his public and private roles. What the boy wants to see, the king must prevent or at least control. When Pentheus agrees to Dionysus' plan—to go to Cithaeron alone and in disguise—he gives up his role as king. It is the boy who is killed, as is made clear in Agave's mourning recognition. The play's final movement hardly discusses Pentheus the king, the man with ultimate political authority. It is a lament for a murdered boy: one who was caught where he did not belong, and was too cruelly punished for his misdeed.

However, Dionysus first presents Pentheus with a political challenge. But Pentheus cannot maintain his political response. His original impulse—to call out the troops and put down civil disorder—evaporates when Dionysus offers to take him to Cithaeron. The double nature of Dionysus' activities are clear in the Chorus. The mysteries are sweet, but they are politically and socially disruptive:

> Blessed, blessed are those who know the
> mysteries of god.
> Blessed is he who hallows his life in the worship of god,
>   he whom the spirit of god possesseth, who is one
>   with those who belong to the holy body of god.
>
> [...]
>
> to the mountain!
>   to the mountain!
> where the throng of women waits,
> driven from shuttle and loom,
> possessed by Dionysus!
>
> [...]
>
> He is sweet upon the mountains. He drops to the earth
>   from the running packs.
> He wears the holy fawn-skin. He hunts the wild goat
>   and kills it.
> He delights in the raw flesh.

The city cannot withstand such dancing. The threat of Dionysus is real, and the authorities must act.

4.

Pentheus is authority in Thebes. He is king. He is a boy. The collision between Pentheus and Dionysus is the heart of *The Bac-*

chae. But it is no usual dramatic collision. To Pentheus, Dionysus is a political threat, a religious faker, and a personal affront. But to Dionysus, Pentheus is a young boy—a love object. Yet what can satisfy the blond cousin who, by virtue of divinity, can have whatever he wishes whenever he wishes it? This ancient riddle can be put several ways: (1) How can there be desire when the desired object is immediately and always available? (2) For the infant whose world is a perfect organization of immediate gratification, can there be any pleasure? (3) If all is pleasure, how is pleasure known?— what can we measure it against?

The blond cousin is neither an intellectual nor a medieval scholastic, and thus these problems never present themselves to him abstractly. His dancing from Lydia through Thebes acts them out. He has taught his dances and rituals, but he is not satisfied. He wishes honor in Thebes. He gets it at a terrible price, but will not be satisfied. He sees Pentheus and wonders what game will suit the encounter. Dionysus' problem is to make the seduction of Pentheus sufficiently difficult and complicated to be pleasurable.

The conflicts between Pentheus and Dionysus are unique in dramatic literature. They run in one direction only. Dionysus taunts and enrages Pentheus, the better to have him. Dionysus' object is not to "reveal" himself (as he proclaims in the play's prologue) but to "hold himself back," prolonging what ecstasy he may feel. There is a coolness about the blond cousin. He does not share the frenzy he engenders in his Bacchantes; he does not himself murder Pentheus. His language is measured and calm, detached and laced with riddles. He has so surpassed himself that the infantile lusts he represents are of no interest to him. He wishes to provoke them in others; his gratification will come in the union-of-murder between mother and son.

Thus the blond cousin's initial disguise is the metaphor of his psyche. This proxy god provokes a proxy passion to destroy a proxy king. And when Agave dances in with Pentheus' head, she does not know with whom she is dancing. *Dionysism* is the property of others—the blond cousin himself can have none of it. He must lead his dancers forever, never dancing with them. He is always outdistancing his lusts. Not able to consent to be a man in fact (as did

Christ), Dionysus can experience none of the rhythms of men. The mystery unravels itself: the blond cousin of stupendous sensual possibility has no access to the pleasures he releases. He is a prisoner of the very divinity he seeks to reveal. More than anything he wishes to worship himself. But the one possibility denied to god is self-worship (Christianity needed its Trinity). *The Bacchae* shows Dionysus trying to become the mortal blond cousin so he might enjoy Pentheus. But he cannot turn the trick.

5.

What exactly are the relationships between Dionysus and Pentheus? Here we can be helped by Eric Berne, who in the introduction to *Games People Play* and throughout *Transactional Analysis in Psychotherapy* develops models of social interaction. According to Berne, there are three personality modes: Parent (P), Adult (A), Child (C). A complimentary transaction is one between two persons operating within the same modes; a crossed transaction is one between two persons operating within different modes. Thus A speaks to B as a parent would to a child; B responds as a child would to a parent—this is a complimentary transaction; if, however, B responds as an adult would to an adult, the transaction is crossed. Most conflicts result from crossed transactions. Furthermore, Berne argues, several transactions can occur simultaneously because there are several levels of consciousness (and unconsciousness). Whenever Pentheus and Dionysus meet face to face, several transactions are taking place. There are three basic transactions which determine Pentheus' relationship to Dionysus:

(1) *Social:* The Blond Cousin versus the Young King

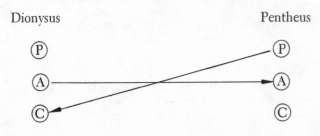

Public Domain

Pentheus treats Dionysus as a sovereign would an intruder. Dionysus, however, does not play the role of the humble suppliant but that of the riddler. Because Dionysus will not submit to the authority of the king, the transaction is crossed. This is the visible action of the first agon between Dionysus and Pentheus. It is not all that is going on, however.

(2) *Universal*: The God versus the King

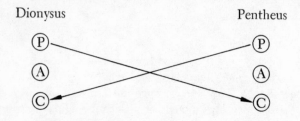

This is the heart of the conflict. Dionysus is a god and as such treats all mortals as children; Pentheus is a king and as such treats all persons within his domain as children. The situation is ironic because both Dionysus and Pentheus are children themselves. Each is right with regard to the other but neither is correct with regard to himself. Infuriated by the answers Dionysus gives him, Pentheus orders the blond cousin imprisoned. Dionysus is careful to answer *not* as the blond cousin, but as the god:

PENTHEUS. I shall cut off your girlish curls.
DIONYSUS. My hair is holy.
     My curls belong to god.
PENTHEUS. Second, you will surrender your wand.
DIONYSUS. You take it. It belongs to Dionysus.
PENTHEUS. Last, I shall place you under guard and
     confine you in the palace.
DIONYSUS. The god himself will set me free
     whenever I wish.

[. . .]

PENTHEUS. Seize him. He is mocking me and Thebes.
DIONYSUS. I give you sober warning, fools:
     place no chains on me.

PENTHEUS. But I say: chain him.
And I am stronger here.
DIONYSUS. You do not know
the limits of your strength. You do not know
what you do. You do know who you are.
PENTHEUS. I am Pentheus, the son of Echion and Agave.
DIONYSUS. Pentheus: you shall repent that name.

Why does Dionysus allow himself to be shorn, stripped of his thyrsus, and jailed?

Because underneath the struggles between blond cousin and young king, god and man, is a third set of transactions—a *collaboration* of love.

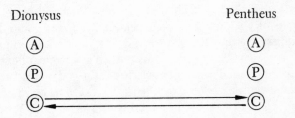

The two young boys trade dares, excite each other, play games for keeps. This operation—the underlying sexual collaboration of *The Bacchae*—becomes very clear in the third and last agon between Dionysus and Pentheus. Dionysus is free, and Pentheus is enraged. He threatens to send his army to attack the women reveling on Cithaeron. Dionysus warns against such folly:

If I were you,
I would offer him a sacrifice, not rage
and kick against necessity, a man defying god.

But then, quite suddenly, Dionysus changes his tone and offers friendly advice.

Friend, you can still save the situation.

[. . .]

Would you like to see their revels on the mountain?

Pentheus admits he would "pay a great sum to see the sight."
Dionysus asks him why he is so curious. Pentheus cannot really
answer. He protests that he would be sorry to see the women drunk
—but still he would like to watch the orgies. Dionysus offers to help.
Their conflict is forgotten. Pentheus goes into the palace to costume
himself as a woman and Dionysus awaits his return, assuring the
Chorus that the "great price" Pentheus will pay for seeing the
Bacchantes will be death. When Pentheus returns, Dionysus ad-
justs his costume, ironically mocking him. What has happened is
that both Pentheus and Dionysus have found ways to indulge their
pleasures: Pentheus by transvestitism and voyeurism, Dionysus by
relentless mockery. Each cooperates completely with the other.
Dionysus arranges for Pentheus to see the women but dressed so that
the young king looks (in Dionysus' words) "exactly like one of the
daughters of Cadmus." Thus cooperating, the king goes off to his
dismemberment and the god to wherever. There is one important
detail: as soon as Pentheus appears dressed as a woman he sees that
horns have sprouted from Dionysus' head: the god is at last revealed.
The blond cousin has been satisfied (as satisfied as he can be) and
now the god can witness the brutal climax of the masquerade.

6.

But why a masquerade at all? Surely it is a thin disguise that
Dionysus wears. Everyone in Thebes except Pentheus seems immediately to recognize that the blond cousin is no mere mortal.
The audience surely knows. Euripides takes no trouble whatsoever
to make this disguise convincing. In fact, none of the disguises in
The Bacchae—a play of disguises—is convincing. Cadmus and
Teiresias are dressed as women; Agave dances in with Pentheus'
head claiming it is a young lion; Pentheus is dressed as a Bacchante
but specifically led through the streets by Dionysus so that he is
"the laughingstock of Thebes."

Disguises are usually worn to fool others. But those in *The
Bacchae* fool only the person disguised. Dionysus hopes that his
disguise as the blond cousin will help him experience the sensual
pleasures of men. Agave deceives herself about whom she has killed.

Cadmus and Teiresias think they are honoring the god. Pentheus wants to be led through the heart of the city because, as he says, "I, alone, of all this city, dare to go." These are all masks. Each disguise hides from the masked person what he is actually doing, who he is. But it hides this truth—relative and subjective as it is—from no one else. Furthermore, the play does not resolve the conflicts arising from these contradictory truths. The city is destroyed, the population scattered. No new order is established, no convincing reason offered to explain what has happened. Ultimately, each character is unmasked. Dionysus is shown to be a god, Pentheus a fool, Cadmus and Teiresias old men whose gestures are self-serving, Agave the murderer of her son. But these "realities" are no more "true" than the masks which concealed them. *The Bacchae* reveals and hides at many levels simultaneously. There is no "center of things" where the truth lies still.

The masking gives to *The Bacchae* an air of farce and celebration. This infuses all the action. As in much of Euripides, the tragic action is woven with threads of farce: old men dressed as women, a young boy spying on his mother's sexual adventures, a god who wishes to experience human lust. *Orestes*, written at about the same time as *The Bacchae*, is more openly farcical. But there much of the farce is in the dialogue in the form of wit and irony. In *The Bacchae* the basic situation is farcical. The relentlessness with which this situation is followed through transforms the farce into tragedy.

7.

Pentheus is killed. Agave discovers what she has done. The story is over.

Not quite. Dionysus returns, unsatisfied as always. He proclaims that Agave and her sisters are to be exiled in "expiation of the murder you have done"—a murder engineered by the god himself, relished by him, and therefore, one would suppose, sanctioned. (Either Pentheus is a blasphemer and deserves death, or he is not and Dionysus is evil and wrong. Dionysus, of course, plays it both ways. To the god, Pentheus was a blasphemer and deserved death; for the sake of punishing others, Pentheus was innocent and his death a "murder.") Cadmus and his wife are to be changed into serpents, later to lead an army against their native Hellas. Thebes is effectively destroyed: there is no more ruling family. Teiresias is not mentioned and one concludes that the blind prophet is excused from punishment. But why him and not Cadmus? Cadmus protests. "We implore you. We have done no wrong. [. . .] Gods should be exempt from human passions." Exactly. And that is why Dionysus is continuously pumping himself up to excesses. Feeling nothing human, he cannot judge by what distance his acts exceed human responses—like the deaf man trying to speak in a normal voice. "I was blasphemed," Dionysus says. And anyway, "Long ago my father Zeus ordained these things." The ultimate evasion.

At this point we must look behind the play at Euripides. Writing *The Bacchae* from exile in Macedonia at the very end of his life, employing his full arsenal of ritual farce, satire, parody, melodrama, wild physical action—what could that old Euripides think he was doing? And why the implausible ending, which, like the end of his *Orestes*, wraps everything up while resolving nothing? We know that Euripides was bitter, that he thought Athens was headed for ruin. We know also that Dionysian cults from the East were becoming popular in Athens. Surely Euripides was saying something to his fellow Athenians. He was foreseeing the end of fifth-century civilization. The constant references of the Chorus to "tradition" and "custom" are ironic: they speak of Dionysus, admittedly a new god. All custom is turned on its head, and the very meaning of tradition is blurred. Dionysus can appeal to Zeus, but over the heads of how many intermediary—and traditional—deities? Euripides' style and attitude in *The Bacchae* are not much different from Genet's. In both, old values have failed and a synthetic, subjective tradition—an inverted sense of good and bad—creates what William Arrowsmith calls the "turbulence" that marks *The Bacchae* and what Sartre calls the "whirligigs" that mark Genet's plays. Dionysus brings with him an outlaw system of infantile sexuality. It is nothing but a movement that ends in violence. But this violence is ecstasy. In a world where law fails (as it had during the Peloponnesian Wars), lawlessness and chaotic sensuality are attractive. This lawlessness is justified by appeals to the highest authorities, authorities far superior to the rigid, and frequently desperate, authority of the state. The authority of individual and intra-personal subjectivity and the authority of new and powerful gods are together invoked. The politics of ecstasy is a predictable response to a decaying social system. But that does not make it a pleasant phenomenon. From such debauches some societies never awaken.

Dionysian ecstasy does not yield all its promises. Or, rather, it achieves more than it threatens. If repression is the price we pay for civilization, total, public, communal, sensual freedom is civilization's death throe.

The analogues between the situation in *The Bacchae* and our own times are obvious. The logic of *The Bacchae* is inescapable and unconsoling. The state cannot recover its youthful virility. And the young, blond, effeminate god offers nothing but his politics of ecstasy. Dionysus demands gratification here and now. He overturns the traditional values which have become oppressive and only apparently strong (Pentheus' army never marches, and it is made clear that if it were to fight it would lose). The state is worse than weak—it is silly, controlled by a young, prurient king, old men disguised as women, and women driven mad. Patently, poignantly missing from *The Bacchae* are the strong men—Oedipus, Philoctetes, Ajax, Aeschylus' Orestes—who so heroically, if tragically, populate Greek theatre. *The Bacchae* is a play of boys, old men, and women. Such was the mood of Euripides in 407 B.C., when, at the age of seventy-one, in voluntary exile, he wrote his bitter tribute to the Athens he would never see again.

There's Lots of Time in *Godot*

1966

TWO DUETS AND A FALSE SOLO, that's *Waiting for Godot*. Its structure is more musical than dramatic, more theatrical than literary. The mode is pure performance: song and dance, music-hall routine, games. And the form is a spinning away, a centrifugal wheel in which the center—Time—can barely hold the parts, Gogo and Didi, Pozzo and Lucky, the Boy(s). The characters arrive and depart in pairs, and when they are alone they are afraid: half of them is gone. The Boy isn't really by himself, though one actor plays the role(s). "It wasn't you came yesterday," states Vladimir in Act II. "No Sir," the Boy says. "This is your first time." "Yes Sir." Only Godot is alone, at the center of the play and all outside it at once. "What does he do, Mr. Godot? . . . He does nothing, Sir." But even Godot is linked to Gogo/Didi. "To Godot? Tied to Godot! What an idea! No question of it. (*Pause.*) For the moment." Godot is also linked to the Boy(s), who tend his sheep and goats, who are his messengers. Nor can we forget that Godot cares enough for Gogo/Didi to send someone each night to tell them the appointment will not be kept. What exquisite politeness.

Pozzo (and we must assume, Lucky) has never heard of Godot, although the promised meeting is to take place on his land. Pozzo is insulted that *his* name means nothing to Gogo/Didi. "We're not from these parts," Estragon says in apology, and Pozzo deigns, "You are human beings none the less." Pozzo/Lucky have no appointment to keep. Despite the cracking whip and Pozzo's air of big business on the make, their movements are random, to and fro across the land, burdens in hand, rope in place: there is always time to stop and proclaim. In Act I, after many adieus, Pozzo says, "I don't seem to be able . . . (*long hesitation*) . . . to depart." And when he does move, he confesses, "I need a running start." In Act II, remembering nothing about "yesterday," Pozzo replies to Vladimir's question, "Where do you go from here?" with a simple "On." It is Pozzo's last word.

The Pozzo/Lucky duet is made of improvised movements and set speeches (Lucky's has run down). The Gogo/Didi duet is made of set movements (they must be at this place each night at dusk to wait for Godot to come or night to fall) and improvised routines spun out of habits learned long ago. Pozzo, who starts in no place, is worried only about Time; he ends without time but with a desperate need to move. Gogo/Didi are "tied" to this place and want only for time to pass. Thus, part way through the first act the basic scenic rhythm of *Godot* is established by the strategic arrangement of characters: Gogo/Didi (and later the Boy) have definite appointments, a rendezvous they *must* keep. Pozzo/Lucky are free agents, aimless, not tied to anything but each other. For this reason, Pozzo's watch is very important to him. Having nowhere to go, his only relation to the world is in knowing "the time." The play is a confrontation between the rhythms of place and time. Ultimately they are coordinates of the same function.

Of course, Pozzo's freedom is illusory. He is tied to Lucky—and vice versa—as tightly as the others are tied to Godot and the land. In the scenic calculus of the play, rope = appointment. As one coordinate weakens, the other tightens. Thus, when Pozzo/Lucky lose their sense of time, there is a corresponding increase in their need to cover space. Lucky's speech is imperfect memory, an uncontrollable stream of unconsciousness, while Pozzo's talk is all *tirade*, a series of set speeches, learned long ago, and slowly deserting the master actor, just as the things which define his identity—watch, pipe, atomizer—desert him. I am reminded of Yeats' *Circus Animal's Desertion*, in which images fail the old poet who is finally forced to "lie down where all the ladders start / In the foul rag-and-bone shop of the heart." Here, too, Pozzo will find himself (Lucky is already there). Thus we see these two in their respective penultimate phases, comforted only by broken bursts of eloquence, laments for that lost love, clock time.

The pairing of characters—those duets—links time and space, presents them as discontinuous coordinates. Gogo/Didi are not sure whether the place in Act II is the same as that in Act I; Pozzo cannot remember yesterday; Gogo/Didi do not recall what they did yesterday. "We should have thought of it [suicide] a million years ago, in the nineties." Gogo either forgets at once, or he never forgets. This peculiar sense of time and place is not centered *in* the characters, but *between* them. Just as it takes two lines to fix a point in space, so it takes two characters to *unfix* our normal expectations of time, place, and being. This pairing is not unique to *Waiting for Godot*; it is a favorite device of contemporary playwrights. The Pupil and the Professor in *The Lesson*, Claire and Solange in *The Maids*, Peter and Jerry in *The Zoo Story*: these are of the same species as Gogo and Didi. What might these duets mean or be? Each of them suggests a precarious existence, a sense of self and self-in-the-world so dependent on "the other" as to be inextricably bound up in the other's physical presence. In these plays "experience" is not "had" by a single character, but "shared" between them. It is not a question of fulfillment—of why Romeo wants Juliet—but of existence. By casting the characters homosexually, the authors remove the "romantic" element: these couples are not joined because of some biological urge but because of some metaphysical necessity. The drama that emerges from such pairing is intense and locked-in —a drama whose focus is internal without being "psychological." Internalization without psychology is naked drama, theatre unmediated by character. That is why, in these plays, the generic structure of their elements—farce, melodrama, vaudeville—is so unmistakably clear. There is no way (or need) to hide structure: that's all there is. Still, in *Godot*, there are meaningful differences between Vladimir and Estragon, Pozzo and Lucky; but even these shadings of individualism are seen only through the couple: to know one character, you have to know both.

In Aristotelian terms drama is made of the linked chain: action

> plot > character > thought. Connections run efficiently in either direction, although for the most part one seeks the heart of a play in its action (as Fergusson uses that term). These same elements are in *Godot*, but the links are broken. The discontinuity of time is reflected on this more abstract level of structure. Thus what Gogo and Didi do is not what they are thinking; nor can we understand their characters by adding and relating events to thoughts. And the action of the play—waiting—is not what they are after but what they want most to avoid. What, after all, are their games for? They wish to "fill time" in such a way that the vessel "containing" their activities is unnoticed amid the activities themselves. Whenever there is nothing "to do" they remember why they are here: to wait for Godot. That memory, that direct confrontation with Time, is painful. They play, invent, move, sing to avoid the sense of waiting. Their *activities* are therefore keeping them from a consciousness of the *action* of the play. Although there is a real change in Vladimir's understanding of his experience (he learns precisely what "nothing to be done" means) and in Pozzo's life, these changes and insights do not emerge from the plot (as Lear's "wheel of fire" does), but stand outside of what's happened. Vladimir has his epiphany while Estragon sleeps—his perception is a function of the sleeping Gogo. Pozzo's understanding, like the man himself, is blind. Structurally as well as thematically, *Godot* is an "uncompleted" play; and its openness is not at the end (as *The Lesson* is open-ended) but in many places throughout: it is a play of gaps and pauses, of broken-off dialogue, of speech and action turning into time-avoiding games and routines. Unlike Beckett's perfectly modulated *Molloy*, *Waiting for Godot* is designed off-balance. It is the very opposite of *Oedipus*. In *Godot* we do not have the meshed ironies of experience, but that special anxiety associated with question marks preceded and followed by nothing.

What then holds *Godot* together? Time, habit, memory, and games form the texture of the play and provide both its literary and theatrical interest. In *Proust*, Beckett speaks of habit and memory in a way that helps us understand *Godot*.

The laws of memory are subject to the more general laws of habit. Habit is a compromise effected between the individual and his environment, or between the individual and his own organic eccentricities, the guarantee of a dull inviolability, the lightning-conductor of his existence. Habit is the ballast that chains the dog to his vomit. [. . .] Life is a succession of habits, since the individual is a succession of individuals. [. . .] The creation of the world did not take place once and for all, but takes place every day..

The other side of "dull inviolability" is "knowing," and it is this that Gogo/Didi must avoid if they are to continue. But knowledge is precisely what Didi has near the end of the play. It ruins everything for him:

> Was I sleeping, while the others suffered? Am I sleeping now? To-morrow, when I wake, or think I do, what shall I say of to-day? That with Estragon my friend, at this place, until the fall of night, I waited for Godot? That Pozzo passed, with his carrier, and that he spoke to us? Probably. But in all that what truth will there be? [*Looking at Estragon*] He'll know nothing. He'll tell me about the blows he received and I'll give him a carrot.

Then, paraphrasing Pozzo, Didi continues:

> Astride a grave and a difficult birth. Down in the hole, lingeringly, the grave-digger puts on the forceps. We have time to grow old. The air is full of our cries. (*He listens.*) But habit is a great deadener. (*He looks again at Estragon.*) At me too someone is looking, of me too something is saying, He is sleeping, he knows nothing, let him sleep on. (*Pause.*) I can't go on! (*Pause.*) What have I said?

In realizing that he knows nothing, in seeing that habit is the great deadener—in achieving an ironic point of view toward himself, Didi knows everything, and wishes he did not. For him Pozzo's single instant has become "lingeringly." For Pozzo "the same day, the same second" is enough to enfold all human experience; Didi realizes that there is "time to grow old." But habit will rescue him. Having shouted his anger, frustration, helplessness ("I can't go on!"), Didi is no longer certain of what he said. Dull inviolability has been violated, but only for an instant: one instant is enough for insight, and we have a lifetime to forget. The Boy enters. Unlike what happened in the first act, Didi asks him no questions about the appointment. Instead Didi makes statements. "He won't come this evening. [. . .] But he'll come to-morrow." For the first time, Didi asks the Boy about Godot. "What does he do, Mr. Godot? [. . .] Has he a beard, Mr. Godot?" The Boy answers: Godot does nothing, the beard is probably white. Didi says—after a silence—"Christ have mercy on us!" But both thieves will not be saved, and now that the game is up, Vladimir seeks to protect himself:

> Tell him . . . (*he hesitates*) . . . tell him you saw me and that . . . (*he hesitates*) . . . that you saw me. [. . .] (*With sudden violence.*) You're sure you saw me, you won't come and tell me to-morrow that you never saw me!

The "us" of the first act is the "me" of the second. Habits break, old friends are abandoned, Gogo—for the moment—is cast into the pit. When Gogo awakens, Didi is standing with his head bowed. Didi does not tell his friend of his conversation with the Boy or of his insight or sadness. Gogo asks, "What's wrong with you?" and Didi answers, "Nothing." Didi tells Estragon that they must return the following evening to keep their appointment once again. But for him the routine is meaningless: Godot will not come. There is something more than irony in his reply to Gogo's question, "And if we dropped him?" "He'd punish us," Didi says. But the punishment is already apparent to Didi: the pointless execution of orders without hope of fulfillment. Never coming; for Didi, Godot has come . . . and gone.

But Didi alone sees behind his old habits and even he, in his ironic musing, senses someone else watching him sleep just as he watches Gogo: he learns that all awareness is relative. Pozzo is no relativist, but a strict naturalist. In the first act he describes the setting of the sun with meticulous hand gestures, twice consulting his watch so as to be precise. Pozzo knows his "degrees" and the subtle shadings of time's passing. He also senses that when night comes it "will burst upon us pop! like that! just when we least expect it." And for Pozzo, once it is night there is no more time, for he measures that commodity by the sun. Going blind, Pozzo too has an epiphany—the exact opposite of Didi's:

> Have you not done tormenting me with your accursed time! It's abominable! When! When! One day, is that not enough for you,

one day he went dumb, one day I went blind, one day we'll go deaf, one day we were born, one day we shall die, the same day, the same second, is that not enough for you!

Of the light gleaming an instant astride the grave, Pozzo has only a dim memory. He has found a new habit to accommodate his new blindness; his epiphany is false. The experience of the play indeed shows us that there is plenty of time, too much: waiting means more time than things to fill it.

Pozzo/Lucky play a special role in this passing of time that is *Waiting for Godot*'s action. Things have changed for them by Act II. Pozzo is blind and helpless, Lucky is dumb. Their "career" is nearly over. Like more conventional theatrical characters, they have passed from bad times to worse. The rope, whip, and valise remain: all else is gone—Lear and the Fool on the heath, that is what this strange pair suggests to me. But if they are that *in themselves*, they are something different to Gogo/Didi. In the first act, Gogo/Didi suspect that Pozzo may be Godot. Discovering that he is not, they are curious about him and Lucky. They circle around their new acquaintances, listen to Pozzo's speeches, taunt Lucky, and so on. Partly afraid, somewhat uncertainly, they integrate Pozzo/Lucky into their world of waiting: they make out of the visitors a way of passing time. And they exploit the *persons* of Pozzo/Lucky, taking food and playing games. (In the Free Southern Theater production, Gogo and Didi pickpocket Pozzo, stealing his watch, pipe, and atomizer—no doubt to hock them for necessary food. This interpretation has advantages: it grounds the play in an acceptable reality; it establishes a first-act relationship of double exploitation— Pozzo uses them as audience and they use him as income.)

In the second act this exploitation is even clearer. Pozzo no longer seeks an audience. Gogo/Didi no longer think that Pozzo may be Godot (Gogo, briefly, goes through this routine). Gogo/Didi try to detain Pozzo/Lucky as long as possible. They play rather cruel games with them, postponing assistance. It would be intolerable to Gogo/Didi for this "diversion" to pass quickly, just as it is intolerable for an audience to watch it go on so long. What "should" be a momentary encounter is converted into a prolonged affair. Vladimir sermonizes on their responsibilities. "It is not every day that we are needed." The talk continues without action. Then, trying to pull Pozzo up, Vladimir falls on top of him. So does Estragon. Obviously, they can pull Pozzo up (just as they can get up themselves). But instead they remain prone. "Won't you play with us?" they seem to be asking. But Pozzo is in no playing mood. Despite his protests, Gogo/Didi continue their game. It is, as Gogo says, "child's play." They get up, help Pozzo and Lucky up, and the play proceeds. When they are gone, Estragon goes to sleep. Vladimir shakes him awake. "I was lonely." And speaking of Pozzo/Lucky, "That passed the time." For them, perhaps; but for the audience? It is an ironic scene—the entire cast sprawled on the floor, hard to see, not much action. It makes an audience aware that the time is not passing fast enough.

This game with Pozzo/Lucky is one of many. In fact, the gamesmanship of *Waiting for Godot* is extraordinary. Most of the play is taken up by a series of word games, play acting, body games, routines. Each of these units is distinct, usually cued in by memories of *why* Gogo/Didi are where they are. Unable simply to consider the ramifications of "waiting," unfit, that is, for pure speculation (as Lucky was once fit), they fall back on their games: how many thieves were saved, how many leaves on the tree, calling each other names, how can we hang ourselves, and so on. These games are not thematically meaningless, they feed into the rich image-texture of the play; but they are meaningless in terms of the play's action: they lead nowhere, they contribute to the non-plot. Even when Godot is discussed, the talk quickly becomes routinized. At one time Vladimir spoke to Godot. "What exactly did we ask him for?" Estragon asks. Vladimir replies, "Were you not there?" "I can't have been listening." But it is Gogo who supplies the information that Didi confirms: that their request was "a kind of prayer . . . a vague supplication." And it is both of them, in contrapuntal chorus, who confirm that Godot would have to "think it over . . . in the quiet of his home . . . consult his family . . . his friends . . . his agents . . . his correspondents . . . his books . . . his bank account . . . before taking a decision."

Conversation in *Godot* is discussion or argument transformed into routinized counterpoint. Much has been said about the beauty of Beckett's prose in this play. More needs to be said about its routine qualities. Clichés are converted into game/rituals by dividing the lines between Gogo and Didi, by arbitrarily assigning one phrase to each. Thus we have a sense of their "pairdom," while we are entranced by the rhythm of their language. Beckett's genius in dialogue is his *scoring*, not his "book." This scoring pertains not only to language but to events as well. Whatever there is to do is done in duets. By using these, Gogo/Didi are able to convert anxiety into habit. Gogo is more successful at this than Didi. For Gogo things are either forgotten at once or never forgotten. There is no "time-span" for him, only a kaleidoscopic present in which everything that is there is forever in focus. It takes Didi to remind Gogo of Godot, and these reminders always bring Gogo pain, his exasperated "Ah." For Didi the problem is more complex. Gogo says, "no use wriggling," to which Didi replies, "the essential doesn't change." These are opposite contentions; that's why they harmonize so well.

A few words about Time. If waiting is the play's action, Time is its subject. Godot is not Time, but he is associated with it—the one who makes but does not keep appointments. (Could it be that Godot passes time with Gogo/Didi just as they pass it with him? Within this scheme, Godot has nothing to do [as the Boy tells Didi in Act II] and uses the *whole play* as a diversion. Thus the "big game" is a strict analogy of the many "small games" that make the play.) The basic rhythm of the play is habit interrupted by memory, memory obliterated by games. Why do Gogo/Didi play? In order to deaden their sense of waiting. Waiting is a "waiting *for*" and it is precisely this that they wish to forget. One may say that "waiting" is the larger context within which "passing time" by playing games is a sub-system, keeping from them the sense that they are waiting. They confront Time (i.e., are conscious of Godot) only when there is a break in the games and they "know" and "feel" that they are waiting.

In conventional drama all details converge on the center of action centripetally. In *Godot* the action is centrifugal. Gogo/Didi do their best to shield themselves from a direct consciousness that they are at the appointed place at the prescribed time. If the center of the play is Time, dozens of activities and capers fling Gogo/Didi away from this center. But events at the periphery force them back inward: try as they will, they are not able to forget. I may illustrate the structure thus:

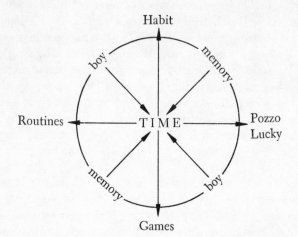

Caught on the hub of this wheel, driven by "re-minders" toward the center, Gogo/Didi literally have nowhere to go outside of this tight scheme. The scenic counterpart is the time-bracket "dusk-darkness"—that portion of the day when they must be at the appointed place. But even when night falls, and they are free to go, our last glimpse of them in each act is:

ESTRAGON. Well, shall we go?
VLADIMIR. Yes, let's go.
They do not move.

As if to underline the duet-nature of this ending, Beckett reverses the line assignments of Act I in Act II.

What emerges is a strange solitude, again foreshadowed by Beckett in his *Proust.* "The artistic tendency is not expansive but a contraction. And art is the apotheosis of solitude." In spinning out from the center, Gogo/Didi do not go anywhere, "they do not move." Yet their best theatrical moments are all motion, a running helter-skelter, a panic. Only at the end of each act, when it is all over for the day, are they quiet. The unmoved mover is Time, that dead identicality of instant and eternity. Once each for Didi and Pozzo, everything is contracted to that sense of Time in which consciousness is possible, but nothing else. To wait and not know *how* to wait is to experience Time. To be freed from waiting (as Gogo/Didi are at the end of each act) is to permit the moon to rise more rapidly than it can (as it does on *Godot's* stage), almost as if nature were to release itself from its own clock. Let loose from Time, night comes all of a sudden. After intermission, there is the next day—and tomorrow, another performance.

There are two time rhythms in *Godot*, one of the play and one of the stage. Theatrically, the exit of the Boy and the sudden night are strong cues for each act (and the play) to end. We, the audience, are relieved—it's almost over for us. They, the actors, do not move —even when the Godot-game is over, the theatre-game keeps them in their place: tomorrow they must return to enact identical routines. Underlying the play (all of it, not just the final scene of each act) is the theatre, and this is exactly what the script insinuates—a nightly appointment performed for people the characters will never meet. *Waiting for Godot* powerfully injects the mechanics of the theatre into the mysteries of the play.

Megan Terry:
The Playwright as Wrighter

1966

Megan Terry doesn't write plays, she wrights them. This cunning homonym indicates a return of the playwright to his original profession. Until the Renaissance, and sporadically since then, the making of plays was not the work of writers (who were poets and had their own profession) but of those who were part of the theatre. Some—Molière, Shakespeare—were actors; others—Brecht, Aeschylus—were directors. All understood that the basic mode of theatre was performance. Few plays were distributed as literary texts in their own time. Even Shakespeare had to wait until he was in his grave seven years before the First Folio appeared. Plays were for playing, and books for reading.

The Renaissance, with its love of documents, changed all that. History was rediscovered and we exist amid the cherished residues of dozens of cultures; no longer can we get through the day without some recourse to the library or museum (at home or institutionalized), some awesome confrontation with a "masterpiece." It's a bit frightening, all that accumulating greatness, and more so in the performing arts than in the others. For the repertory asks to be played and the high-water marks are indeed high. However, recently we have reached a turning point. Renaissance rules and assumptions are no longer that important. Theatre and literature have diverged once again. One need not be a scholar of Antonin Artaud or Bertolt Brecht to recognize that performance, action, and event are the key terms of our theatre—and that these terms are not literary. Surely rhetoric has its place in the theatre, but only as one more differentiated form of action. Megan Terry is one playwright who knows that action is the soul of drama.

Gordon Craig—madman, genius, failure—suggested that Shakespeare wrote by lifting story-segments from English history chronicles or Italian novellas (and elsewhere) and asking his actors to improvise these scenes. A scribe wrote down what the actors said and Shakespeare went home to rework these crude lines into the iambics of his great plays. The actors gave him what no man working alone could get: a living sense of interaction, irony in depth, different linguistic and gestural patterns, simultaneity. Craig's suggestion has logical, if not historical, merit. Shakespeare's plays are unique for their "thickness," the complicated interweave of character, motive, and scene. They work on many levels at once and appeal to a multi-class audience. Their fluidity and busyness is drawn from the streets and an imagination as flexible as electronic circuitry. Shakespeare's plays are free from subjectivity; as Keats noted, the playwright had a "negative capability," an ability to stay out of his plays. If we are to believe Craig, Shakespeare stayed out because he was never in; he assembled, reworked, manipulated, phrased, arranged. But the first lines of the action were shown to him by his actors. Shakespeare's universal imagination is that of the metamorphosing collagist, the great transformer. His gifts and tools included theft.

Surely Megan Terry is not Shakespeare—there are thieves and thieves. But her methods are like those Craig attributed to Shakespeare and her *Viet Rock* is Elizabethan in scope and tone. We see a war unfold, from birth to death, from death back to life; we see both sides, more than two sides; there is irony, parody, seriousness; there are dramatic scenes and music, patter scenes, monologue, pantomime. A grab bag as impertinent as anything the Elizabethans concocted; a conglomeration of styles, sources, and effects. Yet the play has a unity. Why, and where is it?

One seeks Miss Terry not first in her plays or in herself, but in the Open Theatre—that expanding and contracting group, directed by Joseph Chaikin (but not dominated by him), which is laying the groundwork for the American theatre's future. Not the Open Theatre alone, of course: but a way of thinking most clearly exemplified by the Open Theatre, present also in Second City-with-Paul Sills, the Living Theatre, and some other stirrings off Broadway and around the country. Founded in September 1963, the Open Theatre's goals, as defined by Chaikin, are "to redefine the limits of the stage experience, or unfix them. To find ways of reaching each other and the audience." Playwrights are an important part of the Open Theatre. They "suggest forms for us—later these are often written out. These pieces are inspired by the actors' work. You see, there's a give-and-take. After the writer has suggested a form—I don't like 'plot' because these things are often much simpler than a plot—we begin to improvise with them. We select what language to use. Very often this is a 'language' of our own, sounds which communicate. [. . .]The mode of the language depends on the form of the improvisation, its goals, and our own warm-up. [. . .] We're in no hurry." Miss Terry runs a playwright's workshop for the Open Theatre, and V*iet Rock* was developed in that workshop. *Keep Tightly Closed* began as an actors' project for the Open Theatre; *Comings and Goings* is, in Miss Terry's words, "an enjoyment of technique, pure virtuosity on the part of the actors."

These are hints leading us to a method of working that is significantly different from what playwrights have been accustomed to. Miss Terry's plays are made with her actors. They begin as "notions," move through a chrysalis stage of improvisation, become "solidified" in a text, and are produced. But this solidification is not final; the plays themselves, like the performances, evolve. Sometimes, in my opinion at least, they over-evolve—they achieve a balance and then lose it again. I enjoyed the "first" version of V*iet Rock* at the Café La Mama Experimental Theatre Club in New York more than I did its "revised" version at Yale University. But the idea of constant revision is exciting; it puts the playwright on the same ground as the actors, and in the same peril of over-performing. Of course, once the texts have been printed, the plays become "literature," like it or not. But Miss Terry's plays in print do not have the same authority as, say, the texts of Arthur Miller; and this lack of authority is to the plays' advantage. The texts, as Gide would say, remain "pretexts" for productions; their staging should not be a re-creation so much as a reconstruction.

If the basic mood of the Open Theatre is participation, its essential exercise is the "transformation." According to Peter Feldman, who directed the Open Theatre production of *Keep Tightly Closed*, "The transformation is adapted from a Second City Workshop device. [. . .] It is an improvisation in which the established realities or 'given circumstances' (the Method phrase) of the scene change several times during the course of the action. What may change are character and/or situation and/or time and/or objectives. Whatever realities are established at the beginning are destroyed after a few minutes and replaced by others. Then these are in turn destroyed and replaced. These changes occur swiftly and *almost without transition*, until the audience's dependence upon any fixed reality is called into question."

In other words, a transformation is a realistic acting exercise infused with the tensions and strategies of a game. The actor is no longer "playing his reality," but rather "playing with a set of quick-changing realities." The inner rules of realistic acting are surrounded by an outer set of rules which determine the rate and kind of change. Each unit within a set of transformations is (or can be) as "real" as any bit of naturalistic acting; but the quick changes from one bit to another give the overall effect of kaleidoscopic fluidity and scenic explosion. Like many important new techniques, the transformation is simple; it does not make unusual demands on the actor. It merely asks him to give up his conventional, play-long identification with a role. The actor no longer plays out a continuity but a set of inter-related (and sometimes unrelated) actions, each of which is self-contained. He gets from one action to the next not by establishing for himself a logical, motivational connective but by following the "rules of the game" which say that at a certain time, on a certain cue, action A ends and action B begins. It is no more difficult for the actor to make these adjustments than it is for a football player to run with the ball on one play and block for the ball carrier on the next. Transformations do not change acting but the rules governing the use of acting.

In changing these rules, however, new situations are possible for performance and through that for playwrights. If the actor no longer has to make naturalistic connectives between scenes, the playwright, too, can jump from situation to situation, structuring his play on the progression of action-blocs rather than on motivationally connected sequences, each of which is psychologically contained in a larger unit—beat, scene, act, play. The new action-blocs (such as Miss Terry uses in her plays) can relate to each other in pre-logical ways. They can compress, go off on tangents, serve as counterpoint, stop plot development to explore mood, and so on. The device is not expressionistic because it makes no attempt to "represent the mind" of the playwright or the character. Perhaps a few examples from Miss Terry's plays will make the value of transformations clearer.

Act I of *Viet Rock* ends with a Senate Hearing investigating differing attitudes toward the Vietnamese war. Two Senators are running the hearing and a variety of witnesses have been called to testify, among them figures which seem to represent Eleanor Roosevelt, Muhammad Ali (Cassius Clay), General LeMay, the Madonna, and Jesus Christ. After each witness testifies (and several times in the midst of the testimony), the actors playing the roles switch parts. The Madonna becomes a Senator, Ali becomes Jesus, and so on. There is no "reason" for these switches; that is, neither Miss Terry nor the director wished to tell us that the Madonna equals the Senator. What happens is that the audience's usual habit of identifying actor and character is challenged and broken. One watches the action (hilarious, serious parody) and not the actors. And the action of the scenes becomes much clearer because of the breakdown in the actor-character relationship. The American way of "investigation," and the American "consensus," are put to a test. Neither right nor left is spared. And the great "mainstream," which finally carries the scene in triumph, is the most ruthlessly and ironically satirized. Because each actor brings to each bit his own set of gestures and reading of lines, the underlying pattern of the scene emerges more sharply, unmitigated by this or that powerful (or weak) interpretation. One also has the sense, struck home by comparatively few actors, of a national phenomenon: a crowded room, a great variety of Senators and witnesses and observers. All this is achieved with great theatrical economy, without slides, movies, or complicated sets.

In *Keep Tightly Closed* both character and situation change. At one moment there are three men in a cell, linked by murder. Jaspers hired Michaels to hire Gregory to kill Jaspers' wife. Gregory botched the job and all three are serving out life sentences. Shades of the Sheppard murder case, *Deathwatch*, and *No Exit*. Jaspers wants to force Gregory into signing a confession that would exonerate Michaels and Jaspers. The tortures which Jaspers and Michaels put Gregory through are represented by a series of transformations. Gregory becomes an Indian Chief captured by General Custer and one of his soldiers. He is dismembered. Later Gregory becomes Captain John Smith bringing water to two dying members of Smith's expedition in Virginia. The three of them re-enact the murder, with Jaspers playing his own wife. Gregory and Michaels play Jaspers' two young children consoling their father after the murder. And so on. Between these sharp, often satirical scenes the relationship in the cell develops. The three men are locked together; they will not be sprung. The transformations serve several purposes. They explode a routine situation into a set of exciting theatrical images; they reinforce, expand, and explore the varieties of relationships among the three men; they make concrete the fantasies of the prisoners. But these fantasies are shown in a non-psychological way: there is no hint that the transformations are what the characters are thinking. At best, they are what the characters might be thinking were they equipped to think in theatrical terms. As such, the transformations are not naturalistic or expressionistic devices, but active models of the larger situation.

In modern drama we are accustomed to the formula: actor equals character equals life. The audience sees the play and identifies with the characters and the story they enact; a "symbolic reality" is created which metaphorically recapitulates a life-experience. The actor studies his role and seeks means of relating his own psychic and physical gestures to those of the character. In terms popular among today's actors, he seeks a "through line of action" expressed in a set of interrelated and organically developing "objectives," each of which is situated within the "given circumstances" of the play. Thus the audience on one side and the actors on the other try to extend the character into life. Play scripts encourage this task because most plays are recapitulations of possible life-experiences. The modern tendency of valuing individuality as an ideal reinforces this kind of interpretation of theatrical texts. Everything from the "beat" within a scene to the entire play is tied into an organic life-form held together by the interrelation between character and action. The form of a play thus conceived and acted is one of contained and containing boxes in which the "lives" of the characters are axes. Thus there is a harmonious consistency between the parts of the play and between these parts and the play's characters. Characters develop, change strategies, succeed, and fail—all within the context of the "given circumstances" of beat, scene, act, and play.

Transformations introduce an entirely different kind of construction, one with exciting possibilities for the playwright (as Miss Terry knows). The play is no longer a consistent set of interrelated units. It may or may not have an overall harmony in its construction. *Viet Rock, Keep Tightly Closed,* and *In the Gloaming* do, while *Comings and Goings* does not. The basic construction block for *both* playwright and actor is the beat, those discrete units of action which make up a scene. In transformations each scene (sometimes each beat) is considered separately; there is no necessary attempt to relate one scene to the next through organic development: one scene *follows* another but does not logically grow out of it. The relationship between beats, or scenes, is paralogical or prelogical—a relationship of free association or arbitrary cue. Thus, in *Keep Tightly Closed,* when Jaspers, Michaels, and Gregory become Custer, his soldier, and an Indian Chief, they are not actors playing characters who are playing other characters (as the actress playing Claire has Claire play Madame in Genet's *The Maids*), but actors playing soldiers and the Indian directly, as if it were a separate scene entirely. The actors are cued into the Custer-Indian scene through a free association from Jaspers' suggestion of "torture" immediately before the transformation.

TRANSFORMATIONAL STRUCTURE

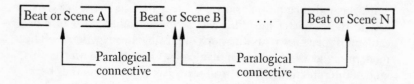

The three scenes are set in the matrix of the play; but the links between the scenes are not organic. One link is an association, the other a technical cue. Miss Terry is able to incorporate transformations into the play by building into her text the same rules which govern transformations as an acting exercise. The actor's way of working and the playwright's coincide. In *Keep Tightly Closed* the characters are continually being transformed into other characters, all based on the play's theme of entrapment, escape, torture, and expiation. The play develops through a set of concrete free associations. Because she worked the play out with the actors, Miss Terry has the advantage of their imaginations. In this play, as in *Viet Rock*, she maintains a real distance between herself and her creation; her "negative capability," it seems to me, is directly related to the way in which she uses her actors as part of the playwrighting process.

One can use transformations without changing the characters; instead, one changes the actors. This is what Miss Terry does in *Comings and Goings*. Here, between beats or in the midst of them, actors are sent in to replace other actors. Miss Terry describes the staging of the play: "A wheel was spun by a disinterested party at intervals of thirty-five to ninety seconds. A name was called out and one actor ran into the play and another actor ran out. I had originally thought the director would sit on one of the benches with the actors and send them in like a coach does at a basketball game." Thus in *Comings and Goings* the scenes may or may not develop organically. If they do not, we add to this scheme the one we saw in *Keep Tightly Closed*. As a matter of fact, *Comings and Goings* is an organic piece playing out variations on the theme of the male-female love relationship. The continual changing of actors, each of whom brings his own interpretation to the part—while it is being played—means that the action will be jolted. There will be no consistent interpretation of roles. In one performance we may see dozens of ways to act the play. The action is pushed this way and that as different actors come onstage. But instead of distracting us from the action, this leads us to see its possibilities more clearly. No longer does an audience identify actor and character (such identification is impossible because the actors keep changing). Instead, most of the audience's attention is divided between the virtuosity of the group of performers (an appreciation of "pure performance") and a close scrutiny of the action which almost seems abstract when stripped of its usual actor-character identification.

Viet Rock uses both kinds of transformations. In the opening scene the actors become, in rapid sequence, a human, primordial flower, mothers and infants, army doctors and inductees, inductees and mothers. In the Senate Hearing scene actors replace other actors within the framework of a single scene. The richness of *Viet Rock* depends largely on the interweave between these two basic modes of transformation. *Viet Rock* thus develops along several lines simultaneously. If it survives the furor over the war (assuming that *we* survive), it will be because the play is a valid artwork independent of its topical references. These references are of course important—they are the concrete bricks with which Miss Terry makes her images and actions; but another set of bricks, used in the same way, would have made as attractive, if thematically different, a play. *Viet Rock* is significant first, therefore, not because it parodies and satirizes a wide range of attitudes relating to the war, but because it uses new theatrical techniques. A relatively small group of actors, trained together, assisting the playwright in every stage of the play's development, are able to portray a world of more than a hundred characters without ever seeming to "double" their roles. In fact, we lose sight of the characters as we become increasingly aware of the steady, rhythmic, and progressive flow of the action. Only a few characters stand out—the Sergeant, the Madonna, Hanoi Hannah; the rest are submerged in the experience of seeing a war scrutinized at home, in the billets, on the battlefield, off duty. This scrutiny has an extraordinary range; it is personal, domestic, political, military; it involves the American soldiers, their families, their leaders, the North and South Vietnamese.

The theme and scope, the variety and density, of *Viet Rock* would have excited Brecht, just as Miss Terry's politics may have disappointed him. Despite the fact that those of the American Left who know *Viet Rock* have welcomed it, the play is non-political. It is a war play and as such it is an anti-war play. But it is not propagandistic or dogmatic. At two points, Miss Terry and the play's production make a political statement, both times directly to the audience. Toward the end an actress steps into the audience saying, "This war is worms. This war is worms invaded by worms. This war is eating away at the boy flesh inside my belly. This war stinks." And at the very end of the play all the actors go into the audience, confronting and touching individuals in the audience. This final gesture throws the problems of the war, its cruelty, inanity, horror, and political shortsightedness directly at the audience. But this final gesture is also elegiac and gentle, a real, physical contact between the quick and the dead, the theatre world and the worldly world. For most of the play Miss Terry represents, and disparages, *all* points of view. *Viet Rock* (like so much of Brecht) is loaded with parody and satire, echoes of popular themes and classic texts. Hollywood movies, advertising catch phrases, political speeches and attitudes, slogans of the Left, Right, and Middle, the soap opera, TV documentaries— all of these, and more, find voice and gesture in *Viet Rock*. But the play is not an exercise of sources; it has very much its own integrity.

This integrity is rooted not only in the thematic and scenic continuity and flow but also in the way Miss Terry fuses performance and text. *Viet Rock* is written, its scenes and actions are concrete, but locked into the text is the fluidity of the transformations from which the play was made. What emerges is a peculiarly powerful unit which is at once loose and tight, free and formed, massive and light. Serious scene and parody, sentimental moment and satire, brutal death and vaudeville gag are all knitted into the complex crossweave of the sudden transformations.

Miss Terry's plays—especially *Viet Rock*—justify the close cooperation between actors and playwright. Attempts in this direction

—notably *Hatful of Rain*—have been disappointing before. I believe it is the addition of the transformation—a major innovation in acting and playwrighting—and Miss Terry's great skill in using transformations both as a source and product that make this cooperative work successful now. *Viet Rock* and *Keep Tightly Closed* both have great scope and depth without claptrap. Miss Terry does not waste time relating her scenes to a realistic organic structure. She moves directly to the center of an action, and switches suddenly from action to action. She has learned how to use the accumulated imagination of the Open Theatre's actors and directors. She must still go home at night and write her scenes; but she does so in the context of the day's explorations. Her opportunities for constructive theft are multiplied. And so are the theatre's.

Pornography and the New Expression

1966

The first question is, Why such a fuss? Sex has been with us since the start, and art nearly that long. They have always been intertwined, sometimes openly and graphically, and more recently in a variety of covert ways. Every society has sought to regulate both sexuality and artistic expression, and to a degree each has succeeded. Freedom, so called, is nothing other than agreement on what to suppress. It becomes a social issue only when opinion diverges. But it is always an artistic issue, because the artistic impulse—to play, expose, and invent—is deeply opposed to the state's urge to conserve and control. We are terribly bothered today because our regulatory systems, our behavior, our expressions, and our tastes are neither harmonious nor static. The problem cuts deep and involves tensions between perception and conception, expression and repression, civilization and its discontented masses. We have always been encouraged to make love and war; but to make love instead of war undercuts the social structure at an intolerably basic level. Such mad fantasies have usually been relegated to religion, where they are neutralized by the Church Militant.

Everyone knows the new expression, but no one knows what to do about it: the "Now" movements among blacks, students, New Leftists, and artists; "God is dead" theology, existential man, automation, electric circuitry, and ontological insecurity; suburban and campus sex (paired and grouped), *Playboy* "sophistication," film nudity. The symptoms of change, exploration, explosion, and implosion are so clear and self-contradictory that one is at a loss to organize them coherently. One wonders if rational discussion suits these phenomena at all. Good is mixed with bad, but standards are so variable that few people can agree on what is good or bad. Previously easy distinctions between the arts and between art and life have blurred. Ann Halprin's dancers act, John Cage's music is visual, and the USCO Group's paintings perform. The synesthesia utopians dreamed of is upon us with disarming repercussions. One need not accept Yeats' happy dread to understand him:

> Things fall apart; the center cannot hold;
> Mere anarchy is loosed upon the world.

It is not the first time.

In *Understanding Media*, Marshall McLuhan suggests that our literary, individualized culture is being tribalized. By that he means that "commitment and participation" are replacing "point of view" as the criteria for evaluating experience. He credits electric circuitry and the media flowing from it—TV, computers, stereo, telephone, telegraph, and so forth—for the "implosive" revolution which has converted the world, in Buckminster Fuller's phrase, into a "global village." McLuhan urges us to disregard the messages sent by these media; his compelling slogan is "the medium is the message." As the storing and exchange of information become major human activities, the quality and intensity of life change. The sequential organization of perceptions that is the basis for a literary view of the world yields to a multi-focused, many-faceted participation in the world. Things no longer come to us one after another, as on the printed page, the assembly line, or in logical thought. They arrive at once, helter-skelter, as a set of organically interrelated phenomena, like a traffic circle or a problem in topological mathematics. One can certainly connect McLuhan's observations with Freud and Einstein. Psychoanalysis and the General Theory of Relativity are both "in depth" grasps of experienced reality. Neither Freud nor Einstein was as interested in mapping as in exploring laws of transformation and relation. As these complicated and sophisticated ideas percolate through our culture, the result is a rejection of classical abstraction (understanding experience by reducing it to other terms) and an urge to "get with it"—to exist inside a situation.

In America, nothing has accelerated this change in context more than TV. According to McLuhan, the TV image is "cool." The tiny lines which are the picture do not provide us with all the information necessary to make figures out of the sensory material. We must participate in the image, constructing out of its many lines the contours of the picture. McLuhan argues that this high degree of participation in making the TV image involves our tactile, rather than our visual, sense: "The TV image in fostering a passion for depth involvement in every aspect of experience [. . .] is, above all, an extension of the sense of touch, which involves maximal interplay of all the senses." We don't so much "watch" TV as "do" TV. A child who receives his perceptual training in front of the video tube is one who is eager to participate in the world. As he matures, he will not make the usual distinctions between life and art, politics and poetics. The specialization of the industrial world—essentially an eighteenth and nineteenth-century world—are replaced by the generalized electric circuit. And rather than be aghast at Berkeley rebels who mess in the administration of the multiversity, or civil rights marchers who occupy private property, we should recognize that these crossovers from learning to doing and from "mine and yours" to "ours" are natural in a world in which there is less and less distinction between categories that once formed the very basis of reality. In McLuhan's words, "Perhaps it is not very contradictory that when a medium becomes a means of depth experience the old categories of 'classical' and 'popular' or of 'highbrow' and 'lowbrow' no longer obtain."

TV affects our perceptions in still another way. TV offers instant, dramatic, and illogical change. The increasingly popular idea of "turning on" refers to more than marijuana or LSD: it is an approach to living that takes its metaphorical cue from TV. The inert tube which is consciousness can be switched into any one of many channels, and these channels can be easily intermixed. And

135

consciousness can do what TV can't—play several experiences simultaneously. The classical rule "each in its own place" now reads "everything in any place."

If one can see the brutal dogs on the streets of Selma and drink Budweiser at home in the same instant, then one can go to Selma and participate personally in someone else's drama, making it one's own, while at home others are watching and drinking beer. Not only are we able to construct conceptual wholes from perceptual fragments, but we are able to move into the center of what we have made. Traditional lags and gaps are healed. Instant communication leads to rapid transportation, both internally and externally. The age-old dream of no wait between impulse and act is today's reality.

However, the freedom thus achieved is largely illusory. More body-conscious—certainly more socially aware than preceding generations—we discover, nonetheless, that the real gaps and lags are built into the human being. Each element of free activity and expression becomes, automatically, an awesome test of our ability to make use of it. A tension is quickly established between a possible and inviting mobility and a stubborn, inborn immobility. Despite TV, and every other prompt and aid, most people sit at home watching someone else's drama. But the awareness that it is possible to go to Selma, or around the corner, or deep inside oneself, is very unsettling.

I think it is from this tension between opportunity and inborn stubbornness—the unique psychic configuration of each individual—that the new expression, including pornography, emerges. A real space has opened up between what we are permitted, even encouraged, to do and what we are. The attempts to fill this space fall as much to fantasy as to real projects. Like the patient on the couch who when told by his analyst to say whatever comes into his head finds he can't say anything, we, as a society and as individuals, fall back into silence or fantasy. Instead of participating, we flee from real involvement and consume, as we go, *The Story of* O and the *Playboy* "philosophy."

Loosed by an image-happy society, a giant bulk of submerged material has surfaced. New work that could not find a commercial sponsor ten years ago is now sought by publishers, film-makers, and stage producers. And classic work long suppressed is now openly sold. We are beginning to understand the difference between masturbatory and celebratory sex; and it may not be long before phallic art becomes as openly popular in our culture as it was in Golden Age Greece. The attention given sado-masochistic work is both a compensation for the long suppression and an indication that we are far from comfortable with our new liberality.

George Steiner, in an article in *Encounter*, deplored our interest in Sade and his cohorts, both past and present. Steiner suggested a causal link between literary sadism and its horrible actuality in Nazi Germany. However, Steiner, like so many others, confuses two symptoms for a symptom and its cause. The spate of sadistic writing in pre-Hitler Germany was not a cause of the Gestapo, but an indication that such impulses were there. The Nazis translated these impulses into facts. Suppressing the literature would have had no effect on the underlying causes of both literature and Nazism. In fact, the literature probably served for a time as a safety valve. Our own pornography is to be condemned because it takes a cheap and totally athletic view of sexual experience. But one ought to look at such pornography the way Freud looked at dirty jokes:

> What these jokes whisper may be said aloud: that the wishes and desires of men have a right to make themselves acceptable alongside of exacting and ruthless morality. And in our days it has been said in forceful and stirring sentences that this morality is only a selfish regulation laid down by the few who are rich and powerful and who can satisfy their wishes at any time without any postponement. So long as the art of healing has not gone further in making our life safe and so long as social arrangements do no more to make it more enjoyable, so long will it be impossible to stifle the voice within us that rebels against the demands of morality.

The answer is not suppression, but the elimination of that "ruthless morality" which drives people to desperate satisfaction. Pornography—and I include in this category everything from dirty pictures to *The Story of O*—is not a release from inhibitions, but a function of them. Surely we should not, as we have done, outlaw these repressive mechanisms. But neither should we admire them as examples of free expression. They are nothing other than the means by which repressive consciousness keeps a restless psyche in tow. And Freud is accurate when he suggests that our consciousness is repressive because of conditioning made necessary by a social order concerned primarily with productivity. Pornography, whether open or underground, is an important weapon in the arsenal of social control. It does not, as Steiner suggests, lead to activity; its tendency is the opposite. The challenge that electric circuitry presents to this control is real. An expressive society would have need for neither pornography nor oppressive controls. Replacing them would be celebratory sexual art and expression: the phallic dances of the Greeks, the promiscuity of Elizabethan England.

The submerged material now available falls into two classes: stuff that uses words once thought obscene; works that show scenes that once were taboo. Although related, the distinction between verbal and scenic expression is a crucial index. For a long time the community's efforts were concentrated against those naughty "Anglo-Saxon" words. This nineteenth-century fight (which continues today in many backwaters) was one of propriety, of "decency" in its social sense. The images which these words conjured up were simply not to be thought, certainly not to be expressed. This was the result of a sexual segregation in which women were property to be used but not exposed to the names these uses were given by males. Once females became something other than chattel, the verbal taboos were soon to go.

But propriety and decency as understood a generation ago (the "dirty little secret" D. H. Lawrence abhorred) are no longer the major issue. We now see things in scenic terms: scope rather than point, and relation rather than incident, form our opinions. And it is the divergent attitudes toward scenic sexuality that I find most interesting. There is a hierarchy in our tolerance, and this seems to say a good deal about us and our art.

Literature is the most free, filmic representation next, and stage presentation least. One can tell everything in a novel, and the writer need have no fear about how graphic his description might be. One can suggest the same things in a film but one rarely sees anything more than sexual foreplay and a pair of naked bodies afterward. The "bold" orgasm scene in A *Stranger Knocks* was of course a fraud.

Even the twilight nudie and sex films are timid—voyeuristic but nothing more. Onstage, one dare do nothing more than kiss and caress. A seemingly strange variation is that one can buy records which appear to be accurate simulations (or realities) of the sounds of lovemaking. And the texts and rhythms of many popular songs are so obviously coital that one wonders how they get on the radio and are sold openly to pre-teens. The fact is that our sexuality is still understood as something visual. The ear is attuned only to catch the "dirty" words; any recorded sentence without them, no matter how suggestive, usually slips by.

The same visual hierarchy applies to nudity. A novelist can describe naked people with as much detail as his words can muster. In films one can show a naked female (but not all of her: the genitals are off limits). Onstage, except in specialized nightclub strip shows, nudity is taboo. Last fall I saw *Poor Bitos* at the Theatre of the Living Arts in Philadelphia. It was an excellent production. In one scene, a character had a breast exposed. The lobby talk—as one might expect—centered on that passing detail. But this same audience (including me) would go home and read *The Story of O* and *Candy* or see *Les Liaisons Dangereuses* at the movies without a second thought.

This hierarchy of tolerance seems related to both the degree and the kind of involvement expected of the reader and viewer. The reader selects his own style of reading; he can put the book down, pick it up, go fast or slow. He is always alone, in a one-to-one relationship with the author. He need tell no one how he felt, or if he felt. The reading experience is therefore the paradigm of secret pleasure; it is an organic relation to an inanimate object. That there are few taboos here is no surprise.

The movie-and-theatre-goer is part of a group. But the most important fact about this group is not its largest unit—the entire audience—but its nuclear units—the "families" of viewers. Book reviewers are sent one copy of the book; film and theatre reviewers are always given two tickets. It is assumed that the film and stage experience is one which we naturally share with a few others who are emotionally close to us. Many of these nuclear groups make up a single audience; and the relationship of performers to audience is not one-to-one—as is usually supposed—but performers to small groups to larger, inclusive group. Why don't we go to the movies and theatre as individuals? Why does it seem natural to insulate ourselves from the whole audience by means of the nuclear group?

The scenic experience is more explosive and empathetic than reading. The energies generated by a film or play, and the rhythms vibrating between performers and audience *in toto*, are counterbalanced by the restraints inherent in the nuclear group. As a whole audience we are encouraged to participate in the performance; as part of the "family" we are warned against complete participation. A compromise emerges as a rigid set of audience conventions: applause, laughter, tears, and coughs are all the physical response permitted. But in a tribal performance, the family, like the individual, is drawn into the larger group; active and total participation is not infrequent —a sanctioned release from strict authority.

In our culture we bring the family with us to the movies or theatre, and even our wildest dramas, say *Lear* and *The Balcony*, are essentially reassuring and passive as we produce them. Were we to go to the movies or theatre without depositing ourselves in the protective envelope of the family, our drama would rapidly become sexualized and orgiastic. A play like Peter Weiss' *Marat/Sade*, as it was produced by the Royal Shakespeare Company, is moving in this direction. But scenic taboos continue in the theatre (less in film) because letting go would be too dangerous: the performance which has traditionally included actors and audience would soon become, as in a tribal dance, one unified activity.

There are some reasons, too, why theatre has more taboos than film. The movie-goer has no control over the rhythm of what he sees. The projector runs on its predetermined schedule. The viewer has to adjust his perceptual rhythm to what he is seeing, and he is constantly reminded that the film is an abstraction. Even as he is engaged by the pictures, he is disengaged by the form of the film and its steady, mechanical unfolding. Film-makers turn this to their advantage, using montage, camera angle, and distance to make the perceptual "reality" of film other than the reality of life. But each effort to make the film less abstract is drawn from the abstract nature of filming: a set of machines that permit editing and dozens of other techniques. And because film art is more abstract than theatre, it is also more sexually permissive. No matter how torrid the love scene, we never feel concerned for the actor. The masterful thing about film is that the actor vanishes into the character, and the character is always (at least perceptually) a fiction, an abstraction.

The unique thing about theatre, of course, is that the actors are *there*. They never vanish into their characters. Like the Christian God who is three-in-one, every actor is two-in-one. It is this double existence that gives him his authenticity as actor. His role in our theatre is not very different from that of his primitive counterpart, who is at once dancer and god. Little overt sexuality is permitted onstage because the audience knows that what happens to the character also happens to the actor. One can understand why physical violence is feigned on stage: there are obligations to tomorrow's performance. But why not have nudity and lovemaking? It cannot simply be that human sexual response is an undependable mechanism. The Greeks, who accepted both sexuality and nudity in public life, maintained a strict decorum in their tragedies. It is that stage performance is always on the verge of tumbling from art back into life. Overt and graphic sexuality would destroy the aesthetic fabric of any performance. How then did Aristophanes manage the love pranks of *Lysistrata?* Aristophanic drama is farce and celebration in a combination that we have lost touch with. Filled with regard for the family, schooled in Renaissance humanism, we are not up to the phallic play of Aristophanes. And it is only within a framework of celebration that sexuality can be both graphic and aesthetic.

Celebratory theatre is returning to our culture in some happenings. Many of these obliterate distinctions between life and art. Once performers are no longer concerned about maintaining their double identities, and audiences accept the invitation to participate in the performance, almost anything can happen. Carolee Schneemann describes her goals in *Meat Joy* this way:

> My kinetic theatre provides for an intensification of all faculties simultaneously [. . .] a mobile, tactile event into which the eye leads the body. [. . .] I assume that senses crave sources of maximum information [. . .] *Meat Joy*, a shifting vision now, relating Artaud, McClure, and French Butcher Shops [. . .] acting and viewing space

interchanged. I see several girls whose gestures develop from a tactile, bodily relationship to individual men and to a mass of meat slices.

Meat Joy is an orgiastic happening linking butcher's beef and women with the phallic meat. Nude or nearly nude bodies are painted, intertwined, and frolicked with. At once intimate and impersonal, it typifies that strange combination of participation and irony that marks much of the new theatre. In some happenings it is difficult to say whether one is attending a performance or a party. Even in more formal works, orgiastic and celebratory material is included within disciplined frameworks, giving the effect of a performance mosaic, some parts of which are expansive and inclusive while others resemble traditional theatre.

Contemporary theatre, in fact, has been affected by the new expression. Jack Gelber's *The Connection*, Kenneth H. Brown's *The Brig*, and Megan Terry's *Viet Rock* are probably the three most important new American plays of the last ten years. (I would add Robert Lowell's *Benito Cereno* to that list—and Lowell's theme, if not his style, is related to my discussion.) Maintaining the scenic taboos, these three plays nevertheless engulf our consciousness, blurring the usual distinctions between performance and reality, audience and stage. Far from being Pirandellian exercises, these plays move in the opposite direction. Pirandello wished to pose insoluble problems: he was the intellectual par excellence. Gelber, Brown, and Terry work rather to make their solutions so unavoidable that they fold the audience into the play. Thus, junk is everywhere, white lines are for crossing, and this ruthless war is our open-eyed choice. The productions of *The Connection*, *The Brig*, and *Viet Rock*—the first two plays done by the Living Theatre, and the last by the Open Theatre, the successor to the Living Theatre in New York—cannot be separated from the plays: the act of writing is so joined to the act of doing that the two become one. The "writer" no longer exists in such a scheme; the craft of making a play becomes a participatory game which involves all the artists and technicians of the theatre and the audience.

Surely happenings, and some of off-Broadway theatre, are not art if judged by traditional criteria. But changes in form elicit changes in criteria. The strategies of Berkeley students and black marchers are not traditional modes of academic behavior or political maneuver in the United States. But the Free Speech Movement, the black freedom movement, and new directions in the performing arts are related. They are all participating forms which value involvement more than "style." This demand for "getting with it" links all the varieties of the new expression.

In *Marat/Sade*, the Marquis speaks of the "revolution of the flesh," which, he says, "will make all your other revolutions seem like prison mutinies." This atavistic, cohesive, and participatory revolution is the new expression. The upheaval has barely begun, and if it ever truly gets moving, we may wish we were safe with Sade in his asylum. The new expression seems pornographic and obscene only when it threatens our sexual taboos. That this is frequent is an index of how much both old and new have invested in sexuality. The least interesting part of the new expression is its literature. At best, publication of new, sexy titles and reissuing of classics are efforts to keep up with change. But Maurice Girodias is hardly Dionysus, and the boldest text is tame in the World of Murray the K. The new expression is a public event, a dramatic shift in scene and context. That is what makes it so disquieting. A society which has been indoors, repressive, and individually protestant is becoming outdoors, expressive, and tribally catholic. And we are never quite certain whether the noise we hear is authentic or merely one more role added to our endless repertory. When authentic, the new expression rejects the sequential logic of print for the simultaneous tumult of experience. We are beginning to see that to "make love, not war" is to go to war against most of what our culture asks of us. The decision in that conflict is not yet clear.

In the woods, a girl hangs upside down from a tree. She is one of five persons dangling from ropes at various spots in the rural New Jersey woodland. From distant places in the damp glen, other persons—searchers—begin calling the names of the five who are hanging. When a name is called, the dangling person who is addressed answers, "Here." Homing in on the sounds, the searchers locate each upside-down caller and quickly cut or rip away his or her clothing.

This is the last part of Allan Kaprow's two-day happening, *Calling*. Kaprow's piece is an example of the "new theatre"—happenings, activities, events, and so on. This new theatre offers us an aesthetic experience for which we have no corresponding critical vocabulary. There is a simple reason why. The new theatre is a genealogical hybrid. Its sources lie in theatre, painting, sculpture, dance, and music. But it is not like opera (another hybrid) or like any of its "parent" arts. Because it is unlike traditional theatre, painting, sculpture, dance, and music, the familiar locutions of these arts cannot either describe what's going on or provide criteria with which to evaluate it. Thus criticism of the new theatre has been mostly opinionated reaction—and angry reaction at that.[1]

---

[1] *By now (1968) an extensive literature on happenings exists, and the impact of the form on the traditional arts is clear. This impact has not been re-*

The difficulty is compounded because the new theatre is not literary and it therefore resists literary summary or analysis. For this reason, I shall avoid detailed descriptions of particular works. I want, instead, to outline salient structural features of the new theatre and to distinguish it clearly from the traditional theatre.

The most efficient way of seeing the differences between the traditional and new theatres is to list them.

TRADITIONAL	NEW
plot	images/events
action	activity
resolution	open-ended
roles	tasks
themes/thesis	no pre-set meaning
stage distinct from house	one area for all
script	scenario or free form
flow	compartments
single focus	multi-focus
audience watches	audience participates, sometimes does not exist
product	process

Obviously not all happenings will contain everything listed under "new," nor will all traditional performances contain everything listed under "traditional." The lists are polar; actual performances tend in one direction or the other.

The traditional theatre works from an organic system of correlations concerning character, story, locale. It involves a series of understandable transformations—changes in outlook and situation —enacted within a contained space which is an accurate metaphor of the conceptual limitations which give traditional theatre its "meaning." Michael Kirby calls such parameters—usually well understood by the audience—the "information structure."[2]

---

stricted to the traditional arts, however. The discothèque, several films, and much of popular music have reacted positively to happenings (or, as Dick Higgins calls it, "intermedia"). There is even one set of university courses, at New York University, specifically addressed to the history, theory, and practice of intermedia. In revising the essay I wrote in 1966, I realized that things have moved rapidly in the two intervening years. However, I think some of the categorical qualities I outlined then are still valid.

[2] Kirby's distinction between performances with information structures

Traditional theatre has an information structure because it is "organic"—an attempt to recapitulate in symbolic terms the actual rhythms and patterns of living. As Susanne K. Langer says:

> Like the distribution of figures on a chessboard, the combination of characters makes a strategic pattern. In actual life we usually recognize a distinct situation only when it has reached, or nearly reached, a crisis; but in the theatre we see the whole setup of human relationships and conflicting interests long before any abnormal event has occurred that would, in actual life, have brought it into focus. [. . .] in the theatre we perceive an ominous situation and see that some far-reaching action must grow out of it. This creates the peculiar tension between the given present and its yet unrealized consequent, "form in suspense," the essential dramatic illusion. [. . .] the sense of past and future as parts of one continuum, and therefore of life as a single reality.[3]

It is precisely this sense of past and future—the "destiny" which typifies drama—that is missing from the new theatre. There the referents to everyday life are purely functions of sounds, textures, and images. No organic development is necessarily suggested. Of course, in the literal sense, no art can be "unlifelike." But the "life of the drama" is one tied closely to our experience as individuals, our sense of "life-career," of an ongoing, sensible, completable journey. On the fringes of this consciousness we perceive irrationalities, we face encounters with others and our environment that are never integrated into our "career patterns," that don't seem to be part of our "destiny." The new theatre plays on these.

The traditional theatre follows a clear line. The new theatre is tangential. It combines associative variations on visual-aural themes, chance permutations, games, and trips (both everyday and psychedelic).

The new theatre is rooted in two seemingly unrelated interests:

---

and matrices (traditional theatre) and those without these limitations (intermedia) is a clear theoretic basis from which to analyze the new theatre. See Kirby's introduction to his Happenings (New York: E. P. Dutton, 1966) and his essay, "The New Theatre," TDR, X, No. 2, 23–43.

[3] Susanne K. Langer, Feeling and Form (New York: Charles Scribner's Sons, 1953), p. 311.

(1) an attempt to bring into celebratory focus the full message-complexity of a downtown street and (2) a playing with modes of perception. John Cage wants to hear a fly buzz. Allan Kaprow exhibits human figures wrapped in tin foil and muslin in Grand Central Terminal. Claes Oldenburg floats persons, balloons, tires, and other colorful debris in a midtown New York pool. Performances are controlled by chance techniques, relieving everyone of the burden of choosing when to do something. (Of course, much scientific experimentation is carried on with the same methodology: a controlled environment in which the "natural object" under study reacts in its "own way.") Shows are often unrepeated and unrepeatable; there have been few runs. Frequently human beings are treated as objects rather than persons, and objects just as frequently take on unexpected life.

In some instances, audience and performer have merged—who is what in a theatre game or street activity? When audiences exist, they are usually left to themselves to "put the thing together" or "make something out of" what's happened. One of the major tasks of traditional theatre is to make the performance meaningful, somehow to relate all the images and actions so that every spectator has a clear sense of what has happened and why. In the new theatre, many spectators cannot see or hear everything that's going on; and if they did they would be hard-pressed to know with any certainty why they have seen what they have seen. The individual spectator is left on his own. The meaning he gets from a performance—if it is clear at all—is his own. No one else may agree with him.

Naturally we are unused to such "chaos." Our society is accustomed to packaging—and to being told before we buy what's under the hood or inside the wrapper. We may often be deceived, but at least we are "told." The fact that we can be so frequently and massively deceived is an index of our desire to be "informed," however incorrectly. We wish to see on the outside what's going on inside. The new theatre runs against this deep cultural tendency—is, in fact, a direct reaction against it. The spectator is not told. Some pieces appear to be put-ons—like Cage's silence—in which we do not get what we expect. But Cage is giving us with his four minutes of silence more than nothing. He is asking us to listen to "silence" with the same care—more care—that we listen to the "noise" of musical instruments. Cage's piece is the coughing, the restlessness, the very heartbeats and breathing rhythms of the audience. Such performances are perceptual educations. They make us aware of our environment—both outer and inner—in new ways.

Perhaps the key distinction between the traditional and new theatres—and one at the very heart of both—is that between playing roles and doing tasks. In playing a role the actor "becomes" a human being other than himself. However, a performer doing a "task" is not playing anyone. He is simply doing something. He need not understand why he is doing it or ask whether the circumstances are such that in everyday life he would be doing what he is doing. He just does it. Because the author of the happening tells him to do it. Or he is given free time and told to do anything he pleases within the space of that free time.

One of the best examples of task-performing is Anne Halprin's *Esposizione*. A huge net was hung from the top of the proscenium of the Venice Opera House and tied to the front of the orchestra pit. During the forty minutes of the dance, the performers were asked to carry heavy burdens of various kinds up the net. They ran from the places where their burdens were stacked, climbed the net, deposited what they brought, climbed back down, got more things, and climbed again. From a traditional viewpoint *Esposizione* was not organic—it "meant" nothing, it wasn't planned so that Halprin or anyone else would know exactly who would be climbing the net when. But from another point of view it was an exceptionally harmonious dance. Done with the urgency the task demanded, the trained bodies of Halprin's troupe coped with a difficult physical situation, one which changed in its particulars from night to night but which necessarily maintained the same overall effect. The organic nature of the dance came from the performers' bodies—the similarity of one human being to another and the ineluctable unity which comes from a group doing roughly the same thing together.

Many happenings are structured the same way. The performers simply do something. Their job is not to build roles or circumstances in which what they are doing is "justified." Motives do not enter in as conscious determinants. The task is everything—whether it is climbing a net, walking from the shallow end of a pool to the deep end, peeling off layers of clothes, or whatever.

The activities are not always without ceremonial meaning. Many of Kaprow's pieces have deep metaphorical evocations—for example, his *Overtime* (1968):

Sundown. (flashlights) 200 straight feet of snow-fence erected in woods. Groundline drawn with powdered chalk. Posted with red flare and marked number 1.

Fence moved next 200 feet, maintaining direction. Groundline drawn. Flare and marker number 2.

Fence moved next 200 feet. Groundline. Flare. Marker 3. (portable radios, food deliveries.)

Process repeated every 200 feet for a mile. Lighted flares maintained along entire line throughout night. Fence removed. Line and markers remaining. Flares out. Sunup.

The announcement for this happening contained the scenario and the following sentence: "Those interested in participating should attend a talk given by Mr. Kaprow at the Main Building Auditorium, The State University of New York at New Paltz, on April 16th, 1968, at 8 P.M." The event is simple enough so that anyone interested can participate. It is ceremonial, ritual-like. It consists of a set of tasks which taken together make an impressive image and an all-night activity. The performance is not designed for an audience. Like Cage's music of silence, Kaprow's happening works on the consciousness of the participants.

Many new theatre pieces are similarly "mysterious." They aim at evoking responses within the audience or participants. These responses are not predictable beforehand. They range from laughter to deep meditation.

Tasks rather than roles, the dissolution of the audience-spectator dichotomy, and a tendency toward a communal, ritualized ceremony—all these diminish the importance of the actor. In the traditional theatre the actor is the major piece of equipment. He is isolated both from the audience and from supportive technology. If there is no such technology—lights, costumes, stage itself—the audience feels cheated. If there is too much, the actor is over-whelmed. But because the new theatre is not actor-centered, there is no minimal or maximal level of technological involvement. Some pieces are entirely technological—forms of electronic music and light shows. Others, like Kaprow's, use very few machines. The partici-pating spectator-performer may be at the center of a piece. Or per-formers may be used as mass, volume, color, and the receptors of images from film, paints, or translucent materials. The scenic reali-ties of the new theatre are absolutely flexible. Some pieces are staged, others are done outdoors in the woods, on highways, or in fields. Some take just a few minutes, others extend over months and may occur simultaneously in diverse locations.

With such extraordinarily variable frameworks, where is the unity? What ties Kaprow's aesthetics to Cage's? This is the major structural question facing us. And it can be answered only by iden-tifying the underlying patterns of all the work that has been called happenings, events, intermedia, theatre of mixed means, and so on. The diversity of names that the new theatre goes by is itself an index of the difficulty of the aesthetic question. If the links between all the elements and examples of the new work were obvious, a single term would have emerged to identify them all.

We can specify three kinds of new theatre. These overlap, are often combined, but are distinct. The first is the technological, essentially electronic event. Its most sophisticated forms include electronic music in an environmental setting—for example, the co-operative work between composer Morton Subotnick and environ-mentalist Anthony Martin. More popular examples of the elec-tronic event are the discothèques, in which the sound and sight environment is combined with the indeterminate behavior of the dancers to form the whole show. Frequently, the technological event is lacking "human intentionality." Cage describes his 1965 concert at Brandeis University:

The performance simply consisted of putting the [90] loops [of pre-recorded] tape on the various [13] machines and taking them off. Doing this, a complex stage situation developed because we had to set up stands around which the tapes would go, and these things were overlapping. The number of loops made it fairly certain that no intention was involved in putting on one rather than another loop. The number of people and the number of machines also created a situation somewhat free of intention.[4]

It would be mathematically easy to calculate the number of permutations Cage's concert permitted. It would be an astronomical sum. The lack of intentionality would be directly proportional to the number of permutations possible measured against the number of people running the machines and the amount of time allotted for the concert. Such calculations would bear out Cage's assertion. Given the framework he set up, intentionality would be almost nil.

The second kind of new theatre also lacks intentionality, but for different reasons. This kind has been most firmly embedded in the public consciousness: the free-for-all happening, the party gone wild. Ken Dewey and Carolee Schneemann have both done a number of these (though they have also done more "structured" events too). The free-for-all happening is roughly sketched in by its author. A group of people is assembled, told to do something; another group is invited to watch and, if they feel like it, participate. The large outlines of the event are known in advance, but the happening may change shape and direction as it proceeds. The planned parts usually consist of simple tasks—such as "You paint her blue over here" and "At ten after nine you ride the motorcycle slowly around the space." Disparate images and activities are gathered in one place for a specified (and sometimes unspecified) duration. What happens, happens.

If the images selected by the author of the happening are unified, this second kind of new theatre can take on elements of celebration or orgy. But it is not an authentic celebration or orgy—it is a model in which the author serves as the "generating society" and the participants as the individuals within that society. Such happenings are designed to evoke and articulate responses within the spectators urging them to become participants—to live out in any way they can the fantasies which the "scene" brings to their awareness.

---

[4] *Michael Kirby and Richard Schechner, "An Interview with John Cage,"* TDR, X, No. 2, 57.

The third kind of new theatre is, in many ways, a combination of the first two. It is not so "cold" as Cage's impersonal concerts or so uncontrolled as a free-for-all happening. This third kind of new theatre may best be described as a "ceremony." Its chief exponents are Kaprow, Kirby, and Robert Whitman. In Kaprow's case, there usually is no audience. The participants are given a simple set of instructions which they are not to improvise on but simply do. Earlier in this essay I cited one of Kaprow's recent happenings of this type. Here is another, called *Arrivals:*

> unused airstrip
> tarring cracks in airstrip
> painting guidelines on airstrip
> cutting grass at airstrip's edge
> placing mirrors on airstrip
> watching for reflections of planes

This was "performed" in April 1968 at Nassau Community College, New York. It, like much of Kaprow's work, has the quality of a secular ritual.[5]

Kirby's work is similar to Kaprow's, except that Kirby almost always has both participants and spectators. Kirby usually works indoors, in a small space, and develops a ritualistic relationship to that space. His *Room 706* combines dialogue (not written, but prerecorded from conversations and played back during the performance) and a ceremony-like description and scenic "investigation" of Room 706 at St. Francis College in Brooklyn, where Kirby teaches.[6] Whitman uses film in many of his pieces and delights in what has become a cliché of happenings: projecting images on persons. In *Prune Flat* (1965) a girl stood on stage and her own life-sized color film image was projected onto her. The film showed her getting undressed, as she made the motions of disrobing while, of course, actually taking off nothing. The sequence ended with the girl

---

[5] For a detailed discussion of Kaprow's work, see my interview with him, "Extensions in Time and Space," TDR, XII, No. 3, 153–159.

[6] See Michael Kirby, "Room 706," TDR, XII, No. 3, 141–147.

—still fully dressed—acting as a screen for her own nude body.[7]

All three kinds of new theatre—the technological, the free-for-all, and the ceremonial—share two elements: autonomy and revitalization. I take these as the unifying factors of the new theatre. The kind of autonomy I am speaking of is hard to define. It seems that new theatre goes out of its way to separate images from their normal matrices. We are asked not simply to look at things from a new perspective, but to disengage what is being shown us from the "information structure" that usually makes images meaningful. Where traditional theatre makes connections, new theatre suggests points where disconnections are possible. Images and events are allowed to "be themselves."

This would be the familiar activity of abstraction (or, if one wishes to see it in a negative social framework, reification) were it not for the immediate intercession of the second process, revitalization. The disconnection is made so that the isolated event or image can be seen in itself, and seen as revitalized. Deadened habits, routine images, unused sensibilities, and even places (Kaprow's highways and supermarkets) are reinfused with meaning. The new theatre has a celebratory function. It is not unlike the process familiar to social anthropologists called "nativistic movements."

In a legitimate nativistic movement, a society or social group which feels threatened resorts to archaic patterns and ceremonies in an attempt to recapture the old days and the old ways. Some "revivals" in evangelic Protestantism and some of the more demagogic right-wing political activity in America are clear examples of nativistic movements. Underlying all nativistic movements is the process which says: things aren't what they used to be, let's get back to when things were better—to do this we must create a ceremony (a kind of initiation rite in reverse). These ceremonies are often frenzied. The elements of infantilism and celebration are always present in nativistic movements. The process simplifies complex situations, reducing difficult circumstances into manageable clichés.

It would be incorrect to call the new theatre a nativistic move-

---

[7] *Kirby discusses Whitman's work in detail and relates it to other new theatre uses of film in "The Uses of Film in the New Theatre," TDR, XI, No. 1, 49–61.*

ment. But clearly it shares some of the characteristics. And the infantile, celebratory myth which underlies the new theatre is one which theoreticians of nativistic movements would understand: social reconstruction through sensory awakening. The project is appealing because it is so simple. If people would *see* again, *feel* again —not as they did in the historical past, but as each one of us did as a child—then "things would get better." It is at this infantile, ecstatic, and fantasy level that the new theatre, the hippies before political activation, and the "intellectuals" who sponsor such things as California's Esalen Institute join forces.

But the new theatre is better than the Esalen Institute. Its revitalization process is not without subtlety, irony, complexity, and humor (a quality which most nativistic movements lack in the extreme). And the process of the new theatre is not just an alternation between autonomy and revitalization. Along with revitalization, there is the possibility of new connections: the participant and spectator are given the chance to make metaphors. On the airstrip near Nassau Community College, some students will see new connections between mass transportation, grass, airstrips, mirrors. These connections are not predictable. The ability to make them, and the new theatre's urgency in creating situations in which they can be made, is at the heart of Cage's assertion that he does not want to turn people on to art but into artists. The essential revitalization that much of the new theatre aims for is one which awakens in many individuals their capacity to make metaphors—to see relationships that were either hidden or not there before.

In other words, the difference between a nativistic movement and the new theatre is the special awareness of the artist. This awareness—as it is manifest in the best work of Cage, Kaprow, Kirby, and others—works against a regressive infantilism that washes away all distinctions between good and bad art, past and present, childhood gratification and adult perception. The danger is there, and it should not be underestimated. But no matter how delicate the balance is between revitalization and fantasy, control and freedom, reflection and participation, complexity and simplification—the balance can be maintained. In maintaining it, the new theatre may attain its advertised significance.

Six Axioms for
Environmental Theatre

1968

1. THE THEATRICAL EVENT IS A SET OF RELATED TRANSACTIONS

The theatrical event includes audience, performers, text (in most cases), sensory stimuli, architectural enclosure (or lack of it), production equipment, technicians, and house personnel (when used). It ranges from nonmatrixed performance[1] to highly formalized traditional theatre: from chance events and intermedia to "the production of plays." A continuum of theatrical events blends one form into the next:

"Impure; life"   "Pure; art"

public events ⟷ intermedia ⟷ environmental ⟷ traditional
demonstrations happenings   theatre   theatre

All along this continuum there are overlaps; and within it—say between a traditional production of *Hamlet* and the March on the Pentagon or Allan Kaprow's *Self-Service*[2]—there are contradictions.

---

[1] *Michael Kirby discusses the distinctions between nonmatrixed and matrixed performances in "The New Theatre,"* TDR, X, No. 2, 23–43.
[2] *See* TDR, XII, No. 3, 160–164.

The new aesthetics is built on a system of interaction and transformation, on the ability of coherent wholes to include contradictory parts; in the words of New York city planner Richard Weinstein, "competing independent systems within the same aesthetic frame." Kaprow might even take a more radical position, doing away altogether with the frame; or accepting a variety of frames, depending upon the perspective of the spectator and performer. Surely the frames may change during a single performance, transforming an event into something quite unlike what it started out to be. The end of *Iphigenia Transformed* at Minneapolis' Firehouse Theatre (1966) had Euripides' *dea ex machina* lowered onto the stage, bringing with her four cases of beer. The marriage ceremony that concludes *Iphigenia at Aulis* was performed—followed by a celebration that included the entire audience, a party that lasted for several hours.

The theatrical event is a complex social interweave, a network of expectations and obligations.[3] The exchange of stimuli—either sensory or ideational or both—is the root of theatre. What it is that separates theatre from more ordinary exchanges—say a simple conversation or a party—is difficult to pinpoint structurally. One might say that theatre is more regulated, following a script or a scenario; that it has been rehearsed. Kirby would probably argue that theatre only presents the self in a more defined way than usual social encounters. Grotowski has said that the theatre is a meeting place between a traditional text and a troupe of performers:

> I didn't do Wyspianski's *Akropolis*, I met it. [. . .] One structures the montage so that this confrontation can take place. We eliminate those parts of the text which have no importance for us, those parts with which we can neither agree nor disagree. [. . .] We did not want to write a new play, we wished to confront ourselves.[4]

Indeed, confrontation is what makes current American political activity theatrical. To meet Bull Connor's dogs in Birmingham or

---

[3] *Erving Goffman—a sociologist who looks at behavior from a theatrical point of view—has begun the discussion of expectation-obligation networks in two books:* Encounters *(Indianapolis: Bobbs-Merrill, 1961) and* Behavior in Public Places *(Glencoe: The Free Press, 1963).*

[4] *"Interview with Grotowski,"* TDR, *XIII, No. 1, 44.*

LBJ's troops at the Pentagon is more than a showdown in the Wild West tradition. In the movies, everything would be settled by the showdown. In our politics, contrasts are heightened, nothing resolved. A long series of confrontations are necessary to promote change. The streets of Birmingham and the steps of the Pentagon are visible boundaries, special places of special turbulence, where sharply opposed styles are acted out by both sides; Grotowski's personal confrontation is converted into a social confrontation. Out of such situations, slowly and unevenly, guerrilla, street, and environmental theatre emerge, just as out of the confrontation between medieval ceremony and Renaissance tumult emerged the Elizabethan theatre.

John Cage has offered a most inclusive definition of theatre:

> I would simply say that theatre is something which engages both the eye and the ear. The two public senses are seeing and hearing; the senses of taste, touch, and odor are more proper to intimate, nonpublic, situations. The reason I want to make my definition of theatre that simple is so one could view everyday life itself as theatre. [. . .] I think of theatre as an occasion involving any number of people, but not just one.[5]

I think that Cage's exclusion of taste, touch, and odor is unnecessarily restrictive. In the New Orleans Group's production of *Victims of Duty* (1967) all three "private" senses were important parts of the performance. During a seduction scene perfume was released in the room; frequently the performers touched the audience, communicating to them with hand and body; at the very end of the show, chunks of bread were forcefully administered to the audience by the performers, expanding the final gesture of Ionesco's script.

In situations where descriptive definitions are so open as to be inoperative as criteria for exclusion, one must seek *relational* definitions. Goffman's assertions regarding social organization go right to the heart of the theatrical event:

> [. . .] any [. . .] element of social life [. . .] exhibits sanctioned orderliness arising from obligations fulfilled and expectations realized.[6]

---

[5] "*An Interview with John Cage,*" TDR, X, No. 2, 50–51.
[6] Encounters, op. cit., *p. 19.*

> Briefly, a social order may be defined as the consequence of any set of moral norms [rules] that regulates the way in which persons pursue objectives.[7]

The nature of the expectation-obligation network and the specific set of applicable rules vary widely depending upon the particular performance. The difference between a relational and a descriptive definition is that the second is fixed while the first is self-generating and flexible. Taking a relational viewpoint makes it possible to understand theatre as something more inclusive than literature, acting, and directing. We can integrate into a single, working aesthetic such seemingly disparate events as Kaprow's *Self-Service* and Tyrone Guthrie's *Oresteia*.

Returning to the continuum, at the left end are loosely organized street events—the October 21 March on the Pentagon, activities of the Amsterdam and New York Provos[8]—near the end of the continuum are Kaprow's kinds of happenings (such as *Calling*[9] and those included in *Some Recent Happenings*[10]). In the center of the continuum are highly organized intermedia events—some of Kirby's and Robert Whitman's work, for example—and "conventional" environmental theatre productions. At the far right of the continuum is the traditional theatre. Textual analysis is possible only from the middle of the continuum to the right end; performance analysis is possible along the entire range.

What are the related transactions which comprise the theatrical event?

---

[7] Behavior in Public Places, op. cit., *p.* 8.

[8] A *Provo event is described by John Kifner in* The New York Times *of August 25, 1967. "Dollar bills thrown by a band of hippies fluttered down on the floor of the New York Stock Exchange yesterday, disrupting the normal hectic trading pace. Stockbrokers, clerks, and runners turned and stared at the visitors' gallery. [. . .] Some clerks ran to pick up the bills. [. . .] James Fourrat, who led the demonstration along with Abbie Hoffman, explained in a hushed voice: 'It's the death of money.' To forestall any repetition, the officers of the Exchange enclosed the visitors' gallery in bullet-proof glass."*

[9] *See* TDR, X, No. 2, 202–211.

[10] Great Bear Pamphlet 7 (*New York: Something Else Press, 1966*). *Something Else Press has published many books and pamphlets about intermedia; a great proportion of these includes scenarios and theoretical writings by artists working in intermedia.*

Among performers.
Among members of the audience.
Between performers and audience.

These are the three primary transactions. The first begins during rehearsal and continues through all performances. In Stanislavski-oriented training the heaviest emphasis is given to these transactions; they are, in fact, identified with "the play," and the theory is that if the interaction among the performers is perfected (even to the exclusion of the audience from the performers' attention) the production of the play will be artistically successful. There are many examples showing that this theory is incomplete. It is simply not enough for the performers to work well together. And where that is all they do, the art is one in which the audience merely watches, "visitors to the Prozorov household," as Stanislavski put it.[11] The performer-to-performer transaction is essential, but it is not exclusive; functioning alone, it is not enough.

The second transaction—among members of the audience—is usually overlooked. The decorum of theatre-going is such that the audience has and keeps strict rules of behavior. They do not leave their seats, they arrive more or less on time, they leave during intermission or when the show is over, they display approval or disapproval within well-regulated patterns of applause, silence, laughter, tears, and so on. In some intermedia and environmental theatre, the audience is invited to participate. In events on the far left of the performance continuum, it is difficult to distinguish audience from performers. A street demonstration or sit-in is made up of shifting groups of performers and spectators; and in confrontations between demonstrators and police both groups play both roles alternately and, frequently, simultaneously. A particularly rich example of this occurred during the March on Washington. The demonstrators had broken through the military lines and were sitting-in on the Pentagon parking lot. Those in the front lines sat against the row of troops, and frequent small actions—nudging,

---

[11] For a cogent criticism of this assertion—namely, that an audience at a traditional theatre performance is passive—see Donald M. Kaplan, "Theatre Architecture: A Derivation of the Primal Cavity," TDR, XII, No. 3, 105–116.

exchange of conversation—turned these front lines into focal points. Every half-hour or so, both the front-line troops and the demonstrators were rotated. Demonstrators who were watching the action suddenly became part of it; the same for the troops. Elements of the Pentagon leadership stood on the steps in front of the main entrance, watching the procedure. For someone at home, the entire confrontation was a performance, and everyone—from McNamara at his window to the ad-hoc demonstration leaders with their bullhorns—was acting according to role.

Very little hard work has been done in researching the behavior of audiences and the possible exchange of roles between audience and performers. Unlike the performers, the spectators attend theatre unrehearsed; they bring to the theatre a decorum that has been learned elsewhere but which is nevertheless scrupulously applied here. Usually the audience is an impromptu group, meeting at the place of the performance and never meeting as a defined group again. Thus unprepared, they are difficult to mobilize and, once mobilized, even more difficult to control.

The third primary transaction—between performers and audience—is a traditional one. An action onstage evokes an empathic reaction in the audience which is not an imitation but a harmonic variation.[12] Thus, sadness onstage may evoke tears in the audience or put into play personal associations which, on the surface, seem unrelated to sadness. Conversely, as any performer will eagerly testify, a "good" audience will make for a different quality of performance than a "bad" audience. Good and bad are sliding terms, depending upon the nature of the performance. An active, noisy audience is good for farce but bad for serious plays. The "best" audience is one in which harmonic evocations are present up to, but not beyond, the point where the performers become distracted. The traditional theatre barely explores a part of the full range of audience-performer interaction.

---

[12] *Not only is audience behavior well regulated, but newspaper critics help write the scripts: after reading a review, an audience member frequently knows what he is going to see and how he should respond. His role in the total event is made clear beforehand.*

As well as the three primary interactions there are four secondary ones.

Among production elements.
Between production elements and performers.
Between production elements and audience.
Between the total production and the space in which it takes place.

These are secondary now. They may become primary in a few years. Production elements have been traditionally understood as scenery, costume, lighting, sound, make-up, and so on. With the full-scale use of electronics—film, TV, taped sound, projected still images, etc.—the production elements need no longer "support" a performance. At certain times these elements are more important than the performers. The Polyvision and the Diapolyecran rooms at the Czech Pavilion at Expo 67 introduced new kinds of film and still-image environments that can serve both as background for performers and as independent performing elements.[13]

Briefly, the Polyvision was the total conversion of a medium-size, rather high room into a film and slide environment. Mirrors, moving cubes and prisms, projections both from outside the space and from within the cubes, images which seem to move through space as well as cover the walls, ceilings, and floors all built the feeling of a full space of great flexibility. The 9½-minute presentation used 11 film projectors, 28 slide-projectors, and a 10-track computer tape for programming. The material itself was banal—an account of Czech industry; but, of course, more "artistic" or "meaningful" material could be used in the system. No live performers participated.

The Diapolyecran was not an environment, strictly speaking. It was restricted to one wall and the audience sat on the floor or stood watching the 14½-minute show. Only slide projectors were used. According to the "Brief Description":

---

13 *A complete outline of these techniques can be found in the pamphlet, "Brief Description of the Technical Equipment of the Czechoslovak Pavilion at the Expo 67 World Exhibition," by Jaroslav Frič. One can obtain the pamphlet by writing to Výstavnictví, N.C., Ovocný trh 19, Prague 1, Czechoslovakia. Frič is chief of research and engineering for the Prague Scenic Institute. Both the Polyvision and the Diapolyecran were developed from ideas of Josef Svoboda. Some of Svoboda's work can be seen in TDR, XI, No. 1, 141–149.*

> The Diapolyecran is technical equipment which enables a simulta-
> neous projection of slides on a mosaic projection screen consisting
> of 112 projection surfaces. The surfaces are projected on from be-
> hind and they may be shifted singly, in groups, or all at once. This
> enables one to obtain with still images pictures of motion, and the
> picture groups thus obtained are best characterized as "mosaic
> projection."

Each of 112 slide projectors was mounted on a steel frame that had
three positions: back, middle, forward. The images could be thrust
out toward the audience or moved back from it. The mosaic was
achieved by complex programming—there were 5,300,000 bits of
information memorized on tape; 19,600 impulses were emitted per
second.

The theatre, which has restricted its electronic research to so-
phisticating lighting control (still using old-fashioned fresnel and
ellipsoidal instruments), has not begun to tap the resources suggested by the Czechs. But the key to making technical elements part
of the creative performance is not simply to apply electronics research. The technicians themselves must become an active part of
the performance. This does not necessarily entail the use of more
sophisticated equipment, but rather the more sophisticated use of
the human beings who run whatever equipment is available. The
technicians' role is not limited to perfecting during rehearsal the use
of their machines. During performance itself the technicians should
participate, improvising and modulating the uses of their equipment
from night to night, just as the performers themselves modulate
their roles. Here the experience of discothèques is very instructive.
The rhythm and content of light-shows is modulated to accompany
and sometimes dominate the activity of the musicians and the
spectator-dancers. During many intermedia performances, the technicians are free to choose where they will project images, how they
will organize sound contexts. There is nothing sacred about "setting"
technical elements. If human performance is variable (as it most
certainly is), then a unified effect—if one is looking for that—will be
better assured by a nightly variation of technical means.

Thus possibilities exist for "performing technicians" whose

"language" is the filmstrip or electronic sound and whose range of action includes significant variations in where and what is to be done. The same goes for other technical elements. Traditional separation between performers and technicians is eroding as new equipment encourages either the complete programming of all material (as at the Czech Pavilion) or the nearly total flexibility of bits that can be organized on the spot, during the performance. The "performing group" is expanding so that it includes technicians as well as actors.

Once this is granted, the creative technician will demand fuller participation in performances; and at times during a performance the actor will support the technician, whose activated equipment will be "center stage." A wide-ranging mix is made possible in which the complexity of images and sounds (with or without the participation of "unarmed" performers) is endless. (An interesting extension of this idea happened during the New Orleans Group's presentation of *Victims of Duty*. There, at several points, the performers operated slide machines and sound sources. At these moments the actors were both technicians and role-playing performers; they modulated the technical environment in which they were performing.)

To achieve this mix of technical and live performers, nothing less than the whole space is needed. Bifurcation of space, in which one territory is meted out to the audience and the other to the performers, is inadequate. The final exchange between performers and audience is the exchange of space, the use of audience as scene-makers as well as scene-watchers. This will not result in chaos: rules are not done away with, they are simply changed.

2. ALL THE SPACE IS USED FOR PERFORMANCE; ALL THE SPACE IS USED FOR AUDIENCE

Perhaps the one convention that has endured from Greek times to the present is that a "special place" is marked off within the theatre for the performance. Even the medieval theatre, which moved from place to place on wagons, saw to it that the performers stayed on the wagons and the spectators in the streets. Most of the classical Eastern theatre agrees with the West in this convention. And even simple village folk-plays are acted out in marked-off areas, established for the performance and removed when it is over.

To find instances of the constant exchange of space between performers and spectators we must search among ethnographic reports of nonliterate ritual. There, two circumstances hold our attention. First, the performing group is often the entire population of a village; or, if it is just the adult males, females and children are frequently not permitted to watch. Secondly, these performances are rarely isolated "shows." We understand now that nonliterate ritual theatre is entertainment, and accepted as such by those doing it; but, at the same time, it is something more: an integral part of community life, part of years-long cycle plays which, like the Hevehe cycle of the Orokolo, recapitulate the life experience of each individual.[14]

During these performances the village, or a place near it, is co-opted for the performance. But the performance does not stand still; it ranges over a loosely defined territory. If there are spectators, they follow the performance, yielding to it when it approaches, pressing in on it when it recedes. The Balinese dance filmed by Margaret Mead and Gregory Bateson (1938) shows this spatial give and take, as well as the full use of an ill-defined space. The dancers are highly organized. But they do not feel called on to stay in one spot. They chase the "witch" (Dr. Mead's unfortunate term for the villain of the dance) and are chased by him; they move in and out of the temple and all across the village square. The space of the performance is organically defined by the action. Unlike our theatre, where

---

[14] *The Hevehe cycle takes from six to twenty years. F. E. Williams, who has written an excellent account of it, believes that the cycle has been abbreviated since the advent of Western culture in the Papuan Gulf. It seems to me that the cycle is meant to incorporate the life-span of the Orokolo male. During his life he plays, literally, many roles, each of them relevant ritually, biologically, and socially. See F. E. Williams,* The Drama of the Orokolo *(London: Oxford University Press, 1940). An extensive, if somewhat haphazard, literature of nonliterate theatre exists. Accounts are rarely organized for use by the theatre theorist or aesthetician; however, I have found ethnographic reading to be of utmost value. See my discussions of the Orokolo in "Negotiations with Environment" and "The Politics of Ecstasy," both included in this book.*

the action is trimmed to a space, the Balinese dance creates its own space, moving where it must.[15]

Once one gives up fixed seating and the bifurcation of space, entirely new relationships are possible. Body contact can naturally occur between performers and audience; voice levels and acting intensities can be widely varied; a sense of shared experience can be engendered. Most important, each scene can create its own space, either contracting to a central or a remote area or expanding to fill all available space. The action "breathes" and the audience itself becomes a major scenic element. During *Victims of Duty* we found that the audience would crowd in during intense scenes and move away when the action became broad or violent; they usually gave way willingly to the performers[16] and reoccupied areas after the action had passed by. During the final scene, Nicholas chased the Detective all around the periphery of the large room, stumbling over the audience, searching in the audience for his victim. Nicholas' obstacles were real—the living bodies of the spectators—and the scene ended when he caught and killed the Detective. Had someone in the audience chosen to shelter and protect the Detective an unpredictable complication would have been added, but not one that could not have been dealt with. At several points in the performance, a member of the audience did not want to give up a place in which an action was staged. The performers (in character) had to deal with these people, sometimes forcibly moving them.

These extra tensions may not seem to be a legitimate part of the performance. Surely they are not part of "the play." But the

---

15 *The film,* Dance and Trance in Bali, *is available from the New York University film library.*

16 *On two occasions spectators came to* Victims *with the intention of disrupting the performance. That is an act of bad faith, using a mask of spontaneity to conceal anything but spontaneous participation. One of these occasions led to a fist fight between a disrupter and another member of the audience who was a friend of mine. The disrupter was thrown out, and the show continued without most of the audience being aware that anything unusual had happened. The structure of the performance permitted such events to be accepted as part of the show. The man who came to disrupt and who was thrown out was a newspaper critic. Such are the small but real pleasures of environmental theatre.*

exchange of place implies the possibilities of conflict over space; such conflicts have to be coped with in terms of the performance. They can be turned to a capital advantage if one believes that the interaction between performers and audience is a real and valuable one. In many intermedia performances, the spectators actively participate. Often the entire space is a performing space; no one is just watching.

The exchange of space between performers and spectators, and the exploration of the total space by both groups, have not been introduced into our theatre by ethnographers. Our model is closer to home: the streets. Everyday street life is marked by movement and the exchange of space; street demonstrations are a special form of street life which depend on the heightened application of everyday customs. One marches with or without a permit, an official sanction; in either case, the event is defined by the rules kept or broken. The ever-increasing use of public space outdoors for rehearsed activities (ranging from demonstrations to street theatre) is having its impact on the indoor theatre.

3. THE THEATRICAL EVENT CAN TAKE PLACE EITHER IN A TOTALLY TRANSFORMED SPACE OR IN "FOUND SPACE"

Environment can be understood in two different ways. First, there is what one can do with and in a space; secondly, there is the acceptance of a given space. In the first case, one *creates* an environment by transforming a space; in the second case, one *negotiates* with an environment, engaging in a scenic dialogue with a space. In the created environment transformed space engineers the arrangement and behavior of the spectators; in a negotiated environment a more fluid situation leads sometimes to the performance being controlled by the spectators.

In the traditional theatre, scenery is segregated; one finds it only in that part of the space where the performance is. The construction of scenery is guided by sight-lines; even when "the theatre" is exposed—as in Brechtian scenography—the equipment is there as an indication that "this is not reality." In short, conventional attitudes toward scenery are naive and compromised.

In environmental theatre, if scenery is used at all, it is used all the way, to the limits of its possibilities. There is no segregation of scenery, and if equipment is exposed it is there because it must be there, even if it is in the way.

The sources of this extreme position are not easy to locate. The theatre of the Bauhaus group[17] was not really interested in scenery. They wished to build new organic spaces in which the action surrounded the spectators or in which the action could move freely through space. Most of the Bauhaus projects were never built. Although not a member of the Bauhaus, Frederick Kiesler (1896–1966) shared many of their ideas. Between 1916 and 1924 he designed (but never built) the Endless Theatre, seating 100,000 people. Kiesler foresaw new functions for theatre:

> The elements of the new dramatic style are still to be worked out. They are not yet classified. Drama, poetry, and scenic formation have no natural milieu. Public, space, and players are artificially assembled. The new aesthetic has not yet attained a unity of expression. Communication lasts two hours; the pauses are the social event. We have no contemporary theatre. No agitators' theatre, no tribunal, no force which does not merely comment on life, but shapes it.[18]

These words were written in 1932. In 1930, Kiesler described his Endless Theatre:

> The whole structure is encased in double shells of steel and opaque welded glass. The stage is an endless spiral. The various levels are connected with elevators and platforms. Seating platforms, stage and elevator platforms are suspended and spanned above each other in space. The structure is an elastic building system of cables and platforms developed from bridge building. The drama can expand and develop freely in space.[19]

The Bauhaus group and men like Kiesler sought in the event itself an

---

[17] For a full account of the Bauhaus see O. Schlemmer, L. Moholy-Nagy, F. Molnar, The Theatre of the Bauhaus (Middletown, Conn.: Wesleyan University Press, 1961).

[18] Shelter magazine, May 1932.

[19] Architectural Record, May 1930.

organic and dynamic definition of space. Naturally, such ideas are incompatible with traditional scenic practice. Kaprow suggests an altogether different evolution.

> With the breakdown of the classical harmonies following the introduction of "irrational" or nonharmonic juxtapositions, the Cubists tacitly opened the path to infinity. Once foreign matter was introduced into the picture in the form of paper, it was only a matter of time before everything else foreign to paint and canvas would be allowed to get into the creative act, including real space. Simplifying the history of the ensuing evolution into a flashback, this is what happened: the pieces of paper curled up off the canvas, were removed from the surface to exist on their own, became more solid as they grew into other materials and, reaching out further into the room, finally filled it entirely. Suddenly there were jungles, crowded streets, littered alleys, dream spaces of science fiction, rooms of madness, and junk-filled attics of the mind.

> Inasmuch as people visiting such Environments are moving, colored shapes too, and were counted "in," mechanically moving parts could be added, and parts of the created surroundings could then be rearranged like furniture at the artist's and visitors' discretion. And, logically, since the visitor could and did speak, sound and speech, mechanical and recorded, were also soon to be in order. Odors followed.[20]

Many intermedia pieces are environmental. Only recently have happeners "discovered" the proscenium stage, and a paradoxical cross-over is starting in which the theatre is becoming more environmental, while intermedia is becoming more traditionally theatrical scenically.

Kaprow says that his own route to happenings (a term he coined) was through "action collage"—not the making of pictures but the creation of a pictorial event. In his 1952 essay, "The American Action Painters," Harold Rosenberg described what it means to "get inside the canvas":

---

[20] *Allan Kaprow*, Assemblages, Environments, and Happenings (*New York: Harry N. Abrams, 1967), pp 165–166. A similar history is presented by Harriet Janis and Rudi Blesh in* Collage (*Philadelphia and New York: Chilton, 1962). Kirby disagrees with these accounts; see his* Happenings (*New York: Dutton, 1965). For descriptions and scenarios of many environmental intermedia pieces see Kirby's book and TDR, X, No. 2, special issue on happenings.*

[. . .] the canvas began to appear to one American painter after another as an arena in which to act—rather than as a space in which to reproduce, redesign, analyze or "express" an object, actual or imagined. What was to go on the canvas was not a picture but an event.[21]

It is but one brief step from action painting (or collage) to intermedia. My own interest in environmental theatre developed from my interest in intermedia. My partners in the New Orleans Group—Franklin Adams (painter) and Paul Epstein (composer)—followed the same path. Our first definition of environmental theatre was "the application of intermedia techniques to the staging of scripted drama." A painter's and composer's aesthetics were added to that of a theatre person's; traditional theatrical biases fell by the wayside. We were not interested in sight-lines or in the focused ordering of space. The audience entered a room in which *all* the space was "designed," in which the environment was an organic transformation of one space into another. The spectators found whatever place they could to view the event. In *Victims of Duty* there were "ridges" and "valleys" of carpeted platforms. For those who sat in the valleys vision was difficult; either they did not see all the action or they stood or they moved. Some of the action took place in the valleys, and during these moments only spectators very close to the action could see it.

For *Victims* a large room (about 75 feet square) was transformed into a living-room. But it was not a living-room in which all the elements had a clear or usual function. It was, rather, the "idea of a living-room." In one corner chairs spiraled to the ceiling; at another place there was an analyst's couch; on a high platform a wooden chair sat under a bright overhead light; a small proscenium stage was built against one wall for the play-within-the-play; trapdoors allowed the performers to play underneath the audience; a

---

21 *Included in Rosenberg's* The Tradition of the New *(New York: McGraw-Hill, 1965), p. 25. The quest for sources can become, in composer Morton Feldman's term, "mayflowering" and as such it is an intriguing but not very productive game. However, since I have begun playing that game, let me add that the work of the Russian Constructivists and the Italian Futurists also bears on the history of environmental theatre.*

trapeze permitted them to play over the audience; certain scenes took place in the street outside the theatre or in other rooms adjoining or over the theatre; stairways led to nowhere; technical equipment was plainly visible, mounted on platforms against two walls; the walls themselves were covered with flats and lightly overpainted so that scenes from previous proscenium productions faintly showed through; on the walls graffiti were painted: quotations from *Victims of Duty*. The scenic idea was to use Ionesco's formulation that the play was "naturalistic drama," a parody of the theatre, and a surrealistic-psychedelic-psychoanalytic search.

We did not plan the set. The directors, performers, technicians, and production crews had been working for about a month in the space in which the play was to be performed (we had, by then, been rehearsing for four months). One Saturday afternoon we decided to build the environment. We lugged whatever flats, platforms, stairways, and carpets we could find and worked for ten hours straight. Out of that scenic improvisation came the environment. Very few changes were made during the ensuing weeks of rehearsal. I do not want to make out of this experience a general principle. But surely the close working together on the production by more than twenty people led to a felt knowledge of what the environment should be.

The very opposite of total transformation of space is found space. The principles here are very simple: (1) the given elements of any space—its architecture, textural qualities, acoustics, and so on—are to be explored, not disguised; (2) the random ordering of space is valid; (3) the function of scenery, if used at all, is to point up, not disguise or transform, the space; (4) the spectators may suddenly and unexpectedly create new spatial possibilities.

Most found space is found outdoors or in public buildings that cannot be tampered with.[22] Here the challenge is to acknowledge the environment and turn it to your advantage. The American proto-

---

[22] *It's rather sad to think about the New York Shakespeare Festival. A stage has been built in Central Park which does its best to take an indoors setting outdoors. When the Festival moves around the city, it brings its incongruent equipment with it—like the visit of an old, dear, outdated aunt.*

type for this kind of performance is the freedom march and confrontation. The politics of these marches and confrontations have
been discussed. Their aesthetics deserves more than passing attention. The streets were dangerous for black people, the highways were
not free, and state governments inhospitable. The sit-ins had explored
small indoor spaces; the freedom rides had claimed the interiors of
buses as they passed through the countryside. But the ultimate gesture was the march of thousands in the streets and across miles of
highway. The aesthetic fallout of that large gesture is that the
streets are no longer places which one uses only to get from here to
there. They are public arenas, testing grounds, stages for morality
plays.

Later demonstrations modeled themselves on these early examples. The American-Roman façade of the Pentagon was the
proper backdrop for a confrontation between anti-war youth and
troops. Draft centers and campuses are other natural focal points.
What is happening at these places is more than political agitation.
Ceremonies are being performed. To adapt a phrase from Goffman,
these are the places where some people act out their reality. This
reality is social and political—therefore, it is no accident that the
themes of most street and guerrilla theatre have been political.

I helped plan and direct a series of events called *Guerrilla Warfare* which was staged at twenty-three locations throughout New
York City on October 28, 1967.[23] Two of the twenty-three performances are worth considering here. One was the 2:00 P.M. performance at the Main Recruiting Center at Times Square and the
other the 6:00 P.M. performance at the Port Authority Bus Terminal.
The Recruiting Center is a place where demonstrations occur frequently. The police are familiar with the routine. However, our anti-
war play attracted a large hostile crowd which closed in on the performers; not threateningly, but aggressively. Some people shouted,
many mumbled their disapproval. Because the play was intentionally
ambivalent (a super-super patriot would think we were for the war),
several teenage kids thought we were American Nazis and from

---

[23] *See "Public Events for the Radical Theatre," in this book, pp. 201–
207.*

that point of view began to question their own support of the war. The performance went swiftly, some of the dialogue was lost in the open air, the performers were not comfortable. We found that the narrow triangular sidewalk, surrounded on all sides by automotive traffic, and further abbreviated by the pressing crowd, made the performance brief and staccato.

Quite the opposite happened at the Port Authority. Here the large, vaulting interior space was suited for sound. The police were not expecting a performance and acted confused until orders from higher up ended the show seconds away from completion. We began all performances by humming and then singing "The Star Spangled Banner." Performers assembled at a central area upon seeing a sight cue and as they gathered they sang louder. In the Terminal the swelling anthem seemed to come from everywhere. Because the commuter crowds were not expecting a performance, at first they didn't seem to believe one was happening. One West Point cadet walked through the performance, paused, and walked away, only to return several moments later, scratch his head, and stay. Finally, when he realized what was being said, he walked off in disgust. A large crowd gathered; they were curious rather than hostile and they kept their remarks low, questioning each other about what was going on. Since we were standing in front of the Greyhound ticket booths, just next to the escalators, and alongside a display Ford automobile, the performance had a strange surrealism to it. But, at the same time, it was far from esoteric. More than in any other location, the Terminal performance—if a bit long—was direct and meaningful. Here, where people want to get home, in the bland, massive institutional architecture of our culture, was the place where a symbolic confrontation could take place.

It is possible to combine the principles of transformed and found space. Once a space has been transformed, the audience will "take their places." Frequently, because there is no fixed seating and little indication of how they should sit, the audience will arrange themselves in unexpected patterns; and during the performance these patterns will change, "breathing" with the action just as the performers do. The audience can thus make even the most cunningly transformed space into found space; it is not possible for the director to block the actors' movements in this kind of situation. The performers should take advantage of audience mobility, considering it a flexible part of the performance environment.

4. FOCUS IS FLEXIBLE AND VARIABLE

Single-focus is the trademark of traditional theatre. Even when actions are simultaneous and spread across a large stage (for example, the more than 200-foot proscenium of the Palais de Chaillot in Paris), the audience is looking in one direction. A single glance or a simple scan can take in all the action, even the most panoramic. And within these panoramic scenes, there are centers of attention, usually a single focal point, around which everything else is organized. The response of one perceptive spectator may be the response of all.

The environmental theatre does not eliminate this practice. It is useful. But added to it are two other kinds of focus, or lack of focus. In *multi-focus* more than one event—several of the same kind, or mixed-media—happens at the same time, distributed throughout the space. Each independent event competes with the others for the audience's attention. The space is organized so that no spectator can see everything. The spectator must move or completely refocus his attention to catch everything that is going on. It is not really the principle of the three-ring circus. In multi-focus, events happen behind and above and below the spectator. He is surrounded by a variety of sights and sounds. However, it is not necessary for the density of events to be "thick." Multi-focus and sensory-overload are not equivalent terms, though at times they are coincident. Sparse, scattered, low-key, and diverse events may be offered simultaneously. Sensory-overload leads to a feeling of a small space which is exploding because it is so full. A low density of events makes one feel that the space is unspeakably large, barely populated. The range of multi-focus moves from one extreme to the other and includes all intermediate points.

A performance using multi-focus will not reach every spectator in the same way. Individual reactions may be affectively incompatible with one another because one spectator will put events together in a different way than will the man next to him. In multi-focus, the director's job of controlling meaning is turned over to the audience. The performers and technicians control the sensory input (and one works painstakingly on this), but the mix of elements is left to the audience.

In *local-focus*, events are staged so that only a fraction of the audience can see and hear them. During *Victims*, Choubert went into the audience and spoke quietly to three or four persons. He was saying lines from the play, intimate speeches that asked for a small circle of witnesses and an extremely low vocal level. While he was speaking to these few people, another action—on a larger scale—was happening elsewhere. Later, during the bread-stuffing sequence, Nicholas left the central action (which was staged single-focus) and went into the audience, where he picked a young woman at random and began kissing and fondling her. He went as far as he could (and on several evenings a girl was very permissive). He spoke into her ear the private words of lovemaking. He was also listening for his cue—a line by the Detective, who continued the central action of stuffing bread down Choubert's throat. When Nicholas heard his cue, he said to the girl he was kissing, "I'm glad you agree with me." If she had not been cooperative, he said, "I'm sorry you don't agree with me." In either case he left her and rejoined the central action.

Local-focus has the advantage of bringing certain scenes very directly to some members of the audience. A commitment on the part of the performer is possible that cannot be realized in any other way. But what of the other spectators, those who cannot hear or see what's happening? One may offer them their own local actions or a central action. Or—and we used this several times successfully in *Victims*—nothing else is going on. Spectators out of the range of sight and hearing will be aware of some action happening "over there." Some will move to that place; some will look around them at the environment, the other spectators. For those who are neither participating nor trying to participate, the moments of local-focus are breaks in the action when they can recapitulate what has gone on before or simply think their own thoughts. These pauses—these pools of inattention—may draw spectators further into the world of the performance.

Local-focus may be used as part of multi-focus. In this case, certain activities are potentially viewable by all the spectators, while other activities are not. In fact, all focus possibilities can be used alone or in combination.

It is very hard to get performers to accept local-focus. They are habituated to projecting even the most intimate situations and language. They cannot understand why the entire audience should not share these intimacies. But once the performer accepts the startling premise that privacy (of a kind) is possible and proper within a performance and that the close relation between a performer and a very few spectators, or even one, is artistically valid, wide possibilities open. A low range of subtle actions and volume can be used. Real body contact and whispered communication are possible between performer and spectator. Local whirlpools of action make the theatrical line more complex and varied than in traditional performances. The theatre space is like a city in which lights are going on and off, traffic is moving, parts of conversation are faintly heard.

5. ALL PRODUCTION ELEMENTS SPEAK IN THEIR OWN LANGUAGE

This axiom is implicit in the others. Why should the performer be any more important than other production elements? Because he is human? But the other elements were made by men and are operated by them. While discussing the first axiom, I pointed out that technicians should be a creative part of the performance. In the environmental theatre one element is not submerged for the sake of others. It is even possible that elements will be made and rehearsed separately and that the performance itself is the arena where competing elements meet for the first time.

Portions of the performance can be structured traditionally. In that case, production elements function "operatically," all joining together to make one statement. At these times, a pyramid of supportive elements has the performer at its apex. But there are other times when the performer may find himself in the base of the pyramid; and times when there is no pyramid at all, but distinct and sometimes contradictory elements. Many multi-focus situations are structured this way.

The long dialogue between the Detective as father and Choubert as son in *Victims* was played in near darkness with the Detective reading from an almost hidden lectern at the side of a projection booth and Choubert seated among the spectators, his head in his hands. Their dialogue supported two films which were projected alternately and sometimes simultaneously on opposite walls. The dialogue which held the audience's attention was the one between the films.

The performers may be treated as mass and volume, color, texture, and movement—not as "actors" but as parts of the environment.

Grotowski has carried to the extreme the idea of competing elements, contradictory statements. "There must be theatrical contrast," he says. "This can be between any two elements: music and the actor, the actor and the text, actor and costume, two or more parts of the body (the hands say yes, the legs say no), etc."[24]

6. THE TEXT NEED BE NEITHER THE STARTING POINT NOR THE GOAL OF A PRODUCTION. THERE MAY BE NO TEXT AT ALL

One of theatre's most durable clichés is that the play comes first and from it flows the consequent production: the playwright is the first creator and his intentions serve as production guidelines. One may stretch these intentions to the limits of "interpretation," but no further.

But things aren't that way. Plays are produced for all kinds of reasons, rarely because a play exists that "must be done": a producer has or finds money; a group of actors wants a vehicle; a slot in a season needs to be filled; a theatre is available whose size and equipment are suited to certain productions; cultural, national, or social occasions demand performances. Not that we have much to be proud of in most of our productions. Sanctimonious attitudes toward the text, and production practice that preserves the playwright's words, will yield little—particularly when there is a brief

---

[24] *See Eugenio Barba, "Theatre Laboratory 13 Rzedow," TDR, IX, No. 2, 153–165.*

rehearsal period. The repertory—from Aeschylus to Brecht—clogs rather than releases creativity. That repertory will not go away; but need it be preserved, expressed, or interpreted? Cage has put it well:

> Our situation as artists is that we have all this work that was done before we came along. We have the opportunity to do work now, I would not present things from the past, but I would approach them as materials available to something else which we are going to do now. [. . .] One extremely interesting thing that hasn't been done is a collage made from various plays. Let me explain to you why I think of past literature as material rather than as art. There are oodles of people who are going to think of the past as a museum and be faithful to it, but that's not my attitude. Now as material it can be put together with other things. They could be things that don't connect with art as we conventionally understand it. Ordinary occurrences in a city, or ordinary occurrences in the country, or technological occurrences—things that are now practical simply because techniques have changed. This is altering the nature of music and I'm sure it's altering your theatre, say through the employment of colored television, or multiple movie projectors, photo-electric devices that will set off relays when an actor moves through a certain area. I would have to analyze theatre to see what are the things that make it up in order, when we later make a synthesis, to let those things come in.[25]

Cage's attitude—treat the repertory as materials, not models—is tied to his high regard for technology. Grotowski shares many of Cage's views about the text, while taking an altogether different position on technology. But a radical new treatment (some will call it mistreatment) of the text does not depend upon one's attitude toward technology. Grotowski:

> By gradually eliminating whatever proved superfluous, we found that theatre can exist without make-up, without autonomic costume and scenography, without a separate performance area (stage), without lighting and sound effects, etc. It cannot exist without the actor-spectator relationship of perceptual, direct, "live" communion. This is an ancient theoretical truth, of course, but when rigorously tested in practice it undermines most of our usual

---

[25] "An Interview with John Cage," TDR, X, No. 2, 53–54.

ideas about theatre. [. . .] No matter how theatre expands and exploits its mechanical resources, it will remain technologically inferior to film and television.[26]

It is not necessary to choose between Cage and Grotowski. Each production contains its own possibilities. What is striking is that two men who have such diverse attitudes toward technology should stand so close in their understanding of the text's function. Cage says the repertory is material; Grotowski practices "montage": rearranging, extrapolating, and eliminating portions of the text.

These practices flow from the premises of my first axiom. If the theatrical event is a set of related transactions, then the text—once rehearsal begins—will participate in these transactions. It is no more reasonable to expect that the text will remain unchanged than that a performer will not develop his role. These changes are what rehearsals are for. But "change" does not precisely describe what happens. Grotowski's *confrontation* is more accurate. I cited Grotowski at the start of this essay, and hope that by now the richness of his vision is understood.

> [The actor] must not illustrate Hamlet, he must meet Hamlet. The actor must give his cue within the context of his own experience. And the same for the director. [. . .] One structures the montage so that this confrontation can take place. We eliminate those parts of the text which have no importance for us, those parts with which we can neither agree nor disagree. Within the montage one finds certain words that function vis-à-vis our own experiences.[27]

The text is a map with many possible routes. You push, pull, explore, exploit. You decide where you want to go. Rehearsals may take you elsewhere. Almost surely you will not go where the playwright intended. You don't "do" the play; you "do with it"—confront it, search among its words and themes, build around and through it . . . and come out with your own thing.

That is the heart of environmental theatre.

---

[26] *Jerzy Grotowski, "Towards the Poor Theatre," TDR, XI, No. 3, 62.*
[27] *"Interview with Grotowski," TDR, XIII, No. 1, 44.*

Negotiations with Environment

1968

> *Our concept of space makes use of
> the edges of things. If there aren't
> any edges, we make them by creating
> artificial lines* [. . .]. *To us a space
> is empty—one gets into it by inter-
> secting it with lines.*
>
> EDWARD T. HALL
> THE SILENT LANGUAGE

1.

I asked Allan Kaprow why he gave up painting and began to
make happenings. "I was an action painter," he replied, "and I
thought of the large canvas as an arena—a damned fine metaphor
for thinking of yourself as thrashing around in there with the lions.
But, after all, that still is a theatrical space—even if it's as big as
a football field. It doesn't make any difference how large the space
is, it's still a stage. It's pretty comfortable working in the middle,
but as soon as you get to the edges you have to stop; and I didn't
feel like stopping." Kaprow's happenings now range across con-
tinents and sometimes take months to enact. He no longer worries
about the edges of things. But to find and then use indeterminate
space he had first to understand time. A space without edges must
take time: become active.

The Orokolo of New Guinea have a ritual cycle play, the
Hevehe, which has many parts and takes between six and twenty
years to enact in its entirety. The whole village knows the "scenario,"
but most do not live long enough to see it all enacted in order. And
it doesn't make any difference whether the Fire Fight, for example,

is done during the fourth or seventh year. The cycle is organic and flexible; its sequence and density depend on the climate, the economy, the local social organization. As these are modified, or as extraordinary circumstances arise, the cycle gives way—breathing with the Orokolo environment. By the end of the cycle everything is completed. The masks are burned; the large men's house is torn down. Things begin again, after a year-or-two pause. Some pivotal events are done in relentless order and the need for this order may delay the cycle for years—the village cannot proceed until the formally structured events can be done in sequence.

Why this uneven quality that is quite unknown to Western aesthetics? Time is treated differently by the Orokolo. To them it is as malleable as space and material are to us. For them there is a constant and varying interchange between time, events, space, and things. Around certain events time literally "clusters," bunching itself for a climactic release. The parts of the cycle that concern puberty initiation may take place for each boy or girl at any time between the ages of eight and eighteen. At whatever time the rites take place, the youth is transformed into a mature person. His chronology waits until the time is right; not his own biological clock, but the social clock of the community.

Time takes its shape from events, and events are modified by time. When the masks are finished, when the dancers are ready, when the weather is right, when the old leaders are satisfied—then "the time is right." There is an impressive combination of casualness and seriousness—almost the entire surplus wealth of the community is devoted to the ritual theatre. (And by surplus I mean everything that is accumulated beyond subsistence.) It's got to be done, the village leaders say, but we don't know when. The artwork is embedded in everyday activity, inseparable from it, sometimes identical with it.

The construction of the spectacular thirty-foot-high masks (huge frameworks which are worn by the strongest men) goes on in a desultory way in the men's house. The building of the masks is part of the ceremony, and without them the cycle cannot go on. The figures are the gods and demons. And yet the work is not "holy work" in our sense, but informal handiwork. Each man works on his mask; but when he is tired or when some other matter presses, he hangs the mask up and leaves it—perhaps for more than a year. As the designs are woven and paints applied, it becomes clear that the masks are great artworks. But the precepts of Western aesthetics are at a loss to explain the social regulations that guide the designs. Even the haphazard architecture of Chartres Cathedral stuns the modern; the Hevehe masks are of the same order, but more so. There is no urgency, but there is an absolute necessity; there is no articulated plan, but there is an emerging artwork of great delicacy and power. It is as if the Orokolo village as a whole made them, so perfectly do they fit the ritual. And yet the offer of something good to smoke will instantly convert a "workman" into a "loafer." The work must go on, but guided by what rhythm?

The cycle play itself is not so "special" as early ethnographers once thought. The women and children (who cannot participate and must not watch) peep out through the thatch walls and watch the dances anyway; the men, although they become spirits when dressed in the huge masks in which they dance, are frequently called by their names and are roundly criticized if their dancing lacks conviction or skill. The women joke with their husbands immediately after a dance, banter with them, and criticize their performances. The sacred food reserved only for the gods is stolen by young men and either eaten or given to the village elders: food is too valuable to be left to rot, gods or no gods. Clearly the cycle play is an entertainment in our sense. It is an amusement, a pastime, a relief from drudgery, play. At the same time it is the community's most sacred ritual. Our culture has lost, perhaps irretrievably, the Orokolo sense of vulgar sanctity.

For us things are this way or that way; but not all ways at once. Spaces have edges and centers, time has a beginning and an end, art is serious or frivolous. We have a considerable cultural investment in our way of doing things. It is difficult for us to think of new patterns; and when we discover them we are apt to dismiss them as "wrong" or "primitive." Our technological success has filled us with a general confidence (threatened here and there by inadequate operations, but barely touched in its basic assumptions) that is all the more stubborn because one of its best qualities is its ability to accommodate change. Within the framework of our technology we are like the permissive parent: anything can be accepted, incorporated, made to fit.

It is extraordinarily difficult to speak of essential change. Our language customs, our communications, and a highly developed, flexible, and abstract mathematics permit any idea to be "worked out." Viewed this way, there is no escape from tradition; nor is there an easy way to map precisely what the tradition is. We know only that when confronted with a space without edges or a time that clusters around events we are confused; such ideas hardly make sense.

2.

Films are now shot largely on location. Although this is not exactly a new phenomenon, it is a very important one. An acted set of events is situated within a "real" environment. The aesthetic consequences of this seemingly simple activity are widespread. Why should film directors insist on lugging quantities of equipment halfway around the world? Why do *auteurs* like working with non-actors as performers? In what way does working with "real stuff" offer film-makers "better" material? Even the "art films" shown at the Film-Makers' Cinematheque in New York (and certainly most of Andy Warhol's films) have a "non-acted" quality about them. Are these techniques just a further step in the naturalistic movement? Would Zola applaud?

Probably not. Zola assumed that art was *made out of* life; many contemporary artists find it hard to distinguish between art and life. It is not that one can be transformed into the other but that distinctions between the two are increasingly difficult to determine. (Of course, I do not include the immense operation of the ongoing traditionalists.) This deterioration of distinctions does not bode well for aesthetics. As Susan Sontag proclaimed against interpretation, many of today's artists proclaim in their work against art. It is because art has become so identified with artfulness—and the products of art with property—that making art and owning it no longer seem either the proper occupation or the honest goal of artists. The on-location film is the halfway house (the most a large public will now accept) between art as art and life-art.

The environment on location can be edited, distorted by lenses, managed in any number of ways. But there remains a certain irrefrangible kernel. At most the film-maker can negotiate with the environment, asking it to yield something to him. But once the film-maker begins shooting, there is no way—short of scrapping the entire episode—in which he can deny the real environment entry into his artwork. This first, perhaps faltering and almost accidental, step leads to others more radical and less obvious.

Andy Warhol turns his camera on people who live to perform, whose very mode of authenticity is performance. We see the pictures and wonder if these performers are "that way in real life." But the question is meaningless in an existence where, as R. D. Laing points out, people can pretend to be who they really are. The space without edges is also an identity without identification.

3.

Films are shown in movie houses. Warhol's arsenal of superstars can be avoided. But if you had been between Avenues C and D on New York's East Seventh Street, where perhaps seven thousand people live, on September 8, 1967, you couldn't have avoided *The Seventh Street Environment*. Coordinated by Bud Wirtschafter and made by dozens of people—including many residents of the block—the *Environment* combined film, still images, taped and live sound. It had the qualities of block party, documentary, free-for-all, and informational feedback. "It was really a double documentary," Wirtschafter says. "The people on the block took their own footage and still shots, recorded their own sounds, went inside their own apartments, into the stores, out in the streets. And we had some professionals working who also took footage and got sounds."

I was in the street that night. It was an impressive scene. Older people sitting on the stoops were commenting to each other in the way families do when they watch home movies. But the thrill of seeing themselves projected onto huge screens hung across the entire street, out of windows, or just on walls converted the home movie situation into one of Hollywood stardom. Perhaps this is a cheap image to propagate; but for people whose self-image is small indeed it was an identity kick worth having. Kids were dancing to the music of several local bands and enjoying the films; two large projectors were mounted on an equipment truck in the middle of the street, and more than a dozen projectors were working from inside apartments, throwing images through windows and onto outdoor surfaces.

Some of the footage was extraordinarily rich, and much of it was poor by professional standards. But these standards seem beside the point. The overall artwork was one of participation, of converting a very drab street into something alive and celebratory, flooded as it was by so many images and sounds of itself.

Watching, participating myself, I thought immediately of non-literate theatre. *The Seventh Street Environment* had neither the tradition nor the communal craftsmanship of the Orokolo cycle play; but it had the same qualities of celebration, casualness, and necessity. Having participated but once, I wondered if these people would ever forget. Even more important, would they insist on doing it again? Probably not. This kind of art is new to them, as it was to Wirtschafter and his crews. But it tapped the roots of an emerging artform, one long missing in America.

The space of Seventh Street breathed with the images and sounds living in it; the habits of summer open windows and street life were lifted out of their routine and transformed. The environment of the street didn't change, but its possibilities were explored. A found space was found interesting; found people were found alive. Technology was used to celebrate, not exploit, the lives of those who had too frequently and too relentlessly been exploited. To a large degree, the people on Seventh Street made their own *Environment*. I remember especially film footage shot by a twelve-year-old boy. It was of his apartment and his family: a very traditional-looking group of Ukrainians. The family was stiff and formal as they posed for their son's 8mm camera. They looked as if they were posing for the family album. They were—but the family now belonged to the *Environment*.

But this is a complicated discussion and sentimentality shouldn't intrude. The *Environment* was significant art not because it gave all those "poor people" a chance to see themselves as they saw themselves; it was significant because celebration, casualness, non-professionalism, ritual, necessity, and environment confronted one another. The multiplicity and simultaneity of the images, the haphazard coordination of film, sound, apartment and street life made real that special kind of time cluster and edgeless space that is the basis of a newly rediscovered art. An artless art without professional performers; one in which the makers and the watchers were all participating; an art of spatial insideness. An art that cannot be "reviewed" or "criticized." In other words, an event.

4.

But what of the professionals? If there is little else to say about the American professional theatre, one thing is certain, it is irrelevant. There's a quaint comfort in that: irrelevancy is harmless; the theatre's sins are totally those of omission. It's not simply that theatre has been artistically bypassed by film and cheated by TV of whatever hope it had of mass audiences. The artform is irrelevant. Of what use are expensively mounted social parades modeled on Aristotle's "imitation of an action"? Rolf Fjelde has pointed out that the world view of the Renaissance steadily diminished until, with the Theatre of the Absurd, objects were internalized or animated, characterization deteriorated, and the tradition we call "drama" came to an end.

During this past winter in New York, at Tambellini's Gate on Second Avenue at midnight on Fridays and Saturdays, the Ridiculous Theatre Company staged *Big Hotel*. Low camp at its most self-indulgent, *Big Hotel* indicated a turn in theatrical consciousness that finds its highest expression in the work of Poland's Jerzy Grotowski. *Big Hotel* was a parody of *Grand Hotel* (and many films and plays since and before); a transvestite, drag-queen celebration made of farce, gimmicks, old gags, and plotless variations on some basic American themes. Everyone was at the hotel—a rundown place represented scenically by whatever the directors and actors found or made out of the stuff in the theatre—half-painted flats, an open second story, plastic plants, and toy telephones. This was not an artistically designed half-set, but an undesigned hodgepodge. The play's action was similarly undisciplined. Actors came and went, lines were muddled, and frequently enough real spats broke out between the performers. I watched for about an hour and a half, had enough, and left to get some coffee. Then I discovered that I had forgotten my scarf. It was about 2:45 A.M. I half-thought that if I went back to get my scarf the building would be locked. But when I returned not only was the building open, but *Big Hotel* was still being performed. More than that, my hour's absence had deprived me of nothing. The plot had not moved forward, the spats were undiminished, the same characters were going at it with full energy and sloppiness. I had laughed during my first encounter with *Big Hotel*, and now I was flooded with near hysteria. *Big Hotel* was everything theatre art should not be. It was formless, it didn't matter what you saw or didn't see, there was no distinction between actors and characters, time didn't matter.

But there was a strange power to *Big Hotel*. I did not forget it and scenes from it kept intruding on my consciousness. I used it as a measuring stick for other productions. *Pantagleize* by the APA was fun, I thought, but not up to *Big Hotel*; Joseph Papp's *Hamlet* was inventive and struck at some theatrical affectations—but it couldn't touch the liberating qualities of *Big Hotel*. I don't know if I can explain why *Big Hotel* touched the same nerve as the Orokolo cycle play and *The Seventh Street Environment*. *Big Hotel* had the qualities of an autonomous event; it involved its audience but didn't depend on them—even on their presence; some very personal stories were being told, and these concerned the performers, not the play. And yet, overall, a public event was taking place, some kind of deeply authentic reality was being acted out. Product-mad American society yielded to something that was all process. There was no way to use *Big Hotel*. It was superfluous and gratuitous to sublimity.

Big Hotel is the nihilistic, decadent (if you will) way out. It is the pop art of drag queens. Grotowski seeks the very opposite solution; but his work has more in common with *Big Hotel* than with the whole traditional theatre that ranges between these two ex-tremes. In 1959 Grotowski began his relentless pursuit of the "art of the actor." Grounded in the work of Stanislavski, Dullin, Meyerhold, Vakhtanghov, Artaud, and even Delsartre; particularly sensitive to varieties of the oriental theatre (specifically the Peking Opera, the Kathakali, and the Noh), Grotowski describes the goal of his work as "to expose totally the spiritual process of the actor. This is not an egoistic technique based on the actor's enjoyment of his own emotional experience, but rather the revealing technique of trance, an integration of spiritual, psychic, and physical faculties climaxing in a 'penetration' from and by the actor's intimate instinc-tive psyche: the actor in the act of giving himself." Lest this sound opaquely mystical, let me say that I spent four weeks in Grotowski's workshop (which he ran during November 1967 at NYU). The work is precise, physical, and absolutely disciplined. Total silence was demanded of the actors for each five-hour session. Grotowski, assisted by one of the actors from his nine-man troupe, Ryszard Cieslak, took us through a detailed set of psycho-physical exercises and then worked carefully and individually on scenes from Shake-speare.

Grotowski and Cieslak stressed a state of mind that is "a passive readiness to realize an active role, a state in which one does not 'want to do that' but rather 'resigns from not doing it.'" This diffi-cult instruction was a key to Grotowski's method. It has obvious analogues in both Eastern meditation and psychoanalysis, where the analysand is instructed to let his thoughts and associations flow. As many a patient—and all of us in Grotowski's workshop—has dis-covered, the ability to resign oneself from not doing something is extraordinarily difficult to come by. It is not a passive, sleepy state of mind. Nor is it the conscious kind of striving so familiar to goal-oriented Americans. It is a condition all its own, at once rigorous and submissive. What one submits to is not an authority outside oneself, but the inner psycho-physical process. I cannot articulate this process with any real accuracy. It is closely related to what Lévi-Strauss calls the "thoracic rhythms"—breathing, heartbeat. It is a way of tuning in on and then acting from impulses that originate in the psycho-physical unity we in the West too swiftly assign to the mind-body dichotomy. It is, finally, a *unity*, and a response to that unity once it is felt.

Grotowski stresses this part of his work because it is at the center of the "confrontations" that take place between the performer's "mask" and his "self" (this unity) and later between this self and the rhythms of the text. Each of Grotowski's ways of awakening our awareness of this psycho-physical unity were rooted in the physical—in a set of rigorously developed and precisely applied exercises. Once we were grounded in these physical exercises, Grotowski moved to the composition of the role, the construction of form, the expression of signs—to artifice.

> There is no contradiction between inner technique and artifice (articulation of a role by signs). We believe that a spiritual process which is not supported and expressed by a formal articulation and disciplined structuring of the role will collapse in shapelessness. And we find that artificial composition not only does not limit the spiritual but actually leads to it. [. . .] The forms of common "natural" behavior obscure the truth; we compose a role as a system of signs which demonstrate what is behind the mask of common vision: the dialectics of human behavior. At a moment of psychic shock, a moment of terror, of mortal danger or tremendous joy, a man does not behave "naturally." A man in an elevated spiritual state uses rhythmically articulated signs, begins to dance, to sing. A *sign*, not a common gesture, is the elementary integer of expression for us.[1]

The discipline of yoga, the signs cherished by Artaud, the classic texts of the Western theatre—these are Grotowski's building blocks. He is not interested in "doing" a play, but in confronting it.

> [. . .] confrontation with myth rather than identification. In other words, while retaining our private experiences, we can attempt to incarnate myth, putting on its ill-fitting skin to perceive the relativity of our problems, their connection to the "roots," and the relativity of the "roots" in the light of today's experience. [. . .] Only myth—incarnate in the fact of the actor, in his living organism—can func-

---

[1] "*Towards the Poor Theatre,*" TDR, XI, No. 3, *p. 61.*

tion as a taboo. The violation of the living organism, the exposure carried to outrageous excess, returns us to a concrete mythical situation, an experience of common human truth.[2]

When I interviewed Grotowski (typically, for him, it was a four-hour non-stop confrontation, one of the great mornings of my adult education), I was after precise examples of what he meant. Working with him I knew that his method was neither opaque nor mysterious; and yet his vocabulary has overtones of mysticism. It is a clear case of the failure of Western language patterns. Grotowski said:

> Every great creator builds bridges between the past and himself, between his roots and his being. That is the only sense in which the artist is a priest: *pontifex* in Latin, he who builds bridges. It is no accident that Joyce wrote *Ulysses* or that Thomas Mann wrote *Dr. Faustus*. It is rather easy to take a myth and to form one's work around it. If that is all you do it is either an illustration or a travesty. What I prefer are new works which are eternal—I may not even know what objects are being referred to—perhaps Joyce wanted to write his own *Odyssey*—but clearly many things in *Ulysses* are important and private to him. These are invisible and so *Ulysses* is not an illustration or travesty. I am conscious of Joyce in his work, and the result is that his work is part of our world. At the same time something archaic exists in the book and in that sense it is eternal. It's the same with the creativity of the actor. He must not illustrate Hamlet, he must meet Hamlet. The actor must give his cue within the context of his own experience. And the same for the director. [. . .] One structures the montage so that this confrontation can take place. We eliminate those parts of the text which have no importance for us, those parts with which we can neither agree nor disagree. Within the montage one finds certain words that function vis-à-vis our own experiences. The result is that we cannot say whether it is Wyspianski's *Akropolis*. Yes it is. But at the same time it is our *Akropolis*. [. . .] We did not want to write a new play, we wished to confront ourselves.[3]

---

[2] Ibid., *p. 64.*
[3] *"Interview with Grotowski,"* TDR, XIII, No. 1, *p. 44.*

The actor is not the end of Grotowski's system, though he is the single most important component. The artwork is environmental staging: productions in which the texts and the actors confront each other, transform the space, and implicate the audience physically through the application of Artaud's axiom, "the theatre is a concrete space to be filled." Not just that part of the theatre called the stage, but the entire space. In most of Grotowski's productions there is no bifurcation of space, no separate stage. The performers and the audience share the same space, and the action moves among the audience, sometimes directly involving it. Note, however, that this free movement is not random, but architectonic. Grotowski wants to articulate cubic space, to bring all of the space into the performance. The audience occupies some of that space and is a scenic element in itself. Movement through the audience, unusual seating arrangements, lack of seating altogether, spectator viewing from above only—these are some of the ways in which Grotowski explores the total space of the performing area. In *Akropolis* the set is built during the performance, crowding the audience out of its original space. Grotowski's attitudes are tied to his belief in the performance as an organic set of transformations. If the theatre is spatial, if things happen during a performance, then it is only logical that the organization of space should evolve and even radically change during the performance.

Akropolis is a classic nineteenth-century Polish play. It is set in the royal palace at Cracow. During the night of the Resurrection, the tapestries come to life and play out episodes from European and Polish history. It ends with the advent of Christ who leads forth a triumphant procession to liberate Europe. "All very good," says Grotowski, "but the royal palace is not a sanctuary any more and this is not the nineteenth century." Working from the premise that the nineteenth century was "Poland's ruined past [. . .] the cemetery of our civilization," *Akropolis* became Auschwitz, the place where "all nations encountered each other [. . .] all the tribes were there waiting for something, but the Messiah never came for those who were killed." It was an Auschwitz that was very real to some of Grotowski's actors.

We did not wish to have a stereotyped production with evil SS men and noble prisoners. We cannot play prisoners, we cannot create such images in the theatre. Any documentary film is stronger. [. . .] What is Auschwitz? Is it something we could organize today? A world which functions inside us? Thus there were no SS men, only prisoners who so organized the space that they must oppress each other to survive. [. . .] We did not show victims but the rules of the game: in order not to be a victim one must make a victim of someone else. [. . .] The prisoners worked all the time. They took metal pipes that were piled in the center of the room and built something. At the start the room was empty except for the pile of pipes and there was a seating arrangement for the audience. By the end of the production the entire room was filled, oppressed, by the metal. The audience could no longer see. The construction was made of heating pipes. We didn't build a crematorium but we gave the spectators the association of fire. It was indirect. Nevertheless afterwards the spectators said that we had built a crematorium.[4]

Anyone who has seen Grotowski's productions, or even pictures of them, knows how space and events are coordinated to form a unity. It is not the unity of sensory overload in which distinctions are washed away by volume. Rather it flows from the principle (known to the Orokolo) that space, events, and time are not separable; they are three terms for one circumstance, one organic situation. The metal structure of *Akropolis* is that production's objective correlative: "a set of objects, a situation, a chain of events which shall be the formula of that *particular* emotion; such that when the external facts, which must terminate in sensory experience, are given, the emotion is immediately evoked." I can add to Eliot's definition only the qualification that in *Akropolis* the emotion was not "evoked" but literally *built*: the environmental image is in the making during the entire performance; suddenly it "arrives." At that moment the audience knows that the random structure of pipes is a crematorium, although not architecturally resembling one.

---

[4] Ibid., *p. 42.*

5.

LA GRANGE, Ga. (AP)—Mrs. A. Landon Morrow, Sr. was watching the late news program on television and a film report on fighting in Vietnam caught her attention. Suddenly there was a familiar face in battle gear.

She looked, then shouted: "Come quick, Landon, here's our son."

The camera had focused briefly on Specialist/4 Landon Morrow, Jr., a radio operator, as the newsman described fighting in "Operation Manhattan."

As the La Grange couple listened and watched, the newsman described an explosion that had wounded a captain and a radio operator. Then there was a film closeup of a soldier lying on the ground.

"We knew then that was our son," said Mrs. Morrow. "We didn't see the explosion but the next time they put the camera on him he was lying on the ground. There were two or three soldiers working on him. We could tell he was wounded."

The next day the Morrows and their daughter-in-law received telegrams explaining that the 20-year-old soldier had been wounded but would survive.

What does it mean to sit in your living-room and watch your son get shot? Or see Jack Ruby shoot Lee Harvey Oswald? This is theatre without drama, performance without aesthetics. Here the space truly has no edge and the event no single time reference. The Morrows sit down for their evening's entertainment. The war is just another program; sponsored like the rest, managed and presented with aplomb and style. It is not "raw war," but carefully edited—like a good war movie. But then, unexpectedly, the program becomes a home movie they didn't photograph; another episode in the Morrow family. "Come quick, Landon, here's our son." The rest is anguish: reality ruining the entertainment. But for all the others watching—as for the Morrows on some other night—death and wounds are entertainment. At least the newspapers reduce the images to words; the confrontation is not direct. Here the real event is plugged into the La Grange living-room and Landon Morrow, Jr. is shot both in Vietnam and at home.

This new experience is one in which larger spaces can be contained within smaller spaces; in which events occurring at great distances can be immediately experienced; in which the passive observer is abruptly converted into a participant. Reality itself is not validated by experience but by the encapsulated reproduction of experience. The distinctions between "out there" and "in here" are blurred. For the Morrows exactly when was their son wounded? Was it the moment it "actually" occurred, or was it when the Morrows saw it on TV? And when young Morrow comes home will he be a wounded veteran or a neighborhood TV celebrity?

These confusions are with us to stay. They may or may not contribute to an increasing insensitivity to suffering. Surely they will muddle the arts—one of whose traditional functions it has been to remind men of the extremes of suffering and joy. The mimetic function of art is usurped by media capable of offering the real thing. But a reverse flow is begun in which the arts usurp reality's function of providing authentic experience. The confrontation of Grotowski's *Akropolis* and the blatant acting-out of *Big Hotel* are harbingers of an art in which reality is programmed; the experience of acting in Grotowski's troupe is not that of "playing parts" but of engaging one's own profoundest terrors and celebrations. The "actors" of *Big Hotel* are not squeamish about playing themselves. Kaprow shuns professional performers and sets portions of his happenings in supermarkets, on public highways, in motel rooms, in private houses. If everywhere around us a histrionic sensibility conditions living, conversely theatre has adapted the modes of authenticity.

Erving Goffman, one of the pioneer map-makers in this difficult territory, puts it very well in the preface to his *The Presentation of Self in Everyday Life:*

> The perspective employed in this report is that of the theatrical performance; the principles derived are dramaturgical ones. [. . .] In using this model I will attempt not to make light of its obvious inadequacies. The stage presents things that are make-believe; presumably life presents things that are real and sometimes not well rehearsed. More important, perhaps, on the stage one player presents himself in the guise of a character to characters projected by other players; the audience constitutes a third party to the inter-

action—one that is essential and yet, if the performance were real, one that would not be there.

This was written in 1959, and I wonder if Goffman has since changed his mind. The distinctive features he attributes to theatre are precisely those which have eroded so swiftly during the past five years. We have ongoing theatrical activity that is not "make-believe," in which actors present themselves as themselves and not as characters, and in which the audience is either physically involved or nonexistent. Where then does that leave "life"?

6.

Obviously we are not the Orokolo. But the ritual undercurrents of our lives are now more tangible than they have been in centuries. Art is emerging from the protective mantle of aesthetics. Out in the open it faces risks. It may even no longer be treated as art and find itself implicated in larger social patterns. The Orokolo have a theatre only for the observing ethnographer. For the people themselves, the activity of the cycle play is living.

7.

Coordinates come from the outside. They provide an objective measure of a space (or, understood metaphorically, of an activity). A space without coordinates must be "lived in" to be understood. All its references are internal. Activities structured this way generate their own rules. A society with this kind of "in-ness" is truly a community. To make art from the inside—to put away edges and sequences that read "beginning, middle, and end," is to operate with relational rather than descriptive aesthetics. What would appear from the outside to be distortions are "clusters," either of time or of space: events making rather than taking shape. It is precisely this in-ness that pervades the Orokolo, *The Seventh Street Environment*, *Big Hotel*, and Grotowski's troupe. The infrastructure of each is homologous to all the others.

The logic which ties these far-flung examples together is not "rational" but associative. None of these activities is concerned with how one event causes another, but with the ways in which events coincide in time and space and under what conditions an event can be transformed into another event. In the West we are beginning to understand again what we once knew—and what non-literate peoples still know—that it is possible for two or more events to occupy the same space at the same time. This, in fact, is the way everyday experience is structured. Our consciousness is not a well-edited book, but a multi-media overload. Space, time, and events suddenly convert themselves from one thing into another; and the seemingly distinct integers are interchangeable. Transformations take place vertically within a set of simultaneous happenings and horizontally between sets of sequential happenings.

Thus we begin negotiating with our environments. Consciousness is the final arbitration between competing expressions. But art is capable of preconscious or nonconscious expression. Not directly but through two contradictory operations. First, the patterns of a community—as in *The Seventh Street Environment*—are revealed through the process of self-documentation. The culture of a community is its doing; and a perceptive observer can detect the cultural patterns by watching carefully, by looking for the rhythms which underlie activities. It is not so easy, of course, for a participant to make the same observations. The Orokolo are not "conscious" of what they are doing; but their cycle play amply documents and outlines the life of their community. No single artist set out to calculate and expose Orokolo communal life; but like any other long-term and engrossing social activity the cycle play expresses that life. It is in this way that an unself-conscious artistry may create great art. Secondly, conscious efforts may be extended to search out and confront otherwise elusive structures. That is the way Grotowski works. It is perhaps the most productive mode for our own culture. We are not "primitive" and cannot hope to regain the superb elegance of the Orokolo by merely "being ourselves." Our social lives are too hedged in by conscious rules and historical guidelines which have been preserved in our literary traditions. When Grotowski talks of "unmasking" or of "roots," he is speaking of that process by which the individual artist moves through and behind the articulated portion of his tradition into an area that is quite literally ineffable, unspeakable, unarticulated. There discoveries are made which confound what we have been taught. Experience is neither universal nor personal; it is social, arising out of culture patterns particular to a society and reflected in each individual. These patterns are the object of Grotowski's research, and, I believe, the proper boundaries of theatre art.

To conduct this kind of research one must look at the "great texts" as materials out of which new artworks can be built. The confrontation process is the means of constructing the new work. Aristotle's description of art as an "imitation of an action" is modified to read the "exchange of actions." The actions of *Oedipus* or *Hamlet* exist in their own right. The task of the theatre artist is to confront these actions, exchange his own with them, and build an artwork which precisely expresses the mechanics of the transaction. This is not meant to exclude new works, but to suggest that even the newest of the new will inevitably involve a negotiation with the past.

Environment is thus understood as a complex set of relationships between time, space, actions, objects. At each level and during each transaction a negotiation takes place. Interchanges between levels and among particulars within the sets are not only possible but unavoidable. Unless art is to become a static recollection of the past, these negotiations are its very stuff.

I remember when I was very young my Grandpa Schwarz (my mother's father) showed me an old Talmud. It was bound in wood and had a lock on it. He explained that this was because the Talmud was a forbidden book in parts of Europe and anyone found possessing it would be prosecuted. Therefore, Talmuds were disguised to look like small wooden chests. The book itself was like nothing I had ever seen. In the center of each page was a short Biblical text. Around it, in varying geometrical patterns, and spreading out to the very edges of the page, were other texts; comments on the Bible and comments on the comments. One did not read this Talmud straight across, as one reads normal books. One searched in the page, jumped across blocks of print—and centuries—followed different patterns as the mind and eye wished, traced with one's finger the "line of an argument" which might begin early in the Christian era and go weaving across the page, still unresolved and urgent late in medieval times. One recapitulated history, confronted the thinking of many wise men, discovered many contradictory assertions. Or one read it like a spiral unfolding of complicated arguments flowing freely and smoothly through the centuries. The logic of that Talmud is the logic of a space without edges. The book held time, and the only way to read it was from the inside.

Public Events for the
Radical Theatre

1967

*These events are offered to everyone.
They can be performed without
permission, royalty, or author's
credit. The situations can be
changed. If any of them, or parts
of them, turn you on, do them. Or
use them to make your own thing.*

THEORETICAL NOTE. The most creative ages of theatre were those in which plagiarism flourished. I think it was Harold Clurman who said that "the first law of creativity is theft." That is surely true of theatre. Theatre artists deal in events, not texts. The greatest playwrights of the Western tradition (and, it would seem, of every civilization) were not inventors of plots. They stole their situations and often great chunks of dialogue. They stole from each other, from the public domain, from the existing work, from other cultures, from history. They worked as craftsmen, not "poets." They organized events, performers, and things.

There is a special beauty in an art whose extraordinary complexity precludes a uniquely personal creativity.

Words are there, but as secondary elaboration. Therefore, I would like to see a theatre in which creative theft is part of the craft. Only when we remove the texts of plays from the straitjacket of copyright (as production methods are already public domain)—making full-scale collage and reconstruction possible—will theatre find its strength again.

One more thing. There has been a lot of talk about "pure theatre." But purity and the theatrical event are incompatible. The theatre must not retreat to "prepared positions" (as I heard Kenneth Tynan argue, that old Tory). Theatre is an art of permeation and exchange. Its boundaries are ill-defined and far-extended. It includes demonstrations, political rallies, religious festivals, celebrations of daily life. The theatre will be more of an art when it becomes less self-consciously aesthetic. Our models should be the civic celebrations of Athens, the processional pageants of the Middle Ages, the tumultuous simultaneity of Elizabethan life, the embracing rituals of many nonliterate peoples.

1.

"The Stations of the IRT." This is best suited for a city with a subway system. I first thought of it for New York. But it can also be done on bus lines, or in relation to any social scheme—from supermarkets to cafeterias—where the essential activity is passing from place to place.

Begin by reading about the traditional Stations of the Cross, a medieval Christian ritual recapitulating Christ's walk from Jerusalem to Calvary. He stopped at fourteen "stations," and at each an action was performed. He ended hanging from his stick.

This journey to sacrifice has counterparts in many non-Christian cultures. These also should be investigated. And it has counterparts in our daily life. Few of us become gods; but most of us move from place to place, performing our daily rituals, and ending on our sticks. Investigate these ceremonial analogues of daily life: riding to and from work, shopping, waiting in a food line, registering for college, applying for Welfare, military induction, and so on.

Find fourteen performing groups. Make these as varied as possible. Include musical groups (both classical and modern); church groups for whom this exercise will be a strengthening and renewal of old ties; anarchists who believe the old rituals are exhausted; nihilists who see in the tradition something to be mocked and blasphemed; theatre groups; film-makers; students; political activists. Fourteen different views of a central set of events.

Then study the environments in which the events are to take

place. Study these environments carefully and in detail. For example: There are fourteen stations between Sheridan Square and Riverside Chapel on the Broadway-Seventh Avenue line of New York's IRT subway. Each of these stations has its own particular character. All share certain characteristics: steel structures, dirt, noise, heat in the summer, cold in the winter, bad lighting, grimy gray and black coloring, gritty texture, anonymous token-sellers, turnstiles. And the trains—those grim machines so markedly unpleasant that they seem designed for torment—a perfect vehicle for sacrifice. Study the social setting as well as the physical environment. Here thousands of people ride to and fro each day. To some purpose. The time on the subway is usually dead time. The object of the performance: to make that time live.

Each group is assigned a station. They are free to do what they wish within the rules of the game. Those rules stipulate a time limit for the performance and urge some relation between the particular IRT station and the traditional Station of the Cross. For example: Make a film that can be shown from the subway car onto the walls of the tunnel. Make another film that can be shown from the station onto the train as it arrives. Show both films at once so that (1) people in the train watch an image that seems to be static rushing across the wall and slow to a stop and (2) an image that is static and through which the rushing train careens. The people in the station see two films also: (1) the one projected from the train which travels rapidly across the wall, slowing to a stop, and (2) the one projected from the station which is first seen on the wall and then on the arriving train.

Do "The Stations of the IRT" on Easter Eve. Begin around midnight. Make every event last fifteen minutes. (Events can be repeated.) Charge no admission—the price of taking the subway is the price of admission. Let people begin downtown and ride from station to station, slowly proceeding uptown. They will arrive at Riverside Chapel for Easter Dawn services. These too should be special, correlated to the experience of the subway processional.

If your local transit authority will not cooperate, do the event anyway. In New York it costs twenty cents to ride. And Christ went free, didn't he?

2.

"Village." Find a large, open space. Indoors or outdoors. Surround it with four screens, with space at each corner: corridors. Find some puppet-makers, a few actors, a film-maker, and a man who knows sound systems. Get some light wood, some thatch.

Invite an audience to your game. Perhaps it can be done after an evening watching a traditional play. With your audience, begin to build a village. Build it as you would matchstick houses. But build it large—say, each house about three feet high. The spectators have by now become performers. Let the village have homes, churches, markets, dance halls. Populate the village with large puppets and hand puppets. Let the audience play with the puppets, become the puppet characters. Encourage them to involve themselves in village life.

On the four screens show films of village life, world-wide. On the speakers have the sounds—very low—of village life, world-wide. Above all, involve the audience in building and maintaining the life of the village. Have an election campaign, a marriage, births, funerals, bar-mitzvahs. Whatever. Be corny. Enact the daily rituals of village life.

When the audience is involved and enjoying it, bring from a distance the sound of approaching planes. Four actors enter from each of the corridors, dressed as airplanes, and they bomb the village. Show pictures of napalm and other kinds of bombs. Lots of noise. The actors stomp the village to splinters, rip the puppets apart, throw red paint on everyone. Then the actors and technicians leave.

The audience is alone in the wreckage. Thinking their thoughts.

3.

"Guerrilla Warfare." Get a map of your town. A big map. Get some stickpins, and a general staff which includes an organizer, a communications person, map-keeper, some message-runners. If you want to find out what's needed write to the Defense Department for a manual on staff organization. Find a large room and set up your headquarters. Tack your map to the wall. Decide what the centers of communication, transportation, entertainment, and politics are in your town. Find the main roads leading in and out of town; the local newspaper office; the mayor's office and house; the police stations; the radio and TV stations. Whenever you find a key spot put a flag-pin in your map.

Reduce each of the key elements to four: four centers of communication, four main roads, four centers of political power, and so on. Four is the number you will work with in building your model guerrilla war. Get six performing groups. Two will always be in reserve. Decide on an appropriate day for action. Do not do any advance publicity, except for mimeographed sheets announcing the time and places of the first set of events. Have some people ready to "tip the press and media" during the day of performance. Have film crews available to photograph what happens—your war correspondents.

Find a short play. If you want to fit your guerrilla war to the protest against the Vietnam War try Hed's *Kill Viet Cong*, printed in the *Tulane Drama Review*, Vol. X, No. 4. Rehearse the play carefully with all six of your performing groups. Each group may have its own director, and rehearsals may produce significant variations of the same scenario. The directors are part of your general staff. Brief the performers not only on the aesthetics of the event they will enact but on the physical contingencies they may face: eventual arrest, crowd harassment, the difficulty of performing outdoors, the need to scatter if attacked, and so on.

Assign to each group two communications people who will relay information to headquarters by phone. Carefully pick the spots for performance so that a public phone is nearby. Under no circumstances are the communications people to involve themselves in the event directly. They are to report back to headquarters.

P (for performance) Day. 10:00 A.M. Perform the event in four theatres. At the end of the performances announce when and where the next set of performances will take place. Arrange with the theatre owners beforehand for permission to perform. Do not tell them that there will be more performances later in the day.

Noon. Perform in four public areas where permits can be obtained, such as public parks. Do not tell anyone that you will perform later in the day when applying for permits. Use public parks, private lawns (with permission of owners), and so on. At the end of the performance announce when and where the next set of performances will take place.

2:00 P.M. Perform in four areas of political importance. The performances will be accepted as a kind of political protest. Be orderly. Do not provoke the police or bystanders. Perform near the mayor's office, at borough halls, in front of the homes of prominent politicians, at police stations. At the end of the performance announce that there will be more performances later in the day. Do not say where. Keep your reserve groups in readiness.

4:00 P.M. Perform at the centers of communication: in the lobbies of TV stations, at radio transmitters, at newspaper offices. Some of your groups may be arrested or dispersed. Make sure your lines of communication are open back to headquarters. Do not stop performing when first requested to. Later stop, to forestall arrest. Headquarters should make sure that no more than two groups are arrested. These two target groups may persist in performing until arrested. Be orderly when arrested. Keep the charges on the misdemeanor level. Announce nothing at the end of the performances.

6:00 P.M. Perform the play at four centers of public transportation, stopping or disrupting traffic. If groups were arrested at 4:00 P.M., use your reserves now. If none of your groups was arrested at 4:00 P.M. send in your reserves as your groups are arrested. Have the reserves (who have been simple spectators close by) wait a few minutes and then pick up the performance exactly where it was cut off. Again, communication is crucial so that the reserve groups will know precisely when to go in (and where to move to, if the group they are relieving has been arrested in another part of town). You are performing on approaches to bridges and tunnels, in main squares, in arterial thoroughfares. All of the groups may be arrested, including the reserves. If that happens, the event is over. If groups are permitted to perform, once the event is completed they should immediately disband, answering no questions.

Arrested groups should be bailed out by headquarters. But headquarters should not reveal its involvement in the set of events. Headquarters should send "friends" to police stations and jails to post bail. When arrested, the allowed phone call should be to headquarters. Visit your local ACLU for lawyers. Plead innocent to all charges and explain the political nature of the protest in court. Only there reveal the whole structure of the events.

"Guerrilla Warfare" is a model event. It shows through action the movement from aesthetics to sanctioned protest to guerrilla tactics. It pinpoints the vulnerable nerves of the community. It is, however, a nonviolent exercise. The idea is to adapt the form and function of guerrilla warfare to nonviolent protest and to aesthetics. To perform *Kill Viet Cong* on the approaches to the Lincoln Tunnel is an act of civil disruption and protest. Were your actors soldiers it would be an insurrection. As it is, they will, at most, be committing a misdemeanor. But people will get the message.

ENDNOTE. "Guerrilla Warfare" was performed in New York City on October 28, 1967. More than one hundred people cooperated as directors, performers, photographers, and organizers. Many of the details of the scenario were not followed. Headquarters was not highly developed; no arrests were made; there were no performances at tunnel approaches or on bridges. The performance closest to a "disruption" took place at the Port Authority Bus Terminal. I was the director of the overall event, in which five groups participated. Therefore, I am largely responsible for the copout. In retrospect, I wish we had gone all the way. The danger of stopping short of disruption and arrest is that one is not taken seriously.

"Village" was performed in November 1967 in San Francisco under the direction of Gordon Duffy. It was performed in a public park; there were no sound effects or films. The village was built from cardboard boxes, puppets were used, the audience got very involved. The village was bulldozed by trucks (perhaps a more fitting ending, reminiscent, as it is, of American "pacification" in Vietnam). The audience fought for their village and saved parts of it. Perhaps later they realized that other peoples will fight for their villages too.

The Politics of Ecstasy

1968

1.

Truly this is an essay-in-progress. The problem of the relationship between art—particularly the very public art of theatre—and politics, even revolution, is more than difficult. It is impossible. Impossible because a call to action is just that, and in some circumstances it is irresistible. What's the difference if art suffers if by action one can relieve the suffering of human beings; why care about the "structure of an event" if one can contribute to the restructuring of a society? At the same time, I suspect that the American white radical looks toward visions of the apocalypse because he is profoundly bored. We Americans are dandies—sitting in our classrooms, conducting tours through our theatres. This white nation is an anomaly: the rich bitch squatting in the squalor of impoverished neighbors. And when the bitch is slaughtered, who will spare its fleas?

I've written this essay three times. First, it was a lecture I gave at the State University of New York at Buffalo in April 1967. The riots in Newark and Detroit made me rethink it and I wrote a second version in August 1967. I finished the current version of the essay in March 1968. The essay would not have been written at all if I hadn't been invited to contribute to Ned O'Gorman's anthology, *Revolution*.[1] It strikes me as ironic, and perhaps indicative, that a subject which has become so important to me did not come of its own, but had to be elicited.

After accepting O'Gorman's invitation to write I met him, in Harlem at a storefront project. He was decked out in his turtleneck sweater, tall, blond, exuding Princeton. A poet, and a supporter of the revolution. Around him black kids moved, smiling and asking questions. I don't knock O'Gorman, but somehow I saw in him the image of America—perhaps a self-image—the tall nation surrounded by short peoples; the blond among blacks. And in the very way we walk through this world we wear the white man's burden. Next summer, maybe, those black kids will shoot O'Gorman: and he is innocent. The guilty will respond with tanks and flame-throwers.

Enriquez Vargas and Peter Schumann share part of a building in New York's East Harlem. The roof of the building stands immediately adjacent to elevated subway tracks. Several times a week members of Vargas' Gut Theatre and Schumann's Bread and Pupput Theatre stand on the roof with big painted signs. The signs read "Four Months" and then "Three Months." Vargas and Schumann know that gangs are armed in East Harlem (and I suppose in central Harlem too) and that guerrilla war is near. The National Guard and the regular Army have contingency plans mapped out for America's cities—how to fight house-to-house, bombing patterns, interrogation and concentration centers. And I suppose when my book is published the publisher will throw me a "publication party." I'll be there, drinking some martinis (or ginger ale), talking to people, smiling. What will Vargas' and Schumann's signs read?

The deepest frustration of a white radical like me is that I am powerless to change the social structure through any personal action. The "acceptable modes" of protest are ineffectual and guerrilla war means an absolute rejection of whatever comforts I have attained. I am a professor, I have a fine apartment, I enjoy the open pleasures of women and the more or less open pleasures of pot.

---

[1] *New York: Random House, 1968.*

I run a small theatre which claims to be a "guerrilla theatre," but is in fact no such thing—just a radical theatre, moving ahead in exploring certain aspects of environmental staging. I earn from my teaching and writing about $20,000 a year—a very comfortable living. I have had the fantasy of the revolution beginning, crowds storming across Washington Square and entering my apartment building, overpowering the doorman, breaking into apartments. They are on the fifteenth floor, and my apartment will be next. After a few moments' hesitation, fond glances at my hi-fi, this neat electric typewriter, my thousand books, the paintings and prints—after all that—I rush out into the hallway and wait on the fire stairs. As the revolutionary mob storms my door I join them, am among the first. We break the door down together and I collaborate in the pillaging of my own apartment. Fear, not nobility, makes me part of the revolution.

So it is fear—a complicated fear of being left out of history and a simple fear for the body—that generates a good deal of revolutionary feeling among the rich and radical. Intellectually we understand that we cannot ally ourselves with the LBJs; neither have we much respect for the Schlesingers, the Galbraiths, or even the elevated souls who edit and write for *The New York Review of Books*. But we are not black, out of work, bitter, angry in our stomachs. Like Norman Podhoretz, I've made it. But it's ashes in my mouth. The revolutionary fervor has to be pumped up, the anger is not direct but intellectual: it is the revolution of knowledge, the disgust with "culture," and not the upsurge of the disenfranchised.

And it probably won't be until the revolution reaches my door that I will make, irrevocably, the decision that my head tells me is right; right strategically and right ethically. Until that time, I write essays, direct plays, teach classes, sign statements, parade in demonstrations.

A decade ago we were told that America was a novice in international diplomacy and that our ruthlessness was a function of our innocence. As with John Wayne in the movies, sometimes the pursuit of the good resulted in the accidental killing of the wrong guy. Now we know that's not so. John Wayne knew damned well who he was shooting—or as Gilbert Moses has it in his short poem:

> The lie that generated the entire
> Christian religion and the liberal
> illusion of Western Culture seen from
> an oppressed viewpoint.
>
> Forgive them Father,
> They know not what they do.
>
> Sheeeit! Dey know what dey doin'.

We act as we do because we have a political and economic need to exploit. It is in our "national interest" to be in Vietnam. Thus we need a re-examination of those national interests. Such a re-examination, I guess, would make us traitors. We would see that we have acted criminally to protect and increase our wealth; that we have oppressed our own population, and supported oppression abroad—that, by and large, we don't care what happens to the niggers in America's ghettos or the billions of niggers overseas. We need those niggers (of many colors) to keep our industrial machinery going. But if the niggers at home become too much of a pain in the ass we can always kill them.

Knowing this, we find traditional political activity irrelevant, fruitless. Art then becomes a refuge—an activity that can generate its own reason for existing. It changes nothing, but who said art was an instrument for change? At the same time—and it is a last hope as well as a pleasurable diversion—I can conceive of art as sponsoring and provoking change. I can also foresee its renewed functions in a restructured society. I don't leave the revolution to others but stake a modest claim in it—a claim for the theatre, for myself. It would indeed be a rare—but not unthinkable—circumstance for the cultural revolution to precede the physical one. But if so, one must take that revolution seriously and understand its consequences: no more galleries, resident theatres, symphony orchestras with furry subscription audiences, lecture-hall universities. The paraphernalia of our culture must be uprooted and a second renaissance promulgated.

2.

Theatre is acted events, a set of transactions, a visual-verbal participatory game. Theatre is put together much as sports are—

with rules, formalized behavior patterns, skilled performers, special areas set aside for the activity. In nonliterate societies games, sports, theatre, and ritual are all but indistinguishable from each other. Theatre can be celebratory, even orgiastic, and communal. It can channel social energy and redistribute it; it can generate action or neutralize the impulse toward action. In the hands of those who know how to use it, it can be a powerful weapon for public control or, conversely, for radical change.

Most primitive societies are rich in theatrical lore and exercises. The theatre is a natural way to celebrate birth, puberty, marriage, the acquisition or transmission of public power, and death; to commemorate house-building, planting, harvest; to retell events of national importance and personal terror and joy. That we in the West have reduced theatre to a spare-time entertainment does not diminish theatre's potential or exhaust its world-wide traditional functions. And it is becoming increasingly clear that our Western avantgarde is, in world perspective, nothing other than a return to the most traditional theatre. In fact, the Western theatre—from Aeschylus to Ionesco—is not the major theatrical tradition but a very important offshoot—a specialized development of certain aspects of world theatre. We have emphasized story and character at the expense of dance, spectacle, ritual, and communal celebration. We have come to believe that ideas are something separate from the action—something that can be "carried" or "transmitted" by the action. In many other parts of the world, the action is the idea. We have also come to value the written text as an artwork in its own right, and we have developed this tendency so far that we can correctly speak of "dramatic literature" as we speak of poetry, the novel, or the short story. But in most cultures the text does not exist except as part of the performance. Many cultures of course have no written language. But even among those that do—East Indian subcultures, for example—the texts are preserved not to be studied in their own right but to be performed. Even in our own tradition, there have been periods when performance was central. The great medieval cycle plays were pageants, histories, city celebrations, religious affirmations, demonstrations of social solidarity.

The theatre, in performance, structures events and offers transactions the collection of which may reconstitute the perceptions and conceptions of those watching and doing. But what does that mean? Simply, after participating in theatre (as performer or spectator) one sees and understands experience differently. This may not happen, and naturally this reconstitution of experience is the aim of all art. I suggest only that theatre is better equipped for this task than literature because literature demands literacy; it is better equipped than painting and sculpture because these are passive, engaging viewers only through secondary psychological mechanisms. The film can surpass theatre in every way except the most essential: the presence of the live performer. It is, in fact, the recognition by non-theatre artists of theatre's unique possibilities that has led many of them to "theatricalize" their work. Paintings now perform, poets once again sing, film-makers allow their projectionists to move and modify the film-image. The sources of such activities, we know, are not modern but very ancient and they bring within reach again the age-old dream of a single, synthesthetic art.

The theatre of plays in which audience and performers are separated, characters developed along linear paths, and a story told without disruptive variation is the tradition we are most familiar with. It is a tradition wrought over five centuries of European history, with roots in ancient Greek and Roman theatre. It is a Western tradition, closely linked to our own kind of sequential logic and our historic faith in individual destiny. Our logic is causal and assumes that personality, social structures, and experience develop "organically." Such a system has no proper premises to deal forthrightly with "randomness," "disorder," "anarchy," and "simultaneity." We understand these phenomena, but think of them as "unnatural." And thus our understanding is prejudiced. But other cultures have other ways and different systems—systems that include associational and suggestive logic, random development, and patterns that are subjectively (and not necessarily individually) discovered rather than objectively presented.

It seems to me that our culture is presently in transition. It is not simply the movement from one basis to another, but a process of dislocation and rearticulation. Over the past century the physical sciences have steadily expanded the premises of Newtonian mechanics until today physics, mathematics, and astronomy can deal with indeterminacy. The recent history of the arts suggests a similar probing of indeterminacy. And much current theatre—happenings, environmental theatre, places like the Electric Circus—reflect a general dissatisfaction with the tradition. This dissatisfaction is unlike earlier ones. Today's artists are not seeking new truths within the framework of old patterns, but new patterns (and sometimes "truth"—the message—is not an issue at all). Like the English theatre before Marlowe, contending world-views are confronting each other. The Elizabethan theatre was not free of medieval notions, it was not its own thing. Neither will our theatre be free of the renaissance. But a significant change is taking place. At least we know that our traditional way of doing things is not the only way, or even the best way. Our traditional theatre is not the only kind.

3.

One need not look too far to find another kind of theatre. In another essay in this book ("Negotiations with Environment") I discuss the cycle play of the Orokolo, a people who live in southern New Guinea. Here let me describe in detail one element of that cycle play—the Fire Fight:

> The bathers, men, boys, and girls, were seen gathering for a moment about the bright fires by which the scene was illuminated. They seemed to be drying themselves, and as they did so they joined spontaneously in the chorus which rose to tremendous power. But they had something else in view, and this was merely an interlude. All were arming themselves with bunches of dry, inflammable coconut leaves, one in each hand, in readiness for the Fire Fight.

> Now they divided themselves into two parties according as they were associated with the east and west sides of the *eravo* [ritual and communal men's house], and faced each other across the fifty yards of open space directly in front of it. Across this space a rough hurdle of bamboo poles had been hastily run up while the bathing was still in progress, and now it stood as a very flimsy frontier between the two forces.

> Suddenly on the east side all the torches seem to flare up simultaneously, and a moment later those on the west also, making per-

haps 200 in all. The foremost on either side dash forward and shatter their torches on the hurdle, so that they seem to burst into a shower of sparks. Reinforcements charge in regardless. In a moment the barrier is broken down and the two sides mingle in a welter of flames and flying sparks. They pursue one another round and about with screams of laughter, striking, dodging, and clashing their weapons together, while lighted torches, flung spear-fashion from the hand, travel through the darkness in blazing arcs, like meteors. For a few minutes the battle rages in the village, and then with one consent the combatants turn on to the broader spaces of the beach and the black distance is soon alive with darting and circling points of fire. Meanwhile the village constables have been blowing their whistles in a well-meant effort to restore order, though happily they are completely disregarded and their shrill bleats only succeed in adding a frolicsome tribute to the revels. But in a few minutes more the thing is all over. The remaining torches are dashed out on the sands, and all return to the village.[2]

F. E. Williams thinks that the Fight "is possibly to be viewed as a last ritual license in the use of this dangerous element." For now the participants, or some of them, were to receive "a formal gift of fire together with appropriate warnings as to its use." Certain parallels can be drawn between the Fire Fight and some happenings. More directly, is there not a relation between the Orokolo and the celebrating fire-bearers of Watts, Newark, and Detroit? The Orokolo Fire Fight is part of a twenty-year-long cycle play which the Orokolo stage with uneven, but superb, relentlessness. Our urban fire rituals are more primitive.

But is it art? What is art? We cannot live the life of the Orokolo and so cannot appropriate their rituals. The theatre which Antonin Artaud urged on the West in *The Theatre and Its Double* consciously adopted Balinese models and, in many ways, was very close to the Orokolo. Some of the work of Carolee Schneemann, Jean-Jacques Lebel, Allan Kaprow, Robert Whitman, and Michael Kirby come near to both Artaud and the Orokolo. As we move from a long period in which the artist wished to control his artwork into

---

[2] F. E. *Williams*, The Drama of the Orokolo (*Oxford: Oxford University Press, 1940*), *p. 203.*

a period where he wishes instead to instigate art, the Orokolo model (and many other nonliterate models) will become increasingly relevant.

Closer than the Orokolo to our traditional theatre are the Greeks. I fear we have lost forever the Greek chorus which Nietzsche, of all moderns, seems to have understood best. Describing the Dionysian nature of the chorus, Nietzsche observes:

> [. . .] the cultured Greek felt himself absorbed into the satyr chorus, and in the next development of Greek tragedy, state and society, in fact all that separated man from man, gave way before an overwhelming sense of unity which led back into the heart of nature. The metaphysical solace (with which, I wish to say at once, all true tragedy sends us away) that, despite every phenomenal change, life is at bottom indestructibly joyful and powerful, was expressed most concretely in the chorus of satyrs, nature beings who dwell behind all civilization and preserve their identity through every change of generations and historical movement.[3]

Dionysus, Eros, tribalism—the terms vary, depending upon whether you are Nietzsche, Freud, McLuhan, or an ethnographer; even without the terminology, everyone has a sense of what Nietzsche is talking about: "the force that through the green fuse drives the flower." Underneath whatever repressive machinery civilization constructs to keep itself intact, a counterforce of great unifying, celebratory, sexual, and life-giving power continues to exert its overwhelming and joyful influence. At certain times in everyone's life and during certain periods of each society's history this counterforce is activated. It is perhaps improper to speak of it as a "counterforce" since it seems—when active—to be more authentic than the civilization—the specific social inhibitions—it opposes and frequently obliterates. Dionysus' presence can be beautiful or ugly or both. It seems quite clear that he is present in today's America—showing himself in the hippies, in the "carnival spirit" of black insurrectionists, on campuses; and even, in disguise, on the patios and in the living-rooms

---

3 *Friedrich Nietzsche,* The Birth of Tragedy, *tr. Francis Golffing, in* European Theories of Drama, *ed. Barrett H. Clark, rev. Henry Popkin (New York: Crown, 1965), p. 298.*

of suburbia. There is a qualitative link between the Orokolo Fire Fight, the Greek chorus, and our own folk-rock discothèques. LSD is contemporary chemistry, but freaking-out is ancient. I take this special, ecstatic quality to be essentially theatrical.

Freud called this special quality the Pleasure Principle and identified it with art—when it was translated and transmuted by organized fantasy. The difference between art as we know it in the West and theatre as it has traditionally shown itself world-wide is that Western art is individualized while traditional theatre is communal. In its communal forms, theatre is both socially constructive and personally "transcendent" or ecstatic. But our art has long lost this double—and contradictory—function, becoming instead a function of individualism: the Protestant-capitalist ethic. And it is inevitable that the individualization of art leads to its commercialization. Nothing formally distinguishes the labor of the artist from the labor of any other worker—and labor is bought and sold by the piece or by the hour.

It is here that the future of art—particularly the theatre—is linked to the development of social systems that are neither individualizing nor commercialized. That does not necessarily mean that theatre does best in socialist societies—because socialism in this century has not become either manageably tribal or demonstrably uncommercial. At the same time, the success of the theatre in eastern Europe can be related to more than the simple availability of subsidy. And the failure of theatre in America is more than a question of poverty. We simply are not brought up to believe in groups; we are trained toward an individualistic ethic that makes us want to achieve things on our own, by ourselves. These values are inimical to theatre. Theoretically, at least, if their societies find a shape which matches their stated intentions, the theatre of eastern Europe, the Soviet Union and China will be better artistically than our own.

The difference in viewpoint and social function is best grasped in the unargued debate between Nietzsche and Hegel a century ago. Hegel felt that tragedy represented "a self-division and self-waste of spirit, or a division of spirit involving conflict and waste." Nietzsche, as we have seen, finds in the Greek chorus something "indestructibly joyful." (It is perhaps the greatest achievement of renaissance theatre that both tendencies were precariously present; surely it is this double sense of waste and joy that gives Shakespeare's plays their sublimity.) In societies that value individuality above all else, tragedy will seem wasteful; in societies that prize the group above all else, tragedy will seem joyful: a necessary, ruthless celebration.

4.

I suppose the Athenian community that saw *Oedipus* and *Lysistrata* in their original productions (a community, we must remember, that lived several generations before Aristotle) sensed the affirmation—even in terror and satire—which these public events offered. Here in a single, circular arena the whole community came to see its reality enacted. Although we have always known about the topicality and obscenity of Aristophanic comedy, we are just beginning to rediscover an equivalent topicality and sexuality in the great tragedies. Aeschylus, Sophocles, and Euripides did not conceive abstract artworks. Their plays related directly to the social life of Athens. *Oedipus* itself can be better understood as a drama of political choice and sexual entanglement than as one of religious significance. It is hard to grasp this because Aristotle and his Christian interpreters so profoundly distorted our view of Greek culture. For centuries, it was necessary to accept that culture as "pre-Christian," and read into it the asceticism and other-worldliness of a Christianity that developed under the aegis of St. Augustine and St. Thomas. And when that kind of Christianity fell away, the tragedies were reinterpreted in the light of Lutheran and Calvinist Protestantism. It is only very recently—as we begin to experience a revolution of the flesh—that we are able to reinterpret the Greeks. We understand now that nothing the Greeks did in their arts was separate from the fabric of city life and that that life was not organized according to a Christian world-scheme.

Ironically enough, a Christianity infused with pagan European culture reveals the same sense of civic identity which characterized Greek theatre. A communal and cosmographic harmony infused the York and Chester cycles: theatrical events involving townsfolk in panoramas of heaven, hell, and the commonest of men. Acted in

219

the streets, continuing for weeks, these cycle plays unfolded a world history focused on the local community.

The theatres of fifth-century B.C. Athens and medieval Europe were community expressions. Reaffirming certain values, they questioned others, and were merciless toward specific individuals. Aristophanes liked neither Athens' leaders nor the Peloponnesian Wars —and he said so in his plays. Can we understand the society which sponsored these plays, officially sanctioned them?

Were we today to sponsor such communal events we would probably uncover forms and subjects too uncomfortable to permit public sanction. It was the joy of the rioters in Newark and Detroit that most outraged the authorities, who responded with a performance of their own: smashed windows led to smashed skulls. Think, if you will, what it would mean to act out in Harlem, Westchester, Birmingham, or Keokuk cycles of plays which truly represented the hopes and fears of our people, which accurately concretized our mythologies and which steadily cast these hopes, fears, and myths in contemporary forms and activities—avoiding archaic and temporizing devices and seeking in the living values we act the images of our actions. Even to think about such performances measures the repressive mechanisms deeply operative in our lives. Try as we might we would be unable to match the Greeks or the medievals. Our expressions become either mish-mash or bloody riots.

Only the new music—written and performed by small groups— has found appropriate and expressive means. In places where the "new expression" should be most generally expressive—peace marches, demonstrations, be-ins, discothèques, some happenings— we see only degrees of inarticulateness. Generally, we are a society in which artistic expression is thought to be for and to us, but not by us. When the lid comes off and we are given the opportunity to express ourselves, we find that we have very little to say. Or, more precisely, we do not know how to say what we want to say. We toy with nudity, sexuality, political organization, democratized artistic creativity. But we don't get very far. Is it not true that these past ten years have shown us that repression is our style, our myth-maker, and the source of our social order? Begin to remove that repression and we reveal not the "natural man" but groups of people who mill about in confusion. It is a desperate situation socially and a distressing one aesthetically.

During the heyday of rapid industrialization repression was the necessary tool for maintaining a social order that demanded of its people unspeakable sacrifices. Freud, Herbert Marcuse, and Norman O. Brown have described the situation well. But now we are beginning to realize that the "free" programs Marcuse and Brown urge on us are impossible. Repression has become the major ideology of our civilization; destroy it and what is left? After the meticulous rigor of Ibsen we have the amorphousness of happenings; after lynch-law, Detroit. We are beginning to realize that the absence of repression is not the answer because it is not the proper question. The answer lies in what to repress, why, and how—and in the development of a social order that will permit us private liberty and communal expressivity in a context that is anything but anarchistic. It will take us many generations to achieve the balance of the Orokolo villagers who acted out the Fire Fight. And perhaps we will never get there, our habitual civilization and our cops intervening long before.

It is not that our be-ins, marches, demonstrations, and riots are styleless. They all reveal—by both opposition and confirmation—life-cycles which are aggressive and murderously self-destructive. I don't deny that some isolated events show a movement toward authentic celebration. But much as I would like to have it otherwise, the new art and most of our rebellious behavior is a reaction against existing rotten cultural forms and not a self-sustaining new culture.

5.

The problem is clear. An "indestructibly joyful" sense underlies communal theatre: it is the spirit of the Greek chorus, the medieval cycle play, nonliterate ritual, some isolated events in our own culture. A sense of "division and waste" underlies our formal tragedies; and either formlessness or self-destruction characterizes our weak attempts at "free expression." How then might we return to, or discover for ourselves, the "indestructibly joyful"? Certainly not by redoing in traditional ways Greek tragedy or by adopting nonliterate ritual in whole cloth. We cannot suppose we are a culture we are not.

However, certain rituals seem basic enough to touch roots in us just as they express the experience of cultures other than our own. I am director of a small group of performers, some of whom have not had formal training in theatre or any other performance art. Our work stems from experiments of my own and other members of the New Orleans Group (1965–1967) and from a brief month's work I had with Jerzy Grotowski when he visited New York in 1967. The Performance Group (as we call ourselves) meets for intensive five-hour work sessions three times a week. We adhere to a rigid discipline which does not permit laughter, talking, tears; and our byword (adopted from Grotowski) is "surpass yourself." The psycho-physical exercises are essentially Grotowski's—and he got some of his exercises from Artaud, others from Stanislavski, some from Yoga and Kathakali. The principles of his work are outlined in several articles and interviews printed in *TDR*.[4]

In several of our workshops we have come close, I believe, to those life-experience roots that we share with other cultures. Naturally, our expression of them is in terms of our own culture—cultures being men's basic "languages," as learned and as distinct one from another as verbal languages. One night we were in an exercise and a member of the group threw another member to the floor. She was hurt, perhaps seriously. I did not know that she was hurt because the exercise dealt with dying, and many members of the group were groaning and rolling about in pain. Finally after some fifteen minutes, having crawled across the floor from where she had landed, she insisted weakly to me, "Richard Schechner, this is not part of the workshop. I am hurt." I stopped the exercise. An ambulance was called, she was taken to the hospital. While waiting for the medical reports, the rest of us sat and discussed what we would do if Georgie were truly seriously injured. I said that we had to discuss the event in terms of serious injury, because that way the issue of violence was most clearly focused. We came to no sure conclusions, except that

---

[4] TDR, *Vol. VIII, No. 4; Vol. IX, No. 3; Vol. XI, No. 3; Vol. XII, No. 3; Vol. XIII, No. 1. A discussion of Kathakali is in* TDR, *Vol. XI, No. 4.*

personal violence was to be eliminated (at least temporarily) from our work and that the work, no matter what, had to go on. After about an hour's discussion we received word from the hospital that Georgie did not seem to be seriously hurt. There were no fractures, nothing that showed up on an X-ray.

The next time we met, the events of the preceding night were heavy on us all. The man who had thrown Georgie down had a history of violent expression. We were a bit afraid of him. The group was up-tight and something had to be done to relive, recall, and repair the events of the night before. We began an exercise, as we always do, with our basic physical work—head rolls, neck rolls, shoulder muscle control, back rolls, "the cat" (a total exercise modeled after the way a cat rises from sleep, stretches, and flexes all its muscles). The group was divided into four subsections, each working on a mat. Bill, the man given to violence, was working alone on a mat with Margaret, one of the most gentle people in the work-shop, a woman who seemed to have a special understanding of Bill. Georgie was there, sitting on the sidelines watching. For two weeks we had been working with musical instruments. The instruments were randomly distributed. The idea was not to "play the instrument" in any formal way, but to use it as a sound producer. We worked with a bongo drum, a flute, a bugle, some bells, and a tambourine.

As the exercise developed (they are never completely planned out), Bill and Margaret lay embraced on their mat, oblivious to the rest of the group. Without their knowledge I arranged wooden chairs all around their mat so that they were isolated entirely from the others. I distributed musical instruments to the rest of the group, but none to Bill and Margaret. And then I said quietly to the others: "You must sacrifice your best couple, the finest people in your village. You must sacrifice them if you are to live. You must sing and dance them to death."

Slowly, over the next three-quarters of an hour, the three groups with musical instruments began playing and dancing, moving closer and closer to Bill and Margaret. The songs and dances were at first hesitant, but then they took on insistent rhythms, a real form, and a community moved toward the place where a symbolic sacrifice was to occur. Bill and Margaret, hearing the approaching singers and dancers, looked up and saw the chairs. No words were spoken (most of our exercises are nonverbal), but they clearly knew that they were trapped, in a special enclosure, and that they were to be sacrificed. As the other groups—now united into one—moved in, Remi tipped the chairs down so that the space allotted to Bill and Margaret was still smaller. As she tipped each chair, the chant grew louder, more insistent, and Bill and Margaret realized that they had to die. Most of the sacrificing group was gathered around those to be sacrificed. However, four of them (there are fifteen people in the Performance Group) stood to the side, arms locked and in a tight circle, doing a mimetic dance of death, suffering symbolically the death Bill and Margaret were to experience.

The exercise truly took on the form of a theatrical ritual, with all the mystery that implies. It was real and unreal, authentic and acted out. No one was dying, but two people were dying; there was no village, but there was one all the same. The "double" that Artaud speaks of so knowingly in relation to the theatre was there; the "confrontation" that Grotowski insists is at the heart of performing was there.

Bill and Margaret took a good time dying. Margaret died first, but Bill took a long, hard time. The group danced around him, he tried to revive Margaret, the song-chant increased its tempo, but with its volume rising and falling. Finally, Bill died too. A certain justice had been done for the night before. Georgie was in tears.

Then I said to the group: "You must now bring your people back to life. You must revive them so that they can dance the triumph ceremony." I did not know what the triumph ceremony would be. I knew only that Bill and Margaret, having been sacrificed (he for his violence, she for her love of him), must now be brought back to the group, accepted as the group's heroes: the ones who had gone through death and returned. At first, the songs began quietly and everyone touched Bill and Margaret. They touched the two dead ones gently and lovingly. Margaret came back, but Bill did not move. The group became more frenzied and massaged and caressed Bill. He did not respond. Margaret chased the group away from Bill, wishing to revive him herself, knowing (as we later found out from Bill) that mauling, loving as it was, would not bring him back to life.

These minutes were very long, and very frightening for me. I do not know whether or not I believe in trances. That night I did and felt that perhaps we had gone too far. I went over and took Bill's pulse. It was beating strongly and I decided to let the exercise go on. An exercise that had transcended exercises.

After many efforts and much gentleness Margaret revived Bill and she began her dance of triumph. He stood, vacant-eyed, and watched her. He did not move, he did not seem to be seeing her at all. Her dance became more frenzied, and around her the others stood chanting. Bill did not respond, did not dance. Margaret screamed and fell to the floor and Bill toppled over, as if he were entirely inanimate. Margaret revived slowly and began again. This time she succeeded and Bill danced his triumph ceremony with her. The exercise was over—more than two hours after it had begun.

I describe it at such length because I wish to communicate its intensity, its communal nature, its reality. It was ritual, theatre, art; and it was also reality—a species of symbolic reality that I had read about but had never seen. It was the beginning of research into a theatre art for our culture and time; something which at its very base is simply different from the theatre of plays. It was traditional theatre, but a different tradition than that which has functioned in the West since the renaissance.

A similar rebirth ritual is performed by the Asmat tribe in western New Guinea.[5] The ritual is part of a kinship exchange between two families or tribes. It results in the adoption of a couple of one tribe by another and symbolizes the peace that exists between the two groups. Thirty men, naked, lay on the floor of a large hut. Astride them stand eight or ten women, wearing only a loin belt of woven leaves. The woman (or man) chosen for adoption is adorned in long strands of palm-fiber, attached to the head and flowing down almost to the knees. The one to be adopted lies down on top of the men and begins to move slowly down the line, pushed

---

5 For a complete description and photos of this ritual see Tony Saulnier, Headhunters of Papua (New York: Crown Publishers, 1963), pp. 41 ff.

on by the women who are straddling the men. As the adopted one moves, the straddling women begin to move and groan as if they are giving birth. The men undulate slightly. The one being born is given the experience of traveling down the birth canal, across the backs of his or her new tribesmen and between the legs of the tribeswomen. When the journey has been completed—and it can be either an easy or a difficult birth—the adopted one is wrapped in swaddling clothes, the umbilical cord is symbolically cut, and he or she takes a few drops of milk from one of the tribeswomen. This tribeswoman will be the adopted one's "mother." Saulnier reports that "the whole was a very realistic portrayal of a childbirth, the rebirth of two couples from a common mother."

Saulnier is a photographer for *Paris-Match*, not an ethnographer. He and a camera team had come to New Guinea to photograph rites like these. They are sacred rites, and few outsiders have been permitted to see them. The ceremony was performed, but the quality of the film was not very good. What happened next astonished Saulnier, and has a very special meaning for those who are interested in such rituals as theatre.

> We took the risk of asking the Asmats to begin all over again. To our amazement they agreed to everything we asked with great alacrity. [. . .] We spent all Monday filming the two-village adoption ceremony, which the Asmats performed all over again, thoroughly, under good filming conditions. They were not acting: they really lived the ceremony over again.

But they were acting—it was extraordinary acting, the kind in which the performers are entirely committed to the action. This ability to repeat sacred ceremonies, consciously to re-enact them (and not for the sake of gain; the Asmats did not have much contact with Western people, they received little for their performances), should bring to mind an obvious question: is there any difference between ritual ceremonies and fine acting? The techniques are the same. The difference is that those who enact a ritual ceremony believe in it and its consequences; they see it as part of their culture, as a central event in their lives. They are not "professional" actors (though there are some in the tribe more skilled at performance than others, and these skilled performers do most of the dancing, most of the acting). It is a tentative conclusion, but I feel that the structure of performance is universal; that the differences between "ritual" and "theatre" are of social function, not of performance credibility or repeatability. The Asmats can repeat their ceremonies. They cannot lift them out of their social context. To be reborn again is to be reborn again; it is not less real the second time.

6.

Such undertakings for our culture would mean fewer plays and more "events," fewer verbal stories and more "rituals." It would mean the development of modern cycle plays and processions, a diminishing importance for the "professional" theatre—though not a diminishing need for skilled and committed performers. It would also mean a careful re-examination of our great repertory. Because our tradition is written, it has become a burden. An oral tradition quite naturally takes its shape from the changing culture which transmits it. A written tradition, however, trends to solidify and become reactionary. We are in the double bind of redoing our repertory while recognizing, as we submit to season after season of dull new plays, that "dramatic literature" is exhausted. We hope that some new playwright will emerge. But it is a vain hope. The last great period of playwriting included Ibsen, Chekhov, Strindberg, Pirandello, and Brecht. There was a coda with Genet, Beckett, Ionesco. But these "anti-plays" and staged rituals signaled the end of the written theatre. We are now returning to an older tradition— performance.

This older tradition is political in the widest sense. It cannot be created outside of a group, a community; and it cannot function without direct reference to the society in which it is embedded. It does not ignore the repertory, but neither does it "express" it. Performance uses the repertory—as material from which to construct new artworks. The Performance Group is now working on a production of Euripides' *The Bacchae* that treats the text as if it were part of an oral tradition. The play will be performed in a large environmentally articulated space. Only parts of Euripides' text will be used, and these parts will be joined to and set against fragments of other texts. The event will be a dance, an ecstasy, and the audience will perform along with members of the Group. Our Bacchanale will not be completely celebratory: that would not be true to our social context. We hope to explore the "politics of ecstasy" which is so important to many young people today.

This politics of ecstasy brings my discussion full circle. There are many young people who believe that an unrepressive society, a sexualized society, is Utopia. Nudity, free sexual expression, communal rather than family units, "inner space," and sensory overload are becoming political issues. The discothèques—the Palm Gardens, the Fillmore, the Electric Circus—are places of public assembly and direct political action. A new way of living is being demonstrated. But this same ecstasy, we know, can be unleashed in the Red Guards or horrifically channeled toward the Nuremberg rallies and Auschwitz. There, too, at the vast extermination camps, an ecstasy was acted out. The hidden fear I have about the new expression is that its forms come perilously close to ecstatic fascism.

Liberty can be swiftly transformed into its opposite, and not only by those who have a stake in reactionary government. Ritualized experience without the built-in control of a strong social system —an Asmat society or an Orokolo society—can pump itself up to destructive fury. So I must end with an indelicate question. Are we ready for the liberty we have grasped? Can we cope with Dionysus' dance and not end up—as Agave did—with our sons' heads on our dancing sticks?

Index

Index

Index